PSYCHOSOCIAL DISORDERS
IN YOUNG PEOPLE

About the Editors

Sir Michael Rutter is Professor and Head of the Department of Child and Adolescent Psychiatry at the University of London's Institute of Psychiatry, and Honorary Director of the Medical Research Council Child Psychiatry Unit, based at the Institute. He also continues in clinical practice. His research activities include stress resistance in children, developmental links between childhood and adult life, schools as social institutions, reading difficulties, neuropsychiatry and psychiatric epidemiology. His publications include some 30 books, 105 chapters, and over 230 scientific papers. He was elected a Fellow of the Royal Society in 1987 and was a founding member of Academia Europaea in 1988. He was knighted in 1992.

David J. Smith is Professor of Criminology at the University of Edinburgh. He was formerly a Senior Fellow of the Policy Studies Institute, London, and Head of the Social Justice and Social Order Group. He has carried out interdisciplinary social science research in a variety of fields related to public policy: inequality, especially between ethnic or religious groups, crime and criminal justice, and school effectiveness. His books include *Racial Disadvantage in Britain* (1977), *Police and People in London* (1983), *The School Effect* (1989), *Inequality in Northern Ireland* (1991), *Racial Justice at Work* (1991), and *Democracy and Policing* (1994).

PSYCHOSOCIAL DISORDERS IN YOUNG PEOPLE

Time Trends and Their Causes

Edited by

Michael Rutter

and

David J. Smith

Published for
Academia Europaea

by

JOHN WILEY & SONS

Chichester · New York · Brisbane · Toronto · Singapore

Published 1995 by John Wiley & Sons Ltd,
   Baffins Lane, Chichester,
   West Sussex PO19 1UD, England

   Telephone   National   (01243) 779777
               International +44 243 779777

Other Wiley Editorial Offices

John Wiley & Sons, Inc., 605 Third Avenue,
New York, NY 10158-0012, USA

Jacaranda Wiley Ltd, 33 Park Road, Milton,
Queensland 4064, Australia

John Wiley & Sons (Canada) Ltd, 22 Worcester Road,
Rexdale, Ontario M9W 1L1, Canada

John Wiley & Sons (SEA) Pte Ltd, 37 Jalan Pemimpin #05-04,
Block B, Union Industrial Building, Singapore 2057

Library of Congress Cataloging-in-Publication Data

Psychosocial disorders in young people : time trends and their causes
   / edited by Michael Rutter and David J. Smith
      p. cm.
   Includes bibliographical references and index.
   ISBN 0-471-95054-8
   1. Adolescent psychology.   2. Adolescent psychiatry.   I. Rutter,
Michael.   II. Smith, David John, *1941– .
BF724.P76   1995
616.89′022—dc20   95–1906
                                                              CIP

British Library Cataloguing in Publication Data

A catalogue record for this book is available from the British Library

ISBN0-471-95054-8

From camera ready copy supplied by the editors
Printed and bound in Great Britain by Bookcraft (Bath) Ltd
This book is printed on acid-free paper responsibly manufactured from sustainable forestation,
for which at least two trees are planted for each one used for paper production.

Contents

PART III The Target Disorders

PART IV Conclusions

Contributors

Sir Michael Rutter FRS (Editor)

Professor and Head of the Department of Child and Adolescent Psychiatry, Institute of Psychiatry, University of London, England; Honorary Director of the Medical Research Council Child Psychiatry Unit. Member of the Academia Europaea.

David J Smith (Editor)

Senior Fellow and Head of the Social Justice and Social Order Research Group, Policy Studies Institute, London, England.
(Professor of Criminology at the University of Edinburgh, Scotland, from August 1994.)

Gian Vittorio Caprara

Professor, Department of Psychology, Universita degli Studi di Roma 'La Sapienza', Rome, Italy.

René F W Diekstra

Professor, and Chairman, Department of Clinical and Health Psychology; Dean, Faculty of Social Sciences, University of Leiden, The Netherlands.

Eric Fombonne

Research Scientist at the Institut National de la Santé et de la Recherche Médicale, Paris, France. (Senior Lecturer and Honorary Consultant, Department of Child and Adolescent Psychiatry, Institute of Psychiatry, University of London, England, from September 1993.)

David Halpern

Research Fellow, Social Justice and Social Order Research Group, Policy Studies Institute, London, England. (Prize Research Fellow, Nuffield College, Oxford, England, from October 1993.)

Laura E Hess

Postdoctoral Research Fellow, Center for Psychology and Human Development, Max Planck Institute for Human Development and Education, Berlin, Germany. (Paediatric Psychology Fellow, Division of Child Development and Rehabilitation Medicine, School of Medicine, University of Pennsylvania, USA, from September 1992; Assistant Professor, Department of Child Development and Family Studies, Purdue University, West Lafayette, Indiana, USA, from August 1994.)

C W M Kienhorst

Assistant Professor, Department of Clinical and Health Psychology, University of Leiden, The Netherlands.

Nancy Leffert

Research Associate, Institute of Child Development, College of Education, University of Minnesota, and Research Scientist, Search Institute, Minneapolis, USA.

Anne C Petersen

Professor, Vice-President for Research and Dean of the Graduate School, University of Minnesota, Minneapolis, USA. (Deputy Director of the National Science Foundation, USA, from October 1994.)

Lee Robins

Professor, Department of Psychiatry, Washington University School of Medicine, St Louis, Missouri, USA.

Rainer K Silbereisen

Professor, Department of Psychology, Justus Liebig University, Giessen, Germany. (Professor, Department of Human Development and Family Studies, College of Health and Human Development, Pennsylvania State University, PA, USA, from November 1992; Professor and Head of Department of Developmental Psychology, Institute of Psychology, Friedrich-Schiller-University of Jena, Germany, from October 1994.)

Ellen Wartella

Walter Cronkite Regents Chair in Communication and Dean, College of Communication, the University of Texas at Austin, USA.

Erik J de Wilde

Postdoctoral Fellow, Department of Clinical and Health Psychology, University of Leiden, The Netherlands.

Preface

Academia Europaea is an association of individual scholars throughout the whole of Europe, from the Atlantic to the Urals, and covering all disciplines. Among its aims are 'to encourage interdisciplinary and international studies and research', and 'to encourage and assist collaboration between scholars in Europe'. Towards the end of 1990, the Academia established a Study Group to consider the scientific evidence on the question of whether psychosocial disorders in young people had become more, or less, frequent over the last 50 years and to determine how possible causal explanations for any changes found might be tested. The Study Group was also asked to review causal explanations in the light of the evidence currently available and to establish priorities for future research. Although the primary purpose of the Study Group was to advance scientific knowledge, it was expected that the findings would be of interest to governments and other organizations concerned with policy. It should thus help to achieve one of Academia Europaea's further aims, which is 'to provide independent advice on matters of scholarly interest or concern to legislatures, governments, universities, and polytechnics, and to professional, industrial and commercial organizations in Europe'. The Academia made trends in psychosocial disorders one of its highest priorities for international collaborative study because the explanation of these trends is one of the greatest challenges facing science today.

A preliminary workshop of key researchers in the field was held at Marbach Castle in September 1990. The following people were present at that meeting.

Michael Rutter (Chairman) *Institute of Psychiatry, London*

Hans Bertram *Deutsches Jugendinstitut e. V., Munich*

Anders Jeffner *University of Uppsala, Sweden*

Jadwiga Koralewicz *University of Warsaw, Poland*

Anders Lange *University of Stockholm, Sweden*

David Magnusson *University of Stockholm, Sweden*

Karl-Ulrich Mayer *Max Planck Institute for Human Development and Education, Berlin*

Anne Petersen *Pennsylvania State University, USA*

Lea Pulkkinen *University of Jyvaskyla, Finland*

Rainer K. Silbereisen *Justus Liebig University, Giessen, Germany*

David J Smith *Policy Studies Institute, London*

Martti Takala *University of Jyvaskyla, Finland*

Laura Hess (Rapporteur) *Max Planck Institute for Human Development and Education, Berlin*

Klaus Jacobs (in attendance) *former CEO Jacobs-Suchard Corporation, Zurich*

Laszlo Nagy (in attendance) *Johann Jacobs Foundation, Zurich*

This workshop led to the conviction that the problem could be tackled. A Study Group was then established under the chairmanship of Professor Sir Michael Rutter FRS. Funding for the project was provided by the Zurich-based Johann Jacobs Foundation, which concentrates on support for action and research on youth issues. The Policy Studies Institute (PSI) administered the budget, and David Smith at PSI agreed to act as scientific secretary to the Group.

The aim was not to produce a collection of loosely connected papers. Rather, the Study Group was a collaborative enterprise based on a clearly articulated plan. It aimed to tackle a set of well-defined scientific problems in a systematic way, and to make the results accessible to specialists and non-specialists alike. The minimum objective was to gather together the available information on cross-national time trends in psychosocial disorders, to analyse the measurement problems in detail, and to make appropriate comparisons between time periods and countries. To collect and evaluate the evidence in such a systematic way would already constitute an important step forward. It was hoped, in addition, to begin the task of elaborating and testing possible causal explanations of the observed time trends.

The objectives of the study, and the general approach to be followed, were set out at an early stage in a proposal, which established a framework for the inquiry. As a general principle, it was decided that each member of the Study

Group would deal with one subject across all countries for which information was available. Members were therefore chosen as authorities on each of the main subjects that had to be covered. They were drawn from a number of European countries, and from the USA. A conscious effort was made throughout to include findings from Southern as well as from Northern European countries and North America. The findings quoted from Southern Europe are nevertheless relatively few, but that is probably a reflection of the amount of relevant material available within the tradition of the quantitative behavioural sciences.

The Study Group was set up a year after the fall of the Berlin Wall. In principle, it should have covered Eastern as much as Western Europe. In practice, it was too early for that to be possible. There was, of course, a considerable tradition of behavioural science in several of the eastern bloc countries under Communism, but scientific networks were not yet well enough established to enable the Study Group to have full access to that tradition. A distinguished Estonian social scientist, Dr Mikk Titma, was invited to join the Group, and provided an overview of relevant research, which provided a useful background to the inquiry.

The Study Group met four times altogether: twice at Marbach Castle, the Communications Centre of the Johann Jacobs Foundation in Southern Bavaria, through the hospitality of Mr Klaus Jacobs, Chairman of the Foundation; and twice in Geneva, at the headquarters of the International Scout Movement, through the hospitality of the Mr Laszlo Nagy, the Foundation's President. At an early stage, members were asked to produce outlines of their chapters, and later, first drafts. At its meeting in January 1992, when first drafts were considered, the Study Group agreed the overall structure of the report, and the format to be followed by each of the chapters on specific psychosocial disorders and on possible risk factors. The final versions were therefore shaped to an agreed pattern.

Each member of the group had extensive opportunities to comment on successive drafts of the chapters. Near-final versions of each chapter, with the exception of the introduction and conclusions (1, 14 and 15), were submitted to academic referees as well as receiving extensive input from other members of the Study Group. In most cases, three or more referees' reports were obtained. Subsequent revisions took account of these comments and those from the Study Group. Each chapter represents the views of the Study Group and not just those of the individual author.

The editors wrote the two concluding chapters (14 and 15) after inviting and receiving comments from members of the Group on a brief summary of conclusions. Group members were then invited to comment on the full draft, and the final version takes account of the comments received at that stage. It is important to emphasize, therefore, that while the editors were responsible for drafting the conclusions, these too give the conclusions of the Study Group as a whole.

Michael Rutter
David J Smith

Acknowledgements

This book is the work of a Study Group set up by Academia Europaea and funded by the Johann Jacobs Foundation, Zurich. We are most grateful to the Foundation for providing the substantial funds that were necessary. In addition, we thank Klaus Jacobs, the Chairman of the Johann Jacobs Foundation, for his hospitality in making Marbach Castle available to the Study Group for three of its meetings. We are also grateful to Laszlo Nagy, President of the Johann Jacobs Foundation, for making available the Scouts Headquarters in Geneva for three meetings, and for all his help in making the administrative arrangements. Both Klaus Jacobs and Laszlo Nagy gave an impetus to the project from the beginning and helped it along by joining our discussions at meetings.

Throughout the major part of the project, David Smith was a Senior Fellow at the Policy Studies Institute (PSI) in London, which acted as the budget holder for the project. Both the study itself and this book turned out to be far longer and more complex than originally envisaged. This imposed considerable extra burdens on PSI in both financial and human terms. We are grateful to the Institute for its continuing support in the face of these extra loads.

Amanda Trafford at PSI was responsible for the daunting task of copy editing the text and dealing with the many details involved with the insertion of tables and figures. She also played an important role, at an earlier stage, in liaising with the various members of the Study Group. We gratefully acknowledge her substantial contribution.

Our thanks also go to Clare Morgan, who carried out all of the word-processing and the final preparation of many of the figures. We are particularly grateful that she was not overwhelmed by the size and complexity of the task.

Adele Summers at the Institute of Psychiatry acted as Michael Rutter's personal assistant for his work on the project. This involved keeping track of a huge volume of correspondence and papers, and we are grateful for all the work she put into this.

We are grateful to Isobel Bowler, then a Research Fellow at PSI, for the work she carried out on use of the media, which was later incorporated into Chapter 7.

As mentioned in the Preface, all of the chapters (with minor exceptions) were read by several referees. As this was an open process, we are happy to be able to thank the following people for their most helpful comments:

Wladislaw Adamski	Brendan Burchell
Bernard Casey	Lindsay Chase-Lansdale
George Davey Smith	Felton Earls
Griffith Edwards	Glen H. Elder Jr.
Christopher Fairburn	David Farrington
Richard Harrington	Anthony Heath
Assen Jablensky	Renate Köcher
Norman Kreitman	David Lester
Kurt Lüscher	Eleanor Maccoby
Barbara Maughan	Pat Mayhew
Andrew Pickles	Martin Plant
Norman Sartorius	Zena Stein
Myrna M. Weissman	Priya Wickramaratne

The following provided invaluable assistance with papers: Peter Anderson; Guy Cumberbatch; David Docherty; Gill Jones.

FIGURE AND TABLE COPYRIGHT ACKNOWLEDGEMENTS

The authors and editors are grateful to the copyright holders for giving their permission to reproduce the copyright material listed below.

Fig.4.1 Reprinted by permission of The New England Journal of Medicine; 4.2 Author's own copyright; 4.3 Family Planning Perspectives New York; Table 4.1 Authors' own copyright; Table 4.2 Oxford University Press Inc.

Fig.5.1 Campus Verlag Frankfurt am Main; United Nations; 5.2 Elsevier Science; 5.3-5.6 United Nations; 5.7 Reprinted by permission of the Council of Europe; 5.8,5.9 United Nations; 5.10,5.11 Statistics Finland; 5.12 Campus Verlag Frankfurt am Main; 5.13 Family Policy Studies Centre; 5.14 United Nations; 5.15 European Family & Social Policy Unit; 5.16 International Institute for Labour Studies; United Nations; 5.17 European Family & Social Policy Unit; 5.18,5.19 NSPCC.

Fig.6.3-6.5 Springer Verlag GmbH & Co KG; 6.6 University of Chicago Press; 6.7 United Nations; 6.8 Crown copyright; 6.9 University of Chicago Press; United Nations; 6.10,6.11 Crown copyright; 6.18b,c,d Walter de Gruyter & Co; 6.28-6.31 Unesco 1993; 6.33 Princeton University Press; The Twentieth Century Fund; 6.34 The Twentieth Century Fund; 6.35 By permission of Kluwer Academic Publishers; 6.36 The Twentieth Century Fund; 6.42 By permission of Oxford University Press; 6.46,6.49-6.52 LIS at CEPS/INSTEAD.

Table 7.1 European Broadcasting Union; Table 7.2 Screen Digest Ltd.

Fig.8.1-8.4 By permission of Macmillan Ltd; 8.5-8.12 By permission of D.G.Barker; 8.13a&b Presses Universitaires de France; By permission of Macmillan Ltd; 8.14-8.16 Professor Ronald Inglehart; 8.17 Reader's Digest Association Ltd; 8.18 Walter de Gruyter & Co; 8.19 Professor Ronald Inglehart; Dartmouth Publishing Company Limited.

Table 9.1 Crown copyright is reproduced with the permission of the Controller of HMSO; Fig.9.1-3 Interpol; 9.4a-c WHO; 9.5-9.7 Interpol; 9.8,9.9 Academy of Criminal Justice Sciences, Northern Kentucky University; Tables 9.2-9.4 Kluwer Law & Taxation Publishers; Fig.9.10-9.12 Interpol.

Fig.10.1 Routledge; 10.2 Copyright by Alcohol Research Documentation Inc, Rutgers Center of Alcohol Studies, Piscataway, NJ 08855; 10.3,10.4 WHO; 10.5 National Institute for Drug Abuse; 10.6 CAN; 10.7,10.8 Institute for the Study of Drug Dependence; 10.9 Produktschaap voor Gedistilleerde Dranken; 10.10 Dr Karl-Heinz Reuband; 10.11 Bundeskriminalamt Wiesbaden RG12; 10.12 Society for the Study of Addiction to Alcohol and Other Drugs. Publisher: Carfax Publishing Co, PO Box 25, Abingdon, Oxon; 10.13 Plenum Publishing Corporation; 10.14 American Sociological Association, and authors.

Fig.11.1,11.2 Copyright 1989/92 American Medical Association; 11.3 Elsevier Science; 11.4 The Society for Research in Child Development Inc.

Fig.12.1 Copyright 1991 The American Psychiatric Association: reprinted by permission; 12.2 Copyright 1990 Munksgaard International Publishers Ltd Copenhagen Denmark; 12.3 Plenum Publishing Corporation.

Table 13.1 Copyright 1968 Macmillan Magazines Limited; Table 13.2 WHO; Fig.13.1-13.3 WHO; 13.4,13.5 Cambridge University Press; Table 13.3 University of Chicago Press; Leuven University Press; WHO; Fig.13.6 University of Chicago Press; Leuven University Press; WHO; 13.7 WHO; 13.8 Copyright 1986 American Medical Association; 13.9 Copyright 1987 Munksgaard International Publishers Ltd Copenhagen Denmark; 13.10 WHO; 13.11,13.13 American Psychiatric Press; 13.14 British Medical

Association; 13.15 Royal College of Psychiatrists; 13.16,13.17 WHO; Table 13.4 British Medical Association; Fig.13.18 British Medical Association.

EUROSTAT (Office for Official Publications of the European Communities): 5.15, 5.17; 6.19-6.23, 6.44, 6.45, 6.47, 6.48; 9.10.

OECD: 6.1, 6.2, 6.12-6.17, 6.18a, 6.22, 6.24-6.27, 6.32, 6.36-6.41, 6.43; 9.11, 9.12.

PART I

Objectives and Methods

1

Introduction

DAVID J. SMITH and MICHAEL RUTTER

The purposes of this study are to provide a detailed review of the scientific evidence on the question of whether psychosocial disorders in young people have become more, or less, frequent over the last 50 years; to determine how causal explanations for any changes found may be tested; to elaborate possible causal explanations and review them in the light of the evidence currently available; and to establish priorities for future research.

THE TARGET DISORDERS

The psychosocial disorders covered by the inquiry are those that tend to rise or peak in frequency during the teenage years; namely crime, suicide and suicidal behaviour, depression, eating disorders (anorexia nervosa and bulimia), and abuse of alcohol and psychoactive drugs. These disorders are ones that are common but involve a serious malfunctioning of individuals in their social setting. The study is therefore concerned both with individual factors (including the process of individual development) and with social structures and conditions. We have not studied those less common conditions that also increase in frequency during adolescence, but which seem to represent qualitatively distinct disorders apparently less open to broader social influences. Thus, schizophrenia was excluded from the study.

The decision to make disorders the focus of the study, rather than well-being, or the process of normal development, was taken after careful thought. A crucial advantage of focusing on disorders is that these can be defined – even though definitional problems remain substantial – whereas well-being and happiness are extremely vague concepts, open to marked attitudinal biases. There is a large tradition of research on the health of communities and nations that is based on analysis of mortality statistics. Although this approach has its limitations (rate of mortality does not measure quality of life) it has nevertheless proved very fruitful. In a somewhat similar fashion, study of trends and patterns in psychosocial disorders is a way into understanding the causes of social and psychological health.

It can be argued that some, at least, of the behaviours called psychosocial disorders may be functional for the individual or group. For example, it may be that in some areas organized crime provides the best available opportunity for some young people to earn a living and establish a stable pattern of relationships. Nevertheless, this kind of example is highly exceptional, and there is ample evidence that crime is indeed both an individual and a social failure. Similarly, depression, anorexia, bulimia, suicide, suicidal behaviours, and abuse of psychoactive drugs, are rightly called disorders.

It is not necessarily the case that these various psychosocial disorders are all closely linked with one another. It cannot, of course, be assumed that the time trends or causal mechanisms will be the same or even similar. At the same time, there are well-known links between several of the disorders: for example, between use of alcohol or drugs and crime, between depression and suicide, and between depression and eating disorders. There is much to be gained, therefore, by providing an integrated treatment of trends and causal explanations.

AGE GROUPS COVERED

As a rough guide, 'young people' are taken to be those aged 12 to 26. While the focus is on that age group, some of the available data are not age-specific. In any case, each disorder has to be viewed in the context of development throughout the life span.

FOCUS ON TIME TRENDS

From the outset, it was decided to make trends over historic time the focus of the inquiry. This contrasts with the main research tradition in most of these fields, which has concentrated on individual differences and developmental pathways. Statistics on economic conditions have been kept in industrialized countries for many years, as an offshoot of government and regulatory bodies. Since the Second World War, considerable efforts, backed by substantial funding, have been devoted (for example, by the Organization for Economic

Cooperation and Development) to the standardization of economic measures (for example, of unemployment, Gross Domestic Product, and growth) and the production of reliable cross-national statistics. By comparison, little attention has been given to cross-national data on social and psychosocial problems. Partly as a consequence, the potential of the investigation of time trends as a method of research has hardly begun to be exploited by behavioural scientists. The present study was based on the judgement that this avenue will prove to be rewarding.

Chapter 2 argues that causal explanations can be formulated to account for secular trends in the aggregate level of crime or suicide, and can be tested through the application of well-established scientific principles. Of course, it is necessary also to make use of findings on individual differences and developmental processes, although, as argued in Chapter 2, explanations of individual differences may not generalize to the aggregate level: for example, individual differences in height are largely determined by genetic inheritance, whereas the secular trend of increase in average height is probably a result of improved diet. In spite of this caveat, it is often necessary to understand individual developmental processes in order to specify the causal mechanisms that account for change in the frequency of disorders in the community at large.

THE SOCIAL AND ECONOMIC CHANGES REVIEWED

The psychosocial disorders are defined in a fairly restrictive way. By contrast, a wide range of social and economic changes will be considered as possible explanations of trends in the disorders. Among the changes reviewed are:

- the changing pattern of adolescence;
- the increase in life expectancy;
- the long-term reduction in the proportion of young people within the population;
- the postwar baby boom;
- economic growth and improvement in the standard of living throughout the twentieth century, but particularly between 1950 and 1973;
- the substantial improvements in health, housing, and other living conditions;
- the increase in leisure;
- fluctuations in the level of unemployment;
- the increasing instability of family units;
- changes in family structure and functioning;

- the increase in female employment, in particular employment of mothers with young children;
- the growth of the mass media;
- fluctuations in international migration;
- complex changes in moral concepts and values.

This study has compiled a large body of data on cross-national time trends in these social and economic conditions, and summarizes the main conclusions that can be drawn from the research evidence on the causes and significance of such changes. It makes a preliminary assessment of the relationships between wider social and economic changes and trends in the psychosocial disorders. This is enough to indicate that certain hypotheses can probably be ruled out, whereas others are worth investigating more fully. The case for further investigation will be particularly strong where a causal mechanism linking the psychosocial disorder with the social condition can be specified, and where the mechanism is well-understood, and its existence well-established by a considerable body of research.

STRUCTURE OF THE REPORT

The report is divided into four Parts. This first Part sets out the objectives and scope of the study, and discusses the scientific methods that can be applied to the problems in question. Chapter 2, on *Causal concepts and their testing*, is particularly important in establishing the framework of analysis that is to be used in this field.

The chapters in Part II (on changing conditions and individual development) are more diverse, but similarly adopt a critical, analytic, and empiricist schema. Chapter 4 provides a summary of findings on adolescent development, a thread that runs through each of the other chapters. Chapter 5, on the family, provides a detailed summary of cross-national trends in family structures, but also an analysis of the likely significance of these changes for child and adolescent development, and their probable influence on the target disorders. Chapter 6, on living conditions, presents a wide variety of data, much of it in chart form, about change in the twentieth century: the main headings are population and demography (including migration), mortality and life expectancy, the changing economy, changes in housing, social welfare, leisure, and the communications media, and changes in the level of inequality, as indexed for example by the level of unemployment and the proportion of people in poverty.

Chapter 7 provides a rigorous analysis of the evidence for a link between exposure to television and psychosocial disorders, particularly violence. Chapter 8 gives a detailed account of cross-national data on changes in values and moral perceptions, and considers how these complex shifts may be related to certain psychosocial disorders, especially crime.

The third Part comprises five chapters on each of the target psychosocial disorders.

Each of these considers the conceptual problems involved in defining the disorder, and the practical problems of measuring it. It is important to consider, in particular, whether it constitutes a single disorder, or a number of related but heterogeneous disorders; whether there is a sharp discontinuity between normality and the disorder; and whether the disorder overlaps with others.

Each considers trends over time, as far as possible between 1920 and 1990, although a more detailed study of trends is generally possible only for the more recent period. Analysis of trends is based on multiple sources of data across as many nations as possible, with the emphasis on Europe. These analyses show whether trends among young people followed those for the general population, and where possible, separate consideration is given to other sub-groups (for example, males and females). Each chapter discusses the meaning of time trends, in particular whether they reflected change among similar populations, or change in the composition of populations.

These chapters also consider the variation in each psychosocial disorder over the life span, and evaluate possible causal mechanisms underlying such variation. Finally, they review possible causal explanations of change over time in the frequency of the disorders in the light of the available evidence. They evaluate competing hypotheses, rather than putting forward a single favoured theory, and these evaluations make use of empirical findings from multiple sources of data on time trends within nations, differences between nations, and change over time within individuals in relation to specified risk factors.

The fourth Part presents the Study Group's conclusions, first on time trends in psychosocial disorders in young people (Chapter 14) then on possible causal explanations of these trends (Chapter 15).

Full references to the source material are provided throughout the volume. Because the study covers so many diverse fields, it would not be helpful to consolidate the references, which are instead listed at the end of individual chapters.

THE CONCLUSIONS

As already emphasized, the conclusions set out in Chapters 14 and 15 are those of the Study Group as a whole. These chapters constitute a summary and analytical review of the contents of the entire volume. As well as distilling the main findings, they provide pointers to the more detailed information and analysis in the other chapters.

2

Causal Concepts and their Testing

MICHAEL RUTTER

The testing of causal hypotheses is fundamental to the task given to this Study Group. If we are to seek an answer to the question of whether changes in social circumstances in Europe have caused an increase, or change of pattern in, psychosocial disorders in young people, we must have a means of moving from statistical associations to causal explanations. Of course, this need is one that pervades the whole of science. During their undergraduate and postgraduate training, it is drummed into students that correlations do not prove causation and that causal hypotheses can be tested only through carefully controlled contrived experiments in the research laboratory. The experimental method may be expressed simply as the operation of 'waggling' one variable in order to determine if it causes some other variable to 'move', and doing so in such a way as to find out if this 'movement' is brought about systematically and regularly in varying circumstances. Without a doubt, this tactic has proved an extremely powerful one for the testing of causal hypotheses and it constitutes the basis of science. Nevertheless, it has not been a straightforward matter to apply this approach in the field of social and behavioural sciences.

Because very few psychosocial features can be subjected to experiments in the laboratory (either because it is not feasible to manipulate them experimentally and/or because it would be unethical to do so), researchers sometimes slide into the easy, comforting, assumption that causal hypotheses cannot be tested in the social sciences. Clearly, that is an unacceptable position and an unnecessary counsel of despair because methods for testing causal hypotheses are available in the social sciences. Indeed, it is *mandatory* that we seek to test causal postulates in a rigorous manner (Rutter, 1981 & in press). Unless we can use our data to bring about an understanding of causal mechanisms and processes, we have achieved very little and, certainly, we are in no position to recommend interventions of any kind. The solution lies in the search for, and use of, so-called 'experiments of nature' (Rutter, 1981).

The principle is quite straightforward, although the identification of the quasi-experimental conditions that are needed for this purpose is often very difficult. The basic ground rules, or guidelines, for establishing cause and effect relationships were clearly expressed by Bradford Hill (1977). His focus was primarily on biological processes in relation to medical conditions, but with slight modification, they are readily extended to social sciences.

TESTING CAUSE AND EFFECT RELATIONSHIPS

The principles to be applied to the testing of causal hypotheses are most easily outlined in relation to causes as they apply at an individual level. Nevertheless, as we shall see, this is not the only way in which causes should be conceptualized, and some adaptation is needed when applying the principles to the more complex, and somewhat different, causal question of whether widespread social changes in society have caused differences in levels of some kinds of psychosocial problem behaviour.

There are two main problems in the inference of causation from correlation. First, whenever a statistical association is found between a risk factor A and an outcome B, it is always necessary to exclude the possibility that the link is due to the operation of some third variable C that is associated with both A and B (Rutter, 1988). Second, with cross-sectional studies, there is the additional need to determine whether B led to A, rather than the other way round. The laboratory experiment deals with the first issue by systematically altering the antecedent conditions in order to determine if it is indeed A, and only A, that leads to the outcome in question. In order to be sure that is the case, it is necessary to check whether this effect still holds across a wide range of conditions. It is also necessary to contrast the effects of A against an extensive range of alternative possibilities that the effects stem from D, E, F, etc.

The standard solution to these problems with cross-sectional survey data is to undertake some form of statistical analysis to partial out, or otherwise control for, the effects of possible confounding variables. If the association between the risk factor A and the outcome B remains significant after the appropriate statistical controls have been introduced, a possible causal association is inferred. While this is a reasonable initial approach, it suffers from two major limitations: first, the impossibility of ever being entirely sure that all relevant confounding variables have been included and adequately measured; and second, the difficulty of undertaking any really effective statistical adjustment when the important confounding variables distribute very differently between the groups to be compared. It is in these circumstances that the recourse to 'natural experiments' becomes important. The basis of experiments of nature lies in finding broadly comparable groups of individuals, one of which has been exposed to the hypothesized risk variable and one of which has not. This comparison may either involve parallel groups who have undergone different experiences of the same type or, alternatively, the same group followed over a period of time during which there was a period of non-exposure to the risk variable followed by one of exposure to it. Many examples of this kind exist in the literature. For example, Hodges and Tizard (1989a&b) undertook a follow-up of children from a residential nursery comparing those who were adopted into homes of generally somewhat above average qualities as against those restored to their biological parents, most of whom provided disadvantaged rearing experiences. Maughan et al. (1990) studied the effects on pupil progress of the appointment of a new school principal in schools that were in serious trouble prior to that appointment. West (1982) studied the effects on young people's delinquent behaviour of a move from Inner London to other parts of the country. Quinton and Rutter (1988) examined the effects on adult social functioning, in a group of young people who spent most of their upbringing in group foster homes, the quality of their marriage and the characteristics of their spouse.

Of course, with all of these examples, the study of changes in behaviour over time associated with the experience hypothesized to cause change (such as a geographical move or a harmonious marriage to a nondeviant spouse) is reliant on adequate measurement of the behaviour in question. Thus, it is necessary to consider the possibility that the measure of behaviour before the experience did not provide an adequate coverage of the relevant individual characteristics. The point may be illustrated by taking the apparent beneficial effect of marital support in reducing criminal and other antisocial behaviour (Pickles & Rutter, 1991; Laub & Sampson, 1993; Sampson & Laub, 1993). It is necessary to ask whether the apparent change is an artefact of persistent unobserved heterogeneity among individuals in antisocial propensity (Nagin & Paternoster, 1991). In other words, the measure of this propensity may have failed to cover key elements of crime-proneness. So-called 'random-effects' models provide a means of examining this possibility through determining whether the error-terms (i.e. the unexplained measures of variance) are strongly correlated over time. Insofar as they are not, it is unlikely that the change in behaviour is an artefact of unmeasured aspects of the antisocial tendency. In the event, the results of such analyses have been able to confirm the reality of the beneficial effects of marital support (and also job stability) on antisocial behaviour.

Usually, the causal hypothesis regarding risk factor A can be contrasted, and tested against, some alternative causal mechanism. When that is the case, the test of non-replication becomes an important one (Rutter, 1974). The notion is that if there are two alternative risk mechanisms, indexed by risk factors X and Y that are strongly intercorrelated, the prediction may be made that if you can find circumstances in which Y is present, but not X, there should be no effect on the outcome variable if X truly constitutes the causal risk influence. Thus, Rutter (1971) postulated that, if family discord rather than parent-child separation constituted the risk mechanism, separation experiences in harmonious circumstances should not be associated with psychiatric disorder. Empirical findings confirmed that was the case. Similarly, Harris et al. (1986) contrasted the hypothesis that parental loss constituted a psychiatric risk versus the alternative that poor parental care (which often followed loss) constituted the risk mechanism. Their findings indicated that parental loss had no effect on psychiatric risk in the absence of poor parental care. Conversely, however, poor parental care was associated with an increased risk even when it arose for reasons other than parental loss. In other words, it is important to use experiments of nature to test predictions of when effects should *not* be found, as well as ones where effects are to be expected if the causal hypothesis is valid.

With cross-sectional data, even when third variable effects can be ruled out, there is necessary ambiguity on the direction of the causal influence. Prospective longitudinal data are valuable because the time relationship between variables will usually enable the direction of effects to be sorted out. In addition, longitudinal studies carry with them the decided advantage that the confounding variables can be measured nearest to the point of operation of the risk factor, rather than having to extrapolate backwards from data collected at the time of measurement of the outcome. This asset was very important, for example, in testing the hypothesis that school qualities made a causal impact on pupils' educational progress (Rutter et al., 1979). However, longitudinal data have an even more important characteristic; the fact that they provide the opportunity of examining intra-individual changes over time (Farrington, 1988). For obvious reasons, the causal inference is possible on a much stronger basis when it is based on intra-individual change, rather than inter-individual differences. Thus, for example, the hypothesis that unemployment caused an increase in psychological distress could be inferred only rather weakly on the basis of differences in distress levels between people who did and did not have paid employment. The causal inference was much stronger when longitudinal data demonstrated that individuals showed an *increase* in psychological distress when they lost their jobs and that unemployed individuals showed a *reduction* in such distress when they succeeded in obtaining work (see, for example, Patton & Noller, 1984; Kessler et al., 1987; Banks & Ullah, 1988). Similarly, the cross-sectional data in the epidemiological study by Richman et al. (1982) indicating that marital discord and maternal depression were associated with psychiatric disorder in 3-year-old children suggested a possible causal effect. However, evidence from their longitudinal study in which the children were followed to age 8 years, with the finding that children without disorder at age 3 were more likely to develop psychiatric disorder by age 8 if these risk variables were present, provided a much stronger pointer to a causal mechanism.

A caveat is necessary, however, with regard to this use of longitudinal data if the sample has already had prolonged exposure to the risk variable at the first point of data collection. In these circumstances, it may be that those without disorder are systematically different because, for some reason, they have an enhanced resistance to the risk factor. When that is the case, longitudinal relationships are likely to be weaker than cross-sectional ones. Thus, for example, a longitudinal study of children chronically exposed to a parent with active tuberculosis might well show little effect because those children who had not already developed tuberculosis at the beginning of the study (after, say, five years' exposure) may well not have done so because they were immune to the pathogenic organism and, hence, their risk of developing tuberculosis over the next five years would be low. It is important to bear in mind this inherent limitation when dealing with the risks associated with chronic adversities. As the unemployment example illustrated, a reversal test is a great help when examining causal hypotheses. That is, unless exposure to the risk factor brings about a permanent and irreversible change, there should be a reduction in the risk outcome when the risk factor is removed as well as increase in the risk outcome following exposure to the risk variable.

The power of longitudinal data to test competing hypotheses on risk mechanisms is an important one. For example, the evidence that, to an important extent, the increase in psychosocial disorder in children associated with divorce was already present before divorce occurred (Block et al., 1986; Cherlin et al., 1991) was important in indicating that much of the risk was likely to stem from the parental discord and conflict associated with divorce rather than from the breakup of the parental marriage as such. The finding that, following divorce, the risks to young people are a function of the extent to which they are drawn into parental conflict also supports this causal inference (Buchanan et al., 1991). Similarly, the demonstration from longitudinal data that the increase in emotional/behavioural disturbance following children's admission into group foster care was often present *before* admission (St. Clair & Osborne, 1987) indicated that it was likely that the risk lay in the family disturbances associated with the admission into care rather than the care experience *per se*.

Naturally occurring experiments in which changes over time affect some individuals exposed to risk factors and not others may also help in ruling out various causal hypotheses. For example, it has long been clear that divorce leads to a marked reduction in living standards for most women and it was often supposed that this played an important role in the psychological risks for the children. However, the remarriage of mothers usually results in a rapid and marked improvement in financial circumstances. The finding that this has no consistent effect on psychological disturbance in the children, either for the better or the worse, makes it unlikely that impoverished financial circumstances constitute the key risk variable for children in relation to divorce (Hetherington, 1989; Hetherington & Clingempeel, 1992).

Bradford Hill (1977) also laid emphasis on the importance of specifying a possible mediating mechanism and on the biological plausibility that this mechanism might actually be operative. In the arena of psychosocial risk factors, application of the 'biological plausibility' test may not always be easy. There are certainly examples when animal studies allowing tighter experimental control indicate the plausibility of a true causal effect. For example, that is evident in the case of social isolation and stressful separation (Suomi, 1991). However, as the examples already given indicate, additional leverage on the causal hypothesis is always provided by the attempt to move from risk indicators to possible risk mechanisms. Bradford Hill (1977) went on to point out that causal inferences were always strengthened when it was possible to show consistent dose-response relationships. That is to say, if there is a true causal risk effect, it should ordinarily follow that the risk increases in systematic fashion in direct relationship to the degree of exposure to the risk factor. When that is not the case, there must be some doubt on the causal inference. Of course, threshold effects may be operative but they need to be demonstrated and not assumed.

A further requirement in testing causal hypotheses is the crucial scientific requirement of multiple replications. It is a basic requirement in science that no finding, however striking, can be accepted until it is replicated in a different sample by an independent set of investigators. Statistical significance, however great, is no substitute. Statistics are no more than the poor man's guide when having to interpret the results of just one study (Rutter, 1988). Obviously, we are all poor men in that respect and it is necessary that we make appropriate use of statistical procedures, but, equally, it is essential that we are aware of the inevitable limitations in the inferences that can be drawn from any single study, however good, when considered in isolation. An extension of this principle is that the testing needs to be done in such a way as to determine whether the same effect can be found in samples that *differ* markedly in other characteristics. This is an important specification because it is only the repeated replication in varied circumstances that provides convincing evidence that the association is not an artefact of some confounding variable.

Bradford Hill (1977) also added the further criterion that causal inferences are strengthened when it can be shown that the effects are specific, rather than undifferentiated and general. The point is certainly a reasonable one. If a risk variable seems to increase the likelihood of all the ills of modern mankind, this must engender a degree of scepticism about the effects being truly causal. Nevertheless, this is not an easy criterion to apply. In the first place, there are many examples in medicine in which a single factor has quite widespread risk effects that are known to be truly causal. For example, cigarette smoking carries with it a substantially increased risk of lung cancer, coronary artery disease, and of osteoporosis, to mention but three out of a much longer list of consequences. Of course, in this instance, the risks do not derive from the same biological mechanism. Thus, some of the effects stem from carcinogenic elements in the tar products, some from nicotine effects on the blood vessels, and some from carbon monoxide produced by smoking. To that extent, the effects are specific, in spite of the fact that they are multiple. However, this only becomes apparent once one knows what the causal mechanisms are. In the second place, some risk factors operate through mechanisms that tend to have quite widespread consequences. For example, that is likely to be so with risk factors that operate through a negative impact on bodily defences or coping mechanisms. Thus, both severe malnutrition and severe stress involve a combination of specific and more general sequelae. Nevertheless, as already noted, it is always desirable to identify a particular risk mechanism and test for its operation. Usually, this will involve at least a degree of specificity.

Finally, Bradford Hill (1977) argued that for the causal inference to be strong, the association between the risk variable and the problem outcome should also be strong. This is a difficult criterion to apply at a community-wide level when dealing with outcomes that are multifactorially determined and in which the overall effect of each causal factor on total population variance is quite small. Thus, numerous influences, biological and psychosocial, have an effect on cognitive performance and educational attainment but, taken individually, their effect is quite small on the population as a whole. Thus, for example, school effects have sometimes been dismissed on the grounds that they account for only a trivial few per cent of the overall population variance in pupils' scholastic attainments. However, this is not the most appropriate way of considering strength of effects. Strength of effects at the population level is hugely influenced by the number of individuals on whom the risk factor could operate. For example, Down's syndrome accounts for a mere 0.006 per cent of population variance in IQ (Broman et al., 1975). On the other hand, there is a 60 point IQ difference between individuals with and without Down's syndrome, so that its effect on those who happen to have this risk factor is enormous. In parallel, although less dramatic, fashion, it is the case that the overall effect of schooling on final levels of scholastic attainment is quite small in population variance terms, although the consequences of attending a really effective school as against a poor one are very considerable at an individual level in terms of scholastic progress over the years of schooling (Mortimore et al., 1988; Smith & Tomlinson, 1989).

The reason for the difference between these two ways of assessing the strength of effect are several-fold. First, many schools differ little in their qualities, and the effects are only likely to be evident when there is a substantial difference between schools in their qualities as educational institutions. Secondly, for obvious reasons, schools cannot influence children's cognitive development in the years before they start to attend school. For this reason, a substantial proportion of the overall population variance is accounted for by family influences (both genetic and environmental) before school attendance begins. In the Mortimore et al. (1988) study the effects of schools on educational progress were actually substantially greater than the effects of family during the years of schooling, although the overall effects of family were greater because of the importance and strength of effects that were already operative before school attendance began.

The implication of these considerations is that the criterion of a strong effect needs to be considered strictly in relation to circumstances where the risk variable is present in strong degree and has the opportunity of having a maximal effect. If, in these circumstances, there is still only a very weak effect, the causal inference is a much more uncertain one. Of course, the fact that an effect is weak in the context of multifactorial determination does not necessarily mean that there is no true causal impact. Nevertheless, it is usually the case that influences that are truly causal, but have little effect on overall population variance, can be shown to have a substantial effect in circumstances where they are likely to be strongly operative. For example, the effects of variations in exposure to lead in the environment make very little difference to the overall population variance in cognitive performance (Mahaffey, 1985). However, there is reason to suppose that they do have a truly causal effect, albeit one of small degree, because both in human and animal studies, there is a substantial effect of markedly raised lead levels and no evidence of a definite threshold below which no effects are apparent. Radiation risks constitute another example in which a substantial amount of the evidence derives from extrapolation downwards using data from individuals subjected to very high exposure. Accordingly, in determining whether the criterion of strength of effect is met, investigators must search out circumstances where this can be put to the proper test as a result of unusually high exposure to the risk variable, rather than relying on overall estimates of effects on population variance.

SECULAR TRENDS

Our main focus in the chapters that follow will be on the possibility that changes in living circumstances that have taken place in society over recent years have had an effect in increasing the level of psychosocial disorders in young people. The principles to be applied in the testing of causal hypotheses, as outlined above, apply in much the same way to this somewhat different sort of causal hypothesis. In this instance, the cause is hypothesized to operate in creating an overall increase in level of risk, rather than in determining whether this individual, rather than some other one, is affected by the psychosocial problem in question. This difference does have certain implications, however, for research strategies. The need for 'natural experiments' and for replication in different circumstances can be met in two main ways. First, comparisons between nations, or between subgroups within nations, provide the experiment. The need is to find nations that are broadly comparable in other respects but which differ in terms of the social change that is hypothesized to be having the effect on psychosocial disorders. Thus, for example, contrasts may be made between those nations that show rising divorce rates and those that do not; between those with and those without high levels of unemployment in young people; or between those experiencing high levels of civil unrest and those not doing so. If the social change is hypothesized as having a causal influence on psychosocial problems within the nation experiencing that social change, it should follow that the increase in psychosocial problems should *not* be found in nations without the specified social change. Therein lies the natural experiment.

The second source of leverage is provided by the fact that social changes frequently work in both directions if sufficiently long time periods are examined. Thus, aggregate time series methods may test whether the timing of social or economic changes is linked with the timing of changes in delinquency rates or suicide rates or some other behavioural indicator (see Dooley & Catalano, 1980). Such studies have tended to show parallels between rises and falls in unemployment and rises and falls in suicide rates, suggesting a causal connection. However, such analyses involve many methodological problems, not the least of which is the uncertainty of the length of time-lag to use. Thus, for example, should one expect the effect of rising unemployment to be immediate, one year delayed, or five years delayed (see Rutter & Giller, 1983)? These two approaches may, of course, be combined by comparing the *timing* of a rise in psychosocial disorders in two nations, both of which have experienced a change in the hypothesized causal social change but in which the latter change occurred much later in the one country than in the other.

The secular trend equivalent of the test of intra-individual change is the test of whether the effect on psychosocial disorders is seen in the group most affected by social change. Thus, Kreitman (1988) sought to determine whether, during a time of rising unemployment, the increase in attempted suicides was particularly evident in those who were themselves unemployed. It is all too obvious that the testing of causal hypotheses in relation to secular changes in risk factors is no easy matter, but nevertheless it remains important to put causal hypotheses to testing that is as rigorous as can be managed.

The criterion of a plausible mechanism is most easily met by turning to the evidence on intra-individual change. That is to say, associations between social change and rises in problem behaviour are more likely to be causal if it has already been shown that the two are causally connected at an individual level. Accordingly, in the chapters that follow, we will be seeking to examine social change risk factors with respect to the evidence on their impact at an individual level. However, once again, a caveat is necessary. That is, although it is often the case that the mechanisms involved in inter-individual differences are similar to those involved in changes in levels of problem behaviour over time, there is no necessity that they be the same, or indeed even overlap. Thus, they will be different when the social change variables are of a kind that tends to operate without much individual variation across the population as a whole. For example, the factors involved in rises and falls in the overall unemployment rate have very little to do with the factors concerned with individual variations in unemployment (see Rutter & Madge, 1976). Similarly, the availability of alcohol is of little importance in determining whether one person, rather than another, becomes alcoholic. On the other hand, at a community-wide level, the availability of alcohol (as influenced by price and licensing control) has been found to make a difference to overall levels of alcohol consumption and thereby, indirectly, to rates of alcoholism (Royal College of Psychiatrists, 1979). Similar associations have been seen with respect to access to drugs (Rutter, 1979/80). In each of these cases, of course, there is a plausible mechanism, even though it is not one that is of much importance at an individual level.

The 'Ecological Fallacy'

The study of secular trends necessarily involves the use of aggregated data in which group trends or correlations are used to infer associations, and hence by extension mechanisms, that apply at the individual level. In a seminal paper, Robinson (1950) pointed out that there was no necessary connection between ecological (group) correlations and individual correlations, and he gave examples in which they actually had different signs. In other words, it was quite possible to have a strongly positive correlation at the group level but a negative one at the individual level. The attempt to infer individual associations from group data came to be known as the 'ecological fallacy', and many investigators have assumed that ecological correlations are therefore useless for the study of causal mechanisms as they apply to individuals. However, as Hanushek et al. (1974) showed, this assumption is misleadingly negative. Robinson was indeed correct in his demonstration that, within the same dataset, group and individual correlations could differ markedly. However, an appreciation of what these differences mean can often be obtained through the appropriate sample stratification and statistical modelling of the effects. That need, of course, applies also to individual data. Unquestionably, the availability of individual correlations is a considerable asset, and there are special advantages in the combination of group and individual findings but, if appropriately analysed, group data can be highly informative. In that connection, two main points need to be made.

First, the disparity between group and individual correlations can arise because different people are involved in the two effects. For example, there could be a group correlation between say, the percentage of recent immigrants living in an area and the juvenile delinquency rate in that area, in spite of most (even all) recent immigrants being adult and therefore not able to contribute to the juvenile delinquency figures. Such a group correlation could be a consequence, for example, of a tendency for recent immigrants to have to live in socially disorganized or run-down areas that predispose to crime or attract delinquency-prone individuals for other reasons. Another way of expressing the same basic issue is to note that, inevitably, group correlations will be influenced by variations in the composition of subgroups within the total group, and by the uniformity (or lack of it) in the patterns of association within those subgroups. The solution to this problem requires first, careful thought on the range of possible alternative mechanisms that could underlie the pattern of findings that is obtained; second, the availability of an appropriate set of measures that might serve to index those mechanisms; and third, the use of statistical techniques that are well designed to capitalize on such datasets. So far as the last is concerned, the development of multilevel models for variance components analysis has been very helpful (Aitkin & Longford, 1986; Goldstein, 1987). In essence, these simply provide procedures for dealing with the 'nesting' of subgroups within larger groups. For example, this approach is needed in studies of the effects of schools on pupils' scholastic progress because the distribution of pupils (according to ability and family background among other factors) varies between schools and may vary also between classes within schools (see Smith & Tomlinson, 1989).

The second point is that the mechanisms need not be the same at group and individual levels. As Bronfenbrenner (1979) pointed out, influences need to be conceptualized in terms of both individuals and the nested set of ecosystems within which they develop and function (family, community, nation etc.) Thus, it is quite possible for the effects of living in an area that is characterized by a large proportion of old people, or foreign-born individuals, or single men, to be rather different from the personal effects of one's own age, ethnicity, gender or marital status. Furthermore, it is not rare for effects to differ in their impact according to social circumstances. The disentangling of the mechanisms underlying such multivariate influences involving interactions can be both complicated and difficult (see e.g. Rindfuss et al., 1984 for an attempt to do this with respect to secular trends in the age of women at the time they have their first child). However, the problems can be tackled through the appropriate hypothesis-driven analysis of different groups of different time periods in order to test competing explanations on the mechanisms that might be involved.

Age, Period and Cohort Effects

In any consideration of the question of whether or not there has been a recent increase in the rate of psychosocial disorders among young people, it is necessary to differentiate between age (or life span) effects and what have been termed 'period' and 'cohort' effects. The issue has been around in various forms for many years (see Ryder, 1965, and Glenn, 1977) but, for developmentalists, it was highlighted by papers by Schaie (1965) and Baltes (1968) that drew attention to the need for a combination of longitudinal and cross-sectional data if cognitive decline associated with biological ageing was to be differentiated from intergenerational differences in cognitive performance (stemming, perhaps, from marked disparities between generations in access to continuing education).

In brief, *age* effects may be defined as an increase (or decrease) in the risk for some specified disorder as a function of the age of the individual (Ryan et al., 1992). The implication is that, regardless of time-period or geography, there is a regular tendency for risk to vary with chronological age. Thus, the overall risk of death is relatively high in the neonatal period, is low during childhood and early adult life, and rises through old age.

A period effect comprises a variation in risk over time that tends to affect all individuals regardless of age. Thus, over the course of this century there has been a progressive reduction in risk of death, and a progressive increase in life expectancy, in all European countries (Townsend & Davidson, 1982).

A *cohort* effect concerns a variation in risk that applies to all individuals sharing a common experience. Typically, the term has been used to refer to birth cohorts of people born at the same time. Thus, the risk of death was increased (compared with both earlier and later time periods) for young adults who served in the armed forces during the Second World War; the effect was less marked for those above or below the age for military service. However, the cohort need not be defined in birth terms. Thus, there is a cohort effect in risk of death for everyone exposed to severe malnutrition or to the effects of a nuclear explosion (although the relative risks may vary with age among those subject to those hazards).

The need to distinguish between these rather different types of effect is real. Nevertheless, if the differentiation is to be successful, both conceptual and statistical difficulties need to be overcome. The first, and most basic, point is that all three effects concern proxy variables that are meaningless until there is specification of what they are supposed to represent (Mason & Fienberg,

1985). Thus, chronological age, in addition to the mere passage of time since birth, reflects various biological processes (such as those associated with puberty, the timing of which shows considerable individual variation – Rutter, 1979/80); psychological experiences (such as education or dating); and social features (such as having reached the legal age for drinking, or marriage, or criminal responsibility). Chronological age as such is an ambiguous variable because it indexes so many different things (Rutter, 1989a). It serves as a useful pointer to the fact that some feature that is associated with age is having an effect but, in itself, it does not indicate what that feature may be. Of course, non-experimental data may be used to test competing hypotheses on the mechanisms associated with age-indexed effects, once the alternatives have been identified. For example, Cahan and Cohen (1989) contrasted the effects of chronological age and duration of schooling on scholastic attainment by taking advantage of the fact that in many countries children tend to start their schooling at a fixed time of year. As a consequence, there is a twelve-month age range within any one school year or class (who all have the same amount of schooling), and a twelve-month difference in the average age of school classes (so that consecutive school years differ by one year in their duration of education, regardless of the age of the children in the classes). It is easy to see that by comparing within- and between-year variations, the effects of age and schooling can be differentiated; on the whole the latter seemed more influential. Similarly, Kreitman (1988) started with the general finding that suicide rates rose markedly and progressively with increasing age, and with the finding that suicide was also associated with lack of a marriage partner. A more detailed examination showed that, at least after early adult life, the age effect virtually disappeared once marital status had been taken into account. What had, at first, appeared as an effect of age *per se*, was actually a reflection of the fact that older people were more likely to be divorced or widowed.

Cohort effects are subject to precisely the same problem (Rosow, 1978; Ryder, 1965; Elder, 1985; Mason & Feinberg, 1985). For the most part, they have been studied through analyses seeking to determine whether some effect applied specifically to individuals born in the same year. However, as already noted, the concept concerns an effect that is specific to individuals sharing a common experience. Accordingly, it has no meaning until that experience has been specified. Moreover, once it has been specified, the cohort will need to be defined in terms that go beyond mere date of birth. For example, studies have sought to relate schizophrenia to the mothers' experience of influenza while pregnant (Mednick et al., 1988); or cognitive performance to the mothers' experience of famine during gestation (Stein et al., 1972); or delinquency to parental deprivation experienced in the Second World War (Wilkins, 1960; Farrington, 1990); or psychosocial outcomes to the experience of the great economic depression of the interwar years (Elder, 1974) or to army service (Elder, 1986).

However, there is one hypothesized type of birth cohort effect that is not defined by an entirely external independent variable. Easterlin (1980) suggested that young people who are part of an unusually large birth cohort (such as those born during the so-called 'baby boom' after the Second World War) will suffer from the increased competition (for further education, jobs etc.) that stems from being part of an unusually large generation. The various attempts to test this hypothesis have produced somewhat contradictory findings (see, for example, Menard & Elliott, 1990; Steffensmeier et al., 1987, 1992). However, at least some of the disparities appear to be a consequence of differences in methods of data analysis (with effects greater, although still small, when tested directly rather than when examined as part of an overall cohort effect). So far, the tests of the Easterlin hypothesis have been restricted to datasets from just one country. Clearly, the separation of this postulated effect from other influences also impinging on the same cohort will be easier if there are data on birth cohorts from different countries over periods of time in which births have gone both up and down. Thus, in principle, the need is exactly the same as with cohort effects reflecting other types of experiences; namely, to compare across birth cohorts according to their showing or not showing the hypothesized causal experience. Similarly, too, it is desirable to move beyond cohort size as a proxy variable for increased competition and measure this supposed mediating variable instead of just inferring it.

In exactly the same way, period effects have little meaning until the underlying mechanism can be identified. The main *raison d'être* of this Study Group's activities has been the use of inter-country and within-nation variations in the presence, or timing, of secular trends in psychosocial disorders in young people in order to examine possible mediating mechanisms.

The statistical problems derive from the inevitable confounds between age, period and birth cohort effects in any one dataset (Glenn, 1976, 1977; Hagenaars, 1990; Holford, 1983). Age and birth cohort effects are confounded in cross-sectional data for particular age groups; age and period effects in intra-cohort secular trend data; and period and birth cohort effects in trend data for each age level. Since Schaie's (1965) seminal article, it has been assumed by many investigators that the combination of cross-sectional and longitudinal data in a sequential design solve the problem. However, it is clear that the usual decision rules on how to use this combination to remove the confounds do not succeed in their aim (Adam, 1978). Moreover, the rules involve assumptions about linearity of effects and an absence of interactions and, if these assumptions are not met, the problems are further increased (Adam, 1978).

Of course, that is not to argue that hypothesis-led analyses may not do much to separate effects (see, for example, Cross-National Collaborative Group, 1992; Farrington, 1990; Wickramaratne et al., 1989; Lavori et al., 1987). However, as is clear from the conceptual considerations, the way forward has to lie in the application of statistical methods to datasets that include some measurement of the hypothesized mediating variables, together with some specification of the groups on which they are thought to operate. Of course a combination of cross-sectional and longitudinal data will be needed in order to make the necessary distinctions, but they are not sufficient in themselves.

A further constraint with respect to many of the psychosocial disorders considered in this volume is imposed by the lack of contemporaneous measurement across different time periods. That is so, for example, with respect to depression in young people (see Chapter 11). In these circumstances, there has to be recourse to cross-sectional surveys in which people are asked to recall their experience of different disorders over their entire life span. The American Epidemiological Catchment Area (ECA) study provides the best documented, and most extensive, study of this kind (Robins & Regier, 1991). Quite apart from the conceptual and statistical hazards involved in separating age, period and birth cohort effects, there is then the additional problem of taking into account possible biases in retrospective recall. Thus, for example, the apparent increase in depression over time in the ECA dataset could simply reflect a tendency for old people to forget that they were depressed when younger. There is no one solution to this problem but it may be tackled in several different ways. For example, if the secular trend applies to some disorders but not others, and if the disorders showing trends do not differ from those not doing so in their likelihood of being remembered, this argues against a memory artefact (Burke et al., 1991; Ryan et al., 1992).

Another approach is to restrict analyses to younger age-groups on the rationale that any forgetting bias is likely to apply most strongly to old people (Lavori et al., 1987; Ryan et al., 1992). This strategy also reduces the biases that could be introduced by the premature death of affected individuals in earlier birth cohorts. The possible bias introduced by variations over time in concepts of disorder may be tackled by focusing only on the most seriously handicapping disorders (Lavori et al., 1987). These, and other, methodological issues are discussed more fully in Chapter 11 in relation to depression, the disorder most studied in relation to the problem of assessing secular trends from retrospective data.

In summary, although the differentiation of age, period and birth cohort effects has been discussed in the literature mainly in relation to statistical approaches, it turns out that it is no more than a special case of the general issue of testing competing causal mechanisms. If there is anything that is distinctive about the issue, it is the fact that all these effects concern proxy variables, with the consequence that any such testing requires additional measures that reflect the hypothesized mechanism more directly. However, this problem and need are widespread in science. It will be appreciated that, depending on the hypothesized mechanism, it is quite likely that it will apply in varying degrees to age, period *and* cohort effects. When this is the case, it is particularly important not to use statistical techniques that rely on assumptions about linearity and an absence of interactions. Put the other way round, it also follows that once the mediating mechanism is specified, it becomes easier to hypothesize when each different sort of effect should be found if the hypothesis is correct.

CONCEPTS OF CAUSATION

In the discussion so far on the testing of causal hypotheses, we have considered the matter as if the key question could be reduced to a consideration of whether the association between risk factor A and outcome B represented a causal influence of the one on the other. However, the matter is not as simple as that both because many causal pathways involve multiple phases or multiple steps and because it is usual for causation to involve multiple factors that may interact in synergistic ways (Rutter, 1989a; Rutter & Pickles, 1991). In addition, it is important to recognize that it may be as crucial to delineate the pathways leading to exposure to the risk factor as the pathways involved in the causative processes from the risk factor to the psychosocial outcome (Laub & Sampson, 1993; Quinton et al., 1993; Rutter et al., in press; Sampson & Laub, 1993).

The multi-phase causal pathways are clearly evident in psychosocial disorders as diverse as delinquency, drug dependency, and attempted suicide. Thus, there are important individual differences in people's liability to engage in delinquent behaviour. However, most young people engage in at least minor delinquent acts at some time or other during childhood or adolescence (Rutter & Giller, 1983). A smaller proportion show a tendency to engage in repeated delinquent acts of a varied nature over a prolonged period of time. Accordingly, as well as factors involved in the initial initiation of delinquent activities, there is the need to consider factors involved in its persistence in the form of recidivist delinquency. However, whether or not an individual who is prone to delinquency actually commits delinquent acts is also much influenced by opportunity and circumstances (Clarke, 1985). Accordingly, causal factors need to be considered in relation to matters of opportunity, supervision, and deterrents.

Of those with persistent delinquent activities or conduct disturbance in childhood or adolescence, a substantial proportion, but not all, go on to exhibit pervasive and persistent social malfunction in adult life (Robins, 1966, 1978, 1986; Zoccolillo et al., 1992). The likelihood of persistence from childhood to adult life is much influenced by factors operating in childhood. For example, persistence into adult life is more likely in the case of conduct disorders of unusually early onset associated with hyperactivity, attentional problems and poor peer relationships (Farrington et al., 1990; Magnusson & Bergman, 1990). On the other hand, it is also influenced by factors operating in adult life. For example, a harmonious marriage to a non-deviant spouse makes an adverse adult outcome less likely (Quinton & Rutter, 1988; Sampson & Laub, 1993; Zoccolillo et al., 1992). Similarly, the pathways to drug dependency involve an availability and access to drugs, the initial taking of drugs on a sporadic basis for recreational or other purposes, the transition to taking such drugs regularly, becoming psychologically and/or physically dependent on them, and the development of adverse physical and psychological sequelae of drug abuse.

The factors involved in each of these steps is not necessarily the same. For example, Robins et al. (1977), in their study of drug abuse in Americans who served in the armed forces in Vietnam, showed that demographic variables had dramatically different and opposing effects at the beginning and end of the causal chain. Thus, older white men from rural areas were the *least* likely to use narcotics in Vietnam (an adjusted 33 per cent versus 70 per cent in young, inner city blacks), but they were *ten* times as likely to be addicted if they continued the use of narcotics on their return to the US (41 per cent versus 4 per cent). When all steps in this chain were put together into an overall multivariate analysis, demographic variables seemed to have little effect and the atypical users (older whites from outside the inner city) did not seem to be a group particularly at risk. On the other hand, they had an exceptionally high risk at a key point in the causal chain and Robins et al. argued that, for this reason, they might well constitute the most appropriate and hopeful group to target in prevention. In the same way, the pathways to attempted suicide involve predisposing factors in terms of both depression and conduct disorder; the tendency to think of a suicidal act as a mode of response to difficulties (which may be influenced by models in the media – Shaffer & Piacentini, 1994); immediate provoking stresses such as a personal humiliation or disciplinary crisis; the availability of means of attempting suicide; and the opportunity to act in a self-destructive fashion. Once again different causal factors may operate at different points in this causal chain.

Much research into possible causal mechanisms involved with risk of psychosocial disorders has been concerned with the examination of direct and immediate risk effects. Of course, it is important to consider these but it is equally important to recognize both that interactive effects and indirect mechanisms must also be taken into account. Moreover, it is necessary to recognize the possible operation of protective, as well as vulnerability, mechanisms. There are many examples in medicine and biology of vulnerability factors deriving from experiences in childhood that create an increased risk for illness in adult life (Bock & Whelan, 1991). Thus, for example, low birth weight constitutes a substantial risk factor for coronary artery disease in middle age. Similarly, early dietary influences may be involved in programming cholesterol metabolism and in influencing allergic propensities. In the same way, adverse psychosocial experiences in early life have been shown to create an increased risk for psychosocial disorders in adolescence and adult life. For example, poor parental care is associated with an increased predisposition to depressive disorders later (Brown et al., 1986). Sometimes, these early adversities have a direct effect in increasing the liability to later psychosocial disorders but sometimes their effects are indirect and dependent on a mechanism whereby there is an increased susceptibility to later stressful experiences (Rutter, 1991). In the absence of later stressors, the outcome may be good but when stressors are encountered adverse sequelae are more likely than is the case in individuals who have not experienced the earlier vulnerability factors.

This kind of synergistic or interactive or catalytic effect can work also in the opposite direction. That is, there are features that, although not directly beneficial in themselves, create an effect that is protective against stresses and adversities (Rutter, 1990). In the medical arena, this is most dramatically shown in the way in which sickle cell heterozygote status serves to protect individuals against malaria. It is not that having the sickle cell gene is in itself a good thing; indeed, it carries with it important disadvantages. Nevertheless, it is protective against malaria. In the psychosocial arena, adoption may be viewed as having some parallels (although it is very different in other respects). Thus, adoption is not in itself a positive influence. Indeed, it is likely that it carries a slightly increased risk of psychosocial disorders (Maughan & Pickles, 1990). Nevertheless, for children from a severely depriving and damaging family background, it may well be protective.

There are three further considerations that need to be borne in mind in relation to multifactorial, multi-stage pathways of causation. First, as implied in the vulnerability and protective mechanisms already discussed, synergistic effects often occur (Rutter & Pickles, 1991). It is well known that there is substantial individual variation in susceptibility to most risk factors and these must be taken into account in considering risk effects. However, it is not just a question of person-environment interactions of various kinds. It is also the case that psychosocial adversities tend to have a greater impact when they occur in the context of other stresses or adversities (Rutter, 1979/80; Kolvin et al., 1990). Indeed, single stresses or adversities that truly occur in isolation on the whole do not create a markedly increased risk. It is the combination of risk factors that is particularly important. It should not necessarily be expected that the interactions between risk factors, by which their combination tends to have a greater effect than the sum of each considered separately, will be evident in a traditional statistical interaction effect in a multivariate analysis (Rutter, 1983; Rutter & Pickles, 1991). However, as Pickles (1993) has shown, most multi-phase or multi-stage causal chains have an implicit interaction or synergistic effect. As so many causal pathways in the psychosocial arena involve indirect chain effects over long periods of time (Rutter, 1989b; Robins & Rutter, 1990), this consideration is a potentially important one.

Secondly, the impact of risk factors cannot be considered in mechanistic fashion. Humans are thinking, feeling creatures and there is cognitive and affective processing of experiences. The ways in which experiences are interpreted and acted upon is likely to make a difference to their consequences. For example, very early puberty in girls has been shown in several studies to be associated with an increase in norm-breaking behaviour. However, this effect is not the result of some inevitable biological process. To the contrary, the increase in norm-breaking behaviour seems only to occur in girls for whom early puberty leads to their joining an older peer group (Stattin & Magnusson, 1990); the effect is most evident in girls who already showed some propensity to norm-breaking behaviour before puberty; and the effect does not seem to be present in girls attending single-sex schools (Caspi & Moffitt, 1991; Caspi et al., 1993). It seems that the influence of antisocial peers is an important part of the risk mechanism initiated by particularly early puberty.

The third consideration concerns the reasons for individual variation in people's exposure to risk environments (Rutter & Rutter, 1993; Rutter et al., in press). Some people encounter far more than their fair share of stresses and adversities whereas other people go through life with remarkably little in the way of negative experiences. It is clear that these individual variations in risk exposure are not random and it is necessary to consider the causal chains involved in variations in risk exposure as well as in risk effects. These may operate at either the individual or the societal level. For example, it is evident that to an important extent people shape and select their environments. Thus, nearly thirty years ago Robins (1966) showed that antisocial boys had a much increased rate of unemployment, broken marriages, rebuffs from friends, social isolation and other stress experiences in adult life. Similarly, Quinton and Rutter (1988) showed that institution-reared girls had a much increased likelihood of marrying deviant spouses and of having teenage pregnancies. By the ways in which they acted, they tended to increase the likelihood that they would experience further adverse environments. It is not, of course, that they chose negative environments but rather that, inadvertently, they acted in ways that made it more likely that they would encounter a string of adverse environments. Curiously, the causal mechanisms involved in this important set of chain processes leading to risk experiences has been very little studied up to now; it constitutes an urgent priority for future research.

An example of a societal influence that makes it much more likely that some people will experience an unusually high rate of stress environments is the operation of racial discrimination. Thus, White and McRae (1989) showed that young Asian men and young Afro-Caribbean women in the United Kingdom tended to have the highest qualification levels but nevertheless they had among the lowest chances of getting jobs in early adult life. It is apparent that racial discrimination still plays an important role in who is affected by unemployment. The observation serves as a reminder that causation needs to be considered not only in terms of individual differences of overall levels of problem behaviour but also in terms of the pattern of distribution of risk experiences in the population as a whole.

Finally, it is necessary to consider outcomes (and, hence, opportunities for intervention) in terms of the secondary sequelae of psychosocial disorders as well as their occurrence. For example, illicit drug-taking in young people is a cause for concern, not just because of the social impairment directly caused by drug abuse and drug dependence, but also because of some of the secondary consequences of drug-taking. Both the fact that drug-taking in many countries is illegal and also the need to obtain large sums of money in order to purchase drugs, tend to mean that young drug-takers are prone to engage in delinquent activities. Also, the sharing of contaminated needles for injectable drugs has played an important role in the spread of AIDS. Because of this, there has been the development of policies of prescribing drugs to addicts with the aim of avoiding both criminalisation and infection (Strang, 1989). Another example of an action to get people to shift from a less safe drug to a more safe one concerns the attempt to replace the smoking of cigarettes by the chewing of nicotine gum (Jarvis & Russell, 1989).

CONCLUSIONS

In the chapters that follow, we will be seeking to test causal hypotheses with respect to connections between changes in society and increases in the level of certain forms of problem behaviour in young people. As will be evident, the attempt to provide a rigorous examination of possible causal influences is all too frequently frustrated by the lack of relevant data. Nevertheless, the causal hypotheses are potentially testable and we shall seek to draw attention to ways in which this may be done and the data that will be needed to do so. For the reasons that we have sought to review briefly in this chapter, it will often be necessary to consider a range of different causal pathways operating at different phases in chains of risk processes. In so far as we can, we will seek to examine causal pathways involved in variations and exposure to risk environments; individual differences in liability to disorder; the translation of this liability or predisposition into manifest problem behaviour; the course of such problem behaviour over time and variations in the degree to which it becomes recurrent or chronic; and in the secondary adverse effects of the problem behaviour or disorder.

REFERENCES

Adam, J. (1978). Sequential strategies and the separation of age, cohort, and time-of-measurement contributions to developmental data. *Psychological Bulletin 85*, 1309-1316.
Aitkin, M. & Longford, N.T. (1986). Statistical modelling issues in school effectiveness studies. *Journal of the Royal Statistical Society A 149*, 1-43.

Baltes, P.B. (1968). Longitudinal and cross-sectional sequences in the study of age and generation effects. *Human Development 11*, 145-171.

Banks, M.H. & Ullah, P. (1988). *Youth unemployment in the 1980s: Its psychological effects.* London: Croom Helm.

Block, J.H., Block, J. & Gjerde, P.F. (1986). The personality of children prior to divorce: A prospective study. *Child Development 57*, 827-840.

Bock, G.R. & Whelan, J. (eds.) (1991). *The childhood environment and adult disease.* Ciba Foundation Symposium No.156. Chichester: Wiley.

Bradford Hill, A. (1977). *A short textbook of medical statistics.* London: Hodder & Stoughton.

Broman, S.H., Nichols, P.L. & Kennedy, W.A. (1975). *Preschool IQ: Prenatal and early developmental correlates.* Hillsdale, NJ: Lawrence Erlbaum.

Bronfenbrenner, U. (1979). *The ecology of human development: Experiments by nature and design.* Cambridge, MA: Harvard University Press.

Brown, G.W., Harris, T.O. & Bifulco, A. (1986). Long-term effects of early loss of parent. In M.Rutter, C.E.Izard & P.B.Read (eds.) *Depression in young people: Developmental and clinical perspectives*, 251-296. New York: Guilford Press.

Buchanan, C.M., Maccoby, E.E. & Dornbusch, S.M. (1991). Caught between parents: Adolescents' experience in divorced homes. *Child Development 62*, 1008-1029.

Burke, K.C., Burke Jr., J.D., Rae, D.S. & Regier, D.A. (1991). Comparing age at onset of major depression and other psychiatric disorders by birth cohort in 5 US community populations. *Archives of General Psychiatry 48*, 789-795.

Cahan, S. & Cohen, N. (1989). Age versus schooling effects on intelligence development. *Child Development, 60*, 1239-1249.

Caspi, A., Lynam, D., Moffitt, T.E., & Silva, P.A. (1993). Unravelling girl's delinquency: Biological, dispositional, and contextual contributions to adolescent misbehaviour. *Developmental Psychology 29*, 19-30.

Caspi, A. & Moffitt, T.E. (1991). Individual differences are accentuated during periods of social change: The sample case of girls at puberty. *Journal of Personality and Social Psychology 61*, 157-168.

Cherlin, A.J., Furstenberg Jr., F.F., Chase-Lansdale, P.L., Kiernan, K.E., Robins, P.K., Morrison, D.R. & Teitler, J.O. (1991). Longitudinal studies of effects of divorce on children in Great Britain and the United States. *Science 252*, 1386-1389.

Clarke, R.V.G. (1985). Delinquency, environment and intervention. *Journal of Child Psychology and Psychiatry 26*, 505-523.

Cross-National Collaborative Group (1992). The changing rate of major depression: Cross-national comparisons. *Journal of the American Medical Association 268*, 3098-3105.

Dooley, D. & Catalano, R. (1980). Economic change as a cause of behavioral disorder. *Psychological Bulletin 87*, 450-468.

Easterlin R.A. (1980). *Birth and fortune: Impact of numbers on personal welfare.* New York: Basic Books.

Elder Jr., G.H. (1974). *Children of the great depression.* Chicago: University of Chicago Press.

Elder Jr., G.H.(ed.) (1985). *Life course dynamics: Trajectories and transitions, 1968-1980.* Ithaca: Cornell University Press.

Elder Jr., G.H. (1986). Military times and turning points in men's lives. *Developmental Psychology 22,* 233-245.

Farrington, D.P. (1988). Studying changes within individuals: The causes of offending. In M.Rutter (ed.) *Studies of psychosocial risk: The power of longitudinal data,* 158-183. Cambridge: Cambridge University Press.

Farrington, D.P. (1990). Age, period, cohort and offending. In D.M. Gottfredson & R.V.Clarke (eds.) *Policy and theory in criminal justice,* 51-75. Aldershot, Hants: Avebury.

Farrington, D.P., Loeber, R. & Van Kammen, W.B. (1990). Long-term criminal outcomes of hyperactivity-impulsivity-attention deficit and conduct problems in childhood. In L. Robins & M. Rutter (eds.) (1990) *Straight and devious pathways from childhood to adulthood,* 62-81. New York: Cambridge University Press.

Glenn, N.D. (1976). Cohort analysts' futile quest: Statistical attempts to separate age, period and cohort effects. *American Sociological Review 41,* 900-904

Glenn, N.D. (1977). *Cohort analysis.* Beverley Hills/London: Sage.

Goldstein, H. (1987). *Multilevel models in education and social research.* Oxford: Clarendon Press.

Hagenaars, J. A. (1990). *Categorical longitudinal data: Log-linear panel, trends and cohort analysis.* Newbury Park, CA: Sage.

Hanushek, E.A., Jackson, J.E. & Kain, J.F. (1974). Model specification, use of aggregate data, and the ecological correlation fallacy. *Political Methodology,* winter issue, 89-107.

Harris, T., Brown, G.W. & Bifulco, A. (1986). Loss of parent in childhood and adult psychiatric disorder: The role of lack of adequate parental care. *Psychological Medicine 16,* 641-659.

Hetherington, E.M.(1989). Coping with family transitions: Winners, losers, and survivors. *Child Development 60,* 1-14.

Hetherington, E.M. & Clingempeel, W.G. (1992). *Coping with marital transitions.* Monographs of the Society for Research in Child Development, Serial no.227, 57, Nos. 2-3.

Hodges, J. & Tizard, B. (1989a). IQ and behavioural adjustment of ex-institutional adolescents. *Journal of Child Psychology and Psychiatry 30,* 53-75.

Hodges, J. & Tizard, B. (1989b). Social and family relationships of ex-institutional adolescents. *Journal of Child Psychology and Psychiatry 30,* 77-97.

Holford, T.R. (1983). The estimation of age, period and cohort effects for vital rates. *Biometrics 39,* 311-324.

Jarvis, M.J. & Russell, M.A.H. (1989). Treatment for the cigarette smoker. *International Review of Psychiatry 1,* 139-147.

Kessler, R.C., Turner, J.B. & House, J.S. (1987). Intervening processes in the relationship between unemployment and health. *Psychological Medicine 17,* 949-961.

Kolvin, I., Miller, F.J.W., Scott, D.M., Gatzanis, S.R.M. & Fleeting, M. (1990). *Continuities of deprivation? The Newcastle 1000 family study*. Aldershot, Hants: Avebury.

Kreitman, N. (1988). Suicide, age and marital status. *Psychological Medicine 18*, 121-128.

Laub, J.H. & Sampson, R.J. (1993). Turning points in the life course: Why change matters to the study of crime. *Criminology 31*, 301-325.

Lavori, P.W., Klerman, G.L., Keller, M.B., Reich, T., Rice, J. & Endicott, J. (1987). Age-period-cohort analysis of secular trends in onset of major depression: Findings in siblings of patients with major affective disorder. *Journal of Psychiatric Research 21*, 23-35.

Magnusson, D. & Bergman, L. (1990). A pattern approach to the study of pathways from childhood to adulthood. In L. Robins & M. Rutter (eds.) (1990) *Straight and devious pathways from childhood to adulthood*, 101-115. New York: Cambridge University Press.

Mahaffey, K.R.(ed.) (1985). *Diet and environmental lead: Human health effects*. Amsterdam: Elsevier.

Mason, W.M. & Fienberg, S.E. (eds.) (1985). *Cohort analysis in social research: Beyond the identification problem*. New York: Springer Verlag.

Maughan, B. & Pickles, A. (1990). Adopted and illegitimate children growing up. In L. Robins & M. Rutter (eds.) (1990) *Straight and devious pathways from childhood to adulthood*, 36-61. New York: Cambridge University Press.

Maughan, B., Pickles, A., Rutter, M. & Ouston, J. (1990). Can schools change? I: Outcomes at six secondary schools. *School Effectiveness and School Improvement 1*, 188-210.

Mednick, S.A., Machon, R.A., Huttunen, M.O. & Bonett, D. (1988). Adult schizophrenia following prenatal exposure to an influenza epidemic. *Archives of General Psychiatry 45*, 189-192.

Menard, S., & Elliott, D.S. (1990). Self-reported offending, maturation or reform, and the Easterlin hypothesis. *Journal of Quantitative Criminology 6*, 237-267.

Mortimore, P., Sammons, P., Stoll, L., Lewis, D. & Ecob, R. (1988). *School matters: The junior years*. Wells, Somerset: Open Books.

Nagin, D., & Paternoster, R. (1991). On the relationship of past and future participation in delinquency. *Criminology 29*, 163-190.

Patton, W. & Noller, P. (1984). Unemployment and youth: A longitudinal study. *Australian Journal of Psychology 36*, 399-413.

Pickles, A. (1993) Stages, precursors and causes in development. In D.F. Hay & A. Angold (eds.) *Precursors and causes in development and pathogenesis*, 23-49. Chichester: Wiley.

Pickles, A., & Rutter, M., (1991). Statistical and conceptual models of 'turning points' in developmental processes. In D. Magnusson, L.R. Bergman, G. Rudinger & B. Törestad (eds.) *Problems and methods in longitudinal research: Stability and change*, 133-165. Cambridge: Cambridge University Press.

Quinton, D. & Rutter, M. (1988). *Parenting breakdown: The making and breaking of inter-generational links.* Aldershot, Hants: Avebury.

Quinton, D., Pickles, A., Maughan, B. & Rutter, M. (1993). Partners, peers and pathways: Assortative pairing and continuities in conduct disorder. *Development and Psychopathology 5*, 763-783.

Richman, N., Stevenson, J. & Graham, P. (1982). *Pre-school to school: A behavioural study.* London: Academic Press.

Rindfuss, R.R., Morgan, S.P. & Swicegood, C.G. (1984). The transition to motherhood. *American Sociological Review 49*, 359-372.

Robins, L. (1966). *Deviant children grown up.* Baltimore: Williams & Wilkins.

Robins, L. (1978). Sturdy childhood predictors of adult antisocial behaviour: Replications from longitudinal studies. *Psychological Medicine 8*, 611-622.

Robins, L. (1986). The consequences of conduct disorder in girls. In D. Olweus, J. Block & M. Radke-Yarrow (eds.) *Development of antisocial and prosocial behaviour: Research, theories and issues,* 385-414. New York: Academic Press.

Robins, L., Davis, D.H. & Wish, E. (1977). Detecting predictors of rare events: Demographic, family and personal deviance as predictors of stages in the progression toward narcotic addiction. In J.S.Strauss, H.M. Babigian & M.Roff (eds.) *The origins and course of psychopathology,* 379-406. New York: Plenum Press.

Robins, L. & Regier, D.A.(eds.) (1991). *Psychiatric disorders in America: The Epidemiologic Catchment Area study.* New York: Free Press.

Robins, L. & Rutter, M. (eds.) (1990). *Straight and devious pathways from childhood to adulthood.* New York: Cambridge University Press.

Robinson, W.S. (1950). Ecological correlations and the behaviour of individuals. *American Sociological Review 15*, 351-357.

Rosow, I. (1978). What is a cohort and why? *Human Development 21*, 65-75.

Royal College of Psychiatrists (1979). *Alcohol and alcoholism.* London: Tavistock.

Rutter, M. (1971). Parent-child separation: Psychological effects on the children. *Journal of Child Psychology and Psychiatry 12*, 233-260.

Rutter, M. (1974). Epidemiological strategies and psychiatric concepts in research on the vulnerable child. In E.Anthony & C.Koupernik (eds.) *The child in his family: Children at psychiatric risk, Vol.III,* 167-179. New York: Wiley.

Rutter, M. (1979/80). *Changing youth in a changing society: Patterns of adolescent development and disorder.* London: Nuffield Provincial Hospitals Trust; 1980, Cambridge, MA: Harvard Press.

Rutter, M. (1981). Epidemiological/longitudinal strategies and causal research in child psychiatry. *Journal of the American Academy of Child Psychiatry 20*, 513-544.

Rutter, M. (1983). Statistical and personal interactions: Facets and perspectives. In D. Magnusson & V. Allen (eds.) *Human development: An interactional perspective,* 295-319. New York: Academic Press.

Rutter, M. (ed.) (1988). *Studies of psychosocial risk: The power of longitudinal data.* Cambridge: Cambridge University Press.

Rutter, M. (1989a). Age as an ambiguous variable in developmental research: Some epidemiological considerations from developmental psychopathology. *International Journal of Behavioral Development 12*, 1-34.

Rutter, M. (1989b). Pathways from childhood to adult life. *Journal of Child Psychology and Psychiatry 30*, 23-51.

Rutter, M. (1990). Psychosocial resilience and protective mechanisms. In J.Rolf, A.Masten, D.Cicchetti, K. Nuechterlein & S.Weintraub (eds.) *Risk and protective factors in the development of psychopathology*, 181-214. New York: Cambridge University Press.

Rutter, M. (1991). Childhood experiences and adult psychosocial functioning. In G.R.Bock & J.Whelan (eds.) *The childhood environment and adult disease*, 189-200. Ciba Foundation Symposium No.156. Chichester: Wiley.

Rutter, M. (in press). Beyond longitudinal data: Causes, consequences, changes and continuity. *Journal of Consulting and Clinical Psychology*.

Rutter, M. Champion, L. Quinton, D., Maughan, B. & Pickles, A. (in press). Origins of individual differences in environmental risk exposure. In P. Moen, G. Elder Jr. & K. Luscher (eds.) *Perspectives on the ecology of human development*. Ithaca: Cornell University Press.

Rutter, M. & Giller, H. (1983). *Juvenile delinquency: Trends and perspectives.* Harmondsworth, Middx: Penguin.

Rutter, M. & Madge, N. (1976). *Cycles of disadvantage: A review of research.* London: Heinemann.

Rutter, M., Maughan, B., Mortimore, P. & Ouston, J., with Smith, A. (1979). *Fifteen thousand hours: Secondary schools and their effects on children.* London: Open Books; 1980, Cambridge, MA: Harvard University Press.

Rutter, M. & Pickles, A. (1991). Person-environment interactions: Concepts, mechanisms and implications for data analysis. In T. D. Wachs & R. Plomin (eds.) *Conceptualization and measurement of organism-environment interaction*, 105-141. Washington, DC: American Psychological Association.

Rutter, M. & Rutter, M. (1993). *Developing minds: Challenge and continuity across the lifespan.* Harmondsworth, Middx: Penguin; New York: Basic Books.

Ryan, N.D., Williamson, D.E., Iyengar, S., Orvaschel, H., Reich, T., Dahl, R.E. & Puig-Antich, J. (1992). A secular increase in child and adolescent onset affective disorder. *Journal of the American Academy of Child and Adolescent Psychiatry 31*, 600-605.

Ryder, N. (1965). The cohort as a concept in the study of social change. *American Sociological Review 30*, 843-861.

St. Clair, L. & Osborne, A.F. (1987). The ability and behaviour of children who have been 'in-care' or separated from their parents. *Early Child Development & Care 28*, No.3 Special Issue.

Sampson, R.J., & Laub, J.H. (1993). *Crime in the making: Pathways and turning points through life.* Cambridge, MA: Harvard University Press.

Schaie, K.W. (1965). A general model for the study of developmental problems. *Psychological Bulletin 64*, 92-107.

Shaffer, D. & Piacentini, J. (1994). Suicide and attempted suicide. In M.Rutter, E.Taylor & L.Hersov (eds.). *Child and adolescent psychiatry: Modern approaches* (3rd edition). Oxford: Blackwell Scientific.

Smith, D.J. & Tomlinson, S. (1989). *The school effect: A study of multi-racial comprehensives.* London: Policy Studies Institute.

Stattin, H. & Magnusson, D. (1990). *Pubertal maturation in female development.* Hillsdale, NJ: Lawrence Erlbaum.

Steffensmeier, D., Streifel C., & Harer M.D. (1987). Relative cohort size and youth crime. *American Sociological Review 52,* 702-710.

Steffensmeier, D., Streifel, C., & Shihadeh, E.S. (1992). Cohort size and arrest rates over the life course: The Easterlin hypotheses reconsidered. *American Sociological Review 57,* 306-314.

Stein, Z., Susser, M., Saenger, G. & Marolla, F. (1972). Intelligence test results of individuals exposed during gestation to the World War II famine in the Netherlands. *T. Soc. Geneesk 50,* 766-774.

Strang, J. (1989). 'The British system': Past, present and future. *International Review of Psychiatry 1,* 109-120.

Suomi, S. (1991). Early stress and adult emotional reactivity in rhesus monkeys. In G.R. Bock & J.Whelan (eds.) *The childhood environment and adult disease,* 171-188. Ciba Foundation Symposium No.156. Chichester: Wiley.

Townsend, P. & Davidson, N. (1982). *Inequalities in health: The Black report.* Harmondsworth, Middx: Penguin.

West, D. (1982). *Delinquency: Its roots, careers and prospects.* London: Heinemann.

White, M. & McRae, S. (1989). *Young adults and long-term unemployment.* London: Policy Studies Institute.

Wickramaratne, P., Weissman, M.M., Leaf, P.J. & Holford, T.R. (1989). Age, period and cohort effects on the risk of major depression: Results from five United States communities. *Journal of Clinical Epidemiology 42,* 333-343.

Wilkins, L.T. (1960). *Delinquent generations.* London: HMSO.

Zoccolillo, M., Pickles, A., Quinton, D., & Rutter, M., (1992). The outcome of childhood conduct disorder: Implications for defining adult personality disorder and conduct disorder. *Psychological Medicine 22,* 971-986.

3

Individual Development and Social Change

GIAN VITTORIO CAPRARA and MICHAEL RUTTER

As outlined in the opening chapter of this volume, the Study Group was set up to examine possible time trends in psychosocial disorders of a type and severity such that they *might* be influenced by changing social conditions. If the rate of any such disorder is found to have increased over time, the implication is that individuals who would have been normal in a previous era are now showing disorder. This could be because a new risk factor has emerged, because a previously existing risk factor has become more frequent or more powerful, or because changed circumstances have made individuals more vulnerable to the same level of risk factors. In any attempt to unravel the skein of multiple mechanisms that conceivably could be involved, it is necessary to ask ourselves which ones are *likely* to be operative. In later chapters, the issues are discussed with respect to particular types of disorder but, before proceeding to specific risks, we need briefly to consider what is known about the processes involved in abnormal development. The focus of that discussion, of course, needs to be on the possible ways in which knowledge about individual differences and individual functioning might inform the study of trends over time and their possible association with social change. These issues constitute the objectives of this chapter.

First, we present some of the empirically derived general principles and concepts of development that appear relevant for psychopathology (Rutter, 1989). In this regard we place particular emphasis on the flow of individual-environment interactions that mediate the various risk and protective mechanisms for psychosocial disorder. Second, we discuss the role of individual differences as they relate to the causal pathways to problem behaviour and consider their implication for secular trends in rates of disorder. Finally, we address the relationship between 'micro' and 'macro' approaches to the interplay between individuals and their environments in the escalation and de-escalation of problem behaviour over time.

DEVELOPMENTAL PROCESSES AND PSYCHOPATHOLOGY

The rapid and exciting recent developments in molecular genetics and in neurobiology have been accompanied by a major change in the emphasis placed on biological factors in the aetiology of psychiatric disorders. As Eisenberg (1986) noted, the brainlessness of psychiatric concepts in the 1950s and 60s has tended to be replaced by a 'mindlessness' in the concepts of the 1980s and 90s. To a remarkable extent, a focus on the inner working of the psyche and on the psychiatric risks stemming from psychosocial hazards and adversities has been dropped and supplanted by a search for the genes causing mental diseases and for the neurobiological roots of normal and abnormal workings of the mind. At first sight, it would seem that any attempt to relate secular trends in psychosocial disorder to changing patterns of social circumstances is doomed to failure. We need to start, therefore, by asking whether that is so.

It is abundantly clear that it is not, for several rather different reasons (Rutter, 1991). To begin with, even with the major mental disorders (which are outside the scope of this volume), the genetic evidence indicates a substantial role for environmental factors. That is even more the case with the range of disorders considered here. Thus, *non*-genetic factors predominate in the development of the commoner varieties of depression (Kendler et al., 1992) and of conduct disorder or delinquency (DiLalla & Gottesman, 1989). However, there are three other reasons for rejecting a strongly deterministic, biological, view of disorder.

First, the degree to which a disorder is heritable is not a fixed quantity; if environmental circumstances change so will the heritability. Similarly, the role of particular environmental influences will alter if their strength or prevalence changes. For example, exposure to radiation probably plays a relatively minor role in the overall risk for cancer, but its importance was much greater in the residents of Hiroshima and Nagasaki following the dropping of the atomic bomb at the end of the Second World War. Also, general bodily health was not a major factor influencing vulnerability to tuberculosis in most industrialized nations in the 1960s and 1970s; however, the emergence of AIDS has meant that it now constitutes a crucial predisposing factor.

Second, apart from rare Mendelian diseases, genetic factors do not cause disorders in a direct fashion. Rather, they contribute to a multifactorial liability or propensity, sometimes by increasing vulnerability to environmental hazards. Accordingly, environmental risk factors may be very important even in strongly genetic disorders.

Third, the fact that genetic factors predominate in the determination of *individual differences* does not mean that they predominate in changes over time in the overall *level* of a trait or disorder in the general population. Tizard (1975) first made this point forcefully in drawing attention to the massive increase in the average height of British schoolboys in the first half of this century (presumably due to improved nutrition) despite height being strongly heritable. Similar considerations apply to the increase in measured IQ and educational attainments that has taken place in most industrialized societies during the last half-century.

For all these reasons, it is apparent that the importance of biological factors in predisposition to many forms of psychopathology (which is undeniable) does *not* mean that changed social circumstances are likely to be irrelevant in the causes of trends over time in psychosocial disorders. As discussed in the previous chapter, cause is a multifaceted concept and its elucidation needs to recognize that different mechanisms may be involved in different facets.

With that in mind, we need to turn to what is known regarding the processes involved in the development of psychopathology in young people, in order to consider the possible implications for the study of secular trends. In discussing these processes, we deliberately use evidence from studies of normal development as well as of disorders because it is clear that there are continuities, as well as discontinuities, between the two (Rutter & Rutter, 1993).

During the last half-century, there have been major changes in the ways in which developmental processes have been conceptualized (Rutter, 1989). In the 1950s many people viewed the effects of adverse early experiences as permanent and irreversible. As longitudinal studies failed to support that belief (Rutter, 1981b), the pendulum swung to a view that very few effects were lasting and that long-term outcomes were heavily dependent on subsequent life experiences (Clarke & Clarke, 1976). Further research in the 1980s pointed to a more complex mix of both lasting sequelae *and* resilience or recovery (Rutter, 1987c). However, what is important in this partial swinging back of the pendulum is that it reflects evidence pointing to a rather different view of the process of development (Elder, 1991; Rutter & Rutter, 1993). It is not that new evidence has contradicted previous findings, nor that a sensible 'middle of the road' compromise between extreme positions has been achieved. Instead, it has become clear that the questions had been posed in the wrong way. In particular, it has come to be appreciated that it is of very limited usefulness to ask whether early adversities have long-term sequelae that are *independent* of later circumstances. The original answer that, for the most part, they do not, still stands (although some exceptions have been demonstrated). However, the reason why that is not the most appropriate question is that it has been found that one of the key ways in which early adversities lead to lasting sequelae is through their either increasing vulnerability to later environmental hazards, or increasing the likelihood that later environments will be risky ones. The focus needs to be on the range of indirect chain reactions involved in causal processes and in perpetuation of their effects, reactions that reside in the interplay between individuals and their environments (Caprara & Van Heck, 1992; Elder, 1991; Endler & Parker, 1992; Magnusson, 1988, 1990; Rutter & Rutter, 1993).

Because this dynamic interactionist perspective has been misunderstood so frequently, it is necessary to spell out what it means and what the research findings show. Sometimes it has been dismissed as the expression of just a naive truism that people grow up and function in a physical and psychosocial environment and that therefore there must be some form of interplay between persons and their environment. Of course, that must be the case but the concept goes far beyond that simplistic notion. At the other extreme, sometimes it has been thought to mean that environmental and individual causal factors must usually involve some kind of potentiation of each other in terms of the catalytic chemistry of the moment, which will be shown by a statistical interaction effect. As discussed below, personal characteristics do indeed operate in part through their effect on individual differences in susceptibility to environmental variables. However, that is only a small portion of what is meant by person-environment interactions (Wachs & Plomin, 1991; Rutter & Rutter, 1993; Wachs, 1992) and, in any case, they will not necessarily be evidenced in statistical interaction effects. That is because, amongst other things, interaction terms are much influenced by the particular statistical models employed and by the number of individuals in the total population who *could* be affected by the interaction.

So what does an interactionist perspective mean; what sorts of empirical data point to the need to view causal processes in these terms; and why and how does it have implications for the study of secular trends? These are best considered in terms of seven crucial issues: individual differences in vulnerability, shared and non-shared environmental effects, multiple adversities, indirect cumulative chain effects, risk and protective mechanisms, active processing of experiences, and timing of experiences.

Individual Differences in Vulnerability

There is a wealth of evidence from biology, medicine, and social sciences that there are major individual differences in people's susceptibility or vulnerability to almost every type of environmental risk. Thus, it is known that there is a substantial sex difference in young children's vulnerability to physical hazards such as infection or malnutrition (males are more susceptible); that people vary greatly in their ability to handle high fat or high cholesterol diets; that there are substantial individual differences in people's reactivity to allergens; and that people's susceptibility to infections is influenced by their overall physical and mental health at the time (Rutter & Pickles, 1991). We start with these medical examples to underline the fact that individual differences in vulnerability are a biological basic and nothing special to psychosocial adversities. Nevertheless, that basic certainly includes the psychosocial arena. Almost all such adversities tend to have their greatest impact on those who are already psychologically vulnerable and, moreover, their effect is to increase or accentuate those pre-existing predispositions or characteristics – what Elder and Caspi (1990) have termed the 'accentuation principle'. This tendency has been found with factors as varied as unemployment, early puberty, divorce, parenthood, and stressful life events (Rutter & Rutter, 1993). The implication for the study of secular trends is that it must be expected that changing social circumstances are likely to have their greatest impact on groups of people who are already vulnerable. It cannot be expected that risks will be found to apply to everyone. Thus, sometimes commentators have sought to dismiss the possible effects of the media on problem behaviours by noting that adverse sequelae are mainly, or even only, found in small vulnerable subgroups. The crucial point is that that is just what should be expected for most such influences; any one variable is not likely to have a major influence on everyone and hence it is improbable that it will account for more than a very small proportion of population variance. However, for reasons discussed below, that does not necessarily mean that it can play no part in accounting for secular trends in psychosocial disorders.

The biological examples we have chosen also bring out another crucial point; namely that individual predispositions may be powerfully influenced by earlier environmental factors (Bock & Whelan, 1991). The predispositions are 'constitutional' insofar as the vulnerability has become part of the individual's biological make-up but they were nonetheless environmentally determined. Thus, an individual's metabolic capacity to handle cholesterol is influenced by the diets experienced in infancy; and a person's susceptibility to infections is influenced by earlier exposure to the relevant pathogens. The same applies with respect to psychosocial risks. For example, animal studies years ago showed that stresses in early life lead to structural and functional changes in the neuroendocrine system that are associated with individual differences in reactions to later stressors (Hennessy & Levine, 1979). The implications for the study of secular trends is that social factors may operate through their effects on vulnerability rather than through any direct risk effect as such.

Shared and Non-shared Environmental Effects

One of the important recent advances in behavioural genetics has been the finding that, in many circumstances, and for many psychological characteristics, non-shared environmental effects tend to be much more important than shared ones (Plomin & Daniels, 1987). In essence, what this means is that influences that impinge differently on different children in the same family tend to have a greater effect than those that affect all children equally. Thus, scapegoating of one child may be more important than the overall level of warmth or discord in the family (Dunn & Plomin, 1990). Similarly, the finding has drawn attention in a helpful way to the need to consider individual experiences outside the family (for example, stresses at school, peer group, hospital admissions) as well as family-broad circumstances. It is important not to overstate the predominant influence of non-shared effects because the conclusion does not apply to all psychosocial disorders (for example, shared effects are important in conduct disorder and delinquency) and it does not necessarily apply to extreme environmental circumstances (Rutter, 1991; Rutter & Rutter, 1993). Even so, the finding has an important degree of generality.

It might be thought that the finding means that community-wide social changes are not likely to play much role in secular changes in psychosocial disorder. If shared environmental effects are so unimportant overall, how could they make much difference? In fact, although that might seem to be a logical consequence of the finding, it is not, for two rather separate reasons. First, the finding that non-shared *effects* predominate is not equivalent to saying that non-shared *variables* are without influence. To the contrary, the important point is that family-wide influences such as poverty, discord, and parental mental disorder impinge more on some children in the family than on others. The variable is family-wide but the effects vary among the children in terms of the extent to which they are exposed to the influence and in terms of their individual vulnerability (hence, the effect is mainly non-shared in spite of the risk factor being one that impinges on all family members to some degree). By extension, the same applies to community-wide (or nationwide) circumstances. They *can* create serious psychosocial risks but their effects will vary greatly among individuals.

The second consideration is of a rather different kind. Part of the implication of non-shared effects is that *perceived disparities* may be as important (perhaps more important) than absolute levels of deprivation or risk exposure (Dunn & Plomin, 1990). There is a very basic human tendency to compare ourselves with other people whom we regard as relevant to our own social situation. Thus, children are very sensitive to perceived favouritism or scapegoating and, as adults too, we tend to notice whether we are being treated better or worse than other people. Cross-national comparisons with respect to housing conditions bring out this point (Rutter & Madge, 1976). One might expect that the amazing degree of overcrowding that has been widespread in Hong Kong would have had seriously damaging consequences, but the limited available evidence suggests that the ill-effects have not been as great as might have been anticipated. The usual interpretation is that this is because most people are living in similar circumstances and because housing conditions have become progressively better over the years, even though they compare poorly with those that prevail in most of Europe or North America.

The 'lesson' for the study of social change as it applies to secular trends in disorder is that attention must be paid to two key features: the spread of adversity and possible changes in the populations with which people compare themselves (Rutter, 1994). For example, it is apparent that in some countries the social disparities and spread of living standards have tended to increase in spite of an overall improvement in economic conditions and housing circumstances. The psychosocial risks are just as likely to stem from the experience of being worse off, and becoming progressively less well treated, as compared with other segments of the population, than from any absolute low level of income or housing conditions. Similarly, the risks may be affected by changes in our comparison group. Thus, if the poor or unprivileged or oppressed change from an acceptance of their lot as an inevitable part of the social system, to a view that their circumstances are not only worse than those of others but could and should be better, they may suffer psychologically thereby, even though in absolute terms their circumstances are improving. For example, this may be relevant to the immense social and economic upheaval now taking place in Eastern Europe and to the changes involved in the reunification of Germany. It is not being argued that there is evidence to attach weights to the risks accompanying relative and absolute deprivation; regrettably that is largely lacking. However, it is being suggested that it is necessary to take account of spread, as well as level, of social circumstances and to do so with attention to the likely role of perceived disparities.

Multiple Adversities

A variety of studies have shown that, on the whole, single stressful experiences that occur truly in isolation, carry rather low psychosocial risks (Rutter, 1979b; Kolvin et al., 1990; Emery, 1982). Serious risks tend to derive from a *combination* of adversities or stresses occurring at the same time, from meaningful *links* between a current stress and a previous adversity, or from *accumulations* of stresses/adversities over time. For example, in the less good hospital circumstances for children in years gone by, there were few long-term risks from just one admission in the preschool years but there were appreciable risks from two or more admissions, especially in children already suffering from psychosocial adversity (Douglas, 1975; Quinton & Rutter, 1976). The implications for the study of effects of social change that stem from this consideration are twofold: first, that the addition of an extra risk factor may have an overall effect that is greater than its effect on its own, if it increases the rate of multiple adversities; and second, that the spread or distribution in the population of additional risks stemming from social change will influence the extent to which multiple adversities are actually increased.

Indirect Cumulative Chain Effects

As noted above, initial attempts to study the persistent effects of adverse experiences in early childhood, sought to examine these in the rare circumstances when they were independent from later experiences. Thus, there was a focus on children rescued from extreme deprivation and then reared in a better than average environment. Few lasting sequelae were found (although there may be some when the early environment is such as largely to prevent the development of lasting selective attachments – see Rutter, 1981a&b; Hodges & Tizard, 1989a&b; Rutter & Rutter, 1993). However, it is now evident that persistent sequelae *do* occur through the operation of indirect cumulative chain effects (Rutter, 1989). These arise as a result of several different mechanisms. First, one negative experience may make another sort of negative experience more likely. For example, racial discrimination in employment and housing are likely to mean that ethnic groups suffering from the psychological effects of personal discrimination will also experience poorer housing and less good jobs as a consequence (Rutter & Madge, 1976). Similarly, some forms of societal response to delinquent behaviour may make it more likely that such behaviour will continue (Sampson & Laub, 1992; Rutter & Giller, 1983).

Second, some negative experiences will have long-term consequences because they shut off important opportunities. Thus children attending poor schools are more likely to truant, to have weak scholastic qualifications, and to leave school early (Gray et al., 1980). Although there are no *independent* long-term effects of schooling, there are important indirect effects extending into adult life because the weak scholastic qualifications make it more likely that the individuals will land up in unskilled jobs, with not much potential. The same applies to the effects of unusually early puberty in girls in predisposing to school drop-out (Stattin & Magnusson, 1990).

Third, people behave in ways that shape and select their environments (Scarr, 1992; Plomin & Bergeman, 1991). The literature on this topic has focused on genetic effects in determining variations in environmental exposure but that constitutes much too narrow a view of this important process (Rutter & Rutter, 1993). Behaviours that are environmentally determined in large part will also serve to influence exposure to risk environments. Thus, one reason why the institutional girls studied by Quinton & Rutter (1988) tended to have a poor social outcome in early adult life was that they tended to become pregnant as teenagers, leaping impulsively into hasty marriages, often with deviant men. As a consequence, later on they suffered from lack of marital support either because the marriage broke down or because they were in a conflictual, discordant relationship. Similarly, Robins (1966) found that antisocial boys behaved in ways that made it more likely that in adult life they would suffer the stresses of unemployment, lack of social support, rebuffs from friends and repeated marital breakdown. A different example is provided by Newcomb's (1943) study of young women attending Bennington College in the late 1930s. He found that, in an environment that provided relative independence from parental influences, the undergraduates experienced an accentuation of liberal political views. A follow-up a generation later (Alwin et al., 1991) showed that the liberalized graduates tended to choose liberal spouses. As in the entirely different Caspi & Herbener (1990) study, assortative marriage served to reinforce their own attitudes and behaviour.

The relevance of these considerations for the study of secular trends is that there is a need to examine the ways in which social changes may impinge (in positive or negative ways) on these indirect cumulative chain effects. Psychosocial risks may be increased or decreased by effects that prolong or curtail negative chain reactions.

Risk and Protective Mechanisms

The fifth issue constitutes an extension of that consideration through an emphasis on the need to consider both risk and protective mechanisms (Rutter, 1990, 1993). There has been a tendency in the past to view resilience as a characteristic of individuals and protective mechanisms as the result of positive experiences. Both tendencies are at least partially mistaken. Of course, individuals do vary in traits that make resilience in the face of psychosocial adversity more or less likely. However, resilience may derive from compensatory experiences rather than individual traits. Thus, Jenkins and Smith (1990) found that a good relationship with one parent protected children experiencing general family discord. Moreover, such compensatory experiences need not necessarily be present at the time of risk, they may precede or succeed the risk experience. Thus, Stacey et al.'s (1970) findings suggested that previously happy separation experiences (such as staying overnight with friends or grandparents) made it easier for children to cope successfully with the unhappy separation experience of hospital admission. Quinton and Rutter (1988) found that a supportive harmonious marital relationship in adult life did much to mitigate the psychosocial risks that accompanied an institutional rearing in childhood.

The equality of protective mechanisms with hedonically positive experiences is also unduly narrowing. Attention has been drawn already to the animal evidence that early exposure to stress may enhance resistance to later stresses (Hennessy & Levine, 1979). There are suggestions that the same may apply with psychosocial stresses in humans (Rutter, 1981a). The parallel with resistance to infection may not be too far-fetched. People develop resistance, *not* through particularly positive health-giving experiences, but rather through successful coping with the pathogen, either through natural exposure or immunization. Successful coping with psychosocial stresses may be similarly protective (Rutter & Rutter, 1993).

The implication for the study of social change lies in the broadening of concepts of ways in which they might serve to increase or decrease risks. Thus, an increase might come about either through stronger (or more pervasive) risk mechanisms or through weaker (or less pervasive) protective ones.

Active Processing of Experiences

In a previous era there was often an implicit assumption that psychosocial stresses or adversities could be considered as absolutes without reference to either their personal meaning or their cognitive processing by the individual. It is obvious now that that makes little sense (Rutter, 1981a). Of course, there are some extraordinary events (such as shipwrecks or being taken hostage) that are so universally stressful that their meaning and processing are of less importance. However, even with these events there is substantial individual variation in response, variation that is related to how they are perceived and dealt with. Moreover, it is easy to make wrong judgements about which aspects of the situation create the stress. For example, Bourne et al. (1967, 1968) found that helicopter and ambulance medics and special forces troops showed neither behavioural nor physiological signs of stress under battle conditions that carried a substantial risk of death or mutilation. It seemed that the job prestige and gratification, together with high group morale, made an *objectively* stressful situation into a *subjectively* rewarding one. By contrast, the captain and radio operator who remained rather separate from the group *did* show signs of stress. Somewhat similarly, it was generally assumed that the very high rate of heroin use among American servicemen in Vietnam was a consequence of battle stress, but Robins' (1993) careful studies indicated no association with actual combat. Clearly, serving in Vietnam did constitute a major risk experience predisposing to heroin use but the assumption that the risk stemmed from participation in armed combat (and the consequent risk of death) seems to be mistaken.

The same considerations apply to more ordinary stress experiences. Thus, increased pressures at school or work may be felt as a positive challenge to be met and enjoyed or a debilitating burden. Divorce may be experienced as a liberation from a conflictual marriage or a terrible loss because it is felt as a personal failure in an important relationship. The implication for the study of social changes is that the consequences of such changes may be much influenced by how they are perceived and reacted to, and that this may be affected by changing social mores and attitudes (see section below on 'micro' and 'macro' approaches).

Timing of Experiences

The last consideration is that the effects of experiences may well be affected by their timing. In part, this derives from the previous point on the cognitive processing of experiences. Thus, very young infants seem to be less affected by separations from their parents because they have yet to develop the capacity to form enduring selective attachments; school age children are less vulnerable because, although they have gained that capacity, they also have acquired the cognitive capacity to maintain a relationship during a separation. By contrast, one to four-year-olds are most at risk because they have the former but not the latter (Rutter, 1981a&b). Somewhat similarly, Elder (1974) found that younger children were more likely than adolescents to be affected adversely by the great economic depression. It seemed that the older group had acquired greater coping skills and especially were able to be rewarded by taking on additional responsibilities (successfully) in the family. The effects of social change, therefore, are unlikely to impinge on all age groups in equal fashion.

However, there is a potentially even more important consideration in the study of secular change. There has been much discussion with respect to the changes of adolescence with regard to whether it is a good or bad thing to have all the transitions occurring at the same time. Coleman (1978) posed the question of why adolescence is such a relatively untroubled period for so many young people (as empirical findings show that it is – Rutter, 1979a; Coleman & Hendry, 1990) given the many major adaptations required in the transitions of puberty, leaving school, taking up employment, and moving from home. His tentative answer was that it may be easier to cope successfully if these transitions do *not* all take place simultaneously. In the same vein, Simmons and Blyth (1987) found that the sometimes negative emotional effects experienced by girls following transfer to high school were largely apparent when the transfer coincided in time with other stresses or challenges. Nevertheless, it certainly cannot be assumed that neither the spread nor pattern of adolescent transition is of psychological consequence. Indeed, Hurrelmann (1989) has argued that secular trends have altered the pattern of timing for different transitions during the adolescent age period (with, for example, a falling age of puberty and a rising age of school leaving) in ways that may create increased psychosocial risks. Obviously, this is a possibility that requires careful study in any examination of secular trends in psychosocial disorder.

THE ROLE OF PERSONALITY AND OTHER INDIVIDUAL CHARACTERISTICS

Most writings on personality have tended to concentrate on its supposed structure in terms of basic traits, represented in recent times by the so-called 'Big Five' dimensions (Digman, 1990). It has been argued that these involve a substantial genetic component, show very strong temporal stability and are largely uninfluenced by broad environmental features. To the extent that that is so, personality features are likely to be largely irrelevant to any consideration of secular trends. However, it is apparent that behavioural traits constitute only one aspect of personality (Pervin, 1990; Rutter 1987b) and that individual characteristics of various kinds influence development in ways that do have a potential relevance for the study of time trends in psychosocial disorder (Caprara, 1992; Caprara & Van Heck, 1992; Engfer et al., in press).

The Meaning of Trait Stability

The first point to appreciate is that, in itself, the empirical finding of either normative stability (meaning that over time people tend to retain their rank order in the population on a trait) or ipsative stability (meaning a tendency to show a similar pattern over time) tells one nothing about the mechanisms involved or about the nature of the trait (Asendorpf, 1992; Caprara & Van Heck, 1992; Rutter & Rutter, 1993; Sampson & Laub, 1992). In particular, the finding is uninformative on the potential for change in the *level* of the trait, either with or without alteration in social conditions. It is quite possible to have major changes in level in spite of very high correlations over time. For example, antisocial behaviour shows high normative stability over time (Olweus, 1979; Farrington, 1989; Huesmann et al., 1984) but, in spite of that, there is a massive drop in the level of criminal activities after early adult life. This means that those individuals who tend to be more antisocial than most in childhood tend still to be more antisocial in adult life but, even so, in the population as a whole increasing age after the early 20s is accompanied by a substantial reduction in antisocial behaviour. Similarly, age-corrected IQ scores show high correlations over time (indicating high normative stability), but crystallized cognitive skills show a steep rise up to early adult life and fluid cognitive skills (that is, those that rely more on experience and knowledge) go on increasing until middle age.

But, even the finding of normative stability tells one nothing about its origins. Sometimes there is a misleading assumption that continuity and stability must be the ordinary expectation and that it is only discontinuity and change that have to be explained. In fact, that is far from the case; the whole process of biological maturation involves change and, insofar as the process is affected by new experiences, these too will bring about change (Rutter & Rutter, 1993). Of course, the establishment of both neural structure and cognitive sets will also bring about continuity and stability. The biological expectation has to be for a mixture of continuity and discontinuity; both require explanation. Asendorpf (1992) suggested that at least three different mechanisms are likely to contribute to stability (each of these has parallels in the developmental considerations discussed above). First, in keeping with their personality characteristics, children select and shape their environments in ways that accentuate their traits. Second, stability of personality is brought about by consistency in the ways children are viewed by important referent persons. There is a considerable literature indicating how quickly reputations are established and showing their effects in shaping interpersonal interactions, and ultimately, in stabilizing, and enhancing individual behavioural characteristics (Brophy, 1983; Caprara & Zimbardo, 1994; Dodge & Crick, 1990; Dweck & Leggett, 1988; Hymel et al., 1990; Engfer et al., in press). Stability is brought about, therefore, through consistency in societal reactions. Third, there is a substantial tendency for individuals' psychosocial environments to remain relatively constant in their overall balance in spite of differences over time in details of their features. Thus, children who start their lives in disadvantage and adversity are all too likely to be experiencing more than their fair share of negative experiences in adult life. Caspi and Elder (1988) expressed somewhat similar notions in terms of the concept that personal styles of behaviour are maintained through both 'cumulative continuity' (the progressive accumulation of the consequences of their own behaviour) and 'interactional continuity' (meaning the evoking of maintaining responses from others during reciprocal social interaction).

However, it is necessary also to invoke the role of a person's own cognitive/affective set (Bandura, 1986, 1990; Bretherton & Waters, 1985; Brown, G.W. et al., 1990; Caprara et al., 1988; Guerra & Slaby, 1990; Rutter, 1987a&b). Personality involves far more than a collection of traits. Rutter (1987b) suggested that it may be thought of as referring to 'the coherence of functioning that derives from how people react to their given attributes, how they think about themselves and how they put these together into some form of conceptual whole' (454). It is obvious that these self-concepts or cognitive/affective sets carry the potential for both change and stability. Insofar as there are no experiences to alter the concepts, they will serve a self-perpetuating function. However, if later experiences involve such a discontinuity with the past that they result in a change in self-concept they will foster changes in behaviour. Thus, attachment theorists have argued that, to an important extent, early relationships affect later relationships because (from early life) people develop views both of themselves as social beings and of what they may expect of other people in their social relationships (Bretherton & Waters, 1985). Similarly, depression theorists postulate that a lack of affectionate parental care in childhood (together with other psychosocial adversities) creates a vulnerability through its effect in predisposing to a self-image involving low self-esteem, learned helplessness, and a perceived lack of self-efficacy (Brown, G. W. et al., 1990). Personality theorists in the field of delinquency comparably argue that a proneness to engage in violence is supported by a set of beliefs that aggression increases their self-esteem, protects their reputation and avoids a self-image(Caprara et al., 1988; Guerra & Slaby, 1990).

In all of these areas, the importance lies not only in the *actual* coping skills that a person possesses, but also in their own *self-perceptions* of their capabilities. As Bandura (1990) emphasized in putting forward the value of perceived self-control in the exercise of control in avoiding AIDS infection, there is the tripartite need for people to know what actions are likely to be effective, to develop the necessary coping skills to act effectively, *and* to acquire a self-belief that they are able to influence what happens to them. It is *perceived* self-efficacy and not just competence that matters.

It is evident that these considerations have very important implications for the study of the possible effects of social change on secular trends in levels or patterns of psychosocial disorder. First, the high normative stability of personality traits does *not* mean that levels of behaviours associated with those traits are impervious to change. Second, it is necessary to entertain the possibility that social changes may bring about effects on psychosocial disorder as much through their impact on social attitudes, values and expectations as through their direct influence on disorders *per se*. Thus, they may affect patterns of *beliefs and expectations* in the population (or subsegments of it), which in turn will result in the ways people *think* about themselves and how other people *react* to them, which will have consequences for the *constructions* of personality dispositions, and thereby on habits or patterns of *behaviour*.

Patterns of Characteristics

The second major issue with respect to personality dimensions concerns their patterning. From the viewpoint of their implications for psychopathology, it is relevant that it seems that, at least for some traits, the main risk derives from constellations or combinations of traits (Magnusson, 1988; Magnusson & Bergman, 1990). Thus, in the Stockholm longitudinal study (Magnusson, 1988) the risks for adult criminality, substance abuse and psychiatric disorder mainly derived from a subgroup of boys who exhibited the combination of aggression, hyperactivity and poor peer relationships. Once this subgroup was excluded, aggressivity ceased to have any significant protective power. In a similar vein, the developmental prognosis seems to be particularly poor for children exhibiting a combination of social withdrawal and aggression (Mayr, 1992; Asendorpf, 1990a&b; Ledingham & Schwartzman, 1984) – perhaps because this constellation is particularly likely to lead to peer rejection.

An extension of the same consideration is that the behavioural traits of both aggression (Caprara, 1987; Caprara & Pastorelli, 1989, 1992) and anxiety (Endler et al., 1991) cannot be considered as necessarily unitary. Thus, it seems that the overall composite of aggression (incorporating irritability, hostility, tolerance towards violence, and persecutory guilt) may have two basic components: emotional vulnerability and dysphoria; and a lack of concern for others, associated with vindictiveness (Caprara et al., 1992). This combination of characteristics seems to be associated with both peer rejection and impaired social cognition (Caprara et al., 1994) – probably in part through the role of the social reactions that this combination tends to elicit and which predisposes to persistence of the behavioural predisposition (Caprara, 1992). Other investigators too have suggested the need to consider subpatterns of antisocial behaviour (for example, Pulkkinen & Tremblay, 1992; Loeber et al., 1993) although the basis of their subdivisions is not quite the same.

The meaning of these findings regarding constellations of traits is not as yet entirely clear. It could be that the individual components of the constellation are truly discrete and that their combination derives from the effects of cognitive sets and social reactions. If so, the implication would be that social changes that impinge on factors predisposing to their combination could be important in affecting overall psychosocial risk. Alternatively, it could be that the meaning of the constellation differs from that of its components and that it therefore has different biological origins as well as different psycho-pathological effects. Both possibilities need to be borne in mind. In addition, however, it will be important to determine whether secular trends in *levels* of disorder have been accompanied by changes in *pattern* and, if so, whether this has implications for the possible causal influences involved in the changes in level. For example, it is clear that over the past 50 years there have been massive changes in both the accessibility of drugs and public attitudes to their use (at least with some drugs). Does this mean that the factors involved in substance use and abuse have also altered over time? We have here made both the point that constellations of behaviours may have a meaning that is different from just the sum of the individual behavioural components that make up the constellation, and the separate point that apparently homogeneous constellations may in reality be made up of subgroups that differ in their aetiological and prognostic implications. It is important to add that an influential group of investigators (Jessor et al., 1991) have argued that much problem behaviour is best viewed as a unitary whole. Clearly, there is a complex mixture of both communality and heterogeneity in the range of psychosocial disorders considered in this volume and it will be necessary to consider both the possibility that these secular trends have the same origin *and* the possibility that several quite different mechanisms are operative.

Individual Characteristics and Disorder

The main point that emerges from research examining the psychopathological risks associated with individual characteristics is that they are probabilistic, as an element in multifactorial determination, rather than directly deterministic. Thus, marked behavioural inhibition has been identified as a risk factor for anxiety disorders (Hirshfeld et al., 1992). However, it was found that the risks were confined to the subgroup of children who continued to show this characteristic over time (only half the sample) and that this subgroup also had parents with anxiety disorders (who probably represented both a genetic and environmental risk). The association between temperamental difficulties and disruptive behaviour disorders (Maziade, 1989; Prior, 1992) showed that the psychopathological risk mainly applied when there was also family discord or adversity. Similarly, the psychopathological risk associated with hyperactivity mainly derives from its combination with adverse family features (Robins, 1991).

The implication for the study of social change and secular trends in disorder is that if such change affects the psychosocial risks stemming from adverse family circumstances, it is likely, by so doing, to alter the strength of risks associated with particular individual characteristics that predispose to disorder.

There is however, one further implication that needs to be noted. Some individual characteristics seem to carry risks *only* as a result of their social meaning or consequences. For example, unusually early puberty in girls (but not boys) has been found to predispose to increased norm-breaking behaviour only if it leads to the girls becoming part of an older peer group that exhibits norm-breaking mores or values (Stattin & Magnusson, 1990; Caspi et al., 1993). Thus, Caspi et al. (1993) found that the effects were confined to girls in mixed sex rather than all girls schools. Similarly, the fat deposition at puberty in girls that is associated with an increase in eating disorders seems to be a function of the social meaning attached to the change in body shape (Richards et al., 1990). Accordingly, social changes that influence social values and meaning may have psychopathological consequences.

'MICRO-' AND 'MACRO-' APPROACHES

Up to this point, we have considered developmental and personality concepts and findings with respect to their implications for the study of secular trends. We now need to grasp the stick by the other end in order to consider how 'macro-' studies at the societal level relate to 'micro-' studies at the individual level. There are both methodological and substantive implications that go beyond the causal testing considerations discussed in the previous chapter.

Meaning of Measures

One of the key issues that has to inform all studies of secular trends is the concern over whether measures mean the same thing or index the same process at all time periods. It is obvious that at least some do not. Five examples may serve to illustrate the problem. First, the massive fall in infantile mortality that has taken place during the last half-century in all European countries might seem to imply that there should have been a parallel drop in the proportion of babies born with damage deriving from pre- and perinatal biological risk factors (most of which, however, are known *not* to be due to birth injury). In fact, that has not happened (Casaer et al., 1991). There is no question but that improvements in both social conditions and in obstetric/paediatric care have had a hugely beneficial effect. For any given birth weight (or any other risk index), the outlook for babies today is incomparably better than it was even a generation ago. However, the populations are in no way the same. Very low birth weight babies who stood no chance of surviving in the past are today being kept alive; some without handicap and some with. To the extent that those who would have died previously are now living, but with some handicap, they have added to the numbers of biologically damaged children. But these are balanced by the children who would have survived with handicap in the past but who are now normally functioning. The net effect is that there has been little change in the rate of cerebral palsy; we have no satisfactory assessment of whether the proportion with more subtle forms of biological damage has increased or decreased. One further change needs emphasis. In the 1950s and 1960s low birth weight was strongly associated with social disadvantage whereas today it is much less so (especially at very low birth weights). As a result, low birth weight today has a rather different meaning and a rather different set of correlates from those that applied 30 or 40 years ago. These changes over time have been so great that many investigators consider that there is no valid way of combining data on very low birth weight babies over extended time periods. Accordingly, we do not know whether the proportion of babies already biologically damaged at the time of birth has gone up or down over time. What is known, however, is that the fall in infantile mortality over time can *not* necessarily be taken as meaning a fall in the rate of damaged babies.

The second example is provided by illegitimacy, which in many European countries has become very much more frequent since the 1950s (see Chapter 5). Because illegitimacy in the past was well documented as a substantial psychosocial risk factor (see Maughan & Pickles, 1990), it might be supposed that the major increase in illegitimate births must mean a parallel increase in psychosocial risk. However, that may not be so, because the statistics also show that there has been a great rise in the proportion of illegitimate births registered in the name of *both* parents. In the past, it was usually presumed that most instances of illegitimacy represented unwanted, unplanned pregnancies in women without the support of a partner (often in the context of social disadvantage). By contrast a proportion of illegitimate births today represent a deliberate choice by a cohabiting (but not legally married) couple in a stable union. Its meaning is not the same. It needs to be added that this proportion varies among countries according to the prevailing mores; as a result considerable care and caution is needed when making comparisons over time or across countries in illegitimacy rates.

The meaning of ethnic minority status has also changed over time in many European countries. At the time of the inner London surveys circa 1970, about half the children born to parents of Afro-Caribbean origin were themselves born abroad. As a consequence their psychological functioning reflected the living conditions that they experienced abroad as much as (if not more than) those experienced in the UK (see Rutter & Madge, 1976). That would no longer be the case today. Almost all such children have been born in and reared entirely in Britain. However, this change in pattern would not be quite the same in other ethnic minority groups. Caution is, therefore, necessary in making comparisons across different time periods. Thus, it is known that the associations with crime are often very different for first- and second-generation immigrants.

The fourth example is provided by parental divorce which was very much a minority experience at the turn of this century but which now affects at least a third of children in some European countries. The question is whether or not the fact that divorce is now socially more acceptable has reduced the psychosocial risks with which it is associated. The answer in this case is probably not, because the risks seem to stem from the family discord that precedes, accompanies and follows divorce rather than from the event of family breakup as such (Cherlin et al., 1991; Buchanan et al., 1991; Block et al., 1986). However, the lack of change in risk in line with altered social acceptability may not apply to other risk indices.

The fifth example emphasizes that an important light on possible mediating mechanisms may be thrown by changes in the pattern of associations over time. In the first half of this century, coronary artery disease leading to heart attacks was more common in socially advantaged groups whereas today it is much more common in the relatively disadvantaged – the association with social class has completely changed its direction (Barker, 1991). This observation led to a series of studies examining the role of various childhood factors that might have played a part in risk mechanisms. Their findings showed that *low* weight at birth and during the first year of life was associated with a substantially increased risk of heart disease in middle age. Because, in adult life it is *excessive* weight that constitutes a key risk factor, it has been suggested that relative malnutrition in early life may have metabolic effects that render individuals less able to handle overeating later (to express the hypothesis in a rather oversimplified form). The lesson, as already noted from developmental considerations, is that we need to consider both the long-term and immediate consequences of changed social circumstances.

In the last chapter, attention was drawn to the need to examine interconnections between social change and trends in psychosocial disorder through replications across nations and over multiple time periods. The value of this approach, but also the hazards resulting from differences in patterns of findings according to the indices chosen and varying interpretations on their meaning, is well illustrated by the contrasting conclusions of Uhlenberg & Eggebeen (1986) and Furstenberg & Condran (1988) on whether the increasing proportions of mothers in the US workforce has led to a declining well-being of American adolescents.

Macro-Effects on Micro-Variables

Discussions and studies of social phenomena have tended to use rather different concepts and variables according to the level of social reality being considered (Nowack et al., 1990). Thus, psychologists usually focus on the cognition, behaviours and feelings of individuals; family researchers on the dynamics and structure of the family social system; sociologists on the social forces generated by and within groups or organizations; and political scientists on market forces and economic policies at a national level. It is obvious that changes at any of these levels may have important consequences for the life and functioning of individuals. The issue, however, is *how* to make links between these different levels. It may be generally helpful to appreciate that an ecological or systems approach is applicable at all levels, and between all levels (Bronfenbrenner, 1979; Maruyama, 1963). Thus, biologists have long appreciated that changes in one part of a biological (or social) system may set off other changes in more distant parts. In this way, marginal shifts may set in motion larger changes with more radical consequences. However, that does not provide direct guidance on *how* to investigate the interplay between micro-and macro- variables or between layers of nested ecosystems. Macro level influences can make an impact on individual phenomena but in order to obtain an understanding of how this effect is mediated it is crucial to specify *how* the macro-variables may be translated into micro terms (Mason & Fienberg, 1985). That requires that the linkage between levels actually be measured.

One approach is to seek to use variables that extend across levels and to examine their effects within and between subsets. The example of studies of school effectiveness was used in this connection in the preceding chapter. However, the analyses need to include consideration of how group effects may impinge differentially on individuals according to the social subset in which they find themselves. For example, grouping children in school classes according to their level of attainment ('tracking' or 'streaming') makes little or no difference to the mean level of children's educational progress (see Rutter & Madge, 1976). However, which stream or track pupils are placed in *does* make a difference to their progress. Compared with similar fellow pupils in unstreamed classes, those in higher streams do better but those in lower streams do less well.

It may also be helpful to consider *how* changes at one level impinge on the next, just as it is useful at an individual level to consider how one set of variables interconnects with another. An example of the latter type is provided by Conger et al.'s (1992) path analysis of the effects of economic hardship on boys' psychosocial adjustment. The findings showed that, in their sample, the main pathway was from economic pressures to mother's depression to marital conflict and impaired parenting, with only the last of these having a direct effect on the boys. Similarly, Rutter and Quinton (1977) showed that rates of psychiatric disorder among school children in inner London were twice as high as those on the Isle of Wight. Detailed analyses went on to show that the area difference had very little (if any) *direct* effect on children's behaviour. Rather, the effect reflected an area influence on the family and on parents (with higher rates of family discord and parental mental disorder in the metropolis). When like families in both areas were compared, the rates of disorder in the children did not differ. Subsequent analyses went on to demonstrate that the family effect on disorder (reflecting area influences) in adolescents derived from effects already apparent in middle childhood or earlier (Rutter, 1979a).

In considering the interplay between macro-and micro- variables we also need to bear in mind the possibility that the mechanisms operating in some social groups may differ from those applicable in others. Thus, for example, a generation ago, sociologists were very interested in the notion of normative delinquent subcultures in working-class or socially disadvantaged populations. As it turned out, the notion seemed to have very little validity in the UK and the US, at least in the conditions applicable to young people at that time (Rutter & Giller, 1983). However, it may well have greater applicability in parts of Southern Italy where organized crime involving whole families has provided a net of solidarity and consensus within civil society (Barbagallo, 1988). It appears that broad collusions between political, economic and criminal forces have provided channels for influence through the creation and assignment of jobs and positions of power. As a consequence, it seems that there has been a legitimization of crime within this subculture so that the usual generalizations about family influences do not apply in any straightforward way. Systematic study of this situation has been quite limited so far, and it would be premature to seek to infer general principles. Nevertheless, there is the implication that, in studying social trends, there is a need to consider the possibility of subgroups of the population where different politico-economic conditions, or historical circumstances, or social mores mean that risk factors operate in a somewhat different way (at least to some extent).

Two-way Effects Between Macro- and Micro-Variables

Finally, in considering the interplay between macro- and micro-variables, it is important to appreciate that two-way influences are likely to be usual. The possible effects of the mass media on young people's behaviour illustrate the point. Part of the scepticism about the reality of such effects (for example, Freedman, 1984) stems from the fact that what is portrayed in the media reflects attitudes and behaviour in society at large and the fact that, to an important degree, people choose what sort of films or TV programmes they watch. Thus, the very high level of violence portrayed in the media is a function of prevailing conditions in the community and of people's interest in viewing violence. Similarly, individual differences in the extent to which children watch violent programmes is likely to reflect variations in their own propensity to engage in violent behaviour. In order to achieve a valid assessment of the effects of the media on individual behaviours, it is necessary to take account of effects going from individuals to the media. As described in several systematic reviews (see for example, Pearl, 1982; Atkin, 1990; Comstock & Strasburger, 1990; Signorielli, 1990; Brown, J. D. et al., 1990; Phillips, 1989; Jonas, 1992; Gould & Shaffer, 1986) a range of research strategies may be used for this purpose. These include: – laboratory or analogue experiments, changes over time in groups that differ in exposure to media, time trends in relation to highly publicized events, and changes over time in individuals in relation to individual differences in exposure to particular sorts of media. The results of such research provide convincing evidence of the reality of media effects, albeit fairly weak ones overall. Moreover, the findings suggest effects that are pervasive across quite a wide range of behaviours including alcohol use, violence, gender stereotypes, sexual behaviour and suicidal acts (but also including some positive features).

Four main points need to be made about the findings. First, the effects vary according to the ways in which the behaviours are portrayed in the media. For example, it seems to matter whether violence is in realistic situations with which viewers can identify and whether it is shown as pleasurable or problem-solving. The implication is that the effects reflect a variety of mechanisms including social learning, desensitization to the use of violence and an increasing belief that violence is normative and justified. The media are also likely to have an effect on the ways in which people compare themselves with others. Second, children vary in their susceptibility to media influences, with effects tending to be greatest when the media messages are consistent with other influences in children's lives and when their own behavioural propensities coincide with the messages. Third, the causal processes probably operate in indirect causal chain terms such that the macro-influences serve to amplify pre-existing marginal tendencies, with the cyclical interaction serving over time to lead to significant psychosocial disturbance in vulnerable individuals (Caprara & Zimbardo, 1994). Thus, Huesmann (1986) put forward a reciprocal model in which some personal factors (such as poor academic achievement) lead to greater TV watching and others (such as aggressiveness and aggression) to a greater interest in TV violence. Then, viewing violent programmes enhances the encoding of aggressive scripts which, in turn, both increases the likelihood of aggressive reactions to interpersonal conflict and increases identification with TV characters and strengthens the interest in TV violence, so completing the circle.

The fourth point, which is basic to the arguments in this chapter, is that both the methodological issues and the substantive findings on operative mechanisms closely parallel those applicable to the study of individual development. Thus, we referred earlier to the role of reputations in enhancing the stabilization and perpetuation of both aggressive behaviour and peer rejection. Ordinarily, of course, reputation will have been formed initially on the basis of the actual behaviour of young people. Accordingly, it is necessary to use research designs that can separate the effects of reputation from those of actual behaviour (see Hymel et al., 1990). Four main designs have been used: 1) comparison of interpersonal interactions in groups of peers who have not met before (i.e. there are no reputations) and those who know one another (i.e. they bring their reputations with them); 2) comparison of responses to the *same* behaviours according to the reputation of the children exhibiting the behaviour; 3) analogue situations); and 4) study of the effects of reputations that are independent of the subject's own behaviour (because they derive from social group, ethnicity and the like). The findings are clear-cut in indicating that reputations *do* have effects on how children are treated by their peers and suggest that these effects probably play a role in the perpetuation of the behaviour that gave rise to the reputation in the first place. However, research into teacher expectancies (see Brophy, 1983; Blatchford et al., 1989) bring out the additional point that there is little effect from reputations that run counter to observed behaviour; the main influence stems from an enhancement of the latter. Probably, much the same applies to macro-influences. That is to say, they are not likely to make much impact if they are out of step with other influences impinging on the individual and with individual propensities. However, they may have a much greater effect in circumstances in which they can amplify pre-existing characteristics and can enhance other influences operating at the micro-level.

CONCLUSIONS

It is all too apparent that there are many difficulties involved in any study of the possible effects of social change on secular trends in psychosocial disorder in young people. Nevertheless, a consideration of developmental principles, of the mode of operation of individual differences, and of the interplay between macro- and micro- variables does at least provide a few guidelines on some of the possible ways in which mechanisms might operate.

REFERENCES

Alwin, D.F., Cohen, R.L. & Newcomb, T.M. (1991). *Aging, personality and social change: Attitude persistence and change over the life-span.* Madison: University of Wisconsin Press.

Asendorpf, J.B. (1990a). Development of inhibition during childhood: Evidence for situational specificity and a two-factor model. *Developmental Psychology 26,* 721-730.

Asendorpf, J.B. (1990b). Beyond social withdrawal: Shyness, unsociability, and peer avoidance. *Human Development 33,* 250-259.

Asendorpf, J.B. (1992). Beyond stability: Predicting inter-individual differences in intra-individual change. *European Journal of Personality 6,* 103-117.

Atkin, C.K. (1990). Effects of televised alcohol messages on teenage drinking patterns. *Journal of Adolescent Health Care 11,* 10-24.

Bandura, A. (1986). *Social foundations of thought and action.* Englewood Cliffs, NJ: Prentice-Hall.

Bandura, A. (1990). Perceived self-efficacy in the exercise of control over AIDS infection. *Evaluation and Program Planning 13,* 9-17.

Barbagallo, F. (1988). *Camorra e criminalita organizzata in Campania* (Camorra and organized criminality in Campania). Naples: Liguori Editore.

Barker, D.J.P. (1991). The intrauterine environment and adult cardiovascular disease. In G.R. Bock & J. Whelan (eds.) *The childhood environment and adult disease,* 3-10. Ciba Foundation Symposium no. 156. Chichester: Wiley.

Blatchford, P., Burke, J., Farquhar, C., Plevis, I. & Tizard, B. (1989). Teacher expectations in infant school: Associations with attainment and progress, curricular coverage and classroom interaction. *British Journal of Educational Psychology 59*, 19-30.

Block, J.H., Block, J. & Gjerde, P.F. (1986). The personality of children prior to divorce: A prospective study. *Child Development 52*, 827-840.

Bock, G.R. & Whelan, J. (eds.) (1991). *The childhood environment and adult disease.* Ciba Foundation Symposium no. 156. Chichester: Wiley.

Bourne, P.G., Rose, R.M. & Mason, J.W. (1967). Urinary 17-OHCS levels: Data on seven helicopter ambulance medics in combat. *Archives of General Psychiatry 17*, 104-110.

Bourne, P.G., Rose, R.M. & Mason, J.W. (1968). 17-OHCS levels in combat: Special forms 'A' Team under threat of attack. *Archives of General Psychiatry 19*, 135-140.

Bretherton, I. & Waters, E. (eds.) (1985). Growing points of attachment theory and research. *Monographs of the Society for Research in Child Development 209*, (no.1-2). Chicago: University of Chicago Press.

Bronfenbrenner, U. (1979). *The ecology of human development: Experiments by nature and design.* Cambridge, MA: Harvard University Press.

Brophy, J. E. (1983). Research on the self-fulfilling prophecy and teacher expectations. *Journal of Educational Psychology 75*, 631-661.

Brown, G.W. and others, (1990). Self-esteem and depression. I: Measurement issues and prediction of onset. II: Social correlates of self-esteem. III: Aetiological issues. IV: Effect on course and recovery. *Social Psychiatry and Psychiatric Epidemiology 25*, 200-209, 225-234, 235-243, 244-249.

Brown, J.D., Childers, K.W. & Waszcak, C.S. (1990). Television and adolescent sexuality. *Journal of Adolescent Health Care 11*, 62-70.

Buchanan, C.M., Maccoby, E.E. & Dornbusch, S.M. (1991). Caught between parents: Adolescents' experience in divorced homes. *Child Development 62*, 1008-1029.

Caprara, G.V. (1987). The disposition-situation debate and research on aggression. *European Journal of Personality 1*, 1-16.

Caprara, G.V. (1992). Marginal deviations, aggregated effects, disruption of continuity, and deviation amplifying mechanisms. In P.J. Hettema & I.J. Deary (eds.) *Foundations of Personality*, 227-250. Dodrecht: Kluwer Academia Publichor.

Caprara, G.V., Manzy, J. & Perugini, M. (1992). Investing guilt in relation to emotionality and aggression. *Personality and Individual Differences 13*, 77-84.

Caprara, G.V., Mazzotti, E. & Prezza, M. (1988). La percezione della violenza (perception of violence). In Labos (ed.) *Giovani e violenza*, 97-150. Rome: TER.

Caprara, G.V. & Pastorelli, C. (1989). Toward a reorientation of research on aggression. *European Journal of Personality 3*, 121-138.

Caprara, G.V. & Pastorelli, C. (1992). Early determinants and correlates of aggressive behaviour. In A. Fraczek & H. Zumkley (eds.) *Socialization and aggression*, 103-113. Berlin: Springer Verlag.

Caprara, G.V., Pastorelli, C. & Weiner, B. (1994). At-risk childrens' causal inferences given emotional feedback and their understanding of the excuse-giving process: 'When a little may be a lot'. *European Journal of Personality 8*, 31-43.

Caprara, G.V. & Van Heck, G. (eds.) (1992). *Modern personality psychology.* London: Harvester Wheatsheaf.

Caprara, G.V. & Zimbardo, P. (1994). Aggregation and amplification of marginal deviations in the social construction of personality and maladjustment. *European Journal of Personality.*

Casaer, P., de Vries, L. & Marlow, N. (1991). Prenatal and perinatal risk factors for psychosocial development. In M. Rutter & P. Casaer (eds.) *Biological risk factors for psychosocial disorders,* 139-174. Cambridge: Cambridge University Press.

Caspi, A. & Elder Jr., G.H. (1988). Emergent family patterns: The intergenerational construction of problem behaviour and relationships. In R.A. Hinde & J. Stevenson-Hinde (eds.) *Relationships within families: Mutual influences,* 218-240. Oxford: Clarendon Press.

Caspi, A., Lynam, D., Moffitt, T.E. & Silva, P.A. (1993). Unraveling girl's delinquency: Biological, dispositional and contextual contributions to adolescent misbehavior. *Developmental Psychology 29,* 19-30.

Caspi, A. & Herbener, E.S. (1990). Continuity and change: Assortative marriage and the consistency of personality in adulthood. *Journal of Personality and Social Psychology 58,* 250-258.

Cherlin, A.J., Furstenberg Jr., F.F., Chase-Lansdale, P.L., Kiernan, K.E., Robins, P.K., Morrison, D.R. & Teitler, J.O. (1991). Longitudinal studies of effects of divorce on children in Great Britain and the United States. *Science 252,* 1386-1389.

Clarke, A.M. & Clarke, A.D.B. (1976). *Early experience: Myth and evidence.* London: Open Books.

Coleman, J.C. (1978). Current contradictions in adolescent theory. *Journal of Youth and Adolescence 7,* 1-11.

Coleman, J.C. & Hendry, L. (1990). *The nature of adolescence* (2nd edition). London: Routledge.

Comstock, G. & Strasburger, V.C. (1990). Deceptive appearances: Television violence and aggressive behaviour. *Journal of Adolescent Health Care 11,* 31-44.

Conger, R.D., Conger, K.J., Elder Jr., G.H., Lorenz, F.O., Simons, R.L. & Whitbeck, L.B. (1992). A family process model of economic hardship and adjustment of early adolescent boys. *Child Development 63,* 526-541.

Digman, J.M. (1990). Personality structure: Emergence of the five factors model. *Annual review of Psychology 41,* 417-440.

DiLalla, L.F. & Gottesman, I.I. (1989). Heterogeneity of causes for delinquency and criminality: Lifespan perspective. *Development and Psychopathology 1,* 339-349.

Dodge, K.A. & Crick, N.R. (1990). Social information-processing bases of aggressive behavior in children. *Personality and Social Psychology Bulletin 16,* 8-22.

Douglas, J.W.B. (1975). Early hospital admissions and later disturbances of behaviour and learning. *Developmental Medicine and Child Neurology 17,* 456.

Dunn, J. & Plomin, R. (1990). *Separate lives: Why siblings are so different.* New York: Basic Books.

Dweck, C.S. & Leggett, E.C. (1988). A social-cognitive approach to motivation and personality. *Psychological Review 95,* 256-283.

Eisenberg, L. (1986). Mindlessness and brainlessness in psychiatry. *British Journal of Psychiatry 148*, 497-508.

Elder Jr., G.H. (1974). *Children of the Great Depression.* Chicago: University of Chicago Press.

Elder Jr., G.H. (1991). Lives and social change. In W.R. Heinz (ed.) *Theoretical advances in life course research V.* Series title: *Status passages and the life course.* Weinheim: Deutscher Studien Verlag.

Elder Jr., G.H. & Caspi, A. (1990). Studying lives in a changing society: Sociological and personological explorations (Henry A. Murray Lecture Series). In A.I. Rabin, R.A. Zucher & S. Frank (eds.) *Studying persons and lives*, 201-247. New York: Springer Verlag.

Emery, R.E. (1982). Interparental conflict and the children of discord and divorce. *Psychological Bulletin 92*, 310-330.

Endler, N.S. & Parker, J.S. (1992). Interactionism revisited: Reflections on the continuing crisis in the personality area. *European Journal of Personality 6*, 177-198.

Endler, N.S., Parker, D.A., Bagby, R.M. & Cox, B.J. (1991). Multidimensionality of state and trait anxiety: Factor structure of the Endler Multidimensional Anxiety Scale. *Journal of Personality and Social Psychology 60*, 919-926.

Engfer, A., Walper, S. & Rutter, M. (in press). Individual characteristics as a force in development. In M. Rutter & D.F. Hay (eds.) *Development through life: A handbook for clinicians.* Oxford: Blackwell Scientific.

Farrington, D.P. (1989). Early predictors of adolescent aggression and adult violence. *Violence and Victims 2*, 79-100.

Freedman, J.L. (1984). Effect of television violence on aggressiveness. *Psychological Bulletin 96*, 227-246.

Furstenberg Jr., F.F. & Condran, G.A. (1988). Family change and adolescent wellbeing: A re-examination of US trends. In A. Cherlin (ed.) *The changing American family and public policy*, 117-155. Washington, DC: The Urban Institute.

Gould, M.S. & Shaffer, D. (1986). The impact of suicide in television movies: Evidence of imitation. *New England Journal of Medicine 315*, 690-694.

Gray, G., Smith, A. & Rutter, M. (1980). School attendance and the first year of employment. In L. Hersov & I. Berg (eds.) *Out of school: Modern perspectives in truancy and school refusal*, 343-370. Chichester: Wiley.

Guerra, N.G. & Slaby, R.G. (1990). Cognitive mediators of aggression in adolescent offenders, II: Intervention. *Developmental Psychology 26*, 1120-1134.

Hennessy, J.W. & Levine, S. (1979). Stress, arousal, and the pituitary-adrenal system: A psychoendocrine hypothesis. In J.M. Srague & A.N. Epstein (eds.) *Progress in psychobiology and physiological psychology*, 134-178. New York: Academic Press.

Hirshfeld, D.R., Rosenbaum, J.F., Biederman, J., Bolduc, E.A., Faraone, S.V., Snidman, N., Reznick, S. & Kagan, J. (1992). Stable behavioral inhibition and its association with anxiety disorder. *Journal of the American Academy of Child and Adolescent Psychiatry 31*, 103-111.

Hodges, J. & Tizard, B. (1989a). IQ and behavioural adjustment of ex-institutional adolescents. *Journal of Child Psychology and Psychiatry 30*, 53-75.

Hodges, J. & Tizard, B. (1989b). Social and family relationships of ex-institutional adolescents. *Journal of Child Psychology and Psychiatry 30*, 77-97.

Huesmann, LR., Eron, L., Lefkowitz, M. & Walder, L. (1984). Stability of aggression over time and generations. *Developmental Psychology 20*, 1120-1134.

Huesmann, L.R. (1986). Psychological processes promoting the relation between exposure to media violence and aggressive behavior by the viewer. *Journal of Social Issues 42, 125-139.*

Hurrelmann, K. (1989). The social world of adolescents: A sociological perspective. In K. Hurrelmann & U. Engel (eds.) *The social world of adolescents: International perspectives*, 3-26. Berlin/New York: De Gruyter.

Hymel, S., Wagner, E & Butler, L.J. (1990). Reputational bias: View from the peer group. In S.R. Asher & J.D. Coie (eds.) *Peer rejection in childhood*, 156-186. Cambridge: Cambridge University Press.

Jenkins, J.M. & Smith, M.A. (1990). Factors protecting children living in disharmonious homes: Maternal reports. *Journal of the American Academy of Child and Adolescent Psychiatry 29*, 60-69.

Jessor, R., Donovan, J.E. & Costa, F. M. (1991). *Beyond adolescence. Problem behavior and young adult development*. New York: Cambridge University Press.

Jonas, K. (1992). Modelling and suicide: A test of the Werther effect. *British Journal of Social Psychology 31*, 295-306.

Kendler, K.S., Neale, M.C., Kessler, R.C., Heath, A.C. & Eaves, L.J. (1992). A population-based twin study of major depression in women: The impact of varying definitions of illness. *Archives of General Psychiatry 49*, 716-723.

Kolvin, I., Miller, F.J.W., Scott, D.M., Gatzanis, S.R.M., & Fleeting, M. (1990). *Continuities of deprivation? The Newcastle 1000 family study*. Aldershot, Hants: Avebury.

Ledingham, J.E. & Schwartzman, A.E. (1984). A 3-year follow-up of aggressive and withdrawn behavior in childhood: Preliminary findings. *Journal of Abnormal Child Psychology 12*, 157-168.

Loeber, R., Wung, P., Keenan, K., Giroux, B., Stouthamer-Loeber, M., Van Dammen, W.B. & Maughan, B. (1993). Developmental pathways in disruptive child behavior. *Development and Psychopathology 5*, 103-133.

Magnusson, D. (1988). *Individual development from an interactional perspective: A longitudinal study*. Hillsdale, NJ: Lawrence Erlbaum.

Magnusson, D. (1990). Personality research-challenges for the future. *European Journal of Personality 4*, 1-17.

Magnusson, D. & Bergman, L.R. (1990). A pattern approach to the study of pathways from childhood to adulthood. In L. Robins & M. Rutter (eds.) *Straight and devious pathways from childhood to adulthood*, 101-115. Cambridge: Cambridge University Press.

Maruyama, M. (1963). The second cybernetics: Deviation-amplifying mutual causal processes. *American Scientist*, 164-179.

Mason, W.M. & Fienberg, S.E. (eds.) (1985). *Cohort analysis in social research: Beyond the identification problem*. New York: Springer Verlag.

Maughan, B. & Pickles, A. (1990). Adopted and illegitimate children growing up. In L. Robins & M. Rutter (eds.) *Straight and devious pathways from childhood to adulthood*, 36-61. Cambridge: Cambridge University Press.

Mayr, T. (1992). Die soziale Stellung schüchtern-gehemmter Kinder in der Kindergartengruppe (The peer status of shy-inhibited children in the kindergarten-group). *Zeitschrift für Entwicklungspsychologie und Pädagogische Psychologie 24*, 249-265.

Maziade, M. (1989). Should adverse temperament matter to the clinician? An empirically based answer. In G.A. Kohnstamm, J.E. Bates & M.K. Rothbart (eds.) *Temperament in childhood*, 421-435. Chichester: Wiley.

Newcomb, T.M. (1943). *Personality and social change*. New York: Dryden.

Nowack, A., Szamrej, J. & Latane, B. (1990). From private attitude to public opinion: A dynamic theory impact. *Psychological Review 3*, 362-376.

Olweus, D. (1979). Stability of aggressive reaction patterns in males: A review. *Psychological Bulletin 86*, 852-875.

Pearl, D. (ed.) (1982). *Television and behavior: Ten years of scientific progress and implications for the Eighties*. US Department of Health and Human Services. Publ. No. ADD82-1195. Washington, DC: US Government Printing Office.

Pervin, L.A. (1990). Personality theory and research: Prospects for the future. In L.A. Pervin (ed.) *Handbook of personality theory and research*, 723-727. New York: Guilford Press.

Phillips, D.P. (1989). Recent advances in suicidology: The study of imitative suicide. In R.F. Diekstra, R. Morris, S. Platt, A. Schmidtke, & G. Sonneck (eds.) *Suicide and its preventions: The role of attitudes and imitation*, 299-312. Leiden: Brill.

Plomin, R. & Bergeman, C.S. (1991). The nature of nurture: Genetic influences on 'environmental' measures. *Behavioural and Brain Sciences 14*, 373-386.

Plomin, R. & Daniels, D. (1987). Why are children in the same family so different from one another? *Behavioural and Brain Sciences 10*, 1-15.

Prior, M. (1992). Childhood temperament. *Journal of Child Psychology and Psychiatry and Allied Disciplines 33*, 249-279.

Pulkkinen, L. & Tremblay, R.E. (1992). Patterns of boys' social adjustment in two cultures and at different ages: A longitudinal perspective. *International Journal of Behavioural Development 15*, 528-553.

Quinton, D. & Rutter, M. (1976). Early hospital admissions and later disturbances of behaviour: An attempted replication of Douglas's findings. *Developmental Medicine and Child Neurology 18*, 447-459.

Quinton, D. & Rutter, M. (1988). *Parenting breakdown: The making and breaking of inter-generational links*. Aldershot, Hants: Avebury.

Richards, M.H., Boxer, A.M., Petersen, A.C. & Albrecht, R. (1990). Relation of weight to body image in pubertal girls and boys from two communities. *Developmental Psychology 26*, 313-321.

Robins, L.N. (1966). *Deviant children grown up.* Baltimore: Williams & Wilkins.

Robins, L.N. (1991). Conduct disorder. *Journal of Clinical Psychology and Psychiatry 32*, 193-199.

Robins, L.N. (1993). Vietnam veterans' rapid recovery from heroin-addiction: A fluke or normal expectation? *Addiction 88*, 1041-1054.

Rutter, M. (1979a). *Changing youth in a changing society: Patterns of adolescent development and disorder.* London: The Nuffield Provincial Hospitals Trust/Harvard University Press.

Rutter, M. (1979b). Protective factors in children's responses to stress and disadvantages. In M.W. Kent & J.E. Rolf (eds.) *Primary prevention of psychopathology, III: Social competence in children,* 49-74. Hanover, NH: University Press of New England.

Rutter, M. (1981a). Stress, coping and development: Some issues and some questions. *Journal of Child Psychology and Psychiatry 22*, 323-356.

Rutter, M. (1981b). *Maternal deprivation reassessed* (2nd edition). Harmondsworth, Middx: Penguin.

Rutter, M. (1987a). The role of cognition in child development and disorder. *British Journal of Medical Psychology 60*, 1-16.

Rutter, M. (1987b). Temperament, personality & personality disorder. *British Journal of Psychiatry 150*, 443-458.

Rutter, M. (1987c). Continuities and discontinuities from infancy. In J. Osofsky (ed.) *Handbook of infant development* (2nd edition), 1256-1296. New York: Wiley.

Rutter, M. (1989). Pathways from childhood to adult life. *Journal of Child Psychology and Psychiatry 30*, 23-51.

Rutter, M. (1990). Psychosocial resilience and protective mechanisms. In J. Rolf, A. Masten, D. Cicchetti, K. Neuchterlein & S. Weintraub (eds.) *Risk and protective factors in the development of psychopathology,* 181-214. New York: Cambridge University Press.

Rutter, M. (1991). Nature, nurture and psychopathology: A new look at an old topic. *Development and Psychopathology 3*, 125-136.

Rutter, M. (1993). Resilience: Some conceptual considerations. *Journal of Adolescent Health 4*, 626-631.

Rutter, M. (1994). Concepts of causation and implications for intervention. In A. Petersen and J. Mortimer (eds.) *Youth, unemployment and society,* 147-171. New York: Cambridge University Press.

Rutter, M. & Giller, H. (1983). *Juvenile delinquency: Trends and perspectives.* Harmondsworth, Middx: Penguin.

Rutter, M. & Madge, N. (1976). *Cycles of disadvantage: A review of research.* London: Heinemann Educational.

Rutter, M. & Pickles, A. (1991). Person-environment interactions: Concepts, mechanisms and implications for data analysis. In T.D. Wachs & R. Plomin (eds.)

Conceptualization and measurement of organism – Environment interaction,
105-141. Washington, DC: American Psychological Association.

Rutter, M. & Quinton, D. (1977). Psychiatric disorder – ecological factors and
concepts of causation. In H. McGurk (ed.) *Ecological factors in human
development,* 173-187. Amsterdam: North Holland.

Rutter, M. & Rutter, M. (1993). *Developing minds: Challenge and continuity across
the lifespan.* Harmondsworth, Middx: Penguin; New York: Basic Books.

Sampson, R.J. & Laub, J.H. (1992). Crime and deviance in the life course. *Annual
review of Sociology 18,* 63-84.

Scarr, S. (1992). Developmental theories for the 1990s: Development and individual
differences. *Child Development 63,* 1-19.

Signorielli, N. (1990). Children, television and gender roles: Messages and impact.
Journal of Adolescent Health Care 11, 50-58.

Simmons, R.G. & Blyth, D.A. (1987). *Moving into adolescence: The impact of
pubertal change and school context.* New York: Aldine de Gruyter.

Stacey, M., Dearden, R., Pill, R. & Robinson, D. (1970). *Hospitals, children and their
families: The report of a pilot study.* London: Routledge.

Stattin, H. & Magnusson, D. (1990). *Pubertal maturation in female development.*
Hillsdale, NJ: Lawrence Erlbaum.

Tizard, J. (1975). Race and IQ: The limits of probability. *New Behaviour 1,* 6-9.

Uhlenberg, P. & Eggebeen, D. (1986). The declining well-being of American
adolescents. *The Public Interest 82 (Winter),* 25-38.

Wachs, T.D. (1992). *The nature of nurture, individual differences and development
series, Vol. III.* London: Sage.

Wachs, T.D. & Plomin, R. (eds.) (1991). *Conceptualization and measurement of
organism-environment interaction.* Washington, DC: American Psychological
Association.

PART II

Changing Conditions and Individual Development

4

Patterns of Development During Adolescence

NANCY LEFFERT and ANNE C. PETERSEN

INTRODUCTION

Adolescence constitutes a phase of life in which there are particularly marked developmental transitions (Alsaker, in press; Brooks-Gunn & Petersen, 1983; Coleman & Hendry, 1990; Feldman & Elliot, 1990; Hill, 1980; Petersen, 1988; Rutter, 1980). Thus, early adolescence is ushered in by the major hormonal changes that lead on to puberty and which are associated with a tremendous growth spurt (with height gain reaching a velocity that is only exceeded by that in the infancy period) and a virtual restructuring of physique. There are also important increases in cognitive competencies, major developments in social relationships, and gains in social and psychological autonomy. In addition, it is a period that involves many important role transitions. These include leaving school, driving a car, being able to drink alcohol legally, voting, first love affair, first sexual relationship, starting work, and possibly getting married and becoming a parent.

The late teenage years also constitute a period during which many psychosocial disorders increase greatly in frequency, with many reaching a peak prevalence between 15 and 25 years (Rutter, 1990). That is so with respect to most of those considered in this volume: substance abuse, crime, depression, attempted suicide and eating disorders. Several serious psychiatric conditions, such as schizophrenia, which are outside the scope of this volume, also peak in late adolescence or early adult life.

Adolescence in all industrialized societies, and at all times during this century, constitutes a period of life that is full of both opportunity and risk. During the second decade of life, adolescents struggle to confront two critical tasks: to temper the internal and external stressors of this period and to prepare for life as an adult. The first requires the skills to manage the primary, secondary, and contextual changes necessary for the transition from childhood to adult roles. The second is achieved through effective coping with the changes and challenges of adolescence, or at least traversing the period without sustaining damage that could permanently impair adult functioning.

To an important extent, 'the development patterns' of adolescence are ones that are universal in their applicability. Nevertheless over the course of the twentieth century, the meaning of adolescence as a developmental period has changed a great deal. To begin with, there have been major alterations in the social construction of adolescence. These are evident in legislation on compulsory education, in the laws differentiating juvenile from adult offenders, and in legal restrictions on the employment of juveniles. However, they are also apparent in the mass youth consumer market (in clothes, music and entertainment) that came into being after the Second World War, and in the growth of youth cultures. In addition, there have been major changes in the timing of adolescent transitions such as the fall in the average age of reaching puberty, the rise in the average age of completing education, and the earlier initiation of sexual relationships.

This chapter seeks to provide a brief outline of the main developmental transitions that characterize adolescence, together with a discussion of their possible implications for increased or decreased risk for the psychosocial disorders that are typical of the age period. Throughout the chapter, the main emphasis is on those transitions that have changed their meaning or timing during this century and which, therefore, might be relevant in any consideration of possible causal influences contributing to secular trends in disorder.

BIOLOGICAL CHANGE

Pubertal development brings the most striking changes during the adolescent period. Prior to its onset, both boys and girls have children's bodies; within a few short years they mature into the physical appearance of adults. Puberty involves changes in height, muscle and fat tissue in both sexes; breast development and onset of menstruation (menarche) in girls; and voice deepening and growth of facial and body hair in boys. The timing of these changes, as well as their patterning, differs markedly between the sexes. Thus girls generally begin puberty one and a half to two years before boys (Tanner, 1962, 1989). Puberty is accompanied by a marked increase in height in both boys and girls; this increase is an early manifestation of puberty in girls but a late one in boys. In both sexes the spectacular increase in height is accompanied by marked changes in physique, but again, the pattern of changes differs between the sexes. Girls increase in hip width, with substantial accumulation of fat as their growth in height slows down. By contrast, boys show an increase in shoulder breadth and a greater increase in muscle than that experienced by girls. Moreover, many (but not all) boys tend to lose fat, rather than gain it, during this period, although there may be some increase in fat in later adolescence when the height spurt slows down. The net result of these sex differences is that most boys in Western societies welcome and are pleased with the physical changes of adolescence, whereas many girls are unhappy about the acquisition of fat even though they may be glad about other aspects of sexual maturity (Feldman & Elliot, 1990; Petersen, 1988; Rutter, 1980). By the late teens and early twenties, up to half of girls have dieted, usually without success. Dieting is much less frequent in boys who, instead, tend to exercise to improve their strength and physique.

As well as the visible external changes in body shape there are major internal changes in hormone secretion. The first event, which precedes puberty by several years, is the increased secretion of gonadotrophic hormones by the pituitary, which bring about the maturation of the ovaries and testes (Gupta et al., 1975). At about 6 to 8 years, the production of male sex hormones by the adrenal glands increases, with a further sharp increase (especially in boys) a few years later at puberty. The production of female sex hormones shows a parallel increase in girls. The male hormones increase sex drive in both males and females and are also responsible for the rise in pimples, blackheads and acne that follows the increase in oily secretions. There is a great deal of individual variation in both the timing of the onset of these changes and their tempo (Eichorn, 1975; Tanner & Davies, 1985).

Secular Trends in Pubertal Timing

Adolescents today in Western Europe, the United States, and Japan experience puberty earlier than adolescents 100 years ago (Chumlea, 1982; Frisch, 1990; Tanner, 1989). In addition, they grow taller, weigh more, and appear physically more mature than in previous generations of adolescents (Chumlea, 1982).

70

Figure 4.1 Mean or median age of first menstruation (menarche) as a function of calendar year from 1790 to 1980

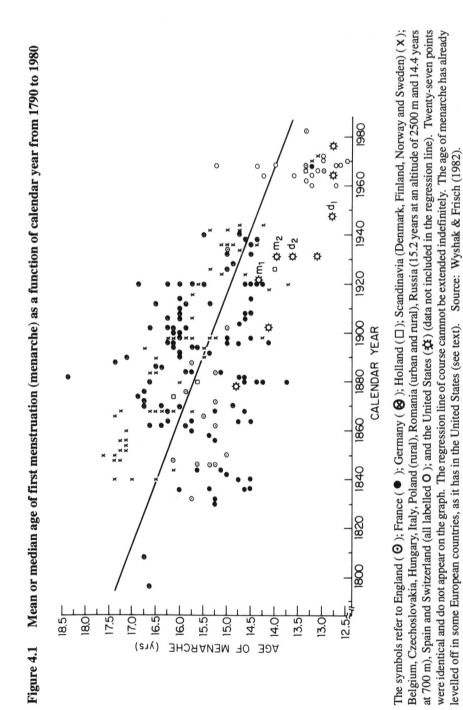

The symbols refer to England (⊙); France (●); Germany (⊗); Holland (□); Scandinavia (Denmark, Finland, Norway and Sweden) (X); Belgium, Czechoslovakia, Hungary, Italy, Poland (rural), Romania (urban and rural), Russia (15.2 years at an altitude of 2500 m and 14.4 years at 700 m), Spain and Switzerland (all labelled **O**); and the United States (✿) (data not included in the regression line). Twenty-seven points were identical and do not appear on the graph. The regression line of course cannot be extended indefinitely. The age of menarche has already levelled off in some European countries, as it has in the United States (see text). Source: Wyshak & Frisch (1982).

The average age of first menstruation has dropped in European and North American populations from somewhere between 15 and 17 a century ago to about 12 or 13 today (Chumlea, 1982; Frisch, 1990; Tanner, 1989) (see Figure 4.1). This decrease amounts to approximately three to four months per decade (Wyshak & Frisch, 1982). During the last few decades, the fall in the age of menarche has either markedly decreased or stopped; the same applies to the increase in height. Although age of maturation is more difficult to discern in boys because of the absence of a discrete event that is easily measured, such as menstruation, findings indicate that the age of male voice deepening has probably decreased from 18 years a century ago to some 14 years of age today (Chumlea 1982; Daw, 1970).

The fall over time in the average age of puberty closely parallels an increase in the average height over the last century and it is clear that improved nutrition has been an important factor in both time trends (Tanner, 1989). However, a lessening in the overall level of disease has probably also played a role (Ellison, 1981; see also Eveleth & Tanner, 1990).

A similar drop in the age of first intercourse has occurred in Europe. Thus, the recent British large-scale national survey (Wellings et al., 1994) showed that the median age of reported first sexual intercourse was 21 years in 55 to 59-year-old women compared with 17 years in 16 to 24-year-olds; the figures for men were closely comparable. Of course, this could reflect the fact that the older adults had to recall an event a much longer time ago. However, repeated cross-sectional surveys show the same trend. Thus, in 1964, 5 per cent of girls in Schofield's (1965) survey had had intercourse by the age of 16 but the figure was 12 per cent in Farrell's (1978) comparable survey a decade later, and 19 per cent in 1990 (Wellings et al., 1994). There can be no doubt that there has been a very substantial increase over the last half-century in the proportion of young people having sexual intercourse by the age of 16. Interestingly, however, the British data suggest a parallel increase over the time in the proportion of people using contraception at first intercourse (although those having first intercourse at 13 to 14 years, are still twice as likely to be unprotected as those having first intercourse in the late teens or early twenties).

Sex Hormone Effects on Behaviour

There are clear connections between increasing levels of male sex hormone and increasing sexual drive in both sexes (Bancroft & Reinisch, 1990; Katchadourian, 1990; Udry, 1979). Regardless of culture, sexual interests and motivation rise markedly with puberty. As a consequence, the initiation into sexual activity rises with age over the adolescent age period in a broadly comparable fashion across countries (see Figure 4.2). By the age of 18 years, some two-thirds of boys and just less than half of girls have had sexual intercourse (Hayes, 1987; Jones et al., 1986; Department of International Economic and Social Affairs, 1988).

Figure 4.2 **Proportion of teenagers who ever had sex by age, for selected countries**

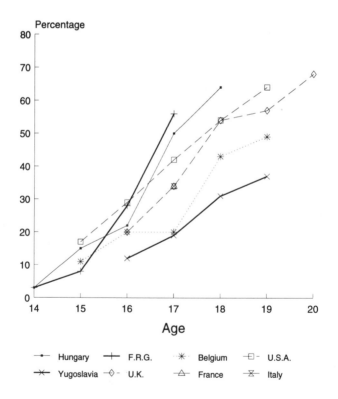

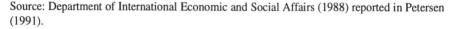

Source: Department of International Economic and Social Affairs (1988) reported in Petersen (1991).

Figure 4.3   **Cumulative percentage of US teenage women who have had premarital sexual intercourse, according to race and year of birth**

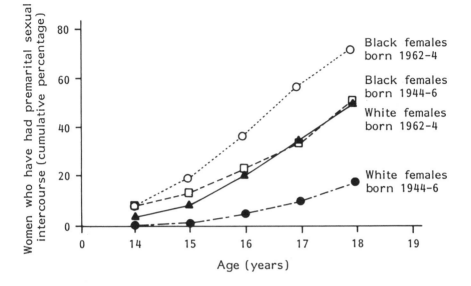

Source: Hofferth et al. (1987).

However, the evidence also shows that sexual behaviour is influenced by sociocultural factors. Within the USA black adolescents become sexually experienced at a much earlier age than their white counterparts (Hofferth et al., 1987 – see Figure 4.3). Poverty, social disadvantage and family disorganization are all associated with an earlier engagement in sexual activities. There are important gender differences, too. Although girls reach puberty some two years earlier than boys, 15-year-old boys are nearly three times as likely as girls to have had sexual intercourse (in both sexes this is usually with older partners). Finally, during the last 50 years or so there has been a marked trend over time for sexual intercourse to begin at an earlier age. Thus, over a mere 20 years the proportion of 18-year-old girls in the USA who had had premarital sexual intercourse doubled. Obviously, this change was too great and too rapid to be accounted for by any secular trend in puberty, particularly as the main increase in sexual activity was at a time when the falling age of puberty was reaching a plateau (Petersen & Leffert, in press).

Surprisingly little is known about hormonal effects on aspects of behaviour other than sexuality (Bancroft, 1991; Susman & Petersen, 1992). In part this reflects methodological problems in the assessment of hormonal levels as indicators of stable individual differences (Halpern & Udry, 1992), but in greater part the ignorance stems from a paucity of longitudinal data in relation to clinically significant disorders (Bancroft, 1991). It seems that male sex hormones have some activating effect on aggression (although the effect is not great), but neither male nor female hormones have a very consistent effect on mood. Moreover, the very limited available data suggest that puberty shows only a rather weak relationship with the rise in depressive disorders during adolescence (Angold & Rutter, 1992).

The onset of menstruation is accompanied in some women by cyclical negative mood changes that tend to be most marked in the days immediately preceding the menses (Bancroft, 1993). It has usually been supposed that these are a direct result of hormonal changes but the evidence on this point suggests that causal mechanisms are more complex than that, with hormonal effects playing some role but not usually a predominant one. There is also only a modest association between the negative mood that is part of the premenstrual syndrome and noncyclical depressive disorders (Bancroft, 1991).

Pubertal Timing and Psychosocial Adjustment

There is a considerable body of research suggesting that individual differences in the timing of puberty are associated with variations in psychosocial functioning (Alsaker, in press; Petersen & Crockett, 1985; Petersen & Taylor, 1980; Rutter, 1980). Pubertal timing has effects on psychosocial adjustment, school achievement, and problem behaviours, but these effects differ between boys and girls.

Early research mainly focused on personality variables (Clausen, 1975; McCandless, 1960) with findings that usually favoured early maturing boys, the differences in girls being less consistent (Jones & Mussen, 1958; Tobin-Richards et al., 1983). More recent research has corroborated the general picture and has contributed to the understanding of the processes involved in these changes (Stattin & Magnusson, 1990).

Early maturing boys tend to be somewhat more self-confident and popular, with more positive body images (Simmons & Blyth, 1987) and higher self-esteem (Blyth et al., 1981). Later maturing boys are less self-assured or popular, generally with more negative self-concepts (Alsaker, in press; Brack et al., 1988). Boys who mature early develop muscle and increased heart and lung capacity earlier; consequently, they are better able to excel at athletics, highly prized in most male groups. Apart from the advantages that may accrue as a result of ability in sports, these boys look more mature. Early maturing boys are more satisfied with their height because they are taller (Simmons & Blyth, 1987) and hence feel more attractive (Tobin-Richards et al., 1983; Simmons & Blyth, 1987).

However, although the advantages experienced by early maturers may persist (Jones, 1965), they do not necessarily stay constant. One small study suggested that, compared with very late maturing boys, early maturing boys may experience a temporary period of being less exploratory, more submissive, more sombre, and yet more quick tempered just after puberty (Peskin, 1967). Not too much should be made of the findings of either persistence or reversal of trends as the results are inconsistent, rely on rather unsatisfactory measures, and derive from a small number of significant findings out of a much larger number of non-significant ones. Early maturation in boys may stand young men in good stead in adolescence, but it has been suggested that it may also reduce the time needed for psychosocial development. This perspective, known as the *stage termination hypothesis* (Petersen & Taylor, 1980), suggests that early puberty cuts short the time available for consolidation and acquisition of skills that characterize the middle childhood years. Evidence to test this hypothesis is not yet available.

The findings for girls also reflect timing differences, although different from those observed in boys. The early studies (Jones & Mussen, 1958) of pubertal timing found that early maturing girls were not popular among, or leaders of, their peers. In addition, it was found that early maturing girls tended to have a more negative body image (Brooks-Gunn, 1987; Dorn et al, 1988; Simmons et al., 1983) compared with later maturing girls, an effect that increases over adolescence (Petersen, 1988). Later maturing girls were more outgoing and self-confident. The effects of context on these issues are obvious. In much of Europe and North America, women currently prize an ideal of thinness (Faust, 1983). A number of studies have supported the association between weight and body image (Blyth et al., 1985; Crockett & Petersen, 1987; Duncan et al., 1985; Garner & Garfinkel, 1980; Silverstein et al., 1986; Stattin & Magnusson, 1990). Cultural values encourage girls to value the long-limbed prepubertal shape. These findings are supported with the exception of some tentative interpretations from Germany (Silbereisen et al., 1989), where apparently a more rounded female figure is considered attractive. This societally -reinforced pursuit of thinness puts girls at additional risk for the development of eating disturbances which, in severe form, may delay puberty (Attie et al., 1987; Sallis, 1993).

Several studies have shown that girls who have an unusually early menarche tend to have more emotional and psychosomatic problems (Aro & Taipale, 1987; Petersen & Crockett, 1985; Stattin & Magnusson, 1990) as well as showing more norm-breaking behaviour (Caspi & Moffitt, 1991; Caspi et al., 1993; Magnusson et al., 1986; Stattin & Magnusson, 1990). Thus, the Swedish longitudinal study found that 14 to 15-year-old girls who reached their menarche before the age of eleven were more likely than other girls to be truant, get drunk, have abortions and take drugs. These effects were shown to be a consequence of some early maturers joining peer groups of older girls. The increased rate of rule breaking did not persist into adult life. The New Zealand longitudinal study of a Dunedin sample indicated that the increase in behaviour problems was largely found in girls clearly showing difficulties before puberty; the effects were also evident only in mixed-sex schools suggesting that the deviant model provided by delinquent boys may have been influential.

Stattin and Magnusson (1990) also found that early maturing girls were less likely to continue their education after the end of compulsory schooling. As a result of opting out of education they landed up in adult life with lower academic qualifications, and with lower occupational attainment.

The findings on the effects of early maturity on boys are much less consistent. Some studies have found that early maturers are more likely to engage in deviant activities (Duncan et al., 1985), but Andersson and Magnusson (1990) found heavy drinking to be more frequent among both early and late maturing 14-year-old boys. As in girls, the effects did not persist into later adolescence.

Pubertal Timing and Scholastic Achievement

The findings on cognitive performance are less clear-cut. UK and US data showed that, on average, early maturing adolescents of both sexes have a slightly higher level of intelligence than late maturers (Newcombe & Dubas, 1987; Tanner, 1989). The differences found were small and the UK difference was evident long before the onset of puberty (see Douglas et al., 1968). US data have indicated that late maturing boys tend to rank lower on standardized achievement tests, on educational expectations held by parents and teachers, and on their own educational aspirations (Dubas et al., 1991; Duke et al., 1982).

Later maturing girls, by contrast, tend to show higher achievement (Dubas et al., 1991; Simmons & Blyth, 1987; Stattin & Magnusson, 1990).

Simmons and Blyth (1987) suggested that, in the United States, later maturing girls are less popular with boys, spend less time in interactions with boys (Crockett & Petersen, 1987), and consequently expend more time and energy on school work. These findings suggest that early maturing girls begin to date earlier (Simmons & Blyth, 1987) and spend less time on school work. As already noted, in Sweden, Stattin and Magnusson (1990) found that early maturing girls were more likely to drop out of education. The lower achievement of late maturing boys is not as well understood. Dubas et al. (1991) suggested that achievement expectations are linked to age-related appearance. Because later maturing boys look immature, adults may perhaps hold lower expectations for their performance and achievement. This speculative suggestion has still to be put to the test. However, it could not account for the lower cognitive levels of late maturers *before* puberty as well as after.

COGNITIVE DEVELOPMENT

In addition to the complex changes occurring as a result of puberty, adolescents develop more advanced cognitive abilities. These changes involve increased ability for abstract reasoning (Inhelder & Piaget, 1958; Keating, 1990). Adolescents are able to think about situations hypothetically (Inhelder & Piaget, 1958) and to use logic in more elaborate ways than younger children. Their ability to make decisions increases (Weithorn & Campbell, 1982). This improved decision-making ability, however, cannot consistently meet the challenges inherent in stressful or novel situations (Linn, 1983). Many of the situations that adolescents face routinely, and which require good judgement, are new to them, such as experimentation with opposite-sex relationships. The fact that adolescents are more likely than adults to be in situations with which they lack experience may render them less able to use their cognitive and decision-making abilities (Crockett & Petersen, 1993). Also, many of the decisions involve emotionally charged issues (Hamburg, 1986), which may add to their difficulty in using mature reasoning and decision-making skills.

DEVELOPMENTS IN SOCIAL RELATIONSHIPS

During adolescence, important changes also occur in the nature and quality of personal relationships, both within and outside the family. As adolescents increase their capacities in other areas, they also increase their ability to develop relationships that are quite different from those of earlier ages. This is true in both peer and family relationships. Over the course of the twentieth century, economic, social, and cultural changes have affected the structure of family and peer relationships.

Family Relationships

Parent-adolescent relationships are often portrayed as being conflictual at best, with a great deal of negative emotion. Thus, early psychoanalytic writings suggested that this conflict was in fact necessary in order to encourage the adolescent's ability to separate from parents (Freud, 1958). However, empirical findings have shown this view to be mistaken. Although there are reports of some temporary distancing during early puberty (Steinberg, 1990), the effects of such distancing are small (Steinberg, 1988). Relationships with parents continue to be important sources of support and closeness for the adolescent (Offer et al., 1981; Youniss & Smollar, 1985) and stressful family relationships are neither universal nor usual (Petersen, 1988; Rutter et al., 1976; Steinberg, 1990).

Although the parent-adolescent relationships remain strong, they undergo a transformation in which the prior expectations of both parents and adolescents about each other's behaviour may be violated. These violations of expectations may occur because the child increasingly needs more autonomy or because the parent increasingly demands that the child should behave more responsibly. As a result, there may be temporary perturbations in the relationship, but most families ultimately reach a concordance of expectations (Collins, 1990; Goodnow & Collins, 1990).

Typically, during adolescence, there is also a gradual shifting of supervision over the adolescent's activities and responsibilities (Maccoby, 1984). In childhood, parents regulate the activities and responsibilities of their children. In adolescence, however, this process evolves into one of co-regulation, with the goal being autonomous functioning by the adolescent upon the transition into adult roles.

Peer Relationships

Peer relationships during adolescence differ from those of middle childhood in quality. Adolescent peer relationships tend to be more intimate than earlier ones, and involve more mutual exchanges of thoughts and feelings, and sharing of activities (Hartup, 1983; Camarena et al., 1990; Youniss & Smollar, 1985).

During the teenage years, adolescents spend more time in association with their peers, out of the direct supervision of their parents (Brown, 1990). Peer relationships also undergo some changes in pattern during adolescence (Crockett & Petersen, 1993). In early adolescence, peer groups or cliques tend to be comprised of same-sex peers. By mid-adolescence the same-sex peer groups and cliques have declined (Crockett et al., 1984; Shrum & Creek, 1987), and been replaced by 'crowds', meaning large cliques generally made up of youths with common interests (Dunphy, 1963). Teens in a specific crowd take on the values of the group as a function of peer influence (Brown, 1989). These groups can be healthy or deviant, the latter contributing to an individual's participation in delinquency, substance use, and inappropriate or potentially harmful sexual activity. The influence of the peer group can affect both the course of development during adolescence as well as future adult roles.

However, it is necessary to question the strength of peer group influences because, to a very large extent, young people (like older adults) choose the peers with whom they associate. The query concerns the extent to which shared behaviours in a clique reflect group influence rather than differential selection of friends. One of the first studies to attempt to separate the two processes was undertaken by Kandel (1978). She studied nearly a thousand friendship pairs at the beginning and end of an academic year. The degree to which friends were more alike at the end of the year than they had been at the beginning indicated peer influence, rather than selection. She concluded that about half of friendship similarity was due to influence and half to selection. More recently, Rowe et al. (1994) have reviewed the evidence as a whole. The findings show the effects of both selection and influence, with selection being somewhat the stronger of the two processes. Interestingly, however, there is no evidence that nonconforming members are excluded from groups or that friends are abandoned when they differ in behaviour.

The further question to consider here is whether peer group influences have increased or decreased over time. There is no good evidence on this point one way or the other but it is possible that the increasing youth culture that has been evident since the Second World War *may* have given greater opportunities for peer group influences to operate.

Sexual Relationships and Love Affairs

Most obviously, of course, adolescence constitutes the age period when young people have their first love relationships and experience their first sexual relationship. As already noted, sexual activities have come to start at a much earlier age over recent decades. Cohabiting relationships have also become much more frequent (see Chapter 5).

Secular Trends in Family and Peer Relationships

In early modern European societies, families served an economic function (Modell & Goodman, 1990). Family members were part of the active agricultural labour force (Chapter 5, this volume; Minge-Kalman, 1978; Modell & Goodman, 1990). Unlike those of today, families were often large; in addition to the nuclear family unit, they included more distant relations, together with people working for or with the family (Chapter 5, this volume; Modell & Goodman, 1990). In earlier times, the attitude towards children tended to be quite different from today. Parents then viewed children as a significant contribution to the labour force; as a consequence, they did not have the same goals as today's parents, many of whom plan their children's education as a preparation for a chosen career (see Chapter 5). For all the potential disadvantages of child labour, it enabled adolescents to work alongside adults in ways no longer possible. While making a necessary contribution to the economy, young people spent many hours daily in association with adults. This kind of youth-adult interaction, absent from our youth culture today (see Chapter 5), provided an opportunity to observe adults performing adult roles, not only in adult 'jobs' but also in the social roles of adulthood.

Industrial advances necessitated increased training for young people (Chapter 5, this volume; Minge-Kalman, 1978); this led to a movement toward mandatory education, and changed the role of children and adolescents in the labour force (Minge-Kalman, 1978). Some scholars suggested that the industrial revolution marked the beginning of a true period of adolescence. Adolescents now have different roles in society from those of adults (Demos & Demos, 1969). Children and adolescents remain in school in order to receive the appropriate training to participate in the industrialized economy;

consequently, they maintain their dependence on their parents through the later part of the second decade of life.

LIFE TRANSITIONS

Love Relationships, Marriage and Child Bearing

Some of the life events and transitions experienced by adolescents derive from the developmental changes just noted. Thus, for most young people, their first love affair constitutes a most important emotional experience and its breakup represents a considerable stress. These events are near-universal in the growing-up process. However, it is necessary to consider whether there have been changes in pattern that might have implications for psychosocial risks. Four changes stand out as potentially important. First, sexual relationships now begin at a much earlier age than they did fifty to a hundred years ago. Second, despite the advent of effective contraception, the rate of teenage pregnancies increased greatly in the 1950s to early 1970s in both Europe and North America (Rutter, 1980); this was evident in major increases in both abortions and illegitimate births to teenagers. It is noteworthy that this *rise* in births to young people occurred at a time when fertility rates in older people were falling. The pattern of births in the United States is markedly different from that in Europe, with teenage pregnancies much more frequent in the USA. This striking difference is *not* due to any difference in level of sexual activity, but rather to a lack of ready availability of contraceptives and family planning advice (Hayes, 1987; Jones et al., 1986). Third, between 1900 and 1960 there was a substantial drop in the average age at marriage in most countries (for example, from 26 to 22 in the UK – see Modell & Goodman, 1990), followed by a rise in the last 30 years. Fourth, in late adolescence and early adult life, young people are very much more likely than those in previous eras to live together. Increasingly, cohabitation is coming to fulfil the role of 'going steady' (Hoem, 1992).

Swedish youth have led the trend toward cohabitation and delayed childbearing (Popenoe, 1987). Forty-four per cent of women born in 1936 – 1940 expressed a preference for cohabitation instead of marriage; this figure increased to 82 per cent of women born in the 1946 – 1950 cohort and 97 per cent of women born between 1956 and 1960 (Hoem, 1992). The annual marriage rates per thousand single Swedish women aged 20-24 dropped from 190 during the mid-1960s to less than 40 during the mid-1980s. Contrary to initial observations, young people *are* choosing to enter into living-together partnerships, but they are doing so without a formal marriage contract. Further, they cohabit at younger ages than youth in previous generations (Hoem, 1992). Cohabitation has also perhaps become a viable option for groups of young people who previously would not have considered a union or marriage (e.g. students).

In some respects, the Swedish example may be useful in coming to an understanding of the complex socio-cultural processes that underlie this major increase in non-marital cohabitation. Swedish society has been a leader in sex education, promotion of contraception, and liberal abortion laws (Hoem, 1992). These features have clearly affected childbearing and may have influenced cohabitation. Perhaps it may also be important that taxation and wages in Sweden do not punish two-income families economically. In addition, the social system encourages and supports two-income families by providing public child care and liberal family leave policies (both maternal and paternal) for single and married parents alike (Hoem, 1992). However, it would be unwise to place too much reliance on these features because the increase in cohabitation has also occurred in many other countries with different social systems (see Chapter 5).

In terms of the implications for disorder, perhaps one key consequence for psychosocial risks is the probably much increased rate of breakdown for non-marital cohabitations. It is known that the rate is increased for couples with children (Popenoe, 1987) and it is very probable that the same applies to those who are childless. If so, this may well constitute an important trend over time for an increase in a crucial source of stress for young people.

Schooling and Further Education

This century has seen a marked extension in the period of education in virtually all Western societies (Chisholm & Bergeret, 1991; Modell & Goodman, 1990; Rutter, 1980). Thus, the end of the period of compulsory education has risen from 12 to 14 years at the turn of the century to 16 to 18 years today. However, these figures underestimate the extension of education. That is because there have been major increases in the proportion staying on at school and in those receiving tertiary education. Thus, in the UK the proportion of children remaining at school after 16 years rose from 12 per cent in 1950 to 32 per cent in 1970. There have been comparable increases in the UK and in other Western countries in the proportion receiving a college or university education.

Chisholm and Bergeret (1991) reported that, in 1990, some two-fifths of 16 to 24-year-olds were still receiving some form of education.

However, although the national variations among educational systems make comparisons difficult, it is clear that countries differ considerably in the length of education usually provided. Compulsory education in the member countries of the European Community ranges from eight to twelve years, with three groups apparent: 1) minimum of eight years (Portugal, Spain and Italy), 2) minimum of nine years (Greece, Ireland, Luxembourg, and Denmark, and 3) ten years or more required (ten in France; eleven in the Netherlands, the United Kingdom, and the former FRG; and twelve in Belgium) (Chisholm & Bergeret, 1991). This produces a range in the age at permissible school-leaving from 14 to 18 years of age.

Apart from compulsory school attendance, enrolment rates reveal interesting cross-national variations. Despite the fact that nine years of schooling are required, 50 per cent of young people in Denmark remain in school by age 19, with the highest percentage of 20 to 24-year olds continuing compared to other countries (Chisholm & Bergeret, 1991). By contrast, the United Kingdom, despite a lengthy compulsory education of 11 years, has only eight per cent of 24-year-olds in full-time education.

These secular trends in duration of education have been accompanied by a somewhat parallel increase in scholastic achievements, at least up to the early 1970s (Rutter, 1980). The educational gains have probably mainly arisen as a result of the opening up of educational opportunities to a much larger proportion of the population. It might be supposed that these educational improvements should have carried benefits but there may well have been accompanying disadvantages. Thus, there has been a progressive reduction in unskilled jobs (see Chapter 6) and an increase in the educational qualifications required for many types of employment. As a consequence, there has been an increase in the *need* for educational credentials. It may well be that educational aspirations have risen as fast, or faster, than achievements. If so, the gap between scholastic ambitions and accomplishments may be as wide as ever.

A further possible concern is that the prolongation of dependence on parents that is inherent in the extension of education may not be wholly desirable. However, whether or not this prolongation *actually* carries psychosocial risks is not known. If it does, the rates of psychosocial disorders should be greater in young people continuing in education than in those entering employment early, but there is no evidence that that is so. Of course, the groups tend to be non-comparable in background characteristics and adequate evaluations of the effects of prolongation of education have yet to be undertaken.

Beginning Employment

As would be expected, the prolongation of education has been accompanied by a substantial rise in the average age of starting full-time paid employment. However, since the late 1970s the transition for many young people has not been from school to work, but from school to unemployment (Table 4.1; also, see Chapter 6). There is no doubt that the experience of unemployment creates

Table 4.1   Youth unemployment percentage rates in 12 OECD countries[1]

	1981	1983	1985	1987	1989
Australia	10.8	17.9	14.3	14.6	10.4
Canada	13.3	19.8	16.3	13.7	11.3
Finland	9.2	10.5	9.1	9.0	6.1
France	17.0	19.7	25.6	23.0	19.0
Germany	6.5	10.7	9.5	8.1	n.a.
Italy	25.8	30.5	33.9	35.5	35.6
Japan	4.0	4.5	4.8	5.2	4.5
Norway	5.7	8.9	6.5	5.3	11.5
Spain	31.1	37.6	43.8	40.2	32.0
Sweden	6.3	8.0	5.8	4.2	3.0
United Kingdom	17.9	23.4	21.8	17.4	8.6
United States	14.3	16.4	13.0	11.7	10.5
Average of countries	13.5	17.3	17.0	15.7	13.9

1.   The term 'youth' refers to the 15-24 age group in all countries except the United States (14-24) and the United Kingdom, Italy, Norway, Spain, Sweden (16-24). Dates and methods of statistical collection vary slightly from country to country. Compiled from Tables in *Labour Force Statistics 1968-1988* (OECD, 1990).

Source: Hess & Petersen (1991).

stress and, at any one time, the unemployed have higher rates of many psychosocial disorders (see Petersen & Mortimer, 1994; Warr, 1987). To some extent, this reflects a selection process whereby young people who have high risk characteristics are more likely to be out of work. However, longitudinal studies show that the successful gaining of employment tends to be followed by a reduction in psychological disturbance; accordingly it may be inferred that unemployment does create increased risks. The risks do not impinge equally on everyone and Hess & Petersen (1991) suggested that the ill-effects may be mitigated by personal beliefs about the reasons for unemployment, social support from family and peers, and an adaptive societal response. Several countries have developed policies and programmes that seek to reduce the increasing marginalization of youth in the labour market (Hart, 1988; Hess & Petersen, 1991). The former Federal Republic of Germany has been particularly successful at keeping youth unemployment low by way of programmes that integrate school and work through on-the-job factory training and 'in-class' preparation (Hess & Petersen, 1991; Oechslin, 1987).

Patterning of Adolescent Transitions

One result of these various secular trends in adolescent transitions is a marked shift in pattern. Thus, at the turn of the century in the UK most young people left school and started work at 14, some years *before* puberty, and some dozen years before marriage. By contrast, nowadays, most people do not leave school until well *after* puberty and many start cohabitation before completing tertiary education. It is not that the process of multiple transitions is necessarily taking longer (the dozen years between starting work and marrying in 1900 is paralleled by the dozen or so years between puberty and economic independence for some young people today). Nevertheless, the pattern of inter-relationships between the different transitions has changed out of all recognition over the course of this century (Hurrelmann, 1989). As in the past, the period of adolescence is characterized by what has been termed 'status inconsistency', but the particular inconsistencies have altered. What is much less clear is whether this has led to an increase or decrease in psychosocial risk. Obviously, there is no 'natural' pattern; equally there are now, as there were in the past, huge individual differences in pattern - between males and females, between ethnic groups, between social strata and between individuals within each of these groups. The question of whether these variations in pattern matter is eminently researchable but, so far, it has not been subjected to systematic empirical study. It may be, too, that the risks derive, not from the particular patterns as such, but from the possibly increased risks that derive from having to cope with multiple challenging or stressful transitions all at once rather than being able to cope with them sequentially one at a time (Coleman & Hendry, 1990). Alternatively, risks may stem from the prolongation of economic dependence on parents rather than from the timing of transitions.

SECULAR TRENDS IN ILLNESS AND INJURY

In most respects, young people today are far healthier and fitter than they were in previous generations (Forfar, 1988). Life expectancy at birth has risen from just over 40 at the turn of the century to about 70 today; infantile (first-year) mortality has fallen dramatically; and the major childhood scourges of fever have been dramatically reduced. Thus, in the UK, in 1911-15 there were 447 deaths per million due to diphtheria in children aged 1 to 14 years whereas in 1976-80 there were none; over the same time-span the deaths due to whooping cough dropped from 385 per million to 0.2, due to gastroenteritis from 488 to 2.7 and due to pneumonia and bronchitis from 1464 to 28.4. Even the rate of accidents has dropped – from 352 to 103. Nevertheless, accidents are now by far the most frequent cause of death in childhood in the UK. The general picture in other European countries is broadly comparable.

Table 4.2   Death rates for teenagers in selected industrialized nations, 1985

	10-14		15-19	
	Male	Female	Male	Female
United States	18.4	7.8	64.1	23.6
Federal Republic of Germany	9.2	4.5	48.4	15.1
France	13.0	5.9	49.9	18.7
Netherlands	7.2	4.8	27.6	9.0
England and Wales	13.9	5.6	35.6	9.9
Sweden	7.0	4.1	35.0	9.9
Canada	16.6	8.3	55.7	21.1
Japan	6.0	2.1	42.5	7.1
Australia	13.1	5.0	67.1	21.3

Death Rates/100,000
Source: Hingson & Howland (1993).

However, the situation in the United States is quite different, with the main contrast lying in the figures for homicide (UNICEF, 1993). Adolescents and young adults in the USA are some 10 to 15 times as likely to die from homicide as in any European country. However, the violent death rate as a whole in young people is much higher in the USA than in Europe (World Health

Organization, 1989; Hingson & Howland, 1993) and it has been rising in recent years (Center for the Study of Social Policy, 1991). Motor vehicle crashes cause nearly three-quarters of accidental deaths among young people in the United States. These rates are greater than those of other countries (Hingson & Howland, 1993). Firearms and a few drownings cause most of the rest of accidental adolescent deaths in the United States. Policies permitting driving at younger ages (usually 15 or 16 years) and the availability of firearms are thought to account for the excess of mortality among young people in the United States (Petersen et al., 1993).

Although, it is important that the exceptionally high rate of violent deaths among young people in the United States does not apply to Europe, there are other continuing health concerns that apply to all industrialized nations. Thus, despite the effectiveness of medical treatments for many sexually transmitted diseases, there was some increase in such diseases (albeit mostly of non-serious varieties) among young people in the 1960s and 1970s (Court, 1976). The rise in the USA seems to have been greater, with a three to fourfold increase in gonorrhoea between 1960 and 1988 among 10 to 19-year-olds (Hechinger, 1992; National Center for Education in Maternal and Child Health, 1990; World Health Organization, 1989). The most serious sexually transmitted disease, of course, is Acquired Immune Deficiency Syndrome (AIDS). Less than 1 per cent of all people with AIDS are adolescents, but adolescents are at considerable risk of contracting HIV because they tend to have multiple sexual partners and unprotected sexual relations. In addition between 1987 and 1989, about a fifth of AIDS-related deaths in the USA were among people 20-29 years old, suggesting that they contracted the disease while in adolescence (Gans, 1990; Hechinger, 1992; Hein & DiGeronimo, 1989). The adolescent's lack of experience with the realities of sexual risk, together with the unavailability of adequate education and health services in some countries, contributes to this risk. Although the rate of AIDS in Europe is far below that in the United States, it is rising, and AIDS is likely to constitute an increasing health hazard for adolescents in the future.

A further concern is that the huge improvements in neonatal care, with the associated major gains in the survival of very low weight babies (Casaer et al., 1991; Forfar, 1988) have not been accompanied by any substantial reduction in the prevalence of cerebral palsy and mental retardation. It seems that the number of infants who now survive in a healthy state instead of being brain-damaged is more or less balanced by a similar number who would have died in the past but now survive as handicapped children.

STRESS EVENTS AND EXPERIENCES

The period of adolescence includes a range of normative life events and experiences that may be stressful as a result of the challenge they present or the adaptations they require. In the previous section of this chapter we considered secular trends in their timing; here we need to discuss whether such normative events may have become more frequent over time or liable to involve more stress. In addition, adolescents are not exempt from the range of non-normative negative life events and experiences that increase the risk of psychiatric disorder as a consequence of long-term psychological threat that they carry (Goodyer, 1990; Haggerty et al., in press; Rutter & Sandberg, 1992; Sandberg et al., 1993). Again, it is necessary to consider whether they have increased over time for young people.

Normative Life Events

Transitions Within Schools

Schooling provides a host of challenging events. These include the major transition from elementary/primary school to secondary/high school, local or national examinations, and the need to achieve entry to the chosen source of further education.

Particular attention has been paid in the US literature to the transition to high school; however, somewhat comparable transitions apply in other countries. When young adolescents move to a more senior school, they tend to have lower status in the new school culture, less say in decision-making, and fewer choices of classes and other activities (Crockett & Petersen, 1993; Feldlaufer et al., 1988). Additionally, when they transfer to secondary school or high school, in many countries students are no longer working in small cooperative groups as they were in primary or elementary grades (Rounds & Osaki, 1982), and their relationships with teachers tend to be less positive (e.g. Hawkins & Berndt, 1985) and more formal (Gullickson, 1985).

Some evidence suggests that this transition in the United States elementary school to middle or junior high school may have negative effects in white girls (e.g. Eccles & Midgley, 1989). School transition affects grade point average, self-esteem, and participation in extracurricular activities (e.g. Simmons et al., 1987) with negative effects increasing with multiple transitions (Crockett et al., 1989). However, these negative effects need to be interpreted in the light of a failure to find them in some studies (Nottelmann, 1987), together with the apparent lack of ill-effects in boys and in black students of both sexes (Simmons & Blyth, 1987). Simmons et al. (1987) concluded that school transitions that occurred at the same time as other challenging or stressful transitions, such as a move to a new neighbourhood, family changes, and the onset of puberty are likely to yield the most negative psychosocial outcomes. The inference is that school transitions coinciding with other changes may be stressful for at least some young adolescents (Simmons & Blyth, 1987; Stattin & Magnusson, 1990). Family changes (for example, divorce, economic instability) can impose a school change on a young adolescent. An early school transition, made alone without the support of the peer group, increases the demands on the adolescent (Stattin & Magnusson, 1990).

These features are not new ones and there has not been any particular secular trend regarding transitions within schooling; accordingly it is unlikely that they have played a significant role in any increase over time in the rate of psychosocial disorders. It is conceivable that school changes may have become somewhat more frequent as a result of increased geographical mobility but evidence on this point is lacking. It is also possible that the stress of school transitions has increased over time as a consequence of their greater coincidence with other stressors. The prolongation of education to a later age, together with the extension of further education to a much higher proportion of the population, will have raised young people's exposure to the challenges of scholastic examinations and the need to seek entry to college or university. It is difficult to know what role this may have played in psychosocial risk. On the other hand, the available evidence (which is quite limited) suggests that such normative life events carry a much lower psychiatric risk than non-normative negative events such as family breakup or rebuffs from friends or assault. On the other hand, education has come to play a greater role in young people's lives and it tends to be perceived as more competitive than in days past. It is possible that this may have added to the level of stress.

Educational Failure

Also, it is well established that educational failure is associated with a much increased risk of psychosocial disorder, particular antisocial behaviour and conduct disorder (see Rutter & Giller, 1983; Maughan & Yule, 1994). There are multiple reasons for this association, only one of which concerns the stresses of educational failure. Nevertheless, there are good reasons for supposing that this constitutes part of the story, if only because it seems that the association greatly reduces after education is completed. Its possible relevance for an increase in psychosocial disorders in young people is that, although educational attainments have risen over time so have expectations and it may well be that the possibilities for educational 'failure' (at least as perceived or experienced) may have increased.

Non-normative Negative Events/Experiences

Divorce and Remarriage

The one stress event that has clearly become *less* frequent over time is the loss of parents through their death during young people's teenage and early adult years. The massive increase in life expectancy this century has greatly reduced this occurrence, although it remains a far from rare event. However, this has been more than counterbalanced by the dramatic increase in divorce rates during the last half-century (see Chapter 5). Rates of divorce vary among European countries. Thus, the UK has the highest rate of divorce, with this affecting one in three marriages (Haskey, 1983; Höhn & Lüscher, 1988), but Sweden has an even higher dissolution rate (meaning the combination of divorces and dissolutions of stable cohabitations – see Cherlin & Furstenberg, 1988; Popenoe, 1987). Nevertheless, there has been a general increase in the breakdown of marriage throughout most of Europe.

The evidence on the risks for psychosocial disorders associated with the experience of parental divorce is reviewed succinctly in Chapter 5 and will not be reconsidered here other than to note that there is indeed an increase in risk (Cherlin et al., 1991; Emery 1982; Hetherington et al., 1992).

However, it is pertinent to consider several specific issues associated with parental divorce. First, it is necessary to note that it is not only divorce that has increased over time; because a high proportion of divorced parents remarry, there has also been a great increase in the proportion of young people experiencing parental remarriage. This is important because of the evidence that this situation, too, carries psychosocial risks (Hetherington et al., 1992). In many respects, parental remarriage brings substantial benefits. Divorced women tend to experience considerable financial difficulties and the addition of income from stepfathers greatly improves that situation. On the whole, mothers gain psychologically from remarriage and this too should have beneficial repercussions for the children. But the research evidence is consistent in its indication that many adolescents are resistant and negative towards step-parents; the resulting conflict and lack of trust often continues for several years and constitutes one source of risk. Moreover, there is some indication that the multiplicity of stressful family transitions (for example, divorce, remarriage, divorce) is itself an index of risk (Capaldi & Patterson, 1991).

Second, it is clear that a substantial part of the risks associated with divorce derive from family conflict rather than the event of breakup as such. This is evident from the finding that the increased level of emotional/behavioural disturbance in children from divorced families is already present *before* the divorce takes place (Block et al., 1986; Cherlin et al., 1991); from the evidence that conflict is a risk factor in intact families (Rutter, 1971, 1991); and from the finding that continuing conflict after divorce constitutes a risk factor (Buchanan et al., 1991; Hetherington et al., 1992; Maccoby & Mnookin, 1992).

Third, it might be supposed that as divorce has become so much more common, the risks to the children might have diminished over time. This would seem to follow either if the risks stemmed from the atypicality of divorced family status, or if divorce was now occurring as a result of lesser degrees of family conflict than in the past and if conflict constituted the main risk factor. However, although systematic comparisons of risk over time are few, there is no evidence that the risks are decreasing (Wells & Rankin, 1991).

Fourth, although adolescents differ from young children in some aspects of their response to parental divorce (for example, they are more likely to disengage and become involved in extrafamilial groups), the overall level of risk does not appear to vary greatly with age. However, the risks associated with parental remarriage seem to be generally greater in early adolescence than either in earlier childhood or the late teenage years when the young people are preparing to leave home (Hetherington, 1989, 1991; Hetherington et al., 1992).

A fifth point is that the risks associated with parental divorce and remarriage apply to a wide range of emotional, behavioural and psychosexual difficulties. The effects on antisocial behaviour are the most striking in both sexes but the risks extend to other forms of disorder as well (Hetherington et al., 1992).

Finally, it is important that there are major individual differences in children's responses, with only a minority developing clinically significant psychosocial disorders. There are several different types of reasons for this individual variation in reaction. Gender differences are not particularly apparent in the adolescent age period although in earlier childhood boys may be more likely to respond adversely (Zaslow, 1988, 1989). The overall level of family conflict in the home and the qualities of parenting are important in divorced families, just as they are in intact ones. Hetherington et al. (1992) concluded that warm, supportive, non-coercive parents who monitored their adolescents' behaviour but granted them considerable autonomy seemed to have the best adjusted children. There is some uncertainty as to whether maternal employment adds to the risks. Possibly it does when the mother's return to work coincides with the divorce, probably it does when mothers are dissatisfied with their work role, and it may be that there are stresses for older daughters when they are expected to take on more housekeeping and child care responsibilities than they are ready for (Galambos et al., 1988; Hilton & Haldeman, 1991). There is also some uncertainty on the extent to which the relative poverty (or at the very least substantial reduction in the standard of living) that so often accompanies divorce adds to the risk. The finding that parental remarriage (which usually markedly improves the financial situation) is *not* associated with a reduction in the psychosocial risks to the children (Hetherington et al., 1992) suggests that probably it does not constitute *the* main direct risk factor. However, there is evidence that low income and poor living conditions impair marital relationships and parenting, and that thereby they increase psychosocial risks indirectly (Conger et al., 1993; Ge et al., 1992). Poverty may also bring about other changes (such as move of home and school) and it seems likely that it adds to the risk even if it is not the principal source of risk (Furstenberg, 1990).

Another key consideration with respect to individual differences, is that family conflict and difficulties do not impinge equally on all children in the family. Not only are children who are caught up in family conflict more at risk (Buchanan et al., 1991) but also there is some evidence that perceived differences in the ways that siblings are treated by their parents may be influential (Dunn & Plomin, 1990; Hetherington et al., 1994). In addition, the quality of the relationship between the siblings may either add to the risk or provide protection from it (Hetherington et al., 1992).

Victimization

The marked rise in crime since the Second World War is discussed in Chapter 9 in terms of its representing a psychosocial disorder or disturbance. However, as shown by data on the rate of being a victim of crime (Mayhew et al., 1992), the same phenomenon means an increase in the experience of being burgled, assaulted or otherwise the object of some criminal act. This rise in criminal victimization applies to all age groups, but adolescents are far from immune, and there is no doubt that this constitutes one form of stress that has increased substantially over the last 50 years. At least in the United States, victimization peaks in adolescence (Earls et al., 1993).

Substance Use and Abuse

In a somewhat different fashion, the rise in the use and abuse of alcohol and drugs over the last half century (see Chapter 10) has created new dilemmas for young people. To begin with, there is a need for adolescents to decide whether or not to engage in this form of risky behaviour. Valid comparisons across time periods are difficult, if not impossible, but it may be that young people today face a greater number of risk decisions as a result of the greater range of opportunities available to them. Of course, risk-taking in the teenage years is not at all a new phenomenon; it is part of human biology as well as being a feature that is subject to cultural influences. But, it is possible that the risk situations today tend to involve more serious hazards. Thus, the heavy use of alcohol and drugs carries with it an increased risk of both crime and suicidal behaviours (see, for example, Windle et al., 1992; Dembo et al., 1991; also Chapters 9 and 10, this volume). Of course, in part, this is a function of the same predisposing characteristics leading to all of these behaviours. Nevertheless, the limited research that has sought to address the issues suggests that the use of alcohol may aggravate the social difficulties and, in doing so, increase the risks of criminal behaviour (Sampson & Laub, 1993).

CONCLUSIONS

Although the research evidence on many key points is much less than one would like, three conclusions seem reasonably firm. First, there are many ways in which the period of adolescence and early adult life is somewhat different from both childhood and later adulthood. Some of these differences suggest that it may be an age period of particular susceptibility to certain societal influences. Thus, educational factors are particularly important at this phase of life; there are key transitions (such as those involving work careers and those involving sexuality, cohabitation and marriage) that are open to disruption; and the effects of parental divorce and remarriage are substantial. Second, there are several respects in which the period of adolescence has changed markedly over the last 50 years. For example, the patterning of transitions has changed considerably as a result of the fall in the average age of reaching puberty, the rise in the age of completing education, and the changing age of marriage together with the growth of non-marital cohabitation. Third, there has been an increase in some forms of negative life events and experiences that are associated with an increased risk for psychosocial disorders and which impinge on young people. Parental divorce and remarriage, together with crime victimization, stand out in that respect. However, in addition, it may be that adolescents today face somewhat more difficult challenges and have to take rather more decisions on risk situations than their counterparts in previous eras.

REFERENCES

Alsaker, F. (in press). Timing of puberty and reactions to pubertal changes. In M. Rutter (ed.) *Psychosocial disturbances in young people: Challenges for prevention.* Cambridge/New York: Cambridge University Press.

Andersson, T. & Magnusson, D. (1990). Biological maturation in adolescence and the development of drinking habits and alcohol abuse among young males: A prospective longitudinal study. *Journal of Youth and Adolescence 19,* 33-41.

Angold, A. & Rutter, M. (1992). Effects of age and pubertal status on depression in a large clinical sample. *Development and Psychopathology 4,* 5-28.

Aro, H. & Taipale, V. (1987). The impact of timing of puberty on psychosomatic symptoms among fourteen- to sixteen-year-old Finnish girls. *Child Development 58,* 261-268.

Attie, I., Brooks-Gunn, J. & Petersen, A. C. (1987). A developmental perspective on eating disorders and eating problems. In M. Lewis & S. M. Miller (eds.) *Handbook of developmental psychopathology,* 409-420. New York: Plenum Press.

Bancroft, J. (1991). Reproductive hormones. In M. Rutter & P. Casaer (eds.) *Biological risk factors for psychosocial disorders,* 260-310. Cambridge: Cambridge University Press.

Bancroft, J. (1993). The premenstrual syndrome – a reappraisal of the concept and the evidence. *Psychological Medicine.* Monograph Supplement 24.

Bancroft, J. & Reinisch J. M. (eds.) (1990). *Adolescence and puberty.* New York: Oxford University Press.

Block, J. H., Block, J. & Gjerde, P. F. (1986). The personality of children prior to divorce: A prospective study. *Child Development 57,* 827-840.

Blyth, D. A., Simmons, R. G., Bulcroft, R., Felt, D., VanCleave, E. F. & Bush, D. M. (1981). The effects of physical development on self-image and satisfaction with body-image for early adolescent males. In R. G. Simmons (ed.) *Research in community and mental health 2,* 43-73. Greenwich, CT: JAI Press.

Blyth, D. A., Simmons, R. G. & Zakin, D. (1985). Satisfaction with body image for early adolescent females: The impact of pubertal timing within different school environments. *Journal of Youth and Adolescence 14,* 227-236.

Brack, C. J., Orr, D. P. & Ingersoll, G. (1988). Pubertal maturation and adolescent self-esteem. *Journal of Adolescent Health Care 9,* 280-285.

Brooks-Gunn, J. (1987). Pubertal processes and girls' psychological adaptation, In R. Lerner & T.T. Foch (eds.) *Biological-psychosocial interactions in early adolescence*, 123-153. Hillsdale, NJ: Lawrence Erlbaum.

Brooks-Gunn, J. & Petersen, A. (eds.) (1983). *Girls at puberty: Biological and psychosocial perspectives*. New York: Plenum Press.

Brown, B.B. (1989). The role of peer groups in adolescents' adjustment to secondary school. In T. J. Berndt & G. W. Ladd (eds.) *Peer relationships in child development*, 188-216. New York: Wiley.

Brown, B. B. (1990). Peer groups and peer cultures. In S. S. Feldman & G. R. Elliott (eds.) *At the threshold: The developing adolescent*, 171-196. Cambridge, MA: Harvard University Press.

Buchanan, C. M., Maccoby, E. E. & Dornbusch, S. M. (1991). Caught between parents: Adolescents' experience in divorced homes. *Child Development 62*, 1008-1029.

Camarena, P., Sarigiani, P. & Petersen, A. C. (1990). Gender specific pathways to intimacy in early adolescence. *Journal of Youth and Adolescence 19*, 19-32.

Capaldi, D. M. & Patterson, G. R. (1991). Relation of parental transitions to boys' adjustment problems: 1. A linear hypothesis; 2. Mothers at risk for transitions and unskilled parenting. *Developmental Psychology 27*, 489-504.

Casaer, P., de Vries, L. & Marlow, N. (1991). Prenatal and perinatal risk factors for psychosocial development. In M. Rutter & P. Casaer (eds.) *Biological risk factors for psychosocial disorders*, 139-174. Cambridge: Cambridge University Press.

Caspi, A., Lynam, D., Moffitt, T. E. & Silva, P. A. (1993). Unraveling girl's delinquency: Biological, dispositional, and contextual contributions to adolescent misbehavior. *Developmental Psychology 29*, 19-30.

Caspi, A. & Moffitt, T.E. (1991). Individual differences are accentuated during periods of social change: The sample case of girls at puberty. *Journal of Personality and Social Psychology 61*, 157-168.

Center for the Study of Social Policy (1991). *Kids count data book: State profiles of child well-being*. Greenwich, CT: Annie E. Casey Foundation.

Cherlin, A. J. & Furstenberg Jr., F. F. (1988). The changing European family: Lessons for the American reader. *Journal of Family Issues 9*, 291-297.

Cherlin, A. J., Furstenberg Jr., F. F., Chase-Lansdale, P. L., Kiernan, K. E., Robins, P. K., Morrison, D. R. & Teitler, J. O. (1991). Longitudinal studies of effects of divorce on children in Great Britain and the United States. *Science 252*, 1386-1389.

Chisholm, L. & Bergeret, J. M. (1991). *Young people in the European Community: Towards an agenda for research and policy*. Luxembourg: Report of Commission of the European Communities Task Force Human Resources, Education, Training, and Youth.

Chumlea, W. C. (1982). Physical growth in adolescence. In B. B. Wolman, G. Stricker, S. J. Ellman, P. Keith-Spiegel, D. S. Palermo (eds.) *Handbook of developmental psychology*, 471-485. Englewood Cliffs, NJ: Prentice-Hall.

Clausen, J. A. (1975). The social meaning of differential physical and sexual maturation. In S. E. Dragastin & G. H. Elder Jr. (eds.) *Adolescence in the life cycle: Psychological change and social context*, 25-48. London: Halsted Press.

Coleman, J. C. & Hendry, L. (1990). *The nature of adolescence* (2nd edition). London/New York: Routledge.

Collins, W.A. (1990). Parent-child relationships in the transition to adolescence: Continuity and change in interaction, affect, and cognition. In R. Montemayor, G.R. Adams & T. Gullotta (eds.) *Advances in adolescent development, Vol II: The transition from childhood to adolescence: A transitional period?*, 85-106. Newbury Park, CA: Sage.

Conger, R. D., Conger, K. J., Elder Jr., G. H., Lorenz, F. O., Simons, R. L. & Whitbeck, L. B. (1993). Family economic-stress and adjustment of early adolescent girls. *Developmental Psychology 29*, 206-219.

Court, S. D. M. (1976). *Fit for the future: Report of the Committee on Child Health Services*. London: HMSO.

Crockett, L. J., Losoff, M. & Petersen, A. C. (1984). Perceptions of the peer group and friendship in early adolescence. *Journal of Early Adolescence 4*, 155-181.

Crockett, L. J. & Petersen, A. C. (1987). Pubertal status and psychosocial development: Findings from the Early Adolescence Study. In R.M. Lerner & T.T. Foch (eds.) *Biological-psychosocial interactions in early adolescence*, 173-188. Hillsdale, NJ: Lawrence Erlbaum.

Crockett, L. J. & Petersen, A. C. (1993). Adolescent development: Health risks and opportunities for health promotion. In S. G. Millstein, A. C. Petersen & E. O. Nightingale (eds.) *Promoting the health of adolescents: New directions for the twenty-first century*, 13-37. New York: Oxford University Press.

Crockett, L. J., Petersen, A. C., Graber, J. A., Schulenberg, J. E. & Ebata, A. T. (1989). School transitions and adjustment during early adolescence. *Journal of Early Adolescence 9*, 181-210.

Daw, S. F. (1970). Age of boys' puberty in Leipzig 1727-49 as indicated by voice breaking J.S. Bach's choir members. *Human Biology 42*, 87-89.

Dembo, R., Williams, L., Getreu, A., Genung, L., Schmeidler, J., Berry, E., Wish, E. D. & La Voie, L. (1991). A longitudinal study of the relationships among marijuana/hashish use, cocaine use and delinquency in a cohort of high risk youths. *Journal of Drug Issues 21*, 271-312.

Demos, J. & Demos, V. (1969). Adolescence in historical perspective. *Journal of Marriage and the Family 31*, 632-638.

Department of International Economic and Social Affairs (1988). Adolescent reproductive behavior: Evidence from developed countries. *Population Studies 109*. (Special issue).

Dorn, L. D., Crockett, L. J. & Petersen, A. C. (1988). The relations of pubertal status to intrapersonal changes in young adolescents. *Journal of Early Adolescence 8*, 405-419.

Douglas, J. W. B., Ross, J. M. & Simpson, H. R. (1968). *All our future: A longitudinal study of secondary education*. London: Peter Davies.

Dubas, J.S., Graber, J.A & Petersen, A.C. (1991). The effects of pubertal development on achievement during adolescence. *American Journal of Education 99*, 444-460.

Duke, P. M., Jennings, D. J., Dornbusch, S. M. & Siegel-Gorelick, B. (1982). Educational correlates of early and late sexual maturation in adolescence. *Journal of Pediatrics 100*, 633-637.

Duncan, P., Ritter, P., Dornbusch, S., Gross, P. & Carlsmith, J. (1985). The effects of pubertal timing on body image, school behavior, and deviance. *Journal of Youth and Adolescence 14*, 227-236.

Dunn, J. & Plomin, R. (1990). *Separate lives: Why siblings are so different.* New York: Basic Books.

Dunphy, D. (1963). The social structure of urban adolescent peer groups. *Sociometry 26*, 230-246.

Earls, F., Cairns, R. B., Mercy, J. A. (1993). The control of violence and the promotion of nonviolence in adolescents. In S. G. Millstein, A. C. Petersen & E. O. Nightingale (eds.) *Promoting the health of adolescents: New directions for the twenty-first century*, 285-304. New York: Oxford University Press.

Eccles, J. S. & Midgley, C. (1989). Stage/environment fit: Developmentally appropriate classrooms for early adolescents. In R. E. Ames & C. Ames (eds.) *Research on motivation in education, Vol. III: Goals and cognition*, 139-186. San Diego: Academic Press.

Eichorn, D. H. (1975). Asynchronization in adolescent development. In S. E. Dragastin & G. H. Elder Jr. (eds.) *Adolescence in the life cycle: Psychological change and social context,* 81-96. Washington, DC: Hemisphere.

Ellison, P. T. (1981). Morbidity, mortality and menarche. *Human Biology 53*, 635-644.

Emery, R. E. (1982). Interparental conflict and the children of discord and divorce. *Psychological Bulletin 92*, 310-330.

Eveleth, P. B. & Tanner, J. M. (1990). *Worldwide variation in human growth* (2nd edition). Cambridge: Cambridge University Press.

Farrell, C. (1978). *My mother said ... the way young people learn about sex and birth control.* London: Routledge & Kegan Paul.

Faust, M. S. (1983). Alternative constructions of adolescent growth. In J. Brooks-Gunn & A. C. Petersen (eds.) *Girls at puberty: Biological and psychosocial perspectives*, 105-125. New York: Plenum Press.

Feldlaufer, H., Midgley, C. & Eccles, J. S. (1988). Student, teacher, and observer perceptions of the classroom environment before and after the transition to junior high school. *Journal of Early Adolescence 8*, 133-156.

Feldman, S. S. & Elliot, G. R. (1990). *At the threshold: The developing adolescent.* Cambridge, MA: Harvard University Press.

Forfar, J. O. (ed.) (1988). *Child health in a changing society.* Oxford: Oxford University Press.

Freud, A. (1958). Adolescence. *Psychoanalytic study of the child 13*, 255-278.

Frisch, R. E. (1990). The right weight: Body fat, menarche, and ovulation. *Ballière's Clinical Obstetrics and Gynaecology 4*, 419-439.

Furstenberg Jr., F. (1990). Coming of age in a changing family system. In S. S. Feldman & G. R. Elliott (eds.) *At the threshold: The developing adolescent,* 147-170. Cambridge, MA: Harvard University Press.

Galambos, N. L., Petersen, A. C. & Lenerz, K. (1988). Maternal employment and sex typing in early adolescence: Contemporaneous and longitudinal relations. In A. E. Gottfried & A. W. Gottfried (eds.) *Maternal employment and children's development: Longitudinal research,* 155-189. New York: Plenum Press.

Gans, J. E. (1990). *America's adolescents: How healthy are they? Vol. I: Profiles of adolescent health series.* Chicago: American Medical Association.

Garner, D. M. & Garfinkel, P. E. (1980). Socio-cultural factors in the development of anorexia nervosa. *Psychological Medicine 10,* 647-656.

Ge, X., Conger, R. D., Lorenz, F. O., Elder Jr., G. H., Montague, R. B. & Simons, R. L. (1992). Linking family economic hardship to adolescent distress. *Journal of Research on Adolescence 2,* 351-377.

Goodnow, J. J. & Collins, W. A. (1990). *Development according to parents: The nature, sources, and consequences of parents' ideas.* Hillsdale, NJ: Lawrence Erlbaum.

Goodyer, I. (1990). *Life experiences, development and childhood psychopathology.* Chichester: Wiley.

Gullickson, A. R. (1985). Student evaluation techniques and their relationship to grade and curriculum. *Journal of Educational Research 79,* 96-100.

Gupta, D., Attanasio, A. & Raaf, S. (1975). Plasma estrogen and androgen concentrations in children during adolescence. *Journal of Clinical Endocrinology and Metabolism 40,* 636-643.

Haggerty, R. J., Garmezy, N., Rutter, M. & Sherrod, L. R. (eds.) (in press). *Stress, risk and resilience in children and adolescents: Processes, mechanisms and intervention.* New York: Cambridge University Press.

Halpern, C. T. & Udry, J. R. (1992). Variation in adolescent hormone measures and implications for behavioural research. *Journal of Research on Adolescence 2,* 103-122.

Hamburg, B. (1986). Subsets of adolescent mothers: Developmental, biomedical and psychosocial issues. In J. B. Lancaster & B. A. Hamburg (eds.) *School-age pregnancy and parenthood: Biosocial dimensions,* 115-145. New York: Aldine de Gruyter.

Hart, P. E. (1988). *Youth unemployment in Great Britain.* Cambridge: Cambridge University Press.

Hartup, W. W. (1983). Peer relations. In P. H. Mussen (ed.) *Handbook of child psychology 4,* 103-196. New York: Wiley.

Haskey, J. (1983). Remarriage of the divorced in England and Wales: A contemporary phenomenon. *Journal of Biosocial Science 15,* 253-271.

Hawkins, J. & Berndt, T. J. (1985, April). *Adjustment following the transition to junior high school.* Paper presented at the biennial meeting of the Society for Research in Child Development. Toronto, Canada.

Hayes, C. . (ed.) (1987). *Risking the future: Adolescent sexuality, pregnancy, and childbearing*, Vol. I. Washington, DC: National Academy Press.

Hechinger, F. M. (1992). *Fateful choices: Healthy youth for the 21st century*. New York: Carnegie Corporation of New York.

Hein, K. & DiGeronimo, T. F. (1989). *AIDS: Trading fears for facts. A guide for young people*. Mount Vernon, NY: Consumers Union.

Hess, L. E. & Petersen, A. C. (1991). *Narrowing the margins: Adolescent unemployment and the lack of a social role*. Manuscript prepared for Academia Europaea and the World Scout Bureau.

Hetherington, E. M. (1989). Coping with family transitions: Winners, losers, and survivors. *Child Development 60*, 1-14.

Hetherington, E. M. (1991). Presidential address: Families, lies, and videotapes. *Journal of Research on Adolescence 1*, 323-348.

Hetherington, E. M., Clingempeel, W. G. together with Anderson, E. R., Deal, J. E., Hagan M. S., Hollier, E. A., Lindner, M. S. (1992). Coping with marital transitions. *Monographs of the Society for Research in Child Development 57*, nos. 2-3.

Hetherington, E. M., Reiss, D. & Plomin, R. (1994). *Separate social worlds of siblings: The impact of nonshared environment on development*. Hillsdale, NJ: Lawrence Erlbaum.

Hill, J. (1980). *Understanding early adolescence: A framework*. Chapel Hill, NC: Center for Early Adolescence.

Hilton, J. M. & Haldeman, V. A. (1991). Gender differences in the performance of household tasks by adults and children in single-parent and two-parent, two-earner households. *Journal of Family Issues 12*, 114-130.

Hingson, R. & Howland, J. (1993). Promoting safety in adolescents. In S. G. Millstein, A. C. Petersen & E. O. Nightingale (eds.) *Promoting the health of adolescents: New directions for the twenty-first century*, 305-327. New York: Oxford University Press.

Hoem, B. (1992). Early phases of family transition in contemporary Sweden. In M. K. Rosenheim & M. F. Testa (eds.) *Early parenthood and coming of age in the 1990s*, 185-199. New Brunswick, NJ: Rutgers University Press.

Hofferth, S. L., Kahn, J. R. & Baldwin, W. (1987). Premarital sexual activity among US teenage women over the past three decades. *Family Planning Perspectives 19*, 46-53.

Höhn, C. & Lüscher, K. (1988). The changing family in the Federal Republic of Germany. *Journal of Family Issues 9*, 317-335.

Hurrelmann, K. (1989). The social world of adolescents: A sociological perspective. In K. Hurrelmann & U. Engel (eds.) *The social world of adolescents: International perspectives*, 3-26. Berlin/New York: Walter de Gruyter.

Inhelder, B. & Piaget, J. (1958). *The growth of logical thinking from childhood to adolescence*. New York: Basic Books.

Jones, E. F., Forrest, J. D., Goldman, N., Henshaw, S., Lincoln, R., Rosoff, J. I., Westoff, C. F. & Wulf, D. (1986). *Teenage pregnancy in industrialized countries:*

A study sponsored by the Alan Guttmacher Institute. New Haven, CT: Yale University Press.

Jones, M.C. (1965). Psychological correlates of somatic development. *Child Development 56*, 899-911.

Jones, M. C. & Mussen, P. H. (1958). Self-conceptions, motivations, and interpersonal attitudes of early and late maturing girls. *Child Development 29*, 491-501.

Kandel, D. B. (1978). Homophily, selection, and socialization in adolescent friendships. *American Journal of Sociology 84*, 427-436.

Katchadourian, H. (1990). Sexuality. In S. S. Feldman & G. R. Elliott (eds.) *At the threshold: The developing adolescent*, 330-351. Cambridge, MA: Harvard University Press.

Keating, D. P. (1990). Adolescent thinking. In S. S. Feldman & G. R. Elliott (eds.) *At the threshold: The developing adolescent*, 54-89. Cambridge, MA: Harvard University Press.

Linn, M. (1983). Content, context, and process in reasoning during adolescence: Selecting a model. *Journal of Early Adolescence 3*, 63-82.

Maccoby, E. E. (1984). Middle childhood in the context of the family. In W.A. Collins (ed.) *Development during middle childhood: The years from six to twelve,* 184-239. Washington, DC: National Academy of Sciences Press.

Maccoby, E. E. & Mnookin, R. H. (1992). *Dividing the child: Social and legal dilemmas of custody.* Cambridge, MA: Harvard University Press.

Magnusson, D., Stattin, H. & Allen, V. (1986). Differential maturation among girls and its relation to social adjustment in a longitudinal perspective. In P. Baltes, D. Featherman & R. Lerner (eds.) *Life span development and behavior 7*, 136-170. Hillsdale, NJ: Lawrence Erlbaum.

Maughan, B. & Yule, W. (1994). Reading and other learning disabilities. In M. Rutter, E. Taylor & L. Hersov (eds.) *Child and adolescent psychiatry: Modern approaches* (3rd edition), 647-665. Oxford: Blackwell Scientific.

Mayhew, P., Aye Maung, N. & Mirrlees-Black, C. (1992) *The 1992 British Crime Survey.* A Home Office Research and Planning Unit Report. London: HMSO.

McCandless, B. R. (1960). Rate of development, body build and personality. *Psychiatric Research Reports 13*, 42-57.

Minge-Kalman, W. (1978). The industrial revolution and the European family: The institutionalization of 'childhood' as a market for family labor. *Comparative Studies in Society and History 20*, 454-468.

Modell, J. & Goodman, M. (1990). Historical perspectives. In S. S. Feldman & G. R. Elliott (eds.) *At the threshold: The developing adolescent*, 93-122. Cambridge, MA: Harvard University Press.

National Center for Education in Maternal and Child Health (1990). *The health of America's youth.* Washington, DC: Author.

Newcombe, N. & Dubas, J. S. (1987). Individual differences in cognitive ability: Are they related to timing of puberty? In R. M. Lerner & T. T. Foch (eds.) *Biological-psychosocial interactions in early adolescence: A life-span perspective,* 249-302. Hillsdale, NJ: Lawrence Erlbaum.

Nottelmann, E. D. (1987). Competence and self-esteem during transition from childhood to adolescence. *Developmental Psychology 23*, 441-450.

Oechslin, J. (1987). Training and the business world: The French experience. *International Labour Review 126*, 653-667.

Offer, D., Ostrov, E. & Howard, K. I. (1981). The mental health professional's concept of the normal adolescent. *Archives of General Psychiatry 38*, 149-152.

Organization for Economic Cooperation and Development (1990). *Labour Force Statistics, 1968-1988*. Paris: Author.

Peskin, H. (1967). Pubertal onset and ego functioning: A psychoanalytic approach. *Journal of Abnormal Psychology 72*, 1-15.

Petersen, A. C. (1988). Adolescent development. *Annual review of psychology 39*, 583-607.

Petersen, A. C. (1991). *American adolescence: How it affects girls*. The 1991 Gisela Konopka Lecture, University of Minnesota, Minneapolis.

Petersen, A. C. & Crockett, L. J. (1985). Pubertal timing and grade effects on adjustment. *Journal of Youth and Adolescence 14*, 191-206.

Petersen, A. C. & Leffert N. (in press). What is special about adolescence? In M. Rutter (ed.) *Psychosocial disturbances in young people: Challenges for prevention*. Cambridge: Cambridge University Press.

Petersen, A. C. & Mortimer, J. T. (eds.) (1994). *Youth unemployment and society*. New York: Cambridge University Press.

Petersen, A. C., Richmond, J. B. & Leffert, N. (1993). Social changes among youth: The United States experience. *Journal of Adolescent Health 14*, 33-41.

Petersen, A. C. & Taylor, B. C. (1980). The biological approach to adolescence: Biological change and psychological adaptation. In J. Adelson (ed.) *Handbook of adolescent psychology*, 117-155. New York: Wiley.

Popenoe, D. (1987). Beyond the nuclear family: A statistical portrait of the changing family in Sweden. *Journal of Marriage and the Family 49*, 173-183.

Rounds, T. S. & Osaki S. Y. (1982). *The social organization of classrooms: An analysis of sixth-and-seventh grade activity structures*. (Report EPSSP-82-5). San Francisco: Far West Laboratory.

Rowe, D. C., Woulbroun, E. J. & Gulley, B. L. (1994). Peers and friends as nonshared environmental influences. In E. M. Hetherington, D. Reiss & R. Plomin (eds.) *Separate social worlds of siblings: The impact of nonshared environment on development*, 159-173. Hillsdale, NJ: Lawrence Erlbaum.

Rutter, M. (1971). Parent-child separation: Psychological effects on the children. *Journal of Child Psychology and Psychiatry 12*, 233-260.

Rutter, M. (1980). *Changing youth in a changing society: Patterns of adolescent development and disorder*. Cambridge, MA: Harvard University Press.

Rutter, M. (1990). Changing patterns of psychiatric disorders during adolescence. In J. Bancroft & J.M. Reinisch (eds.) *Adolescence and puberty*, 124-145. New York: Oxford University Press.

Rutter, M. (1991). A fresh look at 'maternal deprivation'. In P. Bateson (ed.) *The development and integration of behaviour*, 331-374. Cambridge: Cambridge University Press.

Rutter, M. & Giller, H. (1983). *Juvenile delinquency: Trends and perspectives.* Harmondsworth, Middx: Penguin.

Rutter, M., Graham, P., Chadwick, O. & Yule, W. (1976). Adolescent turmoil: Fact or fiction? *Journal of Child Psychology and Psychiatry 17*, 35-56.

Rutter, M. & Sandberg, S. (1992). Psychosocial stressors: Concepts, causes and effects. *European Journal of Child and Adult Psychiatry 1*, 3-13.

Sallis, J. F. (1993). Promoting healthful diet and physical activity. In S. G. Millstein, A. C. Petersen & E. O. Nightingale (eds.) *Promoting the health of adolescents: New directions for the twenty-first century*, 209-241. New York: Oxford University Press.

Sampson, R. J. & Laub, J. H. (1993). *Crime in the making: Pathways and turning points through life*, Cambridge, MA: Harvard University Press.

Sandberg, S., Rutter, M., Giles, S., Owen, A., Champion, L., Nicholls, J., Prior, V., McGuinness, D. & Drinnan, D. (1993). Assessment of psychosocial experiences in childhood: Methodological issues and some illustrative findings. *Journal of Child Psychology and Psychiatry 34*, 879-897.

Schofield, M. (1965). *The sexual behaviour of young people.* London: Longman.

Shrum, W. & Creek, N. H. (1987). Social structure during the school years: Onset of the degrouping process. *American Sociological Review 52*, 218-223.

Silbereisen, R. K., Petersen, A. C., Albrecht, T. & Kracke, B. (1989). Maturational timing and the development of problem behavior: Longitudinal studies in adolescence. *Journal of Early Adolescence 9*, 247-268.

Silverstein, B., Peterson, B. & Perdue, L. (1986). Some correlates of the thin standard of bodily attractiveness for women. *International Journal of Eating Disorders 5*, 895-905.

Simmons, R. G. & Blyth, D. A. (1987). *Moving into adolescence: The impact of pubertal change and school context.* Hawthorne, NY: Aldine de Gruyter.

Simmons, R., Blyth, D. & McKinney, K. (1983). The social and psychological effects of puberty on white females. In J. Brooks-Gunn & A.C. Petersen (eds.) *Girls at puberty: Biological and psychosocial perspectives*, 229-272. New York: Plenum Press.

Simmons, R. G., Burgeson, R., Carlton-Ford, S. & Blyth, D. A. (1987). The impact of cumulative change in early adolescence. *Child Development 58*, 1220-1234.

Stattin, H. & Magnusson, D. (1990). *Paths through life, Vol. II: Pubertal maturation in female development.* Hillsdale, NJ: Lawrence Erlbaum.

Steinberg, L. (1988). Pubertal maturation and parent-adolescent distance: An evolutionary perspective. In G. Adams, R. Montemayor, and T. Gullotta (eds.) *Biology of adolescent behavior and development, Vol I: Advances in adolescent development*, 71-97. Beverly Hills, CA: Sage.

Steinberg, L. (1990). Autonomy, conflict, and harmony in the family relationship. In S. S. Feldman & G. R. Elliott (eds.) *At the threshold: The developing adolescent*, 255-276. Cambridge, MA: Harvard University Press.

Susman, E. J. & Petersen, A. C. (1992). Hormones and behavior in adolescence. In E. R. McAnarney, R. E. Kreipe, D. P. Orr & G. D. Comerci (eds.) *Textbook of adolescent medicine*, 125-130. Philadelphia: W.B. Saunders.

Tanner, J. M. (1962). *Growth at adolescence* (2nd edition). Oxford: Blackwell.

Tanner, J. M. (1989). *Foetus into man: Physical growth from conception to maturity* (2nd edition). Ware: Castlemead Publications.

Tanner, J. M. & Davies, P. S. W. (1985). Clinical longitudinal standards for height and height velocity for North American children. *Journal of Pediatrics 107*, 317-329.

Tobin-Richards, M. H., Boxer, A. M. & Petersen, A. C. (1983). The psychological significance of pubertal change: Sex differences in perceptions of self during early adolescence. In J. Brooks-Gunn & A. C. Petersen (eds.) *Girls at puberty: Biological and psychosocial perspectives*, 127-154. New York: Plenum Press.

Udry, J. R. (1979). Age at menarche, at first intercourse, and at first pregnancy. *Journal of Biological Science II*, 411-433.

UNICEF (1993). *The progress of nations 1993*. New York: Author.

Warr, P. (1987). *Work, unemployment and mental health*. Oxford: Clarendon Press.

Weithorn, L. A. & Campbell, S. B. (1982). The competency of children and adolescents to make informed treatment decisions. *Child Development 53*, 1589-1598.

Wellings, K., Field, J., Johnson, A. & Wadsworth, J. with Bradshaw, S. (1994). *Sexual behaviour in Britain: The national survey of sexual attitudes and life styles*. London: Penguin.

Wells, L. E. & Rankin, J. H. (1991). Families and delinquency: A meta-analysis of the impact of broken homes. *Social Problems 38*, 71-89.

World Health Organization (1989). *The health of youth: Background document for technical discussions, May 1989*. Geneva: Author.

Windle, M., Miller-Tutzauer, C. & Domenico, D. (1992). Alcohol use, suicidal behaviour, and risky activities among adolescents. *Journal of Research on Adolescence 2*, 317-330.

Wyshak, G. & Frisch, R. E. (1982). Evidence for a secular trend in age of menarche. *New England Journal of Medicine 306*, 1033-1035.

Youniss, J. & Smollar, J. (1985). *Adolescents' relations with mothers, fathers, and friends*. Chicago: University of Chicago Press.

Zaslow, M. J. (1988). Sex differences in children's responses to parental divorce: 1. Research methodology and postdivorce family forms. *American Journal of Orthopsychiatry 58,* 355-378.

Zaslow, M. J. (1989). Sex differences in children's responses to parental divorce: 2. Samples, variables, ages, and sources. *American Journal of Orthopsychiatry 59*, 118-141.

5

Changing Family Patterns in Western Europe: Opportunity and Risk Factors for Adolescent Development[1]

LAURA E. HESS

INTRODUCTION

The last few decades have brought global changes that are of growing concern to scientists and technologists, and to the general public (Cooperrider & Pasmore, 1991). On the psychosocial plane, the world has been undergoing rapid transformations, in populations, migration, and social institutions (Sinha, 1991). Macroscopic changes in the structure and culture of societies have continuously altered the family's shape and structure, its extension or size, and its functioning and relevance to the individual and the collective society (Hoffmann-Nowotny, 1987). Moreover, rapid technological advances have transformed the meaning of work and the roles associated with it (see Chapter 6), making it increasingly difficult for individuals to achieve the position they desire, and contributing to the growing uncertainty about the nature and course

1. The bulk of this chapter was completed while the author was a Postdoctoral Research Fellow in the Center for Psychology and Human Development of the Max Planck Institute for Human Development and Education, Berlin, Germany. The author wishes to thank the Computer Graphics Department of the Max Planck Institute for their assistance in the preparation of figures. In addition, the author is extremely grateful to Lindsay Chase-Lansdale, and to Eleanor Maccoby, for their careful and insightful comments on an earlier version of this chapter. Finally, special thanks go to Michael Rutter and David Smith, for their support of my involvement in the Study Group, and throughout all stages of the manuscript.

of individual life courses, and the nature and course of commitment to the modern family (Schmid, 1984).

Changes in the structure and function of the family, which remains the social institution exerting the most control over the psychosocial development of humans across the life span (Amato & Keith, 1991; Lerner & Spanier, 1978; Maccoby & Martin, 1983), pose potential risks, as well as opportunities for positive growth, in the socialization of children growing up in these new family forms, and ultimately for the future of modern society. The goal of this chapter is to examine the historical evolution of the family in Europe (with an emphasis on Western European countries), and, in turn, the impact of these structural and functional changes on the socialization of youth embedded in these families. Research on the effects of changes in family structure and function is important to consider, not only for understanding how changes in the family context may influence individual development, but also to make informed decisions as to how best to intervene (in terms of social policy decisions and individual and family interventions) to help promote healthy development among adolescents, family members, and society in general. It is useful to begin with a brief examination of how the modern Western European family came into being.

Evolution of the Family in Western Europe

How the modern family evolved is the subject of long-standing debate among family historians and sociologists (Janssens, 1986). Many historians and sociologists have adopted a structure-function approach (Parsons & Bales, 1953). According to this perspective, three historical phases of the European family can be identified: the early modern period (from the Renaissance to the end of the eighteenth century); the industrial revolution, which began during the nineteenth century and peaked with the 'golden age' of the bourgeois family in the latter half of the twentieth century; and the post-modern era, from the late 1960s to the present. A synopsis of family characteristics during each of these historical periods follows.

The Family in Early Modern Europe

Society of early modern Europe was predominantly based on agricultural production. Families formed the basic unit of economic production (Modell & Goodman, 1990), requiring all members of the family to be active labourers (Franklin, 1969; Minge-Kalman, 1978). Families were therefore often quite large, and households often included servants or kin beyond the nuclear family to supplement the workforce. However, many scholars have argued that the stem family, comprising several generations in a single household, was *not* the predominant pattern (Laslett, 1972; Modell & Goodman, 1990).

Children contributed significantly to the family economy, and learned at an early age – by working alongside older family members - the roles they would play as adults. However, they were not the hub of family life, and emotional investment in young children was low by today's standards (Minge-Kalman, 1978). Some historians have attributed this to the high infant and child mortality rates of the period (Stone, 1977; in Minge-Kalman, 1978). Families often 'farmed out' youths (usually between 12 and 15 years of age) to live with and work for other families in the community, a practice that not only provided youths with special training, but also helped to limit potential intergenerational conflicts (e.g. sexual misconduct) that might emerge at this stage of development (Modell & Goodman, 1990).

European Families During the Industrial Revolution

The first major transition that took place in European families was set in motion by the industrial revolution in the nineteenth century. Industrialization signalled a movement away from rural agricultural households and towards urban dwellings, and changed the basic roles of the family from a kinship-based institution of production, to one of consumption and preparation of children (through socialization and support of their education) for entering a labour force whose demand for skilled workers was increasing (Künzel, 1974; Minge-Kalman, 1978; Stolte-Heiskanen, 1975). The need for a skilled workforce, a result of technological advances during the industrial revolution, led to a growing concern for mass education, in order 'to discipline the next generation for factory labour' (Minge-Kalman, 1978: 458). This concern for education led to the passing of laws that made elementary education mandatory, rescued children from factories, and extended the period during which children were dependent on their parents from the age of five or six to the late teens or even early twenties, where families supported the higher education of their offspring (Minge-Kalman, 1978). As succinctly put by Demos and Demos (1969), the concept of adolescence is a relatively recent phenomenon. The industrial revolution also brought about a transition to more isolated traditional nuclear or bourgeois families, with households headed by a married man, who was most often tied to a business or industry that took him away from the home, leaving the mother with the primary responsibility for maintaining the household and socializing the children (Modell & Goodman, 1990).

For the last several decades, scholars have debated what was the effect of the industrial revolution on the existence of multi-generational or extended families in Europe. The traditional view is that industrialization led to the separation of the home from the workplace, leading in turn to structural differentiation, and a movement away from extended multi-generational or 'stem' families, and towards more isolated nuclear families (Parsons & Bales, 1953). However, many scholars have criticized this perspective, suggesting that the nuclear family preceded industrialization, and that the stem family was never the dominant form in some countries of Europe, particularly England (Aries, 1962; Laslett, 1972; in Creighton, 1980). Still others have disputed these claims, and have argued that Laslett and others employed too narrow a criterion for defining stem families by relying strictly on residence in a single household, and not considering that families go through stages of extension and constriction throughout their developmental life cycle (Berkner, 1972; Creighton, 1980; Fitzpatrick, 1983; Kertzer, 1989; Shanks, 1987). More recently, Laslett himself has given in to these arguments to some degree, admitting that while nuclear households were more prevalent in Northern and Western Europe, complex or extended family households were common in Southern Europe throughout the nineteenth century (Laslett, 1983).

This debate highlights a methodological limitation in historical analyses of family structural change in general: the confusion of the concepts of family and household, or the failure to specify the relationship between family structure and domestic living arrangement (Creighton, 1980; Shanks, 1987). Creighton (1980) argued that the criterion that should be used to distinguish family structures is the nature of property rights (or inheritance pattern), and that stem families are distinguishable by the rule of impartible inheritance (that is, inheritance by only one child, usually the eldest son). Thus, while nuclear households may have been widespread throughout Europe prior to the industrial revolution, much of the population of Europe was organized through a stem family structure. The system of impartible inheritance meant that the chosen heir usually postponed his marriage until he succeeded to his father's property. Other children were often given support in other ways, such as dowries (especially for daughters who, once married, were excluded from further inheritance), or financial support for apprenticeship or schooling (Creighton, 1980; Shanks, 1987). Non-inheriting sons who remained at home also could not marry, because the family of origin usually could not afford to support an additional family (Shanks, 1987). The predominant pattern of delayed marriage in Europe prior to the industrial revolution provides further evidence that stem family organizations were prevalent. However, this method of passing family property from one generation to the next led to a variety of living arrangements (Creighton, 1980), including the nuclear family household, where the heir to the land waited to marry until the father died or retired; the three-generation household (the retired parents, the heir and his wife, and the grandchildren); and the extended family, where the son and his wife and children took over the main household, and the retired parents or widowed mother lived in a separate dwelling close by (often on the same property, or even under the same roof in a divided house).

The European Family in the mid-Twentieth Century

Many historians have labelled the period following the Second World War as the 'golden age' of the family, in which the traditional or bourgeois family grew throughout industrialized countries to its peak in the 1960s (Trotha, 1990). The modal nuclear family in this era consisted of the 'breadwinner' father, the non-employed mother, and their biologically related children. Since the 1970s, most industrialized countries have experienced a second major transition in family forms, brought on by what many sociologists have referred to as increasing differentiation and individualization (Durkheim, 1933), and have labelled the 'post-modern' era. An accelerated rate of social change is the hallmark of this post-industrial era. The pressures caused by social changes have shaken relationships among family members: children have become more likely to challenge parental authority; to live on their own for prolonged periods of time; and to put off making permanent commitments (via traditional marriages) to their partners; such commitments are less likely to last long under these conditions of change (Schmid, 1984). Thus, post-modern society is characterized by a diversification in family forms; there are trends away from traditional nuclear families, and towards cohabitation and postponement of marriage, together with increases in single-parent and stepfamily households, and decreases in family size (Cseh-Szombathy, 1990; Fend, 1990).

The primary focus of this chapter will be on the changes in family patterns that have occurred since the Second World War. There is evidence that the structural components of families are undergoing rapid transformations, including the dissolution of 'traditional' two-parent nuclear families, and that children and adolescents embedded in these families are increasingly likely to experience multiple transitions in the structure and functioning of their families of origin and procreation throughout their lifetimes. Before turning to the structural changes in family patterns in Western Europe, it is important to recognize the methodological limitations that are inherent in such cross-national comparisons.

METHODOLOGICAL ISSUES

Most family demographers and historians rely on census listings and government statistics for source material on the dynamics of family households over time (Janssens, 1986). Problems inherent in these materials create methodological obstacles to making valid comparisons of family forms across historical time periods or geographic regions.

It is important to draw attention to the limitations of the available evidence, not all of which can yet be overcome. For instance, there has recently been growing concern among sociologists about the practice of classifying families into socioeconomic groups according to a traditional view of the family – that is, using only the male's occupation and income (as the head of household) to determine social class (Graetz, 1991; Leiulfsrud & Woodward, 1987). Thus, more recent classifications of family socioeconomic status have sometimes utilized both male and female earnings, whereas earlier data usually did not include women's earnings in their determination of social class: this makes historical comparisons extremely difficult. The calculation of family size has also varied greatly across national and historical contexts; at some periods and in some regions, only cohabiting relatives have been counted as family or household members, whereas at other periods or in other regions servants and other non-relatives have also been included.

Furthermore, census takers in many European countries have only recently begun to compile data on non-marital or consensual unions. In addition, although an analysis of all the intra-country variation in family forms is beyond the scope of this chapter, it is important to recognize that different regions within a country, for example Northern as compared with Southern Italy, can exhibit drastically different family patterns, and that annual statistics may conceal seasonal fluctuations, for example in employment patterns.

Perhaps most importantly, the family unit is not a stable entity, but rather changes its form in response to significant life events such as birth of additional children; economic gains and losses due to changing employment situations of either parent; changes in the parental unit as a consequence of marriage, divorce, or remarriage; and the launching of children out of the home into education or employment). Thus, a description of the families in existence at any one moment catches them all at various points in their development; their form at any particular time is partly a function of their stage of development, and partly a response to conditions and events in historical time, such as the rate of unemployment, or the level of educational opportunities.

These are just a few of many sources of threats to the validity and reliability of demographic data on family structural change. In sum, the cross-national variation in the compilation of family demographics, paired with the secular changes within countries in the categorization of family forms, make cross-national and historical comparisons of family change quite difficult at times. Thus, extreme caution must be made in interpreting regional and historical variation in family patterns. With these caveats in mind, the section that follows compares recent historical trends in family demographic patterns across countries in Western Europe. Wherever data are available, an attempt will be made to place these recent historical changes in the context of longer-term secular trends.

DEMOGRAPHIC TRENDS IN FAMILY PATTERNS

Several demographers have documented regional consistencies throughout European countries in terms of changes in family structure. Whereas there is of course both inter- and intra-country variation in type of family structure, for many of the categories of the demographic variables to be reviewed, European countries in three distinct geographic regions have experienced similar changes in family patterns: the most traditional countries – typified by largely agriculturally-based economies, high fertility, high and early marriage rates, and larger and extended families – consist of Southern Europe and Ireland; next come the majority of Western European countries, where the traditional nuclear family remains the dominant form but is nonetheless on the decline; and finally, the Northern European countries, which are similar in their abundance of non-traditional or 'post-modern' family structures, with high rates of cohabitation, high divorce rates, and higher proportions of women in the labour force (Gaspari 1980; Keilman, 1987). Based on these regional patterns, Western European countries were grouped in the following manner (whenever sufficient data permitted):

1. *Northern Europe*, comprising Denmark, Finland, Norway, and Sweden;
2. *Western Europe*, including Austria, Belgium, France, the former German Democratic Republic and the Federal Republic of Germany, the Netherlands, Switzerland, and England & Wales; and
3. *Southern Europe and Ireland*, consisting of Greece, Italy, Portugal, Spain, and Ireland.

A more detailed examination of the historical trends in these diverse family forms will highlight some of the regional consistencies and inconsistencies throughout Europe.

Fertility

Much of current knowledge on historical changes in European fertility can be credited to the work of the European Fertility Project, begun in 1963 at the Office of Population Research at Princeton by Ansley Coale, and compiling demographic statistics on fertility change in all countries of Europe, from the pre-industrial era (as early as 1800) up to 1960 (Coale & Watkins, 1986). The total fertility rate, or TFR, is an estimate (based on prevailing age-specific birth rates and mortality rates) of the number of children a woman would have if she survived throughout the childbearing years, and is a commonly-used proxy for tracing trends in family size over time. Coale (1986) summarized the demographic transition in total fertility rates from the pre-industrial era through 1960 as follows:

The demographic transition in Europe was a transition from approximate balance of birth and death rates at moderately high levels to approximate balance at very low levels. Pre-industrial populations had moderately high mortality because uncertain food supplies and unavoidable disease made low mortality unachievable; fertility was only moderately high [circa four to five children per woman] because of low proportions married and birth intervals that are extended by various [naturally occurring] factors [e.g. prolonged breast-feeding of babies]. Couples married late, or postponed the next pregnancy for self-interested reasons, such as waiting until attaining the economic position to form a viable household [traditionally via inheritance of the property from the father to the son] or extending the interbirth interval until the survival of the most recently born would not be jeopardized....Except among special subpopulations, such as the nobility, fertility in most of Europe did not fall until about 1870, despite the gradual decline in mortality. The sole national exception was France, where the TFR by 1870 was 20 percent lower than in 1800. After 1870, fertility fell in every country;...The decline in TFR from 1900 to 1930 was at least 30 percent in every country except France, which had progressed so far in its transition by 1900...From 1930 to 1960, TFR rose...in all of Northwestern Europe. The principal basis of this increase was a large reduction in age at marriage – a partial abandonment of the long-established West European pattern of late marriage and avoidance of marriage (28-29).

Trends in total fertility rates since 1950 are presented in Figure 5.1 for Northern Europe, Western Europe, and Southern Europe and Ireland. Given the prevalence of low mortality, the replacement level of the total fertility rate is approximately 2.1 children per woman (Bourgeois-Pichat, 1987). Between the mid-1920s and the end of the Second World War, fertility rates were below replacement throughout most of Europe (Sardon, 1990). After the war (around 1950), the 'baby boom' boosted European fertility to well above the replacement level in all countries, although there was quite considerable heterogeneity between countries, with the highest values in Ireland, the Netherlands, and Portugal; and the lowest levels in Austria and the former Federal Republic of Germany (Calot & Blayo, 1982). Total fertility rates in most European countries remained stable or increased slightly, until they reached their peak around 1965. The only decrease in total fertility was in Finland. Ireland's total fertility rate was significantly higher than most other countries, with more than four children per woman.

Around 1965, a sudden break in the trajectory of the total fertility rate occurred in all countries, with Greece the only exception (Calot & Blayo, 1982). This sudden decline was more pronounced in the countries of Northern Europe, Western Europe, and England & Wales, and moderate or more gradual in Ireland and most Southern European countries. However, since 1975, nearly all Western European countries (except for Ireland and Spain) have fallen below the 2.1 replacement level necessary to maintain the population at its current size. The Federal Republic of Germany (former West Germany) is the forerunner in this regard, with fertility rates at an historically unprecedented low (TFR of 1.29 in 1985), followed closely by the countries of Northern Europe.

Figure 5.1   Trends in lifetime total fertility rates

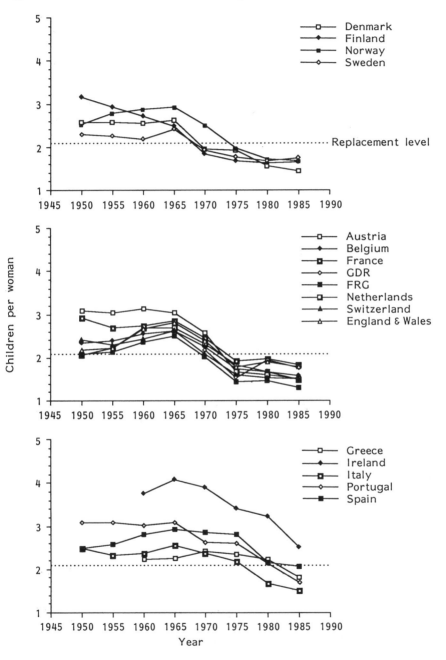

Source: Höpflinger (1987); UN Demographic Yearbook (1986).

Family Size

These declines in fertility signify a gradual decline in the size of nuclear families throughout Europe (with Ireland and Southern Europe once again lagging furthest behind). Paralleling the trends in fertility patterns, the mode of the distribution of family size reached its peak around 1965 for most European countries. Following this, there was a sharp decline in the number of families with over three children, an increase in the number of families with two children, and a more gradual increase in families with only one child or none at all (Sardon, 1990). France serves as a useful sample case, because it currently lies somewhere in the middle of the two family size extremes – Germany and Northern Europe for small families; Southern Europe and Ireland for larger families. Looking at marriage cohorts in France, the number of families with one or two children more than doubled: from 26 per cent in 1950 to 58 per cent in 1975; at the same time, the number of large families - with 5 or more children – was drastically reduced: from 36 per cent in 1950 to only 5 per cent in 1975; the average number of siblings per family has thus declined to less than half that 25 years ago (Blayo, 1984; in Chesnais, 1985).

The number of childless couples has grown significantly in recent years for several Western European countries, especially Austria, Germany, Switzerland, England, and the Netherlands (Chesnais, 1985). However, for Northern Europe, the trend is more towards postponement of childbearing rather than a significant increase in childlessness (Ostby, 1989).

As Figure 5.2 demonstrates, most European women still do desire children. The most common desire is for two children, although well over one third of women in Belgium, Great Britain, and the Netherlands express a desire to remain childless. The pattern for Sweden is quite similar to the general trend presented in Figure 5.2. Almost all Swedish women want to have children, and the ideal family size is most commonly two children; 10 per cent of women favour a single child, whereas 25 per cent prefer three children (Popenoe, 1987). The movement away from large families and towards small nuclear families may be the most dominant single feature of family structural change in this century (Sardon, 1990).

In sum, recent trends suggest a general decline in size of nuclear families, and a movement towards postponing childbearing for a growing number of couples throughout Europe. However, it is important to realize that such aggregate national statistics fail to capture the substantial variations in family size within countries. Although most governments of Europe do not compile family size data according to ethnic group membership, such a breakdown would reveal considerable diversity. In Great Britain, for example, the 1991 Census showed that the average (mean) household size was substantially higher among certain ethnic minorities than among the white population. Thus, mean household size was 2.43 among white people, 4.22 among South Asians, 2.59 among black people, and 2.96 among Chinese people and other groups. Within the South Asians, household sizes were particularly high for Bangladeshis (5.34) and Pakistanis (4.81) (Owen, 1993: Table 1: 1). Evidence from earlier studies (Smith, 1977; Brown, 1984) has shown that these larger household sizes arose partly because young people within the child-rearing

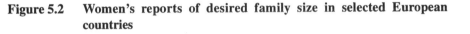

Figure 5.2   Women's reports of desired family size in selected European countries

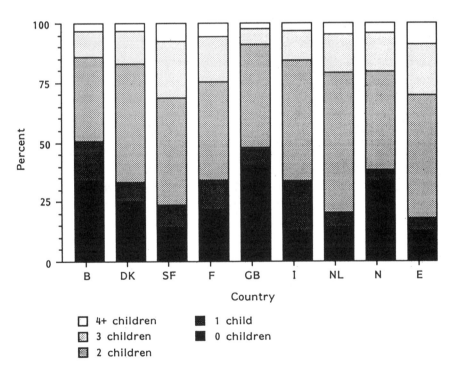

Source: World Fertility Survey data reported in Calhoun (1991).

age bands were a larger proportion of the ethnic minority than of the white population, partly because a relatively high proportion of ethnic minority households consisted of extended families, and partly because rates of fertility among ethnic minorities were relatively high, reflecting the rates in the countries of origin. In 1988-90, the mean number of dependent children per family unit in Britain was 2.0 for both Pakistanis and Bangladeshis, 2.2 for Indians, 0.7 for Afro-Caribbeans, and 0.5 for white people (Jones, 1993: Table 2.12: 29). However, the same studies have also shown that rates of fertility of migrants tend to accommodate fairly quickly towards the prevailing rates in Britain, and the minority group with the largest household size (Bangladeshis) is the one that arrived in Britain most recently. More generally, while members of certain ethnic or socioeconomic groups may be more likely to maintain larger families, the trend throughout Europe is towards smaller numbers of offspring. The decline in total fertility is closely related to changes in reproductive behaviour, which is discussed next.

Reproductive Behaviour

A brief look at indicators related to reproductive choices and behaviours among women may shed additional light on the decline in total fertility. First of all, as Figure 5.3 indicates, there has been an overall shrinking and convergence in birth rates from 1950 to 1958. The only exceptions to this trend can be found in Greece, and in the former German Democratic Republic. In every other country, the most substantial reduction in birth rates has been among 20 to 24-year-old women, suggesting that women are now much more likely to have fewer children during late adolescence than they were around 1950. The peak among 25 to 29-year-olds has also become more pronounced, providing evidence for a postponement in childbearing for a growing number of young adult women. Births to teenage women (15 to 19-year-olds) has also fallen slightly in recent years.

Trends in teenage births are illustrated in Figure 5.4. Northern Europe was the first region to experience a decline in teenage childbirths, after a peak around 1965. The peak for Western Europe was slightly later, around 1970, and now most countries have reduced their teenage childbirth rates to a level commensurate with Northern Europe (the former GDR had the highest rate of all, and the rates in England & Wales and in Austria are currently the highest in Western Europe). The more traditional (and Catholic) countries of Southern Europe and Ireland have lagged farthest behind in the reduction of teenage childbirth, which began to decline there only in the late 70s to early 80s.

Figure 5.3   Birth rates by age of mother

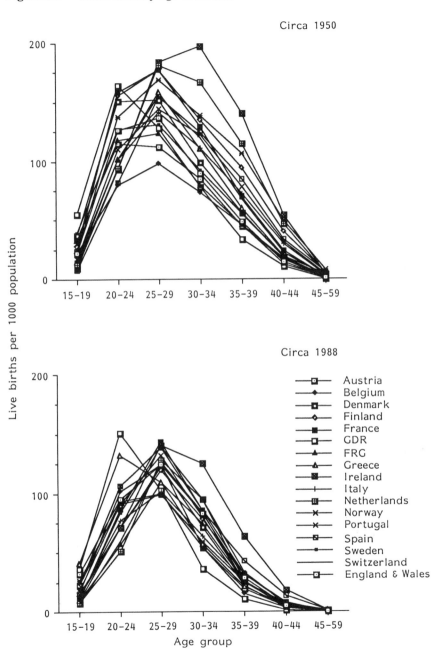

Source: UN Demographic Yearbooks (1978 HS; 1986)

Teenage fertility is much higher in the United States than in virtually every country of Europe. Although there is a large discrepancy between births to white and to African American teenage women (with a higher rate among African Americans), white teenagers in the USA still have much higher rates of pregnancy, live births, and abortion than those in Western Europe (Wallace & Vienonen, 1989). For instance, pregnancy rates for 15 to 19-year-old women were 96 per 1,000 in the USA (86 for whites only), versus 45 for England & Wales, 35 for Sweden, and 14 for the Netherlands (Jones et al., 1985; in Wallace & Vienonen, 1989).

One additional factor in women's reproductive behaviour is their access to birth control via contraception and abortion. The 1960s ushered in significant technological advances in terms of modern methods of contraception, several of which (e.g. the birth control pill and the intra-uterine device, or IUD) became widely used in the 1970s. These medical advances helped to emancipate women by giving them the power to place limits on their own fertility, thus opening up new opportunities for personal growth and financial independence (Chesnais, 1985).

Despite advances in contraceptive techniques, unwanted pregnancies do still occur. As indicated previously, this problem has become quite severe among teenagers in the United States (Hayes, 1987). For personal or medical reasons, women sometimes choose to have an abortion. Figure 5.5 shows the rate of legal abortions per 1,000 women aged 15-44. As this figure illustrates, legal abortions are much more prevalent in Northern Europe, although the United Kingdom is the leader in Western Europe. Taking a closer look at fertility in Sweden and Finland, the drop in fertility can be linked to 1970s legislation that guaranteed free family planning services to all women, including sex education, access to free or low-cost birth control, and free abortion services (Wallace & Vienonen, 1989). This government intervention has led to a significant reduction in unwanted teenage pregnancies, as well as a gradual decrease in the teenage abortion rate in both countries (Wallace & Vienonen, 1989). To illustrate the contrast between the Northern European situation and the teenage pregnancy crisis in the United States, the abortion rate (per 1,000 15 to 19-year-old women) for the period 1980-1981 in the United States was 44.4, well over twice the rate in Sweden (20.7) and in Finland (17.8). Total abortion rates follow a similar pattern: 849, 328, and 202 abortions per 1,000 live births for the USA, Sweden, and Finland, respectively (Wallace & Vienonen, 1989).

Figure 5.4　　Trends in births to teenage (15 to 19-year-old) women

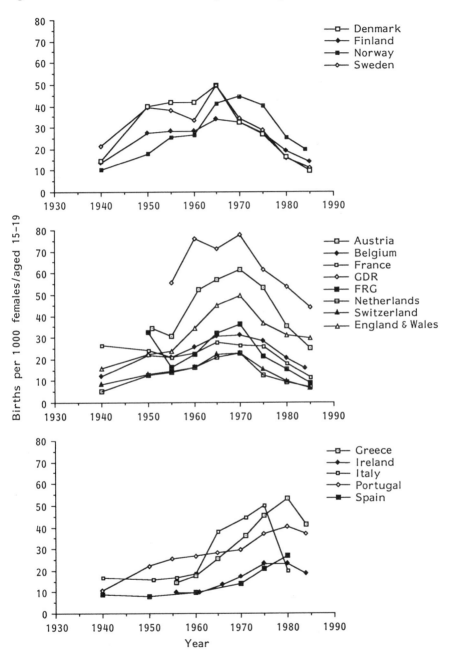

Source:　　UN Demographic Yearbooks (1949/50; 1978 HS; 1986).

Figure 5.5   Legal abortion rates by age groups

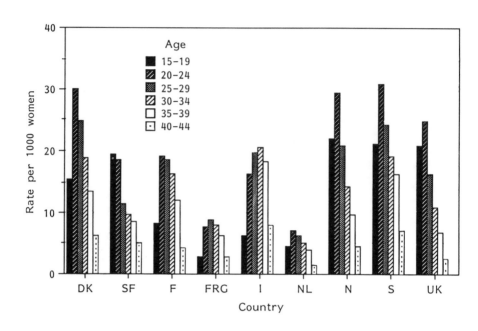

Source: UN Demographic Yearbook (1989).

Figure 5.6 represents a breakdown of the total abortions performed on women of specific age categories. The proportion of abortions that are performed on teenagers is smallest in Italy (7 per cent); this may reflect a preponderance of traditional Catholic families with strong views against birth control. It seems likely that unwanted teenage pregnancies are most likely to be carried to term in Italy, and most likely to be aborted in Finland and the UK.

Taking all of these factors into account, the overall decline in fertility throughout Europe can be linked to improvements in medical technology (e.g. birth control and contraception); to an increasing acceptance of premarital sexual involvement, and legislation that has made contraceptive methods more acceptable and accessible; to postponement of marriage and refusal to marry and have children on the part of an increasing number of women; and to an increase in the number of couples who choose to remain childless (Hoffmann-Nowotny, 1987; Leridon, 1981; Ostby, 1989). In turn, these choices have led to a shrinking in family size, and the disappearance of large families. Fortunately, there is no real danger of European families disappearing, since the majority of women still hope to have children. Nevertheless, the circumstances under which families are formed and develop are changing significantly.

Figure 5.6   Proportions of legal abortions performed on women in three age groups

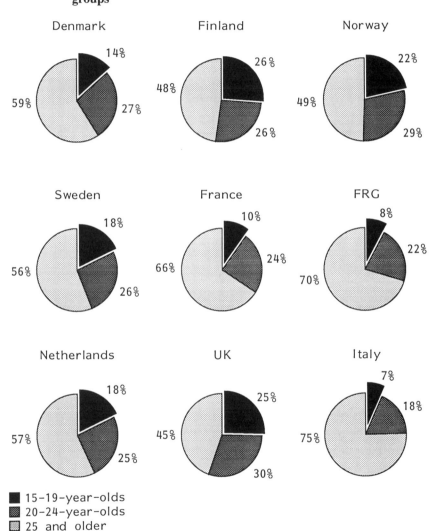

15-19-year-olds
20-24-year-olds
25 and older

Source: UN Demographic Yearbook (1989).

Household Composition: Extended Families and Kinship Networks

As pointed out previously, the industrial revolution ushered in a decline in mortality and fertility. This transition was also accompanied by changes in the size and structure of households throughout Europe (Select Committee of Experts on Household Structures, 1990). Figure 5.7 depicts recent trends in average household size across Northern, Western, and Southern Europe and Ireland. As the figure illustrates, all countries of Europe have witnessed an overall shrinking in household size over the last several decades. However, the rates of change in household size vary considerably by geographic region. The most recent data for the household characteristics of average size and proportion of single-person households follow a pattern quite similar to the general fertility pattern. In general, the smallest households can be found in countries having the lowest fertility rates, including Germany, Sweden, and Denmark: these have an average household size below 2.5 people; have a proportion of single-person households of over 30 per cent; and have over 10 per cent of the total population living alone (Chesnais, 1985). Norway and the remaining countries of Western Europe closely approach this pattern: the average household size ranges between 2.6 and 2.7 members; the proportion of single-person households runs from 20 to 30 per cent; and 8 to 10 per cent of the total population lives alone (Chesnais, 1985). Once again, Ireland and Southern Europe lag significantly behind: the average household size is 3 to 4 people; the proportion of one-person households is from 10 to 20 per cent; and only 5 per cent of the total population lives alone (Chesnais, 1985).

How does the general decline in average household size relate to the existence of multi-generational households and the strength of kinship networks across Europe? Since the industrial revolution, there has been a gradual decline in the prevalence of multi-generational households in Europe (Keilman, 1987). Historians have linked this shift away from three-generation households to decreases in fertility, to urbanization, and to the decrease in agricultural households. Despite increased life expectancy, the number of three- or four- generation households has dropped considerably in the past few decades. In West Germany, for instance, the proportion of multi-generational extended households dropped by roughly 50 per cent from 1961 to 1982, such that in the 1980s less than 5 per cent of all West German children grew up in households with both their parents and their grandparents (Keilman, 1987). Whereas vertically extended family households are shrinking in virtually all countries, the Southern European countries and Ireland have lagged behind in

Figure 5.7   Trends in average household size

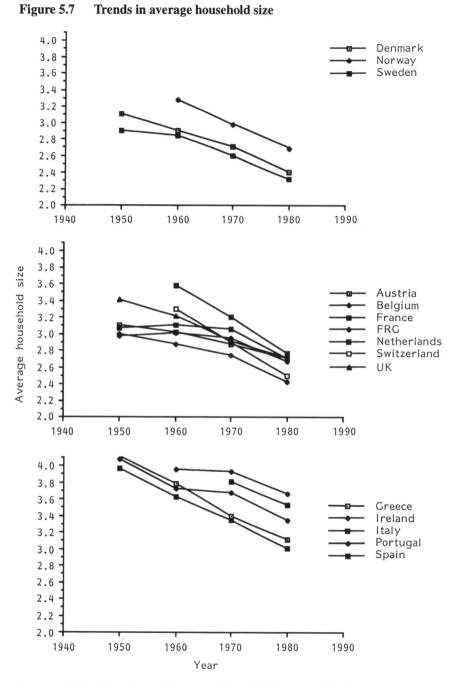

Source: Select Committee of Experts on Household Structures (1990).

this trend (i.e. these countries have had a much higher proportion of extended families), which many sociologists have linked to the higher proportion of families subsisting on agriculture in these countries, and to their more traditional values (Segalen, 1985; Sgritta, 1988). Nevertheless, recent studies of family structures in Ireland (Berger & Berger, 1984; Fogarty et al., 1984; Hannon & Katsiaouni, 1981; in Walsh, 1991) and in Italy (Sgritta, 1988) have documented a significant decline in the proportion of traditional multi-generational extended rural families, and have attributed this change largely to the increased urbanization, industrialization, and technological advances of the 1970s and 1980s.

There is evidence that in many European countries, although kinship networks among family members who migrated to the cities and among those who remained in rural areas were less active at the height of the industrial revolution than formerly, technological advances have helped to strengthen kinship networks again in recent years. For example, Segalen (1985) examined kinship networks in limited rural and urban areas of France, and drew the following conclusions:

> During a long time period, dating perhaps to the XVth century, but that can be actually described for the XVIIIth to the XXth centuries, kinship was embedded in a wider category of relationships that can be dubbed economic; and kinship networks provided for many aspects of economic and social intercourse (23) ... During the XIXth century, we know that internal migrations were sometimes organized through kinship networks... During the 1930s, kindreds were quite efficient in helping migrants into a job, and through family lines we can read the various migrations (27) ... Migrants leaving in the wake of industrialization and urbanization that took place very late in France [1950s] more or less severed their links with the villages where they were born. Cars and telephones were scarce, holidays shorter than at present, and salaries rather low. All these reasons explain why during the 1950s to 1970s there was a period of time when kinship relations between migrants and kin left at birthplaces were not as active as they are today (24) ... Links between migrants and kin in the village of origin are much more active than they were 20 years ago. Higher salaries have made it possible to acquire second houses, cars have been bought, highways have extended throughout the country, and holidays are numerous, without speaking of telephone contacts. Thus relations between migrants and their kin of origin are very active (25).

There is additional evidence that the decline in extended family households is not associated with a dearth of relationships with non-nuclear family relatives (D'Costa, 1985). In Britain, Kiernan and Wicks (1990) pointed out that the main form of child care for preschool children is with relatives, who provide more than two-thirds of all care (maternal grandmother caregivers are most common among full-time employed mothers). Keilman (1987) noted that 30 per cent of children born in the Netherlands in 1981 could be expected to have a living great-grandmother at the age of 10. D'Costa (1985) documented several studies that have shown that the presence of grandparents, and even great-grandparents, was common for a growing number of children in France (roughly 40 per cent of 21-year-olds still had both parents and at least two grandparents). Moreover, over 50 per cent of married children lived within 20 kilometres of their parents' home, and visited their families of origin at least weekly; three-quarters of families surveyed were satisfied with the frequency of visits with grandchildren (Roussel, 1976; Gökalp, 1978; in D'Costa, 1985).

While countries in Europe are experiencing declines in the proportion of extended multi-generational households, extended life expectancy, along with improvements in transport and communications have made interaction with relatives more frequent (Williams, 1983). However, if one considers the fertility trends reviewed in the previous section, as mothers have fewer children, future generations will experience a marked decrease in the size of their kinship networks, or number of collateral relatives (Behnam, 1990). In addition, the increasing life expectancies will lead to a more prolonged and pronounced experience of 'intergenerational squeeze,' in which the obligation to care for ageing parents along with children rests on the shoulders of fewer and fewer siblings and cousins. If the present is any indication of the future, this strain will be greatest for women, since they assume more responsibility for daily taking care of their children, and of their own and their husbands' ageing parents, (Dwyer & Seccombe, 1991; Finch & Mason, 1990). Sinha (1991) has argued that these trends have already led to a weakening of the role of extended families in providing care and support for the elderly.

Marriage

Traditionally, marriage and family have been closely interrelated, because marriage was usually seen as the first step towards forming a family. While this still holds for the majority of people, a growing number of young persons are postponing marriage and family formation, and opting for alternative living arrangements. Figure 5.8 depicts the trends in legal marriages for Western European countries from 1920 to 1988. Because these are rates of marriage per 1,000 population of all age groups, fluctuations over time may actually

Figure 5.8   Trends in legal marriage rates

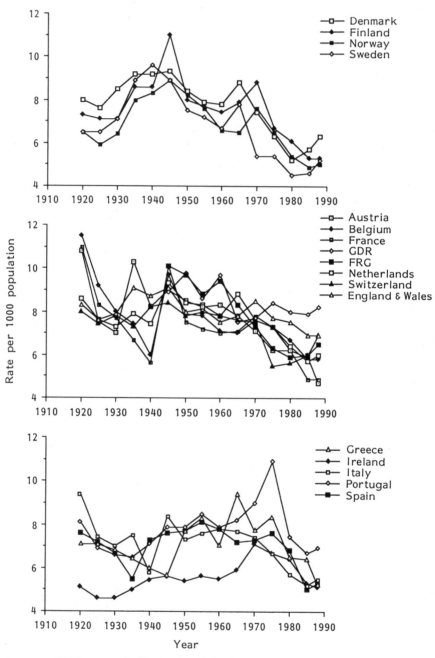

Source: UN Demographic Yearbooks (1968; 1982; 1988).

reflect changes of marital timing. As the figure illustrates, in nearly all European countries, the rate of marriage reached its peak towards the end of the 1960s and beginning of the 1970s, and since then has been on the decline in most countries (Boh, 1989; Hoffmann-Nowotny, 1987). In keeping with the trends in fertility, this decline has been most rapid in Northern Europe (although Denmark and Sweden experienced a slight increase in the overall rate of marriage across the 1980s), followed closely by several Western European countries (note the increasing diversity among Western European countries over the past two decades, with Austria and France witnessing the most rapid decline, and former East and West Germany experiencing slight increases throughout the 1980s). Once again, the countries of Southern Europe have lagged behind in their legal marriage trajectories, with most countries exhibiting gradually increasing rates of marriage until the early to mid-1970s (especially Ireland and Portugal). Up until 1970, when this difference disappeared, Ireland could be distinguished from all other countries of Europe by its low marriage rate; this arose from traditional stem family inheritance patterns, especially among agricultural households, which often led to lengthy postponements of marriage (Fitzpatrick, 1983; Shanks, 1987). However, by 1988, the countries of Southern Europe (with the exception of Portugal) had experienced drastic declines in legal marriages, making their marriage rates commensurate with those of Northern Europe.

At least for the countries of Northern and Western Europe, part of this decline in marriage rates can be explained by the trends in average age at first marriage, as plotted in Figure 5.9. Between 1960 and 1965 all countries saw a fall in age at marriage. In Northern European countries, and also the GDR, people began postponing marriage after 1965, whereas young adults in Western Europe continued to marry at younger ages until 1975, and in Southern Europe and Ireland, the average age at first marriage began to bottom out only in the early to mid-1980s. As Figure 5.10 demonstrates, the vast majority of males remain unmarried throughout their adolescence, and adolescent females have recently begun to catch up with their male counterparts (with Northern European women marrying latest). Interestingly, adolescent men and women in Southern Europe and Ireland are apt to marry later than most men and women in Western Europe. Once again, this provides support for the notion that countries with larger agricultural bases tend to follow traditional family patterns (on which males and females marry later, often waiting to inherit the family farm or business).

128

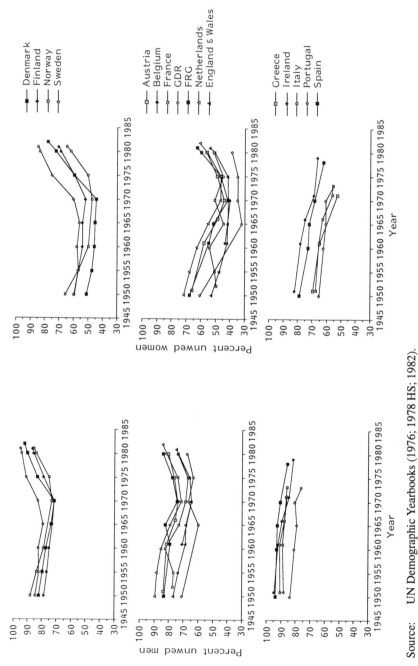

Figure 5.9   Trends in proportion of never married 20 to 24-year-old males and females

Source: UN Demographic Yearbooks (1976; 1978 HS; 1982).

Figure 5.10 Trends in men's and women's average age at first marriage

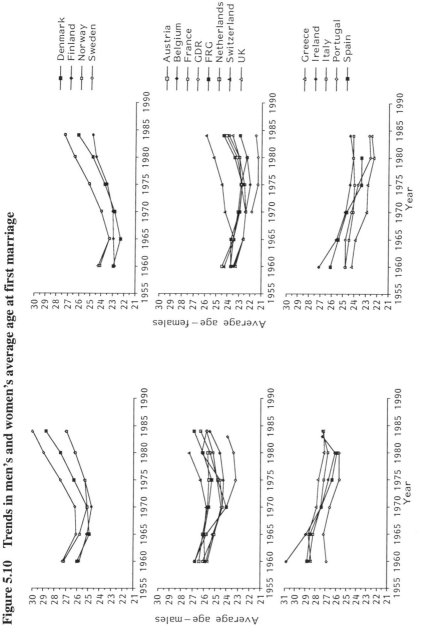

Source: Hoffmann-Nowotny (1987).

On the whole, these trends suggest a waning interest in the institution of marriage, due perhaps to the fact that adolescents entering adulthood are increasingly postponing marriage, or opting for alternative 'consensual unions' (Boh, 1989; Eldridge & Kiernan, 1985). Thus, for a growing number of young people, traditional marriage is being replaced (at least temporarily) by living together, or cohabitation.

Cohabitation

The declining propensity to marry in most European countries has been accompanied by increases in non-marital cohabitation (Chesnais, 1985; Keilman, 1987; Kiernan & Estaugh, 1993; Sardon, 1990; Schmid, 1984). This transition has not occurred, however, at the same time and rate throughout Europe. The precursors of the modern cohabitation patterns can be traced back to before the nineteenth century (Rindfuss & VandenHeuvel, 1990). For instance, in medieval England, what was later labelled 'common-law marriages' were allowed, due mainly to the fact that many remote rural areas were void of justices or clerics to preside over official marriage ceremonies (Arnold, 1951; Houlbrooke, 1984; in Rindfuss & VandenHeuvel, 1990). In the early twentieth century, cohabitation was firmly established in Sweden as well (Hoem & Rennermalm, 1985; Trost, 1979; in Rindfuss & VandenHeuvel, 1990).

Data on trends in cohabitation are quite sketchy, making cross-national comparisons difficult. One source of the problem in compiling such statistics is the operationalization of the term, which, as Hoffmann-Nowotny (1987: 127) pointed out, can include a wide variety of living arrangements: for example, two co-residing people unwilling or unable to marry; two people intending to marry who may or may not have decided on the date; two people who more or less live together but still maintain separate households (and therefore are counted in statistical terms as single persons). Many European countries count only legal marriages, and do not compile official statistics on cohabitation, thereby ascribing all cohabiting people to the category of single persons, whereas a few countries have recently attempted to distinguish between legally married versus cohabiting consensual unions (e.g. Sweden; Popenoe, 1987). Figure 5.11 depicts recent trends in cohabitation for some selected European nations.

Figure 5.11   Recent trends in non-marital cohabitation in selected European countries

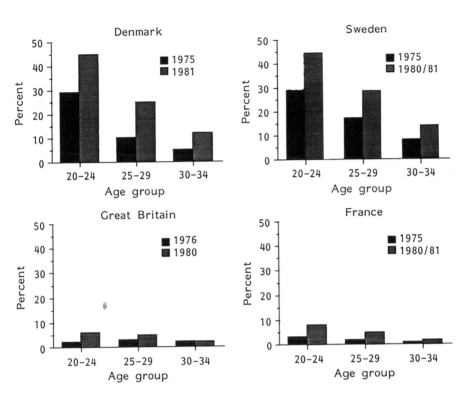

Source: Höpflinger (1985), in Hoffmann-Nowotny (1987).

The forerunners in this living arrangement are the Northern European countries, especially Sweden and Denmark (Boh, 1989; Hoffmann-Nowotny, 1987; Keilman, 1987). In fact, experts suggest that Sweden has the highest non-marital cohabitation rate among all industrialized nations, and that the vast majority of Swedes now cohabit before marriage (Hoem & Rennermalm, 1985; Popenoe, 1987). Even though the marriage rate was the highest in Europe in the last two decades, cohabitation was also quite prevalent in the former German Democratic Republic, where Boh (1989) estimated that roughly 25 per cent of women aged 18 to 35 lived with their partners without being legally married. In the former Federal Republic of Germany, the number of cohabiting couples nearly quadrupled from 1972 to 1982; there was an almost tenfold increase among 18 to 25-year-old cohabiting couples over the same time span (Zimmerman, 1985; in Hoffmann-Nowotny, 1987). Cohabitation is growing in the Netherlands, France, and Britain as well, but is still considerably less prevalent than in Sweden and Denmark (Boh, 1989; Kiernan, 1988). Nevertheless, the proportion of British 16 to 19-year-olds in unions who were cohabiting, rather than married, rose from 13 per cent in 1980 to 62 per cent in 1989; the comparable figures for 20 to 24-year-olds were 11 per cent to 32 per cent (Kiernan & Estaugh, 1993). Ireland and the countries of Southern Europe are the furthest behind in this regard. As the trends in Figures 5.7 to 10 illustrate, marriage is losing ground, and cohabitation is definitely on the rise in Western and Northern Europe. However, as Figure 5.11 also illustrates, the proportion of people who are living together outside marriage does decrease with age. Although it is problematic to draw conclusions from cross-sectional data about individual change over time, these trends suggest that even in Northern Europe, the majority of couples do eventually leave their cohabitation phase, either by breaking up or by getting legally married.

However, recent findings suggest that cohabiting couples constitute three rather different groups (Kiernan & Estaugh, 1993). First, there are youthful childless couples who have never married – so-called 'nubile cohabitants'. For the most part, these unions are short-lived, lasting only two to three years before converting to marriage or resulting in breakup. Increasingly, cohabitation is becoming a normal transitional phase before marriage. Thus, whereas 30 per cent of French women marrying in 1974-76 had cohabited before marriage, by 1980-82, 65 per cent had done so. However, from the point of view of the experiences of young people, it is likely to be relevant that there is a relatively high rate of breakup of non-marital cohabitations, with repeated broken cohabitations not uncommon (although good data on both these features are lacking). As a result, it is probable that, since the 1960s, there has been a marked increase in the proportion of older adolescents and young adults experiencing the stress of broken love relationships with cohabiting partners.

The second group of cohabiting couples comprises those who have previously been married; these are generally similar to reconstituted families formed after remarriage, but those unmarried are more likely to be in receipt of welfare maintenance than their married counterparts.

The third group consists of never-married couples with children. These cohabiting couples differ from married couples in several important respects. First, their relationships seem to be much more unstable and prone to dissolution; thus, a Swedish study showed a breakdown rate that was three times as great (Popenoe, 1987). Second, despite a small, highly educated, relatively affluent subgroup, the large majority live in disadvantaged economic circumstances – a much higher proportion than among the married with children (Kiernan & Estaugh, 1993; McRae, 1993). This is a rapidly growing group of young adults, as shown by the trends in extramarital childbearing.

Figure 5.12 depicts the trends in births to unmarried women since 1900. One difficulty in interpreting these trends is that illegitimate births are defined in legal terms (as births to unmarried women) throughout Europe, such that it is impossible to distinguish how many of these births are accounted for by single women versus women living with the father of their child. Nevertheless, an examination of the historical trends indicates that most countries of Europe experienced fairly stable or slightly increasing levels of births to unmarried women (hovering at or below ten per cent), until the Second World War, after which illegitimate births bottomed out in the 1960s, and began an upward trend after 1970, surpassing the turn of the century percentages by the 1980s. A curious exception to this pattern is Austria, where a marked peak in illegitimate births was reached in 1930, and had not been surpassed by the early 1980s.

Another sharply contrasting pattern can be found for Sweden and Denmark. The patterns of births to unmarried women in these countries suggest that expecting the birth of a child is no longer much of a motivation to get married (Hoem & Hoem, 1988; Popenoe, 1987). Well over 40 per cent of children were born to unwed mothers in 1980 in both Denmark and Sweden, representing a more than twofold increase since 1970.

Nevertheless, these trends illustrate that, aside from Denmark and Sweden, where nearly half of the children are born to unmarried parents, the vast majority of European couples who wish to have children still do so through the convention of marriage (see Figure 5.13). Although an estimated 30 to 40 per cent of all children in Europe (approaching 50 per cent in some countries) are conceived outside marriage, a minority of women remain unmarried by the time the child is born (Boh, 1989). Nave-Herz (1981: 11; in Boh, 1989) reported that the prevailing attitude among women in the Federal Republic of Germany is that children should not be born into non-legalized marriages, which seems to be consistent with the thoughts of prospective parents throughout most European countries. Less than ten per cent of cohabiting couples in the former West Germany have children, and, where they do, only

Figure 5.12   Trends in births to unmarried women

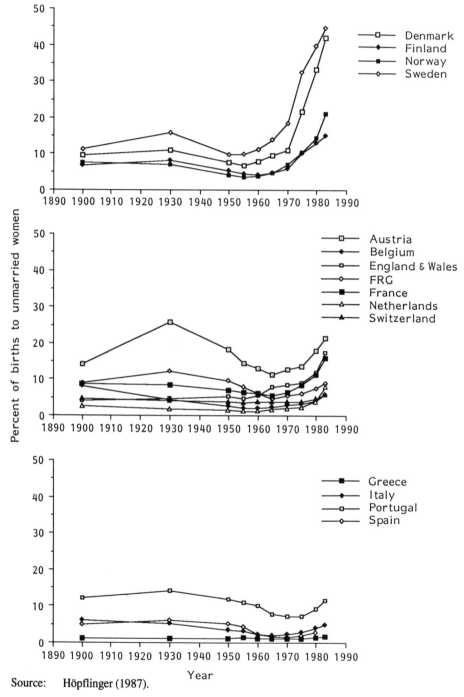

Source: Höpflinger (1987).

roughly one third of the children are biologically related to both members of the couple (Keilman, 1987). Leridon (1990) pointed out that from 1983 to 1985 in France, the fertility rate among cohabiting young couples (ages 20-24) was less than half the rate for married couples, which suggests that most couples postpone having children while cohabiting. Thus, although a growing number of people begin their lives together as cohabitees, the vast majority of people still find it worthwhile to marry eventually. Especially if the woman becomes pregnant, or the couple plans for a child, the partners are highly likely to legalize the union (Boh, 1989; Hoffmann-Nowotny, 1987; Keilman, 1987; Kiernan, 1988).

Figure 5.13   Extra-marital births (per 100 births)

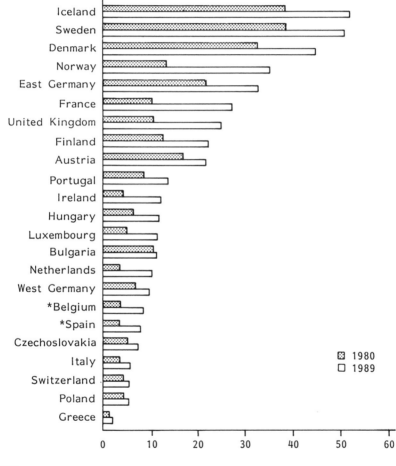

* 1987
 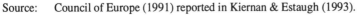
Source: Council of Europe (1991) reported in Kiernan & Estaugh (1993).

As suggested above, fertility among cohabiting couples is significantly lower than that among married couples, such that the increasing propensity to cohabit may be contributing to the declining fertility levels throughout Europe (Chesnais, 1985). However, many European countries may witness significant increases in couples with children who choose not to legally marry in the future, especially as cohabiting couples' parental rights become more widely recognized. In Germany and Britain for instance, births to unwed parents can now be registered in the name of both the mother and the father, protecting the legal rights of parents and children regardless of marital status. Evidence from Britain suggests that a growing number of couples are opting to have children outside the confines of marriage (Kiernan, 1988; Office of Population Censuses and Surveys, 1990). The percentage of live births inside marriage in Britain dropped from 91 per cent in 1975 to 72 per cent in 1990 (Office of Population Censuses and Surveys, 1990). While the proportion of live births to single mothers increased from 5 to 8 per cent over the same time period, the marital status of these mothers often changes quite rapidly. For instance, nearly 40 per cent of single mothers who solely registered their newborn babies between 1978 and 1981 had legally married by the time of the census in 1981 (Kiernan, 1988). The largest increase of all births outside marriage from 1975 to 1990 was in the percentage of births registered jointly (by both parents): an increase from 4 per cent to 18 per cent (Office of Population Censuses and Surveys, 1990). Joint birth registration policies have been in practice for quite some time in Denmark and Sweden. Popenoe (1987: 176) explained that 'the concept of children born out-of-wedlock was dropped from all Swedish legislation in the early 1970s (the term *illegitimate* was dropped in 1917), and children of such unions have exactly the same rights as do children of married unions'. As other countries begin to shape their social policies along similar lines, cohabitation and family formation outside marriage is likely to continue to grow throughout most of Western Europe in the future (Sardon, 1990).

Marital Dissolution

Measuring the dissolution of marriages across Europe by relying on comparisons in divorce rates is becoming more and more problematic, for several reasons. First of all, since 'not every breakdown of a marriage ends in divorce,' marital disruptions that do not lead to divorce go largely unaccounted for in most countries (Künzel, 1974: 384). Moreover, couples are much more likely to live separately for prolonged periods in countries with stringent or non-existent divorce laws (i.e. Southern Europe and Ireland). Finally, the increasing tendency towards cohabitation as an alternative to marriage means that divorce rates in countries with high proportions of cohabiting couples (e.g. Sweden and Denmark) underestimate the actual rate of dissolved unions (Popenoe, 1987). Thus, the trends in divorces are highly dependent on the ease or difficulty with which couples can legally acknowledge or dissolve their unions.

Figure 5.14 lists the trends in divorce rates across Western Europe over the last five decades. As is illustrated in the figure, divorce was quite uncommon in the early part of the twentieth century. Except in Southern Europe, there was a slight increase in divorces just after the Second World War, then divorce rates stabilized or declined slightly in most countries, until the mid-1960s in Northern Europe, and late 1960s to early 1970s in most countries of Western Europe, marking the end of the 'golden age of the family.' The data available for Southern Europe indicate that divorce was very rare throughout most of this century – it was illegal in Italy until 1970, and remains a very lengthy process of prolonged separation (Sgritta, 1988). Rates of divorce have only recently begun to increase slightly in Greece, and have even decreased slightly in Italy. Thus, divorces in Southern Europe are currently at a level nowhere near the rates of Western and Northern Europe, although as mentioned previously, stringent divorce laws in these regions may lead to under-representation of dissolved marital unions. In fact, even in Ireland, where divorce remains illegal, separation rates are increasing, and have exceeded widowhood as the leading cause of single parenthood (Clancy, 1984; in Walsh, 1991).

The turning point in divorce rates in Western and Northern Europe seems to have come when the law was changed. When most countries in Europe made divorce easier in the late 1960s to early 1970s by no longer requiring evidence of violation of matrimonial vows or harmful mistreatment, and moving towards 'no-fault' policies and mutual consent (Boh, 1989; Burns, 1992; Dieleman & Schouw, 1989; Haskey, 1983; Kiernan, 1988) rates of divorce increased substantially. However, they levelled off or even declined slightly in the mid to late seventies in Northern Europe, as well as in the Federal Republic of Germany, although it is difficult to determine how far this is because of the increasing rates of cohabitation in these countries (see Hoem & Hoem (1988) for a discussion of factors in declining divorce rates in Sweden). Thus, although Britain currently has the highest divorce rate in Western Europe (Kiernan, 1988), experts suggest that Sweden's high non-marital cohabitation rate (which has been shown to have a much higher breakup rate than marriage), in combination with its high divorce rate, places Sweden as the leader in family

138   *Laura E. Hess*

Figure 5.14   Trends in divorce rates

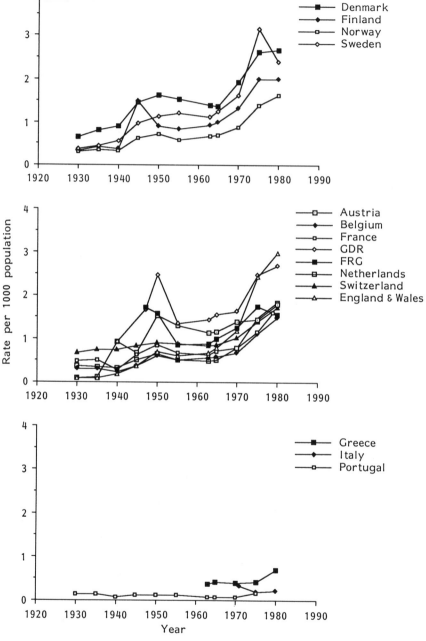

Source: UN Demographic Yearbooks (1958; 1982).

dissolution (Cherlin & Furstenberg, 1988; Popenoe, 1987). For the same reason, the rate of family dissolution may be equally high in Denmark. Recent estimates of the likelihood that marriages will end in divorce are one in three for England and Wales (Haskey, 1983), an increase from a rate of 7 per cent in the early 1950s (Kiernan, 1988); one in three for the former Federal Republic of Germany, an increase from one in eight in 1960 (Höhn & Lüscher, 1988); compared to one in two for the United States (Haskey, 1983). In sum, all indications are that the rate of European family dissolution (whether due to separation or divorce) has increased steadily since 1960, has reached a high-level plateau in Northern Europe, and is unlikely to diminish in the near future.

Single-Parent Families

The increase in divorce rates over the last two decades has been paralleled by an increase in families headed by a lone parent in most countries of Europe. The only known exception to this is the Netherlands, for which Keilman (1987) presented data showing a decline in single-parent families across the last three decades (from 10 per cent in 1960 to 7 per cent in 1985). Whereas single-parent households have existed throughout the history of Europe, the death of a spouse was the main cause of such living arrangements, until the 1970s, when divorce replaced widowhood as the leading cause (Keilman, 1987).

Figure 5.15 presents data from the 1989 European Community (EC) Labour Force survey on the percentage of households with children under age 18 headed by single parents for select EC countries (Roll, 1992). According to this definition, Northern Europe had by far the highest proportion of single-parent households (31 per cent for Denmark), while most countries of Western Europe hovered around 12 per cent (with the UK standing out at 15 per cent). Southern Europe and Ireland have the lowest percentage (ranging from 9 per cent in Ireland to 5 per cent in Greece). One important limitation of these estimates is that these data do not exclude lone parents who are cohabiting, and thus the percentages are most likely overestimates of actual lone parents (especially in countries with large proportions of cohabiting couples such as Denmark). Proof of this can be found in estimates from the mid-1980s which defined lone parents as those not living in a couple. On this definition, Denmark's proportion of single-parent families dropped to 14 per cent, equal to that of the UK; figures from 1990-91 indicate that more recently the UK figure of 19 per cent has actually exceeded Denmark's estimate of 15 per cent (Roll, 1992). As Figure 5.15 also illustrates, the vast majority of single-parent families are headed by women. The proportion of single-parent households that are headed by a father never exceeds 3 per cent for any EC country.

Not surprisingly, changes over time in single-parent households follow a pattern quite similar to the trends in divorce rates. In Great Britain, for instance, one-parent families comprised 13 per cent of all British families with dependent children in 1984, a twofold increase over the 6 per cent level in 1961 (Kiernan, 1988). This figure rose to 15 per cent by 1989 (Roll, 1992). As illustrated in Figure 5.15, the majority of these are mothers.

Figure 5.15   Percentage of households consisting of single parents with children under 18

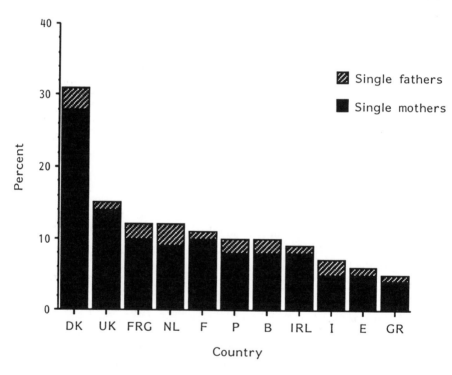

Source: EC Labour Force Survey (1989); in Roll (1992).

However, the trends in extramarital childbirth presented earlier indicate that there has also been an increase in women who choose to have a child on their own, without marrying (the declines in teenage childbirth presented in the fertility section suggest that increasingly, single women are having fewer unwanted births). It is important to recognize that the proportion of single, never-married mothers in a given country may be clouded by government policies on extra-marital registration of babies: some women who are cohabiting may go on government record as single mothers. Keeping this in mind, the proportion of never-married mothers rearing a child in Britain was 23 per cent of all single-parent families in 1982-84 (Kiernan, 1988). Germany also witnessed a sharp increase in single-parent families; their number increased by 24 per cent from 1972 to 1985 in the former West Germany (Höhn & Lüscher, 1988). The former German Democratic Republic experienced sharp increases in single-parent families as well, due increasingly to births to unwed mothers: this percentage rose from 17.3 in 1978 to 29.2 in 1982 (Rueschemeyer, 1988).

Unfortunately, when couples choose to dissolve their marriage, children are usually involved. In Britain, which currently has the highest divorce rate among Western European nations, over half of divorced couples (55 per cent in 1985) have at least one child under the age of 16 (Kiernan, 1988). In West Germany, 30 per cent of divorced women have a child under 18 living with them (Höhn & Lüscher, 1988). Roughly two-thirds of all divorces in Sweden involve children under the age of 18 (Popenoe, 1987). The estimate for the United States in 1979 was 60 per cent (Popenoe, 1987); projections are that nearly half of all American children alive today will experience the divorce of their biological parents by their eighteenth birthday (Furstenberg & Peterson, 1983; Bumpass, 1984; in Hoffmann-Nowotny, 1987).

The proportion of children who had experienced parental divorce rose steeply from the early 1970s to the early 1980s, especially in the countries in Europe with the highest divorce rates. In 1971, proportions of 7-year-old children who experienced parental divorce were 6 per cent in Sweden; and roughly 4.5 per cent in England & Wales, Switzerland, and (formerly West) Germany. A decade later (1981), the proportions for 7-year-olds were 12 per cent in Sweden and in England & Wales; 9 per cent in Switzerland; and 6 per cent in Germany (Festy, 1985). Eighteen per cent of all households with children were headed by single parents in Sweden in 1980 (Popenoe, 1987), a percentage second only to Britain for all Western European countries. Although the USA still maintains the highest proportion of single-parent households (the proportion grew from 21 per cent in 1980 to 24 per cent in

1984, with current rough estimates around 25 per cent), African American mothers make up the majority of these families (52 per cent in 1980), such that the proportion of single-parent white families (17 per cent in 1980) is lower than in the Swedish population, which contains very few people of African heritage (Popenoe, 1987).

In the light of increases in family dissolution, there has been growing interest in identifying both protective and risk factors for divorce. In terms of risk factors, several experts have demonstrated an association between early marriage and parenthood and increased likelihood for divorce (Festy, 1985; Gibson, 1973; Haskey; 1983; Künzel, 1974). Recent evidence from Sweden indicates that women who marry early have nearly double the rate of divorce than those who marry later; in Britain, estimates are that the risk of divorce increases 16 per cent with every year by which age at marriage is lowered (Bennett et al., 1988). Premarital pregnancy has also been associated with a higher susceptibility to divorce (Menken et al., 1981; Morgan & Rindfuss, 1985; Teachman, 1982; Bennett et al., 1988). In Sweden, women who have a baby prior to marriage have a 50 per cent higher divorce rate than women who marry childless (Bennett et al., 1988). Studies have also indicated that childless couples or couples with a low number of children have less stable marriages, and that families with greater numbers of children are more apt to remain married (Künzel, 1974), although this may be confounded by the fact that women in large traditional families are less likely to work, and therefore may be more financially dependent on their husbands. For instance, in a West German study, a comparison of couples married five to nine years revealed that those with no children were nearly four times as likely to divorce as those with three or more children; couples with one child were twice as likely to divorce as families with three or more children; and couples with two children experienced roughly 50 per cent more divorces than did couples with three or more children (Festy, 1985). However, Festy (1985) has also shown that building a rather large family (i.e., 3 children or more) within a short time-span is associated with higher probabilities of divorce; the link between large family size and divorce becomes less significant as duration of marriage increases. Finally, the few studies that exist on the effects of premarital cohabitation on subsequent marital stability suggest that 'trial marriage' does *not* increase the likelihood of maintaining successful legal marriages (Bennett et al., 1988; Hoem & Hoem, 1988). In Sweden, for instance, the divorce rates for couples who cohabited prior to marriage were found to be nearly 80 per cent higher than for those who do not, although the likelihood of divorce among previously cohabiting couples declined with duration of the marriage, and after eight years became indistinguishable from the probability for couples who married without premarital cohabitation after eight years (Bennett et al., 1988). The trend towards lengthier postponement of marriage and childbearing, and the increased educational aspirations of women are sources of optimism. Studies in the United States have found that an increased level of education reduced the likelihood of divorce (Menken et al., 1981; Morgan & Rindfuss, 1985; Teachman, 1982; in Bennett et al., 1988). Finally, the above findings suggest that the likelihood of divorce is reduced as the age of marriage advances, and that postponing childbirth until after marriage may also serve as a protective factor against marital dissolution.

Although the proportion of single-parent households is growing throughout Europe, largely as a result of dissolved marriages, nevertheless, single-parent households are usually not a permanent family living arrangement.

Remarriage

Accompanying the growing rates of divorce throughout Western and Northern Europe have been increases in subsequent marriages among divorced persons. In England & Wales, for example, the proportion of marriages in which at least one spouse was previously divorced rose from one in twelve in 1970 to one in five in 1980 (Haskey, 1983).

While remarriage is an increasingly common phenomenon, it is not growing at the same rate as are divorces in most of Europe. The number of (legally remarried) stepfamilies are increasing at a lower rate than are the number of marital dissolutions or breakups of consensual unions. In several countries – including England & Wales, France, Sweden, and Switzerland – the rate of remarriage for women reached a peak during the 1960s, and dropped sharply during the 1970s, indicating a growing interval between divorce and remarriage, especially among younger divorcees (Haskey, 1983; Hoffmann-Nowotny, 1987).

Throughout European countries, divorced men are more likely to remarry than are divorced women; a difference that increases with age (Haskey, 1983; Hoffmann-Nowotny, 1987). A strong factor in this may be that, as indicated previously, the vast majority of divorcing fathers do not have custody of their children.

There has also been a growing tendency for divorced persons to cohabit rather than remarry. In Britain in 1984, for instance, 20 per cent of divorced women and 17 per cent of separated women were cohabiting, compared to only 12 per cent of never-married women, and 4 per cent of widowed women

(Kiernan, 1988). Thus, similar to the increases in 'trial marriages' through cohabitation, there appears to be a growing inclination to 'try out' family life with a potential step-parent before committing to a remarriage.

Given this tendency to try out stepfamily life prior to marrying, along with the fact that remarrying adults are older, and that at least one of the partners has prior experience of marriage, one might expect that remarriages would be less likely to dissolve than first marriages. Disappointingly, available evidence suggests that this is not the case. Studies from the United States dating back to the early 1950s have consistently documented that divorce rates of remarriages exceeded rates among first marriages (Monahan, 1952; White & Booth, 1985; in Hoffmann-Nowotny, 1987). Similarly, data from the early 1980s in England & Wales show that the divorce rate among divorced women who remarry is double that recorded for wives who were single prior to marriage, and that this higher risk remains fairly constant regardless of the age at which women remarry (Festy, 1985). White and Booth (1985) argued that the presence of stepchildren – which is most likely among remarrying women as opposed to men – is a key factor in the high instability of stepfamilies (in Hoffmann-Nowotny, 1987). Thus, children who are subjected to divorce of their natural parents are even more likely to experience divorce of their mother and a step-parent, should their mother remarry.

Maternal Employment

With increasing industrialization, the separation of the occupational sphere from the family sphere resulted in a decrease in the role of women as producers alongside their husbands, for example, on the family farm, and a diminution in the proportion of married women whose role was solely that of housewife (Künzel, 1974). Industrialization alongside higher educational attainment of women, and higher divorce rates (and single-mother families) has thus led to a steady increase throughout Europe in the proportion of mothers working independently of their families. Many scholars consider this development to be the most significant of all changes in family patterns (Boh, 1989; Kiernan 1991; Land, 1979).

It is quite difficult to make comparisons of trends in female employment patterns within and between national boundaries. A commentary on the changing role of men and women fifteen years ago still holds true today (Sullerot, 1977; in Land, 1979):

That the world of work has been built up, planned and designed for and by men is apparent as soon as one endeavors to describe the situation of working women in statistical terms. Definitions vary from one country to another: in some countries the unpaid wives of farmers, businessmen and skilled craftsmen working in the family enterprise are considered to be unemployed.... A particular society will count accurately only what is in its view important, and the statistical haziness surrounding female employment proves that the economic role of women has long been regarded as marginal (74-75).

Additional evidence for the inaccuracies in cross-national comparisons of female economic activity rates can be found in the fact that there is wide diversity within and between countries in the proportion of the day spent by women in paid employment (Kronick & Lieberthal, 1976). Only very recently have countries begun to dichotomize female employment into part-time versus full-time work, making comparisons of trends over time quite difficult. Moreover, in some countries, persons employed part-time are considered part of the economically active population, while in others, they are considered inactive. Non-comparability due to such differences have serious implications for the validity of cross-national comparisons in female employment statistics.

Keeping these caveats in mind, trends over the past three decades in the employment of women are presented separately for several European countries in Figure 5.16. The trends that emerge from these plots converge quite nicely, although at various rates across time and between European regions. In the earliest year plotted (usually around 1960) female participation in the labour force generally increased rapidly between the ages of 15 to 19, to reach a peak between the ages of 20 and 24; it declined rapidly between the ages of 25 and 29 to remain on a low plateau from the age of 35 to 59, and dropped again steadily after that. Ireland and Southern Europe (especially Spain) have maintained this traditional profile over the past three decades, offering additional evidence that the primary role of women as mothers and housewives changed relatively little over the thirty years from 1960 (note however that change in Italy and Portugal was more marked from the early 1970s to the early 1980s). Although information on trends in women's employment patterns for the Netherlands across this time-span was incomplete, Jallinoja (1989: 108) has demonstrated that maternal employment in the Netherlands is more similar to the traditional patterns found in Southern Europe and Ireland, in that at least 60 per cent of young married women were not employed outside the home in 1960, 1970, and 1980.

Figure 5.16   Trends in female employment across age groups

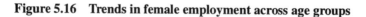

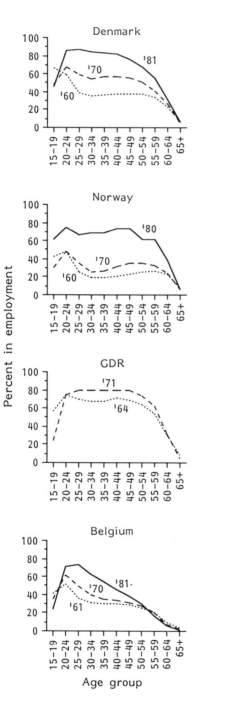

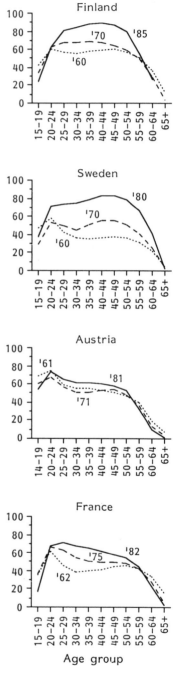

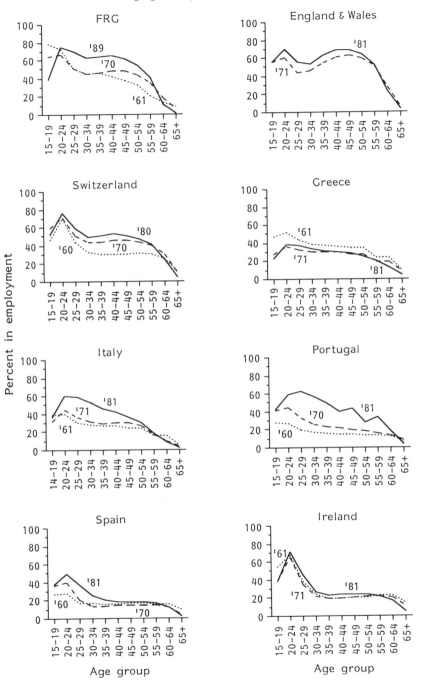

Source: Paukert (1982); UN Demographic Yearbooks (1964; 1973; 1979; 1984; 1988).

Beginning with the 1970s, in most countries of Western and Northern Europe, declines in labour force participation after marriage (or age 20-24) became less drastic, and employment in the middle-age groups – especially between the ages of 35 to 54 – began to rise, forming another peak, followed by another more gradual decline from 55 to 59. The 'M-shaped curve' typical of the 70s – see Norway, Sweden, France, FRG, England & Wales – illustrates the typical trend of that era for women to re-enter the labour force after raising their children (Paukert, 1982: 321). Note also that Finland and the former German Democratic Republic experienced only a minimal drop in female employment during the childbearing years in the 1960s, and that this drop had vanished by the early 1970s. In the remaining Western and Northern European countries, the M-profile was flattened considerably in the early 1980s. In the countries with high rates of female employment, such as all the countries of Northern Europe, the new profile of the 80s can be characterized by an 'inverted U-shape curve, resembling the male activity curve, although still remaining at a slightly lower level ' (Paukert, 1982: 321).

Although every country of Europe has witnessed an increase (of varying magnitudes) in the percentage of women in the labour force over the past three decades, the overall level of female employment remains considerably lower than that of male employment, which suggests that paid work for women is still considered in most countries to be secondary (or supplementary) to the role of men as the primary bread-winners (Land, 1979). According to the 1989 Labour Force Survey at least 95 per cent of men who had not reached retirement age were economically active throughout Western Europe (Roll, 1992). Moreover, it can be said of countries exhibiting a decline in female economic activity during the child-bearing years – including all of Western Europe (except the former GDR) and Southern Europe and Ireland – that most women interrupt their careers with the onset of children, although the length of this interruption is growing shorter in most of Western Europe.

Figure 5.17 shows the proportions of mothers with children under 18 employed full-time versus part-time, for all women as well as just for single mothers. As the top histogram illustrates, less than half of all mothers work full-time in the majority of EC member countries (except for Portugal). Mothers are more likely to be working part-time than full-time in Germany, the Netherlands, and the United Kingdom. The most striking contrasts between full-time versus part-time employment can be found in the Netherlands, where only 5 per cent of all mothers are employed full-time, and conversely, in the countries of Southern Europe, where 5 per cent or less of all mothers have part-time jobs. Thus, the movement towards greater proportions

Figure 5.17 Proportions of mothers with children under 18 who are in employment

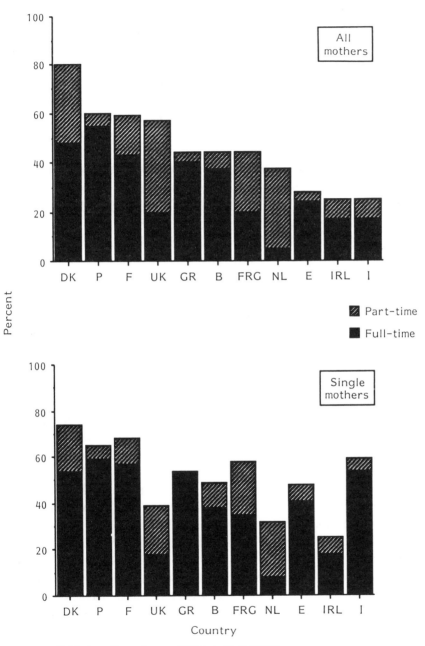

Source: EC Labour Force Survey (1989); in Roll (1992).

of working mothers does not seem to be significantly slower in Southern Europe. The poor economic situation in these Southern European countries would suggest that many of these women may work out of economic necessity (Roll, 1992). Comparing the bottom histogram (single mothers only) with the top histogram (all mothers), single mothers are more likely to be employed than all mothers in most countries. However, evidence from the UK suggests that there is little difference between single mothers and married mothers (39 per cent vs. 42). Finally, as can be seen in the bottom histogram, single mothers are somewhat more likely to be employed full-time, except in the Netherlands and the UK, where they are more likely to have part-time jobs.

Recent estimates suggest that Sweden has the highest percentage (85 per cent) of mothers of young children (under age 7) in the workforce of all Western European nations (Popenoe, 1987); the estimate for Norway approached 60 per cent by 1980, and France's level exceeded 60 per cent by 1975 (Paukert, 1982). However, Sweden also had the highest percentage of mothers working part-time in 1982: over 45 per cent (Boh, 1989). This may be largely due to legislation that guarantees Swedish parents the right to work part-time (six hours per day), for as long as eight to twelve years after their child's birth (Popenoe, 1987). Thus, even in countries with high levels of female labour force participation, it appears that a substantial proportion of European mothers with children and adolescents still at home work only part-time (especially in Sweden, the UK, the Netherlands, and Germany).

Turning back to the profiles in Figure 5.16, the presence of even a minor dip (or 'shallow M') would suggest that mothers drop back in their rate of employment somewhat, at least for some portion of their children's lives. Michel (1989) offered some additional clarification, and maintained that the presence of children reinforces the traditional division of gender roles among most European husbands and wives, by keeping women out of full-time employment.

Researchers have found many demographic correlates with increases in female employment. Changes in fertility patterns have been most closely associated with trends in employment (Vannoy, 1991). An inverse relationship exists, such that larger numbers of children are associated with lower employment rates (Kronick & Lieberthal, 1976; Schmid, 1984). By comparing these employment trends with the trends in fertility (see Figure 5.1) and average age at marriage (Figure 5.9), it becomes clear that those countries with low fertility and longer postponement of marriage are also likely to have high rates of female economic activity.

However, the theoretical linkage between lower fertility and maternal employment has generated considerable controversy as to which causes which (Chesnais, 1985; Joshi et al., 1985; Lehrer & Nerlove, 1986; Michael, 1985; Waite & Stolzenberg, 1976). Waite & Stolzenberg (1976) provided empirical evidence that the main direction of causality is likely to flow from increased labour force participation to limitations on fertility, rather than the converse. However, clearly there are influences in both directions. Thus, the birth of twins is followed by an immediate reduction in maternal employment but an increase later in the life cycle (Rosenzweig & Wolpin, 1980). The particular pattern depends on many factors – including the husband's earning power, the availability of child care, and the availability of part-time work and employment close to the home. Trends suggest that adolescent women throughout Europe are increasingly choosing to postpone marriage and have fewer children, due in part to their efforts to achieve more in the world of work via higher educational attainment (Schmid, 1984). But it seems that the likelihood of leaving the labour force upon the birth of a child is somewhat higher among women of higher socio-economic and educational backgrounds (Lehrer & Nerlove, 1986). This possibly explains further the slight 'dip' in the 'inverted U' profiles for many European countries (see Figure 5.16). Unfortunately, women's commitment to a successful career often exacts a price in terms of marital instability (Vannoy, 1991). Several studies in the United States have found high occupational attainment of women to be associated with marital dissolution, especially if the wife's job approaches or surpasses the status and earning potential of her husband's (Hornung & McCullough, 1981; Houseknecht & Spanier, 1980; Philliber & Hiller, 1983; Kronick & Lieberthal, 1976). All in all, throughout the bulk of Western European countries recent years have been marked by increasing labour force participation, especially among married women and women with children.

Physical and sexual abuse

One of the most striking features of the period since the Second World War has been the widespread recognition of the high prevalence of the physical and sexual abuse of children, and the appreciation that such abuse constitutes a risk factor for psychiatric disorders in adolescence and early adult life (Skuse & Bentovim, 1994; Smith & Bentovim, 1994). In some quarters, abuse has been seen as a new pandemic and it is necessary to consider whether it has in fact become more frequent and, if so, whether it may have played a role in any rise in psychosocial disorders in young people.

The physical abuse of children is, of course, far from a new phenomenon (Zigler & Hall, 1989); concerns over its occurrence led to the setting-up of various national societies for the prevention of cruelty to children just over a hundred years ago. Nevertheless, it is fair to say that it was not until Kempe et al. (1962) coined the term 'battered child syndrome' in the early 1960s, and described its medical manifestations, that professionals and the general public became aware of its high frequency. The general recognition of sexual abuse is even more recent, with an upsurge of reporting of cases in the United States in the 1970s followed by a similar upsurge in Europe a few years later. Registers began to be set up and it is these that provide the most systematic data on trends over time.

The Dutch register data showed a threefold increase in the incidence of abuse between 1974 and 1983 (Pieterse & Van Urk, 1989) but this was due to an upsurge in cases of neglect and of sexual abuse. There was actually a decline in the number of cases of physical harm. It may be inferred that the overall rise was probably a consequence of a broadening of the definition of abuse combined with a growing recognition of sexual abuse.

Figures 5.18 and 5.19 show the findings over the two decades from 1970 from the registers set up by the National Society for the Prevention of Cruelty to Children in the UK (Creighton, 1992). It is clear that there has been a huge rise in the 1980s in the number of children placed on their registers, but the great majority of these fell into the 'grave concern' category. The 'fatal and serious injury' category showed a much smaller rise. Because the latter are likely to have been regularly registered over the whole of the time period, it is probable that these will provide a better index of time trends. It may be concluded that the peak in the early 1970s represented a backlog of cases brought to notice through the setting-up of registers, that there is no indication of any substantial change in rate between the mid-1970s and the mid-1980s but that there may have been some increase in the late 1980s. It is also probably relevant that the England and Wales figures show no increase in infant homicide rates between the 1950s and the mid-1980s (Marks & Kumar, 1993).

With respect to sexual abuse, there are several North American surveys in the 1980s that have employed similar methods and which can be compared with the Kinsey survey in the 1940s. When, so far as possible, like is compared with like, it appears that some 10 to 12 per cent of girls experienced sexual abuse at both time periods, with no evidence of an increase over time (Feldman et al., 1991). Whether the same applies in Europe is not known.

Figure 5.18 Registration, injury, sexual abuse and grave concern rates by year, 1975-1990

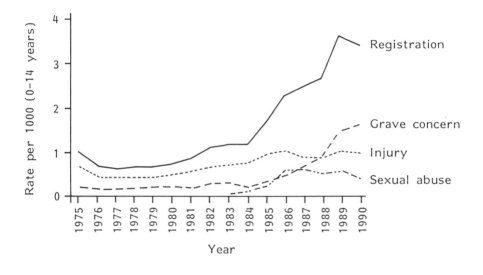

Source: Creighton (1992).

Another approach to time trends is provided by recourse to retrospective data based on the recall of adults of different ages. Few such data are available but those that have been published on sexual abuse (Anderson et al., 1993; Wyatt, 1985) give no indication that younger women are more likely than older women to have experienced abuse. There are many methodological considerations in assessing abuse (Wyatt & Peters, 1986) and these negative findings do not necessarily rule out an increase over time in the experience of abuse. However, equally, they provide no convincing evidence of a recent pandemic of abuse.

Abusing experiences do constitute risk factors for later psychological disorders (Skuse & Bentovim, 1994; Smith & Bentovim, 1994) but it is doubtful whether such experiences have played more than a very minor contributory role in a rise in such disorders over the last 50 years.

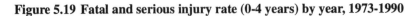

Figure 5.19 Fatal and serious injury rate (0-4 years) by year, 1973-1990

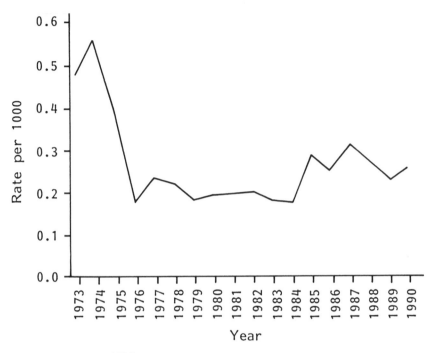

Source: Creighton (1992).

Summary

The preceding review of demographic trends has helped to elucidate the linkage between macro-level societal changes (for example, increasing industrialization and modernization) and increasing complexities in family patterns that have occurred over the past several decades in countries of Western Europe. While the data point to considerable regional diversity, a few general trends can be summarized for European countries. Keilman (1987) offered the following conclusions regarding the evolution of families in Europe:

> The individual has much weaker ties with traditional families nowadays than a few decades ago. Children are more often involved in a divorce; when they leave the parental home, they relatively often live on their own, or in non-marital cohabitation. Nevertheless, such a living arrangement is often a prelude to marriage, and only in Sweden and Denmark is it a full alternative to marriage

for the majority of cohabitants. In the rest of Europe, marriage usually occurs as soon as a child is desired or expected. Yet an increasing number of children are born outside wedlock. The character of this non-marital fertility is, however, different from that of the 1960s: a shift has taken place from 'accidents' to 'planned' births....In the future we shall witness a substantial increase in the prevalence of non-traditional living arrangements. There will be fewer marriages, more voluntarily childless couples, and more consensual unions (also among the elderly). The high marriage propensities at young ages in the 1960s were replaced by consensual unions in the 1970s. Extrapolating this trend one might expect that an increasing number of cohabitants will view their life style as a full alternative to a legal marriage (322-323).

Examining these relationships across both historical time and geographic regions of Western Europe has helped to demonstrate that changes in the socio-political and economic settings in which families are embedded are inextricably and reciprocally related to changes in the structure or function of the family. A wide body of research in developmental psychology suggests that such family changes are, in turn, bidirectionally related to the development of individual family members.

The focus of the next section is on the impact of these transitions on the lives of adolescents embedded in families undergoing such changes. Although the bulk of research evidence on this next topic stems from the United States, the results are relevant to Europe, given the rapid rate of family change experienced there in recent decades.

ADOLESCENTS' EXPERIENCES OF CHANGING FAMILY PATTERNS

Most decisions to change the pattern of family life in a significant way, including for example the mother taking a job, a move to a different area, the dissolution of one family and later the formation of another, are taken by one or both parents, yet they require readjustment in the lives of all family members. As Glick (1988) pointed out:

The costs and benefits from changes in family behaviour – more divorce, remarriage, cohabitation, lone living, and lone parenting – are not distributed equally among those who are affected. Many of those involved are more resilient than others during changes; some can take fragile marital [or cohabital] relationships in stride more easily than others; and some can withstand pressures to marry (or divorce) [or cohabit (or separate)] more effectively than others (871).

Children and adolescents are often vulnerable during periods of family reorganization. However, some young people thrive under very adverse family conditions, whereas some extremely stable families have adolescents with multiple psychosocial problems. Development in adolescence, and throughout the life span, is determined by the characteristics of the individual, by the individual's ability to change the environment, and by the social and physical conditions in which the individual is embedded (Baltes, 1987; Hinde, 1987; Lerner, 1984; Lerner & Kauffman, 1985).

This section examines research into the dynamic interactions between the developing child and the developing social setting. It focuses, in particular, on the impact of family structural change – as indicated by maternal employment, family migration, parental divorce, and remarriage – on family functioning, and on the development of adolescents. To put this discussion in proper perspective, it is useful to begin with a brief description of changes in family life that typically occur when children make the transition to adolescence (see also Chapter 4).

The Impact of the Transition to Adolescence on Family Relationships

One of the primary tasks of adolescence is to make the transition from dependence to self-reliance and responsibility (Hess et al., in press). Most human developmental theorists recognize the growth of personal identity or self-concept as the key process in this transformation (Erikson, 1955, 1968; Gunnar & Collins, 1988; Lerner & Foch, 1987). However, many different kinds of developmental change occur during adolescence, including biological change brought about by the onset of puberty (Paikoff & Brooks-Gunn, 1991; Petersen & Taylor, 1980), cognitive advances associated with the transition from concrete thinking to more abstract reasoning (Keating, 1990; Piaget, 1972), and changes in the nature of interactions with peers of the same and of the opposite sex (Steinberg, 1987). Paikoff & Brooks-Gunn (1991) reviewed evidence which suggests that the self concept of the adolescent is modified in interaction with this combination of changes and that the effects of the various factors on adolescent behaviour and parent-adolescent relationships are most likely mediated by contextual factors, including gender of the parent and child, family structure, and ethnicity. Furthermore, the rites of passage from childhood to adulthood are becoming more poorly defined, as adolescents mature physically at younger ages (the average age of pubertal onset has dropped from 14.2 to 12.5 since the beginning of this century), and enter the adult world of work and family at older ages; this has led to less clear roles for both parents and adolescents (Hess et al., in press; Quinn et al., 1985).

These multilevel changes are associated with renegotiation of roles and responsibilities within the family system, which often leads to increased conflict between young adolescents and their parents (Petersen, 1988; Quinn et al., 1985; Steinberg, 1981). Part of this conflict may stem from the inability of adolescents around the ages of 10-15 to reason abstractly, and to take the perspective of their parents (Piaget, 1958), and from the tendency on the part of some parents to 'tighten the reins,' or place higher demands on their physically maturing child for adult-like behaviour (Rapoport, 1991). Parent-adolescent conflicts most often revolve around everyday issues, such as the adolescent's complaints about too few privileges and freedoms as well as too many chores and responsibilities (Montemayor, 1983). These disputes reach peak levels during early adolescence (age 10-14), when youngsters are striving to become more peer-oriented and independent from their parents; may remain high during mid-adolescence (age 15-16), when many adolescents favour interaction with and support from their peer group over their parents; and eventually dissipate throughout late adolescence, as parents and their children learn to accept and appreciate each other as unique and responsible adults (Blum, 1985; Hill & Holmbeck, 1986; Paikoff & Brooks-Gunn, 1991).

Several characteristics of adolescents have been found to influence the feedback they receive (in terms of socialization) from their parents. For example, Steinberg (1988) has provided evidence that as adolescents approach the pubertal apex, conflict with parents intensifies, and that this heightened conflict is more likely to be experienced with daughters than with sons. Further evidence for gender-specific socialization exists, in that adolescent boys are more likely to be encouraged to be independent and responsible in the public sphere (and more likely to be punished for transgressions), whereas teenage girls are encouraged to be emotionally expressive, but are also more closely supervised and restricted from access to social activities (Davies, 1984; in Rapoport, 1991). In addition, several studies have found that siblings within the same family often – because of differences in individual characteristics such as age, personality, and temperament – receive differential treatment from their parents, and that such differential treatment can lead to increased dissatisfaction and conflict (Brody et al., 1992; Harris & Morgan, 1991; McHale & Pawletko, 1992; Stocker et al., 1989).

Despite the heightened conflict and the desire to associate more with peers and separate from the family, most adolescents still rely heavily on their families for emotional support and guidance, and place a high value on having good relationships with both parents (Burke & Weir, 1978; Kandel & Lesser, 1972; Noller & Callan, 1986; Richardson et al., 1984). Thus, the developmental task for parents of adolescents is to provide their children with strong emotional support and a sense of belonging in the family, while at the same time recognizing their increasing maturation and independence (Blum, 1985). Most researchers agree that family relationships characterized by emotional warmth and parental involvement foster positive psychosocial adjustment in adolescent children, as shown by more positive relationships with peers, higher academic achievement, and a sense of autonomy and self-esteem (Bell et al., 1988; Cooper et al., 1983; Hirsch, 1985; Hunter & Youniss, 1982). What then is the implication for the psychosocial adjustment of children of the change towards small families and the disappearance of large families throughout Europe? Furthermore, how does the trend towards increased turbulence associated with family dissolution, remarriage, changes in parental employment, and family relocation, influence parent-child relations, and affect the well-being of adolescents and their families?

Family Size

Past research has demonstrated that the well-being of children is influenced in large part by the structure and functioning of their families. However, there is also a growing literature which shows that the number and ages of children can significantly influence the marital satisfaction of parents, which, in turn, can affect the future stability of family structures (Hernandez, 1986). Spanier and Lewis (1980), in their review of research during the 1970s, conclude that marital satisfaction tends to decline as a consequence of the transition to parenthood. Several subsequent studies have found that childless married couples report higher marital satisfaction than couples with children, and that this negative relationship grows somewhat stronger with increasing numbers of children (Abbott & Brody, 1985; Glenn & McLanahan, 1982; Polonko et al., 1982). However, as discussed above, childless couples are nevertheless more likely to divorce. It seems that the arrival of children may increase family strains but still somewhat deter couples from dealing with their problems through seeking divorce. Marini (1980) found that a premarital pregnancy, the number of children, and the age of the youngest child were all negatively related to parental satisfaction (although the premarital pregnancy had no impact on fathers' satisfaction). The negative effect of number of children on marital satisfaction may be greater for women who are employed full-time than for other women, due in large part to increased demands on their time (Glenn & McLanahan, 1982). However, Gove and Geerken's (1977) research indicates that with increases in family size, non-employed wives tend to report more feelings of loneliness, and have a higher incidence of psychiatric symptoms such as depression, anxiety, and irritability than do employed wives or husbands. These researchers also report that the negative impact of family size on adjustment tends to decrease as children grow older, which contradicts Marini's (1980) findings.

A great body of research has been generated on the relationship between family size and the cognitive and intellectual development of children. However, many studies have been limited by their inability, due in great part to insufficient sample sizes, to control for important variables including parental socio-economic status, child birth order and intervals between births, and parental age or stage in the family life cycle (Chesnais, 1985).

National surveys conducted in Scotland (in 1953), and in France and the Netherlands (both in 1973) were designed to address these problems (see Chesnais, 1985). These three studies found no significant differences in intellectual performance (IQ) among one-child, two-child, three-child, or four-child families; only children who had four or more siblings were likely to fall substantially behind in intellectual achievement (a pattern that was more evident in economically deprived families). Contributing factors to this decline in IQ among children from large families included economic pressures and associated declines in housing, poorer nutrition, lack of maternal care or involvement, and lack of parental planning and insight into their family's future. Several North American studies have provided evidence that the presence of larger numbers of siblings in a family is somewhat negatively associated with psychological well-being (especially among males), and that this negative relationship is most pronounced with regard to educational achievement and attainment (Alwin & Thornton, 1984; Blake, 1981a; Glenn & Hoppe, 1982; Mott & Haurin, 1982; in Hernandez, 1986). Studies of the impact of family size on physical maturation and health status are less common, but existing evidence suggests that children with many siblings tend to be less physically mature (smaller, lighter), which has been linked to nutritional deficits, less frequent use of medical services, decreased intervals between births, and births to older mothers (Chesnais, 1985). Given the predominant pattern across Europe of a trend towards one- or two-child families, large family size does not seem to be an important risk factor for physical or cognitive deficits among the majority of European children.

However, it could be suggested that the increased likelihood of growing up as an only child might have consequences on psychosocial adjustment. All else being equal, parents of small families have more resources (financial, emotional, and intellectual) to devote to their children than do parents of large families (Blake, 1981b; Mott & Haurin, 1982). Despite the fact that single children may have an advantage of receiving more adult attention and interaction, the large-scale European studies discussed above failed to find significant cognitive gains for single children (Chesnais, 1985). On the contrary, single children's absorption into the adult world may exact a price in terms of increased difficulty of interaction with same-age peers (Chesnais, 1985). Miller and Maruyama's (1976) study of 1,750 North American grade school children showed that first-born children were less popular among peers than later-born children, but first-born only children were not differentiated from those who were eldest in a multi-child family. Blake's (1981a) review of the literature, and the results of her own study on the long-term adjustment of only children helped to dispel the popular belief that only children may be at a disadvantage. The only significant difference found was that only children were somewhat less likely to grow up through age 16 with both parents. She also found that people who had grown up with no siblings were equally or even more likely to rate themselves as generally happy, and satisfied with their health, leisure activities, and jobs.

In sum, most studies have failed to find significant differences in terms of psychological well-being and educational achievement between children with no siblings and those with one or two. However, children raised in large families do seem to be more at-risk for lower achievements and adjustment, perhaps because the large numbers of children dilute parents' emotional and financial resources. The presence of children seems to detract from marital satisfaction, an effect that is more pronounced in families with several children. Encouragingly, marital satisfaction has been found to improve after the youngest child has moved through adolescence. While the demographic data reviewed previously show that the divorce rate is higher among childless couples than among couples with children, the growing number of parental divorces experienced by children today suggests that many parents are increasingly unable or unwilling to overcome their feelings of dissatisfaction with their marriage. The impact of parental divorce and remarriage on children and adolescents is reviewed next.

Divorce and Remarriage

A great deal of research has been conducted on the impact of marital breakdown and parental remarriage on children's psychosocial development. Several reviews of this extensive literature have been published (see Amato & Keith, 1991; Barber & Eccles, 1992; Cherlin et al., 1991; Emery, 1982; Wallerstein, 1991). The divorce literature can be broken down into two main categories: first, studies that have focused primarily on short-term consequences of marital dissolution (these are the majority); and second, later studies that have examined the effects of divorce and remarriage on children and adolescents' long-term adjustment. The short-term consequences of divorce and remarriage are reviewed first, followed by a review of the long-term consequences for adolescents' own family formation.

Short-term Consequences of Parental Divorce

In the period immediately surrounding separation and divorce, most family members experience emotional distress and disrupted functioning (Hetherington et al., 1982; Wallerstein & Kelly, 1980). Single-parent mothers, usually absorbed with their own problems of recovering emotionally and surviving financially often communicate more poorly, are less affectionate, and less supportive and sensitive to the needs of their children than mothers in partnerships. Part of the reason single parents are restricted in the amount of time and and energy they can devote to their children is that they have often just taken a full-time job (Amato & Keith, 1991). In the initial readjustment phase, single mothers are also often more restrictive and punishing, and make fewer demands for maturity, than mothers in intact families. Correspondingly, children (particularly boys) often refuse to comply with the mother's wishes and act out hostile feelings (Hetherington, 1988; Wallerstein & Kelly, 1980).

The financial loss that commonly accompanies the breakdown of a marriage makes adjustment more difficult. Divorce often pushes single mothers below the poverty line (Duncan & Hoffman, 1985; Weitzmann, 1985; in Amato & Keith, 1991). Weiss (1984) matched the family income level of intact families to the pre-divorce level of single-parent families, and found that five years after women and children had experienced a divorce, their family incomes were, on average, one half the size of those of intact families. During the 1980s, the incomes of single-parent families were reduced in many countries by cuts in welfare payments while at the same time housing costs increased (Burns, 1992). In Britain, for example, the percentage of single parents relying on

Supplementary Benefit or Income Support (for only the very poorest) rose from 40 per cent in the 1970s to 60 per cent in 1991 (Kiernan & Wicks, 1990). Economic hardship has been associated with poor child nutrition and health (Williams, 1990), with a lack of materials and support at home to facilitate educational achievement (Amato & Keith, 1991), and with moves to neighbourhoods with poorly financed or inadequate educational programmes and services for children (McLanahan, 1989). Rising economic pressures can also lead to depressed feelings, as well as to anger and hostility on the part of parents and children (Elder et al., 1992). Finally, economic loss has been associated with entrance into deviant subcultures during adolescence (Voydanoff & Majka, 1988; in Amato & Keith, 1991). However, although income loss significantly contributes to family hardship in single-parent families, even when income is controlled children from divorced families are still psychologically worse off than their counterparts from intact families, suggesting that other factors in addition to economic loss are important (Amato & Keith, 1991).

Short-term longitudinal studies have indicated that most mother-child relationships tend to improve and largely stabilize within two to three years following parental separation (Hetherington, 1988; Wallerstein & Kelly, 1980). However, research has also shown that if the parental discord and conflict that precipitated the divorce continue afterwards or if adjustment to the new situation is compounded by new stressors, children and adolescents are more likely to continue to have problems of maladjustment (Buchanan et al., 1991; Camara & Resnick, 1988; Forehand et al., 1988; Kline et al., 1991). Especially as adolescents develop the cognitive abilities to empathize with and take the perspective of their parents, they are more likely to experience guilt and depressive feelings stemming from a sense of being 'caught' between uncooperative custodial and non-custodial parents (Buchanan et al., 1991). Although many studies have found that children experiencing parental divorce are likely to have poorer adjustment than children from intact families (Chase-Lansdale & Hetherington, 1990; Kiernan, 1992), a great deal of inconsistency exists in the literature, due in part to the fact that studies often fail to control for age level of the child, timing of divorce, and socioeconomic status of the families involved. Amato and Keith (1991) conducted a meta-analysis of 92 available studies of the effects of divorce on children's psychosocial adjustment to try to sort out these inconsistencies, and estimated (via calculation of effect sizes) the net impact of parental divorce on children's well-being, as determined by the following domains: school achievement, conduct, psychological adjustment, self-concept, social adjustment, mother-child relations, and father-child relations. Their findings yielded significant negative effects of parental divorce across all domains of well-being. However, the effect sizes across the studies reviewed were generally weak, and the few studies that considered time since divorce found that conduct and adjustment problems dissipated somewhat over time. In addition, the authors concluded that gender differences were not as pronounced as had been thought: the consequences were no more severe for boys than for girls. The strongest negative effects on post-divorce adjustment were found for children in late childhood through middle adolescence, and weakest effects among college-age students. Finally, compared with studies conducted in the United States, the relatively few studies of children of divorce conducted outside the USA reported more conduct problems, poorer psychological adjustment, and more impaired parent-child relations. Amato and Keith (1991) attributed this finding to the higher prevalence rates in the United States, which may make divorce less stigmatizing for US children than for children living in countries where divorce is less common. If this argument is valid, one might find less severe consequences of divorce on child and adolescent adjustment in Northern Europe and Britain, countries which currently have the highest divorce rates in Europe. Obviously, comparative research on the impact of divorce across countries of Europe is necessary to confirm this hypothesis.

Several studies converge on the tenet that marital disruption negatively influences child adjustment primarily due to the conflict that occurs between parents before, during, and after the separation (Amato & Keith, 1991; Block et al., 1986; Buchanan et al., 1991; Kline et al., 1991). In one of few longitudinal studies of its kind, Block et al. (1986) showed that children whose parents were originally married and then subsequently divorced during the course of the study were already showing signs of adjustment problems before the divorce occurred. Similarly, Cherlin et al. (1991) reviewed national longitudinal datasets of children of divorce in Britain and in the United States, and found that a substantial portion of behaviour problems and school achievement difficulties in children were visible before the parents separated (an effect that was stronger for boys than for girls). Amato and Keith's (1991) meta-analysis of data from nine independent samples found strong support for the role of conflict in predicting psychosocial adjustment: children in high-conflict intact families exhibited significantly lower levels of well-being than did children in low-conflict intact families or children in divorced families. These studies in combination suggest that, regardless of family structure, high levels of parental conflict place children at risk for increased problem behaviours and decreased well-being; children may benefit from life in a single-parent family if it results in a reduction of parental and familial conflict.

While the preceding review provides convincing evidence that single-parent families present a high-risk situation for parents and children, not all the effects need to be negative. Single parents, lacking an adult companion to share their experiences, often turn to their teenage children as an ally in running the household and in providing emotional support. Because of this link, such teenagers may experience greater maturity and responsibility, and in turn, feel and perform more competently, both at home and at school, than their peers who live with both parents (Csikszentmihalyi & Larson, 1984). In effect, they make the transition to adulthood before their peers. It is commonly the girls of single-parent families who show the increase in positive experience. This presumably is because the single parent at home is almost always the mother, and the mother-daughter relationship tends to be more emotionally close and supportive than does the mother-son (Csikszentmihalyi & Larson, 1984; Hetherington, 1988). Single mothers also tend to rely on daughters more for emotional support, and give daughters and sons more adult responsibilities, and more say in family decision-making, than do mothers in intact families; this may lead to fewer family conflicts (Amato, 1987; Asmussen & Larson, 1991; Weiss, 1979).

Short-term Consequences of Parental Remarriage

The most marked and consistently positive influence of remarriage on family functioning may be the rapid improvements in standard of living brought about by the increase in family income provided by the stepfather (McLanahan & Bumpass, 1988). Duncan (1984) found that among US children whose mother remarried, real family income increased from 1971 to 1978 by an annual average of 9.5 per cent.

Despite the improvements in daily living brought about by the increase in family income, the introduction of a step-parent into the home requires major readjustments on the part of all family members, which often leads to increased tensions in the family. Step-parents often have a particularly difficult time adjusting to their new role. Several studies have pointed out unique demands and stressors on stepfathers, which are not experienced by fathers in intact families: feelings of ambiguity or confusion in their role as a parent and disciplinarian; distant or conflictual relationships with stepchildren; conflicts with former and present spouses over legal, financial, and childrearing matters;

feelings of split loyalties between their stepchildren and (usually non-resident) biological children (Furstenberg, 1987; Hetherington et al., 1985; Schwebel et al., 1991). These stressors can lead to decreased satisfaction and increased emotional distance on the part of the stepfather, and increased spousal and familial conflict (Bray, 1988; Schwebel et al., 1991). The inability to resolve such issues may ultimately lead to separation and divorce – an event that is even more common among stepfamilies than intact families (Glick, 1984).

Several studies have suggested that girls often have more difficulty in adjusting to a step-parent than do boys, and that they exhibit more behaviour problems than do girls in intact families (Amato & Keith, 1991; Bray, 1988; Brand et al., 1988; Hetherington, 1988; Hetherington et al., 1985; Wallerstein et al., 1988; Vuchinich et al., 1991). However, in their most recent study, Hetherington and Clingempeel (1992) failed to find that girls in stepfamilies were more likely to do poorly; regardless of gender, young adolescents in their sample were exhibiting more behaviour and adjustment problems if their parents had divorced or remarried than if they had remained intact (in general, there were no significant differences between adolescents from single-parent versus stepfamilies). Where gender differences have been found, they have been linked to the fact that daughters may harbour more resentment towards their mothers and stepfathers for changing the dynamics of the close mother-daughter relationship that existed while the mother remained single, and to the difficulty both daughters and stepfathers face in establishing an appropriate level of intimacy in the light of young adolescent girls' increasing sexuality (Hetherington, 1988; Vuchinich et al., 1991).

With increasing time (usually after the first two or three years), stepfamilies can develop satisfying and supportive parent-child relationships that are often indistinguishable from those found in intact or single-parent families (Amato, 1987; Kurdek & Sinclair, 1988). However, as mentioned previously, Hetherington and Clingempeel (1992) found that early adolescents experiencing remarriage showed marked behaviour problems and difficulties in parent-child relations, and that these problems did not show significant improvement in the two years following remarriage. Furthermore, although Steinberg (1987) did not find evidence of more parental control among stepfamilies than among single-parent families, Amato (1987) found that stepfathers became more involved with their adolescent stepchildren (in terms of support, punishment, and control) over time, which led to heightened feelings of emotional closeness or cohesion on the part of stepfathers and their stepchildren. These somewhat inconsistent results lead to the conclusion that adjustment to life in a stepfamily is often a slow and arduous process, and that considerable work remains to be done in order to fully understand the nature of stepfamily relationships over time.

Long-term Consequences of Parental Divorce and Remarriage

Recent research that has examined the long-term consequences of divorce and remarriage for adolescents and young adults has cast considerable doubt on previous research (e.g. Hetherington, 1988; Wallerstein & Kelly, 1980) that suggested that the negative impact of family reorganization on children's adjustment was only temporary. This newer research has yielded evidence that for some adolescents, delayed effects of parental divorce and remarriage in childhood or early adolescence may emerge in late adolescence (Wallerstein, 1991).

The long-term direct effects appear to be stronger for late adolescents' family formation behaviour than for other indices of behavioural adjustment. Several US studies have found that women who spend a portion of their childhood in single-parent families are more likely to engage in early sexual intercourse, to leave the single state and enter cohabitation, to marry and bear children early, to give birth before marriage, and to have their own marriages result in divorce (Glenn & Kramer, 1987; Hogan & Kitagawa, 1985; McLanahan & Bumpass, 1988; Newcomer & Udry, 1987; Thornton, 1991). Wallerstein et al. (1988) found somewhat lower educational attainment among older adolescents after parental divorce, due largely to the fact that many fathers failed to pay child support so that the children could either not afford to go to college at all, or else were taking longer to complete their education because of having to work part- or full-time to support themselves. These authors also found delayed effects in the domain of interpersonal intimacy, although only for a minority of subjects (who were most often women). These women were more hesitant to get involved in committed relationships, and were prone to have multiple short-term sexual partners. Kiernan (1992) has provided evidence from Britain that family disruption (due to death or divorce), followed by parental remarriage, was linked to earlier home-leaving, earlier school-leaving, and earlier entrance into the labour market, among males and females. For the men in this study, having lived in a stepfamily was also linked to entering partnerships and becoming a father at younger ages. For the women, the experience of family disruption (regardless of whether or not their mothers remarried) appeared to be the key impetus for entering partnerships and having children (within or outside the confines of marriage) prior to age

20 (although women in stepfamilies were somewhat more likely to marry than to cohabit).

These long-term effects are cause for considerable concern. Some demographic changes will tend to cause a further increase in the rate of marital disruption: among these are earlier age of marriage or cohabitation and increased incidence of premarital or early pregnancy. Against this, the overall declines in age at first marriage, increases in female employment, and declines in teenage birth rates provide sources of careful optimism. Perhaps in the future, as young women opt for living alone, extending their educational careers and planning for employment, they will make more mature and careful choices with regard to forming commitments and bearing children, which may in turn lead to a greater likelihood of stable family lives.

Maternal Employment

Recent studies of maternal employment have attempted to identify the underlying processes that link maternal employment status to child and adolescent outcomes. Two of the key links in this indirect path between employment status and child adjustment have been maternal role satisfaction and the quality of mother-adolescent relations (Lerner & Galambos, 1985). Whether a mother is or is not employed outside the home, role satisfaction seems to be the strongest predictor of positive parent-child interactions (Hoffman, 1989). Nevertheless, several studies have indicated that the employed mothers reported better physical and mental health (Baruch et al., 1987; Gove & Geerken, 1977; Haavio-Mannila, 1986), and greater satisfaction with their lives than did non-employed mothers (Gold & Andres, 1978a & b; Hoffman, 1974, 1979).

Maternal satisfaction is largely dependent, however, on the degree of role strain experienced in trying to balance the competing demands placed on women (Spitze, 1988). These stressors come from multiple sources, including husbands, children, ageing parents needing care, and the workplace (Kandel et al., 1985; Williams et al., 1991). Role strain is more common for single mothers, who do not have support from a spouse in meeting these competing demands (Hilton & Haldeman, 1991). Furthermore, in keeping with the evidence that single mothers rely on daughters more than sons, when single mothers feel overburdened, they are more likely to overload daughters rather than sons with household tasks (Hilton & Haldeman, 1991). These increased demands to be responsible for housework, during a stage in their development when many adolescents are seeking to be less involved at home and more involved in social activities with peers, can also lead to heightened parent-child conflicts, and to feelings of isolation from the peer group.

Even if the husband is present in the home, he usually contributes far less than his wife in terms of care for children and household chores such as laundry, meal preparation, and cleaning (Menaghan & Parcel, 1990; Nave-Herz, 1989). In recent years, values have shifted towards more paternal involvement, and although the majority of fathers have yet to actualize these ideals, change is gradually headed towards a more equitable balance of labour between marriage partners (Hiller & Philliber, 1986; Pleck, 1985). To the extent that fathers and other family members do assist in such daily activities, mothers experience less strain and have more time to be involved in mutually satisfying (and less conflictual) relationships with their children (Bird & Ratcliff, 1990; Furstenberg, 1988; Williams et al., 1991).

Some slight detrimental effects of maternal employment on adolescents have been found, but for the most part they are not a direct result of working or non-working. Maternal employment is commonly (at least initially) associated with a decrease in parental supervision (Richardson et al., 1989). Insufficient monitoring of adolescents on the part of parents, in turn, is related to involvement in deviant or high-risk behaviours (Dornbusch et al., 1985; Maccoby, 1958) and to poorer grades in reading and mathematics (Heyns & Catsambis, 1986; Milne et al., 1986). Thus, it is not the employment status per se, but rather the quality of parental involvement in the supervision of their children's activities that is most predictive of negative adolescent behavioural outcomes.

The amount of time mothers spend in paid employment is inversely related to the amount of time and energy they can spend supervising and providing support for their adolescent children. Heyns and Catsambis (1986) found that full-time mothers' employment was more detrimental to adolescents' achievement than was part-time employment, and that an erratic job history (or intermittent employment) was more damaging than continued labour force experience.

Maternal employment has been found to have positive effects on adolescents as well. As indicated earlier, employed mothers of adolescents are often happier, more satisfied with their roles, and more likely to exhibit warmth and encourage independence and egalitarian sex-role attitudes in their children than are non-employed mothers (Galambos, 1985; Hoffman, 1979). Adolescents are also given more household responsibilities when their mothers are employed, and this has been found to contribute to their positive self-esteem (Smokler, 1985; in Lerner & Hess, 1988). Adolescent daughters of working mothers have been found to be more outgoing, independent, motivated towards occupational achievement, and better adjusted on social and personality measures than daughters of non-employed mothers (Hoffman, 1979; Lerner & Hess, 1988). In addition, both sons and daughters of employed mothers are less likely to show sex-role stereotypes than children from families in which the mother is not employed (Hoffman, 1979). Fewer sex-typed attributes have been found to be closely related to early adolescent behavioural flexibility and positive self-image (Galambos et al., 1985; Lamke, 1982; Massad, 1981). Furthermore, these attitudes may lead to more egalitarian relationships in adulthood, and may ultimately result in women being accorded recognition and respect for the work they do, both in and outside the family, which bodes well for the stability of family relationships in the future (Land, 1979; Vannoy, 1991).

In sum, the evidence so far fails to support consistent positive or negative effects of mothers' employment status *per se* on the behavioural, academic, or psychosocial development of children and adolescents. When negative effects are found, they are most likely to be the result of a lack of maternal involvement and supervision, or of negative (conflictual) mother-child interactions, rather than work status alone. Although working mothers are likely to provide positive models for egalitarian sex-role attitudes and career achievement in both daughers and sons, it is continued parental involvement (i.e., close monitoring and open communication) that seems to offer the most protection against adolescent problem behaviours.

Family Migration and Ethnic Minority Families

Political and economic changes at several levels of society, ranging from the local community, to the relations among countries, indirectly affect family life through their impact on migration (Behnam, 1990). When economic, political, or social changes exert pressures on parents, they often lead to decisions to move to another country.

Unfortunately, there is a dearth of comparative research on the prevalence rates and psychosocial consequences of changes in family structure among ethnic minority children and adolescents. Paikoff and Brooks-Gunn (1991), in their review of parent-child relations at puberty, summarized the challenges facing researchers interested in better understanding interethnic variation in family relationships during adolescence:

Research on minorities has tended to focus on problematic outcomes (e.g., teenage pregnancy and juvenile delinquency) rather than normative developmental processes and relational changes. It is also more difficult, time consuming, and less methodologically clean to investigate families of diverse racial and ethnic backgrounds in psychological studies that often rely on small samples, in relation to the standards of other social science disciplines. Another problem is that the traditional classifications of ethnic groups do not capture all relevant cultural differences, as is illustrated by differences between Hispanics of Puerto Rico, Mexico, and the Virgin Islands (60).

As this quotation suggests, very little is known about the variability in parent-child relations and child and adolescent socialization that may exist among ethnic minorities. However, some research has been done on the role of the family in helping or hindering the adjustment of immigrating children and adolescents to the majority culture. The consequences of moving depend on many factors, such as the attitudes of the majority of people in the new environment, the economic and housing situation, the degree to which the migrating family's cultural and ethnic background is represented in the new context and the amount of social support provided by friends and relatives (Spencer & Dornbusch, 1990). The minority adolescent is forced to decide how much he or she values and wants to identify with the cultural characteristics of his or her own ethnic group; and how important it is to have positive relationships with the larger society and people of diverse ethnic backgrounds (Phinney et al., 1992). As minority adolescents mature cognitively, they become very sensitive to the evaluations of them and their ethnic group made by the majority culture (Spencer & Dornbusch, 1990). This heightened sensitivity may exact a price in terms of feelings of incompetence and marginalization, which, depending upon the amount of support available from family, friends, or other key adults, may lead to maladaptive coping behaviours (Hess et al., in press).

One of the key sources of stress for minority adolescents is differential socialization that may occur in the two key institutions through which culture, knowledge, and behaviour is transmitted: the family and the school (Gökalp, 1984). As Gökalp (1984) pointed out, success in school (which is also a key to entering the job market) is based on the immigrant's ability to excel in writing and speaking the host country's language, as well as understanding mathematical concepts. This pressure from teachers, as well as the pressure to conform with the peer group, may push adolescents to abandon behaviours stemming from their culture of origin that set them apart.

Parents often react negatively to such behaviours, and sometimes become more restrictive towards their adolescent children, trying to protect them from societal and peer pressures that conflict with family and minority group values (Nauck, 1989; Spencer & Dornbusch, 1990). For instance, Nauck's (1989) study of Turkish immigrant families in Germany found that Turkish parents tended to exert more authoritarian control and protectiveness over their adolescent sons and daughters (with more highly-educated parents decreasing their control somewhat) than did German parents. Daughters of Turkish immigrants were most likely to be strictly controlled, and to be saddled with a large portion of the family household tasks. In German families, protectiveness and control of sons decreased with age, whereas control of both adolescent daughters and sons was less authoritarian among more educated parents. Conflict often escalates if adolescents continue to give the demands of the school and peer group preference. By contrast, adolescents who choose to conform to the cultural values of their family may run the risk of being rejected by their peers, which impacts upon their feelings of competence and self-worth. Although Nauck's (1989) study clearly does not apply to all immigrant families and ethnic minorities, it does suggest that minority adolescents may experience more pressure at home than do non-minority adolescents. Also, it appears that the role strain experienced by minority adolescent girls may be greater than that of their male counterparts. However, immigrant and ethnic minority families also can be a source of support and pride for their adolescent children. They can serve as a buffer against racist and destructive messages from the majority culture, providing alternative role models and points of view (Barnes, 1980; in Spencer & Dornbusch, 1990). In addition, since extended families and larger kinship networks are more common among ethnic minorities, adolescents can lean on other relatives for support and guidance that are often unavailable (because of geographical distance) to many non-minority adolescents. Furthermore, many parents and other adult relatives of minority adolescents do recognize the importance of succeeding in school for their children's economic future, and they often are very supportive and involved in their children's educational pursuits (Dornbusch et al., 1987; Marjoribanks, 1991). Finally, immigrant minority adolescents can also positively influence their parents, by offering them a window into the social world of the majority culture that might otherwise be closed to them.

Summary

Variables such as ethnicity, family size, marital status, and socioeconomic status, broadly characterize the home environment, and therefore the type of living arrangements adolescents may experience. These structural variables may indeed impose constraints on the ways in which adolescents may interact with their family members. However, such marker or status variables are seldom directly linked to adolescent developmental outcomes (Baltes et al., 1980; Baltes & Schaie, 1973; Bronfenbrenner, 1979; Bronfenbrenner & Crouter, 1983). Instead, they most often exert their influence via alterations in the psychosocial aspects of family relations, or by changes in family functioning (Kurdek & Sinclair, 1988; Martens, 1984). The studies reviewed provide consistent evidence that the family structural changes marked by marital dissolution and reorganization place children and adolescents at significantly higher risk for short-term problems in psychosocial well-being, as well as for long-term difficulties in forming and maintaining families of their own. Where such direct effects have been found, the challenge facing researchers is to identify the underlying *processes*, or the more proximal variables related to family socialization patterns, as well as individual adolescent characteristics such as cognitive ability, coping style, maturation, that may be more closely associated with adolescents' psychosocial adjustment.

CONCLUSIONS

This chapter has attempted to integrate historical evidence on macrosocial change and regional variation in changes in family structure throughout Europe, and to examine the impact of such changes on adolescent development in the family. The value of placing these cross-national comparisons in a historical context (Elder, 1984) was brought out by the fact that for most demographic indicators, the secular trends in Northern Europe tend to serve as a road map for the countries to the South, with several countries of Western Europe in close pursuit of their neighbours to the North, and Southern European countries just recently beginning the journey towards substantial change in family structure. However, the data also illustrate that although the trends of changes in Western European family patterns certainly show a tendency towards convergence, the actual course of change varies considerably from one country to another (Chesnais, 1985). Therefore, it is by no means certain that all countries are inevitably bound to follow the course laid out by Northern Europe. Nevertheless, the demographic data reviewed do seem to illustrate the usefulness of examining closely the social and cultural conditions in Scandinavia, where these family structural transitions have been most marked. If current trends in Europe continue, more and more children and adolescents in the future can expect: to grow up as a single child or with very few siblings; to experience maternal employment; parental divorce and/or remarriage; to postpone leaving home (especially young people who are economically disadvantaged and unemployed); to live alone for a greater portion of their lives (either before uniting with a partner or in their extended old age); to cohabit as a transition to marriage; to have several cohabitations that break down; to postpone marriage or refuse to marry and have children; and to choose planned single-motherhood or parenthood outside marriage (Chesnais, 1985).

The discussion of the linkage between family structural change and family functioning and adolescent psychosocial development demonstrated that transitions such as moving, divorcing, remarrying, or leaving or entering the labour force are sources of stress that require adaptation and reorganization on the part of all family members. The degree of risk these family changes pose to the psychosocial well-being of adolescents, is, in most cases, dependent upon the nature of family functioning, in terms of the degree of intrafamilial conflict, and the amount of involvement and emotional support between adolescents and parents. Regardless of family structure, families with high levels of parental discord or with distant and unavailable parents often function less effectively (Block et al., 1986; Grych & Fincham, 1990; Hetherington, 1988; Rutter, 1971). Living with both parents is no guarantee that fathers and mothers will be 'emotionally present' and invested in the socialization of adolescents (Harris & Morgan, 1991; Lasch, 1979). Mounting evidence on risk factors for psychosocial problems during adolescence converge on the tenet that young people embedded in families characterized by high levels of conflict, or by parents who are not able to provide adequate supervision, effective discipline, and emotional support have an increased risk of experiencing a range of psychosocial disorders, including school problems and academic failure (Rutter, 1985); school drop-out and unemployment (Hess et al., in press); decreased feelings of self-competence and poor peer relationships (Cooper & Ayers-Lopez, 1985); antisocial behaviours and criminality (Mednick et al., 1987; Reid & Patterson, 1989); malnutrition and eating disorders (Bailey, 1991; Garmezy, 1991); alcohol and substance abuse

(Barnes, 1977; Foxcroft & Lowe, 1991; McDermott, 1984); early sexual activity and unwanted pregnancy (Barnett et al., 1991); and depression and suicide (Rubenstein et al., 1989). Such ineffective parenting can be found in all family structures, and in all ranges of socioeconomic and ethnic groups (Lamborn et al., 1991). Even adolescents who have supportive, involved, and financially secure parents may become susceptible to such problem behaviours as pressures from peers, school, and sexual maturation mount. However, adolescents in families experiencing parental separation or divorce, economic loss, maternal employment, parental remarriage, a move to a new area and a new school, may be most at risk for exhibiting maladaptive coping behaviours (Frydenberg & Lewis, 1991; Garmezy, 1991; Patterson & McCubbin, 1987; Rubenstein et al., 1989; Simmons & Blyth, 1987).

The evidence is reassuringly strong however, that many children, adolescents, and adults have the resilience to overcome periods of stressful family change (Rutter, 1987). Protective factors that enable adolescents to deal effectively with adverse family circumstances can be grouped into three sets of variables (Garmezy, 1985, 1987; Werner, 1989; in Garmezy, 1991):

First, the use of external sources of support can help compensate during times of family instability. Family changes, along with the developmental changes associated with the adolescent period, do not occur in a vacuum. Peer relationships become more salient during adolescence, but despite the increased influence of peers, teenagers and parents maintain quite similar values and ethical beliefs throughout adolescence (Brown, 1990; Chapter 8, this volume). However, studies have indicated that adolescents may rely on peers more when support from parents is lacking, as is often the case during periods of family reorganization and high parent-child conflict, and may thereby be more susceptible to antisocial peer pressure (Collins, 1990; Steinberg, 1987; Dornbusch et al., 1985). In addition, schools – the second key institution in which adolescents are embedded – have a profound influence on the adolescent experience. As suggested by Paikoff & Brooks-Gunn (1991), although numerous studies have found an association between family characteristics such as family structure and parental discipline and involvement and adolescents' school achievement (Entwisle, 1990; Spencer & Dornbusch, 1990), we still know little about the way in which adolescents' daily school experiences (such as their relationships with teachers) shape their interactions with family members at home, or about how family experiences shape adolescents' relationships with teachers and strategies for seeking help (both scholastic and interpersonal) at school. Nevertheless, increased involvement in social institutions outside the family – whether structured through youth organizations, schools, sports clubs, churches, local businesses, or community agencies – may increase adolescents' interactions with supportive peers and adult role models, and can decrease feelings of isolation and marginality (Hess et al., in press).

A second key factor is the degree to which adolescents have close affectional ties to family members (for instance grandparents or siblings, if a parent is emotionally unavailable). Regardless of family constellation, low family conflict and high family cohesion is most conducive to healthy adolescent adjustment, including positive self-esteem and motivation to achieve academically, high goal directedness, and low severity of psychopathology (Kurdek & Sinclair, 1988).

The final set of protective variables relate to features within the individual, such as temperament (e.g. activity level and reactivity), intelligence and cognitive abilities, and social and communication skills. These intra-individual characteristics modify the effects of contextual conditions, and provide the basis for adolescents to influence persons and events around them, and the course of their own and their family's development in the future (Lerner & Busch-Rossnagel, 1981).

The findings on the changes in family patterns that have occurred in Western Europe over the last half-century now need to be brought together in order to consider their possible relevance as explanatory variables for any increases in psychosocial disorders that may have taken place in young people over the same time period. To begin with there is one change, a reduction in the proportion of children living in very large families, that might be expected to bring benefits, although whether it has in fact done so is not known. Second, there is another change, an increase in maternal employment, that is probably relatively neutral in terms of its implications for disorder. It would be likely to carry disadvantages if it was accompanied by a worsening in the care provided for young children but there is no evidence that that has been the case (although data on this point are very weak). However, any ill-effects should be least evident in countries with good family support and child care systems (such as Sweden – Burns, 1992) and most evident in countries where those are in short supply or of poor quality. The decrease in multi-generational households is less likely to be negative in its effects because the evidence indicates that there has been no reduction in close relationships within the extended family, or in the help with child care provided by grandparents.

Third, some secular trends have gone in both directions over the last 50 years, and some have varied greatly among countries. Thus, births to teenage mothers increased during the 1950s and 1960s but declined in most countries over the last two decades. Similarly, the abortion rate in young women rose and then fell over roughly the same period. Insofar as both teenage pregnancies and abortions constitute psychosocial stressors, their effects on psychosocial disorders in young people should have been maximal some 20 years ago and least evident in the last decade.

Fourth, there are some risk factors that do have definite implications for psychosocial disorders but for which there is doubt on whether their incidence has increased over the last half-century; this applies to both sexual abuse and physical child abuse. The negative evidence is more impressive with respect to sexual abuse in that neither retrospective reports nor repeated surveys suggest any marked increase in spite of the much greater public awareness of the phenomenon. Case register data for physical abuse are consistent with some increase, especially perhaps in the last decade, but they do not support the stereotype of a massive rise in the maltreatment of young people.

Fifth, there is one feature, a marked rise in nonmarital cohabitation, that might carry psychosocial risks but the extent to which it does so is quite unknown. It is unlikely that cohabitation in itself carries any increase in risk but, if (as seems probable) such cohabitations mean that young people today are much more likely than their predecessors to experience recurrent breakdowns in important love relationships (together with the practical disruptions that are so often involved), that could carry important risks. If so, their effects should be most evident in the late teens and twenties rather than in childhood or early adolescence.

Finally, there is a set of features associated with psychosocial risk that have increased markedly since the Second World War; namely, a period of single parent upbringing, and the experience of parental divorce and remarriage. There is evidence that these experiences carry some risk in their own right and hence their increase might well play a role in the parallel increase in psychosocial disorders. However, the research findings also indicate that the greater risk derives from the family conflict that precedes and follows parental divorce. In that connection, the key question is whether there has been an increase over time in family conflict. The alternative is that the rise in divorce simply means that people today are more likely to turn to divorce for lesser degrees of marital conflict or disharmony. There is no direct evidence that could resolve that issue. However, there are two findings that suggest that the increase in divorce probably does index an increase in psychosocial risk (perhaps as a result of increased family conflict). First, it seems that the association between parental divorce and psychosocial disorders in the young people involved is probably as great today as it was a generation or more ago when divorce was less frequent (Amato & Keith, 1991). Second, contemporaneous studies of divorce provide ample evidence of substantial conflict both before and after the breakup of the marriage. Regrettably, the 'civilized' concept of a harmonious agreed decision to part, with the interests of the children foremost, does not apply to the majority of divorces today. Accordingly, it seems likely that the increase over time in parental divorce and remarriage may well mean an increase in risks for the children involved.

REFERENCES

Abbott, D. A. & Brody, G. H. (1985). The relation of child age, gender, and number of children to the marital adjustment of wives. *Journal of Marriage and the Family 47*, 77-91.

Alwin, D. F. & Thornton, A. (1984). Family origins and the schooling process: Early versus late influence of parental characteristics. *American Sociological Review 49*, 784-802.

Amato, P. R. (1987). Family processes in one-parent, stepparent, and intact families: The child's point of view. *Journal of Marriage and the Family 49*, 327-337.

Amato, P. R. & Keith, B. (1991). Parental divorce and the well-being of children: A meta-analysis. *Psychological Bulletin 110*, 26-46.

Anderson, J. C., Martin J. L., Mullen P. E., Romans S. E. & Herbison G. P (1993). The prevalence of sexual abuse experiences in a community sample of women. *Journal of the American Academy of Child and Adolescent Psychiatry 32*, 911-919.

Aries, P. (1962). *Centuries of childhood.* London: Jonathan Cape.

Arnold, J. C. (1951). *The marriage law of England.* London: Staples Press.

Asmussen, L. & Larson, R. (1991). The quality of family time among young adolescents in single-parent and married-parent families. *Journal of Marriage and the Family 53*, 1021-1030.

Bailey, C. A. (1991). Family structure and eating disorders: The family environment scale and bulimic-like symptoms. *Youth & Society 23*, 251-272.

Baltes, P. B. (1987). Theoretical propositions of life-span developmental psychology: On the dynamics between growth and decline. *Developmental Psychology 23*, 611-626.

Baltes, P. B., Reese, H. W. & Lipsitt, L. P. (1980). Life-span developmental psychology. *Annual Review of Psychology 31*, 65-110.

Baltes, P. B. & Schaie, K. W. (1973). On life-span developmental research paradigms: Retrospects and prospects. In P. B. Baltes & K. W. Schaie (eds.) *Life-span developmental psychology: Personality and socialization.* New York: Academic Press.

Barber, B. L. & Eccles, J. S. (1992). Long-term influence of divorce and single parenting on adolescent family- and work-related values, behaviors, and aspirations. *Psychological Bulletin 111*, 108-126.

Barnes, E. J. (1980). The black community as the source of positive self-concept for black children: A theoretical perspective. In R. Jones (ed.) *Black psychology*, 106-130. New York: Harper & Row.

Barnes, G. M. (1977). The development of adolescent drinking behavior: An evaluative review of the impact of the socialization process within the family. *Adolescence 12*, 571-590.

Barnett, J., Papini, D. & Gbur, D. (1991). Familial correlates of sexually active pregnant and nonpregnant adolescents. *Adolescence 26*, 457-472.

Baruch, G. K., Biener, L. & Barnett, R. C. (1987). Women and gender in research on work and family stress. *American Psychologist 42*, 130-136.

Behnam, D. (1990). An international inquiry into the future of the family: A Unesco project. *International Social Science Journal 126*, 547-552.

Bell, L. G., Cornwell, C. S. & Bell, L. G. (1988). Peer relationships of adolescent daughters: A reflection of family relationship patterns. *Family Relations 37*, 171-174.

Bennett, N. G., Blanc, A. K. & Bloom, D. E. (1988). Commitment and the modern union: Assessing the link between premarital cohabitation and subsequent marital stability. *American Sociological Review 53*, 127-138.

Berger, B. & Berger, P. (1984). *War over the family*. New York: Penguin.

Berkner, L. (1972). The stem family and the developmental cycle of the peasant household: An eighteenth century Austrian example. *American Historical Review 77*, 398-418.

Bird, G. W. & Ratcliff, B. (1990). Children's participation in family tasks: Determinants of mothers' and fathers' reports. *Human Relations 43*, 865-884.

Blake, J. (1981a). Family size and the quality of children. *Demography 18*, 421-442.

Blake, J. (1981b). The only child in America: Prejudice versus performance. *Population Development Review 7*, 43-54.

Blayo, C. (1984). *Les françaises et la reproduction depuis 1946. Colloque Franco-Soviétique, 1984.* Paris: Presses Universitaires de France.

Block, J. H., Block, J. & Gjerde, P. F. (1986). The personality of children prior to divorce: A prospective study. *Child Development 57*, 827-840.

Blum, R. W. (1985). The adolescent dialectic: A developmental perspective on social decision-making. *Psychiatric Annals 15*, 614-618.

Boh, K. (1989). European family life patterns – a reappraisal. In K. Boh, M. Bak, C. Clason, M. Pankratova, J. Qvortrup, G. B. Sgritta & K. Waerness (eds.) *Changing patterns of European family life: A comparative analysis of 14 European countries*, 265-298. London: Routledge.

Bourgeois-Pichat, J. (1987). The unprecedented shortage of births in Europe. In K. Davis, M. S. Bernstam & R. Ricardo-Campbell (eds.) *Below-replacement fertility in industrial societies: Causes, consequences, policies*, 3-25. London: Cambridge University Press.

Brand, E., Clingempeel, W. G. & Woodward, K. B. (1988). Family relationships and children's psychological adjustment in stepmother and stepfather families. In E.

M. Hetherington & J. D. Arasteh (eds.) *Impact of divorce, single parenting, and stepparenting on children*, 299-324. Hillsdale, NJ: Lawrence Erlbaum.

Bray, J. H. (1988). Children's development during early remarriage. In E. M. Hetherington & J. D. Arasteh (eds.) *Impact of divorce single parenting, and stepparenting on children*, 279-298. Hillsdale, NJ: Lawrence Erlbaum.

Brody, G. H., Stoneman, Z. & McCoy, K. J. (1992). Associations of maternal and paternal direct and differential behavior with sibling relationships: Contemporaneous and longitudinal analyses. *Child Development 63*, 82-92.

Bronfenbrenner, U. (1979). *The ecology of human development*. Cambridge, MA: Harvard University Press.

Bronfenbrenner, U. & Crouter, A. C. (1983). The evolution of environmental models in developmental research. In W. Kessen (ed.) *History, theory and methods, Vol. I: Mussen Handbook of Child and Adolescent Psychology* (4th edition), 357-414. New York: Wiley.

Brown, B. B. (1990). Peer groups and peer cultures. In S. S. Feldman & G. R. Elliott (eds.) *At the threshold: The developing adolescent*, 171-196. Cambridge, MA: Harvard University Press.

Brown, C. (1984). *Black and white Britain: The third PSI report*. London: Heinemann Educational.

Buchanan, C. M., Maccoby, E. E. & Dornbusch, S. M. (1991). Caught between parents: Adolescents' experience in divorced homes. *Child Development 62*, 1008-1029.

Bumpass, L. (1984). Some characteristics of children's second families. *American Journal of Sociology 90*, 608-623.

Burke, R. J. & Weir, T. (1978). Sex differences in adolescent life stress, social support, and well-being. *Journal of Psychology 98*, 277-288.

Burns, A. (1992). Mother-headed families: An international perspective and the case of Australia. *Social Policy Report 6*, 1-22.

Calhoun, C. A. (1991). Desired and excess fertility in Europe and the United States: Indirect estimates from World Fertility Survey data. *European Journal of Population 7*, 29-57.

Calot, G. & Blayo, C. (1982). Recent course of fertility in Western Europe. *Population Studies 36*, 349-372.

Camara, K. A. & Resnick, G. (1988). Interparental conflict and cooperation: Factors moderating children's post-divorce adjustment. In E. M. Hetherington & J. D. Arasteh (eds.) *Impact of divorce, single parenting, and stepparenting on children*, 169-195. Hillsdale, NJ: Lawrence Erlbaum.

Chase-Lansdale, P. L. & Hetherington, E. M. (1990). The impact of divorce on life-span development: Short and longterm effects. In R. M. Lerner & D. L. Featherman (eds.) *Life span development and behavior*, Vol. XI, 105-150. Hillsdale, NJ: Lawrence Erlbaum.

Cherlin, A. J. & Furstenberg Jr., F. F. (1988). The changing European family: Lessons for the American reader. *Journal of Family Issues 9*, 291-297.

Cherlin, A. J., Furstenberg Jr., F. F., Chase-Lansdale, P. L., Kiernan, K. E., Robins, P. K., Morrison, D. R. & Teitler, J. O. (1991). Longitudinal studies of effects of divorce on children in Great Britain and the United States. *Science 252*, 1386-1389.

Chesnais, J. C. (1985). The consequences of modern fertility trends in the member states of the Council of Europe. *Population Studies 16*. Strasbourg: Council of Europe.

Clancy, P. (1984). *The changing family*. Dublin: Family Studies Unit.

Coale, A. J. (1986). The decline of fertility in Europe since the eighteenth century as a chapter in human demographic history. In A. J. Coale & S. C. Watkins (eds.) *The decline of fertility in Europe*, 1-30. Princeton, NJ: Princeton University Press.

Coale, A. J. & Watkins, S. C. (eds.) (1986). *The decline of fertility in Europe*. Princeton, NJ: Princeton University Press.

Collins, W. A. (1990). Parent-child relationships in the transition to adolescence: Continuity and change in interaction, affect, and cognition. In R. Montemayor, G. Adams & T. Gullotta (eds.) *Advances in adolescent development, Vol. 2: From childhood to adolescence: A transitional period?*, 85-106. Newbury Park, CA: Sage.

Cooper, C. R. & Ayers-Lopez, S. (1985). Family and peer systems in early adolescence: New models of the role of relationships in development. *Journal of Early Adolescence 5*, 9-21.

Cooper, C. R., Grotevant, H. D. & Condon, S. M. (1983). Individuality and connectedness in the family as a context for adolescent identity formation and role taking skill. In H. D. Grotevant & C. R. Cooper (eds.) *New directions for child development: Adolescent development in the family*, 43-59. San Francisco: Jossey-Bass.

Cooperrider, D. L. & Pasmore, W. A. (1991). Global social change: A new agenda for social science? *Human Relations 44*, 1037-1055.

Council of Europe (1991). *Recent demographic developments in Europe*. Strasbourg: Council of Europe Press.

Creighton, C. (1980). Family, property and relations of production in Western Europe. *Economy and Society 9*, 129-187.

Creighton S. J. (1992) *Child abuse trends in England and Wales 1988-1990; and an overview from 1973-1990*. London: NSPCC.

Cseh-Szombathy, L. (1990). Modelling the interrelation between macro-society and the family. *International Social Science Journal 126*, 441-449.

Csikszentmihalyi, M. & Larson, R. (1984). *Being adolescent: Conflict and growth in the teenage years*. New York: Basic Books.

Davies, L. (1984). *Pupil power: Deviance and gender in school*. London: Palmer Press.

D'Costa, R. (1985). Family and generations in sociology: A review of recent research in France. *Journal of Comparative Family Studies 16*, 319-327.

Demos, J. & Demos, V. (1969). Adolescence in historical perspective. *Journal of Marriage and the Family 31*, 632-638.

Dieleman, F. M. & Schouw, R. J. (1989). Divorce, mobility and housing demand. *European Journal of Population 5,* 235-252.

Dornbusch, S. M., Carlsmith, J. M., Bushwall, S. J., Ritter, P. L., Leiderman, P. H., Hastorf, A. H. & Gross, R. T. (1985). Single parents, extended households, and the control of adolescents. *Child Development 56,* 326-341.

Dornbusch, S. M., Ritter, P. L., Leiderman, P. H., Roberts, D. F. & Fraleigh, M. J. (1987). The relation of parenting style to adolescent school performance. *Child Development 58,* 1244-1257.

Duncan, G. J. (1984). *Years of poverty, years of plenty.* Ann Arbor: Institute for Social Reseach, University of Michigan.

Duncan, G. J. & Hoffman, S. D. (1985). A reconsideration of the economic consequences of marital disruption. *Demography 22,* 485-498.

Durkheim, E. (1933). *The division of labor.* New York: Free Press. (Original work published 1893.)

Dwyer, J. W. & Seccombe, K. (1991). Elder care as family labor: The influence of gender and family position. *Journal of Family Issues 12,* 229-247.

Elder Jr., G. H. (1984). Families, kin, and the life course: A sociological perspective. In R. D. Parke (eds.) *Advances in child development research: The family,* 80-136. Chicago: University of Chicago Press.

Elder Jr., G. H., Conger, R. D., Foster, E. M. & Ardelt, M. (1992). Families under economic pressure. *Journal of Family Issues 13,* 5-37.

Emery, R. E. (1982). Interparental conflict and the children of discord and divorce. *Psychological Bulletin 92,* 310-330.

Eldridge, S. & Kiernan, K. (1985). Declining first-marriage rate in England and Wales: A change in timing or a rejection of marriage? *European Journal of Population 1,* 327-345.

Entwisle, D. (1990). Schools and adolescence. In S. S. Feldman & G. R. Elliott (eds.) *At the threshold: The developing adolescent,* 197-224. Cambridge, MA: Harvard University Press.

Erikson, E. H. (1955). Ego identity and the psychosocial moratorium. In H. L. Winter & R. Kotinsky (eds.) *New perspectives in juvenile delinquency.* Washington, DC: US Department of Health, Education, and Welfare.

Erikson, E. H. (1968). *Identity: Youth and crisis.* New York: Norton.

Eurostat (1989). *EC Labour Force Survey.* Luxembourg: Author.

Feldman, W., Feldman, E., Goodman, J. T., McGrath, P. J., Pless, R. P., Corsini, L. & Bennett, S. (1991). Is childhood sexual abuse really increasing in prevalence? An analysis of the evidence. *Pediatrics 88,* 29-33.

Fend, H. (1990). *Sozialgeschichte des Aufwachsens [The social history of growing up].* Frankfurt am Main: Suhrkamp.

Festy, P. (1985). *Divorce, judicial separation and remarriage.* Population Studies 17. Strasbourg: Council of Europe.

Finch, J. & Mason, J. (1990). Filial obligations and kin support for elderly people. *Ageing and Society 10,* 151-175.

Fitzpatrick, D. (1983). Irish farming families before the First World War. *Comparative Studies in Society and History 25*, 339-374.

Fogarty, M., Ryan, L. & Leo, J. (1984). *Irish values and attitudes*. Dublin: Dominican Publications.

Forehand, R., Long, N. & Brody, G. (1988). Divorce and marital conflict: Relationship to adolescent competence and adjustment in early adolescence. In E. M. Hetherington & J. D. Arasteh (eds.) *Impact of divorce, single parenting, and stepparenting on children*, 155-167. Hillsdale, NJ: Lawrence Erlbaum.

Foxcroft, D. R. & Lowe, G. (1991). Adolescent drinking behavior and family socialization factors: A meta-analysis. *Journal of Adolescence 14*, 255-273.

Franklin, S. H. (1969). *The European peasantry: The final phase*. London: Methuen.

Frydenberg, E. & Lewis, R. (1991). Adolescent coping: the different ways in which boys and girls cope. *Journal of Adolescence 14*, 119-133.

Furstenberg Jr., F. F. (1987). The new extended family: Experiences in stepfamilies. In K. Pasley & M. Ihinger-Tallman (eds.) *Remarriage and step-parenting: Current research theory*, 42-61. New York: Guilford.

Furstenberg Jr., F. F. (1988). Good dads, bad dads: Two faces of fatherhood. In A. J. Cherlin (eds.) *The changing American family and public policy*, 193-218. Washington, DC: Urban Institute Press.

Furstenberg Jr., F. F. & Peterson, J. L. (1983). The life course of children of divorce. *American Sociological Review 48*, 656-668.

Galambos, N. L. (1985). *Maternal role satisfaction, mother-adolescent relations, and sex-typing in early adolescent girls and boys*. Unpublished doctoral dissertation, The Pennsylvania State University, University Park.

Galambos, N. L., Petersen, A. C., Richards, M. & Gitelson, I. B. (1985). The Attitudes Toward Women Scale for Adolescents (ATSWA): A study of reliability and validity. *Sex Roles 13*, 343-354.

Garmezy, N. (1985). Stress-resistant children: The search for protective factors. In J. E. Stevenson (ed.) *Recent research in developmental psychopathology* (Journal of Child Psychology and Psychiatry Book Supplement No. 4, 213-233). Oxford: Pergamon.

Garmezy, N. (1987). Stress, competence, and development: Continuities in the study of schizophrenic adults, children vulnerable to psychopathology, and the search for stress-resistant children. *American Journal of Orthopsychiatry 57*, 159-174.

Garmezy, N. (1991). Resiliency and vulnerability to adverse developmental outcomes associated with poverty. *American Behavioral Scientist 34*, 416-430.

Gaspari, C. (1980). Characteristics of family structure, sociopsychological stress, and economic achievement: An international comparison (Merkmale der Familienstruktur, sozialpsychologische Belastung und wirtschaftliche Leistung: Ein internationaler Vergleich). *Zeitschrift für Klinische Psychologie und Psychotherapie 28*, 43-56.

Gibson, C. (1973). Social trends in divorce. *New Society 25*, 6-8.

Glenn, N. D., & Hoppe, S. K. (1982). Only children as adults: Psychological well-being. *Journal of Family Issues 5*, 363-382.

Glenn, N. D. & Kramer, K. B. (1987). The marriages and divorces of the children of divorce. *Journal of Marriage and the Family 49*, 811-825.

Glenn, N. D. & McLanahan, S. (1982). Children and marital happiness: A further specification of the relationship. *Journal of Marriage and the Family 44*, 63-72.

Glick, P. C. (1984). Marriage, divorce, and living arrangements: Prospective changes. *Journal of Marriage and the Family 39*, 5-13.

Glick, P. C. (1988). Fifty years of family demography: A record of social change. *Journal of Marriage and the Family 50*, 861-873.

Gökalp, A. (1984). Migrants' children in Western Europe: Differential socialization and multicultural problems. *International Social Science Journal 36*, 487-500.

Gökalp, C. (1978). Le réseau familial. *Population 33*, 1077-1093.

Gold, D. & Andres, D. (1978a). Developmental comparisons between adolescent children with employed and nonemployed mothers. *Merrill-Palmer Quarterly 24*, 243-254.

Gold, D. & Andres, D. (1978b). Developmental comparisons between 10-year-old children with employed and nonemployed mothers. *Child Development 49*, 75-84.

Gove, W. R. & Geerken, M. R. (1977). The effect of children and employment on the mental health of married men and women. *Social Focus 56*, 66-76.

Graetz, B. (1991). The class location of families: A refined classification and analysis. *Sociology 25*, 101-118.

Grych, J. H. & Fincham, F. D. (1990). Marital conflict and children's adjustment: A cognitive-contextual framework. *Psychological Bulletin 108*, 267-290.

Gunnar, M. M. & Collins, W. A. (eds.) (1988). *Transitions in adolescence: Minnesota symposia on child psychology* (Vol. XXI). Hillsdale, NJ: Lawrence Erlbaum.

Haavio-Mannila, E. (1986). Inequalities in health and gender. *Social Science Medicine 22*, 141-149.

Hannon, D. & Katsiaouni, L. (1981). *Traditional families? From culturally prescribed to negotiated roles in farm families*. Dublin: Dominican Publications.

Harris, K. M. & Morgan, S. P. (1991). Fathers, sons, and daughters: Differential paternal involvement in parenting. *Journal of Marriage and the Family 53*, 531-544.

Haskey, J. (1983). Remarriage of the divorced in England and Wales – A contemporary phenomenon. *Journal of Biosocial Science 15*, 253-271.

Hayes, C. D. (ed.) (1987). *Risking the future: Adolescent sexuality, pregnancy, and childbearing*. Washington, DC: National Academy Press.

Hernandez, D. J. (1986). Childhood in sociodemographic perspective. *Annual Review of Sociology 12*, 159-180.

Hess, L. E., Petersen, A. C. & Mortimer, J. T. (in press). Youth unemployment and marginality: The problem and the solution. In A. C. Petersen & J. T. Mortimer (eds.) *Youth unemployment and society*. New York: Cambridge University Press.

Hetherington, E. M. (1988). Parents, children, and siblings: Six years after divorce. In R. A. Hinde & J. Stevenson-Hinde (eds.) *Relationships within families*, 311-331. Oxford: Clarendon Press.

184 *Laura E. Hess*

Hetherington, E. M. & Clingempeel, W. G. with Anderson, E. R., Deal, J. E., Hagan,
M. S., Hollier, E. A., Lindner, M. S., Brown, J. C., Rice, A. M., Bennion, L. D.,
O'Conner, T. G., Eisenberg, M. & Maccoby, E. E. (1992). Coping with marital
transitions: A family systems perspective. *Monographs for the Society for
Research in Child Development 57*, 5.

Hetherington, E. M., Cox, M. & Cox, R. (1982). Effects of divorce on parents and
children. In M. E. Lamb (ed.) *Nontraditional families,* 233-288. Hillsdale, NJ:
Lawrence Erlbaum.

Hetherington, E. M., Cox, M. & Cox, R. (1985). Long-term effects of divorce and
remarriage on the adjustment of children. *Journal of the American Academy of
Child Psychiatry 24*, 518-530.

Heyns, B. & Catsambis, S. (1986). Mother's employment and children's
achievement: A critique. *Sociology of Education 59*, 140-151.

Hill, J. P. & Holmbeck, G. N. (1986). Attachment and autonomy during adolescence.
Annals of Child Development 3, 145-189.

Hiller, D. & Philliber, W. (1986). The division of labor in contemporary marriage:
Expectations, perceptions, and performance. *Social Problems 33*, 191-201.

Hilton, J. M. & Haldeman, V. A. (1991). Gender differences in the performance of
household tasks by adults and children in single-parent and two-parent, two-earner
families. *Journal of Family Issues 12*, 114-130.

Hinde, R. A. (1987). *Individuals, relationships, and culture: Links between ethology
and the social sciences.* Cambridge: Cambridge University Press.

Hirsch, B. J. (1985). Adolescent coping and support across multiple social
environments. *American Journal of Community Psychology 13*, 381-392.

Hoem, B. & Hoem, J. M. (1988). The Swedish family: Aspects of contemporary
developments. *Journal of Family Issues 9*, 397-424.

Hoem, J. M. & Rennermalm, B. (1985). Modern family initiation in Sweden:
Experience of women born between 1936 and 1960. *European Journal of
Population 1*, 81-112.

Hoffman, L. W. (1974). Effects of maternal employment on the child: A review of
the research. *Developmental Psychology 10*, 204-229.

Hoffman, L. W. (1979). Maternal employment: 1979. *American Psychologist 34*,
859-865.

Hoffman, L. W. (1989). Effects of maternal employment in the two-parent family.
American Psychologist 44, 283-292.

Hoffmann-Nowotny, H. J. (1987). The future of the family. In *European Population
Conference*, 113-200. Helsinki: Central Statistical Office of Finland.

Hogan, D. P. & Kitagawa, E. M. (1985). The impact of social status, family structure,
and neighborhood on the fertility of black adolescents. *American Journal of
Sociology 90*, 825-855.

Höhn, C. & Lüscher, K. (1988). The changing family in the Federal Republic of
Germany. *Journal of Family Issues 9*, 317-335.

Höpflinger, F. (1985). Changing marriage behavior: Some European comparisons.
Genus XLI 1-2, 41-64.

Höpflinger, F. (1987). *Wandel der Familienbildung in Westeuropa [Family developmental transitions in Western Europe].* Frankfurt: Campus Verlag.

Hornung, C. A. & McCullough, B. C. (1981). Status relationships in dual-employment marriages: Consequences for psychological well-being. *Journal of Marriage and the Family 43*, 125-141.

Houlbrooke, R. A. (1984). *The English family 1450-1700.* London: Longman.

Houseknecht, S. & Spanier, G. (1980). Marital disruption and higher education among women in the United States. *Sociological Quarterly 21*, 375-389.

Hunter, F. T. & Youniss, J. (1982). Changes in functions of three relations during adolescence. *Developmental Psychology 18*, 806-811.

Jallinoja, R. (1989). Women between the family and employment. In K. Boh, M. Bak, C. Clason, M. Pankratova, J. Qvortrup, G. B. Sgritta & K. Waerness (eds.) *Changing patterns of European family life*, 95-122. London: Routledge.

Janssens, A. (1986). Industrialization without family change? The extended family and the life cycle in a Dutch industrial town, 1880-1920. *Journal of Family History 11*, 25-42.

Jones, E. F., Forrest, J. D., Goldman, N., et al. (1985). Teenage pregnancy in developed countries: Determinants and policy implications. *Family Planning Perspectives 17*, 53-63.

Jones, T. (1993). *Britain's ethnic minorities.* London: Policy Studies Institute.

Joshi, H. E., Layard, R. & Owen, S. J. (1985). Why are more women working in Britain? *Journal of Labor Economics 3*, S147-176.

Kandel, D. B., Davies, M. & Raveis, V. H. (1985). The stressfulness of daily social roles from women: Marital, occupational and household roles. *Journal of Health and Social Behavior 26*, 64-78.

Kandel, D. B. & Lesser, G. S. (1972). *Youth in two worlds: United States and Denmark.* San Francisco: Jossey-Bass.

Keating, D. P. (1990). Adolescent cognitive processes. In S. Feldman & G. R. Elliott (eds.) *At the threshold: The developing adolescent*, 54-89. Cambridge, MA: Harvard University Press.

Keilman, N. (1987). Recent trends in family and household composition in Europe. *European Journal of Population 3*, 297-325.

Kempe, C. H., Silverman, F. N., Steele, B. F., Droegemueller, W., & Silver, H. K. (1962). The battered child syndrome. *Journal of the American Medical Association 181*, 4-11.

Kertzer, D. I. (1989). The joint family household revisited: Demographic constraints and household complexity in the European past. *Journal of Family History 14*, 1-15.

Kiernan, K. E. (1988). The British family: Contemporary trends and issues. *Journal of Family Issues 9*, 298-316.

Kiernan, K. E. (1991). *The respective roles of men and women in tomorrow's Europe.* Paper presented at the Human Resources in Europe at the dawn of the 21st Century International Conference. Luxembourg (November).

Kiernan, K. E. (1992). The impact of family disruption in childhood on transitions made in young adult life. *Population Studies 46*, 213-234.

Kiernan, K. E. & Estaugh, V. (1993). *Cohabitation: Extra-marital childbearing and social policy*. London: Family Policy Studies Centre.

Kiernan, K. E. & Wicks, M. (1990). *Family change and future policy*. London: Family Policy Studies Centre.

Kline, M., Johnston, J. R. & Tschann, J. M. (1991). The long shadow of marital conflict: A model of children's postdivorce adjustment. *Journal of Marriage and the Family 53*, 297-309.

Kronick, J. C. & Lieberthal, J. (1976). Predictors of cross-cultural variation in the percentage of women employed in Europe. *International Journal of Comparative Sociology 17*, 92-96.

Künzel, R. (1974). The connection between the family cycle and divorce rates: An analysis based on European data. *Journal of Marriage and the Family 36*, 379-388.

Kurdek, L. A. & Sinclair, R. J. (1988). The adjustment of young adolescents in two-parent nuclear, stepfather, and mother-custody families. *Journal of Consulting and Clinical Psychology 56*, 91-96.

Lamborn, S. D., Mounts, N. S., Steinberg, L. & Dornbusch, S. M. (1991). Patterns of competence and adjustment among adolescents from authoritative, authoritarian, indulgent, and neglectful families. *Child Development 62*, 1049-1065.

Lamke, L. K. (1982). The impact of sex-role orientation on self-esteem in early adolescence. *Child Development 53*, 1530-1535.

Land, H. (1979). The changing place of women in Europe. *Daedalus 108*, 73-94.

Lasch, C. (1979). *The culture of narcissism*. New York: Warner Books.

Laslett, P. (1972). Introduction: The history of the family. In P. Laslett & R. Wall (eds.) *Household and family in past time*, 1-89. Cambridge: Cambridge University Press.

Laslett, P. (1983). Family and household as work group and kin group: Areas of traditional Europe compared. In R. Wall, J. Robin & P. Laslett (eds.) *Family forms in historic Europe*, 513-563. Cambridge: Cambridge University Press.

Lehrer, E. & Nerlove, M. (1986). Female labor force behavior and fertility in the United States. *Annual Review of Sociology 12*, 181-204.

Leiulfsrud, H. & Woodward, A. (1987). Women at class crossroads: Repudiating conventional theories of family class. *Sociology 21*, 393-412.

Leridon, H. (1981). Fertility and contraception in 12 developed countries. *Family Planning Perspectives 13*, 93-96.

Leridon, H. (1990). Extra-marital cohabitation and fertility. *Population Studies 44*, 469-487.

Lerner, J. V. & Galambos, N. L. (1985). Maternal role satisfaction, mother-child interaction, and child temperament: A process model. *Developmental Psychology 21*, 1157-1164.

Lerner, J. V. & Hess, L. E. (1988). Maternal employment influences on early adolescent development. In M. D. Levine & E. R. McAnarney (eds.) *Early adolescent transitions*, 69-77. Lexington, MA: D. C. Heath.

Lerner, R. M. (1984). *On the nature of human plasticity.* New York: Cambridge University Press.

Lerner, R. M. & Busch-Rossnagel, N. A. (1981). *Individuals as producers of their development: A life-span perspective.* New York: Academic Press.

Lerner, R. M. & Foch, T. T. (eds.) (1987). *Biological-psychosocial interactions in early adolescence: A life-span perspective.* Hillsdale, NJ: Lawrence Erlbaum.

Lerner, R. M. & Kauffman, M. B. (1985). The concept of development in contextualism. *Developmental Review 5*, 309-333.

Lerner, R. M. & Spanier, G. B. (eds.) (1978). *Child influence on marital and family interaction: A life-span perspective.* New York: Academic Press.

Maccoby, E. (1958). Children and working mothers. *Children 5*, 83-89.

Maccoby, E. & Martin, J. (1983). Socialization in the context of the family: Parent-child interaction. In E. M. Hetherington (eds.) *Handbook of child psychology*, 1-101. New York: Wiley.

Marini, M. M. (1980). Effects of the number and spacing of children on marital and parental satisfaction. *Demography 17*, 225-242.

Marjoribanks, K. (1991). Ethnicity, family environment and social-status attainment: A follow-up analysis. *Journal of Comparative Family Studies 22*, 15-23.

Marks, M. N. & Kumar, R. (1993). Infanticide in England and Wales. *Journal of Medical Sciences and the Law 33*, 329-339.

Martens, P. L. (1984). School-related behavior of early adolescents: In search of determining factors. *Youth and Society 15*, 353-384.

Massad, C. M. (1981). Sex role identity and adjustment during adolescence. *Child Development 52*, 1290-1298.

McDermott, D. (1984). The relationship of parental drug use and parents' attitude to adolescent drug use. *Adolescence 19*, 89-97.

McHale, S. M. & Pawletko, T. M. (1992). Differential treatment of siblings in two family contexts. *Child Development 63*, 68-81.

McLanahan, S. S., (1989). Mother-only families: Problems, reproduction, and politics. *Journal of Marriage and the Family 51*, 557-580.

McLanahan, S. S. & Bumpass, L. (1988). Intergenerational consequences of family disruption. *American Journal of Sociology 94*, 130-152.

McRae, S. (1993). *Cohabiting mothers: Changing marriage and motherhood?* London: Policy Studies Institute.

Mednick, B., Reznick, C., Hocevar, D. & Baker, R. (1987). Long-term effects of parental divorce on young adult male crime. *Journal of Youth and Adolescence 16*, 31-45.

Menaghan, E. & Parcel, T. L. (1990). Parental employment and family life: Research in the 1980s. *Journal of Marriage and the Family 52*, 1079-1098.

Menken, J., Trussell, J., Stempel, D. & Babakol, O. (1981). Proportional hazards life table models: An illustrative analysis of sociodemographic influences on marriage dissolution in the United States. *Demography 18*, 181-200.

Michael, R. T. (1985). Consequences of the rise in female labor force participation rates: Questions and probes. *Journal of Labour Economics 3*, S117-146.

Michel, A. (1989). The impact of marriage and children on the division of gender roles. In K. Boh, M. Bak, C. Clason, M. Pankratova, J. Qvortrup, G. Sgritta & K. Waerness (eds.) *Changing patterns of European family life: A comparative analysis of 14 European countries*, 173-188. London: Routledge.

Miller, N. & Maruyama, G. (1976). Ordinal position and peer popularity. *Journal of Personality and Social Psychology 33*, 123-131.

Milne, A. M., Myers, D. E., Rosenthal, A. S. & Ginsburg, A. (1986). Single parents, working mothers, and the educational achievement of school children. *Sociology of Education 59*, 125-139.

Minge-Kalman, W. (1978). The industrial revolution and the European family: The institutionalization of 'Childhood' as a market for family labor. *Comparative Studies in Society and History 20*, 454-468.

Modell, J. & Goodman, M. (1990). Historical perspectives. In S. S. Feldman & G. R. Elliott (eds.) *At the threshold: The developing adolescent*, 93-122. Cambridge, MA: Harvard University Press.

Monahan, T. P. (1952). How stable are remarriages? *American Journal of Sociology 58*, 280-288.

Montemayor, R. (1983). Parents and adolescents in conflict: All families some of the time and some families most of the time. *Journal of Early Adolescence 3*, 83-103.

Morgan, S. P. & Rindfuss, R. R. (1985). Marital disruption: Structural and temporal dimensions. *American Journal of Sociology 90*, 1055-1077.

Mott, F. L. & Haurin, R. J. (1982). Being an only child: Effects on educational progression and career orientation. *Journal of Family Issues 3*, 575-593.

Nauck, B. (1989). Intergenerational relationships in families from Turkey and Germany. An extension of the 'Value of Children' approach to educational attitudes and socialization practices. *European Sociological Review 5*, 251-274.

Nave-Herz, R. (1981). *Changing family patterns in the Federal Republic of Germany*. National Report.

Nave-Herz, R. (1989). Tensions between paid working hours and family life. In K. Boh, M. Bak, C. Clason, M. Pankratova, J. Qvortrup, G. Sgritta & K. Waerness (eds.) *Changing patterns of European family life: A comparative analysis of 14 European countries*, 159-171. London: Routledge.

Newcomer, S. & Udry, J. R. (1987). Parental marital status effects on adolescent sexual behavior. *Journal of Marriage and the Family 49*, 235-240.

Noller, P. & Callan, V. J. (1986). Adolescent and parent perceptions of family cohesion and adaptability. *Journal of Adolescence 9*, 97-106.

Office of Population Censuses and Surveys. (1990). Perinatal and infant mortality: Social and biological factors. *Mortality Statistics, Series DH3 no. 24*.

Ostby, L. (1989). The diffusion of modern contraception in Norway and its consequences for the fertility pattern. *European Journal of Population 5*, 27-43.

Owen, D. (1993). *Ethnic minorities in Great Britain: Housing and family characteristics*. 1991 Census Statistical Paper 4. Warwick: University of Warwick, Centre for Research in Ethnic Relations.

Paikoff, R. L. & Brooks-Gunn, J. (1991). Do parent-child relationships change during puberty? *Psychological Bulletin 110*, 47-66.

Parsons, T. & Bales, R. (1953). *Family, socialization and interaction process.* Glencoe: Free Press.

Patterson, J. M. & McCubbin, H. I. (1987). Adolescent coping style and behaviors: Conceptualization and measurement. *Journal of Adolescence 10*, 163-186.

Paukert, L. (1982). Personal preference, social change or economic necessity? Why women work. *Labor and Society 7*, 311-331.

Petersen, A. C. (1988). Adolescent development. *Annual Review of Psychology 39*, 583-607.

Petersen, A. C. & Taylor, B. C. (1980). The biological approach to adolescence: Biological change and psychological adaptation. In J. Adelson (ed.) *Handbook of adolescent psychology*, 117-155. New York: Wiley.

Philliber, W. W. & Hiller, D. V. (1983). Relative occupational attainments of spouses and later changes in marriage and wife's work experience. *Journal of Marriage and the Family 45*, 161-170.

Phinney, J. S., Chavira, V. & Williamson, L. (1992). Acculturation attitudes and self-esteem among high school and college students. *Youth & Society 23*, 299-312.

Piaget, J. (1958). *The growth of logical thinking from childhood to adolescence.* New York: Basic Books.

Piaget, J. (1972). Intellectual evolution from adolescence to adulthood. *Human Development 15*, 1-12.

Pieterse, J. J. & Van Urk, H. (1989). Maltreatment of children in the Netherlands: An update after ten years. *Child Abuse and Neglect 13*, 263-269.

Pleck, J. H. (1985). *Working wives / working husbands.* Beverly Hills, CA: Sage.

Polonko, K. A., Scanzoni, J. & Teachman, J. D. (1982). Childlessness and marital satisfaction. *Journal of Family Issues 3*, 545-573.

Popenoe, D. (1987). Beyond the nuclear family: A statistical portrait of the changing family in Sweden. *Journal of Marriage and the Family 49*, 173-183.

Quinn, W. H., Newfield, N. A. & Protinsky, H. O. (1985). Rites of passage in families with adolescents. *Family Process 24*, 101-111.

Rapoport, T. (1991). Gender-differential patterns of adolescent socialization in three arenas. *Journal of Youth and Adolescence 20*, 31-51.

Reid, J. B. & Patterson, G. R. (1989). The development of antisocial behavior patterns in childhood and adolescence. *Adolescence 3*, 107-119.

Richardson, J. L., Dwyer, K., McGuigan, K., Hansen, W. B., Dent, C., Johnson, C. A., Sussman, S. Y., Brannon, B. & Flay, B. (1989). Substance use among eighth-grade students who take care of themselves after school. *Pediatrics 84*, 556-566.

Richardson, R. A., Galambos, N. L., Schulenberg, J. E. & Petersen, A. C. (1984). Young adolescents' perceptions of the family environment. *Journal of Early Adolescence 4*, 131-153.

Rindfuss, R. R. & VandenHeuvel, A. (1990). Cohabitation: A precursor to marriage or an alternative to being single? *Population and Development Review 16*, 703-726.

Roll, J. (1992). *Lone parent families in the European Community.* London: European Family and Social Policy Unit.

Rosenzweig, M. R. & Wolpin, K. I. (1980). Life cycle labor supply and fertility: Causal inferences from household models. *Journal of Political Economy 88,* 328-48.

Roussel, Louis. (1976). *La famille après le mariage des enfants.* INED: Travaux et Documents No. 78. Paris: Presses Universitaires de France.

Rubenstein, J. L., Heeren, T., Housman, D., Rubin, C. & Stechler, G. (1989). Suicidal behavior in 'normal' adolescents: Risk and protective factors. *American Journal of Orthopsychiatry 59,* 59-71.

Rueschemeyer, M. (1988). New family forms in a state socialist society: The German Democratic Republic. *Journal of Family Issues 9,* 354-371.

Rutter, M. (1971). Parent-child separation: Psychological effects on the children. *Journal of Child Psychology and Psychiatry 12,* 233-260.

Rutter, M. (1985). Family and school influences on behavioural development. *Journal of Child Psychology and Psychiatry 26,* 349-368.

Rutter, M. (1987). Psychosocial resilience and protective mechanisms. *American Journal of Orthopsychiatry 57,* 316-331.

Sardon, J. P. (1990). Cohort fertility in member states of the Council of Europe. *Population Studies 21.* Strasbourg: Council of Europe.

Schmid, J. (1984). The background of recent fertility trends in the member states of the Council of Europe. *Population Studies 15.* Strasbourg: Council of Europe.

Schwebel, A. I., Fine, M. A. & Renner, M. A. (1991). A study of perceptions of the stepparent role. *Journal of Family Issues 12,* 43-57.

Segalen, M. (1985). Family change and social uses of kinship networks in France. *Historical Social Research 34,* 22-29.

Select Committee of Experts on Household Structures. (1990). Household structures in Europe. *Population Studies 22.* Strasbourg: Council of Europe.

Sgritta, G. B. (1988). The Italian family: Tradition and change. *Journal of Family Issues 9,* 372-396.

Shanks, A. (1987). The stem family reconsidered: The case of the minor gentry of Northern Ireland. *Journal of Comparative Family Studies 18,* 339-361.

Simmons, R. G. & Blyth, D. A. (1987). *Moving into adolescence: The impact of pubertal change and school context.* Hawthorne, NY: Aldine de Gruyter.

Sinha, D. (1991). Rise in the population of the elderly, familial changes and their psychosocial implications: The scenario of developing countries. *International Journal of Psychology 26,* 633-647.

Skuse, D. & Bentovim, A. (1994). Physical and emotional maltreatment. In M. Rutter, E. Taylor & L. Hersov (eds.) *Child and adolescent psychiatry: Modern approaches,* 209-229. Oxford: Blackwell Scientific.

Smith, D. J. (1977). *Racial disadvantage in Britain.* Harmondsworth, Middx: Penguin.

Smith, M. & Bentovim, A. (1994) Sexual Abuse. In M. Rutter, E. Taylor & L. Hersov (eds.) *Child and adolescent psychiatry: Modern approaches* (3rd edition), 230-251. Oxford: Blackwell Scientific Publications.

Smokler, C. S. (1985). *Self-esteem in pre-adolescent and adolescent females.* Unpublished doctoral dissertation, University of Michigan.

Spanier, G. B. & Lewis, R. A. (1980). Marital quality: A review of the seventies. *Journal of Marriage and the Family 42*, 825-839.

Spencer, M. B. & Dornbusch, S. M. (1990). Challenges in studying minority youth. In S. S. Feldman & G. R. Elliott (eds.) *At the threshold: The developing adolescent,* 123-146. Cambridge, MA: Harvard University Press.

Spitze, G. (1988). Women's employment and family relations: A review. *Journal of Marriage and the Family 50*, 595-618.

Steinberg, L. D. (1981). Transformations in family relations at puberty. *Developmental Psychology 7*, 833-840.

Steinberg, L. D. (1987). The impact of puberty on family relations: Effects of pubertal status and pubertal timing. *Developmental Psychology 23*, 451-460.

Steinberg, L. D. (1988). Reciprocal relation between parent-child distance and pubertal maturation. *Developmental Psychology 24*, 1-7.

Stocker, C. M., Dunn, J. & Plomin, R. (1989). Sibling relationships: Links with child temperament, maternal behavior, and family structure. *Child Development 60*, 715-727.

Stolte-Heiskanen, V. (1975). Family needs and societal institutions: Potential empirical linkage mechanisms. *Journal of Marriage and the Family 37*, 903-916.

Stone, L. (1977). *The family, sex and marriage in England 1500-1800.* New York: Harper & Row.

Sullerot, E. (1977). The changing roles of men and women in Europe. In *The changing roles of men and women in modern society: Functions, rights and responsibilities.* New York: United Nations.

Teachman, J. D. (1982). Methodological issues in the analysis of family formation and dissolution. *Journal of Marriage and the Family 44*, 1037-1053.

Thornton, A. (1991). Influence of the marital history of parents on the marital and cohabitational experiences of children. *American Journal of Sociology 96*, 868-894.

Trost, J. (1979). *Unmarried cohabitation.* Västeras, Sweden: International Library.

Trotha, T. v. (1990). On the change of the family (Zum Wandel der Familie). *Kölner Zeitschrift für Soziologie und Sozialpsychologie 42*, 452-473.

United Nations (1950). *Demographic Yearbook 1949/50.* New York: Author.

United Nations (1959). *Demographic Yearbook 1958.* New York: Author.

United Nations (1965). *Demographic Yearbook 1964.* New York: Author.

United Nations (1969). *Demographic Yearbook 1968.* New York: Author.

United Nations (1974). *Demographic Yearbook 1973.* New York: Author.

United Nations (1977). *Demographic Yearbook 1976.* New York: Author.

United Nations (1979). *Demographic Yearbook 1978* (Special issue: Historical supplement). New York: Author.

United Nations (1980). *Demographic Yearbook 1979.* New York: Author.

United Nations (1984). *Demographic Yearbook 1982.* New York: Author.

United Nations (1986). *Demographic Yearbook 1984.* New York: Author.

United Nations (1988). *Demographic Yearbook 1986.* New York: Author.

United Nations (1990). *Demographic Yearbook 1988.* New York: Author.

United Nations (1991). *Demographic Yearbook 1989.* New York: Author.

Vannoy, D. (1991). Social differentiation, contemporary marriage, and human development. *Journal of Family Issues 12,* 251-267.

Voydanooff, P. & Majka, L. C. (1988). *Families and economic distress.* Newbury Park, CA: Sage.

Vuchinich, S., Hetherington, E. M., Vuchinich, R. A. & Clingempeel, W. G. (1991). Parent-child interaction and gender differences in early adolescents' adaptation to stepfamilies. *Developmental Psychology 27,* 618-626.

Waite, L. J. & Stolzenberg, R. M. (1976). Intended childbearing and labor force participation of young women: Insights from nonrecursive models. *American Sociological Review 41,* 235-252.

Wallace, H. M. & Vienonen, M. (1989). Teenage pregnancy in Sweden and Finland: Implications for the United States. *Journal of Adolescent Health Care 10,* 231-236.

Wallerstein, J. S. (1991). The long-term effects of divorce on children: A review. *Journal of the American Academy of Child and Adolescent Psychiatry 30,* 349-360.

Wallerstein, J. S., Corbin, S. B. & Lewis, J. M. (1988). Children of divorce: A 10-year study. In E. M. Hetherington & J. D. Arasteh (eds.) *Impact of divorce, single parenting, and stepparenting on children,* 197-214. Hillsdale, NJ: Lawrence Erlbaum.

Wallerstein, J. S. & Kelly, J. B. (1980). *Surviving the breakup: How children and parents cope with divorce.* New York: Basic Books.

Walsh, W. M. (1991). Irish middle class life in transition. *Journal of Comparative Family Studies 22,* 107-110.

Weiss, R. S. (1979). Growing up a little faster: The experience of growing up in a single-parent household. *Journal of Social Issues 35,* 97-111.

Weiss, R. S. (1984). The impact of marital dissolution on income and consumption in single-parent households. *Journal of Marriage and the Family 46,* 115-127.

Weitzman, L. J. (1985). *The divorce revolution.* New York: Free Press.

Werner, E. E. (1989). High-risk children in young adulthood: A longitudinal study from birth to 32 years. *American Journal of Orthopsychiatry 59,* 72-81.

White, L. K. & Booth, A. (1985). The quality and stability of remarriages: The role of stepchildren. *American Sociological Review 50,* 689-698.

Williams, D. R. (1990). Socioeconomic differentials in health: A review and redirection. *Social Psychology Quarterly 53,* 81-99.

Williams, G. R. (1983). Child protection: A journey into history. *Journal of Child Clinical Psychology 12,* 236-243.

Williams, K. J., Suls, J., Alliger, G. M., Learner, S. M. & Wan, C. K. (1991). Multiple role juggling and daily mood states in working mothers: An experience sampling study. *Journal of Applied Psychology 76,* 664-674.

Williams, R. G. A. (1983). Kinship and migration strategies among settled Londoners: Two responses to population pressure. *The British Journal of Sociology 34*, 386-415.

Wyatt, G. A. (1985) The sexual abuse of Afro-American and White-American women in childhood. *Child Abuse and Neglect 9*, 507-519.

Wyatt, G. A. & Peters, S. D. (1986). Methodological considerations in research on the prevalence of child sexual abuse. *Child Abuse and Neglect 10*, 241-251.

Zimmerman, G. (1985). Nichteheliche Lebensgemeinschaft – Alternative zu Ehe und Familie? [Nonmarital cohabitation – alternative to marriage and family?]. Short version of a paper presented at the workshop, *Lebenslauf und Familie [Life course and family]*, May 30 - June 1. Bielefeld, FRG.

Ziglèr, E. & Hall, N. W. (1989). Physical child abuse in America: Past, present, and future. In D. Cicchetti & V. Carlson (eds.) *Child maltreatment. Theory and research on the causes and consequences of child abuse and neglect*, 38-75. New York: Cambridge University Press.

6

Living Conditions in the Twentieth Century

DAVID J. SMITH

INTRODUCTION

The twentieth century has seen unprecedented change in the economies of countries throughout the world. The scale of economic growth can best be expressed by considering the total value of goods produced, as measured by the gross domestic product (GDP) at constant prices. In the 16 advanced economies that belong to the Organization for Economic Cooperation and Development (OECD), GDP per head of population increased nearly sixfold in real terms between 1900 and 1987. Over the same period the increase was more than threefold in Asia, nearly fivefold in Latin America, and more than sevenfold in the USSR (Maddison 1989). Economic growth has led to far-reaching changes in styles of life: for example, richer diet, more spacious housing with better facilities, greater mobility through both public and private transport, better communications, more information and entertainment through the cinema, broadcasting and printed matter. In the developed countries, an increasing proportion of growing national earnings has been spent on public services; and levels of education, health, and life expectancy have all increased. The proportion of the workforce engaged in agriculture has declined from about half to about one in twenty, and reduced working hours have left more leisure for private and cultural pursuits.

The changes brought about by economic growth are of such great magnitude that they have profoundly altered the living conditions of all sections of the population. By contrast, the power relationships between different groups, and the pattern of distribution of wealth among them, have remained far more stable. In the late twentieth century, life expectancy and health still varies widely between social classes in the economically advanced countries. In the 1980s, as in the 1930s, a substantial minority were unemployed, and there was a radical difference in present experience and in future life chances between the unemployed and their families and those in work. Although there is some historical tendency for incomes to become more evenly distributed as economies grow, changes in distribution are far less rapid than increases in production. Hence there remains a problem of poverty at the heart of the most advanced economies.

It would not be surprising to find that these fundamental economic changes have had an important influence on the nature and extent of the problems experienced by young people. Nevertheless, the nature of any such relationship can only be guessed at until there is a better understanding of the mechanisms that link economic structure with social stress. The same economic changes may be associated with a large number of social changes, which interact in a complex way. For example, economic growth leads to the satisfaction of basic needs – better diet, housing and health – which might be expected to increase people's well-being and reduce their level of stress. On the other hand, it is also associated with many other changes, such as the concentration of the population in towns and cities, the lengthening of the period of education and of adolescence, a widening of horizons among young people, who receive more and more information about the world and the possibilities open to them, and an increase in choice and spending power among many sections of the youth population. Satisfaction of basic needs may therefore be accompanied by a wider vision of possibilities and an increase in expectations, and the transition to adulthood may become longer and more difficult to negotiate. In short, economic growth is associated with many different developments, some of which increase whereas others reduce the pressure on young people.

The task of this study as a whole is to describe secular changes in psychosocial problems among young people and to take the first steps towards formulating and testing theories to account for such changes. The purpose of this chapter is to review the massive changes in living conditions that provide possible explanations of changes in psychosocial problems. For the most part, the chapter will simply describe these social and economic changes. Discussion of their explanatory significance is contained mainly in the later chapters on the problem behaviours, and in the overall conclusions. A more refined analysis of the relationships between changes in living conditions and in psychosocial problems remains a project for the future, but even a preliminary review can eliminate many hypotheses.

The strategy adopted at this early stage is to identify phases of development, differences between nations, and variations between nations in the timing of development. The intention is to highlight opportunities for testing fairly simple theories about the influence of economic change. For example, it may be thought that unemployment has an important influence on crime. As will be shown in detail later, there was a high rate of unemployment in many of the OECD countries in 1926-27, in 1931-38, and in the 1980s, whereas between 1950 and 1972 the rate was much lower; secondly, certain of the OECD countries have consistently maintained much lower rates of unemployment than the others. This provides some opportunity for testing at a crude level the idea that high unemployment is associated with high rates of crime. At a first glance the theory receives little support, since the pre-war period of high unemployment was a period of low crime rates, whereas the postwar period of high unemployment was a period of high crime rates; and certain of the low-unemployment countries (Japan and Switzerland) have low crime rates, whereas others (Austria and Sweden) do not.

This kind of reasoning is crude because many different factors are involved in any social change, so that a more detailed analysis would be required to test any particular theory. However, in most cases that detailed stage of analysis has not yet been reached. The purpose of this chapter is to prepare the ground for it by setting out the main facts of economic change.

The first main section on *demography* describes the increase in population and in life expectancy in the developed countries, and the reduction in the size of the youth population as a proportion of the total. The next section, on *economic development*, describes the rapid but uneven growth of the Western economies over the present century; divides this pattern of growth into phases of development; describes the massive shift from agriculture to manufacturing and services; and shows how development was accompanied by a large increase in public expenditure on health, housing, education, income maintenance, and social services.

The third section, on *standard of living*, turns from economic change in the abstract to consider concrete changes in conditions of life; it covers, in particular, ownership of consumer durables, standards of housing, level of education, health, and patterns of leisure.

The fourth main section, on *inequality*, considers whether the increased output of the economy has come to be distributed more or less evenly among the groups varying in power within the population. This provides the background needed for testing the many theories that suggest that the distribution of resources is a more important determinant of psychosocial problems than the average level of prosperity.

DEMOGRAPHY

Growth of population and increasing life expectancy are closely allied to economic development. Some light is shed on the reasons for this link by considering the wide differences in life expectancy between social classes in a society at any one time. If psychosocial problems are regarded as analogous to health problems, then one of the largest questions raised is why economic development is accompanied on the one hand by improving health and declining mortality, and on the other by increasing rates of crime, suicide, depression, and drug abuse.

Population

Population growth between 1820 and 1987 is shown on a logarithmic scale for nine of the OECD countries in Figures 6.1 and 6.2. Figure 6.1 covers the four large countries of Western Europe – France, the Federal Republic of Germany, Italy, and the United Kingdom – which by 1987 had all reached similar populations of 50 to 60 million.[1] However, they reached this similar destination through widely divergent routes. France already had a population of over 30 million in 1820, whereas West Germany was half that size, and Italy and the UK two-thirds. In France, there was only gradual population growth between 1820 and 1900, and virtually no growth for the first half of the present century; but since 1950, France has experienced far more rapid population growth than at any other time in its recorded history.

In Germany, by contrast, population growth, starting from a much lower base, was rapid between 1820 and 1900, so that by 1900 the population of France and West Germany was about the same. From 1900 to 1950 there was a period of slower growth, followed by a period of rapid growth between 1950 and 1970, then after 1970 an actual decline. Italy and the UK showed a steadier pattern of growth over the period of 167 years, although the population of the UK grew more rapidly than the population of Italy in the first half of the period, and less rapidly in the second.

---

1. The population figures are adjusted to present national boundaries, or in the case of Germany to the boundaries of the Federal Republic before unification.

Figure 6.1   Population: selected countries, 1820-1987: adjusted to present-day boundaries

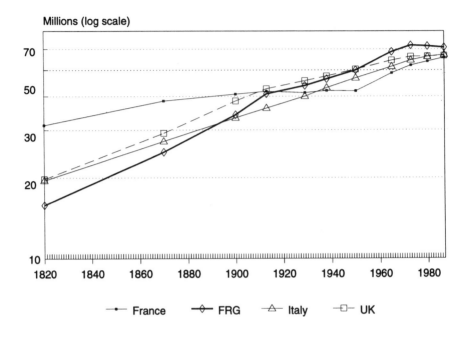

Source: Maddison (1989).

Figure 6.2 covers the two largest OECD countries – the USA and Japan – together with three of the smaller countries of Western Europe. In 1820, the population of the USA was about 10 million compared with Japan's 30 million. In the 100 years from 1820, the population of the USA increased more than tenfold to reach well over 100 million. It then grew at a lower rate, except for a spurt in the 1950s, to reach about 250 million by 1987. Growth of population in Japan was slow over the 100 years from 1820; the population of the USA overtook that of Japan in the 1860s, and before 1900 it was twice the size. However, in the present century Japan's population has grown much more rapidly than before, to reach about 120 million in 1987.

Comparing Figures 6.1 and 6.2, it is clear that the populations of both Japan and the USA have grown far more quickly than the populations of the four major European countries. The difference is, of course, most marked in the case of the USA, a country built out of mass immigration. However, immigration has not been a major factor in Japan, which remains an ethnically homogeneous country. In 1820, the population of Japan was about the same as that of France, then the most populous of the European countries, but by 1987 Japan's population was about two and a half times that of France, West Germany, Italy, or the UK.

Figure 6.2   Population: selected countries, 1820-1987

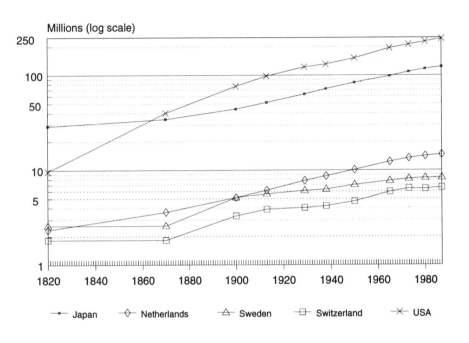

Source: Maddison (1989).

The Netherlands, Sweden and Switzerland had populations of around 2 million in 1820. Since 1900, population growth has been much more rapid in the Netherlands than in the other two countries, so that the population of the Netherlands is now about twice as large, at around 15 million, as that of Sweden (just over 8 million) or Switzerland (6 million).

Death Rates and Life Expectancy

One factor in the growth of population during the nineteenth and twentieth centuries was a decline in death rates and an increase in life expectancy. This may have particular significance for a study of youth and its problems, since a longer life allows more room for adolescence to be considered as a separate phase.

The death rate is defined as the proportion of a group who die in a 12-month period. Since death rates vary widely according to age, for most practical purposes they have to be quoted for specific age groups. Figure 6.3 charts death rates in Sweden from 1755 to 1975 among young adults (men and women aged 20-24, and aged 25-29). It is striking that the sharp and consistent decline in death rates in the present century (from 1915 to 1955) had no precedent in recorded history. In fact, the death rates for young adults in 1915 (at between 600 and 800 per 100,000 for the various groups) were not much lower than they had been 160 years earlier, yet by 1955 they had declined to 50-120. Further declines after 1955 were slight.

Figure 6.3   Age-specific death rates: Sweden, 1751-1975

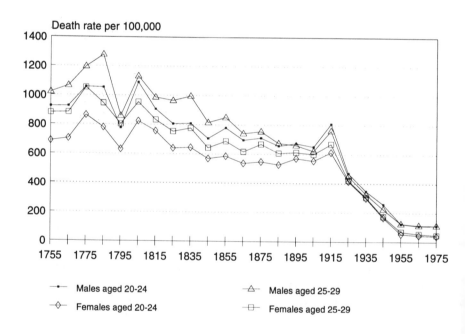

Source: Lancaster (1990).

The historical run of data available for Sweden is exceptionally long, but data for several other European countries also show that the persistent decline in death rates began in the last quarter of the nineteenth century or in the first quarter of the twentieth.[2] The present century has therefore seen an unprecedented transformation in the number of years young people can expect to live.

Figure 6.4   Expectation of life: England and Wales

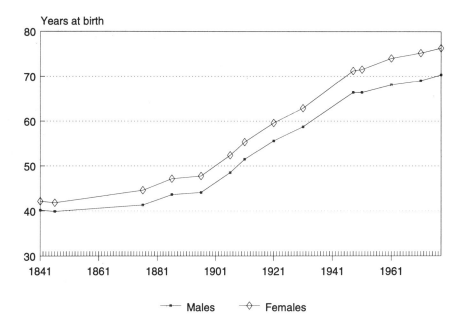

Source: Lancaster (1990).

In order to demonstrate this more precisely, life tables can be used to calculate the complete expectation of life, that is, the average length of life that a person of a given age will live. Figure 6.4 shows expectation of life at birth in England and Wales from 1841 to 1978. Over the whole period, expectation of life rose from 40 to 70 years for males, and from 42 to 76 for females. There

---

2. Lancaster (1990) summarized information on this point for France, Sweden, Norway, the UK, Australia and New Zealand (29, Table 3.6.1). For the 25-34 age group, the beginning of a persistent decline in death rates dates from 1886 in France, 1881 in Sweden, 1906 in Norway, 1871 in the UK, 1886 in New Zealand, and not later than 1891 in Australia.

was little increase until 1881, while the main part of the increase occurred between 1895 and 1948; the rate of increase after 1948 was much slower than in the previous half-century. Furthermore, a considerable part of the increase in recent years reflects a sharp decline in perinatal mortality.

Figure 6.5   Expectation of life: Japan, and England and Wales

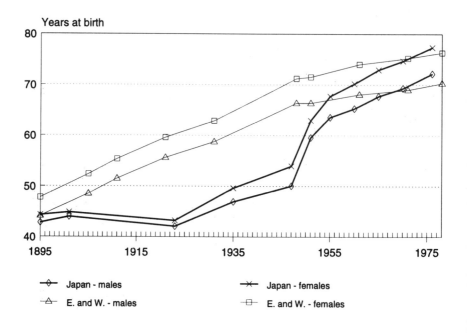

Source: Lancaster (1990).

Figure 6.5 shows a striking difference between the historical pattern of change in expectation of life in Japan compared with England and Wales. Before 1920, there was no increase in expectation of life in Japan: in fact, there was some decline between 1900 and 1923. Over that same period, expectation of life was already rising steadily and steeply in England and Wales. Between 1923 and 1947, expectation of life rose at about the same rate as in England and Wales, but over this period the gap between the two countries remained about 17 years. For ten years from 1947 onwards there was a remarkably sharp rise in expectation of life in Japan, and major increases continued up to the 1970s, when Japan overtook England and Wales. Broadly this pattern reflects earlier industrialisation in Britain and modest economic growth over a long period, compared with later industrialisation in Japan, and explosive economic growth from the early 1950s onwards. In terms of the shape of the curve, Japan and Britain are at two extremes among the developed countries. If youth problems are associated with such historical changes, then it should be possible to observe differences between the two countries in the shape of the curves of development of youth problems over time.

For all of the developed countries, as for Japan and Britain, death rates generally (for all age groups aggregated) have declined only slightly since 1960, and hence complete expectation of life at birth has increased only slowly in recent years. There has, nevertheless, been a dramatic reduction in infant mortality in developed countries since around 1950. In France, for example, the death rate (per 10,000 per annum) among males across all age groups declined only modestly from 133 in 1948 to 112 in 1976; but over the same period the death rate among male infants aged less than one year declined from 615 to 140 (Lancaster, 1990: 394, Table 38.5.1). This is the typical pattern for Western European countries.

Income, Inequality and Life Expectancy

The comparison between England and Wales and Japan suggests a connection between mortality and economic development. More systematic research has confirmed that there is a close relationship between gross national product per head and life expectancy (Marsh, 1988). 'In 1984 few countries achieved an average life expectancy at birth of 70 years or more until gross national product per head approached a threshold of almost $5,000 a year' (Wilkinson, 1992:168). However, beyond that threshold, the relationship is comparatively weak: although economies continue to grow, and life expectancy continues to increase, there is little systematic relationship between these two developments. Thus, among 23 developed countries that are members of the Organization for Economic Cooperation and Development (OECD), Wilkinson (1992) found a correlation coefficient of only 0.38 between life expectancy and gross national product per head in 1986-7. He found virtually no correlation between the *increases* in gross national product per head and in life expectancy over the 16 years from 1970 onwards.

On the other hand, for developed countries there is evidence of a strong correlation between equality of income distribution and life expectancy. For nine countries covered by the Luxembourg Income Study, Wilkinson (1992) found a correlation of 0.86 between life expectancy and the share of income going to the bottom seven-tenths of families. Gross national product per head is also significantly related to life expectancy, in combination with equality of income distribution, but the relationship is far weaker. On three separate sets of data, Wilkinson has also demonstrated a fairly strong relationship in developed countries between *increases in* equality of income distribution during the 1970s and early 1980s and *increases in* life expectancy (correlation coefficients between 0.47 and 0.73).

At the same time, there is cross-sectional evidence of a curvilinear relationship between income and health or life expectancy; as income increases from its lowest point, health and life expectancy at first increase rapidly, but once a certain income level is reached, these increases level off, and as income increases beyond a certain point, health and life expectancy actually decline slightly. All of this evidence suggests that life expectancy is greatly increased by raising income, but only up to a certain threshold. At earlier but not at later stages of economic development, increases in gross national product have the effect of raising a substantial body of people above the threshold beyond which their life expectancy is improved. Among developed countries, increases in gross national product no longer have that effect, but there are still people below the threshold, and they may be raised above it by redistribution of income.

Marmot and Davey Smith (1989) have carried out a detailed evaluation of the contrasting trends in life expectancy in Britain and Japan over the past 30 years. For Japanese males, life expectancy at birth rose from 63.6 years in 1955 to 75.2 years in 1986, an increase of 18 per cent; for British males, life expectancy rose from 67.5 years in 1955, considerably higher than the Japanese figure, to 71.9 years in 1984-86, considerably lower than the Japanese figure, an increase of only 7 per cent. The figures for females show a closely similar contrast. After reviewing a number of possible explanations of the difference, Marmot and Davey Smith concluded that the increasing equality of income distribution in Japan over this period, contrasted with the increasing inequality of income distribution in Britain, is probably the most important factor.

There is also a strong and well-established relationship between social class and mortality (Davey Smith et al., 1990a). In Britain in 1981, the age-standardized mortality ratio was 2.4 times as high for the lowest as for the highest of five social classes. Being a home owner, having access to a car, and having a high educational level are also associated with higher life expectancy, and these relationships are all partially independent of one another. Studies focused on specific hierarchies such as the civil service or the army, in which each grade is relatively homogeneous, have found still greater contrasts in life expectancy (Davey Smith et al., 1990b; Lynch & Oelman, 1981). Broadly similar social class differences in mortality have been found for a number of other European countries (Davey Smith et al., 1990a). Data from the British longitudinal study based on the censuses of 1971 and 1981 have now shown that downward social mobility does not account for these differentials (Goldblatt, 1988, 1989); this excludes the possibility that people come to occupy a low social class as a consequence of ill health. It has been argued that differences in life styles between social classes are unlikely to account for more than a small part of the differences in mortality (Davey Smith et al., 1990a). Probably the main part of the explanation lies in differences between social classes in living conditions over which people have little control: for example, housing, environment, working conditions, and the physical and other demands of the job itself.

Taken together, these findings demonstrate that inequality in developed societies is strongly associated with mortality. It will be important to establish whether it is also associated with psychosocial problems.

Age Structure of the Population

One factor that may be expected to have an important influence on the extent of youth problems is the age structure of the population. In the case of crime and other deviant behaviour which is characteristic of young people and much less common among other age groups there are particularly strong reasons to expect age structure to be important. First, there is the direct compositional effect: that is, crime will increase where younger people, who are most likely to commit crime, form an increasing proportion of the population, and *vice versa*. Second, it may be thought that crime will be more easily controlled where the younger age groups are a small minority, so that the norms and social controls of the older majority are more likely to prevail. The same kind of reasoning might be applied, although perhaps with rather less force, to a number of other problem behaviours of youth. Alternatively, the implications of age structure can be approached from the perspective of economics. Easterlin (1968) argued that competition would be greater among members of larger as compared with smaller age cohorts, so that members of 'baby boom' generations would tend to be at a disadvantage in a variety of ways.

A consequence of the long-term changes in rates of mortality is, of course, that young people now form a smaller proportion of the population than they did in the past, so long-term changes in age structure should help to explain a decline in crime and other youth problems rather than an increase. In Western

Figure 6.6   **Age distribution: USA**

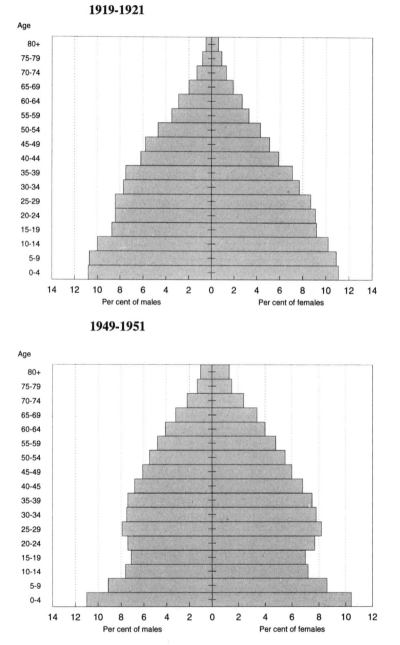

1919-1921

1949-1951

Source: Keyfitz & Flieger (1968).

Figure 6.7   Age distribution: USA

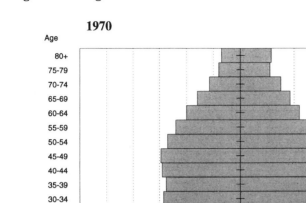

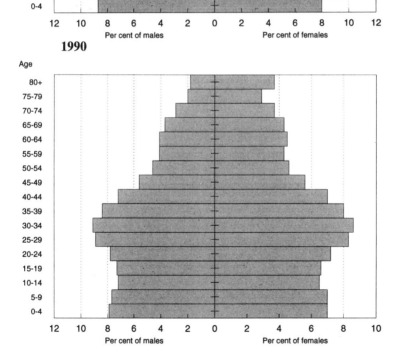

Source: UN (1991).

European countries and America, superimposed on the long-term trend towards an ageing population, there has been a short-term 'bulge' of children born in the years immediately following the Second World War. Figures 6.6 and 6.7 illustrate both the long- and short-term patterns of change for the USA by showing its age pyramids at four points in the present century, starting in 1919-21 and ending in 1990. Comparing the beginning and end of the period, there is a major difference in age structure. The pyramid for the early part of the century has a broad base and a fine point, showing that young people predominated and the numbers in older age groups fell off rapidly. By contrast, the pyramid for 1990 has a much narrower base and a thicker apex, showing a more even distribution across the age groups, and a much lesser predominance of young people.

The progress of the short-term bulge can be seen in the three later pyramids. In 1949-51 the very base of the pyramid is extended, showing a bulge of children aged 0-4. By 1970, this bulge has moved upwards, peaking among the 10-14 age group, and by 1990 the largest bulge is among those aged 30-34.

Most countries in Western Europe also experienced a postwar bulge in birth rate, but the timing and extent of these short-term changes varied considerably between countries. Figure 6.8 shows age pyramids for England and Wales at three points in the present century. The long-term trend towards an ageing population is again shown by the narrowing base and thickening apex of the pyramids, but the 1981 pyramid also shows two bulges rather than one: the first of people aged 30-34 in 1981 (the immediate postwar baby boom), and the second of people aged 10-19 in 1981 (the baby boom of the 1960s). The short-run differences between the USA and England and Wales are quite large, and similar differences occur between various Western European countries.

This last point is illustrated by Figure 6.9, which shows the youth share of the population at ten-year intervals from 1920 to 1990 for six European countries. In the longer term, young people (aged 15-29) have come to form a decreasing proportion of the population in all six countries, although this change is smaller in France and the Netherlands than elsewhere. However, there is considerable variation between countries in the pattern of change since 1960. In England and Wales, for example, the youth share of the population increased between 1960 and 1990, whereas in Italy it declined by a similar quantity.

It is an interesting question whether or not the short-term changes in the size of the youth population are large enough to have an important effect on the extent of youth problems and the capacity of the wider society to control or deal with them. A comparative study by the OECD (1986: 106-133) showed

Figure 6.8   Age distribution: England and Wales

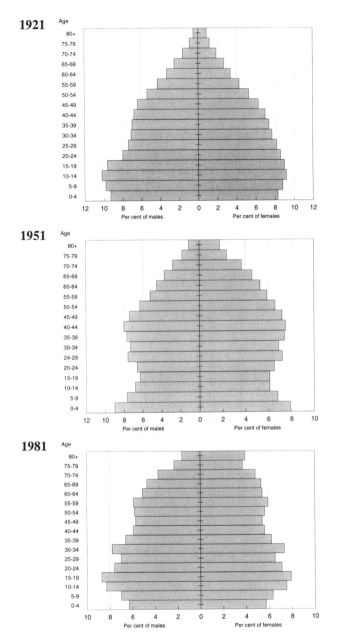

Source: Censuses of population.

that economic opportunities are reduced for members of large youth cohorts: this is reflected both in a decline in relative youth earnings, and an increase in unemployment, and there is, in addition, a trade-off between these two effects. However, in many of the high unemployment countries, the increase in the relative size of the youth cohort occurred well before the big rise in unemployment in the second half of the 1970s. Thus, generational crowding had an influence in increasing the level of youth unemployment in the 1960s and 1970s, but it hardly helps to account for the rising levels of youth unemployment in high unemployment countries from the late 1970s onwards. It would be possible to carry out similar research to analyse the relationship between the size of the youth cohort and psychosocial problems, but no analysis of this kind has yet been reported.

Figure 6.9   Youth share of population: percentage of population aged 15-29

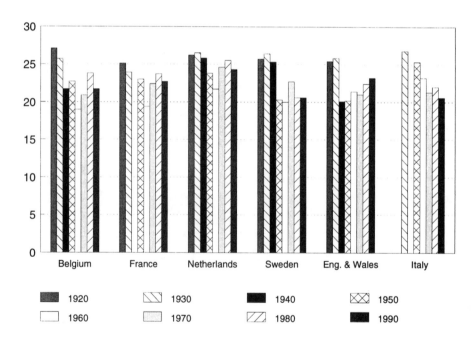

Source: Keyfitz & Flieger (1968); UN (1991).

Immigration

Much of history is the story of the migration of populations, and international migration has continued on a large scale in the nineteenth and twentieth centuries. (See Castles & Miller, 1993, for a general summary of population movements over the past 200 years.) Countries such as the United States, Canada, Argentina, Australia, and New Zealand were, of course, formed from mass migration in relatively modern times. For example, an estimated 54 million people migrated to the United States between 1820 and 1987 (Borjas, 1990: 3). Substantial population movements also arose from the transportation of slaves: an estimated 15 million people were transported from Africa to the Americas before 1850 (Appleyard, 1991: 11). Later, the aftermath of colonialism tended to produce migration systems (Kritz et al., 1992) leading to a flow of population from the former colonies to the European countries that had colonized them; these systems consist of a number of historical, economic, and political linkages that facilitate migration.

There was considerable international migration within Europe during the nineteenth and early twentieth centuries. An estimated 6.8 million Italians went to other European countries between 1876 and 1920, mainly to France, Switzerland, and Germany (Cinanni, 1968: 29). 'As Western Europeans went overseas in the (often vain) attempt to escape proletarianization, workers from peripheral areas, like Poland, Ireland and Italy, were drawn in as replacement labour for large-scale agriculture and for industry' (Castles & Miller, 1993: 53-55). Industrialization brought with it a vast movement of population from the countryside to the towns within each European country, but in addition it caused a considerable flow of international migration.

There was a great movement of population from Ireland to Britain during the nineteenth century, so that by 1851 Irish people formed 3 per cent of the population in England and Wales and 7 per cent in Scotland (Jackson, 1963). An estimated 120,000 Jews came to Britain as refugees from the pogroms in Russia between 1875 and 1914 (Castles & Miller, 1993: 55). The Irish were British subjects from the outset, and the Jews rapidly became British subjects, so both groups had full political rights, but both remained identifiable for many years, occupied inferior social and economic positions, and were subject to discrimination.

Foreign labour played a major role in German industrialization (Castles & Miller, 1993). In the late nineteenth century, there was a substantial movement of population from the East to the industrial Ruhr valley. By 1913, an estimated 164,000 of the 410,000 Ruhr miners were of Polish origin, although they had Prussian, and later German citizenship (Stirn, 1964: 27). There was further migration of 'foreign Poles' to do the agricultural jobs vacated by the 'German Poles'. By 1890, this was regulated so as to prevent the 'foreign Poles' from settling permanently, which meant that their wages could be kept low (Castles & Miller, 1993: 57). As well as the Poles in the East, there were large numbers of Italian workers in Southern Germany, and some Belgians and Dutch. In 1907, there were 950,000 foreign workers in the German Reich (Castles & Miller, 1993: 57): the total foreign population must have been higher than that, although 'the authorities did their best to prevent family reunion and permanent settlement'.

Migration has been particularly important in the creation of modern France, apparently because birth control became effective there much earlier than elsewhere in Europe. Birth rates fell sharply after 1860, and comparatively few people left the countryside to work in large-scale industry in the towns, so that industrialization could only proceed through the recruitment of workers from abroad (Castles & Miller, 1993: 58). According to Noiriel (1988: 308-18), the French labour market has been regularly fed by immigration from the 1860s onwards, and without immigration, the French population today would be 35 million instead of over 50 million.

Immigration into European countries was substantially reduced during the interwar period, but the major exception here was France, where the demographic deficit had been increased by the First World War. France set out to recruit labour from Poland, Italy, and Czechoslovakia, but most immigrants probably arrived spontaneously. Just under two million foreign workers entered France from 1920 to 1930, and by 1931, there were 2.7 million foreigners in France, making up 6.6 per cent of the total population (Castles & Miller, 1993: 61). During the depression of the 1930s, the immigration policy was reversed, and foreign workers were subject to discrimination and deportation.

More systematic information on immigration into European countries is available for the period since the Second World War. Peach (1993) has suggested that immigration into Europe and across European borders in the postwar period falls into three categories.

- First, people returning or expelled from former colonial territories or displaced because of the movement of national boundaries at the end of the war: there were about 16 million migrants in Europe within this group.
- Second, migration of workers and their dependants, either from one European country to another (for example, from Turkey to West Germany), or from former colonial territories to the European countries that had

colonized them (for example, from India and the West Indies to Britain. Peach (1993) has estimated that there were about 12 million migrants of this kind in Western Europe in 1990.

- Third, 'the new wave of asylum seekers, fleeing upheavals mainly in the former socialist countries, but also crises elsewhere in the world' (Peach, 1993: 1). According to the statistics compiled by SOPEMI (1992), these numbered about 2 million from 1980 to 1991.

In more detail, the patterns of postwar migrations are highly complex, and social scientists have only recently begun to develop theories to explain them (Kritz et al., 1992). The consequences of these extensive population movements are diverse, and hard to summarize. Some immigrants and their descendants have tended to form distinct ethnic groups that have maintained a separate identity for many years, whereas others have tended to be assimilated relatively quickly. To the extent that immigrants are not immediately assimilated, migration of course increases cultural diversity. All immigrants have tended to occupy a specific socio-economic niche, at least for a time, to do jobs that indigenous workers refuse, and to exist in disadvantaged and stressful social conditions. In a number of European countries, but most notably in West Germany, immigrants had limited political rights for a long period, and limited rights to social welfare. Hammar (1990) has proposed the term 'denizens' to describe the large group of foreign citizens in European countries who have gained permanent residence rights, but not the full political and social rights that go with citizenship. Groups of immigrant origin, especially those that are identifiable by their appearance, have been subject to substantial discrimination since the Second World War. This is well-documented in Britain (Smith, 1977; Brown & Gay, 1986) but is probably widespread also in France, Germany, and elsewhere in Europe. Nevertheless, vast numbers of former migrants and their descendants are no longer identifiable or noticeable as such within the populations of European countries. For example, the Irish ancestry of millions of British people is seldom noticed, and nor is the Italian ancestry of millions of French people. On the other hand, people of Caribbean and Indian origin are easily identifiable and often subject to racial discrimination in Britain, as are people of North African origin in France.

Counting migrants poses substantial conceptual problems, because the political rights and patterns of life of different migrant groups vary so widely. Those that become 'ethnic minorities' or 'racial minorities' may remain identifiable indefinitely, as is the case with many Jews. Those that assimilate may 'disappear' in less than a generation. The concept of an 'ethnic minority' refers to a tradition that the people concerned acknowledge, and that forms a part of their own definition of their identity. Social research in Britain, and in a few other European countries, has used that concept as a framework of analysis, but elsewhere in Europe – most notably in France – this approach is emphatically rejected, because the official ideology is one of assimilation. Consequently, it is not possible to count and compare the numbers belonging to ethnic minority groups within the populations of European countries. Official statistics in Britain use country of birth as the criterion for defining immigrants (as opposed to members of ethnic minority groups, many of whom were born in Britain). The advantage of such a definition is that country of birth at least remains stable during a person's lifetime. However, elsewhere in Europe statistics are compiled on the basis of nationality, so that effectively immigrants are equated with foreigners. The disadvantage with this approach is that people cease to be counted as immigrants once they acquire the nationality of their country of residence, so that immigrants may disappear from the statistics while remaining highly identifiable in real life.

For the purpose of comparing European countries, therefore, the only available information is the population of foreign nationality. Figure 6.10 shows the trends since the Second World War in the foreign population for eight European countries. The most striking feature is the growth of the foreign population in West Germany from less than half a million just after the war to over 5 million in 1990. In France, the foreign population after the Second World War was already substantial (just under 2 million), but it rose from 1955 to reach over 3.5 million by 1980. Immigration to Britain in the postwar period was also very substantial, although this is understated by the figure, because most of the migrants from former colonial territories had British nationality before they came. The 1991 census in Britain showed that about 6 per cent of the population belonged to ethnic minority groups; a large proportion of these originated from the Indian sub-continent, and a smaller proportion from the Caribbean and from Africa.

Figure 6.11 shows the foreign population in 1990 as a proportion of the total population for 12 European countries. This illustrates the wide variations even between neighbouring countries. For example, foreigners are a much higher proportion of the population in France than in neighbouring Italy, and much higher in Sweden than in neighbouring Finland. The extraordinarily high proportion of foreigners in Switzerland is particularly notable. This reflects a deliberate and controlled policy of recruiting foreign labour, without offering permanent residence in most cases.

Figure 6.10 Foreign population (millions)

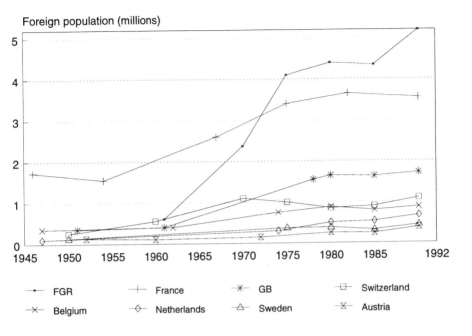

Foreign population (millions)

1945	1950	1955	1960	1965	1970	1975	1980	1985	1992

—•— FGR   —+— France   —*— GB   —⊟— Switzerland

—✕— Belgium   —◇— Netherlands   —△— Sweden   —✕— Austria

Source: Haskey (1992).

It is likely that patterns of migration will have some connection with trends in psychosocial disorder, for at least three reasons. First, rates of the disorders may vary between national and cultural groups, and such differences may persist among migrant populations. For example, as shown in Chapter 13, rates of suicide among migrants in the United States tend to reflect the rates in the countries of origin. Second, the process of migration and the disadvantaged position of migrants in the adopted country may increase the risk of psychosocial disorder among them. Third, migration may bring about changes in society at large, for example increased competition, an injection of energy and social resources, increased cultural diversity, and periods of turbulence.

Very little is known about the indirect effects of migration on society at large (the third category above). With regard to the direct effects on the migrants themselves (the first two categories) these are certainly important, but they cannot form any substantial part of the explanation of the substantial increases in psychosocial disorders that are discussed in later chapters. That is because the populations of recent migrant origin, although substantial, are nevertheless

David J. Smith

relatively small minorities of the total populations of European countries (with the exception of Switzerland). Hence, even where psychosocial disorders are more common among migrants than among others (and this does not apply by any means to all disorders or to all groups) this could only make a small contribution to the large increases in the disorders observed since the Second World War.

Figure 6.11   Foreign population (percentage)

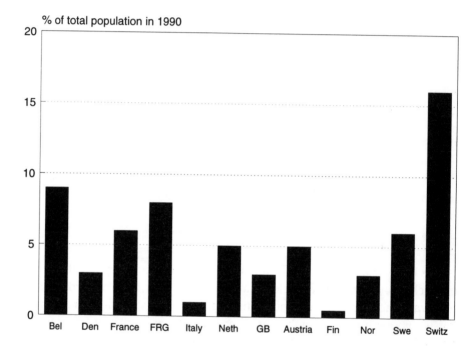

Source: Haskey (1992).

Whether migration has any relation at all to trends in psychosocial disorders is a question that remains to be investigated. The large differences in migration patterns between European countries give some scope for a natural experiment to test the theory that there is such a relationship.

ECONOMIC GROWTH

The total value of goods produced, captured by the internationally standardized concept of gross domestic product (GDP), provides a single summary measure of output, and a time series of GDP figures provides a measure of economic growth. A measure of this kind is, of course, at a high level of abstraction. It is only applicable at the national level (whereas regional differences within nations may be very important). The goods produced as part of GDP are extremely heterogeneous: they include public and private services as well as manufactured goods, so for example policing and the armed services are included, along with health, education, and hairdressing.[3] However, because there are broad similarities in the structure of all developed economies, it is useful to have a single summary figure, which turns out in practice to be strongly related to many aspects of social life: for example, as pointed out in the last section, at earlier stages of economic development there is a close relationship between growth in GDP and expectation of life.

Although there is not space here for a detailed description of the components of economic change, the treatment of GDP will be amplified by a discussion of changes in the structure of employment, in the share of the public sector in the total economy, and in public expenditure on social goods. More concrete changes in standard of living will be considered in the following main section.

Gross Domestic Product

GDP, the output of the whole economy, can be defined in any of three ways: it is the sum of value added in different sectors (for example, agriculture, industry, services); it is the sum of final expenditure (for example, by consumers, investors, and government); and it is the total of incomes from wages, rents, profits, and so on. In the postwar years, the statistical offices of most governments have estimated GDP according to a standardized system for which guidelines have been laid down jointly by the OECD and the United Nations. Fairly refined methods have been developed for expressing GDP at constant prices, and for converting the values from national currencies into

---

3. Illegitimate services, such as prostitution, and products, such as street heroin, are largely excluded from the official figures, however.

international dollars on the basis of purchasing power and not exchange rates.[4] For present purposes attention is focused on standard of living rather than the absolute size of an economy: hence it is appropriate to quote GDP in international dollars per head of the population.

This measure is shown in Figure 6.12 over the present century for three groups of countries: the advanced economies belonging to the OECD, selected Asian countries, and selected countries in Latin America. A logarithmic scale is used, so that a straight line indicates a steady rate of growth. For the OECD countries, the pattern is one of slow growth up to 1950, rapid growth from 1950 to 1973, then slower growth (though still faster than in the period up to 1950). By 1987, GDP per head of population was on average 5.6 times as high in OECD countries as it had been in 1900. At the beginning of the century, *per capita* GDP was 2.4 times as high in the OECD countries as in the Latin American sample, and 3.7 times as high as in the Asian sample. The pattern of growth in the Latin American countries was similar to that in the OECD countries, except that levels of growth after 1950 were lower: consequently, the gap between OECD and Latin American countries had widened from 2.4 times in 1900 to 3.4 times in 1987. The pattern of growth in the Asian countries was, however, markedly different. Growth up to 1929 was slower than in the OECD countries, and there was negative growth between 1929 and 1950. Between 1950 and 1973, growth in the Asian countries was at about the same rate as in the OECD countries, but after 1973 the growth rate in the Asian countries increased, whereas in the OECD countries it declined. The net result is that the Asian countries were further behind the OECD countries in 1987 than they had been in 1900, but since 1973 they had been narrowing the gap.[5]

These statistics are all taken from Angus Maddison's study of *The world economy in the 20th century* (1989). Maddison argues that there have been four phases of development in the present century. The first phase, the liberal world order to 1913, was the tail end of a long period of 'respectable and sustained growth' in the advanced OECD countries going back to 1820. The second phase, which Maddison calls 'conflict and autarky' lasted from 1913 to 1950 and encompassed three major 'system shocks': the two world wars, and the Great Depression of 1929-32. 'The unifying characteristics of this period were international disharmony, slow growth in GDP and trade and an

---

4. Exchange rates mainly reflect purchasing power over tradeable goods and services, and are subject to a good deal of fluctuation as a result of capital movements.

5. GDP *per capita* was 3.7 times as high in the OECD countries as in the Asian countries in 1900, and 5.2 times as high in 1987, but in between it had been 7.4 times as high in 1973.

absolute fall in foreign investment. There was a sharp decline in the status and influence of European countries and the emergence of the United States as an economic superpower.' The third phase was the 'golden age' of 1950-73, when a new liberal world order was established on a much sounder institutional and political basis than after the first world war. 'The golden age saw a growth of GDP and GDP *per capita* on an unprecedented scale in all parts of the world economy, a rapid growth of world trade, a reopening of world capital markets and possibilities for international migration.' The fourth phase, starting from 1973, was one of growth deceleration and accelerated inflation, except that the Asian countries have bucked the general trend.

Figure 6.12 GDP per capita: three groups of countries, 1900-1987

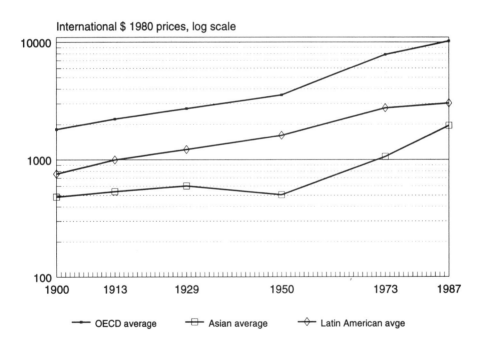

Note: Asia: Bangladesh, China, India, Indonesia, Pakistan, Philippines, S. Korea, Taiwan, Thailand
           Latin America: Argentina, Brazil, Chile,Colombia, Mexico, Peru.

Source: Maddison (1989).

Maddison was able to show that whether the OECD countries or developing countries are considered, these four phases can be clearly distinguished in the trends for four quantitative measures: GDP, GDP *per capita*, volume of exports, and inflation. Figure 6.13 shows changes in GDP *per capita* for selected European countries, Japan, and the USA. In 1987, the four major European countries (top panel) had reached a similar level of GDP *per capita* by rather different routes. In 1900, GDP *per capita* was substantially higher in the UK than in France, West Germany, or Italy, but growth during the 'golden age' was substantially faster in France, Germany and Italy than in the UK, so that by 1973 the four countries had reached a similar standard of living. Between 1900 and 1987, GDP *per capita* in Italy increased by 6.7 times, and the rates of growth in France and Germany were similar; over the same period, however, GDP *per capita* increased in the UK by only 3.3 times.

GDP *per capita* in the USA was already higher than in any European country by 1900, and the US economy has shown sustained growth throughout the century, with comparatively small changes between the four phases (bottom panel of Figure 6.13). Japan, by contrast, is at the opposite extreme. It started the century at a far lower level of GDP *per capita* than the USA or the major European countries, showed better growth than most other countries up to 1929, then an actual decline in GDP *per capita* between 1929 and 1950; this was followed by a dramatic reversal during the 'golden era' 1950-73, when Japan produced a far higher rate of growth than any other economy; although the rate of growth was sharply reduced from 1973 onwards, it was still higher than for the USA or most European countries.

Two of the smaller prosperous countries of Europe, Sweden and Switzerland, showed a pattern of growth over the century similar to that of the USA, though Sweden tended to catch up with Switzerland, and Switzerland with the USA. The Netherlands, by contrast, showed a far more uneven pattern of development, with a more severe setback in the years following the Great Depression.

Figure 6.14 presents essentially the same results in the form of annual average compound growth rates. This illustrates more clearly the wide differences between growth rates in each of the four phases, and between the rates for different nations in the same phase. Particularly noteworthy are the relatively even growth rates achieved by the USA over the four phases, the extremely uneven growth rates over the four phases in Japan, and the high growth rates, especially in the golden era, in Japan, Germany, Italy and France.

Figure 6.13   GDP per capita: selected countries, 1900-1987

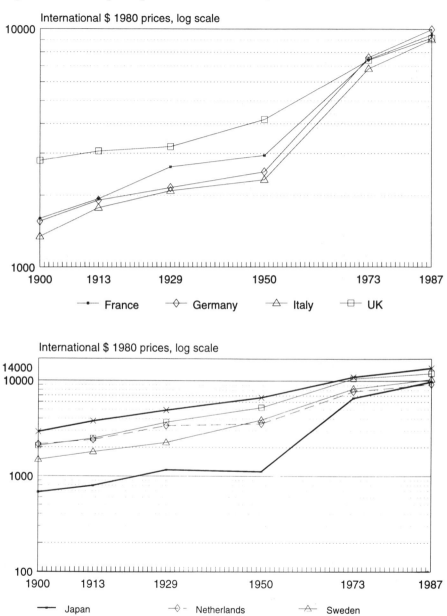

Source: Maddison (1989).

Figure 6.14   Per capita real GDP growth: selected countries, 1900-1987

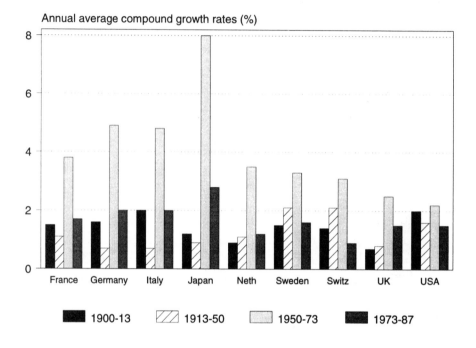

Source: Maddison (1989).

Structure of Employment

Before the industrial revolution, most employment was in agriculture. A major structural change associated with economic growth is a decline in the proportion employed in the agricultural sector, and an increase in the proportion employed in the industrial sector and, later, in the service sector. Figure 6.15 illustrates this trend of development for the OECD countries from 1870 onwards. By 1870, the process of industrialization was already well under way in many of these countries, so the earlier stages of the transformation fall outside the period. At the beginning of the period, agriculture accounted for about half of employment, while industry and services each accounted for about a quarter. By 1987, agriculture accounted for 6 per cent of employment, services for 64 per cent, and industry for 30 per cent. The main feature, therefore, is the growth of employment in the services sector, and the decline of employment in agriculture. Employment in industry, which had been increasing up to 1870, continued to increase up to 1950, but then declined again, so that it accounted for a similar proportion of all employment in 1987 as just over 100 years before.

Figure 6.15 Structure of employment: OECD countries, 1870-1987

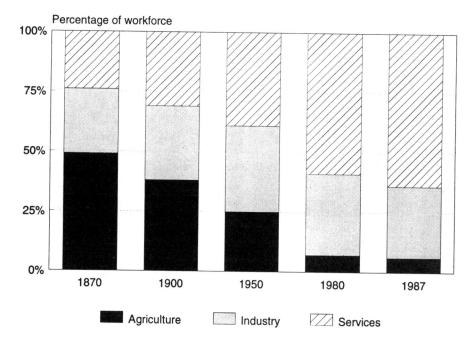

Source: Maddison (1989).

This broad change in the structure of employment, and particularly the decline of employment in agriculture, signals fundamental social change, including migration from villages to towns and cities. The timing of these changes varied considerably between the OECD countries. Figure 6.16 (top panel) shows that as late as 1950 there was wide variation between countries in the proportion working in agriculture from 5 per cent in the UK, which pioneered the industrial revolution, to 48 per cent in Japan, which became a great industrial nation only during the golden era 1950-73. Besides Japan, the other countries still having a substantial proportion of employment in agriculture in 1950 were Italy and Austria, while other countries besides the UK which already had only a small proportion in agriculture were Belgium, the USA, and the Netherlands. By 1980, (bottom panel of Figure 6.16) the

Figure 6.16   Structure of employment: selected countries

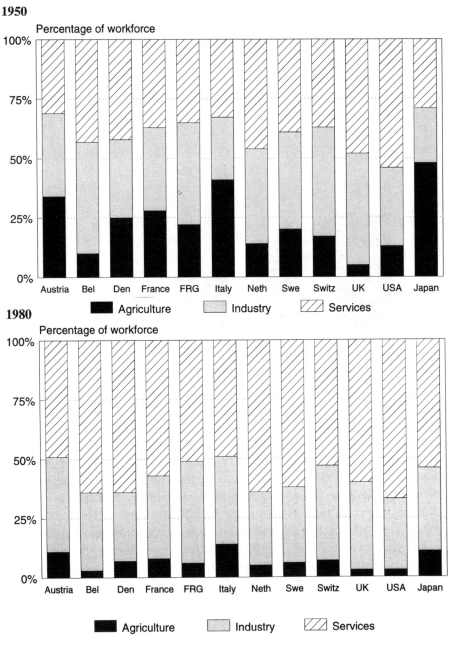

1950

Percentage of workforce

1980

Percentage of workforce

Source: Maddison (1989).

Figure 6.17 Structure of employment: selected countries, 1950 and 1980

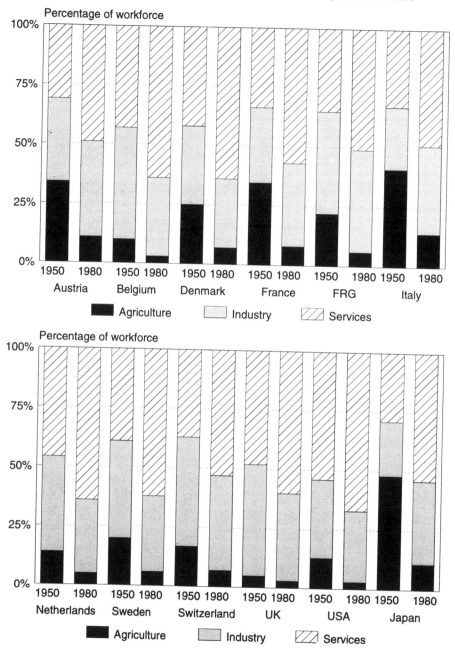

Source: Maddison (1989).

David J. Smith

proportion employed in agriculture was low in all of the OECD countries: the highest figure was 14 per cent for Italy. The proportion working in industry was by 1980 fairly similar for all of the countries shown, but there was considerable variation in the proportion working in the service sector: from 67 per cent in the USA at one extreme to 49 per cent in Austria and Italy at the other.

Figure 6.17 presents the same data in a different way, so as to highlight the change in the structure of employment within each country over the 30 years from 1950. The largest changes over this period were in Japan, Italy, France and Austria. The structure of employment was most stable in the UK and the USA, which had industrialized earliest.

One of two approaches might be taken in attempting to relate this fundamental aspect of economic structure to social problems. The first approach would be to make comparisons between countries according to the proportion in agriculture, services, and industry at any given time. For example, it would be useful to consider whether there were differences between social problems in Japan and the UK in 1950 that might be associated with the large difference between the two countries in the proportion working in agriculture at that time. The second approach would be to compare countries in terms of the rate of change over a given period in the structure of employment. For example, it would be useful to consider whether *over the period from 1950 to 1980* there were differences between social problems in Japan and the UK that might be associated with the much higher rate of change in Japan in the structure and nature of employment.

Public Expenditure

Over the present century there has been a very substantial rise in government expenditure as a proportion of GDP in the developed countries. Figure 6.18a shows the government share of expenditure from 1913 to 1986 for six countries: France, Germany, Japan, the Netherlands, the UK and the USA. Taking the average for these six countries, government expenditure rose from 12 per cent of GDP in 1913 to 46 per cent in 1986. Over the same period, GDP rose on average more than fivefold in these six countries, so government expenditure in 1986 was about 21 times as high in real terms as it had been in 1913. In Germany and Japan, and to a lesser extent in France and the Netherlands, there was a marked rise in government expenditure in the 1930s associated with preparations for war. This bump in the 1930s is superimposed on a generally sustained rise in government expenditure as a proportion of GDP throughout the century.

There are, however, important differences between the six countries on this measure, and the differences tended to become greater during the course of the century. They first of all diverged during the war preparations of the 1930s, then came closer together after the Second World War, and drew further apart from the 1950s onwards. After the period of militarism in the 1930s, government expenditure was proportionately lower in Japan than in the other countries. In the USA government expenditure as a proportion of the total remained throughout the century consistently lower than in other countries except Japan. In the Netherlands, government expenditure started low in 1913, but from the beginning of the golden age it grew very quickly, and from 1958 onwards remained consistently higher than in the other five countries. There was also a notably rapid growth in government expenditure in France in the fourth phase of development, from 1973 onwards.

Figure 6.18a Government share of GDP: total government expenditure as percentage of GDP

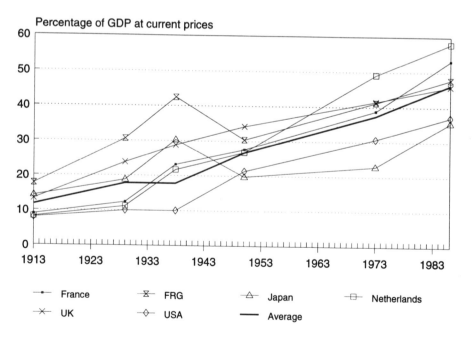

Source: Maddison (1989).

Social Expenditure

According to Maddison, 'after the early postwar nationalisations, there was no rise in the share of employment in public enterprise, and all the Western countries remained basically capitalist'. The rise in government expenditure 'was due largely to increases in social security and spending on merit wants such as education and health' (1989: 69). The increase in social expenditure is certainly striking. Figure 6.18b shows total public expenditure on social objects as a proportion of GDP for eight European countries in the postwar period. Social expenditure's share of GDP increased in the 30 years from 1950 by at least two-thirds in all eight countries, and for several a threefold increase was recorded. There were wide differences between countries on this measure at the beginning of the period, and by the end of the period these differences had increased still further. Thus, in 1980 social expenditure was 20 per cent of GDP in Switzerland, at one extreme, compared with 40 per cent in the Netherlands, at the other. The largest rises in social expenditure as a share of GDP took place in the ten years starting in 1966.

Figure 6.18b Social expenditure as share of GDP

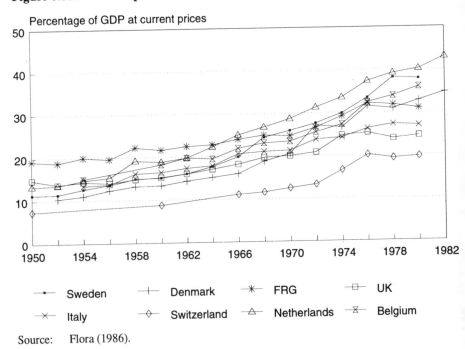

Source: Flora (1986).

229

Figure 6.18c Social expenditure at constant prices

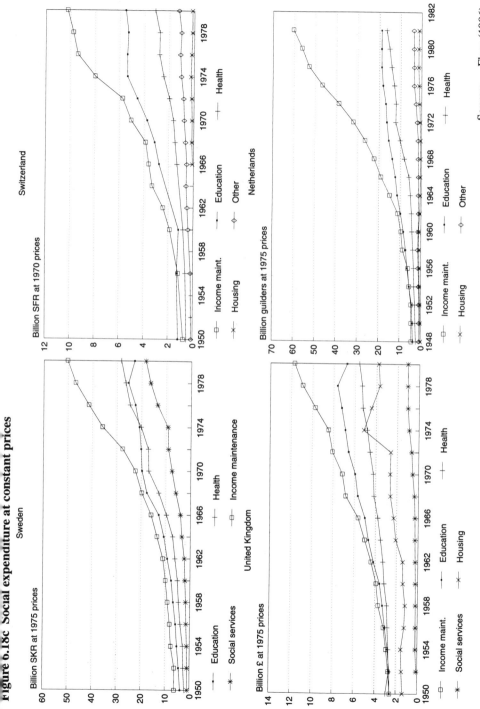

Source: Flora (1986).

Of course, GDP itself was also rising rapidly over this period. Consequently there were very large rises in social expenditure in absolute terms (after allowing for inflation). These changes are illustrated for four European countries in Figure 6.18c, which shows four or five main categories of social expenditure separately.[6] In all four countries, much the largest increase was in income maintenance, which by 1980 also accounted for much the largest share of total social expenditure. There were also substantial increases in education and health expenditure in all four countries over the period, although there are many detailed differences between the countries in the patterns of increase. Social services and housing represented generally smaller expenditures, although the pattern of expenditure on housing in the United Kingdom was unusual, in being relatively high, and rising rapidly then falling again during the 1970s.

STANDARD OF LIVING

Consumer Durables

A more concrete indication of the progress of economic growth is provided by statistics on ownership of specific goods such as cars, telephones, and television or radio sets. Figure 6.19 shows the number of passenger cars per 1,000 inhabitants for a selection of seven European countries, together with Japan and the USA, from 1956 onwards. The most striking feature is that high levels of car ownership began much earlier in the USA than elsewhere. In 1956, there were over 300 cars per 1,000 inhabitants in the USA, compared with about 100 in Sweden, the country having the highest car ownership outside of the USA at that time. Also, the level of car ownership by 1989 reached a considerably higher level in the USA than in any European country.

Japan rapidly accelerated towards its present position as a world economic power from the 1950s onwards, so it is not surprising that levels of car ownership were low in Japan in the 1950s and 1960s. However, even in 1989, car ownership in Japan continues to be lower than in the major European economies, and less than half of the level in the USA. This shows that car ownership is not just a function of overall economic development. One other important factor is geographical scale: the large distances in the USA partly

---

6. Expenditures are expressed in the national currencies, so comparisons of absolute expenditures cannot be made between the four countries, although the pattern of increase can be compared.

explain high car ownership there, whereas the high density of population in the habitable parts of Japan means that distances are short and the roads crowded. A second factor is the state's transport policy, which in Japan has strongly supported a high quality public transport infrastructure, whereas in the USA it has allowed privately owned railways to wither away.

Figure 6.19   Cars: selected countries, 1956-1989

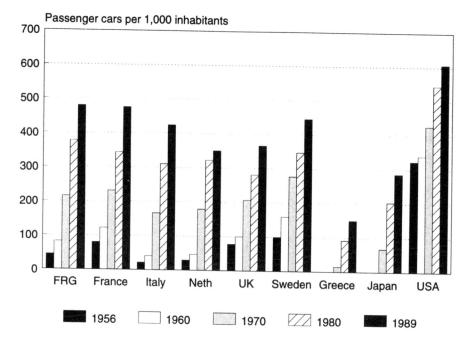

Source: Eurostat, *Basic statistics of the community.*

Differences between the four major European economies in the timing of growth in car ownership and the eventual levels reached are not striking. On the other hand, the pattern in a late-developing European economy such as Greece is entirely different: in fact, the level of car ownership reached in Greece by 1989 is similar to the level reached by 1960 in Sweden. This illustrates the completely different way of life in European countries where economic development is at a relatively early stage.

Figure 6.20   Telephones: selected countries, 1956-1989

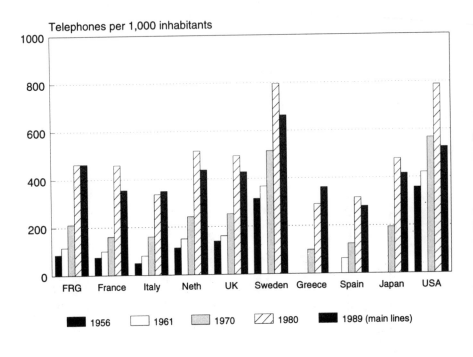

Source: Eurostat, *Basic statistics of the community.*

Telephone ownership shows a broadly similar pattern to car ownership in terms of change over time (see Figure 6.20).[7] In most European countries, the growth in telephone ownership began in the 1950s, but the most rapid growth was in the 1970s. This growth started considerably earlier in the USA, and also in Sweden, than elsewhere. Levels of telephone ownership in Japan are similar to those in the most highly developed European economies. Growth of telephone ownership in a late-developing European country such as Greece

---

7. Unfortunately, there is a break after 1980 in the series of statistics shown in Figure 6.20. Up to then they show the number of *telephones*, whereas after 1980 they show the number of *main lines* (a considerably smaller figure). Figure 6.21 shows a different (and more useful) statistic, the proportion of households with a telephone; but this is only available for 1980 and 1985.

was much later than in the major European economies, but has progressed more quickly than car ownership. By 1985, the proportion of households with a telephone (Figure 6.21) had reached around 90 per cent for several European countries (the Netherlands, France, Denmark, Germany).

Figure 6.21   Households with a telephone: EC countries in 1980 and 1985

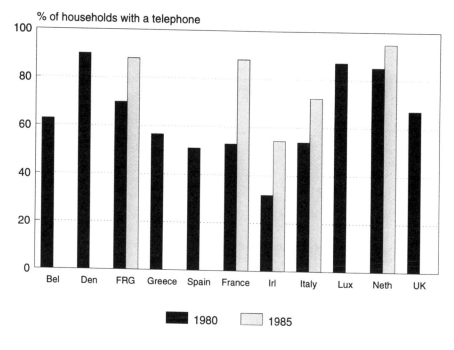

Source: Eurostat (1991).

Housing

Housing conditions are an important dimension of standard of living, in which there have been dramatic changes over the postwar period (see Figure 6.22). Around 1950 there were substantial differences in housing conditions between the USA and the UK, on the one hand, and the great majority of European countries on the other. The proportion of dwellings having a bathroom was 71 per cent in the USA and 62 per cent in the UK; otherwise, the highest figure in mainland Europe was for West Germany (32 per cent). Sweden (28 per cent) and the Netherlands (27 per cent) had reached a stage of development similar to West Germany in this respect, but other European countries were far

Figure 6.22

Bathrooms: various countries, 1950-1981

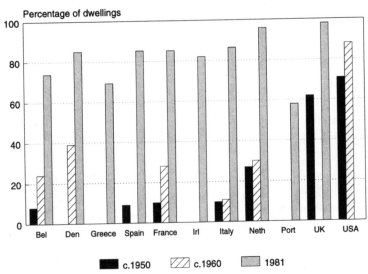

Source: Eurostat, *Basic statistics of the community.* Eurostat (1991).

Density of occupation in principal residences

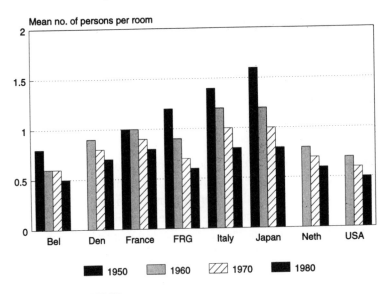

Source: OECD (1986b).

behind, for example France and Italy (both 10 per cent). Some improvement had already occurred by around 1960, but the major transformation of housing amenities in the advanced European countries happened in the 20 years from 1960. By 1981, the great majority of dwellings had a bath or shower in the more advanced European countries, while even in later developing countries the proportion was well over half (Portugal 58 per cent, Greece 69 per cent). One feature of this pattern is that in the second wave of European development, as exemplified by Greece and Portugal, housing conditions are being given priority over car ownership: by contrast, in the first wave of development, car ownership began to rise sharply in France, for example, at a time when few flats or houses had a bathroom.

There was also a substantial reduction in the number of persons per room in the 30 years from 1950 (bottom panel of Figure 6.22). These changes had the effect of making the developed countries more alike in terms of density of occupation in 1980 than they had been in 1950. While the figure shows the average number of persons per room, there were also substantial reductions in the proportion of families living at very high densities: for example, in Japan the proportion of families living at a density of more than 1.5 persons per room declined from 27 per cent to 9 per cent in the ten years from 1968 (OECD, 1986b).

Health

The large postwar increases in public expenditure on health services are illustrated in Figure 6.18c. While health expenditure increased in the 1950s, in most European countries these increases became steeper from the early 1960s onwards.

Some crude indication of the development of medical services is given by statistics on the number of doctors and hospital beds (Figure 6.23). In most European countries, there was a modest rise in the number of doctors (in relation to the population) in the 10 years from 1960, followed by enormous increases in the 15 years from 1970. The most common pattern was a more than twofold increase between 1960 and 1985. By contrast, increases in the UK were far more gradual. Statistics currently available for the USA and Japan are incomplete, but they also indicate a far more gradual increase than in most European countries. The most recent statistics (for 1985) show very considerable variations between European countries in the number of doctors per 1,000 population from 4.2 in Italy, at one extreme, to 1.5 in the UK, at the other. While the low figure for the UK reflects a unique, and probably efficient,

Figure 6.23

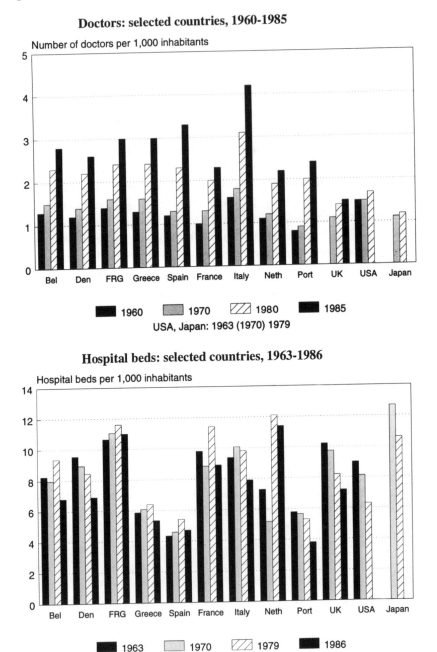

Doctors: selected countries, 1960-1985

Number of doctors per 1,000 inhabitants

■ 1960　▨ 1970　▨ 1980　■ 1985
USA, Japan: 1963 (1970) 1979

Hospital beds: selected countries, 1963-1986

Hospital beds per 1,000 inhabitants

■ 1963　▨ 1970　▨ 1979　■ 1986

Source:　Eurostat, *Basic statistics of the community.* Eurostat (1991).

method of health service organization, these differences do correspond to variations in consumption of health services in some sense.

Trends over time in the number of hospital beds are entirely different. The most common pattern is of a decline from 1963 to 1986, but with some increase in the intervening years. However, in some countries (Denmark, Portugal, the UK, and probably the USA and Japan) the number of hospital beds per head of the population has declined steadily over this period. The one major exception is the Netherlands, where the number of hospital beds increased sharply between 1973 and 1980, but then declined slightly. The overall decline in most countries probably reflects major changes of policy in the care of the long-term sick and mentally ill, with an increasing preference for 'care in the community' rather than in hospital; and perhaps also increasing efficiency in the use of hospital beds in general and acute wards, together with a reduction in the time spent in hospital by patients undergoing various procedures. For reasons such as these, the number of hospital beds is probably a poor indicator of consumption of health services.

However, expenditure on health care, and the volume of available health care resources, is not closely related to the population's level of health, especially in developed countries (Canadian Institute for Advanced Research, 1992). Japan again provides a particularly striking example. As mentioned in an earlier section, life expectancy is high in Japan and has increased rapidly in recent years, yet expenditure on health care in Japan is lower than for many other developed countries, whether it is expressed as a proportion of GDP or converted to international dollars at purchasing power parities (Marmot & Davey Smith, 1989). Indeed, it can be argued that in developed countries further increases in expenditure on health care are likely to reduce the potential for increasing the health of the population. Much health care fails to address the *causes* of morbidity, so that growing health care budgets divert expenditure from broader policies that may have preventive potential. Yet more strongly, it can be argued that many kinds of health care, including some expensive treatments using high technology, are harmful or inappropriate (Canadian Institute for Advanced Research, 1992).

Historical studies have for long shown that at earlier stages of economic development, improvements in health and life expectancy were brought about mainly by environmental change, public health measures and changes in life styles rather than by improvements in medical treatment. There are some striking differences in health and life expectancy between developing countries today. Costa Rica, Sri Lanka and Kerala (India) have much lower levels of infant mortality than Pakistan, Afghanistan or Morocco, although all of these countries have similar levels of income *per capita*. The decisive factor may be the extent to which women have control over their lives; there is evidence that in the countries with lower infant mortality, education and support services are stronger, and have succeeded in giving women and children more autonomy.

There are large social class differences in health as well as life expectancy in all nations that have been studied (Canadian Institute for Advanced Research, 1992). These differences of course persist in developed countries long after the main barriers to access to health care have been removed, so standard of health care is certainly not the main causal factor. There is evidence, as mentioned in an earlier section, that reducing the social class differences themselves (for example by moving towards a more equal income distribution) may reduce the class differences in health. For example, in Sweden, where income differences between social classes are smaller than in most other developed countries, the gradient in mortality rates between social classes is also less steep. The change towards a more equal income distribution has taken place in Sweden over a period of around 50 years. It is particularly telling that among older cohorts the gradient in mortality between social classes remains steep, showing a long-lasting effect of the historical income distribution (Canadian Institute for Advanced Research, 1992).

There are large differences in health not only between the top and bottom social classes, but also between classes close to the top of the scale (Marmot & Theorell, 1988; Marmot et al., 1987). These differences are stable and present in widely different societies with different disease patterns, hence they are not connected with any specific disease, but arise from much more general causes. US data show that these social class differences are found among adolescents as well as among the general population (Klerman, 1993). The broadest explanation that has been put forward is that health differences arise from differences in autonomy between social classes, both at work and in other social contexts. That is probably the best way of explaining differences in health between different grades of affluent British civil servants. American research has found that a perception of control over one's life is strongest among adolescents in the highest socio-economic quartile (Klerman, 1993), but the specific relationship between autonomy and health has not been tested among young people.

Other factors that have been shown to be related to health are working conditions, unemployment, physical environment, and early childhood development. The long-term secular change in health and life expectancy is probably related to changes in all of these conditions.

Education

In the advanced economies, there has been a steady increase throughout the century in the level of education of the population as a whole. The statistic chosen to illustrate this trend in Figure 6.24 is the number of years of education per person aged 15 or over, expressed in equivalent years of primary education, where each year of secondary education counts for 1.4 years of primary education, and each year of higher education counts for 2 years.[8] For four out of the five major economies illustrated (France, Germany, the UK and the USA), this statistic stood at 7 or 8 in 1913, while it was considerably lower (around 5) for Japan. By 1983, it had risen to 12 or 13 for four of these countries, but to a considerably higher level (16) for the USA. In round numbers, therefore, years of education nearly doubled in the major economies between 1913 and 1983.

Figure 6.25 gives a rather more detailed picture of change between 1950 and 1980 by showing separately the average years of secondary and higher education. Years of higher education grew substantially over this period in all five countries, although the rise was smaller in the UK than elsewhere. In absolute terms, the number of years of higher education was substantially higher in the USA than in the other countries both in 1950 and in 1980. By 1980, the number of years of secondary education was much the same in all five countries, but there had been substantial differences in 1950. There was particularly rapid growth in secondary education in Japan, from a low base in 1950. In Germany, there was little growth from a high 1950 figure.

This historic increase in level of education is clearly closely allied to economic development. Very broadly, there are two types of theory. On the one hand there is the idea that education enhances the skills needed in production, and therefore directly influences economic activity and social welfare. This idea has been developed as 'human capital theory' by Becker (1964) and others. On the other hand, there is the idea that education has an allocative function: it is used as a criterion to decide which individuals should do which jobs, but not necessarily because the education itself enhances their productivity. Econometric studies seem to support the view that educational attainment is a variable influencing economic performance, but the results of such studies are open to more than one interpretation (OECD, 1989: 47-93).

---

8. These weights were chosen by Maddison (1989) on the basis of an economic analysis of the increment in earning power attributable to years of education at the three levels.

There is no need to choose between the human capital theory and the allocative theory of education. A reasonable view is that educational attainment both increases the potential for economic growth and determines the distribution of well-being from growth.

Figure 6.24   Years of education: per person aged 15 and over, in equivalent years of primary education

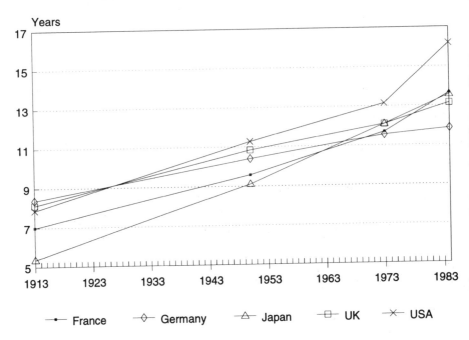

Equivalent in primary years: secondary, 1.4; higher, 2.

Source: Maddison (1989).

Economic growth and the growth of education are, of course, associated with fundamental changes in the structure of employment: with the decline of agriculture, the growth of services, and the expansion of higher occupations (managerial, administrative, technical, scientific, and professional). In line with that analysis, levels of education in all countries are higher among those in the expanding higher occupations than among others, and lowest among those working in agriculture (OECD, 1986b).

Figure 6.25 Years of secondary and higher education: persons aged 15-64 in 1950 and 1980

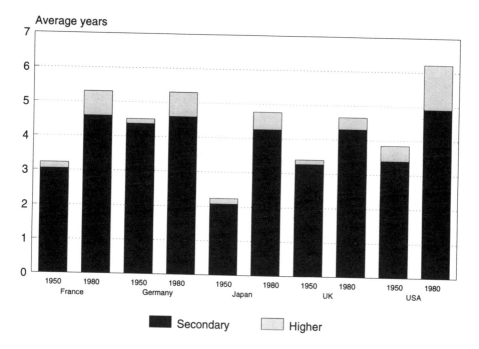

Source: Maddison (1989).

The increase during the present century in the average number of years spent in education has brought about a transformation in the phasing of adolescent development. As argued in a later chapter, the transition to adult status has been pushed to a later and later age; also, it can be argued that because of the increasing length of education, transitions to adult status in different domains such as work, family, and leisure have tended to occur at increasingly different times, so that the whole transition process has become less coherent. Even over a short period of 11 years starting in 1975, changes in the proportion of young people enrolled in educational establishments were radical (see Figure 6.26). In the Netherlands, for example, the enrolment rate among 19-year-olds rose from 31 per cent in 1975 to 53 per cent in 1986, while among 21-year-olds the rate increased from 14 per cent to 32 per cent. The effect of these changes is that at the age of 19 about half of the population are involved in education in the advanced European countries, and between 20 and 30 per cent at the age of 21. Although detailed historical statistics are not available, only a tiny

David J. Smith

Figure 6.26 Enrolment rates

At age 17

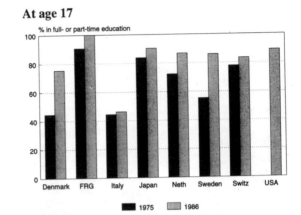

At age 19

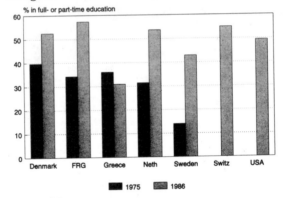

At age 21

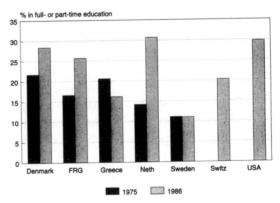

Source: OECD (1990).

fraction of the population within these age groups was still in education before the Second World War.

Leisure

In all European countries, and in the USA, there has been a substantial reduction in the number of hours worked during the present century (see Figure 6.27). In Japan, working hours have declined considerably less, and remain at a distinctly higher level than in Europe or the USA. Taking France as an example, the hours worked per working person in a year have declined from about 2,700 in 1900 to about 1,500 in 1986. In Japan, by contrast, working hours have declined from about the same figure at the turn of the century as in France (2,700) to around 2,200 in 1986. The timing and extent of this reduction in working hours is very similar for all countries shown except Japan.

Figure 6.27   Hours worked: selected countries, 1900-1986

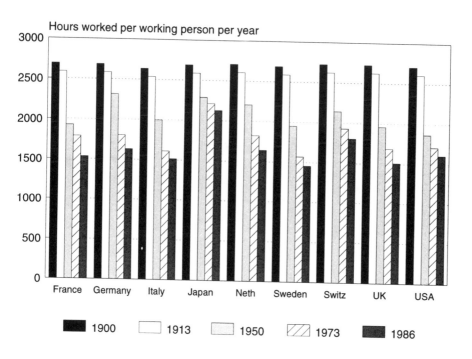

Source: Maddison (1989).

David J. Smith

This substantial increase in leisure has made time available for a whole range of activities, including the mass media and reading. It has not, unfortunately, been possible to find a long run of data on cinema attendance, but it is clear that in Europe and the USA the cinema reached its peak in the 1930s when working hours were rapidly declining. The data available, which start in 1965 (see Figure 6.28) show a steady decline in cinema attendance in developed countries up to 1987, accompanied by a steady increase in developing countries. Over the same period, the number of radio and television receivers was steadily increasing both in the developed and developing countries, although the penetration of radio and television had, of course, reached far higher levels in the developed than in the developing countries (see Figure 6.29). By 1988, in developed countries there was one radio receiver to each inhabitant, and one television set to every two inhabitants.

Figure 6.28   Cinema attendance, 1965-1987

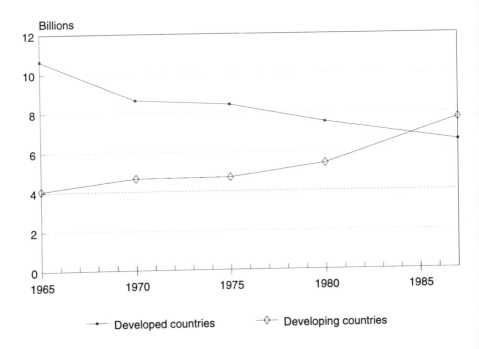

Source: UNESCO, *Statistical Yearbook.*

Figure 6.29   Radio and TV receivers: developed and developing countries, 1965-1988

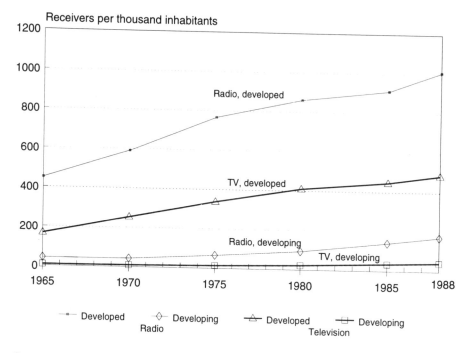

Source: UNESCO, *Statistical Yearbook*.

More detailed statistics (Figure 6.30) show that the timing of the introduction of television varied considerably between developed countries.[9] In the USA and the UK, a significant minority of the population had television sets by 1953, whereas most European countries reached a similar stage around 1960. Over a ten-year period starting in 1955, the major European economies reached the point where about half of the population had access to television, and after another ten years nearly all had access to it.

---

9. In interpreting Figure 6.30 it is important to note that the figures given for the USA refer to individual receivers, while those given for the other countries refer to licences, where there is normally one licence for a household regardless of the number of individual receivers. In Japan in 1985 there were 580 receivers per 1,000 population, compared with 261 licences, which implies a roughly 2:1 ratio. The US histograms have been scaled accordingly in the Figure.

Figure 6.30   TV licences or receivers: selected countries, 1953-1988, per thousand inhabitants

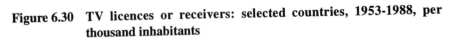

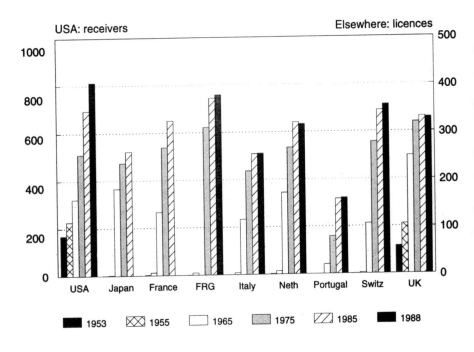

Source: UNESCO, *Statistical Yearbook.*

During the period of growth in the mass media, there has also been rapid growth in the number of book titles published (see Figure 6.31). In the developed countries, this growth levelled off after 1980, while in developing countries it continued in absolute terms, but levelled off in relation to population.

Information on the use of leisure time is available for a number of developed countries in the late 1970s or early 1980s, although little or no information is yet available about change over time. These data derive from time budget surveys which differ for example in the categories of activity used, but the OECD (1986b) has compiled comparative tables from the available results, which at least permit rough comparisons between countries. The OECD define free time as what is left over after deducting the time allotted to essential needs (sleep, meals and personal hygiene), household and family activities, and work or study. Among the countries surveyed, free time accounted for between 22 and 29 per cent of the 168 hours of the week for the population as a whole.

Men had more free time than women, whether those with or without paid employment were considered.

Figure 6.31 Number of book titles published: developed and developing countries, 1955-1988

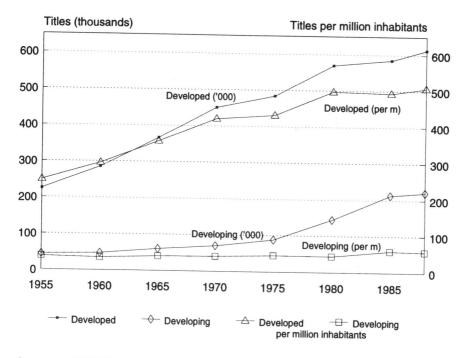

Source: UNESCO, *Statistical Yearbook.*

The six main leisure time activities shown in Figure 6.32 take up about 80 per cent of free time between them. In order of importance they are watching television, social contacts, reading, recreation (physical and sports activities), organized meetings, and cultural activities. As shown by the figure, there appear to be substantial differences between countries in the use of free time. Particularly notable is the large amount of time spent watching television in Japan, and to a lesser extent in the USA. Japan has an exceptionally low incidence of social problems (such as crime) that are sometimes linked with media influences, but an exceptionally high level of television watching.

In most countries, young people spend less time watching television than older people, but more time in social contacts, recreation, and cultural activities. Time spent on reading tends to increase with age, particularly among those aged 65 or more.

Figure 6.32   Free time activities: late 1970s

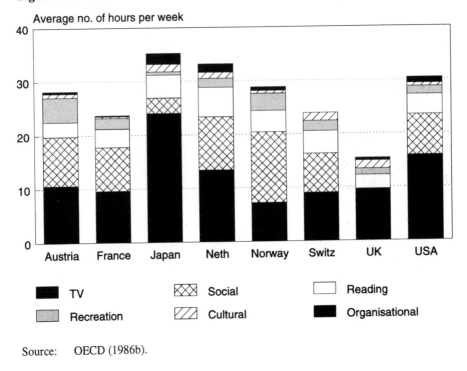

Source: OECD (1986b).

INEQUALITY

So far this chapter has documented the massive changes that have occurred during the present century in conditions of life for the population as a whole in the advanced industrial countries. Sustained economic growth has brought about large increases in the average standard of living, and fundamental changes in the structure of the economy and the pattern of leisure time pursuits. The analysis has not yet considered whether these changes have affected all sections of the population equally, and in particular whether the increased output of the economy has come to be distributed more or less evenly among the more and less powerful groups within the population.

Of course, it is clear, particularly from statistics on concrete elements of life-style such as ownership of television sets or proportion of dwellings with a bathroom, that economic growth has profoundly affected all or nearly all of the population: for example, it has changed the number of years they can expect to live, the kinds of jobs they do, the kind of accommodation they live in, the way they travel about, how they do their shopping, the kind of medical attention available to them, and the way they obtain information and entertainment.

On the other hand, it is equally clear that substantial inequalities remain in Western societies, for example according to whether or not a person (or someone in the family) has a job, and according to the level of individual (or family) income. Most sociological analysis would suggest that differences in status and power between specific groups, relative privilege, and relative deprivation, have a more fundamental influence on behaviour than conditions of life in absolute terms (see, for example, Runciman, 1966). As we have seen, this view is supported by analysis of variations in health and life expectancy according to income and social class. In any case, the very concepts of standard of living and poverty, when applied to individuals or groups, are incapable of definition except in relation to some prevailing norm.

In seeking to understand changes in youth problems, therefore, it is important to consider trends in inequality in Western societies during the present century of unprecedented economic growth. Two aspects of inequality will be considered here: unemployment, and poverty, or more broadly, income distribution.

Unemployment

For several reasons, unemployment is perhaps the single clearest cause or example of inequality in advanced societies. First, employment, unlike income, is not distributed across individuals in infinitely varying quantities: instead, each individual is either in work or out of work. At most periods, the great majority of those who are seeking work are in work, so that the unemployed form a minority who are totally excluded, for a short or long period, from all of the benefits provided by employment. Second, in advanced societies, paid employment is central to most social transactions: it provides income, activity, social role, social relationships outside the family, and a focus for personal identity. A huge body of evidence from research over the postwar period shows that deprivation of employment over a long period causes miseries and problems of many kinds for individuals and their families.[10] Against that background, it will be important to examine the evidence on links

---

10. For a summary of this evidence, see White (1991).

between unemployment and specific youth problems. This section aims to provide a general description of transnational differences and secular change in unemployment during the present century, with some discussion of the causes of these differences and changes. Links between unemployment and specific youth problems will be considered in later chapters.

Definition of Unemployment

During the postwar period, the International Labour Office (ILO) has developed an internationally agreed definition of unemployment, which has led to increasing standardisation of statistics available from national sources. In very broad terms, the unemployed are those who are available for work, and seeking work, but who are not currently employed for a wide variety of reasons (dismissal, suspension, temporary or indefinite lay-off, change of status, e.g. previously employer, retired, or in full-time education). In order to arrive at an unemployment rate, the number of unemployed people is expressed as a percentage of the economically active population. Even after the ILO's attempts to standardize the definition, there remain detailed differences in definitions that give rise to the need for some caution in making transnational comparisons of absolute unemployment rates. Comparisons of changes in unemployment rates between countries are likely to be more robust.

The Interwar Period

For the period before the Second World War, the problems of arriving at comparable statistics are far greater. Eichengreen and Hatton (1988) gave the following account of the development of the concept of unemployment.

> Though the existence of worklessness had been recognised for centuries, it was not until the 1890s that the term unemployment gained widespread currency.... [in Britain]. This 'discovery' of unemployment can be traced to a combination of factors. First, the growing complexity of the labour market and of its industrial relations drew attention to employment conditions. Second, social surveys linked poverty and moral degradation to low-wage labour and intermittent employment. Third, the depression of the 1890s created growing awareness of the cyclical character of employment opportunities and led ultimately to the recognition that unemployment was an economic phenomenon or 'problem of industry' rather than one of individual inadequacy (3-4).

Widespread recognition of the problem of unemployment emerged at the same time in the United States as in Britain, but rather later in France. By the end of the second decade of the present century, unemployment as an aggregate, along with others like inflation and the trade cycle, was firmly established. As Eichengreen and Hatton (1988: 5) put it, 'The alarming rise in the number of unemployed that occurred in the wake of the First World War in nearly every country reinforced this awareness.' Nevertheless, aggregate unemployment statistics available for the interwar period provide a highly imperfect measure of the phenomenon. The main sources of information are trade union reports and statistics collected in the operation of public and private unemployment insurance schemes. The available statistics mostly relate to unemployment in industry, and provide little information about unemployment in agriculture or services. However, Galenson and Zellner (1957) have constructed a series of estimates of industrial unemployment rates in the interwar years for ten countries, and Lebergott (1964) has made similar estimates for the United States. Galenson and Zellner's estimates incorporate adjustments to improve comparability between countries. Maddison (1964) arrived at estimates of economy-wide unemployment rates by adjusting ILO statistics on the registered unemployed to a labour force basis.

Figure 6.33 compares the industrial unemployment rates from Galenson and Zellner with the economy-wide rates estimated by Maddison, taking in each case an average for the years 1921-29 and 1930-38. The differences between the two sets of estimates are dramatic. For Denmark, Germany, the Netherlands and Sweden, Maddison's economy-wide estimates are less than half of the estimates of industrial unemployment rates, and for the other countries too they are considerably smaller. Eichengreen and Hatton have argued, however, that Maddison's estimates for the 1930s are likely to be too low for various reasons.[11] They concluded that the actual economy-wide rates probably lie somewhere between the industrial rates and Maddison's estimates for the aggregate. In spite of these problems of definition and measurement, the available data are informative, since 'economic fluctuations in the 1930s were large enough to dominate all but the largest changes in coverage and eligibility' (Eichengreen & Hatton, 1988: 10). It has been shown, however, that in countries where industrialization was relatively recent, estimates of

---

11. 'The census benchmarks from which Maddison's series were extrapolated typically failed to adequately enumerate underemployment in agriculture and services, particularly of family members (especially women) on farms and in small businesses and of those on temporary lay-off in industry. Younger workers who had never had a job and older workers for whom retirement was a respectable alternative were similarly underenumerated' (Eichengreen & Hatton, 1988: 10).

David J. Smith

unemployment rates are particularly open to error because of chronic and unregistered underemployment in rural areas.

Figure 6.33   Estimates of interwar unemployment: industrial compared with economy-wide

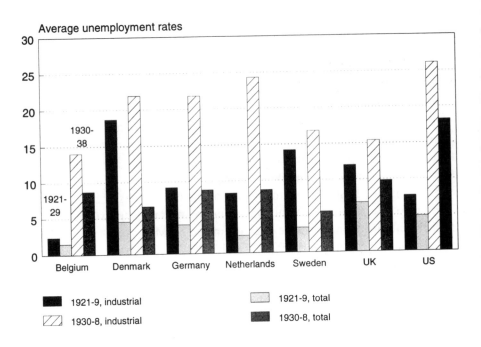

Source: Industrial: Galenson & Zellner (1957); economy-wide: Maddison (1964).

Maddison's estimates of economy-wide unemployment rates for 1913 to 1960 are shown in Figure 6.34; the estimates of unemployment in industry quoted by Eichengreen and Hatton for 1920 to 1939 are shown in Figure 6.35. The trends over time shown by the two sets of estimates are closely similar, although at any one time the relative position of countries is frequently different on the two measures. Taking the industrial unemployment rates (Figure 6.35) as the main point of reference, it is clear that the time series pattern differed greatly across countries. In the US[12] there was a pattern of stable and relatively low unemployment in the 1920s (following a short peak

---

12. Also in Australia and Canada, although these data are not shown in the Figure.

Figure 6.34 Unemployment rate: selected countries, 1913-1960

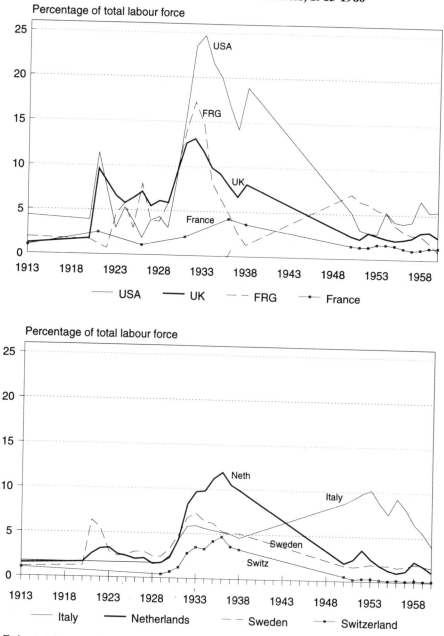

Percentage of total labour force

Estimated from partial statistics; for problems of comparability, see text.

Source: Maddison (1964).

at the end of the First World War), a steep rise in unemployment between 1929 and 1932, then a strong and steady decline. The pattern of unemployment in Germany was distinct by virtue of the sharp peak and dramatic fall in the 1930s. For the other countries, unemployment remained fairly level throughout most of the 1920s, then rose more gradually from 1929 to a lower peak in 1932, before falling only gradually.

Estimates of unemployment rates by age have also been compiled for six countries during the 1930s (Eichengreen & Hatton, 1988: 33, Table 1.9).[13] The patterns varied in a complex way from one country to another, but only in the USA and Australia was the unemployment rate substantially higher among younger than among older age groups. Broadly speaking, whereas youth unemployment rates in the 1980s and 1990s greatly exceeded unemployment rates for adults aged 25 and over, this was not the case in the interwar period. There is evidence that this apparent difference arises at least partly because youth unemployment was underrecorded in the pre-war period; nevertheless, there has been a genuine change in the age composition of the unemployed, as youth unemployment has become more sensitive to fluctuations in the economy.

The rise of unemployment in the Great Depression was accompanied by a rise in the average duration of unemployment. 'In the UK, where in September 1929 78.5 per cent of applicants for benefit or assistance had been out of work for less than three months and only 4.7 per cent for more than a year, by 1936 only 55 per cent had been unemployed for less than three months and fully 25 per cent for more than a year' (Eichengreen & Hatton, 1988: 38). There is strong evidence, too, for an increase in the duration of spells of unemployment during the 1930s in both Australia and the USA. Younger workers seem to have experienced relatively high rates of turnover but lower spell durations. In contrast, older workers typically suffered longer durations, largely accounting for their high unemployment rates.

The effects of unemployment were serious, although living standards probably remained higher than 30 years before because of economic growth, and because rudimentary social security systems now provided some relief. The effects on health and vitality are difficult to identify (for example, in statistics of mortality), but social and psychological effects have been well established through some classic pieces of research (Eisenberg & Lazarsfeld (1938), Jahoda et al. (1972). As Eichengreen and Hatton put it, 'even though the majority continued to search actively for work, the atrophy of skills, loss

---

13. For the most part these estimates derive from the censuses of population.

Figure 6.35   Unemployment rates in industry: selected countries, 1920-1939

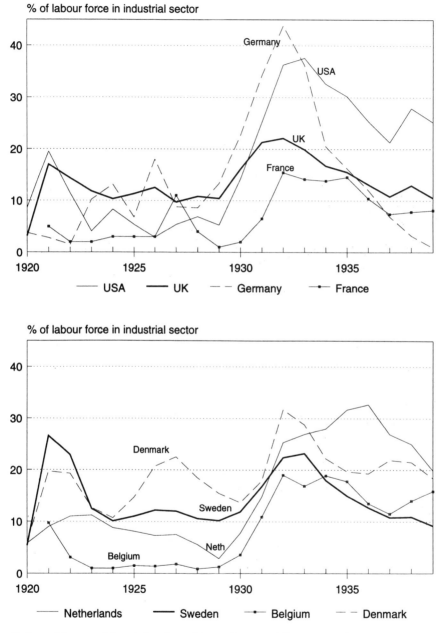

Estimated from partial statistics; for problems of comparability, see text.

Source: Eichengreen & Hatton (1988).

of morale and possibly declining health as well as loss of contacts left them at a severe disadvantage' (1988: 51).

The Postwar Period

From about 1948 until the beginning of the 1970s there was a period of very low unemployment in most developed countries. Economic historians agree (Maddison, 1982; van der Wee, 1986) that nervousness set in at the end of the 1960s, when it became clear that the US dollar could no longer cope as the bedrock of the world financial system. Confirmation of this came in 1971, when the USA unilaterally cancelled the gold-dollar convertibility standard. The world's finances were still in turmoil when, in November 1973, the leading oil-producing countries succeeded in imposing a huge rise in crude oil prices (a quadrupling) upon the rest of the world. This first 'oil shock' of 1973 was repeated in 1979 as a result of the Iranian political crisis. It is now clear that it was not the actual increase in energy costs that caused subsequent problems, but the shock waves which ran through the world financial systems as they were required to manage huge new flows of funds and debts.

Equally important as background to the high unemployment of the 1980s was the upsurge of wage demands throughout many Western countries in the late 60s and early 70s, which resulted in a growth of wage-induced inflationary pressures. Trade union bargaining power had been growing steadily in the postwar period, in Britain as in many other countries. Now unions were learning to anticipate inflation and build a provision for it into their wage claims, so that real wages would continue to increase. To avoid the dangers of instability, many governments imposed public budget cuts and swingeing increases in interest rates for borrowers. With economies already stagnating through low profitability and productivity, partly brought about by wage pressures and partly by the slowdown in international trade, such actions were bound to precipitate recession and unemployment. The period of mass unemployment of the 80s and its aftermath had begun.

During the decade from 1973 to 1983, the unemployment rate in the OECD area rose from 3.5 per cent to 9 per cent; it then fell slowly each year to reach 7.5 per cent by 1988 before the onset of another recession. The changes in unemployment rate in selected individual countries are charted in Figure 6.36. From this it is clear that the OECD average conceals remarkable differences between countries in their experience of recession. This can be illustrated still more clearly by charting the difference between the aggregate rate of unemployment in 1988 and 1973 (Figure 6.37). This chart shows that in the

Figure 6.36   Unemployment rate: selected countries, 1950-90

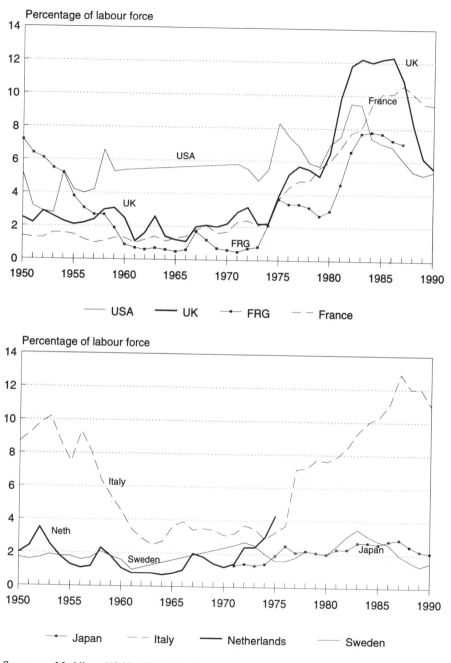

Source: Maddison (1964); OECD, *Labour force statistics*.

David J. Smith

majority of OECD countries unemployment in 1988 remained substantially higher than before the onset of the first postwar recession, but in a few countries it had returned almost to pre-recession levels.

Figure 6.37   Rise in unemployment rate: OECD countries, 1973-1988

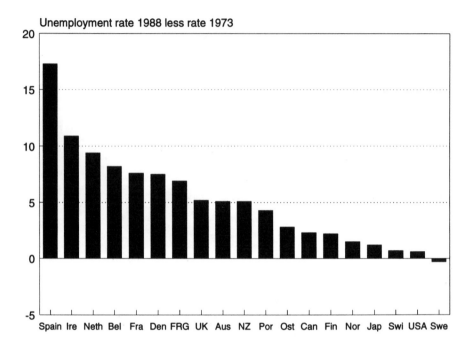

Source: OECD (1989).

In bringing together its recent research on these issues, the OECD (1989) distinguished between three groups of countries.

1. In the first group unemployment rates have been brought down almost to their 1973 levels. Two more specific categories can be distinguished. The first category includes *Japan* (where the unemployment rate was 2.5 per cent in 1988 compared with 1.3 per cent in 1973) and those European countries where unemployment has for many years been low and stable, namely *Austria, Finland, Norway, Sweden* and *Switzerland*. In these European low-unemployment countries, the rate was 2.6 per cent in 1988 compared with 1.3 per cent in 1973. The second category includes the *United States* and *Canada*, where the unemployment rate was about twice

as high as in the European low-unemployment countries or Japan, but had almost returned to its 1973 level.

2. In a second group of countries, unemployment was, by 1988, still close to its peak rate. This includes most European countries (*France, Germany, Italy, the United Kingdom, Belgium, Denmark, Ireland, the Netherlands, Portugal* and *Spain*). In these high-unemployment countries, the rate rose steeply from 2.7 per cent in 1973 to 10.6 per cent in 1983, and then remained at the same level. In some countries the increase was far more extreme: in Spain, for example, the rate was 2.2 per cent in 1973 compared with 19.5 per cent in 1988.

3. In *Australia* and *New Zealand* unemployment has remained much higher than at the beginning of the 1970s, but not as high as in the second group of countries. Also, the rate began to fall substantially in *Australia* after 1983.

Uneven rates of unemployment across countries reflect, in part, different growth of output. In the low-unemployment countries, average GDP growth accelerated from a little over 2 per cent over the period 1973-83 to about 4 per cent after 1983. In the high-unemployment group, growth picked up to only around 2.5 per cent. The labour-intensity of growth also differed considerably among countries. Expansion was most labour intensive in North America. Not only did output grow rather more slowly in low-unemployment European countries than in North America, but employment expanded more slowly still (at about 0.5 per cent a year). For most of the countries in the high-unemployment European group, employment in 1988 was still below the 1973 level: the notable exceptions were *Italy* and *Portugal*.

A number of the OECD's surveys of individual countries have examined the role of international mobility in changes in the supply of labour. In *Switzerland*, the supply of immigrant labour has been controlled as a method of adjusting to changes in the labour market (OECD, 1985): as a result, *Switzerland* is the only country where the labour force actually fell (by almost 3 per cent) in the period 1973-83, following the same trend as employment. Migration has also been an important counter-cyclical adjustment mechanism in *New Zealand*. A resumption of large-scale emigration from *Ireland* prevented unemployment from rising still higher. In the case of *Portugal*, however, migration aggravated the unemployment problem, as the massive return of Portuguese from former colonies after 1974 coincided with the international recession.

The Distribution of Unemployment in the Postwar Period

Region. There are considerable disparities between unemployment rates within each region in OECD countries. This can best be shown by ranking regions within each country according to unemployment rate, then comparing regions containing the top and bottom quarter of the labour force on this criterion. In smaller countries the ratio between the unemployment rates for regions in the top and bottom quarters is usually below 2; for the five largest European countries, Japan, and the USA the ratio is about 2. Both in Europe and Japan, unemployment rates tend to be higher in peripheral than in central regions. This centre versus periphery effect is evident among the regions within a particular country, not among the regions of a number of countries considered together. This suggests that within each country there is a pull towards the capital or other large city which is stronger than any pull towards centres outside the national boundaries. There is no centre-periphery pattern of this kind in the USA. Regional differentials increased during the 1980s in a majority of the OECD countries. In Finland, France, Italy, the UK and the USA, the rise followed a certain fall in differentials during the 1970s.

Sex. The following summary is based on analysis of unemployment rates in 1973, 1983 and 1990 in eight OECD countries: France, Germany, Italy, Japan, Spain, Sweden, the UK, and the USA. In four of the eight countries (France, Germany, Italy, and Spain) the rate of unemployment in 1990 was higher among women than among men, and for three of these countries, the exception being Germany, the difference was substantial. In the United Kingdom, the rate of unemployment was substantially higher among men than among women. In the remaining three countries (Japan, Sweden and the United States) the male and female unemployment rates were closely similar. These differences between countries are probably connected with differences in the social security systems, which may or may not encourage married women who cannot find a job to withdraw from the labour market.

The increase in the rate of unemployment between 1973 and 1983 was substantially higher among women than among men in the United Kingdom, and somewhat higher in Spain and Italy. In the case of the United Kingdom, however, this result is probably spurious, being caused by a radical understatement of female unemployment in the 1970s due to non-registration. The increase in the rate of unemployment was substantially higher among men than among women only in Germany.

These trends should be seen in the context of changing patterns of female participation in the workforce. Sweden and Japan show the highest rates, while the Southern European countries, Italy and Spain, show the lowest ones. In all eight countries the female participation rate has increased; these increases have been most marked in Sweden and Japan, but there have also been sharp increases from a low base in Italy and Spain. Male participation rates have tended to decline in all eight countries, but these declines have been substantial only in France and Spain, as a result of state policies encouraging early retirement during the recession.

Age. As stated in an earlier section, there was no consistent tendency in the interwar years for young people to suffer higher unemployment rates than older people; in fact, in the majority of countries, the highest rates were among older men. A different pattern of age differences has emerged in the postwar period. When age is plotted against unemployment rate, in the great majority of countries the resulting curve is in the shape of a 'reverse J': unemployment rates are highest for youths, then decline with age, then remain fairly flat for the prime age groups. At the other end of the age spectrum, at least in some countries, the unemployment rate increases for people aged 55-59 (OECD, 1988: 26-29). A number of factors have been suggested to account for the relatively high level of youth unemployment. As recent entrants to the labour market, young people are highly mobile between jobs and, therefore, more likely to experience a number of spells of unemployment before settling into a more permanent career. Demographic developments may also be important: members of the 'baby boom' generation faced increased competition with their contemporaries. On the demand side, the competitive position of young compared with older workers varies widely between countries, depending on the system of youth training and the associated wage structures.

Unemployment rates for the 16-19 age group are strongly affected by government schemes and associated counting rules in Labour Force Surveys: for example, in the UK the rate of unemployment for males aged 16-19 apparently declined from 32.3 per cent in 1983 to 6.8 per cent in 1990, largely as a result of government programmes that took youths out of the group counted as unemployed (see Figure 6.38, top panel).

Another factor is the wide variation between countries in the proportion of young people who are counted as part of the labour force (Figures 6.40 and 6.41). Broadly speaking, the countries with *high* rates of youth unemployment are ones in which a relatively *small* proportion of young people are counted as

David J. Smith

Figure 6.38   Youth unemployment rates, 1973-1990: selected OECD countries

Males aged 16-19

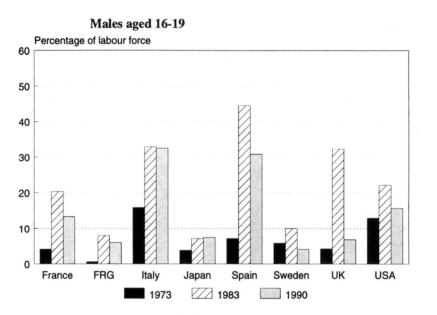

Females aged 16-19

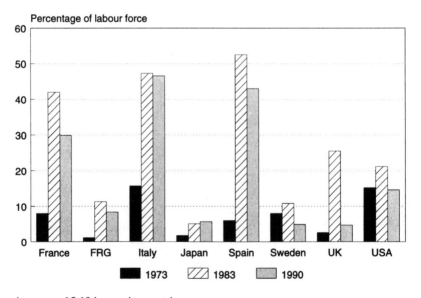

Age range 15-19 in certain countries.

Source: OECD, *Labour force statistics.*

Figure 6.39 Youth unemployment rate, 1973-1990: selected OECD countries

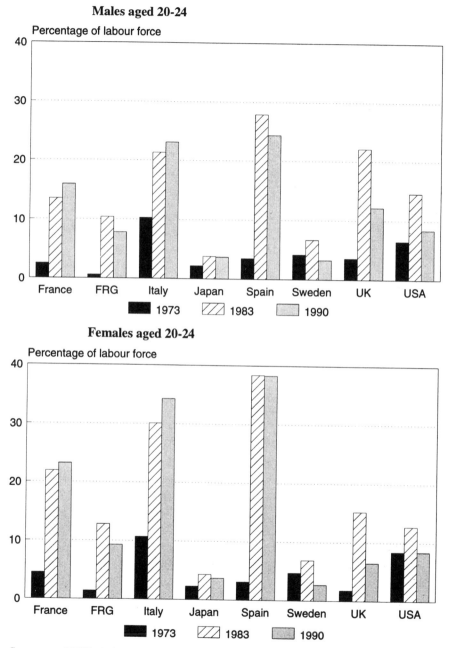

Source: OECD, *Labour force statistics.*

part of the labour force. On the one hand this means that variations between countries in youth unemployment are less marked when expressed as a proportion of the whole age group than as a proportion of the labour force. On the other hand it means that the countries with high youth unemployment are extremely unsuccessful, compared to those with low rates, in absorbing young people into the labour force. In countries such as Italy, Spain and France relatively few young people are actually in work: most are either unemployed or defined as outside the labour force.

Changes in rates of unemployment in eight countries between 1973, 1983 and 1990 are shown in Figures 6.38 and 6.39 for the youngest age group (15-19 or 16-19) and for those aged 20-24. At the peak of unemployment, in 1983, the rate for males aged 16-19 reached 45 per cent in Spain and around 33 per cent in Italy and in the UK. The rate for this age group did not exceed 10 per cent in Germany, Japan, or Sweden. In 1983, the rate of unemployment for the 16-19 age group was well over twice the total rate in the case of all OECD countries except Germany; the ratio between the 16-19 rate and the total rate was particularly high in Italy. By 1990, when there had been a substantial decline in the total rate of unemployment from its peak in 1983, the rate for the 16-19 group remained much higher than the total rate in most countries.

Rates of unemployment for the 20-24 age group tend to be somewhat lower than for youths aged 16-19, but in many countries they are around twice as high as for all age groups. Germany is again the major exception: there youth unemployment rates are only slightly higher than the overall rate. In Spain and Italy, unemployment among males aged 20-24 remained at well over 20 per cent from 1983 onwards, and among females it remained at over 30 per cent. The rates in France were also high – around 15 per cent for males, and around 20 per cent for females – and showed no decline between 1983 and 1990. In the UK, unemployment rates among this age group reached high levels in 1983 (22 per cent among males, 14 per cent among females) but then sharply declined. These rates were considerably lower in the USA and Germany, and much lower still in Sweden and Japan. In this age group, the rate of participation in the labour force is around two-thirds to three-quarters in most countries (see Figure 6.41), so the high rates of unemployment reached in many countries affect a large proportion of the total age cohort.

Occupation. Statistics collected for eight major industrial nations by the OECD show that in all except Germany the rate of unemployment is considerably higher among manual than among non-manual workers (OECD,

Figure 6.40   Unemployment and participation rates: selected OECD countries 1990

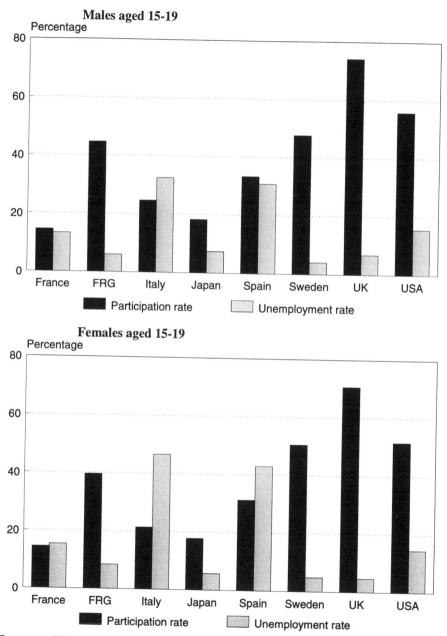

Source: OECD, *Labour force statistics.*

**Figure 6.41   Unemployment and participation rates: selected OECD countries
1990**

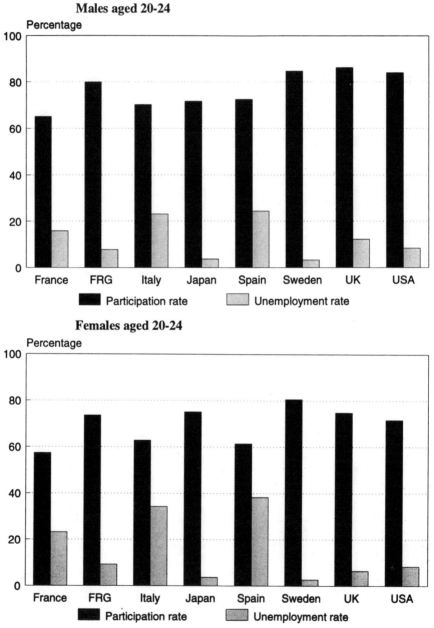

Source: OECD, *Labour force statistics*.

1987: 84-90). Concentration of unemployment among manual workers is particularly strong in the United Kingdom. It is worth briefly considering the dynamics underlying these differences in the aggregate unemployment rate. A study of the inflow into unemployment (Daniel, 1990) shows that two-thirds of male and one half of female entrants have come from manual jobs. Furthermore, among the remaining female entrants the majority have come from routine service and clerical jobs which it is now customary (in the UK) to classify as 'working class' positions (see, for example, Goldthorpe, 1983). A study of the long-term unemployed (White, 1983) showed that 80 per cent of males had come from manual occupations, while virtually all the females had come either from manual or from lower service or clerical occupations. Further, the minority of white-collar workers in long-term unemployment have been shown to be untypical in having exceptionally low levels of educational qualification (White, 1983; see also White & McRae, 1989). Accordingly, those in long-term unemployment in the recessionary period of the 1980s could be generally characterized as 'from lower occupations and/or lower-qualified'.

Explanations of High Unemployment Since 1973

Since the late 1960s the world economic order has been increasingly turbulent, with an international financial system in almost continuous difficulty, unprecedented variations in the price of energy, and rising expectations of workers in industrial nations leading to new bargaining behaviour. In a general review of the determinants of unemployment, White and Smith (1994) concluded that the primary causes of unemployment can reasonably be assigned to these pressures and to the incapacity of governments, severally and collectively, to manage them in a way that maintains steady growth. Yet this is barely to be counted an explanation since it fails to show why there has been a remarkable divergence in the 1980s between industrialized nations that have contained unemployment at very low levels, and others that have experienced persistent high unemployment. Low unemployment countries include some free market economies, where wage fixing is highly decentralized, and some corporatist economies, where wage fixing is highly centralized and social welfare systems highly developed.

There is strong evidence from international comparative research that the central reason for divergence between the two groups of countries is wage rigidity: the failure of wages in the high unemployment countries to adjust downwards quickly to compensate for a sudden increase in aggregate unemployment. In creating such wage rigidity, wage pressures caused by trade union and worker power may have some importance. At least equally important are the policies of leading employers in the labour market, particularly their strategies of productivity enhancement through work intensification, and their learned dependence upon wage incentives to achieve their goals.

The concentration of unemployment among young people, manual workers, and people with low educational attainment requires further explanation. It has been argued that relatively high youth unemployment arises from an unfavourable combination of wage structures and training arrangements. The apprenticeship system in German-speaking countries has been uniquely successful in overcoming these problems and delivering a low relative rate of youth unemployment. Within this system, young people receive clearly defined training and obtain widely recognized and transferable qualifications while in a job; the incentive to employers to take on apprentices within this framework is that their wages are very low.

Education and occupation do more than explain the distribution of unemployment between social groups. The reason is that educational and class barriers not only determine the distribution of unemployment, thereby working to the disadvantage of the uneducated and the manual worker, but also reduce the capacity of the economy to adapt, and thereby limit growth and total welfare. A class analysis of unemployment may be capable of integrating a number of explanations: it is particularly valuable in drawing attention to the role of the system of educational qualification in accentuating vertical divisions between occupations and in obstructing the mobility needed for adaptation to economic pressures and shocks.

The idea that there is a growing underclass of people increasingly detached from the labour market is supported by only limited evidence as yet. Any such group is a consequence, not a cause, of the period of persistent high unemployment, and is much too small to explain the fundamental changes that have arisen in the functioning of the labour market since 1973.

Poverty and Distribution of Income

The idea of poverty presents itself as an appeal, as a call for action. In Piachaud's words, 'the term "poverty" carries with it the implication and moral imperative that something should be done about it' (1987: 161). Although it is an indispensable notion, it is also vague and flexible. This is equally true in many other fields of social enquiry. There can be no single, unambiguous measure of poverty any more than there can be a single, unambiguous measure of crime. There can, however, be a number of informative indicators, which can be usefully deployed in many kinds of discussion.

Distribution of income is a much wider notion, and one that is much more neutral or ambivalent in its policy implications. Liberal economists and philosophers argue that a considerable degree of inequality of income may be justified if it contributes to the welfare of everyone including the poorest (Rawls, 1972). The same writers would not argue that poverty can be justified in a similar way. Distribution of income is just a fact, whereas the idea of poverty incorporates a judgement about the level of income in relation to need. At a technical level, the poor are not simply those towards the bottom end of the income distribution, because income has to be evaluated in relation to circumstances.

In practice, trends in the level of poverty can be established only for recent years, from the mid-1970s onwards. It is worth considering income distribution as well, so as to have a longer run of data.

It is important to consider poverty and income distribution as possible explanations of changes in the nature and extent of youth problems; but the nature of any such relationship is less evident than might at first appear. It is easy to show that the poor are more subject to a variety of problems (including ill-health and high mortality) than the affluent; and broadly the explanation for that pattern is that lack of material resources is associated with a poor physical and social environment, with stressful working conditions, and with a lack of autonomy; it makes survival more difficult, and also makes it more difficult for people to build up the personal resources (physical, educational, social) needed to overcome their problems. However, it does not follow that increasing affluence will necessarily reduce youth problems. There are many complicating factors.

First, poverty is in part relative (this point is discussed in greater detail below). Increasing affluence may or may not be associated with a decline in the proportion of people who are relatively poor.

Second, much will depend on the detailed shape of the relationships involved. If, for example, certain youth problems are associated mostly with extreme poverty, then reducing extreme poverty could be a good way of reducing their incidence. If, however, there is a smooth and gradual curve, such that every increment in resources (relative to the mean) is associated with a small reduction in certain youth problems, then any conceivable income distribution would have the potential for causing these problems.

Third, certain problems – for example, many kinds of property crime – are particularly associated with affluence. More generally, new sets of tensions and difficulties arise in affluent societies compared with those in societies at earlier stages of economic development. Hence, differences between poor and affluent groups within a developed society do not necessarily predict differences between poorer and more affluent whole societies, since the pattern of social and economic relationships changes with economic growth.

Finally, poverty may be a factor in deciding *who* has problems at any one time, without influencing the total extent of problems. Relationships of this kind certainly exist in other fields. For example, men who are unemployed are far more likely to be arrested by the police than men who are in work; but it is much less clear that the level of arrests rises and falls with the level of unemployment.

The vague and flexible idea of poverty encompasses an absolute notion (having so few resources as to make survival doubtful) and a range of relative notions, which vary, for example, according to the breadth of the comparisons that we choose to make. Although there can be an absolute notion of poverty, we operate with relative notions most of the time. It may be of some importance that our ideas of poverty are relative in two distinct ways.

1. The nature and quantity of resources needed to achieve any given objective – for example, to survive – vary according to the economic and social structure. For example, a person living in the suburbs of Los Angeles would starve to death without a motor car, because a car is needed to travel to the supermarket to buy food. By contrast, a person living in Pimlico (London) can walk to the shops in a few moments, and a French peasant grows most of his own food and only has to go to the shops occasionally. Thus poverty is relative to the economic and social structure in that the resources needed to meet basic needs vary according to that structure.

2. In Townsend's phrase (1979), poverty is relative to the 'customs, activities and diets comprising society's style of living'. Social structures, the pressure of norms and expectations, create self-standing needs. In California the person who does not have access to a motor car is an outcaste, even if he or she is not starving through not being able to get to the shops.

Hence there are in principle two distinct ways in which our ideas of poverty are relative to particular norms and social structures, and this again shows that there is a plurality of standards underlying our notions of what poverty is. In more concrete terms, three types of measure of poverty will be referred to in what follows.

a) *Budget standard.* This consists in defining budget standards for different types of expenditure. Groups of experts are required to make professional judgements as to what needs to be spent for food, clothing, transport, housing, heating, etc. This was the approach pioneered by Seebohm Rowntree in his studies of poverty in York. Although it is often described as an attempt to define poverty in absolute terms, in fact the judgements are made in the context of a particular society at a particular time, and they change in response to change in the pattern of consumption. In fact, Rowntree radically changed his budget standard from one study to the next. The US government still uses the budget standard approach to define the official poverty line.

b) *Income relative to the national average.* This is now the approach most commonly used by poverty researchers, for example by those involved in the Luxembourg Income Study. Income per person is, however, adjusted depending on family size.

c) *Standard food share approach.* The basic principle is to infer from analysis of empirical data a level of income at which people will, in practice, spend enough on food to have an adequate diet.

As will appear, international comparisons of levels of poverty produce very different results depending on which of these approaches is adopted. Until recently, the focus of interest among campaigners against poverty has tended to be within their own country, and researchers providing evidence to back these campaigns have tended to argue for a relative income definition, because they wish to highlight continuing relative deprivation in the midst of economic growth. However, if the focus is shifted to international comparisons, then a relative income approach will understate differences between countries, whereas a budget standard approach will highlight poverty in less developed countries far more clearly.

Long-term Trends in Income Distribution

The most important international study of changes in income distribution is by Harold Lydall (1968). Reasoning from basic economic principles, Lydall argued that the two main determinants of the inequality of earnings in existing and past societies are the distribution of education, and the proportion engaged in agriculture. The more unequally education is distributed, and the higher the proportion engaged in agriculture, the more unequal will be the distribution of earnings. He adduced a wide range of evidence from international comparisons and changes over time which tends to show that these predictions are fulfilled. It is a corollary of Lydall's theory that in many cases economic development is associated with a reduction in the inequality of earnings, since growth is associated with the reduction of the agricultural sector and the widening of educational opportunity.

Figure 6.42   Pre-tax income dispersion c. 1960: male non-farm full-time workers

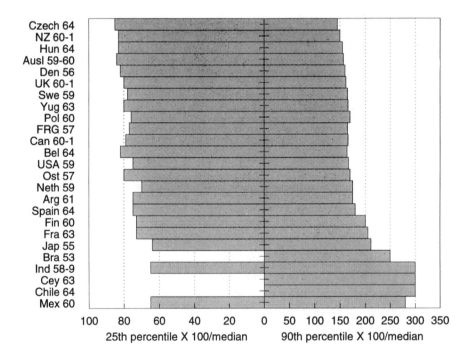

For explanation, see text.

Source: Lydall (1968).

A recent analysis based on a larger number of countries supports the association between development and income equality. 'Equality of income distribution... increases sharply with economic development, up to a level of about $3,500 per capita; but above that threshold, there is virtually no further rise... In 70 percent of the nations with a GNP per capita below $3,500, the top tenth of the population got more than one-third of the total income (in some cases as much as 57 percent). In *none* of the nations with a GNP per capita above $3,500 did the top tenth of the population get more than one-third of the total income' (Inglehart, 1990: 250).

Other analyses have produced broadly similar results. Figure 6.42, derived from Lydall, shows the dispersion of pre-tax income around 1960 for 25 countries. The left half of the chart shows the 25th percentile (working upwards from the bottom of the distribution) as a percentage of the median – a measure of the proportion of workers who were relatively poor. The right half shows the 90th percentile as a percentage of the median – a measure of the proportion who were relatively rich. Among these 25 countries, the five then having the most unequal distribution of earnings were all at an early stage of economic development: Mexico, Chile, Ceylon, India and Brazil. Among the more developed countries, this analysis understates the differences according to political system, because it shows pre-tax earnings.

Figure 6.43, derived from Maddison (1989), gives two measures of the dispersion of the pre-tax income of households around 1970 in 16 countries. The left half shows the Gini coefficient, which attempts to summarize dispersion by a single statistic.[14] The higher the coefficient, the more dispersed is the distribution. The right half of the chart shows *per capita* income of the top decile as a multiple of *per capita* income in the bottom two deciles, so it is a measure of the gap between earnings at the top and bottom of the distribution. On both measures, the dispersion of pre-tax income is greatest for the Latin-American countries. There is no clear-cut difference between the average of the six Asian countries and the average of the five OECD countries. Within the OECD countries, there was by 1969 a notably low dispersion of income in Japan (then in its period of explosive growth), and a relatively large dispersion in France and the USA.

---

14. About half a dozen other single statistic measures are used in the literature. No single measure can adequately summarize the pattern of dispersal, because so many different comparisons are possible between any two distributions. The main shortcoming of the Gini coefficient is that it emphasizes differences towards the middle of the distribution, and de-emphasizes differences at the extremes.

David J. Smith

It is harder to establish that this cross-sectional pattern reflects a longitudinal trend. Reliable data are for recent periods and relate to economically advanced countries, which have shown little increase in income equality in the last 30 years (as we shall see later, there has been increasing inequality at least in the UK). That is what should be expected if the relationship between development and income equality is curvilinear, with diminishing further increases in equality once a threshold of development has been reached. However, there is evidence that both the USA and Japan moved towards substantially greater income equality during their period of fastest economic development. 'Conversely, Taiwan, South Korea, Singapore, and Hong Kong all have made dramatic leaps from poverty to prosperity only recently – and all have shown substantial increases in income equality' (Inglehart, 1990: 250).

Figure 6.43   Dispersal of pre-tax income c. 1970: households

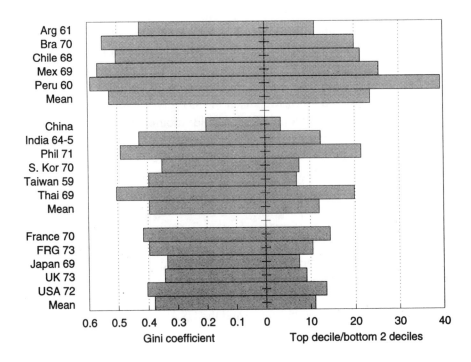

For explanation, see text.

Source: Maddison (1989).

For any period earlier than about 1960 data on changes in the dispersion of wages or incomes over time are hard to find. In considering long-term trends, Lydall relied, for the most part, on data about skill differentials, for example the ratio between wage rates for skilled and unskilled workers in the building trades and in manufacturing. For a period of about 20 years from 1950, direct information on income dispersion is available from a study by Sawyer (1976).

In the USA skill differentials fell very substantially between 1907 and 1960. A separate analysis of earnings in 141 occupations (Keat, 1960) showed that the variation fell by about one third between 1903 and 1956. Another analysis by Keat showed that earnings in teaching professions declined radically compared with average earnings in manufacturing over a similar period: for example, high-school teachers' salaries fell from 288 per cent of the manufacturing wage in 1904 to 136 per cent in 1953. Putting this together with more direct evidence on dispersion of earnings for part of the period, Lydall concluded that most of the change took place between 1939 and 1949, and that there was little change during the present century before the Second World War.

Between 1947 and 1972, Sawyer found little change in dispersion of earnings in the USA, but there was a small loss of share by the lowest five deciles.

Evidence on skill differentials in the UK shows much less change during the years 1900 to 1960 than in the USA. The long-term trend is towards smaller differentials, although a rapid decline in differentials during the First World War was partly reversed during the early postwar period. Information on the dispersion of all earnings over the period is highly incomplete, but consistent with a picture of gradual overall decline. More comprehensive information is available from about 1950 onwards. One source (the 'Blue Book') shows a slight trend towards greater equality from 1949 to 1973. Another (the Family Expenditure Survey) shows an increasing degree of inequality from 1957 to 1973, although it has been shown that this is partly because of changes in household composition.

Unusually full information is available for Sweden. Between 1920 and 1930 there was an increase in dispersion that was more marked for men than for women. From 1930 to 1960 there was a dramatic decline in dispersion for men, and a smaller decline for women: for example, the 95th percentile of earnings for male manual workers fell from 217 per cent of the median in 1930 to 158 per cent in 1960. This coincided with a period of sustained economic growth.

The limited evidence available for Germany and France suggests that there was little change in the dispersion of earnings in the first 60 years of the century. In France, there is clear evidence of increasing equality between 1956 and 1970, which Sawyer believed was associated with the decline of the agricultural sector. In the Federal Republic of Germany, there is evidence of an increase in equality over the whole period 1950 to 1973, but all of this increase occurred in the earlier part of the period (1950-1960), while there was a slight reversal of the trend in the later part.

In Japan, there were some changes in skill differentials during the war years (including 1936-39, when Japan was at war), but over the whole period 1924 to 1958 there is no evidence of an overall decline in differentials or dispersion of earnings. However, in the 15-year period from 1956 there is evidence of a substantial decline in dispersion, coinciding with the period of explosive economic growth. To a considerable extent, this reflects a reduction in the differences in earnings between different sizes of establishment; Lydall concluded that it could therefore be interpreted as a movement towards a more unified labour market. The case of Japan provides particularly good support for Lydall's general theory. As Lydall put it, 'the history of Japan is a classic example of a country which was transformed from a backward, predominantly agricultural, economy into an advanced industrialized economy within the space of a hundred years'. As the result of a deliberate and determined policy, the educational standards of the mass of the population were transformed during the first 60 years of the century, and over a similar period the late and dramatic shift from agriculture to industry and services occurred. As predicted by Lydall's theory, these changes were accompanied by a radical reduction in the dispersion of earnings. For the period 1962 to 1972, the Japanese Family Earnings Survey (which excludes the agricultural sector) shows a further increase in equality of earnings.

Comparing Relative and Absolute Poverty

For the period from 1975, more detailed information is available than for earlier periods which makes it possible to compare the level of poverty on a common definition in different countries, and to study change over time in the level of poverty within countries. The following section considers the evidence on change over time since 1975 in the extent of poverty. Before coming to that discussion, it is necessary to consider the implications of using different methods of defining a poverty line.

Figure 6.44   Relative and absolute poverty rates: ten EC countries around 1980

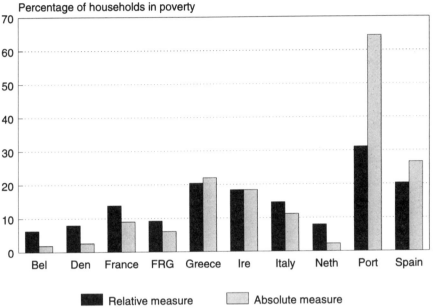

Percentage of households in poverty

■ Relative measure   ▨ Absolute measure

Relative: below 50 per cent of mean equivalent expenditure
Absolute: based on standard food share of 35 per cent; see text

Source: Teekens & Zaidi (1990).

Teekens and Zaidi (1990) illustrated the contrasting results of adopting an absolute compared with a relative measure of poverty, using data for ten EC countries around 1980-85. Their method of arriving at an absolute poverty line was complex in detail, but the line was defined as the level of household income at which food accounts for 35 per cent of expenditure.[15] However, those calculations were merely the background to the choice of a single poverty line expressed in ECUs, which was then applied (after conversion according

---

15. They also considered two alternative levels, where food accounts for 30 per cent, and for 40 per cent of expenditure, but for simplicity only the middle of the three definitions is considered here. In principle, the food share should be chosen in such a way that households in which food accounts for that proportion of expenditure, or a smaller proportion, are ones obtaining an adequate diet. (As total expenditure rises, so expenditure on food rises, and diet improves, but food as a share of total expenditure declines.) In practice, Teekens and Zaidi have not been able to carry out such an evaluation, so the choice of food share, and hence of poverty line, is arbitrary.

Figure 6.45 **Absolute poverty line of 2360 1980 ECUs: as a percentage of median expenditure per adult equivalent**

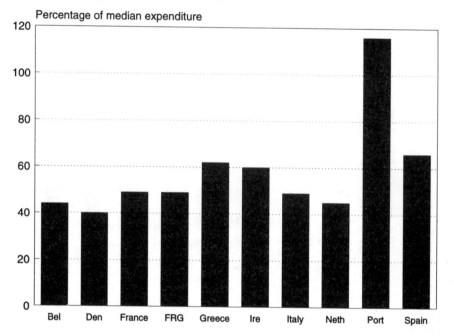

For explanation, see text.

Source: Teekens & Zaidi (1990).

to purchasing power parities) to all of the countries considered. Relative poverty was defined as anything below 50 per cent of mean household expenditure, except that expenditure was weighted according to a well-established method to reflect household composition. The weighting reflects the fact that the amount of expenditure required per person to maintain a household depends on its composition.[16]

Figures 6.44 and 6.45 show the results of adopting these two different poverty definitions. In Portugal, Spain, and to a lesser extent Greece, there is a much higher proportion in poverty on the absolute than on the relative definition. In the most advanced countries covered (France, Germany, Italy, the Netherlands, Denmark, Belgium), the proportion in poverty is much higher

16. The currently most widely accepted equivalence scale, which is recommended by the OECD's work on social indicators, assigns a weight of 0.7 to each adult other than the first, and a weight of 0.5 to each child.

on the relative than on the absolute definition. Figure 6.45 shows that the absolute poverty line is a much larger proportion of median expenditure in the less developed than in the more developed countries. These analyses make the rather obvious point that on any absolute (single transnational) standard Portugal is a poorer country than the others considered, and therefore has a higher proportion of poor people. They also illustrate the less obvious point that on a standard of poverty relative to the national mean, too, there is a higher proportion in poverty in the less developed European countries than in the more developed ones; but in the case of the relative standard, these differences are far less extreme.

Figure 6.46 illustrates the results of another comparison, by Suesser (1988), between an absolute and relative standard of poverty. The relative standard is much the same as before, although in this instance it is defined by reference to median (rather than mean) equivalent income (that is, weighted according to household composition, as before). The absolute standard used in this case was the official US poverty line, which is defined by reference to the income needed to buy a basket of goods regarded as necessities.[17] The analysis does not, unfortunately, include any late-developing country such as Portugal, so the pattern of differences between countries is less dramatic than before. Countries in which the proportion in poverty was considerably higher where the relative rather than the absolute definition was used are Canada, Switzerland and the USA; countries for which the opposite is true are France, Germany, Norway and the UK. Only France and Germany are covered by both of the analyses shown in Figures 6.44 and 6.46; for these two countries, the comparison between the relative and absolute measures runs in opposite directions on the two analyses, probably because the specific absolute poverty lines have been drawn at different points.

Both of these analyses showed substantial differences in the early 1980s in the proportion in poverty even between highly developed countries. From the analysis shown in Figure 6.46, the proportion below the US poverty line was around 5 per cent in Sweden, 7 per cent in Germany, and between 11 and 14 per cent in France, the UK, the USA and Australia. Variations in the proportion below the relative poverty standard are even greater: from around 5 per cent in Sweden, Norway and Germany, through 8 or 9 per cent in France and the

---

17. In more detail, this measure of absolute poverty includes all persons with adjusted incomes below the official US government three-person poverty line, converted to other currencies using OECD purchasing power parities, where adjusted incomes are computed using the US poverty line equivalence scales.

UK, and 12 per cent in Australia and Canada, up to 17 per cent in the USA.
There is a rather low correlation between the proportion in relative and absolute
poverty, although Sweden is bottom and the USA nearly top on both measures.

Figure 6.46   Relative and absolute poverty c. 1980: Luxembourg Income Study

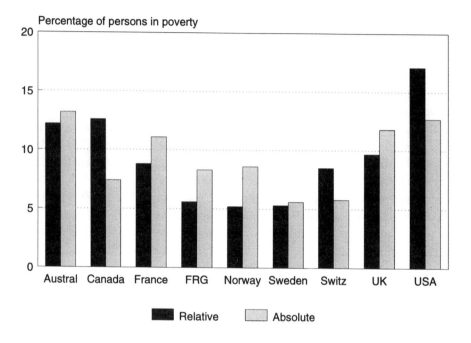

Relative: below half of median adjusted national income
Absolute: below US government three-person poverty line

Source: Suesser (1988).

Recent Trends

The rather limited available information on recent trends in poverty uses
definitions relative to national average incomes. O' Higgins and Jenkins
(1990) provided comparisons for the 12 EC countries in or around 1975, 1980
and 1985. Poverty was defined as less than 50 per cent of mean equivalent
income (with the usual weightings according to household composition).[18]

---

18. Using the OECD equivalence scales.

The findings (Figure 6.47) show a sharp and consistent increase in the proportion in poverty in the UK over this period; there were also increases in Denmark, Ireland and Portugal. Two countries, France and Greece, registered a decline in the proportion in poverty over this period, and in both cases this decline occurred during the first five years. There was little or no change over the whole period in the remaining countries (Belgium, Germany, Italy, Luxembourg, the Netherlands, and Spain). In the EC as a whole there was a slight increase in the proportion in poverty over the whole period.[19]

Figure 6.47   Poverty rates 1975-1985: European Community

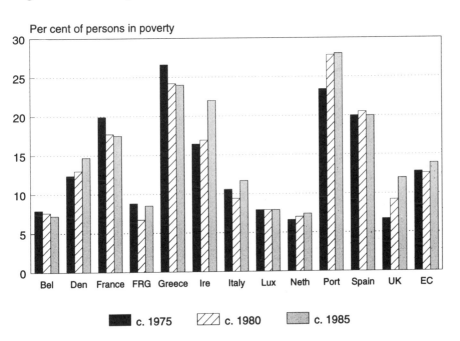

Poverty is defined as less than 50 per cent of average equivalent income: see text.

Source   O'Higgins & Jenkins (1990).

The findings for the UK fit with a large body of other information which shows that the distribution of incomes became more unequal during the late 1970s and 1980s. For example, the increase in real income between 1979 and

---

19. Source: *The First Report from the Social Security Committee*, London: House of Commons, 1992.

1988 was 2 per cent for those at the fifth percentile of the distribution, compared with 22 per cent for those at the 45th percentile, so the income of the affluent increased much more rapidly than the income of the poor over this period.

Comparing the results for c. 1985 in Figure 6.47, the earlier pattern is confirmed: that is, the least developed countries (Portugal, Greece and Spain) had the highest proportions in relative poverty. The countries with the lowest proportions in poverty were the Netherlands, Belgium, Germany and Luxembourg. The proportion in poverty in France was high, particularly in relation to the high level of GDP in that country.

Figure 6.48   Persons in poverty in FRG 1963-1986: definition: below 50 per cent of mean adult equivalent disposable income

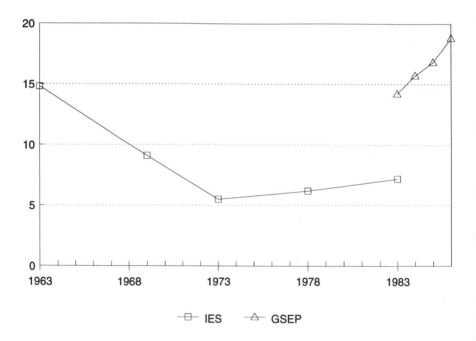

IES: Income and Expenditure Surveys. GSEP: German Socio-Economic Panel.
Break in series in 1983.

Source: Hauser & Semerau (1990).

Figure 6.48 summarizes the results of an analysis by Hauser and Semerau (1990) of trends in relative poverty in the Federal Republic of Germany. One source of data was used for 1963 to 1983, and another for 1983 to 1986. The two sources produce markedly different results for 1983, where the two series overlap, probably because the first source underrepresents low-income households. In spite of this problem, the results can be used to establish trends over time. Between 1963 and 1973, the proportion in relative poverty declined sharply and steadily from 15 to just over 5 per cent. There was then a more gradual rise between 1973 and 1983, where the break in the series occurs. However, from 1983 to 1986 the rise in the proportion in poverty became much sharper. The probable implication is that the level of poverty had risen again by 1986 to something like the 1968 level.

Hauser and Semerau's analysis also showed a much higher proportion of 'foreign' than of 'German' households in poverty (38.2 compared with 17.4 per cent in 1986).

Green et al. (1990) have analysed change in the dispersion of earnings between 1979 and 1987 for Germany and five countries outside the EC (the USA, Canada, Sweden and Australia). The results, which are summarized in Figure 6.49, are confined to male heads of household aged 25-54. For all of these countries, they show a slow decline over the period in the share of earnings going to the bottom quintile; this decline is steepest in Canada, and most gradual in Sweden.

Change over time in the distribution of earnings in recent years has been more intensively analysed for the USA than for any other country. Henle and Ryscavage (1980) found that the trend in earnings inequality for men was upwards between 1958 and 1977. In a later study (1990) they found that in the 1980s, earnings inequality increased not only among men, but among women as well, and among whites, black men and Hispanics considered separately, and among workers in various occupations and industries.

In conclusion, there is a considerable body of evidence to show that over the long term income disparities tend to be reduced as economic development progresses, at least during the phases involving a switch from agriculture to industry and services and the introduction of mass education. In line with this historic trend, income disparities are currently greatest in countries at an early stage of economic development. At the same time, there are substantial differences both in income dispersion and in the incidence of poverty among countries now at an advanced stage of economic development. Some of the most successful economies (Japan, Sweden) are among those having low income disparities and a low incidence of poverty, while others (the USA, France) are among those having high income disparities and incidence of poverty. Although the long-term historic trend in the advanced economies has been towards greater equality of income, this trend has clearly been reversed in a number of these countries, notably the USA, the UK and Germany, in recent years.

Figure 6.49   Change in share of aggregate earnings: male heads of household aged 25-54 c. 1980 and 1986

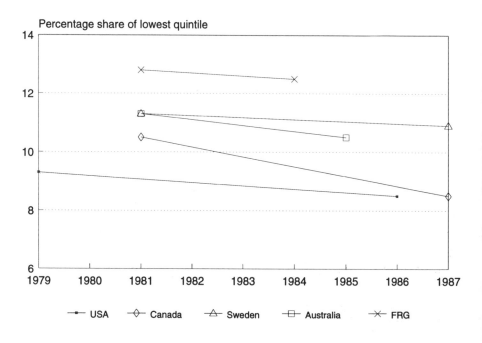

Source: Green et al. (1990).

Poverty Among Children and Among Single Parent Families

Before transfers through taxation and social security systems, the young and the old are the groups most at risk of poverty. Countries differ substantially in the way that poverty varies with age, because of the contrasting effects of national social transfer policies. On the basis of data from the Luxembourg Income Study, Figure 6.50 shows the proportion in relative poverty for three broad age groups: 0-17, 18-64, and 65 or more. The rate of poverty is high for both children and old people in the US, Australia and Canada; it is extraordinarily high for old people in the UK. In the remaining countries

(France, Germany, Norway, Sweden and Switzerland) the poverty rate is held to 10 per cent or less for all three age groups, although the rather high rate of poverty among old people in Germany is notable. By contrast, an extremely small proportion of old people in Sweden are poor.

Figure 6.50 Proportion in relative poverty c. 1980: children, adults and old people; Luxembourg Income Study

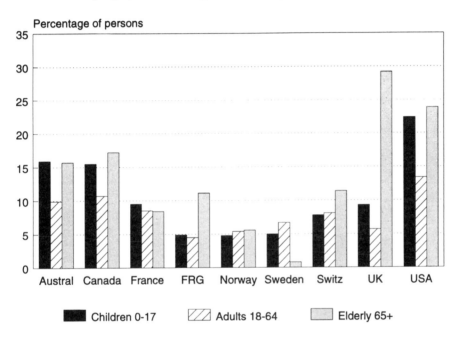

Relative poverty: adjusted income below half the median adjusted national income

Source: Suesser (1988).

There is a very high rate of poverty among single-mother households. Figure 6.51 shows relative poverty rates for three countries – the USA, Germany and Sweden – among single-mother and two-parent households, according to the number of children. The rates for single-mother households (solid lines) are altogether higher than for two-parent households (dotted lines) except in the case of Sweden, where poverty rates are uniformly low. Poverty rates tend to increase with the number of children in the household (illustrated by the upward slope of most of the lines). The graph shows data for the USA at two different points in time: 1979 and 1986. Poverty among both single-mother and two-parent households increased over that period. By 1986, the poverty rate in single-mother households with two children was nearly 60 per cent in the USA, compared with around 12 per cent for two-parent households with two children. From findings such as these it is clear that the increase in many countries in the number and proportion of single-mother households must be a cause of increasing poverty.

Figure 6.51   Relative poverty among two-parent and single-mother households

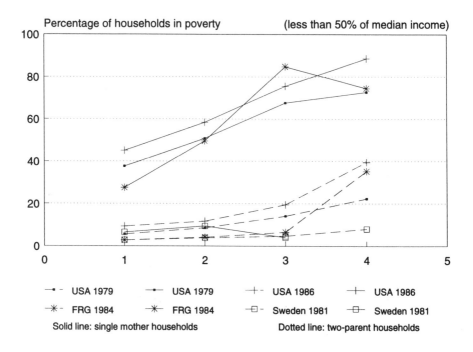

Source: Sørensen (1990).

Figure 6.52 shows some broadly similar statistics for a wider range of countries c. 1980. The percentage of children in poverty varies widely between single-mother and two-parent families in each of the nine countries, although in the case of Sweden and Germany the rates even for children in single-mother households are low. The countries having the highest rates of relative poverty among children in single-mother households are Australia, the USA, and Canada; these rates are also fairly high in the UK and the Netherlands.

Figure 6.52   Relative poverty of children in two-parent and single-mother families

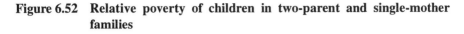

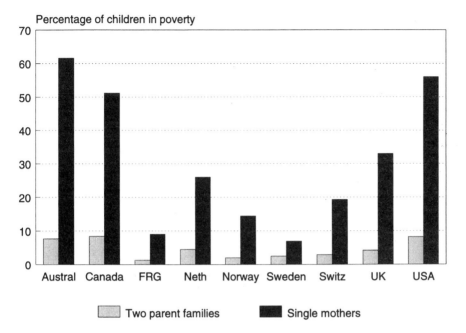

Relative poverty: in families with adjusted income less than 50 per cent of the median.

Source: Rainwater (undated).

CONCLUSION

The twentieth century has been a period of rapid and massive change in the economies of the more advanced countries and in the living conditions of their inhabitants.

All of these countries have experienced large increases in population and in life expectancy. Because these changes were closely associated with economic development, they occurred much earlier in the UK, which pioneered the industrial revolution, than in Japan, which entered on its explosive period of growth around 1950. As life expectancy has grown, so the young have come to form an increasingly small part of the total population, although certain cohorts, such as those belonging to the baby boom of the late 1940s, have been much larger than average.

From the second half of the nineteenth century onwards, there have been large flows of migrants into a number of European countries, most notably Germany, France, and Britain. After a period of reduced immigration in the interwar years (except into France) there have again been substantial flows of immigrants in the period since the Second World War. Although the total flows are very large, many of the migrants from earlier periods have been largely assimilated, so that the populations in European countries that are identifiably foreign, or belong to an ethnic minority group, form relatively small proportions of the total national populations (except in Switzerland). Little is known about the possible indirect effect of immigration on the total society (and hence on the incidence of psychosocial disorders). There must be some direct effect, because the rates of certain disorders are known to vary between national and ethnic groups. However, this cannot account for major time trends, because identifiable foreign or ethnic minority groups are not a large enough proportion of the population in any European country (except Switzerland) for the direct effect to be large.

The total output, expenditure, or consumption of the OECD countries, as captured by GDP, increased by a factor of six between 1900 and 1987. The pattern of growth was, however, highly uneven. There was, first, a phase of steady growth up to 1913; second, a phase of conflict and low growth from 1913 to 1950; third, the 'golden era' of 1950-73 when GDP grew at an unprecedented rate; and, fourth, a phase of slower growth and accelerated inflation from 1973, heralded by the first increase in oil prices. Rates of growth varied widely between countries, the explosive growth of the Japanese economy between 1950 and 1973 being the most remarkable feature.

A major structural change associated with economic growth is a decline in agriculture and an increase in industry and, later, services. The share of employment taken by agriculture fell in the OECD countries from about half in 1870 to 6 per cent in 1987. This broad change (which was well under way in many countries before the beginning of the present century) is associated with the massive growth of population in towns. The timing of the shift from agriculture to services varies widely between the developed countries.

These patterns provide a number of opportunities for testing the relationships between economic growth and social problems. The most obvious point is that if a major increase in standard of living either increases or reduces specific problems, then the extent of these problems should have changed substantially during the course of the present century in all developed countries. A second point is that if there is a relationship between standard of living and social problems, then OECD countries should be much more similar to each other in terms of the extent of their social problems at the present time than they were at the beginning of the century. A third point is that there should have been rapid change in the incidence of social problems during or soon after the periods of most rapid economic growth. In particular, changes in the incidence of social problems should have been most evident during the 'golden era' 1950-73 or soon after, and these changes should have been particularly marked in the high growth countries: that is, in Japan, and to a lesser extent in France, Germany and Italy. On the other hand, changes associated with low rates of growth should have been most evident in the period between 1929 and 1950, especially in Japan and the Netherlands.

In principle, another opportunity for research is provided by the switch from agriculture to industry and services, and the associated concentration of population in towns and cities. The problem here is that in many countries these changes were largely accomplished before the period for which data about youth problems are available.

Since the Second World War developed countries have greatly increased their expenditure on income maintenance, health, education, and social services. The largest category of expenditure is income maintenance; this is associated with a reduction of inequality of income, and has to some extent reduced the inequalities caused by the return of mass unemployment in the 1980s.

The 'golden era' saw explosive growth in key consumer products such as cars, telephones and television sets. Improvement in housing conditions was also dramatic. Health and life expectancy continued to improve, but both continued to be strongly related to income and class inequalities. Neither the pattern of change over time in health and life expectancy, nor the differences between countries at any one time, nor the class differences, can be explained by standards of health care. Health and life expectancy are, however, improved by other conditions associated with economic growth, such as improvements in physical conditions at home and at work, improvements in the wider physical environment, changes in diet and life styles, changes in the nature and organisation of work, and improved social support and education leading to greater autonomy at work and at home, especially for women.

There have been substantial increases over the century in the average number of years of education. Whereas at the beginning of the century education beyond the age of 14 was for only a tiny minority, by 1986 half of the population aged 19 in developed countries was enrolled at an educational establishment. A consequence of this change is that although young people in any defined age band now form a much smaller proportion of the population than formerly, the phase of youth now extends over a wider age band than previously. The growth of education effectively means that the transition to adulthood, at least in some of its aspects, is postponed until later. Also, it has been argued that the different transitions to adulthood – for example, in the domains of work, social life, and the family – have become less synchronized and therefore less coherent, and that adolescents increasingly face an extended period during which their identity is precarious because they have adult status in some domains but not in others. Another consequence of the growth of education is that whereas 50 years ago most young people lacked educational qualifications, now qualifications of some sort are rapidly becoming the norm, so the substantial minority who fail to obtain any are increasingly regarded as deviant.

There has been a large expansion of leisure time during the present century. Much free time is spent watching television, although young people watch less than older people do. Many social problems are popularly associated with media influences, but time spent watching television is highest in Japan, where many of the social problems are at their lowest.

Over the longer term, the process of economic development is strongly associated with a reduction of inequality of income, but once a threshold of development has been crossed, the link between further increases in GDP and inequality becomes weak. A major cause of inequality for the developed countries in the present century was the mass unemployment of the 1930s. The return of mass unemployment in the 1980s reversed the trend towards increasing equality in developed countries, although some of the effects were cushioned by the substantial income maintenance systems that were now in place. In certain developed countries, such as the USA, the UK, and West Germany, there is evidence of a recent increase in income inequality which is unconnected with unemployment. This will, in time, provide the opportunity for testing the theory that increasing inequality is associated with specific youth problems.

Although unemployment rose sharply in all developed countries in the early 1980s, in some it fell back towards its earlier rate, while in others it persists at a high level. Rate of unemployment is strongly related to level of education, and to occupation or social class. In the interwar period, youth unemployment rates tended to be lower than for older people, whereas in the 1980s and 1990s, youth unemployment rates greatly exceeded unemployment rates for adults aged 25 and over. Hence youth unemployment has become a much larger problem in recent years than ever before.

For a relatively recent period (starting around 1975) accurate information about income is available in a form that allows close comparisons to be made between countries. These comparisons produce widely different results depending on whether an absolute standard of poverty is used, or a relative standard (by reference to the national average). In Portugal, Spain and Greece, there is a much higher proportion in poverty on the absolute than on the relative definition. In the most advanced countries, the opposite is true. However, even when a relative standard is used, there is a higher proportion in poverty in the less developed European countries than in the more developed ones. On a relative standard, the proportion in poverty consistently increased from 1975 to 1985 in the UK, Denmark, Ireland and Portugal. A similar increase occurred in West Germany between 1983 and 1986. Also, dispersion of incomes increased in the USA, Canada and Australia between 1979 and 1987. Thus the long-term trend towards greater equality of income has been reversed in a number of developed countries in recent years.

Single-mother households are far more likely to be in poverty than two-parent households, and it is clear that the increase in many countries in the number and proportion of single-mother households must be a cause of increasing poverty.

Overall, this complex pattern of change in the twentieth century offers a rich field for testing hypotheses on the relationships between economic development and living conditions on the one hand, and social problems on the other. The main difficulty, of course, is that the many different changes are closely interconnected, so that there is a temptation to invoke a hopelessly vague concept such as 'modernization'. The challenge is to find ways of disaggregating the results and disentangling the effects of different specific changes in living conditions. The history of the twentieth century offers many opportunities for doing this, since the process of development was far from uniform. The many research strategies reviewed in an earlier chapter are available to study the specific effects of the living conditions described here.

REFERENCES

Appleyard, R. T. (1991). *International migration: Challenge for the nineties.* Geneva: International Organization for Migration.
Becker, G. S. (1964). *Human capital: A theoretical and empirical analysis with special reference to education.* New York: Columbia University Press.

Borjas, G. J. (1990). *Friends or strangers: The impact of immigration on the US economy.* New York: Basic Books.

Brown, C. & Gay, P. (1986). *Racial discrimination: 17 years after the Act.* London: Policy Studies Institute.

Canadian Institute for Advanced Research (1992). *The determinants of health.* Toronto: Author.

Castles, S. & Miller, M.J. (1993). *The age of migration: International population movements in the modern world.* London: Macmillan.

Censuses of Population (OPCS). Ten-yearly. London: HMSO.

Cinanni, P. (1968). *Emigrazione e imperialismo.* Rome: Riuniti.

Daniel, W. W. (1990). *The unemployed flow.* London: Policy Studies Institute.

Davey Smith, G., Bartley, M. & Blane, D. (1990a). The Black report on socioeconomic inequalities in health 10 years on. *British Medical Journal 301,* 373-377.

Davey Smith, G, Shipley, M. J. & Rose, G. (1990b). The magnitude and causes of socio-economic differentials in mortality: Further evidence from the Whitehall study. *Journal of Epidemiology and Community Health 44,* 265-270.

Easterlin, R. A. (1968). *Population, labor force and long swings in economic growth: The American experience.* New York: National Bureau of Economic Research.

Eichengreen, B. & Hatton, T. J. (1988). Interwar unemployment in international perspective: An overview. In B. Eichengreen & T. J. Hatton (eds.). *Interwar unemployment in international perspective.* Dordrecht: Centre for Economic Policy Research/Kluwer.

Eisenberg, P. & Lazarsfeld, P. F. (1938). The psychological effects of unemployment. *Psychological Bulletin 35,* 358-390.

Eurostat. *Basic statistics of the community,* annual. Luxembourg: Author.

Eurostat (1991). *A social portrait of Europe.* Luxembourg: Author.

Flora, P. (ed.) (1986). *Growth to limits: The Western European welfare states since World War II: Vol.4: Appendix, bibliographies,tables.* Berlin/ New York: Walter de Gruyter.

Galenson, W. & Zellner, A. (1957). International comparison of unemployment rates. In National Bureau for Economic Research, *The measurement and behaviour of unemployment,* 439-580. Princeton: Princeton University Press.

Goldthorpe, J. H. (1983). Women and class analysis: In defence of the conventional view. *Sociology 17,* 465-488.

Green, G., Coder, J. & Ryscavage P. (1990). *International comparisons of earnings inequality for men in the 1980s.* Luxembourg: Luxembourg Income Study Working Paper 58.

Hammar, T. (1990). *Democracy and the nation state.* Aldershot, Hants: Gower.

Haskey, J. (1992). The immigrant populations of the different countries of Europe: Their size and origins. *Population Trends 69,* 37-47.

Hauser, R. & Semerau, P. (1990). Trends in poverty and low income in the Federal Republic of Germany 1962/63 – 1987. In R. Teekens & B. M. S. van Praag (eds.) *Analysing poverty in the European Community,* 313-333. Luxembourg: Eurostat.

Inglehart, R. (1990). *Culture shift in advanced industrial society.* Princeton: Princeton University Press.

Jahoda, M., Lazarsfeld, P. F. & Zeisch, H. (1972). *Marienthal.* London: Tavistock.

Jackson, J. A. (1963). *The Irish in Britain.* London: Routledge & Kegan Paul.

Keat, P. G. (1960). Long-run changes in occupational wage structure 1900-1956. *Journal of Political Economy 68,* 584-600.

Keyfitz, N. & Flieger, W. (1968). *World population: An analysis of vital data.* Chicago: University of Chicago Press.

Klerman, L. V. (1993). The influence of poverty on health-related behaviors in adolescents. In S. G. Millstein, A. C. Petersen & E. O Nightingale (eds.) *Promoting adolescent health,* 38-57. New York: Oxford University Press.

Kritz, M. M., Lim, L. L. & Zlotnik, H. (1992). *International migration systems: A global approach.* Oxford: Clarendon Press.

Lancaster, H. O. (1990). *Expectations of life: A study in the demography, statistics and history of world mortality.* Berlin: Springer.

Lebergott, S. (1964). *Manpower in economic growth.* New York: Gordon & Breach.

Lydall, H. (1968). *The structure of earnings.* Oxford: Clarendon Press.

Lynch, P. & Oelman, B. J. (1981). Mortality from coronary heart disease in the British army compared with the civil population. *British Medical Journal 283,* 405-407.

Maddison, A. (1964). *Economic growth in the West.* New York: The Twentieth Century Fund; London: George Allen & Unwin.

Maddison, A. (1982). *Phases of capitalist development.* Oxford: Oxford University Press.

Maddison, A. (1989). *The world economy in the 20th century.* Paris: OECD.

Marmot, M. G. & Davey Smith, G. (1989). Why are the Japanese living longer?. *British Medical Journal 299,* 1547-1551.

Marmot, M. G., Kogevinas, M. A. & Elston, M. (1987). Social/economic status and disease. *Annual Review of Public Health 8,* 111-135.

Marmot, M. G. & Theorell, T. (1988). Social class and cardiovascular disease: The contribution of work. *International Journal of Health Sciences 18,* 659-674.

Marsh, C. (1988). *Exploring data.* Cambridge: Polity Press.

Noiriel, G. (1988). Le creuset français: Histoire de l'immigration XIXe-XXe siècles. Paris: Seuil.

O' Higgins, M. & Jenkins, S. P. (1990). Poverty in the EC: 1975, 1980, 1985. In R. Teekens & B. M. S. van Praag (eds.) *Analysing poverty in the European Community,* 187-211. Luxembourg: Eurostat.

Organization for Economic Cooperation & Development. *Labour force statistics,* annual. Paris: Author.

Organization for Economic Cooperation & Development (1985). *OECD employment outlook, 1985.* Paris: Author.

Organization for Economic Cooperation & Development (1986a). *OECD employment outlook, 1986.* Paris: Author.

Organization for Economic Cooperation & Development (1986b). *Living conditions in OECD countries: A compendium of social indicators.* OECD Social Policy Studies No. 3. Paris: Author.

Organization for Economic Cooperation & Development (1987). *OECD employment outlook, 1987.* Paris: Author.

Organization for Economic Cooperation & Development (1988). *OECD employment outlook, 1988.* Paris: Author.

Organization for Economic Cooperation & Development (1989). *Economies in transition.* Paris: Author.

Organization for Economic Cooperation & Development (1990). *Education in OECD countries 1987-88: A compendium of statistical information.* Paris: Author.

Peach, C. (1993). *Emerging trends and major issues in migration and ethnic relations in Western and Eastern Europe.* Paper given at a UNESCO-CRER seminar. Warwick: University of Warwick, Centre for Research in Ethnic Relations.

Piachaud, D. (1987). Problems in the definition and measurement of poverty. *Journal of Social Policy 16,* 147-164.

Rainwater, L. (undated). *Inequalities in economic well-being of children and adults in ten nations.* Luxembourg: Luxembourg Income Study Working Paper 19.

Rawls, J. (1972). *A theory of justice.* Oxford: Oxford University Press.

Runciman, W. G. (1966). *Relative deprivation and social justice: A study of attitudes to social inequality in twentieth-century England.* London: Routledge & Kegan Paul.

Ryscavage, P. & Henle, P. (1980). The distribution of earned income among men and women, 1958-77. *Monthly Labour Review,* April, 3-10.

Ryscavage, P. & Henle, P. (1990). Earnings inequality accelerates in the 1980s. *Monthly Labour Review,* December, 3-15.

Sawyer, M. (1976). Income distribution in OECD countries. *OECD economic outlook: Occasional studies.* Paris: OECD.

Smith, D. J. (1977). *Racial disadvantage in Britain.* Harmondsworth, Middx: Penguin.

SOPEMI (1992). *Trends in international migration: Continuous reporting system on migration.* Paris: OECD.

Sørensen, A. (1990). *Single mothers, low income, and women's economic risks: The cases of Sweden, West Germany and the United States.* Luxembourg: Luxembourg Income Study Working Paper 60.

Stirn, H. (1964). *Ausländische Arbeiter im Betrieb.* Frechen/Cologne: Bartmann.

Suesser, J. R. (1988). *Quelques eléments de comparaison internationale sur les revenus.* Luxembourg: Luxembourg Income Study Working Paper 30.

Teekens, R. & Zaidi, A. (1990). Relative and absolute poverty in the European Community. In R. Teekens & B. M. S. van Praag (eds.) *Analysing poverty in the European Community,* 213-250. Luxembourg: Eurostat.

Townsend, P. (1979). *Poverty in the United Kingdom.* Harmondsworth, Middx: Penguin.

United Nations (1991). *Sex and age distributions of population: The 1990 revision.* Population Studies No. 122. New York:Author.

UNESCO. *Statistical Yearbook*, annual. Paris: Author.

van der Wee, H. (1986). *Prosperity and upheaval: The world economy 1945-1980.* New York: Viking.

White, M. (1983). *Long-term unemployment and labour markets.* London: Policy Studies Institute.

White, M. (1991). *Against unemployment.* London: Policy Studies Institute.

White, M. & McRae, S. (1989). *Young adults and long-term unemployment.* London: Policy Studies Institute.

White, M. & Smith, D. J. (1994). 'The causes of persistently high unemployment'. In A. J. Petersen & J. Mortimer (eds.) *Youth unemployment and society.* Cambridge: Cambridge University Press.

Wilkinson, R. G. (1992). Income distribution and life expectancy. *British Medical Journal 304*, 165-8.

7

Media and Problem Behaviours in Young People[1]

ELLEN WARTELLA

In the constellation of factors that influence the social behaviour of adolescents – personality, peers, family, school, social background – the mass media seem to occupy a central role primarily in popular theorizing about the problems of youth, and less so in the academic literature on adolescent development. However, concerns about the effects of mass media on youth have been part of the social commentaries accompanying the introduction of each new technology of this century – film, radio, television and video (Wartella & Reeves, 1985); and this agenda of public concerns has given rise to social science research on the topic of media effects on children and youth.

Moreover, the social concerns about the effects of media on youth seem everywhere alike, and this can only accelerate as the international market-place of media products becomes ever more global and homogenized across national boundaries. Critics are concerned that young people spend too much time with media products that are too violent, commercialized, and of inappropriate morality (see Huston et al., 1992).

Although several countries (such as France and Canada) do have limits on the importation of foreign films or television programmes, a global cultural market now exists in which films made in, say, Ireland, are marketed elsewhere in Europe as well as in the Americas, Asia and Australia. European productions increasingly are competing with and even replacing the dominant American share of the market-place of the 1980s; nonetheless American television, film and music still predominate throughout the Western world. Throughout Europe the standards of aesthetic tastes or expectations for television dramatic

1. The section on use of the media within this chapter is distilled from a longer report by Isobel Bowler, then a Research Fellow at the Policy Studies Institute. The substantial contribution made by Isobel Bowler to the chapter is gratefully acknowledged.

fare, films, popular music and videos, are also increasingly homogenized. Like armies of old, cultural products now traverse western industrialized democracies. Multinational media conglomerates like Berlusconi (Italy), Rupert Murdoch (Australia, England and the United States) and Bertelsmann (Germany), and the American television networks, assure a comparability of content no matter what the nationality of the producer or the audience.

It is into such a global international media market-place, heavily promoting cultural products saturated with violence, sexuality and commercialism, that young audiences throughout Europe are increasingly drawn. The privatization of European television during the past decade has only speeded up this process. Against this backdrop, it is important to examine the theory that increasing exposure to harmful influences through the media may be among the causes of an increase over time in the incidence of psychosocial disorders among young people. The first part of this chapter briefly summarizes the evidence on the use of media by young people in European countries, with particular emphasis on television. The second part critically reviews the evidence on the effects of media exposure on problem behaviours in young people, including aggression, suicide, drug use, nutrition and eating disorders. It seems reasonable to examine – indeed it would be unreasonable not to examine – the heavily American-dominated literature on media effects as well as the relevant European literature on the same topic.

USE OF MEDIA

Long-term Trends

As detailed in Chapter 6, in developed countries there was a decline in cinema attendance from the time when statistics first became available in 1965, accompanied by an increase in the number of radio and television receivers. In the USA and the UK, a significant minority of the population had television sets by 1953, whereas most European countries reached a similar stage around 1960. Over a ten-year period starting in 1955, the major European economies reached the point where about half of the population had access to television, and after another ten years, nearly all had access to it. On average, Europeans now spend between two and three hours a day watching television (the figure varies between countries), which amounts to between 13 and 19 per cent of their waking lives. That total exposure has remained fairly constant since about 1975, having risen to that point from zero 20 years earlier. The

introduction of television between 1955 and 1975 clearly constitutes one o
the major social changes of the twentieth century.

Table 7.1   Availability of televisual media: 1988-89

Country	Households 1000s	Percentages of households with				
		TV	Colour TV*	2 + TVs*	VCR	Satellite Cable
Austria	2831	97	99	30	30	23
Belgium	3610	96	90	21	33	90
Denmark	2205	97	95	23	37	52
Finland	2120	95	92	30	45	32
France	22000	94	X	23	36	–
GFR	24600	97	95	18	31	X
Germany '91	31054	X	X	X	X	26
Ireland	1045	94	88	15	25	–
Italy	20276	99	85	39	19	–
Netherlands	6025	97	97	21	47	77
Norway	1900	96	97	26	48	29
Portugal	2715	92	60	7	X	–
Spain	11120	99	88	34	32	–
Sweden	3863	93	95	28	52	32
Switzerland	2600	94	97	12	40	70
UK	21700	97	93	47	54	7

*   Expressed as a percentage of TV households
–   Represents figures below 10 per cent
X   Represents missing data

Source: European Broadcasting Union (1990).

Since television was introduced, the terrestrial channels have been regulate(
in all European countries.   Whether such channels are state-owned
privately-owned, or run by quangos like the BBC, the content of the
programmes is subject to much greater restrictions than those applying, fo*
example, to books or magazines. The development of new technologies from
the 1980s onwards tended to create audiovisual products that were
decreasingly subject to regulation.   By the end of the 1980s, videorecording
machines were present in about half of households in a number of Europear
countries such as the UK, Sweden, Norway, the Netherlands (see Table 7.1)

The proportion of young people having access to video machines is probably higher than this. For example, in the UK in 1990, 89 per cent of children aged 11-14 had a video machine in the home, compared with 72 per cent of the total population aged 7 or over (Cinema & Video Audience Research, 1991). Satellite and cable television were also spreading rapidly, although the timing of their introduction varied considerably between European countries. It seems likely that the spread of these new technologies will increasingly loosen control over the content of material seen by children and young people.

Quality and Comparability of Audience Research Data

Every country in Europe has a system for finding out what people watch on television. In broad terms, three types of method are used to collect information on viewing from population samples. First, there are various electronic metering systems. These are used to register when each television set (and in some countries, videorecording machine) is switched on; also, viewing data for individuals may be recorded through a remote-control handset. None of these methods can record whether an individual is actually watching the screen, or attending to the programme. Second, there is the 'roster recall method', whereby people are interviewed and shown a list of yesterday's or last week's television programmes and asked to tick the ones they remembered viewing. Third, there is the diary method, which was the one most commonly used in Europe until the mid-1980s. Individuals in the sample are asked to record their viewing in a log on a daily basis: this task of course becomes more difficult as the number of channels increases.

Because telemetric research is driven by the demands of the advertising industry, much of it has no direct relevance to the present study. Methods are continually updated in order to meet the needs of advertisers and programmers, so that the scope for assessing change over time is severely curtailed. In addition, the scope for comparison between countries is limited by differences in the basic methods used, in the sample profiles, the times of year at which measurements are taken, and the age groups for which data are presented.

For these reasons, only limited data on change over time in exposure to television are available, and accurate cross-national comparisons cannot be made.

Exposure to Television

Table 7.2 gives some basic information about the channels available in European countries in 1989/90 and (bearing in mind the above caveats about method) the average (median) number of minutes spent viewing terrestrial television channels each day for the general population. This average was around two to three hours for most countries. Daily viewing time in Switzerland was apparently very low (median 60 minutes); it was high in Spain, Italy, and the UK.

There is a well-reported pattern of television use with age, which is fairly similar for all European countries. There is a steady increase in television viewing time from the ages of around 2 to 8 years old. This is followed by a period of relative stability between the ages of 9 and 13. Time spent in front of the television then decreases to reach its minimum level in late adolescence. In early adulthood, the level rises, and then remains relatively constant up to retirement age, when it increases to new heights. The British data (Broadcasters' Audience Research Board, 1990) can be used to illustrate that pattern. In 1989, median daily viewing was 212 minutes for all age groups (aged 4 and over), but was substantially lower than this for children and adolescents. In more detail, the medians were 149 minutes for those aged 4-7, 154 minutes for those aged 8-11, 166 minutes for those aged 12-15, and 149 minutes for those aged 16-24. The more recent British surveys do not disaggregate the 16-24 age group, but earlier surveys showed that viewing was lowest among those aged 16-19 (142 minutes in 1981) and rather higher among those aged 20-29 (156 minutes) (BBC Broadcasting Research, 1982). A similar pattern was shown for countries such as Sweden (Sveriges Radio, 1991), Finland (Erholm & Silvo, 1984) and Belgium (RTFB, 1990). In Norway (NRK, 1991) the differences between age groups were less marked, although the basic pattern was similar.

People in lower socio-economic groups tend to watch considerably more television than those in higher groups. For example, British data for 1989 showed an average weekly viewing of 30 hours 57 minutes among people in semi-skilled or unskilled manual occupational groups, compared with 17 hours 36 minutes among those in professional and managerial groups (Day & Cowie, 1990). Lukesch (1987) found that children at a Gymnasium (the most academic of the three types of school in Germany) read significantly more and watched significantly less than those at other types of school. Rosengren and Windahl (1989) showed that in Sweden time spent viewing was related both to socio-economic group and to sex among children aged 11-15: the level of viewing was higher among working-class than middle-class children, and higher among boys than among girls, so the level was highest of all among working-class boys.

Table 7.2 Television channels and average viewing time: European countries, 1989/90

	TV channels (A)	(B)	Pay channels	Imported programme share (%)	Median daily viewing (minutes)
Austria	2	(5)	7	X	113
Belgium	6	(9)	6	53.5	133
Denmark	2	(6)	11	46.0	98
Finland	3	(X)	7	50.0	125
France	6	(X)	–	15.0	128
GFR	3	(3)	12	53.0	131
Ireland	2	(4)	5	60.0	174
Italy	4	(X)	–	45.8	185
Netherlands	4	(9)	12	38.3	108
Norway	1	(2)	1	62.3	107
Portugal	2	(X)	–	X	155
Spain	3	(X)	–	42.5	209
Sweden	2	(2)	4	55.0	105
Switzerland	5	(X)	2	64.8	60
UK	4	(0)	–	20.0	185

A = indigenous TV channels, B = cross border TV channels which are able to be received by more than 10 per cent households viewing
Pay channels: number of pay channels with at least 10 per cent of households as subscribers – not necessarily indigenous stations
X represents missing data

Sources: Screen Digest (February 1991); European Broadcasting Union (1990).

The major change in exposure to television came with the introduction of the medium between about 1955 and 1970. As set out in an earlier section, accurate time series data are not available because of changes in audience measurement methods, but there may have been some increase in viewing since 1970 in some countries. For example, in Britain the median daily viewing time was found to be 148 minutes in 1973 for people aged 5 or over (BBC Broadcasting Research, 1974), compared with 212 minutes in 1989 (Broadcasters' Audience Research Board, 1990). On the other hand, viewing time in Sweden apparently remained stable between 1976 and 1989 (Sveriges Radio, 1991).

Video, Satellite and Cable Television

The viewing data quoted above refer to terrestrial television channels. Because of the spread of videorecording machines from the early 1980s onwards and the introduction of satellite television in the 1990s, the range of audiovisual material available to young people has already vastly increased, and will continue to increase in the future. Unfortunately, information about the time spent watching the newer audiovisual media is very patchy. The timing of the introduction of videorecording machines varied considerably between European countries: in 1988/89, the proportion of households with a videorecording machine ranged from 19 per cent in Italy, 25 per cent in Ireland, and 32 per cent in Spain, to 52 per cent in Sweden and 54 per cent in the UK (see Table 7.1). Households with children were more likely to acquire videorecording machines than other households. In Great Britain in 1989, 74 per cent of households with children, and 80 per cent of those with two or more children, had videorecording machines (Social Trends 1991 21, Table 10.5).

Although detailed data are not available, it is clear that up to 1990 the terrestrial television channels accounted for a high proportion of all viewing time. By 1990, video had made considerable inroads in some countries, but was still dwarfed by television. For example, in Britain in 1990, 22 per cent of the population aged 7 and over had watched video during the previous week, whereas over 90 per cent had watched a terrestrial television channel (Cinema & Video Audience Research, 1991). The impact of satellite television is still more recent. Swedish data for 1990 show that on average people spent 91 minutes a day watching terrestrial television channels, 13 minutes watching satellite television, and 5 minutes watching video (Sveriges Radio, 1991; population aged 3 and over). Up to about 1990, therefore, if exposure to audiovisual material was related to psychosocial disorders in young people, then the influence must have been through terrestrial television channels, and not through the newer electronic media.

What Young People Watch

Children do not just watch television designed for children. Indeed the most popular programmes amongst children are, in many countries, not children's programmes at all. Soap opera, comedy and game shows feature in the children's top ten in all the European countries for which such charts were available (UK, Switzerland, West Germany, France, Netherlands). It seems from examining the charts that children's tastes are moving closer to those of adults earlier than might have been imagined. There is a clear differentiation between the 8-11 year olds and the 4-7 year olds, with the latter watching more adult programming (Eurodience, 1990).

It is extraordinarily difficult to describe or analyse the content of television programmes, because of the complexity of the material, and because so many different conceptual frameworks are possible and conceivably appropriate, depending on the purpose of the analysis. Concern has most often been expressed about the level and frequency of violence in television programmes. Of course, on any coherent theory, the influence of such violent episodes must depend on their meaning in the context of the drama, narrative, or other form; yet the available quantitative data consist merely of crude counts of violent incidents classified according to severity, but without any consideration of how they would be perceived and understood in the context.

Content analysis of violence on television has been carried out predominantly in the United States. For over two decades American researchers have devised and applied measures of violent 'content' of programmes. One of the best known of these is George Gerbner's violence index which came out of his 1968 'cultural indicators' project (Gerbner, 1969, 1972). A problem of this type of work is that the measurements of violence are necessarily subjective. Gunter (1985) identified three problems of measurement: first, the definition of 'violence' used; second, the sample of programmes analysed; and third, the weighting of the violence index employed. The data presented here, therefore, should be treated with caution.

Since Gerbner's work in the USA, there have been several studies in European countries of violence on television. Direct comparison of most of these studies with Gerbner's US study, or indeed with each other, is problematic. Cumberbatch et al. (1988: 14) noted that 'the time periods sampled vary from one study to another while eccentric decisions seem to have been taken on the program genres to be included or excluded'.

The overall rates of violence found by the cultural indicators team in the USA have remained 'remarkably constant' over the years. 'An average of 5 or 6 acts of overt physical violence per hour menace over half of all major characters' on prime time television at least (Gerbner et al., 1980). The rates of violence per programme average 4.81 for prime time television (8pm to 11pm) and 5.77 for weekend daytime. Gerbner et al. (1980) reported an overall rate of 7.5 violent acts per hour.

A study in Germany reported 8.6 violent acts per hour in an analysis of 261 hours of 'entertainment' studied (Stuttgarter Nachrichten, 1986). From the Netherlands, Bouwmann and Strappers (1984) reported 5.8 violent episodes an hour in an analysis of 105 episodes of dramatic fiction programmes. In the UK, Cumberbatch et al. (1987) analysed more than 2,000 programmes in 1986 and reported violence during prime time at only 2.5 violent acts per hour. This rate is under half that reported in most other countries.

A second measure of violence is the proportion of broadcast programmes containing violence. The figures for the USA (80 per cent) and the Netherlands (80 per cent) are far higher than those for the UK (56 per cent) (Cumberbatch et al., 1987). Cumberbatch et al. (1988) pointed out that the low rate for Britain must be seen in the context of a relatively small proportion of broadcast television being devoted to dramatic fiction. This genre, in particular 'action adventure series', contains (along with film) more violence than does soap opera or situation comedy (Wober, 1988). Nineteen per cent of the 2,078 programmes analysed by Cumberbatch et al. (1987) fell into the category of dramatic fiction. This fifth of their sample contributed over three quarters (81 per cent) of all violence coded. The proportion of dramatic fiction in other countries is generally higher. For example, 23 per cent of the programmes in the Dutch study fell into this category (Bouwmann & Strappers, 1984) and in 1982 Finnish output was approximately 26 per cent dramatic fiction (Erholm & Silvo, 1984). Rosengren and Windahl (1989) estimated that 25 per cent of output in Sweden was in either film or fiction.

Although choice is constrained by the programming schedules, individuals can still exercise discretion over what they watch. Both Rosengren and Windahl (1989) in Sweden and Wober (1988) in Britain found that children were drawn to dramatic fiction programmes. These findings replicate those in other studies (for example, Comstock et al., 1978; Lyle & Hoffman, 1972; McLeod & Brown, 1972). In the Swedish study the three genres of programme that rated most highly in the children's list of preferences were detective/crime, films and serials. These programme types also attracted high audiences.

Wober (1988) found in Britain that the youngest age group in his sample (10 to 15-year-olds) were more drawn to items that contained violence than to those that did not. He also examined consistency of use of certain types of programmes by age. He found that there were substantial and significant correlations indicating that people who watched a great deal of a particular programme type in one week also watched that type more heavily in another week than did light consumers of the programme type. Even at the youngest age surveyed (4-6) certain individuals showed a consistent tendency to watch adventure action programmes.

Analysing the number of items of different kinds viewed per week, Wober found that children aged 10-12 consumed, on average, 2.9 episodes of adventure action out of a total diet of 35.5 episodes (four weeks surveyed, 1985/6). Comparable figures for adults were between 1.6 and 2.3 episodes out of around 31 episodes watched. However, these figures are means. Wober suggests that whereas some people will watch little if any of this genre, for others it will comprise around one half of their total viewing diet.

The proportion of television output that is of US origin varies between European countries. Cumberbatch and colleagues (1988) reported that the primary difference between US and UK programmes shown on British television was in the quantity of violence they contained. American programmes made up only 15 per cent of the 2,078 programmes coded by Cumberbatch et al. (1987) but contributed 31 per cent of the violent acts coded.

Summary

On average, people in Europe spend between one fifth and one seventh of their waking lives watching television, so the introduction of the medium between 1955 and 1970 clearly constitutes one of the major social changes of the twentieth century. Children and adolescents watch less television than adults, but their viewing time is still substantial. Although videorecording, satellite, and cable television will vastly increase the variety of audiovisual material available, in 1990 terrestrial television channels still accounted for a high proportion of viewing time in all European countries. Therefore, in the period 1955 to 1990, it is terrestrial television channels rather than other audiovisual materials that might, in principle, have had an influence on psychosocial disorders in young people. Although there are some differences between European countries in time spent watching television, in the timing of the growth of viewing from the 1950s onwards, and in the content of television programmes, the similarities are much more striking than the differences. Therefore, while television might, in principle, be connected with a general increase in psychosocial disorders in the postwar period, it probably could not contribute to an explanation of cross-national differences.

EFFECTS OF MEDIA ON PROBLEM BEHAVIOURS

The remainder of this chapter briefly summarises the evidence on the impact of media on adolescent problem behaviours such as aggression, suicide, drug use, nutrition and eating disorders. It considers in turn the major theoretical accounts of the links between media exposure and problem behaviours, the empirical evidence for such links, and the questions that remain to be addressed in this field.

The Effects of Media Violence on Aggressive Behaviour

By far the most heavily studied domain of potential media effects on behaviour is that of the influence of media violence. Particular attention over the past 40 years has been paid to the impact of television violence on adolescent aggression. More than a thousand studies in the United States (Comstock, 1990) and dozens within Europe have been devoted to this topic. One of the earliest studies of children and television in England, Himmelweit et al.'s (1958) study of the introduction of television into British society, addressed just this problem. Furthermore, several recent summaries of the whole body of research, as well as a national commission review of violence in the United States (National Research Council, 1993), have recently been reported (Comstock & Paik, 1991; Huston et al., 1992). Distilling decades of laboratory, survey and field experimental studies, the current reviews conclude that there is a correlation between violence viewing and aggressive behaviour, a relationship that holds even when a variety of controls are imposed (for example age of subject, social class, education level, parental behaviour, attitudes towards aggression) and tends to hold across national boundaries (see, for example, Belson, 1978, for research in England, and Huesmann et al., 1984b, in Finland).

As Comstock and Paik (1991) have noted, a variety of meta-analytic studies of violence research (for example Andison, 1977) have demonstrated that the effects of exposure to television violence on aggressive behaviour of adolescents and young adults is *best* illustrated in experimental research. However, as a plethora of critics have noted (see, for instance, Cumberbatch & Brown, 1989), laboratory studies are fraught with serious challenges to external validity: most importantly, the experimental setting and the measures of violent behaviour used there are simply too far removed from the real interpersonal setting of teenagers' lives. Moreover, the moderating forces of real social situations, presence of adults and authority figures, and opportunities for the adolescent to delay responses, are very real. Thus, it may be that laboratory studies overestimate the frequency, severity and likelihood of violent response to television violence.

Consequently, studies with greater ecological validity (for example survey, longitudinal panel studies and even field experiments) offer more compelling evidence of the relationship between attention to media violence and adolescent violent behaviour. These will be considered in turn.

The best known of the European field studies of violence and adolescents is Belson's (1978) survey of more than 1,500 12 to 17-year-old adolescents in London. This was a particularly carefully constructed survey, with great care taken in drawing the sample and measurement preparation. Belson measured 13 different types of violence (for example violence that is 'in a good cause' as against violence that is 'horrific', as well as criminal actions of the real world such as attacking someone with a tyre lever); he also developed detailed measures of the adolescent viewing of different kinds of television fare (for example sports, news, comedies, cartoons), and exposure to violent fare in other media such as newspapers, film and comic books. Further, he carefully matched respondents in his sample when comparing heavy and light violence viewers on various dependent measures. He found, for instance, that heavy violence viewers committed more acts of serious antisocial behaviour (7.48 acts in previous six months) compared to light viewers of television violence (5.02 acts), but even less serious acts of antisocial behaviour showed statistically significant differences between heavy and light television violence viewers. Furthermore, Belson found that this pattern of correlations between exposure to violent fare and antisocial behaviours held when other media were examined as well (film and comics). Belson (1978:15) concluded that:

> The evidence gathered through this investigation is very strongly supportive of the hypothesis that high exposure to television violence increases the degree to which boys engage in serious violence. Thus for serious violence boys: (i) heavier viewers of television violence commit a great deal more serious violence than do light viewers of television violence who have been closely equated to the heavier viewers in terms of a wide array of empirically derived matching variables; (ii) the reverse form of this hypothesis is not supported by the evidence.

As Comstock and Paik (1991) noted, the importance of the Belson study is that he found a relationship in the real world between viewing media violence and serious, criminal behaviour on the part of adolescent boys.

The weakness of the Belson study, however, was that because it was cross-sectional, it could not demonstrate a causal relationship between exposure to media violence and violent behaviour, nor could it show the direction of the causation. Belson assumed that exposure to media violence caused the boys to behave violently, but it is possible that boys inclined to violence sought out violent television programmes to watch. More convincing evidence of causal relationships can be provided by longitudinal studies. Eron and colleagues' longitudinal study of adolescents in the United States found a relationship between viewing television violence and real-world aggressive behaviour. For instance, boys' viewing of television violence at age 8 predicted these boys' aggressive behaviour at age 18, and more importantly, predicted serious criminal behaviour at age 30 (Eron, 1982; Eron et al., 1972; Huesmann et al., 1984a). Indeed, Huesmann and colleagues (1984) found that children whose peers rated them as more aggressive at age 8 were more likely to be convicted of serious crimes by age 30. These researchers argued that aggression is a stable trait and reported a 0.46 correlation between age 8 aggression scores and age 30 criminality. These major longitudinal studies suggested that early viewing of television violence is at least one factor contributing to adolescents' and young adults' aggressive behaviour.

Importantly, this same research team has carried out similar longitudinal studies in four other countries (Australia, Finland, Poland and Israel) which parallel the US study (see Huesmann & Eron, 1986). Again, the data *across nations* support the conclusion that viewing televised violence leads to aggressive behaviour and not *vice versa*. However, it should be noted that the overall levels of violence viewing varied considerably across the countries studied. The one US longitudinal study (Milavsky et al., 1982) that did not support the assertion that television violence viewing causes later aggressive behaviour has been vigorously criticized on methodological grounds, and indeed the data themselves have been reinterpreted to support a causal explanation (Cook et al., 1983; Comstock & Paik, 1991).

More recently, Rosengren and Windahl (1989) reported on a decade's research in Sweden on children and adolescents' media use. Included are longitudinal data on television use and effects. Using teacher ratings of children's aggressiveness, Rosengren and Windahl (1989:219) reported that:

> In grade 5, at the age of 11, those who watched more than two hours of TV a day while in preschool, tend to have a level of aggressiveness rated almost twice as high as those having watched less TV while in preschool, even after control for aggressiveness in preschool, as well as for a number of other relevant variables.

Lately, there is evidence from a recent natural field experimental study conducted in Canada and reported by Williams (1986). She examined children's aggressive behaviour (which measured both verbal and physical aggression) before and after the introduction of television in a Northern Canadian town. Initially, she compared the children in the no-television town with children in two other towns with established television. Although there was no difference in aggressive behaviour among the children in the three towns at the time before television was introduced, after two years of television, children in the town that formerly had no television showed significantly higher levels of verbal and physical aggression than did children in the other two towns.

Limitations on the causal relationship are generally of the following types. First, children and adults who are *predisposed* towards violence are more likely to respond to television violence (see, for example, Comstock & Paik, 1991). Secondly, variations in the *portrayal* of the violence also can influence the effect. In particular, Comstock (1990) noted that there are three other major contingencies. Violence that was rewarded, shown as unjustified, and close to real life or pertinent to the viewer increased the likelihood of influencing behaviour. And importantly, the longitudinal studies suggest that early exposure to television violence is associated with antisocial behaviours even up to 20 years later. Moreover, there is variation in the *effect size* found: Comstock (1990) reported that an analysis of 22 different surveys found that effect sizes varied between 5 and 15 per cent. Nonetheless, the *cause* of the correlation is not so clearly agreed upon (National Research Council, 1993:106):

> There is debate about the underlying causal relationship. The correlations may reflect the joint effect of greater exposure to television violence and a heightened potential for violent behaviour, both resulting from poor parental supervision. It may also be that children with high potential for violent behaviour select violent material to watch. There is also debate about permanence of any direct effect, about the importance of whether the television violence is punished or rewarded and about the behavioural effects of frustration that might be activated by compelling changes in children's television viewing patterns.

Two major theories have been proposed to account for this correlation. First, there is the social learning theory originally proposed in the 1960s by Bandura (1977), who focused on the imitative effects of television; a variation on the theory by Berkowitz (Berkowitz & Rawlings, 1963) stressed the disinhibitory effects of television violence. This idea that viewing can be a disinhibition mechanism – that viewing television violence can reduce constraints on viewers' pent-up aggressive behaviour – has been perhaps the most widely studied and widely cited theoretical explanation for violence effects.

A second theoretical explanation is proposed by Zillman's (1982) arousal and Drabman & Thomas's (1974) desensitization hypothesis. Both these hypotheses propose that television violence is an arousing stimulus which when viewed in heavy amounts over time can actually desensitize heavy viewers such that each subsequent exposure to violence on television becomes less arousing. Eventually, it has been argued, such desensitization leads to more callous attitudes toward real-world violence (Donnerstein et al., 1987).

It is quite likely that these are not competing theories of television violence effects; both may be operative. Indeed, since the 1960s and 1970s when the earliest research on Bandura's social learning theory was conducted, increasingly elaborate theories of television violence have been offered. For instance, from Berkowitz's early theorizing about the disinhibitory effects of media violence, he (Berkowitz, 1984) has now developed a very rich and elaborated view of how media portrayals of violence stimulate associative networks or cognitive scripts or thoughts. When primed by a real world situation, a media-related script sparks an acting out of an aggressive behaviour. This theoretical reformulation, then, tries to account for instances when real-world aggressive behaviour does not imitate media portrayals of aggression, but may nonetheless be stimulated by the media portrayal. In this formulation, media portrayals of violence are important in initially implanting ideas about aggression. That is, violence from television is 'encoded' in the cognitive map of viewers, and subsequent viewing of television violence helps to maintain these aggressive thoughts, ideas and behaviours. Over time such continuing attention to television violence thus can influence people's attitudes toward violence and their maintenance and elaboration of aggressive scripts. Finally, the arousing aspect of viewing media violence can stimulate the actual production of violent behaviour on the part of viewers. In this elaborated theory, it is not television violence alone that causes violent action. Rather media violence is one environmental factor that may contribute to the maintenance of a stable pattern of aggressive behaviour in children and adults. Other environmental factors that may frustrate and victimize the child also reinforce aggressive behaviour. Here, Huesmann's (1986:138-139) account is relevant:

> Aggressive scripts for behaviour are acquired from observation of media vi-
> olence and aggressive behaviour itself stimulates the observation of media
> violence. In both childhood and adulthood, certain cues in the media may trigger

the activation of aggressive scripts acquired in any manner and thus variables may mitigate or exacerbate these reciprocal effects. However, if undampened, this cumulative learning process can build enduring schemes for aggressive behaviour that persist into adulthood. Thus, early childhood television habits are correlated with adult criminality independently of other likely causal factors. Therefore, interventions directed at mitigating the effects of media violence on delinquency and criminality should focus on the preadolescent years.

The view of media violence effects presented here is a distinctly American view and is not without its critics such as Freedman (1984) in the United States and Cullingford (1984) in Britain. Nonetheless it comports with the most recent reviews of the area both in the United States and in Europe, and with reports by American national commissions on media (Huston et al., 1992) and on aggression (National Research Council, 1993). A few comments are in order, however, regarding major European critics of this perspective.

The British reviews by Cullingford (1984) and by Cumberbatch & Brown (1989) help to identify many of the concerns regarding the American media violence research. First, compared to the thousand American studies of media violence effects, only a few dozen European studies have examined television and media violence effects over the past 30 or so years of television. Second, European media, particularly the public broadcasting systems that dominated European television until recently, were never as violent as American television. As is argued above, this circumstance is rapidly changing. As it does, the prior European lack of concern with violent media may well change. Third, at least in the case of these two reviews, European insistence that the conclusions from laboratory studies may be dismissed as externally invalid does not address the overall consistency of the survey and field experimental research which, with a few exceptions (notably the disputed Milavsky et al. study, 1982), are supportive of a causal link between television violence viewing and aggressive behaviour. Fourth, the magnitude of media violence effects has been interpreted as having little social significance in accounting for real-world aggression and violence, at least when measured against social class, ethnic, gender, economic, political and other socio-cultural factors.

Overall, these critics do not undermine the substantial body of convincing evidence to show that television violence is among the causes of real-world violence. However, they are persuasive in arguing that the magnitude of the effects of television violence in comparison with other causes is not well understood, and may be small; and that its influence may in the past have been substantially less in Europe than in the USA, because European television in the past was considerably less violent than US television.

It is difficult to see how more research on the short-term effects of television violence can be beneficial. Continuation of the longitudinal studies, cross-nationally, by Eron and his colleagues, however, could further increase our understanding of the role of media violence in the aggressive behaviour of adolescents. In short, the question that remains is not whether media violence has an effect, but rather how important that effect has been, in comparison with other factors, in bringing about major societal changes such as the postwar rise in crime. Future research should also aim to establish who precisely is most susceptible to media violence, and what sorts of intervention help diminish its influence.

Media Influence on Homicide and Suicide Rates

American sociologist David Phillips has been conducting statistical analyses of the rates of homicide and suicide in various populations. His argument (in keeping with psychologist Albert Bandura's social learning theory) is that human violence is highly susceptible to social influence. Phillip's method is to examine national rates of homicide or suicide following heavy media coverage of such social events as public executions, plane crashes, spectacular murders or multiple suicides. For instance, in one study (Phillips, 1982), he reported an examination of the short-term fluctuations in the homicide rate in London following 22 heavily publicized executions that took place in England between 1858 and 1921. He argued that such public executions have the short-term effect of 'deterring' homicide, but that deterrence is indeed short-term. He found, for instance, that compared to a four-week control period directly prior to a public execution, the number of homicides in London decreased an average of 35.7 per cent the week after a public execution; however, the frequency of homicides increased by a corresponding amount within two to four weeks after the public execution. The study was replicated in the United States by Phillips & Hensley (1984).

Most pertinent to this review is Phillips' study of the effects of media coverage of suicide. Phillips (1974) found that after widely covered suicides of famous people, suicide rates increased. For instance, within a week after Marilyn Monroe killed herself in 1963, national suicide rates jumped 12 per cent. Also, Phillips and Corstensen (1988) found teenagers are particularly susceptible to suicide stories as compared to adults aged 30-39. From a study of 38 stories broadcast between 1973 and 1979, they reported that teenage suicides increased following nationally televised news or features stories about suicides.

These sociologists argued that media coverage of suicides, particularly coverage that spans across media such as on television news, talk shows, newspapers, radio and magazines, acts as a 'natural advertisement' for suicide and influences those teenagers who are already in despair over their social and psychological situation.

In one replication of this latter study in Europe, Schmidtke and Hafner (1988) found an increase in the rate of suicides among West German teenagers following the airing of a television programme showing the suicide of a teenager by jumping under a train; they reported that the number of railway suicides among male teenagers aged 15-19 increased by 175 per cent after the television programme.

Quasi-experimental statistical studies of this kind have been criticized in the US by Baron and Reiss (1985) on the grounds that they pay inadequate attention to time lag between the media event and subsequent homicide or suicide, that they use unsatisfactory definitions of suicide, and that they rely on databanks with sometimes questionable data on the frequency and timing of crimes of violence in the population. In short, these studies are very difficult to conduct and findings from them remain controversial.

At present, the hypothesis that media coverage of suicides, homicides, and other spectacular deaths has a social influence on imitative murder and suicides among teens is very tentative. It may be that such media coverage acts in Phillips' words as 'a national advertisement' triggering actions whose causal roots are found elsewhere in the environment or individual personality. Further replication of Phillips' work across cultures is clearly needed.

Media Influence on Body Image, Nutrition and Eating Disorders

Over the past decade there has been increased concern about the role of media, and in particular television, in influencing adolescents' nutritional choices and eating habits. As one review of the American television portrayals of food and nutrition noted, American television tends to promote fattening foods in the advertisements (snack foods, chocolate, soft drinks) as well as promoting snacking in dramatic programmes, yet most people populating television are slim and healthy (Blum, 1990). In a content analysis of 600 minutes of television commercials and programming, Kaufman (1980) found that nearly half of the 537 television characters she coded were rated as thin or average; moreover, teenagers were never depicted as obese and only 7 per cent were rated as overweight. Nonetheless nearly all (95 per cent) of the television characters were depicted either talking about food, eating food or shown with food. As Kaufman noted: 'the television diet may be unbalanced and fattening but characters in commercials and programmes alike remain slim and healthy' (Kaufman, 1980:37).

Critics of television's role in children's nutrition such as Dietz and Gortmaker (1985) have argued that both television viewing (itself a low-energy activity associated with snacking among American children) and the nutritional messages portrayed there are detrimental to good nutritional habits.

There have not been many studies of the actual effects of media use on nutritional behaviour. Two of the best known are those of Dietz and Gortmaker (1985) and Tucker (1986). Both are survey studies. Dietz and Gortmaker conducted a health survey of more than 15,000 children and adolescents across the United States. They found a strong correlation between viewing television (but not time spent reading or time spent with friends) and obesity, with every hour increase in television viewing increasing the probability of obesity by two per cent. This correlation held when all appropriate controls for family background and environmental factors were introduced. Tucker (1986) examined the relationships among television viewing, physical fitness and nutritional health. He surveyed 406 middle-class teenage boys and found a negative correlation between television viewing and physical fitness. He noted, however, that the direction of causality could not be determined since it may very well be that physically unfit children are more attracted to watching television as a pastime than are more active and physically fit children.

In addition to concerns about television's influence on nutritional behaviours, there is a growing body of evidence suggesting that media portrayals of very thin and healthy young adults may lead adolescents to become dissatisfied with their own body image and to adopt abnormal eating behaviours in an attempt to attain an undesirably thin standard of beauty. Some have suggested that sociocultural pressures (such as the unattainably thin women portrayed through the media) in addition to family pressures and the general socialization of women may play a role in the causation of bulimia and anorexia nervosa (Boskind-White & White, 1983).

Recently, researchers have begun to investigate the influence of the media on the body images of adolescents. For instance, in a longitudinal study of youth in Finland, Rauste and Wright (1989) found that older adolescents were more satisfied with their bodies than were younger adolescents, and that boys at all ages were more satisfied than were girls. She noted 'there seems to be, for each sex, a set of critical features which appear to reflect those culturally determined stereotypes of the ideal female or male body emphasized in books, mass media and advertisements' (Rauste & Wright, 1989:81). For young adolescent females, weight is the critical feature that determines self-satisfaction with their body.

These findings seem to hold cross-nationally as well. Offer et al. (1988: 67-68) found that adolescent boys 'consistently expressed more pride in and positive feelings about their bodies ... Across ten countries, girls much more often reported feeling ugly and unattractive than did boys.' These authors attributed this finding to the obligation placed on women to be attractive in order to attract a mate. Again, Murray (1990) argued that much of adolescent girls' knowledge about eating disorders such as bulimia and anorexia nervosa comes through the mass media of television, newspapers and magazines. In their study of 150 Australian adolescents and young adults, they found that about one third of the females reported that they had used information about eating disorders acquired through media to experiment with their own eating habits.

One experimental study in the United States (Meyers & Biocca, 1992) found that female college students tended to hold distorted body images, and that their estimations of their body size were subject to change. They exposed female students to one of two types of commercial: a commercial oriented towards body image and focusing on ideal, thin female bodies, or a neutral commercial that represented either average weight or neutral characters and did not focus on the bodies shown. Contrary to expectations, Myers and Biocca found that indeed the commercials oriented towards body image did influence the college women's images of their own bodies, but by making the women feel thinner and slimmer. That is, although they found that college women's perceptions of their own body shape could be influenced by only 30 minutes of television programming, the influence was in the opposite direction from that hypothesized. The authors argued:

> The young women may have imagined themselves in the ideal body presented by the advertising. They may have bought the ideal female body sold by the advertising. Our model suggests that a woman's body image is an elastic construct, a compromise between her internalized ideal body and her objective body shape. The young women may have seen the ideal as more attainable and within reach. The commercials invited them to fantasize themselves in their future ideal body ... The commercials' cumulative message of 'You can be thin' may have developed greater feelings of self control in the young women. 'You can be thin' may have been translated as 'I am getting thin' and, maybe, even 'I will be thin.' In the body image measurement task, these subjects may have

consciously or unconsciously projected a self-perceived body image that was closer to the ideal marketed in the commercials, an ideal they had internalized (Myers & Biocca, 1992:127).

Thus, media portrayals of very youthful, slim and healthy people may very well influence adolescents' perceptions of their own body image. Clearly, more needs to be known about the direction of the influence. However, when coupled with poor nutritional messages heavily weighted toward promoting fattening snack and sugared foods, contradictory health messages are promoted through the media. Whether such messages actually predispose to adolescent eating disorders is not at all clear; however, there is some evidence that media images are part of the cultural context that determines adolescent satisfaction with body images and consequently nutritional and eating behaviours.

Media Influence on Alcohol and Drug Use

In a major review of the relationship between US television use and adolescent alcohol use, Atkin (1990) suggested several reasons to expect that television portrayals of alcohol are influential on adolescent drinking: first, there is heavy promotion of alcohol both in commercials and in scheduled programmes. Second, young adolescents are curious about the adult behaviour of drinking alcohol and therefore are motivated to attend to alcohol messages and are more susceptible to the cultivation of positive attitudes toward such drinking behaviour. Third, given their general life state, adolescents may be more susceptible to advertising themes that associate drinking with having fun and getting along with peers.

For the most part, however, research on media influences on alcohol use has been limited to correlational survey research methodologies; it is difficult to ascertain causality from these static surveys. Two key US studies have demonstrated a positive association between media use and alcohol use by adolescents. Strickland (1983) surveyed 772 adolescents from seventh through eleventh grades. He extrapolated exposure to advertising from measures of television viewing of programmes during the previous month after weighting for the presence of beer and wine advertising. In addition, he measured the adolescents' alcohol consumption. Strickland found that advertising had only 'meagre effects' on the adolescents' consumption: the partial correlation between advertising exposure and alcohol consumption was 0.12, after controlling for age, sex, race and total television viewing time; and the standardized regression coefficient in a path model of consumption for advertising was 0.18. A much stronger causal effect was found for having peers who are drinkers (path coefficient of 0.34). This study has been criticized on varied methodological grounds (Atkin, 1990), most importantly for only including in the final analysis students with past drinking experiences, thereby excluding those who will never drink and those who do not drink now but will drink in the future. This may have suppressed the correlations by narrowing the variance in the consumption variable.

The other major American survey by Atkin et al. (1984) was of 665 12 to 17-year-olds. The authors developed an elaborate index of exposure to alcohol advertising, composed of measures of exposure during the previous month to television programmes that frequently carried alcohol advertising, frequency of exposure to certain alcohol brands, and exposure to various product categories and specific television advertisements. The consumption variable was assessed through a detailed instrument to gauge various consumption patterns. This study also measured adolescents' knowledge about alcohol and attitudes towards its use. When various analyses were performed, controlling for demographic characteristics, family and anti-drinking messages, the authors found a modest positive relationship between exposure to alcohol advertising and beer drinking (the regression coefficient for beer was 0.20). Atkin et al. also found that exposure to alcohol advertising was associated with favourable attitudes toward beer drinkers as fun-loving, friendly, manly and young (attributes promoted in American beer advertisements). Strickland (1984) challenged the strength of the causal inference by noting that Atkin et al. may not have controlled for all relevant antecedent variables. Atkin (1990:19) later cautiously reinterpreted his own findings thus: 'the most reasonable interpretation of these data is that beer advertising makes a significant but mild positive contribution to beer drinking among teenagers'.

A survey of 433 Scottish youth aged 10 to 17 was reported by Aitken et al. (1988). They found that young drinkers in the sample identified with the portrayals of drinking in television advertisements for beer, and that such advertisements reinforced these adolescents' under-age drinking patterns.

In another study of adolescent smoking, Aitken and Eadie (1990) reported that under-age adolescent smokers were also influenced in their preferences for different types of cigarette brands. The largest American study of the direct behavioural effects of televised drug messages comes from a massive public service informational campaign to stop drug use: Campaign for a Drug Free America. After five years of monitoring the largest television anti-drug health campaign ever mounted (in 1989 it was the eleventh largest advertising campaign in US television history), Black (1991) reported that specially constructed anti-drug messages were shifting children's, college students' and adults' attitudes against drugs and drug users. The age group showing the least change in drug attitudes was teenagers (Black, 1991).

In short, there is little evidence to suggest that television messages are the cause of under-age drinking or drug use. However, as Walleck (1983) noted, health education campaigns such as public service messages will not succeed in television if the other messages (such as glamorous portrayals of smoking and drinking alcohol) appear throughout dramatic television fare and product advertisements. Clearly, the influence of media portrayals operates within larger networks of environmental, social and psychological factors: all these together influence adolescents' use of drugs and alcohol.

SUMMARY AND CONCLUSIONS

The first section of this chapter concluded that the growth of television from close to zero coverage in 1950 to near universal coverage in 1970 was one of the most striking social changes of the present century. In all developed countries, people spend a substantial proportion of their waking hours watching television, and although exposure is lower among children and, especially, teenagers, than among the general population, it remains very substantial. On any reasonable definition, television in all countries shows a large number of violent acts, although at least until recently the level of violence has been substantially higher on US than on European television. However, the studies that have counted violent acts portrayed say little or nothing about the meaning of these portrayals as perceived by those who watch them. These facts leave open the possibility that the growth of television might be among the causes of a growth of violence in society, as reflected for example in rising crime rates. It seems less likely that television violence could explain cross-national differences in societal violence, except, perhaps, any such difference between the USA and Europe as a whole.

The second part of the chapter has critically examined the evidence from studies designed to test the theory that the media have an influence on problem behaviours. Although in popular debate the mass media have for long been criticized for having a bad effect on the behaviour of young people, the effects of the media are not often seriously addressed in the academic psychological literature on adolescence. The factors more typically thought to be causal are personality, interpersonal relationships within the family, peers, school performance, and a host of other influences in the socio-cultural environment, such as social class and economics. Nonetheless, partly in response to popular concerns, there is a growing body of research on the impact of the media on youth.

The vast preponderance of this research has focused on the influence of media portrayals of violence on adolescent aggression. After more than one thousand studies in the United States and a much smaller number in Europe, one can conclude that there is a positive correlation between viewing television violence and aggression in adolescence. Furthermore, there is evidence from cross-national longitudinal research that heavy viewing of television violence in the early grade school years is associated with criminal behaviour among young adults. Children who are more disposed to violence (such as those living in violent homes and environments) are more likely to be influenced by violent portrayals in the media. In several respects, the effects are also related to the particular ways in which violence is portrayed. Finally, theoretical accounts of the mechanisms through which television violence influences viewers' psychology have become increasingly elaborate over the past 30 years. Current theorizing suggests that portrayals of violence operate to encode, maintain and evoke violent ideas, thoughts and behaviourial scripts in heavy viewers which are later acted out in a variety of settings. The long-term development of aggression as a stable behaviourial pattern among some young people and adults suggests that media violence, while not *the* cause of such violent behaviour, certainly is a likely contributor to such problem behaviours.

When considering other adolescent problem behaviours such as suicides, eating disorders, alcohol and drug use, there is far less evidence about the strength of the relationship between media portrayals and these adolescent behaviours. Partly, this is due to the paucity of research on these topics. Since the same theoretical accounts of adolescent social learning that have been applied to acts of violence may also be applied to modelling of body images, drinking and smoking patterns, it seems likely that media portrayals may be implicated in these areas as well.

In conclusion, the role of mass media as an environmental factor providing adolescents with information about what are appropriate standards of behaviour should not be discounted. No one is likely to say that media are the cause of disordered adolescent behaviour, but neither are media neutral or unimportant as socializers of youth.

REFERENCES

Aitken, P. & Eadie, D. (1990). Reinforcing effects of cigarette advertising on underage smoking. *British Journal of Addiction 85*, 399-412.

Aitken, P., Leathar, D. & Scott, A. (1988). Ten to sixteen year olds' perceptions of advertisements for alcoholic drinks. *Alcohol and Alcoholism 23*, 491-500.

Andison, F.S. (1977). TV violence and viewer aggressiveness: A cumulation of study results. *Public Opinion Quarterly 41*, 314-31.

Atkin, C.K. (1990). Effects of televised alcohol messages on teenage drinking patterns. *Journal of Adolescent Health Care 11*, 10-24.

Atkin, C.K., Hocking, J. & Block, M. (1984). Teenage drinking: Does advertising make a difference? *Journal of Communication 28*, 71-80.

Bandura, A. (1977). *Social learning theory*. Englewood Cliffs, NJ: Prentice Hall.

Baron, J.N. & Reiss, P.C. (1985). Sometime next year: Aggregate analysis of the mass media and violent behaviour. *American Sociological Review 50*, 347-63.

BBC Broadcasting Research (1974). *BBC Broadcasting Research Annual Review I*, 10-13.

BBC Broadcasting Research (1982). *Annual Review of BBC Broadcasting Research Findings 8*, 27-39.

Belson, W.A. (1978). *Television violence and the adolescent boy*. Westmead, England: Saxon House, Teakfield Limited.

Berkowitz, L. (1984). Some thoughts on anti-and prosocial influence of media events: A cognitive-menoassociation analysis. *Psychological Bulletin 95*, 410-27.

Berkowitz, L. & Rawlings, F. (1963). Effects of film violence on inhibitions against subsequent aggression. *Journal of Abnormal and Social Psychology 661*, 405-12.

Black, G. (1991). Changing attitudes toward drug use: The effects of advertising. In L. Donohew, H. Sypher & W. Bukowski (eds.) *Persuasive communication and drug abuse education*, 157-191. Hillsdale, NJ: Lawrence Erlbaum.

Blum, R. (1990). Executive summary. *Journal of Adolescent Health Care 11*, 86-90.

Boskind-White, M. & White, W. (1983). *Bulimarexia: The binge/purge cycle*. New York: W.W. Norton.

Bouwmann, H. & Strappers, J. (1984). The Dutch violence profile: A replication of Gerbner's message system analysis. In G. Melishedk, K. E. Rosengren & J. Strappers (eds.) *Cultural indicators: An international symposium*. Vienna: Verlag der Osterreichischen Akademie Wissenschaften.

Broadcasters' Audience Research Board (1990). *1989 Yearbook*. London: AGB Television Information Systems.

Cinema & Video Audience Research [CAVIAR] (1991). Press release 8. London: Author.

Comstock, G. (1990). Deceptive appearances: Television violence and aggressive behaviour. *Journal of Adolescent Health Care 11*, 31-44.

Comstock, G. A, Chaffee, S., Katzman, N., McCombs, M. & Roberts, D. (1978). *Television and human behavior.* New York: Columbia University Press.

Comstock, G. & Paik, H. (1991). *Television and the American child.* New York: Academic Press.

Cook, T.D., Kendzierski, D.A. & Thomas, S.V. (1983). The implicit assumptions of television: An analysis of the 1982 NIMH report on television and behaviour. *Public Opinion Quarterly 47*, 161-201.

Cullingford, C. (1984). *Children and television.* Aldershot, Hants: Gower.

Cumberbatch, G. & Brown, N. (1989). Violence to television: Effects research in context. *British Journal of Social Psychology 31*, 147-64.

Cumberbatch, G, Jones, I. & Lee, M. (1988). Measuring violence on television. *Current Psychology: Research and Reviews 7*, 10-25.

Cumberbatch, G., Lee, M., Hardy, G. & Jones, I. (1987). *The portrayal of violence on British television.* London: British Broadcasting Corporation.

Day, K. & Cowie, E. (1990). Trends in viewing and listening. *BBC Broadcasting Research Annual Review XVI,* 5-22.

Dietz, W.H. & Gortmaker, S.L. (1985). Do we fatten our children at the television set? Obesity and television viewing in children and adolescents. *Paediatrics 75*, 807-12.

Donnerstein, E., Linz, D. & Penrod, S. (1987). *The question of pornography: Research findings and policy implications.* New York: The Free Press.

Drabman, R.S. & Thomas, M.H. (1974). Does media violence increase children's toleration of real-life aggression? *Developmental Psychology 10,* 418-21.

Erholm, E. & Silvo, I. (1984). *Radio and TV audience patterns, 1976-82.* Report no. 27/1984. Helsinki: RLE.

Eron, L.D. (1982). Parent child interaction, television violence and aggression of children. *American Psychologist 27,* 197-211.

Eron, L.D., Lefkowitz, M.N., Huesmann, L.R. & Walder, L.O. (1972). Does television violence cause aggression? *American Psychologist 27,* 253-63.

Eurodience (1990). Children's television. *Eurodience: European Newsletter of Programmes and Audiences 35,* 7-16.

European Broadcasting Union (1990). *EBU Statistics, Vol. II: Cable & Satellite Yearbook.* Geneva: Author.

Freedman, J. L. (1984). Effect of television violence on aggressiveness. *Psychological Bulletin 96,* 227-246.

Gerbner, G. (1969). Dimensions of violence in television drama. In R. K. Baker & S. J. Ball (eds.) *Mass media and violence.* Washington, DC: US Government Printing Office.

Gerbner, G. (1972). Violence in television drama: Trends and symbolic functions. In G. A. Comstock & E. A. Rubenstein (eds.) *Television and social behaviour, Vol. I: Content and control.* Washington, DC: US Government Printing Office.

Gerbner, G., Gross, L., Morgan, M. & Signorelli, N. (1980). The 'mainstreaming' of America: Violence profile no. 11. *Journal of Communications 30,* 10-29.

Gunter, B. (1985). *Dimensions of television violence.* London: Gower.

Himmelweit, H.T., Oppenheim, A.N. & Vince, P. (1958). *Television and the child: An empirical study of the effects of television on the young.* London: Oxford University Press.

Huesmann, L.R. (1986). Psychological processes promoting the relation between exposure to media violence and aggressive behaviour in the viewer. *Journal of Social Issues 42*, 125-139.

Huesmann, L.R. & Eron, L.D. (1986). *Television and the aggressive child: A cross-national comparison.* Hillsdale, NJ: Lawrence Erlbaum.

Huesmann, L.R., Eron, L.D., Lefkowitz, M.H. & Walder, L.O. (1984a). The stability of aggression over time and generations. *Developmental Psychology 20*, 1120-34.

Huesmann, L.R., Lagerspetz, K. & Eron, L. (1984b). Intervening variables in the television violence-viewing-aggression relation: Evidence from two countries. *Developmental Psychology 20*, 746-75.

Huston, A.L., Donnerstein, E., Fairchild, H., Feshback, W.D., Katz, P.A., Murray, J.P., Rubinstein, E.A., Wilcox, B.L. & Zuckerman, D. (1992). *Big world, small screen: The role of television in American society.* Lincoln: University of Nebraska Press.

Kaufman, L. (1980). Prime time nutrition. *Journal of Communication 30*, 37-46.

Lukesch, H. (1987). Videorecorder und Mediennutzung bei Kindern und Jugendlichen. *Rundfunk und Fernsehen 1987/1*, 92-98.

Lyle, J. & Hoffman, H. R. (1972). Children's use of television and other media. In E. A. Rubenstein et al. (eds.) *Television and social behavior, Vol. IV: Television in day-to-day life: Patterns of use.* Washington, DC: US Government Printing Office.

McLeod, J. & Brown, J. D. (1972). The family environment and adolescent television use. In R. Brown (ed.) *Children and television.* London: Collier Macmillan.

Meyers, P.N. & Biocca, F.A. (1992). The elastic body image: The effects of television advertising and programming on body image distortions in young women. *Journal of Communication 42*, 108-33.

Milavsky, J.R., Kessler, R., Stipp, H.H. & Rubens, W.S. (1982). *Television and aggression: A panel study.* New York: Academic Press.

Murray, S. (1990). Knowledge about eating disorders in the community. *International Journal of Eating Disorders 9*, 87-93.

National Research Council (1993). *Understanding and preventing violence.* Washington, DC: National Academy Press.

NRK (1991). Personal communication from Marit Bakke, Norsk Rijskring Kasting, 0340 Oslo 3.

Offer, P., Oxtrov, E., Howard, K. & Atkinson, R. (1988). *Adolescent self images in ten countries.* New York: Plenum Press.

Phillips, D.P. (1974). The influence of suggestion on suicide: Substantive and theoretical implications of the Werther effect. *American Sociological Review 39*, 340-354.

Phillips, D.P. (1982). Airplane accidents, murder and the mass media: Towards a theory of limitation and suggestion. *Social Forces 58*, 1001-24.

Phillips, D.P. & Hensley, J.E. (1984). When violence is rewarded or punished: The impact of mass media stories on homicide. *Journal of Communication 34*, 101-116.

Phillips, D.P. & Corstenson, L.L. (1988). The effects of suicide stories on various demographic groups. *Suicide and Life Threatening Behaviour 18*, 100-14.

Rauste, R. & Wright, M. (1989). Body image satisfaction in adolescent girls and boys: A longitudinal study. *Journal of Youth and Adolescence 18*, 71-83.

Rosengren, K.E. & Windahl, S. (1989). *Media matter: TV use in childhood and adolescence.* New York: Academic Press.

RTFB (1990). Statistics supplied by the Bureau d'Etudes de la Radio - Télévision de la Communauté Française, Brussels.

Schmidtke, T. & Hafner, W. (1988). The Werther effect after television films: New evidence for an old hypothesis. *Psychological medicine 18*, 665-76.

Screen Digest (1991). February.

Social Trends (1991) 2. London: HMSO.

Strickland, D. (1983). Advertising exposure, alcohol consumption and misuse of alcohol. In Grant, M., Pland, M. & Williams, A. (eds.) *Economics and alcohol: Consumption and controls*, 201-22. New York: Gardner Press.

Strickland, D. (1984). Contents and effects of alcohol advertising, comments on NTIS publication No. PB82-123142. *Journal of Studies on Alcohol 45*, 87-93.

Stuttgarter Nachrichten (7.2.1986). Newspaper report cited in Cumberbatch, Jones & Lee (1988). Measuring violence on television. *Current Psychology: Research and Reviews 7*, 10-25.

Sveriges Radio (1991). Personal communication from Leni Filipson, Swedish Broadcasting Corporation, S-10510 Stockholm.

Tucker, L.A. (1986). The relationship of television viewing to physical fitness and obesity. *Adolescence 21*, 797-806.

Walleck, L.M. (1983). Mass media campaigns in a hostile environment: Advertising as anti health education. *Journal of Alcohol and Drug Education 28*, 51-63.

Wartella, E. & Reeves, B. (1985). Historical trends in research on children and the media: 1900-1960. *Journal of Communication 15*, 118-133.

Williams, T.M. (ed.) (1986). *The impact of television: A natural experiment in three communities.* New York: Academic Press.

Wober, M. (1988). The extent to which viewers watch violence-containing programmes. *Current Psychology: Research and Reviews 7*, 43-57.

Zillman, D. (1982). Television and arousal. In D. Pearl, L. Bouthilet & J. Lazar (eds.) *Television and behaviour: Ten years of scientific progress and implications for the eighties*, 53-76. Washington, DC: US Government Printing Office.

8

Values, Morals and Modernity: the Values, Constraints and Norms of European Youth

DAVID HALPERN

INTRODUCTION

This chapter explores generational differences in self-expressed values across time and across countries. It relates these findings to broader changes in the form and organization of societies across the same period. The underlying theme is an attempt to understand the nature and form of the social processes that guide and constrain behaviour.

The chapter is in three sections. First, there is a brief summary of some of the theories that have been proposed to explain the relationship between changes in modern societies and in the values and norms of the individuals within them. The methodological problems involved in appraising these theories empirically are discussed. Second, data are presented on generational differences in self-reported values and attitudes from across Europe. The data are drawn from a number of sources. Methodological problems involved in inferring attitudes and behavioural orientations from survey data are explored. The third part considers the relationship between changes in self-reported attitudes and broader changes in the form and structure of post-industrial societies.

Late Modernity and the 'Moral Fabric'

It is a common assertion that many contemporary problems, especially those of youth, stem from a decay in the 'moral fabric' of modern societies. Related assertions are that people no longer have a sense of community, that we are living in increasingly selfish and materialist societies where all that matters is money, that a generation gap has opened up, that today's youth no longer hold the moral values of previous generations, and that the basic consensus about what is right and wrong is collapsing. Similar comments are made in most historical periods, for example this one from eleventh-century England:

> The world is passing through troubled times. The young people have no reverence for their parents: they are impatient of all restraint; they talk as if they alone knew everything, and what passes for wisdom with us is foolishness for them. (Peter the Hermit, eleventh century; quoted in Raven (1952).)

Similar anxieties are expressed in academic writings, and by authors from both ends of the political spectrum. It has been argued that modern life has undermined many of the sources of influence that sustained traditional systems of ethics and morality. Two institutions have been seen as having fared particularly poorly in recent times: the traditional, locally embedded community, and the church.

Many sociologists have held that efficient but impersonal modern societies compare unfavourably with older societies in which communal values were stronger. For example, according to Berger et al. (1974: 142), mass society and large-scale bureaucracy have resulted in the 'collective and individual loss of integrative meanings' and the breaking down of older forms of community. From this viewpoint, the modern individual, having no clear or absolute reference points for values or meaning, is existentially 'homeless' and exposed to a plurality of 'life-worlds' (62). Similarly, writers such as Horkheimer (1974) and Habermas (1987) have maintained that organized capitalism and the transformation of goods and services into commodities have undermined traditional forms of community and personal relations.

Many writers, assuming that the influence of the church has declined dramatically, have wondered what will become of the ethics that the church supported. Freud raised this question in his *New Introductory Lectures*. Discussing the religious world-view, he wrote:

> Its doctrines bear the imprint of the times in which they arose... Its consolations deserve no trust. Experience tells us the world is no nursery. The ethical demands on which religion seeks to lay stress need, rather, to be given another basis; for they are indispensable to human society and it is dangerous to link obedience to them with religious faith. ('A Weltanschauung?' (Freud, 1933:168); *New Introductory Lectures on Psycho-Analysis, Standard Edition, Vol. XXII*, 1964).

One of the questions that this chapter will address is whether the influence of the church has actually declined, and if it has, whether this decline has been associated with a parallel decline in the 'ethical demands' it has supported in the past.

Closely related to sociological accounts of the contrast between traditional and modern societies are sociological models of urban life. Cities have been described as the symbol of modernity, and their development has been regarded as undermining traditional forms of moral influence. Writing at the turn of the century, Simmel argued that the scale of cities, and the division of labour and domination of money associated with urban life, inevitably led to a blunting of feelings (or alienation) and to indifference towards the needs of others (Saunders, 1986). Since Simmel's time, when most people in the world lived in the countryside, the proportion of the world's population living in cities has risen rapidly. In the more developed countries, the proportion of people living in an urban setting rose from 53.6 per cent in 1950 to 72.4 per cent in 1985, and it is expected to rise to about 79 per cent by the year 2000. The corresponding levels for the developing countries were 17.3 per cent in 1950, 31.7 per cent in 1985, and a predicted 44 per cent in 2000 (United Nations, 1986). By the year 2000 over half of the world's population are expected to be living in urban areas (Salk & Salk, 1981).

A model of urban life proposed by urban ecologists remains influential. In an essay on 'Urbanism as a Way of Life', Wirth (1938) argued that the characteristics of the city – size, density, and heterogeneity – imply a level of mix and differentiation amongst city dwellers that deeply undermines the bonds of kinship, neighbourliness and community. Without community or consensus, competition, exploitation and formal controls would come to replace the bonds of solidarity that otherwise hold people together. Wirth thought that the social and economic conditions of the city would reinforce a 'moral disorder', producing competitiveness, indifference and a predatory orientation towards others (Krupat, 1985). Although some have since developed counter arguments that highlight the more positive aspects of urban living and modern life (Geller, 1980; Fisher, 1982), Simmel's and Wirth's views continue to be reflected in the work of many contemporary sociologists and social psychologists. Some have maintained, for example, that city dwellers have to cope with vast numbers of anonymous others and consequently have to find ways of avoiding being overloaded by social encounters (Lofland, 1973; Milgram, 1977). The principal strategy that city dwellers have learnt, it is argued, is to disregard the demands of the world of strangers around them.

In sum, the carriers of modernization, such as bureaucracy, urbanization, education, and the mass media, are all presumed to bring with them a diversification and relativization of beliefs. It is held that these developments have tended to undermine the ability of the locally embedded church and community to determine the values of their members, and have exposed individuals to a plurality of world-views and value systems. It is, further, held that these developments have undermined the perceived rationality of reciprocal obligations and have replaced them with an economics and rationality of the individual (Hirsch, 1977). Hence, on this view the processes of modernization have heralded two central psychological changes: first, the erosion of structures of authority and meaning embedded in a wider community; and second, the development of a belief in the efficacy and value of the self (Westen, 1985). Modern individuals, amidst the diverse and often contradictory values that are presented to them, must find their own identity and choose their own values. The construction of the self and the values selected to compose it becomes 'a reflexive project' (Giddens, 1990). In such a project, the particular values of a previous generation cannot be presumed to have any special place.

The foregoing discussion is not, of course, a comprehensive review of writings on modernization, but merely illustrates how popular concerns about modernity and its relationship to moral values are reflected in the writings of academics. One expert opinion may be unduly influenced by particular circumstances, or by a particular piece of research, or a particular method of doing social science. For example, the influential but extremely negative view of urban life presented by Wirth (1938) emerged from the Chicago of the 1920s and 1930s, a city in a period of rapid and unchecked growth attempting to cope with a large influx of ill-prepared rural migrants. Perhaps if Wirth had been living in another city or at another time, he would have formed a different view (Krupat, 1985). It would be interesting to establish whether in fact consistent views about modernization are expressed by a number of experts from different countries and social contexts.

An 'experiment' employing just such a method was conducted as part of a recent project by the Centro Studi Investimenti Sociali (CENSIS) sponsored by the Italian Ministry of Foreign Affairs for Italy's six-month Presidency of the European Economic Community (Angeli, 1991). Eighty-five 'experts' from across Europe were presented with a grid of hypothesized social processes, and after evaluating the grid itself, the experts were asked to evaluate the extent to which the processes applied and had occurred in their country. Trends that most experts across countries believed were strongly established included increasing 'acquisitiveness' (the propensity to acquire material goods as a means of self-expression); increasing 'search for quality' (the expression of discriminating demands); and increasing 'individualism' (the placing of the individual at the centre of the system of values and behavioural choices, and the following of individual convictions rather than external models).

This study shows that there is a convergence of academic opinion about certain trends, but it cannot show whether these opinions are founded on fact, or merely reflect a popular sociological myth.

Operationalizing the Concepts

In order to explore the relationship between modernity and values further, it is necessary to find ways of defining or operationalizing the concepts used by theorists so that they can be tested by empirical research. An immediate difficulty is that many of these concepts describe processes that are not directly observable, but may only be inferred from the results of direct observation. However, this is a problem that is not unique to the social sciences: it does not constitute a reason for abandoning attempts at empirical validation (Latour, 1987; Goldman, 1986). The solution lies in specification of the measures that may be supposed to tap the latent construct and in the use of the appropriate statistical techniques to deal with the fact that all such measures are likely also to reflect other (unwanted) constructs (see Rutter & Pickles, 1990). If we wish to argue that there are coherent processes such as 'modernization', 'secularization' or a trend towards 'individualism', then we must demonstrate that the hypothesized markers of the processes are all pointing in the same direction. For the process of modernization, markers could include levels of wealth as measured by Gross National Product *per capita*, the proportion of the population living in urban areas, productivity levels, the proportion of the population working in agriculture, and the development of transport infrastructures (see Chapter 6). The fact that these markers are very highly correlated across countries and across time suggests that they are closely interrelated and may be symptomatic of a relatively coherent underlying process (Maddison, 1989).[1] Yet there is a strong sense in the sociological

---

1. The fact that there existed many significant differences between traditional societies (the starting point of the process), and that many differences continue to exist between the more industrialized nations, does not mean that we cannot speak of the transformative process ('modernization') as coherent (Westen, 1985). Similarly, the term modernization does not necessitate thinking of either more, or less, developed nations as superior.

literature that these processes are not only economic in their manifestations and consequences, but are also closely tied to changes in lifestyles, to changes in individuals' orientations to others, and, of course, to changes in values. Examples of markers of changes in lifestyles and orientations might include falling fertility rates, changing levels of cohabitation, divorce and single-parent families, and increasing levels of reported crime, all of which have shown marked changes over recent years and all of which are broadly associated with the more affluent and developed nations (see Chapters 6 and 7).

However, the hypothesis that the conditions of late modernity have been associated with significant value shifts can, in principle, be tested relatively directly. If modernization is associated with major shifts in world-view then these shifts should show in differences across generations and across time in large-scale social attitude surveys. *Are* the moral values of young people today very different from those of previous generations? *Have* the values of society really changed? *Are* modern societies uncaring when compared to those of the past? *Has* there been a collapse in consensus? *Are* society and the young becoming awash in a sea of anarchic moral relativism and selfish individualism? The bulk of this chapter will attempt to answer these questions with reference to a series of international social attitude surveys, but before turning to this evidence it is helpful to make an important distinction.

The Nature of Values and Constraints: the Distinction Between Formal and Informal

In seeking to understand what guides and constrains behaviour, it is useful to make a distinction between the *formal* and *informal* domains. The *formal* refers to norms, values and sanctions that are public and explicit, and enforced by visible institutional mechanisms. The most obvious examples are those in the realm of law. The *informal* refers to norms, values and sanctions that are private, and maintained by less explicit mechanisms such as subtle social pressure. Examples of informal codes might include politeness, honour, or how to conduct oneself in a particular setting. If we are to discuss changes in values then we must recognize that they exist in both domains.

It is also important to note that the norms that exert the most powerful influence over behaviour are not necessarily formal ones. Formal rules, even when enforced by public and manifestly severe sanctions, are often broken (see Chapter 9). Yet there are many internalized and informal rules that are almost never broken, despite the absence of explicit sanctions. 'Manners' are an example. In most industrialized cultures it is almost unheard of for an individual to defecate in company, say while at the dinner table. In a private house it is not illegal, yet the force of the norm that prevents us doing so is incredibly strong. The norm is of course an internalized one: external sanctions are no longer required for its enforcement. Individuals act as if they know 'how to go on' (Wittgenstein, 1958), or in other words, they act as if their behaviour is guided by complex sets of rules, scripts and schemata (Lindsay & Norman, 1977). These rules are internalized to the extent that they become inseparable from the self, even to the person in question (Goffman, 1959). The extent of the internalization is seen most clearly when a social rule is broken, such as when a person responds unusually in a routine social interaction, for example, as in Garfinkel's famous breaching experiments (Garfinkel, 1963, 1967; Heritage, 1984) or in Milgram's New York subway experiment where subjects simply had to ask 'may I have your seat?' (Milgram & Sabini, 1983). In these studies subjects found the violation of subtle social rules and expectancies extremely disturbing, and very powerful sanctions – both internal and external – were employed.[2] Furthermore, people act as if their behaviour is guided by rules and schemata even though these rules may never have been articulated to them or by them in an explicit form (McClelland & Rumelhart, 1986). The socialization process is very important in the acquisition of social norms (Myers, 1990).

The most effective rules are those that are internalized, and are reinforced by subtle pressures rather than by institutional mechanisms. The most visible set of explicit rules enforced by dedicated mechanisms is the law. Compliance with the law varies very widely from one kind of law to another. Probably the most important factor determining the level of compliance is whether the law corresponds to internalized values and to informal sanctions. There is, of

---

2. In Garfinkel's breaching experiments, subjects were engaged in a game of tick-tack-toe (similar to noughts and crosses), but after the subject had made the first move, the experimenter erased the subject's mark and moved it to another cell while avoiding making any indication that what he was doing was unusual. Most subjects reacted extremely strongly to this violation of expectations. In a more realistic variant of the method, students were asked to engage an acquaintance in an ordinary conversation but then to insist that the person clarify the sense of some commonplace remark. For example:

The victim waved his hand cheerily.

S: How are you?

E: How am I in regard to what? My health, my finance, my school work, my peace of mind, my...

S: (Red in the face and suddenly out of control.) Look! I was just trying to be polite. Frankly, I don't give a damn how you are (Garfinkel, 1963: 222).

In the vast majority of cases, breaches were rapidly and powerfully sanctioned.

course, a complex interplay between the effectiveness of formal sanctions on the one hand and internalized values ('morals') and informal social pressures on the other. Effective law enforcement depends on internalized values (for example, witnesses volunteering to come forward), but equally the effectiveness of law enforcement influences what the internalized values are (for example, failure to enforce parking regulations is connected with the fact that few are ashamed of breaking them).

Even after allowing for such interactions, it would certainly be wrong to assume that most rules, even those that are public and formal, are complied with because of formal policing and enforcement. People normally act in caring and considerate ways towards others not because of formal rules or sanctions, but because of their own values and informal schemata about what is, and is not, appropriate behaviour.

CHANGES IN SELF-REPORTED VALUES ACROSS TIME AND ACROSS COUNTRIES

This section of the chapter provides an exploration of cross-national generational differences in values based on data drawn from a number of international social attitude surveys. The principal sources are the surveys conducted by the European Value Systems Study Group, the Eurobarometer series sponsored by the Commission of the European Communities, and the Eurodata surveys conducted by Gallup and sponsored by Reader's Digest. Background statistics on Gross National Products, levels of urbanization, and proportions of the labour force employed in agriculture are principally from World Bank data.

Methodological and Interpretive Pitfalls

There are a number of methodological and interpretive pitfalls that need to be kept in mind when attempting to make inferences from attitude surveys, and especially where differences between generations and between countries are concerned.

Right at the start, there is the problem of deciding what should be asked. The range of possible questions is limitless, so the process of selection has an enormous influence on the conclusions reached. When we read the results of a social attitude survey we are seeing the values of the public refracted through the priorities of the survey designers, who tend to focus in their questioning on attitudes and values that are currently at the centre of political and academic debate. Researchers are disinclined to include questions likely to elicit universal agreement or disagreement, not only because they are apt to consider such questions to be uninteresting, but also because they may not think of them at all: such questions will not be 'on the agenda'.

Consequently, surveys rarely or never ask questions about whether it is right or wrong to cheat on a friend, to sexually abuse a child or indeed, to defecate at the dinner table. This highlights a fundamental limitation of survey research. Although surveys may give us an accurate picture of the level of consensus or disagreement on a particular issue, they have limited ability to establish levels of consensus or homogeneity of belief in the very general sense.

The second set of methodological pitfalls concerns the translation of survey items from one country and language to another. When items are translated, nuances of meaning may be changed, and the subsequent differences in responses across countries may be less the result of actual or cultural differences than of linguistic differences. A classic example is the interpretation of the long-standing finding that there exist large and consistent national differences in levels of happiness and self-reported satisfaction with life as a whole (Inglehart, 1990). Over the period of the Eurobarometer surveys from 1973 to 1988, the Danes and the Dutch have consistently reported very high levels of life satisfaction, while other nationalities such as the French and Italians have consistently reported very low levels of satisfaction. Fortunately, Switzerland provides an opportunity for distinguishing between linguistic and national differences. It was found that the French, German, and Italian speaking Swiss all express substantially higher levels of satisfaction than the French, Germans and Italians with whom they share a language. A similar pattern is seen for the Belgians (Inglehart, 1990).

Yet the best way to overcome the problems involved in the interpretation of items that have been translated across countries and languages is to sidestep them altogether by concentrating on comparisons within countries. Where (as in the present study) the focus is on differences across generations and across time, the problems involved in translation are much reduced.

A third difficulty is that there is not yet a long run of data for repeated social attitude surveys, so that in order to find out about changes over time and differences between generations, cross-sectional surveys have to be analysed by age. This leads to the familiar problem of distinguishing between secular change (or period effects), age effects, and cohort effects (see Chapter 2; and for a further discussion in connection with depression, Chapter 11). In broad terms, if a difference in values is found between a younger and older generation, there are three possible interpretations. The first is that the difference between generations reflects their point in the life cycle (age effect) and that when the younger generation has reached the present age of the older generation they too will hold the views of the present older generation. On the second and third interpretations, the generation has formed different (but stable) values compared with the earlier generation. If this reflects a change in values that will continue to affect successive generations, it is a secular change; if it is the result of common experiences shared by this particular generation, it is a cohort effect.

As discussed in Chapter 2, from any given set of cross-sectional data, it is not possible in formal mathematical terms to distinguish between the three types of effect, and there are also difficulties in interpreting longitudinal data. However, when background knowledge of the social processes involved is combined with survey data, one interpretation often becomes more plausible than the others.

A fourth difficulty that can arise in the interpretation of social attitude data is that even if the wording of a question remains constant over time, its meaning may have changed. This is an especially serious problem in political attitude surveys, where subjects are asked questions about their attitudes towards parties and policies that keep changing in nature. Similar problems can arise in questions designed to tap moral issues. For example, the following question has been included in the British Social Attitudes surveys. 'A man gives a five pound note for goods he is buying in a big store. By mistake, he is given change for a ten pound note. He notices, but keeps the change.' The proportion of people who said he had done nothing wrong and that they would act the same way themselves has increased over time. Although this might be taken as evidence that British people had become more selfish, an alternative explanation might be that the value of a five pound note fell over the period, so that the meaning of the question changed, and the hypothesized act became a less serious one.

There is no simple solution to this difficult problem. To a large extent, each question must be considered on its own merits. When questions are carefully worded, the problem can be reduced, but because the meanings of questions must be grounded in a continually changing social context, they are bound to change to some extent. Researchers should make explicit the way they use their own life experience and wider knowledge to help choose between interpretations.

The Relationship Between Attitudes and Behaviour

This chapter is primarily about values and attitudes, but these will only have relevance to the pattern of psychosocial disorders to the extent that there is some relationship between attitudes and behaviour. There are several classic studies indicating that people often don't do what they say they will do. Perhaps the most famous was conducted in the United States by LaPiere (1934). LaPiere accompanied a young Chinese couple as they called on 251 restaurants, hotels and other establishments. They were refused service only once. After a delay of a few months, LaPiere sent a letter to each establishment asking: 'Will you accept members of the Chinese race as guests in your establishment?' Over 90 per cent of the 128 establishments that replied said that they would *not* accept Chinese as guests, even though they had, in fact, done so.

During the 1960s and early 1970s there was widespread discussion about the frequent inability of expressed attitudes to predict behaviour. Wicker (1969) reviewed several dozen studies covering a variety of people, attitudes and behaviours. He concluded:

> Taken as a whole, these studies suggest that it is considerably more likely that attitudes will be unrelated or only slightly related to overt behaviour than that attitudes will be closely related to actions. Product-moment correlation coefficients relating the two kinds of responses are rarely above .30, and are often near zero (65).

How can this be explained? Since the time of Wicker's review it has become clear that the ability of expressed attitudes to predict behaviour depends on a number of methodological and social factors. First of all, social factors affect the original expression of the attitude, particularly if the attitude concerns a socially sensitive issue. For example, it has been found that male college students revealed significantly more hostile attitudes towards racial minorities and towards women's rights when they thought that their answers would be checked by a lie detector, strongly suggesting that their normal responses did not represent their underlying attitudes (Jones & Signall, 1971; Jamieson & Zanna, 1983). This makes it extremely difficult to appraise the accuracy of attitudes expressed about socially sensitive issues, especially if the survey is not anonymous. Second, the ability of an expressed attitude to predict behaviour is greatly influenced by the compatibility of the measures employed. It is difficult to predict the occurrence of a specific behaviour from the expression of global attitudes, or indeed, the expression of global attitudes from the occurrence of a specific behaviour. However, aggregate measures of attitudes typically predict aggregate measures of behaviour fairly well (Ajzen, 1988). Third, attitudes are more likely to predict behaviour if the individual has thought about the attitude a great deal (for example, as in voting intentions) or if the individual is reminded of the original expression of the attitude at the time of the behaviour. One way this can be achieved is by making individuals more self-aware either at the time when the attitude was expressed or at the time when the behaviour is elicited. Hence, for example, it has been found that attitudes were significantly more likely to predict behaviours where people could see themselves in a mirror either at the time when the attitude was expressed or at the time when the behaviour occurred (Carver, 1975; Pryor et al., 1977). Fourth, and perhaps most importantly, social influences greatly affect the expression of a behaviour. Ajzen and Fishbein (1977; Ajzen, 1988) have expressed this phenomenon as a theory of 'planned behaviour'. An individual's preparedness to engage in a particular behaviour is determined by at least three major factors:

* their own attitude towards the behaviour;
* their perceptions of the attitudes of *others* towards that behaviour; and
* their perception that the behaviour will lead to the desired outcome.

Ajzen has shown that predictions based on these factors combined can predict an individual's behaviour significantly better than the individual's attitude alone.

In summary, the current literature shows that attitudes predict behaviour best when:

* the attitude is specific to the action;
* the individual has thought through, is aware of, and committed to, the expressed attitude; and
* when other social influences are minimized.

However, it is also important to note that an individuals' behaviour is influenced by the perceived attitudes of others (the social norm). This means that the attitudes expressed by a whole population can have indirect as well as direct effects on behaviour: the expressed attitude of an individual not only predicts that person's behaviour but also, in so far as it contributes to a social norm, tends to predict the behaviour of others. This is one of the reasons why the behaviour of a population can be easier to predict than the behaviour of an individual.

The European Values Survey, 1981

In the late 1970s, an initially informal group of natural and social scientists, theologians, philosophers and opinion researchers, came together to form what became known as the European Value Systems Study Group. The group was formally established as a Foundation in 1978, and in March to May 1981 the group conducted a massive cross-national survey of values. This study, the European Values Survey (EVS) 1981 provides a useful starting point for an exploration of cross-national differences in values. A detailed analysis of the original EVS data for ten Western European nations was published in 1986 (Harding et al., 1986).

In the original study, the ten Western Nations were: Belgium, Denmark, Eire, France, Great Britain, Italy, Netherlands, Northern Ireland, Spain, and West Germany. The age range sampled was 18 upwards. (There are very few social attitude surveys that include samples of young people below the age of 18, although an exception is the work of Furnham & Gunter (1989) for Britain.) Probability sampling methods were used in six countries, and quota sampling in four. The sample sizes were about 1,200 in each country, with the exception of Northern Ireland where it was around 300. A booster sample of 200 young adults aged 18-24 was provided for each country. The total number of interviews was 12,463.

Cross-national Tolerance of Morally Debatable Acts

A central element of the questionnaire consisted of a list of 22 'morally debatable behaviours', such as lying in your own self-interest, under-age sex, cheating on tax, married men and women having an affair, buying stolen goods, and joyriding. For each item, respondents were asked: 'Please tell me for each of the following statements whether you think it can always be justified, never be justified or something in between...' Respondents were then asked to rate how justifiable they thought each action was on scale ranging from 1 for 'never justified' to 10 for 'always justified'.

Overall, there was widespread agreement between countries over which acts were most and least justifiable. For example, the least justifiable of the acts in eight out of the ten countries was 'taking and driving away a car belonging to someone else' (joyriding). The two exceptions were Spain and Italy where political assassination was regarded as even less justifiable. The most justifiable of the acts in seven of the ten countries was 'killing in self-defence'. The exceptions were Denmark and West Germany, where divorce had the highest justifiability score, and Holland where homosexuality had a higher justifiability score.

Some countries were generally more tolerant than others, as measured by their average justifiability scores. The countries that tended to be most tolerant were (in descending order) France, Holland, and Denmark. The least generally tolerant countries were Northern Ireland, Eire, and Italy (see Figure 8.1). However, general ratings of tolerance give only a part of the picture. Some countries were far more tolerant of certain acts than others, so the overall rating depends to some extent on which items are included in the scale used to measure tolerance. For example, concerning the issue of divorce, Denmark was the most tolerant country of the ten. Yet for the issue of 'keeping money that you have found' Denmark was the least tolerant of the ten. Of course, similar contrasts exist on the level of the individual: individuals may be tolerant about certain issues but intolerant about others. A more powerful method is needed to make sense of these complex patterns.

Figure 8.1   Average tolerance levels for morally debatable acts

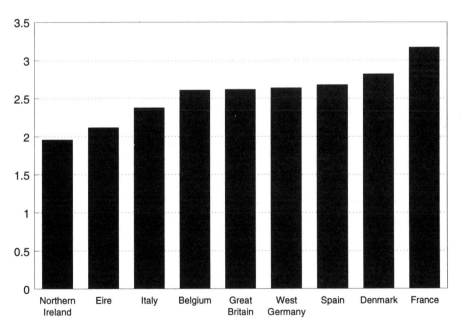

Source: European Values Survey (1981) reported in Harding et al. (1986).

The method used by these researchers was factor analysis, a statistical technique designed to simplify sets of associations between large numbers of supposedly related variables into smaller numbers of inferred underlying variables. The technique has been most widely used in psychometric studies on personality and intelligence where researchers have attempted to infer underlying personality traits from the pattern of inter-correlations within a wide range of attitudes and self-reported behaviours. Cattell, a figure closely associated with the technique, described factor analysis as the search for 'concomitant variation': if different behavioural manifestations covary then this might be accounted for by a shared underlying trait (Cattell, 1965).

Figure 8.2   National differences in perception of morality

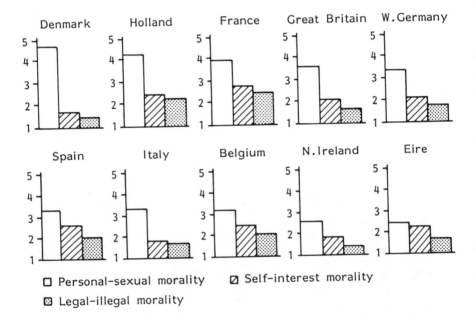

Calculated from mean scores from each factor area, higher scores indicating greater tolerance, lower scores greater strictness (maximum = 10, minimum = 1).

Source: Harding et al. (1986).

Applying factor analysis to the twenty-two 'morally debatable' behaviours used in the European Values Survey, Harding et al. (1986) found that the pattern of variance could be described by three underlying factors. A very similar three-factor solution applied across all ten countries. The strongest of the factors was labelled 'personal-sexual morality' because it reflected attitudes towards prostitution, divorce, homosexuality and abortion, suicide, euthanasia, killing in self-defence, and married men and women having an affair. This means that within each country, individuals' level of tolerance towards say, prostitution, tended to be closely related to their level of tolerance towards say, homosexuality, divorce or euthanasia. The second underlying factor was labelled 'self-interest morality'; it reflected elements of cheating or dishonesty such as 'buying something you knew was stolen', 'cheating on tax if you have the chance', and 'avoiding a fare on public transport'. The third factor was labelled 'legal-illegal morality' because it covered acts that were clearly beyond the law such as 'taking and driving away a car belonging to someone else', 'political assassination', and 'someone accepting a bribe in the course of their duties'.

Although the items tended to cluster into these three factors in all ten countries, the relative weight given to the factors in each country varied markedly. For example, countries such as Great Britain, West Germany and Eire were all approximately equal in their tolerance on the self-interest dimension, but Eire was far less tolerant than Great Britain or West Germany on the personal-sexual dimension. Perhaps even more strikingly, Denmark was found to be highly tolerant in the personal-sexual domain, yet was found to be among the least tolerant in the self-interest domain (see Figure 8.2). Clearly, countries that are high on one of the factors are not necessarily high on the others. As we shall see, this finding has proven to be very resilient. An extremely consistent trend was found across generations (see Figure 8.3). For all three moral factors, increasing age was associated with greater moral strictness (lower levels of tolerance). A higher level of education (itself strongly associated with youth) was found, independently of age, to be associated with higher levels of tolerance. This trend was strongest for the personal-sexual factor and somewhat less consistent for the self-interest and legal-illegal factors.

Those who described themselves as more left-wing and those who described themselves as atheist or not religious tended to be more tolerant. The association with religious belief was particularly strong on the personal-sexual factor. Relative to religion, political affinity was found to have a stronger association with the self-interest and legal-illegal factors.

Figure 8.3   Moral judgements by age

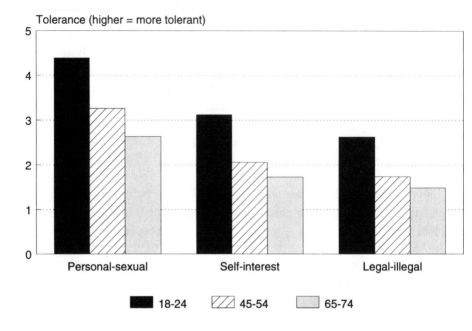

N = 1901, 2058, 1457.

Source: European Values Survey (1981) reported in Harding et al. (1986).

Other Generational Differences in Values

Differences were found between the young and old in a wide range of other values as well as in tolerance for morally debatable acts. One of the strongest differences between young and old was found in orientation to religion (see Figure 8.4). Younger people were much less likely to attend church regularly, less likely to report traditional religious beliefs (belief in God, life after death, sin), less likely to have confidence in the church's ability to provide answers to social, moral or spiritual problems, and less likely to describe themselves as religious in a more general sense (describe self as a religious person, get comfort and strength from religion, or pray).

The European Values survey also included items asking about respect for the Ten Commandments. Again, young people were significantly less likely to describe the Ten Commandments as applying to themselves than older people, but the size of this difference differed substantially according to the specific Commandment. In general, respect for the 'moral' Commandments (IV-X) was much higher than respect for the 'religious' Commandments (I-III): the proportions who said they applied to themselves was 74 and 42 per cent respectively.

Figure 8.4   Religious values and behaviour by age

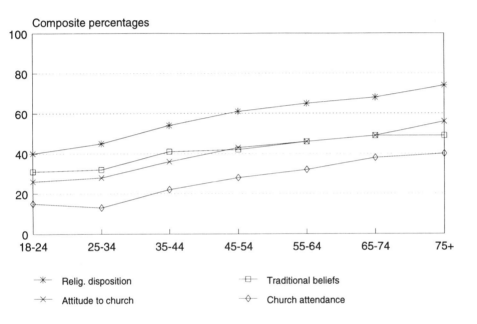

Composite percentages

| Relig. disposition | Traditional beliefs |
| Attitude to church | Church attendance |

Source: European Values Survey (1981) reported in Harding et al. (1986).

A surprising aspect of these results was the enormous difference between the proportions of people saying that the Commandments applied to themselves and the proportions saying they applied *to most people.*[3]   There was a very strong tendency for the majority of people to see themselves as moral (in the sense of respecting the Ten Commandments, or at least the last

---

3. The exact wording of the question was: 'Here is a card on which are the Ten Commandments. Please look at them and tell me, for each one, whether it still applies fully today, whether it applies today to a limited extent, or no longer really applies today (a) for yourself, and (b) to most people?'

seven) while simultaneously regarding most people as not respecting them. This may shed some light on the historical tendency of most generations to see the world in a state of moral decline. It can probably be explained by a phenomenon described by social psychologists as 'the fundamental attribution error' (Myers, 1990). When explaining the behaviour of others, individuals show a strong tendency to underestimate the importance of situational factors and to overestimate the importance of personal factors (Ross, 1977). When individuals analyse their own behaviour they tend to make the reverse error; they overestimate the importance of situational factors and underestimate the importance of personal factors. When we see someone else transgress, we locate the cause of the act within that person – for example, in their lack of respect for the prescriptions embodied in the Commandments. When we ourselves transgress, we locate the cause in the situation and consider the transgression as an exception rather than a 'falsification' of our values.

Younger people differed from older people in their views on a number of other matters. Younger people were more prepared to protest (sign petitions, attend demonstrations, occupy buildings) and tended to be more left-wing (self-rated). Younger people were more demanding of work; they rated almost all aspects of jobs as being more important than older people including: pleasant people to work with, generous holidays, meeting people, opportunity to use initiative, good chances of promotion, and good pay. The only aspects of a job that were rated as significantly more important by older people were security and that the job be respected by people in general. Perhaps because of these higher expectations, younger people were also less satisfied with their jobs.

Young people also differed from old people in their attitudes towards marriage and family. Younger people were more likely to agree 'that marriage is an outdated institution', more likely to approve 'if a woman wants to have a child but not a stable relationship with a man', were less likely to agree that 'to grow up happily a child needs a home with both a father and a mother', and were more tolerant of all reasons for divorce. Some national differences existed. The French and Spanish were particularly likely to see marriage as outdated and the Irish and Germans were least likely to describe it as such. The Italians were most likely to feel that a child needs both parents to grow up happily, and the Danes and British least likely. Widest disagreement existed over approval of a woman having a child outside marriage, most approval coming from the Danes and the French and least from the Irish. Young people were more tolerant of variants in sexual behaviour, such as homosexuality, having affairs, and prostitution. They were considerably more likely to agree with the statement 'Individuals should have complete sexual freedom without being restricted': at the extremes of the age distribution, 42 per cent of 18 to 24-year-olds, compared with 6 per cent of those aged 75 or more, agreed with the statement. However, when asked about which factors were important for a successful marriage there was considerable agreement between age groups. For example, the proportion describing 'mutual respect and appreciation' as very important was around 83 per cent for all age groups. Factors rated as relatively more important by young people were a 'happy sexual relationship' and 'living apart from your in-laws', and factors rated as relatively more important by older people included 'faithfulness', 'children' and shared backgrounds and beliefs.

Finally, turning to the values that people saw as important to foster in children, all age groups agreed that qualities such as honesty, tolerance and respect for others, good manners, and feelings of responsibility were very important. Honesty was seen as the most important quality to be developed in children in all ten countries except Spain where 'feeling of responsibility' and 'good manners' were seen as more important. The young tended to give relatively more weight to qualities such as independence, determination, and imagination. Older people tended to give more weight to qualities such as obedience, hard work, thrift, and religious faith.

Overview and Comments

In Harding et al.'s (1986) analysis, at least three moral dimensions were identified as describing the pattern of values across countries, the sexual-personal, the self-interest, and the legal-illegal. Countries that were high in tolerance on one of the factors were not necessarily high on another.

However, the number and relative strength of factors depends not only on the pattern of associations between the variables, but also the number and types of variables included and, to some extent, on the type of solution specified by the researcher (number of factors, type of rotation, and whether or not the factors are allowed to be statistically related or not).

When a principal components analysis is used on the whole survey, one very strong overall factor emerges (Inglehart, 1990). More than 40 attitudes showed significant loadings on this dimension, with a very similar pattern emerging within each society when analysed separately. The items that loaded most strongly on this dimension were concerned with traditional religious beliefs such as belief in God and in heaven, and acceptance of the first three Commandments. The highest-loading item on this factor was respondent ratings on a scale from 1 to 10 of the importance of God in their life. However, the items loading on this factor were not exclusively religious. Other positively loading items included believing in the unjustifiability of abortion, divorce, extramarital affairs, prostitution, euthanasia, homosexuality, or under-age sex (all these items had loadings stronger than 0.5 on the factor). Items from Harding et al.'s self-interest and legal-illegal factors also load on this one 'super-factor': these items include considering it unjustified to fight the police, to use marijuana, to buy stolen goods, to keep found money, to avoid paying the fare on public transport, and to cheat on taxes. From Inglehart's work, therefore, it seems that there is an underlying factor around which a very large number of values cluster, but particularly religious and sexual ones. This factor appears to relate to the acceptance or rejection of a relatively unitary belief system – the traditional Judaeo-Christian value system.

Returning to the Harding et al. study, it can be confirmed that if countries were ranked in order of their personal-sexual tolerance, this correlated very highly with the rated importance of God by the respondents from that country. The relationships between the self-interest and legal-illegal factors and the super-factor (traditional Judaeo-Christian beliefs) are less clear.

Turning to the differences between young and old, the most striking themes that run through the generational differences in the 1981 European Values Survey are that the young are more tolerant in general, less respectful of traditional values or rules, and more demanding of autonomy and control. This pattern of findings could be explained by a secular change (or period effect) – a rise in individualism and a shift away from traditional and religious values affecting all age groups; or by an age effect – a tendency for people's values to change as they grow older; or possibly by a cohort effect, if values are strongly influenced by some experience such as a type of education that all members of a given cohort have in common. This issue cannot be resolved with cross-sectional data alone, so the discussion now shifts to a focus on data from surveys that have been repeated at intervals.

Findings from Repeated Cross-national Surveys

Findings on change over time in self-rated values are chiefly available from three repeated cross-national surveys: the EVS surveys carried out in 1981 and 1990, the annual Eurobarometer surveys from 1973-1990, and the Reader's Digest Eurodata surveys carried out in 1963, 1969 and 1990. Shortly after the first EVS survey of ten European nations, surveys were conducted in a number of other countries; data from all of these surveys are included in the comparisons below. The Euro-Barometer and Reader's Digest surveys are far more limited in the range of questions asked, but they have the advantage of having been carried out over a longer time span. The sampling methods used in these surveys were very similar to that described above for the EVS 1981 survey.

The discussion below brings together the findings for each of the following value fields:

PERSONAL
sexual/personal
civic
   self-interest
   legal-illegal

RELIGIOUS
orientation
belief

WORK
materialism/postmaterialism
workplace
protest proneness

Changes in sexual-personal values

At present, analysis of the 1990 EVS must be based on the initially published results. A fuller interpretation must await publication of more detailed results, or secondary analysis of the data. As explained in an earlier section, the factor score of tolerance with respect to personal-sexual values was found to be strongly related to age. Looking first at the findings for Europe, these show that both in 1981 and in 1990, there was a regular relationship with age, such that younger age groups were more tolerant than older ones (see Figure 8.5a). The only departure from regularity was that there was little or no difference between the attitudes of the two youngest age groups (18-24 and 25-34) either in 1981 or in 1990. Whichever age group is considered, people in that age group were more tolerant in 1990 than people within that same age group in 1981 (see again Figure 8.5a). This demonstrates that in Europe there was an overall, secular shift towards greater tolerance. This shift was, however, considerably less marked for the two youngest age groups than for the four older ones.

Figure 8.5   Personal-sexual values: Europe

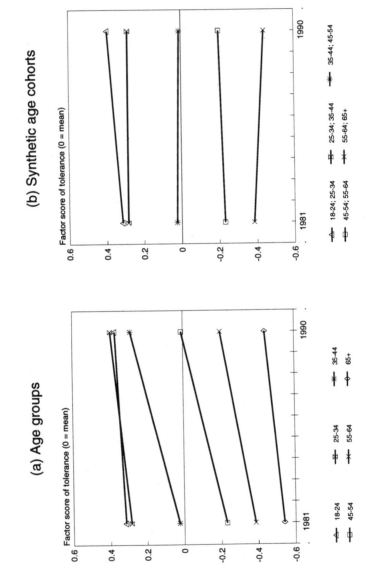

(a) Age groups

(b) Synthetic age cohorts

1981 + 1990 mean.

Source: European Values Survey reported in Barker (1991).

The EVS consists of two snapshot surveys, but synthetic age cohorts can be constructed by comparing answers given in 1981 by people aged 18-24 with those given in 1990 by people aged 25-34, and so on. The results for Europe are presented in that form in Figure 8.5b. A minor source of inaccuracy is that the gap between the surveys was nine years, whereas the age groups each comprise ten years, but the analysis still gives a fairly good impression of the direction of change. It can be seen that in Europe there was no consistent shift in views over the nine-year period for the five synthetic cohorts. For the three middle cohorts (those aged 25-34, 35-44, and 45-54 in 1981) the lines are more or less flat, indicating little or no change. For the youngest group (those aged 18-24 in 1981) there was some increase in tolerance over the nine-year period, whereas for the oldest group (those aged 55-64 in 1981) there was some decrease.

It seems, therefore, that the differences between age groups in level of tolerance arise not because people become less tolerant as they grow older, but because over the second half of the century, each successive European generation has been more tolerant than the previous one. However, this interpretation must remain tentative, because there are as yet only two data points. Also, the somewhat divergent results for the youngest and oldest of the synthetic cohorts suggest that there may be some more complex pattern of change taking place, which cannot be adequately described until more results become available.

The results for North America again showed a regular relationship between tolerance in the personal-sexual sphere and age, both in 1981 and in 1990 (see Figure 8.6a). Again, the only departure from regularity was that there was little difference between the attitudes of the two youngest age groups. Also, members of each age group in 1990 were considerably more tolerant than members of that same age group in 1981, demonstrating a secular shift towards greater tolerance over this period. However, the results for the synthetic age cohorts show a different pattern in North America (Figure 8.6b) from that shown in Europe (Figure 8.5b). In North America, the level of tolerance shown by each synthetic age cohort increased between 1981 and 1990, and the regularity of the pattern is striking. In North America, therefore, unlike Europe, there seems to have been a tendency over this nine-year period for people to become more tolerant in the personal-sexual domain as they became

Figure 8.6   Personal-sexual values: North America

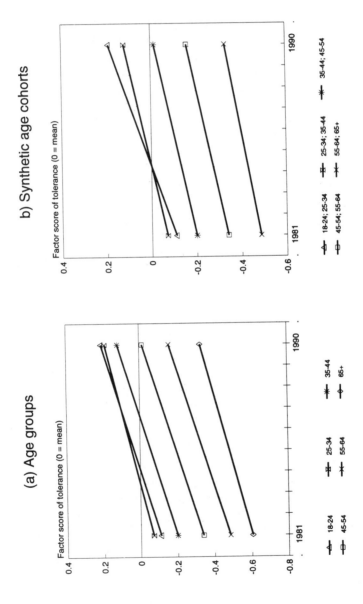

(a) Age groups

b) Synthetic age cohorts

Factor score of tolerance (0 = mean)

1981 + 1990 mean.
Source: European Values Survey reported in Barker (1991).

older; this is in addition to the overall secular shift towards greater tolerance, which is a common result for Europe and North America.[4]

Changes in Self-interest and Legal-illegal Values

Analyses of the 1981 EVS showed that countries that were relatively tolerant on the sexual-personal factor were not necessarily tolerant on the other two factors, self-interest and legal-illegal morality. This pattern has been confirmed by the 1990 EVS. While the Southern European countries (and Ireland) tended to be less tolerant in the sexual-personal domain than the Scandinavian countries, this pattern was reversed for 'civic morality' – the self-interest and legal-illegal factors combined.[5] In terms of civic morality (buying stolen goods, accepting bribes, joyriding) the Scandinavian countries were substantially less tolerant than the Southern Europeans. Northern European and North American countries were somewhere in between, in terms of civic tolerance, with the North Europeans tending to be slightly more tolerant than the Americans.

As in the case of personal-sexual morality, the results showed a regular pattern of differences between age groups, such that younger people were more tolerant of acts of self-interest and illegality (Figures 8.7a and 8.8a). Differences between the younger age groups (between those aged 18-24 and 25-34, and between those aged 25-34 and 35-44) were particularly marked, whereas differences between older age groups were smaller.

The results suggest that there was little or no secular change in tolerance of acts of self-interest and illegality over the nine-year period from 1981. When results for each age group in 1981 are compared with those for that same age group in 1990, the differences are small and inconsistent for both Europe and North America, although there is perhaps a slight suggestion of a marginal

---

4. Another reason why it can be very important to look for changes within age bands and within cohorts, is that the changing demographic profile of industrialized nations can mask (or create) changes in the values of cohorts if marked generational differences in values exist. For example, if the proportion of young people in the population today is lower than that of ten or twenty years ago (which it is), and if young people tend to be far more tolerant (in all periods) than older people, then even if there were no cohort effects whatsoever (in other words, today's young people were equally tolerant as yesterday's) then there would appear to be a general shift towards reduced tolerance due to the shift in the average age of the whole population.

5. In the initial results so far released, self-interest and legal-illegal factors have been collapsed into a single dimension (Barker, 1991). It is not yet clear whether this has been done for simplicity or because the factors were no longer found to be independent.

350

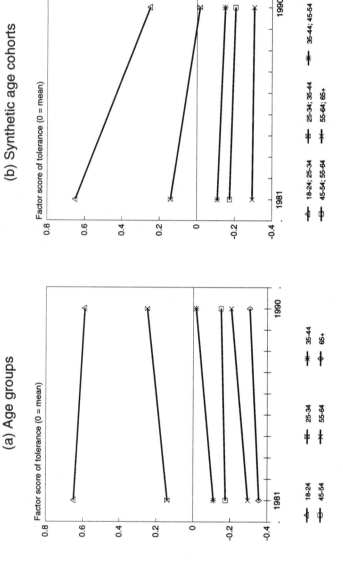

Figure 8.7 (Anti)-civic values: Europe

1981 + 1990 mean.

Source: European Values Survey reported in Barker (1991).

secular increase in tolerance over the nine-year period in the latter case (Figure 8.7a and 8.8a).

In both Europe and North America, the synthetic age cohorts showed a decline in tolerance of acts of self-interest and illegality, although this decline was much more marked for the youngest cohort (aged 18-24 in 1981), and to a lesser extent for the next one (aged 25-34 in 1981) than for the older cohorts (see Figures 8.7b and 8.8b). Because there are only two data points, these results cannot be interpreted with confidence, but they are consistent with the theory that young people start by being tolerant of acts of self-interest and illegality, but tend to grow out of these attitudes over a period of ten or twenty years. That interpretation would fit well with the age-crime curve: the rate of offending peaks in the teenage years, then falls steeply up to the age of 25 and less steeply thereafter (see Chapter 9).

While the results for Europe as a whole show no consistent secular shift in level of tolerance for self-interested and illegal acts, the pattern of change varies considerably between countries. There was a shift towards greater tolerance in those countries that had previously been least tolerant of self-interested and illegal acts – the Northern European and Scandinavian countries. In Southern Europe, where tolerance for self-interested and illegal acts tends to be higher, tolerance levels have fallen. If continued, this pattern of change will tend to bring attitudes in different European countries closer together.

The longer run of Reader's Digest surveys provides evidence that attitudes towards acts of self-interest have changed in a different way from attitudes towards acts that are clearly illegal. Respondents were asked to what extent they approved or disapproved of 'people who, on finding a lost article, keep it for themselves'. This is a well-worded question as it contains no references that would change its meaning or weight across time. In 1969, the average proportion of the population disapproving of such acts across sixteen European nations was 88 per cent, the lowest level being 85 per cent in France, and the highest being 94 per cent in Sweden. The proportion of young people disapproving was lower, but only slightly: 86 per cent of 18 to 24-year-olds disapproved compared to the average of 88 per cent (Reader's Digest, 1970). In 1990, the average proportion of the population disapproving was 68 per cent. In every single country without exception, the proportions disapproving of acts of finders-keepers had fallen. Analysing the results by age shows that this enormous shift appears to be largely the result of a period effect: all age groups have become more tolerant of finders-keepers, although the youngest generation remain the most tolerant of all. The shift has been smallest in the

Figure 8.8   (Anti-)civic values: North America

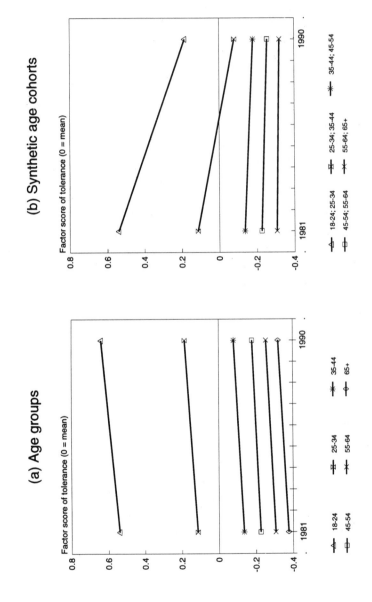

(a) Age groups

(b) Synthetic age cohorts

1981 + 1990 mean.
Source: European Values Survey reported in Barker (1991).

Scandinavian countries, hence it is the Scandinavian countries (Norway, Sweden, Denmark and Finland) that remain most disapproving of people who keep lost articles for themselves.

Yet when the questions about more serious or illegal acts are considered, a very different pattern of change arises. Average levels of disapproval of people who evade taxes and of people who drive after drinking have remained virtually unchanged (disapproving of tax evaders: 65 per cent in 1969, 66 per cent in 1990; disapproving of driving after drinking: 92 per cent in 1969, 91 per cent in 1990). People had actually become more critical of those who broke the speed limit, although it should be added that speed limits have tended to be raised over the period. The Scandinavians were again the most likely to disapprove of such acts, although on tax evasion there had been some convergence, with the Scandinavians becoming slightly less disapproving and the Southern Europeans more disapproving. These results suggest that people have not become more tolerant of illegal acts in general, but that they may have become more tolerant of certain acts of self-interest that are not, as such, illegal.

The earlier section showed that there has been a considerable overall shift in levels of tolerance in the personal-sexual domain. The findings on civic values are more complex. The EVS findings show little or no change over the nine-year period from 1981 on a broadly-based aggregate measure, although there was a slight increase in tolerance of anti-civic acts in North America. However, the Reader's Digest surveys, which cover the 21-year period from 1969, suggest that civic values should be split into two components. The results show that there has been some shift towards greater tolerance of acts of self-interest, but little or no shift towards greater tolerance of illegality. These shifts in civic values seem to reflect secular change superimposed on change throughout the life cycle. Clearly, future analysis of the EVS should distinguish more clearly between acts of self-interest and illegality.

Religious Orientation and Formal Religious Beliefs

Analyses of the 1981 EVS showed that a very strong factor could be extracted relating to acceptance or rejection of the traditional Judaeo-Christian value system (Inglehart, 1990). Other values, particularly sexual-personal ones, were also found to load strongly on this factor. Large generational differences were found, with the young considerably less likely to describe themselves as having a religious orientation (taking comfort from religion, describing themselves as religious) or to report believing in traditional religious doctrines (God, life after death, heaven).

Figure 8.9   Assent to religious beliefs: Europe

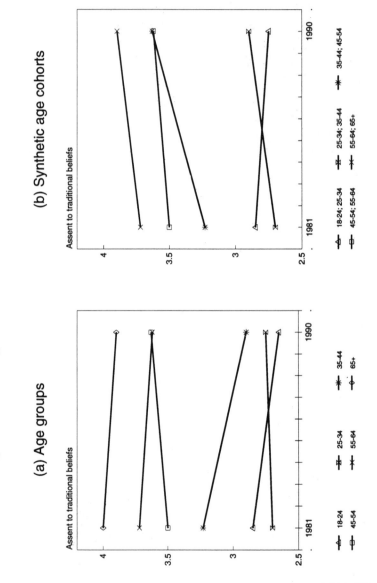

(a) Age groups

(b) Synthetic age cohorts

1981 mean = 3.3, 1990 mean = 3.1.

Source: European Values Survey reported in Barker (1991).

On the basis of the limited findings so far available, it seems that there has been a modest secular shift away from religious beliefs between 1981 and 1990 both in Europe and in North America. (The items included in the religious beliefs scale are belief in God, life after death, a soul, the devil, hell, heaven, and sin.) Comparing the beliefs of each age group in 1981 with the beliefs of that same age group in 1990, a decline in beliefs was shown for four out of the six age groups in Europe (see Figure 8.9a) and for five out of the six in North America (see Figure 8.10a). The two age groups in which religious beliefs, if anything, slightly increased in Europe were those aged 45-54 and 25-34. The one age group showing, if anything, a slight increase in religious beliefs in North America was those aged 65 or more. Overall, levels of religious belief were much higher in North America than in Europe both in 1981 and in 1990.

The results for synthetic age cohorts show that, in Europe, four out of five of the groups showed an increasing level of religious belief over the nine-year period from 1981; the one group that showed a declining level of belief was the youngest (those aged 18-24 in 1981) (see Figure 8.9(b)). In North America, by contrast, all five of the synthetic age cohorts showed a declining level of belief over the nine years starting in 1981 (see Figure 8.10(b)). In broad terms, therefore, there has been a slow secular decline in religious beliefs both in North America (where the level of belief is relatively high) and in Europe (where it is relatively low). In North America, there is also evidence of a decline in religious belief with increasing age, whereas in Europe there is evidence of an increase in belief with age, except for the youngest cohort. Of course, these trends will become much clearer when more data points are available.

Religious orientation, as opposed to religious belief, has been defined in analyses of the EVS as taking comfort in religion, describing oneself as religious, and taking moments of prayer. Comparing the same age groups in 1981 and 1990, we find that in Europe religious orientation declined for all six age groups, but much more strongly for the younger than for the older ones (see Figure 8.11a). This demonstrates, in Europe, a fairly marked secular decline in religious orientation. In North America, however, there was no clear pattern of secular change over the nine-year period from 1981. Among North Americans aged 18-24, religious orientation was considerably lower in 1990 than it had been in 1981, whereas among those aged 65 and over, it was considerably higher. Changes for the four age groups in the middle were smaller, but indicate overall a slight decline (see Figure 8.12a). One consequence of this pattern of change is that there has been a widening of differences between age groups in North America in terms of religious

Figure 8.10   Assent to religious beliefs: North America

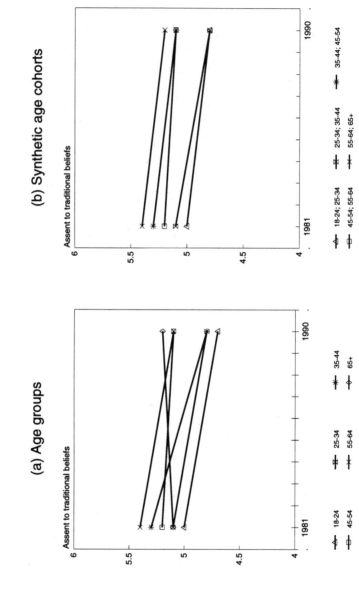

(a) Age groups

(b) Synthetic age cohorts

1981 mean = 5.2, 1990 mean = 5.0.

Source: European Values Survey reported in Barker (1991).

Figure 8.11 Religious orientation: Europe

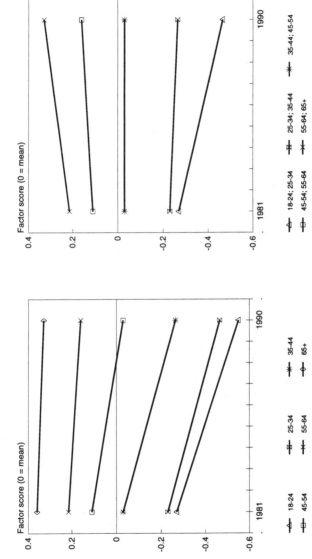

(a) Age groups

(b) Synthetic age cohorts

1981 + 1990 mean.

Source: European Values Survey reported in Barker (1991).

orientation between 1981 and 1990. The same is true for Europe, but to a lesser extent.

The results for synthetic age cohorts suggest that, in Europe, religious orientation has tended to decline with increasing age among the younger to middle cohorts, but to increase among the older cohorts (see Figure 8.11b). The results for North America show the same general pattern, although it is only the youngest cohort (those aged 18-24 in 1981) whose religious orientation actually declined with age. The next cohort (aged 25-34 in 1981) remained about level over the nine-year period, whereas the other three cohorts showed an increase in religious orientation (see Figure 8.12b). These results suggest that there is a parting of the way between the generations in religious orientation, with the older generations becoming more oriented towards religion as they grow older whereas the younger generations are doing the reverse.

Some of the EVS findings on religious beliefs are perhaps surprising. The impression given by the sociological literature is that religious orientations and beliefs - and especially traditional (formal) Judaeo-Christian beliefs - have been thoroughly undermined by the secular values of advanced industrial societies. Yet as the EVS data clearly show, religious beliefs appear to remain extremely resilient: of Europeans, 77 per cent still believe in God, 68 per cent still believe in the soul, 58 per cent believe in sin, and 52 per cent believe in the after life (the figures for North America are even higher, 92, 89, 82, and 74 per cent respectively). Although it is true that national differences exist, with highest levels of belief (and religious orientation) in the US and Ireland, followed by Southern and then Northern Europe, and with lowest levels of belief in Scandinavia, religious beliefs are still generally very high. For example, a majority of the population believes in God in every country except Sweden, and a majority define themselves as religious persons in every country except Sweden, Norway and France. Long term data from other surveys confirm the resilience of traditional beliefs (see Figures 8.13a & b). However, formal involvement in the church is much lower. Ashford and Timms (1992) reported that in 1981 the proportion of Europeans who attended church weekly was 49 per cent; by 1990 this figure had fallen to only 29 per cent. (These figures are the averages of ten European nations.) The drop in the proportion of 18 to 24-year-olds attending church weekly was more dramatic still, falling from 43 per cent in 1981 to only 18 per cent in 1990. Barker (1991) reported that the proportion of Europeans who were actively involved in the church (who attended church at least once a month and who were a member of or active in religious organizations) stood at 9 per cent. Of the fourteen European

Figure 8.12 Religious orientation: North America

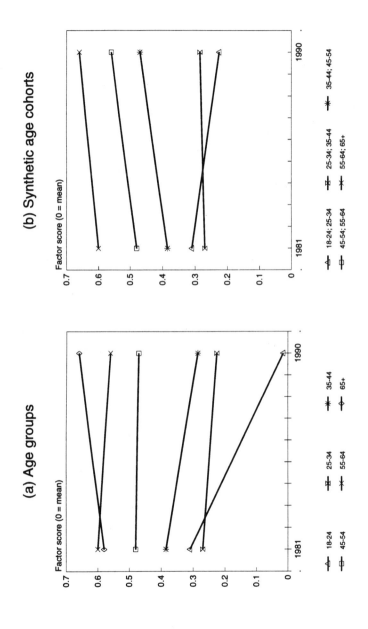

(a) Age groups

(b) Synthetic age cohorts

1981 + 1990 mean.
Source: European Values Survey reported in Barker (1991).

countries surveyed in the 1990 EVS, in only two – the Netherlands and Northern Ireland – did this core membership exceed 20 per cent. The figure for North America was 31 per cent. There was a cross-national trend across age groups, younger people being much less likely to be actively involved in the church than older people, and much more likely to be completely uninvolved.

So the question remains, why, despite the dramatic decline in levels of church attendance and formal religious involvement, have expressed religious beliefs (such as belief in God) proved so resilient? A small part of the answer may lie in the pattern of demographic shifts, which has meant that the elderly (who are the most likely to believe religious doctrines) have gradually come to constitute a larger and larger proportion of the population. Yet this demographic change cannot alone explain the degree of resilience of religious beliefs. Another probable explanation is that the definition of the concepts has changed. People today, and especially young people, are relatively happy for the church to pronounce on matters concerned with the third world, human rights, and the environment, but they are far less happy about the church's pronouncements about sexual relations or family life (Ashford & Timms, 1992; De Moor, 1991). It would seem that the type of God that people choose to believe in today is a far more personal and less empowered character than the God of previous generations. Many of the religious concepts that have withstood the enormous changes of the twentieth century have done so because they have been sufficiently flexible to have been reworked into more secular and metaphorical forms. The third reason why certain religious concepts may have proved so resilient is that their bases may be more psychological than spiritual. For example, in terms of subjective experience, the concept of 'sin' is almost inseparable from that of guilt. Similarly, perhaps the reason why the concept of God has proved so resilient is not that it accurately describes the nature of the cosmos, but that it encapsulates something about subjective experience - the subjective experience of significant internalized others from early childhood. Perhaps even the resilience of concepts such as 'heaven' and the 'after-life' should be understood in psychological terms: they defend internal moralities and motivations, and protect us from the harsh realities of the present (Freud, 1933).

Figure 8.13

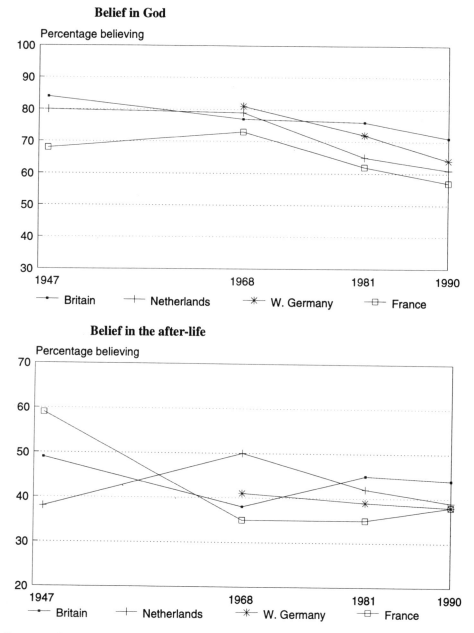

Belief in God

Percentage believing

Britain   Netherlands   W. Germany   France

Belief in the after-life

Percentage believing

Britain   Netherlands   W. Germany   France

Source: Stoetzel (1983); Harding (1986).

Changes in Material Values, Work Attitudes and the Willingness to Protest

Postmaterialism?

One of the most influential ideas to have arisen out of research on cross-national social attitudes is the hypothesis that, since the Second World War, there has been a major intergenerational shift away from 'materialist' towards 'postmaterialist' values among the publics of the advanced industrial societies. This 'postmaterialism' hypothesis was proposed in the early 1970s by Ronald Inglehart (Inglehart, 1971 & 1977), who has since spent many years building up evidence to support the hypothesis. However, as we shall see, Inglehart's thesis is also vulnerable to a number of serious critiques.

Inglehart's theoretical framework is closely related to the theory of human motivation proposed by the psychologist Abraham Maslow. Maslow postulated that humans had a hierarchy of five basic needs, which were (in order of strength): basic physiological needs (food, water etc.), safety, belongingness and love, esteem, and self-actualization (Maslow, 1954 & 1968). He argued that when people have satisfied needs at the lower levels of the hierarchy, they then move on to attempting to satisfy their needs at the next level. Inglehart translated Maslow's ideas into what could be described as a nested scarcity hypothesis: that people place the greatest subjective value on those things that are in relatively short supply – this depending on socio-economic conditions – with priority given to those things lower on the hierarchy of needs. In other words, in times of relative economic hardship, people prioritize lower level (material) needs, but in times of economic plenty, they prioritize higher level (non-material or postmaterial) needs. Inglehart added to this a second hypothesis – a 'socialization hypothesis' – that the relationship of the socio-economic environment to value priorities is not an immediate one, but involves a substantial time lag, a person's basic value priorities reflecting the conditions that prevailed during their pre-adult years.

One source of Inglehart's evidence for the postmaterialism hypothesis was longitudinal Japanese data showing the proportion of the Japanese public agreeing with the statement: 'In bringing up children of primary school age, some think that one should teach them that money is the most important thing.' In 1953, 65 per cent of the Japanese public agreed that financial security was the most important thing, but by 1978, this figure had fallen to only 45 per cent (and to 43 per cent in 1983). In every year, the youngest age group (20 to 24-years-old) was least likely to agree with the statement. This change was largely accounted for by a shift in values across cohorts; later cohorts brought up in times of relative prosperity were substantially less likely to agree that financial security was the most important thing. The values of each cohort remained relatively stable as individuals grew older, so the overall shift appeared to be due to generational replacement. A second source of Inglehart's evidence was cross-sectional survey data from six European nations showing that similar generational differences existed within Europe. People were asked what they personally considered the most important goals among the following:

A. Maintain order in the nation
B. Give people more say in the decisions of the government
C. Fight rising prices
D. Protect freedom of speech.

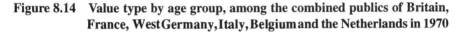

Figure 8.14 Value type by age group, among the combined publics of Britain, France, West Germany, Italy, Belgium and the Netherlands in 1970

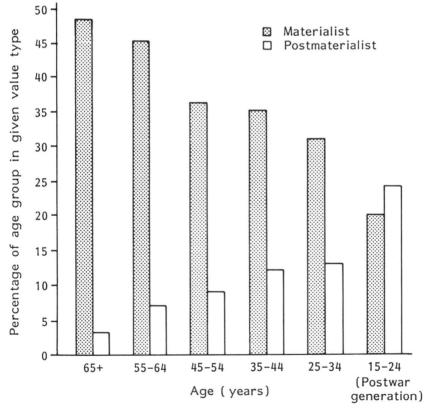

Source: Inglehart (1990).

People who gave priority to both A and C were described as 'materialists', and those who gave priority to B and D were described as 'postmaterialists'. Those who gave priority to a combination were described as 'mixed'. Inglehart found that younger people, compared to older people, were far less likely to be materialists and far more likely to be postmaterialists (see Figure 8.14) (Inglehart, 1977 & 1981).

Figure 8.15   Value priorities of eight age cohorts across six West European publics, 1970-1988

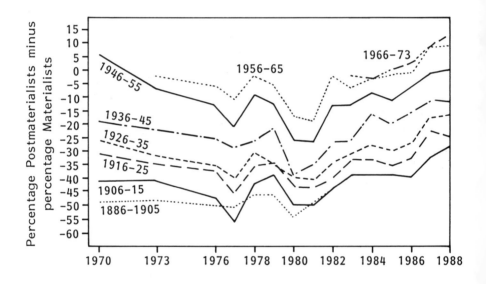

Based on data from representative national samples of publics of France, Great Britain, West Germany, Italy, Belgium and the Netherlands, interviewed in European Community surveys of 1970 and 1973 and Euro-Barometer surveys 6 through 29 (total N = 190,129).

Source: Inglehart (1990).

The postmaterialism scale (now expanded to 12 items) has been regularly incorporated into the Eurobarometer surveys conducted since 1970. This has enabled the construction of a time series of attitudes on the postmaterialism scale (Inglehart, 1990). The time series data show that despite some period effects, individual cohorts have been largely consistent in their value priorities

– the more recent the cohort, the more 'postmaterial' its orientation (see Figure 8.15). The Eurobarometer surveys have continued to document clear differences between the value priorities of the generations as measured by the postmaterialism scale (Abramson & Inglehart, 1992), and analyses by other researchers have similarly confirmed the remarkable stability of the value priorities of differing generations as measured by the scale (De Graaf et al., 1989). Inglehart and his colleagues now claim to have recorded similar differentials between the value priorities of earlier and later cohorts across all Western European countries (Inglehart, 1990), in the USA, Canada and Mexico (Inglehart, 1991), in Hong Kong (Ho, 1985) and even in Poland (Inglehart & Siemienska, 1988). The only countries where the generational difference has seemed to be less clear have been in Japan and China. In Japan, the meaning of some items and their relation to one another and to the materialism-postmaterialism scale were somewhat different to that in the West. In particular, the item 'friendlier, less impersonal society' (translated as 'a society with harmonious human relations') which correlates strongly with other postmaterial items in the West and is strongly endorsed by the young, was more endorsed by the older generation in Japan. This seems to highlight something very interesting about the uniqueness of Japan among the industrialized nations (for Japan's exceptional record of low and stable crime rates, see Chapter 9). Provisional evidence from a small Chinese sample outside Hong Kong suggests that young people in China were more materialist than were the older generation (Ho, 1985), but this result could reflect the relative poverty of the Chinese and does not therefore contradict Inglehart's general thesis.

The postmaterialism thesis suggests that young people today are less materialist than previous generations. Furthermore, it suggests that as nations become more affluent, the changes in values that this affluence brings among the younger generation actually undermine the value system that originally led to that economic growth. If the level of postmaterialism (the percentage of materialists minus the percentage of postmaterialists) for different countries in the early eighties is plotted against those countries' levels of affluence in 1950 (gross national product per capita, 1950) then a broad negative relationship is found ($r = -0.59$). The countries that were richest in 1950 were the countries where postmaterial values were most common in the 1980s (see Figures 8.16 (a) & (b). However, the countries that had the highest growth rates (in the period 1965-1984) were those with the most materialist values ($r = 0.54$).

The postmaterialism thesis has been criticized on both theoretical and methodological grounds, especially the bolder claim that postmaterialism is at the centre of a contemporary culture shift and a dominant cause behind it. First, Inglehart has been highly criticized for his failure to explore alternative interpretations of the data he presents (Witherspoon & Jowell, 1992). He has shown a strong tendency to impute causality to patterns of correlations, and may, therefore, have over-emphasized the causal relevance of postmaterialist values in the process of change. For example, Inglehart has stressed the patterns of association between postmaterialist values and other types of values such as less traditional religious beliefs and more liberal attitudes towards

Figure 8.16(a) Economic development and the decline of materialist values

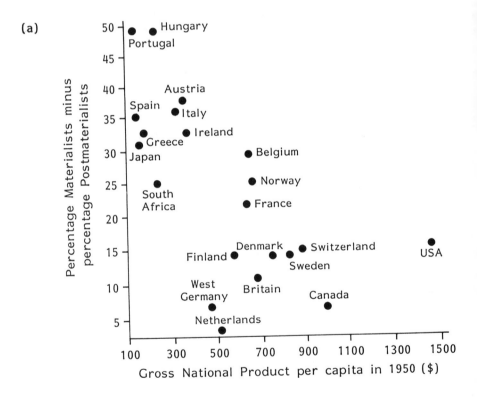

Value priorities data from World Values survey, 1981: Eurobarometer surveys 19-25 (1982-1986); and Political Action, 1974. Gross National Product per capita calculated from *UN Statistical Yearbook*, 1958 (New York: 1959).

Figure 8.16(b) Materialist values and economic growth, 1965-1984

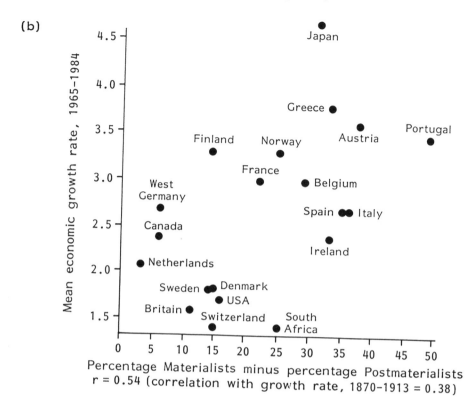

Growth rates 1965-1984 from *World Development Report*, 1986 (Washington: World Bank, 1986). Growth rates 1870-1913 from Angus Maddison, *Economic Growth in Japan and the USSR* (London: Allen and Unwin, 1969).

Source: Inglehart (1990).

sexual behaviour and gender relations. However, it is not clear why postmaterialism should be given such a privileged position in the analysis as opposed to, say, age, education, or religious values. In terms of the ability of the materialist-postmaterialist thesis to explain economic growth, some might argue that there are other hypotheses that can explain this, notably the idea of a cultural 'work ethic' (Giorgi & Marsh, 1990). Second, doubts have been expressed about the validity of the postmaterialism scale itself. Is it really measuring what Inglehart has claimed? There is always a danger that when questionnaire items are referred to by a single global term a certain amount of semantic slippage can occur. The postmaterialism scale does not attempt to measure the absolute strength of respondents' material values, but rather the strength of these values *relative* to those of others in the scale. This means that an alternative interpretation of the generational differences as measured by the scale could be that younger generations are just as materialist as older generations, but that it is their political expectations that have changed. In other words, younger generations may be more concerned about freedom of speech, political participation and so on, yet equally concerned about material issues. Data presented by Flanagan (1982) support this view. Flanagan re-analysed Japanese data (part of which Inglehart had used in formulating his original hypothesis) and concluded that although there had been important value shifts over the previous three decades, this pattern of value change was better understood in terms of a shift from 'authoritarian' to 'libertarian' values rather than one from materialism to postmaterialism. When seen from this point of view, the demonstration by Inglehart (1990) that the period effects in postmaterial values correspond very closely to levels of inflation suggests that the materialist part of the 'postmaterialism' scale might not, in fact, be responsible for the generational differences on the scale. Inglehart's data could instead be interpreted as suggesting that economic conditions (notably levels of inflation) have direct and short-term effects on economic priorities, but that the underlying generational differences (and overall cultural shift) actually result from changes in political culture. In order to save the postmaterialist thesis, one would need to demonstrate that today's young people really are more prepared to prioritize non-material goals over material ones. As we shall see below, there is little evidence that this is so.

Changes in Work Values

As already noted, in the 1981 EVS, the young were found to be generally more demanding than the old in terms of the aspects of jobs that were thought to be important. The direction of change since then has generally emphasized this trend. The main factors that were more likely to be rated as more important in 1990 were (figures in brackets indicate per cent change): a job that's interesting (+7), a job that meets one's abilities (+7), a job in which you can achieve something (+6), a responsible job (+6), good pay (+5), and an opportunity to use initiative (+4). Factors that were rated as less important in 1990 were: good job security (-3), generous holidays (-2), not too much pressure (-2), and a useful job for society (-1).

The pattern of change provides little support for the postmaterialism thesis. There is no evidence that Europeans have become less concerned with material remuneration for their work. In fact, the reverse appears to be happening: people appear to be becoming more concerned about pay and promotion, and if anything, less concerned about the job's usefulness to society. However, these changes are overshadowed by the rapidly increasing emphasis being given to the importance of intrinsic interest, personal development and responsibility. In a recent paper, Harding (1992) analysed the changing patterns of emphasis given to different aspects of jobs in the 1990 EVS as compared to the 1981 EVS. He concluded that the main change that has occurred is that people have developed a stronger desire to use their own initiative coupled with increased expectations of flexible and equitable remuneration – or in other words, pay for performance. This shift in values is captured in responses to a hypothetical case put to subjects in the EVS. Subjects were asked to imagine the situation of two secretaries of the same age and doing practically the same job, but one of whom discovers that the other is more highly paid (the actual amount has been adjusted for inflation between the two surveys). The better paid secretary, however, is quicker, more efficient, and more reliable at her job. Subjects were then asked, 'In your opinion, is it fair or not fair that one secretary is paid more than the other?' In 1981, 59 per cent of Europeans said that this was fair, but this figure had risen to over 70 per cent in 1990.

Higher expectations seem to be the reason why Europeans have become less satisfied with their work: levels of work satisfaction have fallen across Europe since 1981 (except for Belgium), the fall being particularly large in the Netherlands (-10) and Britain (-8).

Overall, the picture of change for work values suggests not that people have become less materialistic, but that they have become more demanding. Consequently, pay is not enough: people today – and especially young people – expect work to be interesting *and* well paid.

Willingness to Protest

The 1990 EVS showed that over the previous ten years, people had become more willing and more likely to become involved in protest. In 1990 people were more likely to report being willing to engage in political action and were more likely to report having done so than in 1981, and this increase in 'protest proneness' was found both across Europe (Barker, 1991) and in North America

(Inglehart, 1991).[6] Young people were particularly likely to be willing to engage in protest and to have already done so, but all cohorts had become more protest-prone since 1981. Hence the 45 to 54-year-olds of 1990 were more willing to get involved in political action than the 18 to 24-year-olds of 1981.

Given that protest proneness was particularly high amongst young people and those with postmaterial values (Inglehart, 1991), perhaps this gives us a further clue as to what the changes measured by the 'postmaterialism' scale are tapping. It could be that the scale measures an expanding political awareness rather than any reduced emphasis on material goods. It will be recalled that the postmaterial items are things like 'give people more say in the decisions of government', 'protect freedom of speech' and 'give people more say in how things are decided at work and in their community'. The pattern that seems to emerge out of the larger picture on value change is not the de-emphasis of materialism but the even stronger and emerging emphasis of individual empowerment, equitable remuneration and a broader and more sceptical political awareness. This conclusion is also supported by data on attitudes towards institutions. Young people have less confidence than older generations in most institutions including the church, the armed forces, the educational system, the trade unions, the police and the civil service, and confidence in all of these institutions has fallen since 1981 (Ashford & Timms, 1992). Clearly, this evidence is more consistent with Flanagan's suggestion of a shift from authoritarian to libertarian values than with Inglehart's postmaterialism thesis.

Racial Prejudice

As minority issues are one of the themes examined in this volume, a brief summary of the evidence on prejudice is presented. However, as mentioned earlier, self-expressed attitudes do not always predict behaviour, and this is

---

6. The exact wording of the question was: 'I'm going to read out some different forms of political action that people can take, and I'd like you to tell me, for each one, whether you have actually *done* any of these things, whether you might do it or would never, under any circumstances, do it?'

	Have done	Might do	Would never do	DK
A) Signing a petition				
B) Joining in boycotts				
C) Attending lawful demonstrations				
D) Joining unofficial strikes				
E) Occupying buildings or factories.				

particularly true of attitudes and behaviour towards racial minorities. This should be borne in mind when considering the evidence presented below.

Because of the importance of race relations in American politics and social policy, much attitude research has concentrated on racial prejudice, and a great deal of effort has been devoted to the development of accurate measures. Despite the difficulties involved, a number of consistent results have been reported. Both early and recent studies have found prejudice to be associated with political conservatism, general ethnocentrism, absence of intergroup friends, lack of political interest and low educational level (Adorno et al., 1950; Altemeyer, 1981; Pettigrew & Meertens, 1992). Levels of expressed hostility vary markedly across countries. In the 1988 Eurobarometer people were asked: 'Do you personally, in your daily life, find disturbing the presence of people of another nationality?' The proportions saying yes were 17 per cent in Germany, 16 per cent in Belgium and 13 per cent in France to 5 per cent in Spain and Ireland and 3 per cent in Portugal. It is noteworthy that these figures tend to reflect the actual number of non-EC nationals in relation to the population of the individual country (Melich, 1991). However, when a specific and more personal situation was described, far higher proportions of people reported prejudice, although this varied according to the minority group in question. For example, the proportions of the French who would mind having a suitably qualified South East Asian as their boss was 22 per cent but this figure rose to 35 per cent if the new boss was described as North African (Jackson et al., 1991). Similar, but even larger differences were found concerning the possibility of the outgroup person joining the family through marriage: for example, the French show greater hostility to the idea of a North African joining the family (44 per cent minding) than a South East Asian (22 per cent), and the Dutch show greater hostility towards the idea of a Turk joining the family (29 per cent) than a Surinamer (16 per cent).

Most research has found that young people tend to express significantly less prejudiced attitudes than older people. Part of this difference may relate to educational level, but regression analyses suggest that it cannot be reduced to educational differences alone (Pettigrew & Meertens, 1992). However, in an analysis of Dutch, German, French and British samples, Pettigrew and Meertens reported that the strength of this negative association between age and prejudice was stronger in some settings than in others. It was found to be relatively strong in Holland and France, but weaker in Germany and Britain. In fact, their analyses of the Eurobarometer suggested that in Britain the relationship between age and prejudice had become reversed: in other words, younger generations reported more, rather than less, prejudice than older generations. As they pointed out, 'this result suggests ominous difficulties for future British race relations' (12). However, this peculiar British effect was not replicated in the latest British Social Attitudes survey which showed that, as elsewhere, self-reported prejudice tended to be lower in younger age groups, and especially concerning sensitive issues such as marriage to an outgroup member (Young, 1992).

There are few data on long-term time trends, but what evidence there is suggests that the generational differences probably reflect a longer-term trend. The Reader's Digest Eurodata included some repeat questions about the issue of marrying someone of a different racial, religious or educational background. In both 1969 and 1990, younger people were considerably more tolerant than older people of marrying someone from a different background. In 1969, the proportion of Europeans from sixteen nations disapproving of marriage to someone of a different education or class was 19 per cent of all adults. By 1990, the proportion disapproving had fallen to 8 per cent. The level of disapproval decreased in all countries, but fell most rapidly in the countries such as Austria, Spain, West Germany and Luxembourg where the original levels of disapproval were highest. Similar falls occurred in the proportions disapproving of marriage to someone of a different cultural and religious background (25 per cent disapproved in 1969 and 16 per cent in 1990). Against this long-term trend, however, recent Eurobarometer results suggested that, in at least some respects, attitudes have very recently become harsher towards minority groups and especially towards immigrants. In 1988, the proportion of Europeans (EC12) agreeing with the statement that 'the rights of immigrants should be restricted' was 18 per cent, but by 1991 this proportion had risen sharply to 33 per cent. It could be that this particular question reflects a very specific issue, and one closely grounded in current economic difficulties, but this finding cautions against hasty conclusions about long-term trends in racial hostilities.

Are these findings a true reflection of underlying attitudes? It is noteworthy that in the Eurobarometer, when the question was changed from one about *personal* attitudes ('*I* would not mind if...') to one about the attitudes of people in general ('*Most people* would not mind if...') the proportions reporting various forms of prejudice approximately doubled. Clearly, this is reminiscent of the findings on other types of moral and socially desirable self-expressed attitudes: people tend to be far more liberal in their descriptions of themselves than about others. Here the further difficulty arises that as people become more aware of the issues and sensitive to their own behaviour, they may report higher rather than lower levels of prejudice, although their actual behaviour may have become less prejudiced. The generational differences in self-expressed attitudes are certainly consistent with a secular trend towards reduced prejudice, but they are by no means conclusive. Furthermore, it is possible that if economic conditions worsen and youth unemployment rises further, tomorrow's young people may become more rather than less hostile towards perceived outgroups.

One final issue concerning minority groups concerns how their values and attitudes relate to those of the majority. This is potentially a very important issue and one that future research should explore more carefully. It is a popular belief – and one that is sometimes used to justify prejudice – that minority groups hold different and incompatible values to those of the majority. Unfortunately, most current data are poorly placed to analyse such differences as the questionnaires themselves are often quite ethnocentric (the EVS, for example, contains many questions specifically grounded in Judaeo-Christian terminology), and anyhow, the samples of minority groups are often too small for useful analysis. It is to be hoped that future surveys will be worded and designed with minority groups in mind.

The Generation Gap – Transient Effect or Permanent Feature?

Differences in attitudes and beliefs between the generations are represented in popular representations of stormy relationships between adolescents and parents, between 'youths' and the authorities, and between students and the State. If it were possible to show how much of the difference in values between age groups is attributable to period, age, and cohort effects, this would resolve the question whether there is merely a transient difference between these particular generations, or a permanent generation gap between the young and the old. However, from the data currently available, it is not possible to make a reliable or accurate estimate of the size of the three types of effect. A more straightforward approach is to ask people directly about their attitudes to the younger generations and to compare the results across time.

In the Reader's Digest Eurodata surveys, respondents were asked about their attitudes to people aged 16-24. In 1969, 45 per cent of Europeans said that they had a 'mainly favourable' impression of the under-25s and 24 per cent said they had a 'mainly unfavourable' impression of them. In 1990, 59 per cent had favourable impressions of the under-25s, and only 13 per cent had unfavourable attitudes. In fact, in no less than fifteen of the sixteen countries included in both surveys, a higher proportion of people held favourable attitudes to the young in 1990 than in 1969. (The only slight exception was the Netherlands, but even there, the proportion holding *un*favourable attitudes had fallen.) Furthermore, data from the seven countries included in an even earlier Eurodata survey (France, West Germany, Italy, the Netherlands, Belgium, Luxembourg and Britain) showed that attitudes to young people were even less favourable in 1963 than in 1969. The average level of the population favourable to the under-25s (across the seven countries) in 1963 was only 38 per cent, with almost as many – 29 per cent – being mainly unfavourable. The figures for the same seven countries in 1969 were 44 per cent favourable (26 per cent unfavourable), and in 1990 were 56 per cent favourable (and 14 per cent unfavourable) (see Figure 8.17). These figures show how, right across Europe, people have become more favourable towards the younger generation. Generally speaking, the countries that were most favourable to young people in 1969 – the Scandinavian countries plus Ireland – remained among those most favourable to young people in 1990 (r = 0.62), although the gap had closed.

Figure 8.17 Attitude to the under-25s

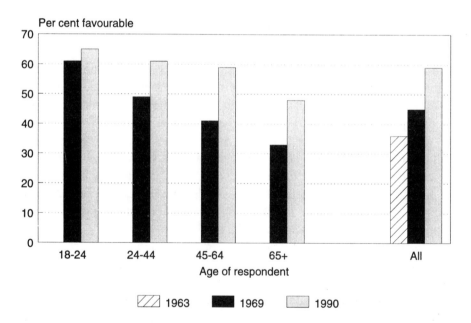

17 European countries; 7 in 1963.

Source: Reader's Digest Surveys: Products & People (1963); Survey of Europe Today (1969); Eurodata (1990).

At least four interpretations of this shift seem plausible. First, it could be that the level of objective behavioural 'problems' associated with young people has fallen, and that changing attitudes simply reflect this phenomenon. However, data presented in the rest of this volume make this an implausible interpretation. Second, it could be that the gap between the beliefs of young and old has substantially declined. As we have already seen, while this may have occurred in some areas, there is evidence of increasing polarization between the beliefs of young and old in many areas, and substantial value differences between age groups persist. Third, it could be that attitudes towards the young have become more favourable not because of an absolute reduction in the level of value differences between the young and old, but because of the widespread increase of tolerance in general. Increasing levels of tolerance have been reported for a whole range of behaviours including marrying out, sexual-personal affairs, and gender relations. Accordingly, it may be that people have learnt to be tolerant towards all kinds of different behaviour and therefore of the young as well. In a closely related fashion, it could be argued that attitudes towards the young have become more tolerant (and favourable) because of a reduction in the level of misunderstanding between the generations, perhaps through greater levels of communication. The misunderstanding is well illustrated by the answers to one of the items included in the 1981 EVS, which asked: 'How much trust do older people have in the young today?' (1 = none, 10 = a great deal). Breaking down the answers to the question by age it was found that the young greatly underrated the level of trust reported by the old. Similarly, the old greatly underrated the level of trust the young reported in the old. The fourth possibility is that modern societies have become more youth-oriented, such that the state of 'being young' itself is now more respected or even sought after. It is certainly possible to think of many examples from the world of advertising and fashion which suggest that being young is what is considered desirable in modern societies, but without further information, this interpretation must remain speculative.

ATTITUDE CHANGE IN A BROADER CONTEXT

Changes in the Informal and Formal Domains

The data presented so far have shown that there have been changes in individual values in a wide range of areas. In general, the attitudes of younger generations have predicted the direction of future change. Perhaps the clearest theme in the data has been a trend towards tolerance and permissiveness, and a move away from more traditional and rigid value systems. People are increasingly unlikely to look to the church for guidance in moral issues, and instead see moral values as determined by individual choices rather than by automatic reference to religious doctrine. This trend has led some to describe today's Europeans as 'moral entrepreneurs' (EVG press release, 1991).

The results of attitude surveys provide strong evidence for the hypothesis of an increase in the strength of individualism reported by the panel of experts in the CENSIS study referred to earlier (Angeli, 1991). The value shift is consistent with other changes in the informal social structures of modern societies (see earlier for a distinction between the formal and informal domains) such as falling church attendance, the move towards smaller average household sizes, the decreasing importance of locality, increasing rates of divorce, and falling rates of fertility. Falling fertility rates are a particularly interesting example: social attitude data suggest that this fall is closely associated with the rise of individualism, as potential parents take control over their own fertility and choose to prioritize their own lives rather than the traditional group norm (having children). (Of 18 to 34-year-old Europeans, approximately one in four men and one in five women agree or strongly agree with the statement 'having children interferes too much with the freedom of parents'.)

However, as discussed earlier, an examination of value shift needs to consider not only changes in the informal domain, but also complementary changes that may have occurred in the formal domain. For whereas it may be argued that the general increase in tolerance and individualism has led to a reduction in consensus about prescriptive rules in the informal domain, this stands in sharp contrast to changes in the formal domain. Over the course of this century there has been a general convergence in the domain of formal and universal rules. This is seen most clearly in the development and ratification of a wide range of international treaties and conventions (Bowman & Harris, 1984) and in the development of international legislative institutions such as the United Nations and the European Economic Community. These developments signal the expansion of formalized rules and sanctions that are intended to apply in generalized ways to generalized others, the prime example being the formalization of the idea of universal human rights. To get a sense of the rapidity of this expansion one can simply look at a volume listing EC legislation by title: the list of EC regulations, directives and decisions made during the 1960s takes up 77 pages, during the 1970s 912 pages, and during the 1980s 1,360. The expansion in legislation has been reflected in a parallel growth in the legal professions (Abel, 1988). It is noteworthy, therefore, that the lower confidence in the church among younger compared with older people is not repeated for all institutions of authority.

Furthermore, the increase in tolerance in the sexual-personal domain and to some extent in the self-interest domain was not matched by an equivalent increase in tolerance in the legal-illegal domain. The generally very permissive Scandinavian countries (Sweden, Finland, Norway, and Denmark) towards whose values other countries appear to be moving, are actually quite strict (and remain so) in terms of their low tolerance of illegal acts. It cannot be concluded, therefore, that there has been a general collapse in values of right and wrong. Although the moral authority of the church may have waned, this has not been paralleled by an increase in tolerance for acts that are recognized as wrong in a legal (secular) sense. The formalization of behavioural codes has been seen far more widely than in legislation. Especially since the Second World War, there has been an expansion in almost every kind of formalized provision within the industrialized nations. There have been enormous cross-national expansions in the formal provision of health care, of primary, secondary and tertiary education, and of welfare in general (Flora, 1986). These expansions are reflected in the size and level of spending of governments across the industrialized world; governments' levels of welfare spending have increased steadily both in absolute terms and in terms of percentage of gross national product (Figure 8.18). The welfare crisis of the 1980s slowed, but did not eliminate, this growth.

Patterns of formal provision – and in particular, formal care – stand in some contrast to the patterns of informal provision and care of traditional systems (Bulmer, 1986). Popular concern over this difference has tended to focus on the way in which formal provision is often experienced as cold, 'uncaring', and institutional, but as a wider analysis shows, informal systems of provision are not without problems (Halpern, 1990). In an informal system of care a person looks after someone literally because they care (and/or because they feel obligated by some form of reciprocity)[7]. In a formal system, care is instead based on some kind of rational appraisal of need. The problem with informal provision is that since it is based on highly personal or local appraisals of need, those persons or groups with fewest resources (those most in need) are also those who are least likely to receive assistance. The problem with formal

---

7. It should be stressed that the 'informal' is not the same as the 'voluntary': providers of care often feel that they have little choice about their role either because of shortfalls in state provision or because of economic factors and the inability to afford any other alternative.

provision, of course, is that there is no necessary personal relationship between the provider and the person in need.

Figure 8.18   Social expenditure as percentage of GDP

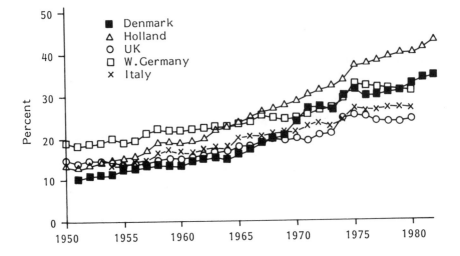

Source: Flora (1986).

Social attitude data appear to reflect both the positive and the negative aspects of the shift from the informal to the formal. Although people may have become more self-interested in some respects (for example, the increasing tolerance of 'finders' keepers'), they have also become more prepared to give to distant others who are in need. This can be seen in Reader's Digest Eurodata asking people about their willingness to pay taxes to help poorer areas. In 1969, 42 per cent of Europeans were prepared to pay higher taxes to help poorer countries outside Europe (and 48 per cent among the under-25s); in 1990, the figure had risen to 47 per cent (and 58 per cent among the under-25s). Similarly, in 1969, 50 per cent of Europeans were prepared to pay higher taxes to help poorer areas within the EC (59 per cent of the under-25s); in 1990 the figure had risen to 61 per cent (67 per cent of the under-25s). The populations of the wealthier countries (as measured by GNP *per capita*) tend to be the most prepared to support paying higher taxes to help poorer countries (r = 0.53).

The increased preparedness of people to help poorer countries has been paralleled by a reduction in the level of nationalism within most countries over the same period (see Figure 8.19), although this decline has been more uneven over the 1980s. This combined evidence suggests that there has been a long-term trend away from national partisanship towards a recognition of the relative needs of poorer countries.

Drawing the various strands together, it seems that we may be witnessing a long-term change in Western European orientations to others. We are seeing the transformation of care and reciprocity from a system of informal obligations to one of formal provisions, and this is evident in both changing social structures and changing values. Some writers have pointed, with some despair, to the darker side of this change, to an apparent failure of the 'enlightenment project' of discovering rational secular foundations for morality, and to its undermining by the nihilist writings of figures such as Nietzsche (MacIntyre, 1981; Barker, 1991). However, perhaps future and more cautious writers will question the pessimism of these conclusions.

> Do I exhort you to love thy neighbour? I exhort you rather to flight from your neighbour and to love of the most distant! ... It is the distant man who pays for your love of your neighbour; and when there are five of you together, a sixth always has to die. (Nietzsche, *Thus Spoke Zarathustra.*)

Whether or not a person sees the apparent decline of the creed 'love thy neighbour' as a bad thing seems to depend on the world-view through which they look, and this in turn seems to depend largely on the generation to which they belong.

The simple thesis that there has been a collapse in the consensus about moral behaviour or appropriate rules of conduct is not supported by the evidence. It would be more accurate to argue that, in the informal domain, there has been a reduction in the pressure to conform to traditional, prescriptive systems of rules, and an increase in tolerance, while in the formal domain, there has been an expansion in the extent and reach of rules.

Figure 8.19   National Pride

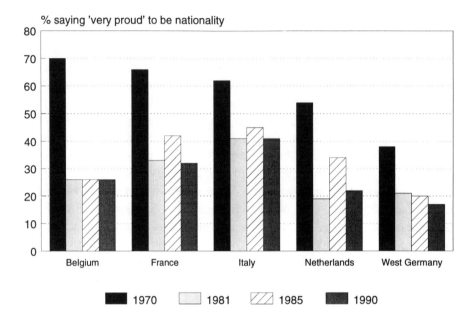

% saying 'very proud' to be nationality

Legend: ■ 1970 □ 1981 ▨ 1985 ■ 1990

Source: European Community Survey (1970); European Values Survey (1981);
           Eurobarometer 24 (1986) reported in Inglehart (1990); European Values Survey
           (1990) reported in Ashford & Timms (1992).

Change as an Interlocking Process

Social and structural change and value change form an interlocking spiral of
change in modern societies, and it is often difficult or impossible to determine
which came first.   An example, albeit a somewhat controversial one, of the
relationship between social and value change has already been mentioned.
Evidence suggests that a particular kind of value system may have provided
the motive force which led to the relative economic success of one nation over
another.   The social and structural change that arises from this economic
success (affluence) then in turn leads to the emergence of a new value system
('postmaterialism', or perhaps more accurately, libertarianism) which
undermines the value system and motive force behind the original economic
success.

A somewhat different, but related, example concerns how a country's economic success may be influenced by the public's belief in the values promoted by its government. Bornschier presented time-series data suggesting that countries that showed the strongest economic growth in the 1960s and 1970s were those that showed the lowest levels of political protest in the previous decades (Bornschier, 1989). This effect persisted after having controlled for the size of the country and the strength of its economy in 1950. Bornschier argued that the effect is due to the perceived legitimacy of the social order: policies (such as redistribution) promoted by governments that are considered just by their publics lead to the long-term economic success of the country concerned. This suggests that states that invest in a system of social order consistent with the values of their populations, for example, by investing in welfare (Korpi, 1985) or by assisting poorer nations, can thereby boost the motivation of their people and the long-term economic success of their nation by creating an atmosphere of legitimacy and civil obedience.

Yet the clearest example of social and value change as an interlocking process can be seen in globalization and the shift away from the values of 'love thy neighbour' towards a more reflexive concern about self and distant others. Young people today are far more global and less local in their world-view than their elders or young people of twenty years ago. A significant factor behind this shift in awareness has presumably been the enormous technological advances of the twentieth century. Communication is easier and cheaper, especially between distant points. Since the 1950s, as detailed in Chapter 6, there have been large increases in the number of television and radio receivers and in the proportion of the population having a telephone.

Levels of travel have increased, especially among the young. Europeans aged 15-24, despite their relative youth, are almost as likely to have visited another European country as those aged 25 or over (67 per cent vs. 69 per cent for the EC 12; Young Europeans, 1987). Private cars have become more common, and other kinds of mobility have increased even faster. The proportion of Europeans who could speak two or more languages was 28 per cent in 1969, but had risen to 42 per cent in 1990 (Reader's Digest Eurodata). It is the young and better educated that strongly lead this trend: within the EC, 52 per cent of young people (15-24) in 1987 spoke at least one foreign language against only 30 per cent of those over 25 (Angeli, 1991). Being able to speak other languages increases the mobility of young people and their access to ideas and values outside the local context still further. Yet perhaps an even more dramatic example of the expansion in mobility and the loosening of the influence of local context is money. Once synonymous with coins of rare metals, then with the less immediately valuable but equally concrete symbols of coinage and bank notes, money has become less and less physical and more and more a matter of the information held in some distant computer. The proportion of Europeans with bank accounts in 1969 was only 38 per cent; in 1990 the proportion was 78 per cent. The processes of modernity are bringing with them unprecedented levels of mobility of every kind.

This mobility of people, capital, information and ideas has led to what some social theorists have called 'disembedding' (Giddens, 1990), the lifting of social relations out of local contexts and their 'restructuring across indefinite spans of time-space'. Mobility and disembedding undermine the influence of local and informal norms and constraints. The waning importance of the church, the undermining of traditional value systems, and the rise of reflexive individualism and the desire for individual empowerment all appear to be results of this loss of influence, and these changes in values all act to reinforce the processes that created them. However, the conditions of modernity are also lending a new force to universal, formal structures, norms and constraints. The processes of modernity embody changes in social structures and values that are mutually reinforcing. Values and the social context create each other, and any policy whether it be aimed at moral, social or economic change has no choice but to take this interdependence in mind.

CONCLUSION

This chapter has attempted to answer a series of questions about generational differences in values that transcend national boundaries. The evidence presented has shown that many differences do exist between the values held by younger and older generations. From the available evidence, reliable and accurate estimates cannot be made of the proportions of these differences that are attributable to secular change (period effect), age effects, and cohort effects. It is clear, however, that secular changes have played an important part.

There appears to be no simple or unitary scale on which the moral values of nations can be ranked. Very broadly, the Scandinavian countries show the highest levels of tolerance on sexual-personal scales, closely followed by Northern Europeans, then the North Americans, and then the Southern Europeans and Ireland. In terms of religious orientations and beliefs, the order is roughly reversed, but with the Americans far more religious than any European nation with the possible exception of Ireland. In the case of tolerance for illegal acts and acts of self-interest, the pattern is more complex, with

Scandinavians tending to be less tolerant and the Southern Europeans tending to be more tolerant, but with this gap closing.

Situating value changes in a broader context, it was argued that the general pattern of change can be characterized as constituting two interrelated elements. First, there has been a reduction in the universality of norms, values and constraints at the informal level. This was manifested by higher levels of individualism (emphasis of individual convictions rather than external models), the development of libertarian (as opposed to authoritarian) values, and higher levels of tolerance in the personal sphere in general. Second, however, there has been an expansion in the extent of norms, values and constraints in the formal domain, most obviously in the legal sphere, but also in many other areas such as health, education, and welfare. These changes are bound up with each other and with the processes of modernity in ways that are self-reinforcing and difficult to separate. These changes appear to be occurring throughout the industrialized world.

Throughout Europe, there is a more positive attitude towards young people today than twenty years ago. Whether this means that the rate of value change is slowing down, and the 'generation gap' closing, or simply that we have become more accustomed to the idea of change that the young bring with them, we will have to wait for future generations to discover.

REFERENCES

Abel, R. L. (1988). *The legal profession in England and Wales.* Oxford: Blackwell.

Abramson, P. R. & Inglehart, R. (1992). Generational replacement and value change in eight West European societies. *British Journal of Political Science 22*, 183-228.

Adorno, T. W., Frankel-Brunswik, E., Levinson, D. J. & Sanford, R. N. (1950). *The authoritarian personality.* New York: Harper & Row.

Ajzen, I. (1988). *Attitudes, personality, and behaviour.* Buckingham: Open University Press.

Ajzen, I. & Fishbein, M. (1977). Attitude-behaviour relations: A theoretical analysis and review of empirical research. *Psychological Bulletin 84*, 888-918.

Altemeyer, B. (1981). *Right-wing authoritarianism.* Winnipeg: University of Manitoba Press.

Angeli, F. (1991). *Social Europe: In search of a common culture.* Rome: Centro Studi Investimenti Sociali.

Ashford, S. & Timms, N. (1992). *What Europe thinks: A study of Western European values.* Aldershot: Dartmouth.

Barker, D. G. (1991). *Changing social values in Europe*. Paper presented to an International Symposium on The unexpected Europe: Implications for the United States, 15 November 1991. University of Maryland.

Berger, P., Berger, B. & Kellner, H. (1974). *The homeless mind*. Harmondsworth, Middx: Penguin.

Bornschier, V. (1989). Legitimacy and comparative economic success at the core of the world system: An exploratory study. *European Sociological Review 5*, 215-230.

Bowman, M. J. & Harris, D. J. (1984). *Multilateral treaties*. London: Butterworth.

Bulmer, M. (1986). *Neighbours: The work of Philip Abrams*. Cambridge: Cambridge University Press.

Carver, C. S. (1975). Physical aggression as a function of objective self-awareness and attitude toward punishment. *Journal of Experimental Social Psychology 11*, 510-19.

Cattell, R. B. (1965). *The scientific analysis of personality*. Harmondsworth, Middx: Penguin.

De Graaf, N. D., Hagenaars, J. & Luijkx, R. (1989). Intergenerational stability of postmaterialism in Germany, the Netherlands and the United States. *European Sociological Review 5*, 183-201.

De Moor, R. (1991). Religion and church in Western countries. Unpublished briefing document. Quoted in D. G. Barker, *Changing social values in Europe*. University of Maryland.

Fisher, C. (1982). *To dwell among friends: Personal networks in town and city*. Chicago: University of Chicago Press.

Flanagan, S. C. (1982). Measuring value change in advanced industrial societies: A rejoiner to Inglehart. *Comparative Political Studies 15*, 99-128.

Flora, P. (1986). *Growth to limits: The Western European welfare states since World War II, Vol. 4: Appendix, Bibliographies, Tables*. Berlin/New York: Walter de Gruyter.

Freud, S. (1933). New introductory lectures on psycho-analysis. In J. Strachey (ed.) (1964) *Volume XXII of the standard edition of the complete psychological works of Sigmund Freud*. London: Hogarth.

Furnham, A. & Gunter, B. (1989). *The anatomy of adolescence: Young people's social attitudes in Britain*. London: Routledge.

Garfinkel, H. (1963). A conception of, and experiments with, 'trust' as a condition of stable concerted actions. In O.J. Harvey (ed.) *Motivation and social interaction*. New York: Ronald Press.

Garfinkel, H. (1967). *Studies in ethnomethodology*. Englewood Cliffs, NJ: Prentice-Hall.

Geller, D. (1980). Responses to urban stimuli: A balanced approach. *Journal of Social Issues 36*, 86-100.

Giddens, A. (1990). *The consequences of modernity*. Cambridge: Polity.

Giorgi, L. & Marsh, C. (1990). The protestant work ethic as a cultural phenomenon. *European Journal of Social Psychology 20*, 499-517.

Goffman, E. (1959). *The presentation of self in everyday life.* New York: Anchor Books.

Goldman, A. I. (1986). *Epistemology and cognition.* Cambridge, MA: Harvard University Press.

Habermas, J. (1987). *The theory of communicative action.* Cambridge: Polity.

Halpern, D. S. (1990). Active citizenship and a healthy society. In *Encouraging citizenship: Report of the Commission on Citizenship.* London: HMSO.

Harding, S. (1992). *Changing expectations and opinions of employees: Results from recent research.* Paper prepared for conference 'Increase motivation, performance and productivity', 24-25 March 1992. London.

Harding, S., Phillips, D. & Fogarty, M. (1986). *Contrasting values in Western Europe: Unity, diversity and change.* Basingstoke: Macmillan.

Heritage, J. (1984). *Garfinkel and ethnomethodology.* Cambridge: Polity.

Hirsch, F. (1977). *Social limits to growth.* London: Routledge &Kegan Paul.

Ho, E. S. (1985). Values and economic development: Hong Kong and China. Ph.D dissertation, University of Michigan. Quoted in R. Inglehart (1990) *Culture Shift.* Princeton, NJ: Princeton University Press.

Horkheimer, M. (1974). *Critique of instrumental reason.* New York: Seabury.

Inglehart, R. (1971). The silent revolution in Europe: Intergenerational change in post-industrial societies. *American Political Science Review 65*, 991-1017.

Inglehart, R. (1977). *The silent revolution: Changing values and political styles among Western publics.* Princeton: Princeton University Press.

Inglehart, R. (1981). Post-materialism in an environment of insecurity. *The American Political Science Review 75*, 880-900.

Inglehart, R. (1990). *Culture shift in advanced industrial society.* Princeton: Princeton University Press.

Inglehart, R. (1991). *Changing values in industrial society: The case of North America, 1981-1990.* Paper presented at the annual meeting of the American Political Science Association in Washington, DC, 29 August – 2 September, 1991.

Inglehart, R. & Siemienska, R. (1988). Political values and dissatisfaction in Poland and the West: A comparative analysis. *Government and Opposition 23*, 440-457.

Jackson, J. S., Kirby, D., Barnes, L. & Shepard, L. (1991). *Institutional racism and pluralistic ignorance: A cross-national comparison.* Paper presented at Le Colloque International Trois Jours Sur Le Racisme, 5-7 June 1991, La Maison de Sciences de L'Homme, Paris.

Jamieson, D. W. & Zanna, M. P. (1983). *The lie detector expectation procedure: Ensuring veracious self-reports.* Paper presented to the Canadian Psychological Association, Winnipeg.

Johnston, M. (1988). The price of honesty. In R. Jowell et al. (eds.) *British social attitudes: The 5th report.* Aldershot: Gower.

Jones, E. E. & Signall, H. (1971). The bogus pipeline: A new paradigm for measuring affect and attitude. *Psychological Bulletin 76*, 349-64.

Korpi, W. (1985). Economic growth and the welfare state: Leaky bucket or irrigation system? *European Sociological Review 1*, 97-118.

Krupat, E. (1985). *People in cities: The urban environment and its effects.* Cambridge: Cambridge University Press.

LaPiere, R. T. (1934). Attitudes vs. actions. *Social Forces 13*, 230-237.

Latour, B. (1987). *Science in action.* Milton Keynes: Open University Press.

Lindsay, P. H. & Norman, D. A. (1977). *Human information processing.* New York: Academic Press.

Lofland, L. (1973). *A world of strangers.* New York: Basic Books.

MacIntyre, A. (1981). *After virtue: A study in moral theory.* London: Duckworth.

Maddison, A. (1989). *The world economy in the 20th century.* Paris: OECD.

Maslow, A. H. (1954). *Motivation and personality.* New York: Harper & Row.

Maslow, A. H. (1968). *Toward a psychology of being* (2nd edition). Princeton, NJ: Van Nostrand.

McClelland, J. L. & Rumelhart, D. E. (1986). *Parallel distributed processing: Explorations in the microstructure of cognition.* Cambridge, MA: MIT Press.

Melich, A. (1991). *Public opinion towards non-EC immigrants in the European Community.* Paper prepared for the Scientific Conference on International Perspectives on Race and Ethnic Relations, 13-15 September 1991, Institute of Social Research, University of Michigan, Ann Arbor, Michigan.

Milgram, S. (1977). *The individual in a social world: Essays and experiments.* Reading, MA: Addison-Wesley.

Milgram, S. & Sabini, J. (1983). On maintaining social norms: A field experiment in the subway. In H. H. Blumberg, A.P. Hare, V. Kent & M. Davies (eds.) *Small groups and social interactions, Vol. 1.* London: Wiley.

Myers, D. G. (1990). *Social psychology.* New York: McGraw-Hill.

Nietzsche, F. (1961). *Thus spoke Zarathustra.* London: Penguin.

Pettigrew, T. F. & Meertens, W. R. (1992). *Subtle and blatant prejudice in Western Europe.* Paper presented at the International Congress on Psychology, July 1992, Brussels.

Pryor, J. B., Gibbons, F. X., Wicklund, R. A., Fazio, R. H. & Hood, R. (1977). Self-focused attention and self report validity. *Journal of Personality 45*, 514-27.

Raven, J. (1952). *Human nature.* London: H.K.Lewis.

Reader's Digest Surveys. *Products and People* (1963); *Survey of Europe today* (1969); *Eurodata* (1990). London: Reader's Digest.

Ross, L. D. (1977). The intuitive psychologist and his shortcomings: Distortions in the attribution process. In Berkowitz (ed.) *Advances in experimental social psychology, Vol. 10.* New York: Academic Press.

Rutter, M. & Pickles, A. (1990). Improving the quality of psychiatric data: Classification, cause and course. In D. Magnusson & L. R. Bergman (eds.) *Data quality in longitudinal research*, 32-57. Cambridge: Cambridge University Press.

Salk, J. & Salk, J. (1981). *World population and human values.* New York: Harper.

Saunders, P. (1986). *Social theory and the urban question,* (2nd edition). London: Hutchinson Educational.

Simmel, G. (1950). The stranger. In *The sociology of Georg Simmel.* New York: Free Press.

Stoetzel, J. (1983). *Les valeurs du temps présent.* Paris: Presses Universitaires.

United Nations (1986). *Report on the world situation.* New York: UN.

Westen, D. (1985). *Self and society: Narcissism, collectivism, and the development of morals.* Cambridge: Cambridge University Press.

Wicker, A. W. (1969). Attitudes versus actions: The relationship of verbal and overt behavioural responses to attitude objects. *Journal of Social Issues 25,* 41-78.

Witherspoon, S. & Jowell, R. (1992). Inglehart's culture shift (book review). *European Sociological Review 8,* 95-98.

Wittgenstein, L. (1958). *Philosophical investigations.* Oxford: Blackwell.

Wirth, L. (1938). Urbanism as a way of life. *American Journal of Sociology 44,* 1-24.

Young, K. (1992). Class, race and opportunity. In R. Jowell et al. (eds.) *British social attitudes: The 9th report.* Aldershot: Gower.

PART III

The Target Disorders

9

Youth Crime and Conduct Disorders: Trends, Patterns, and Causal Explanations

DAVID J. SMITH

INTRODUCTION

In all developed countries except Japan there have been very large increases in the level of recorded crime since the Second World War. A very few crimes, such as murder and financial fraud, are mostly committed by mature adults. However, crimes that make up the bulk of all those officially recorded, that is robbery, theft, burglary, assault, and damage to property, are mainly committed by teenagers and young adults in their twenties. The peak age even for fraud and forgery is 19 (although large-scale frauds are mostly committed by older people). A later section considers the relationship between age and crime in greater detail, and shows that the enormous rise in crime since the Second World War is essentially an increase in misconduct among young people up to the age of 29.

The purpose of this chapter is to review the evidence on trends in crime and patterns of offending, to specify possible causal explanations for the striking rise in crime, most of it committed by young people, and, where possible, to test these against the evidence. The emphasis on explaining trends in aggregate crime (or overall rates and frequencies of offending) makes this approach distinctive.

There are two major traditions of research and writing on crime and conduct disorder, the one springing from psychology, and the other from sociology. More recently, a few writers have started applying the ideas of economics to the field. Psychologists have been concerned to understand why some individuals are disposed towards criminal behaviour or conduct disorder whereas others are not. To a lesser extent, they have also been interested in changes in the same individual's behaviour over the life course. That meant describing patterns of criminal behaviour, showing how those disposed towards crime or conduct disorder are distributed between social and cultural groups, comparing the personal and psychological characteristics of offenders and non-offenders, and studying the process of individual development that leads to normal and to criminal behaviour.

By contrast, the focus of interest for sociologists is social groups, and larger social structures and institutions. Various sociological theories have tried to show how crime can be caused by the social dynamics of groups of adolescents, by the strains arising from inequality between class, age, or ethnic groups, by the stigmatizing effects of the criminal justice system, or by the failure of the usual processes of informal and formal social control.

The distinctive contribution of economics is that it sees crime as the outcome of rational choices, although in a more realistic version, *limited* rationality theory allows that these choices may be made on the basis of partial, faulty, and perhaps misleading information.

It is striking that these three ways of thinking about crime have not been successfully integrated; and that trends over time have not been a major preoccupation for writers in any of the three traditions. This chapter starts from the assumption that several types and levels of explanation are needed; and that ultimately psychology, sociology, and economics should be brought together in an integrated theory. This study as a whole is based on the premise that the analysis of secular trends is a promising and underused research strategy. Any explanation of time trends must specify detailed causal mechanisms involving individual psychology, personal interactions, social structures and meanings, and rational choice. The focus on time trends should therefore not lead to vaguely specified theories at a high level of abstraction (for example, that the rise in crime is caused by wealth, poverty, or moral degeneration) but to the search for well-specified causal mechanisms. By insisting on the need to explain the rise in crime, we add a new test for existing theories, and provide an impetus for the development of better and more integrated ones.

The next two sections discuss the conceptual and measurement issues involved in defining and counting crime, and the well-established relationship between age and criminal behaviour. This clears the way for a summary in the following section of the evidence on trends in crime and cross-national differences. The next three sections review the extensive research evidence on crime and individual development, the personal characteristics of offenders, and the sociocultural patterns associated with offending, for the light that it throws on the mechanisms driving secular change. The following section specifies possible explanations of time trends, and tests them against the available evidence. A final section summarizes the main conclusions and suggests priorities for future research.

CONCEPTUAL AND MEASUREMENT ISSUES

The idea of crime is grounded both in moral judgements and in a legal code. A crime is something that is thought to be morally wrong, and that breaks the law. While the law is a method of deciding, by the application of a system of criteria and rules, whether particular acts were criminal or not, it is also a set of resources for dealing with crime. This has important implications for our conception of what crime is. There are a number of ways of dealing with behaviour found offensive, judged to be morally wrong, and which might possibly be against the law. One way is to report the matter to the police so that it is processed by the criminal justice system, but many other responses are possible. Matters that are reported, and that are classified by the authorities as crime and investigated accordingly, thereby become crimes. Matters that are dealt with in some other way, or ignored, are not treated as crimes. Hence the difference between schoolboy bullying and assault, for example, lies chiefly in the way in which it is dealt with (internally by the school, or externally by the police and courts); and a crime, somewhat tautologically, is something that is referred to the criminal justice system.

Thus, there are three basic elements in the idea of crime: moral wrong, transgression of a legal code, and a decision to use the resources of the criminal justice system to deal with the matter. Of course, many things are regarded as crimes even though they are not referred to the criminal justice system, on the principle that they *might* be. However, where some type of behaviour, such as family violence, is very seldom processed by the official system, it tends not to be perceived as crime. Without any change in the legal code, there can be an increase in the referral of such matters to the system, so that they come to be treated as crimes, where previously they were not. It is harder to think of examples of actions that are no longer normally treated as crimes, although they are formally so: this indicates that the trend is towards expansion rather than contraction of the field of formal regulation (this point is extensively discussed in Chapter 8).

Any method of measuring crime must be bound up with the changing content of legal codes, changing moral perceptions, and changing methods of dealing with offensive behaviour. Different methods of measurement place varying degrees of emphasis on the three main elements. Recorded crime is a count of incidents that have been referred to the authorities, and classified by them as breaking the legal code. Victim surveys report incidents that people know about and remember, and that the surveyors regard as being against the law. This includes many that were not referred to the authorities, although people are still influenced in deciding what to mention in the survey by their conception of what it might be worth reporting to the police. Studies of self-reported offending also cover a wider field than recorded crime. Both victim surveys and self-report studies of offending are subject to biases caused by forgetting and distortion, by mistaking when an event occurred, and by a reluctance to mention certain incidents.

The measurement problems involved in making cross-national comparisons, which are serious, have been carefully enumerated by Mayhew (1992a). She divided the problems in making use of statistics of recorded crime into 'cultural' differences and 'system' differences. 'The nuances of culture are reflected most intangibly in which forms of deviance are "socially" defined as criminal by victims, and which – within wide ranges of discretion it seems – are "officially" so defined by criminal justice agencies. Descriptions of particular systems have documented some official differences, but we have nothing approaching a systematic index.' What limited research there is suggests that there is a wider consensus across countries on social attitudes to crime than might be imagined (Newman, 1976; Scott & Al-Thakeb, 1980), although some researchers have found marked contrasts (Normandeau, 1970). In Mayhew's phrase, 'cultural and system differences intertwine to produce differences in legal codes and their application'. Differences in classification and recording practices also have important implications, and while rules may be open to inspection, extensive research would be needed to discover how they are actually put into practice. It has been shown that *local* rates of recorded crime may vary widely because of enforcement strategy or recording practice (Reynolds & Blyth, 1975; McCleary et al., 1982; Farrington & Dowds, 1985), and this suggests that similar differences between countries are likely. As Mayhew pointed out, 'thresholds for offences involving sexual behaviour or assault can be particularly problematic' but 'even seemingly straightforward offences such as burglary, vehicle theft or homicide can pose problems in comparisons'. There is wide variation in the extent to which less serious offences are counted in official statistics, which means that comparing the total of all recorded offences between countries is particularly perilous. The proportion of offences reported to the police may vary between countries: it has certainly been shown to change over time in the USA. Changes in recording practice can take place because of directives, shifting perceptions among staff, or organizational changes such as computerization that reduce the scope for discretion. An example of the effects of reporting and recording changes is the divergence in England and Wales over a 15-year period in survey-measured trends in burglary, which rose by 17 per cent, and that from recorded offences, which rose by 127 per cent (Mayhew et al., 1989).[1] These changes may be related to increasing house ownership and insurance.

The method followed in victim surveys is to ask respondents whether each of a number of specific things has happened to them over a reference period (often 12 months). The incidents are mostly described in simple language, sometimes without reference to the word describing the corresponding criminal offence. The respondent's description is not tested: for example, someone who says that her purse was stolen will not be asked more detailed questions to explore the possibility that she lost or mislaid it. Victim surveys count many incidents that are not counted in recorded crime: many that are not reported to the police, and others that are reported, but not recorded (for instance, because the police consider they did not amount to a crime). However, many incidents that might sometimes be recorded as crimes are not mentioned in victim surveys, because the respondent did not notice or care about or recall them, or did not want to think of them as crime, or did not want to tell anyone about them. This is particularly true of sexual offences, and of violence between people who know each other well. Thus, for example, the number of domestic assaults reported by the British Crime Survey (BCS) rose by 79 per cent between 1981 and 1991 (Mayhew et al., 1993), but over this period there was an increasing recognition of the importance and seriousness of this type of offence and more explicit efforts by the police to deal with it. The proportion of domestic assaults mentioned to BCS interviewers that were reported to the police rose from one-fifth in 1981 to one half in 1991. This parallel increase in reporting to the police suggests that the increase in domestic assaults shown by the crime survey may at least partly reflect the increasing acceptability of admitting that such incidents occur (Mayhew et al., 1993: 96-7).

---

1. This may overestimate the divergence, because the two different surveys used over the 15-year period were not entirely comparable. The British Crime Survey in 1981-87 shows a 59 per cent increase in burglary versus 38 per cent in comparable recorded offences (Mayhew et al., 1989).

Incidents counted in victim surveys but not in the statistics of recorded crime are offences having identifiable victims that were either not reported or not recorded. Offences counted in statistics of recorded crime but not in victim surveys are chiefly those without any victim or which are generated by law enforcement or regulation: examples are possession of illicit drugs, prostitutes soliciting, obstructing a police officer, and contravention of traffic regulations. Finally, some types of offence are little recorded by either method: examples are corruption, tax fraud, white-collar crime, and contravention of public safety and health regulations.

However, the great bulk of crime revealed by victim surveys is theft, damage to property, and assault, and these are probably the kinds of crime that cause greatest public concern. For England and Wales and for the United States it is now possible to make a close comparison between victim survey results and counts of recorded crime for selected offences of this kind. These findings are shown in Table 9.1. Except for motor vehicle theft, the victim survey counts are higher than the counts of recorded crime by factors of 2.5 or more. The near-universal insurance of motor vehicles accounts for the fact that nearly all thefts of motor vehicles are recorded.

Table 9.1   The ratio of survey to police counts, by selected offences, in England and Wales and the USA

	England and Wales[a]	USA[b]
Motor vehicle theft	1.16	1.29
Burglary	2.44	2.52
Theft from motor vehicles	3.33	.
Vandalism	9.61	.
Robbery	5.90	3.31
Aggravated assault	4.80	3.45
Rape	.	2.56

(a) From the British Crime Survey 1988 (Mayhew et al., 1989:15).
(b) The data derive from the National Crime Surveys (both the Household and Commercial surveys) of 1976.

Source: Mayhew (1992a).

In spite of this wide difference in coverage, the results of victim surveys over time show fairly similar trends to the statistics of recorded crime. The main difference, in both the United States and England and Wales, is that the curves shown by victim survey statistics are flatter and smoother. Between

1981 and 1991, for those crime categories that can be compared, recorded crime in England and Wales nearly doubled, whereas crime as measured by the BCS rose by 50 per cent (Mayhew et al., 1993: 24). A major reason for the discrepancy is an increase in the proportion of violent crimes and acts of vandalism that are reported to the police. The size and direction of the divergence over time between police and survey statistics vary in a complex way between types of offence.

The results from asking people about offences they have committed have been compared with their official convictions. All of the relevant studies show that self-reported offenders are more likely to be official offenders than are self-reported non-offenders, and conversely that official offenders are more likely to be self-reported offenders than are the official non-offenders (Huizinga & Elliott, 1986). Although these results have been taken to demonstrate the validity of the self-report method, another possible interpretation is that those whose offences are officially recorded become more willing to admit their delinquent acts as a result. The most convincing demonstration of the validity of self-report, therefore, is to show, as Farrington (1973, 1989) has done, that self-reported offending *predicts* future convictions among those who are currently unconvicted. At the same time, self-reports yield far more incidents than are counted in official statistics of recorded crime: in fact, many studies show that the absolute probability of a self-reported offender becoming an officially recorded offender is quite low. Unlike victim surveys, self-report studies have not generally been used as a method of estimating the volume of crime. It has been sufficient for the purposes of these studies to show that there is a clear connection between self-reported and official offending.

From this discussion it should be clear that the concept of crime is elusive, and that it is captured by different measures in markedly different ways. Different measures are subject to different influences, and emphasize different elements of the idea of crime - perception of moral wrong, infraction of a legal code, or processing by the criminal justice system. There is a substantial overlap between them, but the interpretation of statistics of recorded crime and of victim survey results has to be hedged around with qualifications.

AGE AND CRIME

Probably the most important single fact about crime is that it is committed mainly by teenagers and young adults. The crime rate increases swiftly to a peak in the teenage years between 15 and 17, then decreases more gradually with increasing age. The pattern can be illustrated by reference to the official statistics for England and Wales (Home Office, 1989) on males convicted by the courts or officially cautioned.[2] In 1988, the number of offences per 100 males was 0.8 for those aged 10, 2.5 for those aged 12, 7.4 for those aged 15, 7.6 for those aged 18, and after that the rate declined steadily.

The statistics just quoted are cross-sectional: they compare the offending rates between boys who have reached various ages in a given year. This kind of comparison confounds period effects (those associated with varying conditions at different periods of historic time) and ageing effects (those associated with the process of human development). During periods of rising crime rates, it is inevitable that the peak crime rate as shown by cross-sectional data will be at an earlier age than that shown by longitudinal data for specific age cohorts. Farrington (1990) has constructed longitudinal data from the official statistics for England and Wales: for example, the life course of the group born in 1951 can be studied by considering offending rates for 10-year-olds in 1961, 11-year-olds in 1962, 12-year-olds in 1963, and so on. As expected, these comparisons show the offending rate peaking at a later age than shown by the cross-sectional comparisons, but always between 15 and 19.

Prospective longitudinal studies provide closely similar findings on the relationship between age and officially recorded offending. In England, the Cambridge Study in Delinquent Development has been a rich source of data on this topic (for a general description of the study, see Farrington & West, 1990). This is a prospective longitudinal study of 411 males who were living in a working-class area of London in 1961-2, when they were first contacted at the age of 8 to 9. Information on offences officially committed by this group was collected through repeated searches at the Criminal Record Office; minor crimes such as common assault (not causing marks or injury), traffic infractions, and drunkenness are not normally recorded there and were therefore excluded. There were 1.7 offences leading to conviction per 100 males at age 10, rising to a peak of 16.8 at age 17, and then falling to 3.0 at age 31, the last age with reasonably complete conviction data. These findings count offences rather than people (the same person may commit many

---

2. These statistics cover indictable offences only (this excludes the least serious ones). If they admit the offence, in some cases offenders may be cautioned rather than prosecuted, and these cases are included. However, since 1985, police forces have increasingly begun to use unrecorded warnings rather than recorded cautions for apprehended juvenile offenders (aged under 17), and these are not, of course, covered by the quoted statistics.

offences). In order to obtain a prevalence rate, it is necessary to count people rather than offences. The cumulative prevalence rate is the proportion of people who have been convicted of one or more offences up to a given age. In the Cambridge Study, the cumulative prevalence rate was 4.9 per cent by the age of 12, 13.1 per cent by the age of 14, 20.7 per cent by the age of 16, 27.0 per cent by the age of 18, 31.2 per cent by the age of 20, and 36.1 per cent by the age of 30 (Farrington, 1990).

Although the Cambridge study is of boys from one particular part of London, and is based on a small sample size, national statistics are remarkably similar. The Home Office has calculated official offending rates of English males born in four randomly chosen weeks of 1953 (Home Office Statistical Bulletin, 1987, 1989). This provides information for the whole of England for males born in the same year as the Cambridge cohort (which is focused on a working-class area of London). The pattern of change in rates of offending by age is closely similar for the national and local cohorts. Also, the national cohort shows a cumulative rate of official offending of 32.6 per cent by the age of 30, only about 3 per cent less than in the inner-city London sample of the Cambridge study. These findings show that in England for a young male to have been convicted of breaking the law is hardly deviant in a statistical sense. Equally striking, however, is the decrease in lawbreaking after the peak at the age of 17. One quarter of the cohort were convicted of an offence between the ages of 13 and 18, compared with 12 per cent between the ages of 27 and 32.

The findings quoted so far relate to officially recorded offending, but a closely similar relationship between age and crime is also shown by the large number of studies based on respondents' accounts of the offences they have themselves committed. The Cambridge study, for example, collected information about offending from self-reports as well as offences officially recorded. Comparisons between self-reports and court records show that the self-reports have a high level of validity; but of course the self-reports provide a wider measure of offending, which is less dependent on the reactions of the police and the courts.[3] At the age of 18, respondents were asked about

---

3. Self-reports may not be completely independent of the reactions of the criminal justice system, however. Whether respondents remember offences, or think them worth reporting, may be influenced by whether the matter came to light, and by whether they were punished. Also, while self-reports have been shown to have validity in general terms, the relationship between self-reported and official offending may perhaps vary in important ways between population groups, with important consequences for example for our understanding of the relationship between crime and ethnic group.

offending in the past three years, while at the age of 32 they were asked about the past five years. Despite this difference in the time window, the proportion who said they had offended decreased very sharply between these two ages. The proportion admitting to one or more of six non-violent offences[4] declined from 45 per cent at the age of 18 to 11 per cent at the age of 32. The proportion who said they had been involved in fights declined from 63 per cent to 37 per cent between these two ages.

The Relative Constancy of the Age-crime Curve

So far, this account of the relationship between age and crime has concentrated on males in England, but the relationship remains much the same for different times, places and social groups. Hirschi and Gottfredson have put forward the extreme view that the relationship is invariant (Hirschi & Gottfredson, 1983; Gottfredson & Hirschi, 1990). Although that is certainly an exaggeration, the level of constancy in the relationship is striking. Thus, Gottfredson and Hirschi (1990) were able to show that the age-crime curve in England and Wales was much the same in 1842-44, in 1903, and in 1965; that the curves were similar for males and females if the rate of offending was standardized to cancel out the large difference at all ages between the sexes; that the curves for the United States and for England and Wales were similar; and that the curves were similar for different ethnic groups in the United States. Studies in many other countries also show a similar relationship: a recent example is the longitudinal study of official offending among a cohort in Stockholm (Wikström, 1990).

In spite of these striking regularities, Farrington (1986) has shown that there are also some potentially significant variations. The crime rate for English males peaked at age 13 in 1938, at age 14 in 1961, and at age 15 in 1983, a rising age that contrasts with the falling age of puberty (see Chapter 4). This raises the possibility that some social change (such as the raising of the school-leaving age) has caused offending to peak at progressively later ages over the present century. Unfortunately, however, the interpretation cannot be straightforward, since the pattern of change for females is different. These changes over time are in any case small. Much larger are the differences according to the type of offence. Clear differences of this kind have been shown from analysis of American official arrest statistics. For example, Cline (1980) divided offences into three broad groups according to the median age of arrest (shown in brackets below).

---

4. Burglary, theft of vehicles, theft from vehicles, shoplifting, theft from slot machines, vandalism.

1. Vandalism (17); motor vehicle theft, arson, burglary, larceny-theft, liquor law violations (18).

2. Handling stolen property (20); narcotic law violations (21); violence, disorderly conduct, prostitution (24); sex offences other than forcible rape and prostitution (26); white-collar offences such as forgery and fraud (26); abuse and neglect of family and children (28).

3. Drunkenness and drunk driving (35); gambling (37).

Wilson and Herrnstein (1985) using FBI figures for 1985 showed a similar change in the pattern of offences by age. Longitudinal studies of officially recorded offending confirm that 'changes in offending patterns with age seen in national statistics... are at least partly due to crime switching by offenders' (Farrington, 1986: 209). The self-report data from the Cambridge study 'showed that most offences peaked during the period fifteen to eighteen, although shoplifting and burglary peaked earlier' (Farrington, 1986: 210).

TRENDS IN CRIME AND CROSS-NATIONAL COMPARISONS

The statistics of recorded crime are the best available indicator of trends in youth crime since the Second World War. For a very recent period, crime surveys are a better source, but the US series started only in the mid-1970s, the British series in 1982, and others more recently still. It is only where there is a suspect that the age of the offender can be recorded, and since detection rates are very low, data on persons arrested, cautioned, or convicted give a partial and biased picture. Because, as shown in the last section, a very high proportion of crimes are committed by young people, the statistics of recorded crime are a better indicator of trends in crimes committed by young people than the statistics on young offenders.

The Longer Historical Perspective

Evidence on trends in the nineteenth and twentieth centuries suggests that there is a U-shaped curve, with high rates of crime and disorder in the early part of the nineteenth centuries, especially in larger cities, falling rates in the latter half of the nineteenth century and the early part of the twentieth century, followed by a large increase after the Second World War.[5] The discussion of explanations for crime, including changes in crime rates, will be postponed until later. It is worth pointing out here that the longer historical trends are not easily explained in terms of broad societal changes such as industrialization or urbanization. Although theories have been put forward to account for historic trends, they rely on speculative assertions about the effects of other social changes, and they cannot be rigorously tested from the available data. It will be more profitable to concentrate on change over a more recent period.

Crime Rates Since the Second World War

The International Criminal Police Organization (Interpol) has reported statistics of recorded crime collected from a range of countries since 1950. Although broad guidelines are given on counting and classification, countries derive the statistics entered on the form from the official statistics available, which are shaped by the national legal code. Hence the statistics provide no more than a rough and ready basis for comparison between countries. Comparison of trends over time between countries may be somewhat more reliable. The crime classification used by Interpol was changed to a more detailed one in 1977. It is possible to make a continuous series from 1950 by aggregating certain of the categories used since 1977. Generally, the results show a smooth trend over this break in classification between 1976 and 1977 when the later categories are aggregated in this way.

Figures 9.1 to 3 and 9.5 to 7 illustrate the trends shown by the Interpol data for selected countries, always expressing recorded crime as a rate per 1,000 population. Figures 9.4a to c show the trends in homicide, expressed as a rate per 100,000 population, from statistics compiled by the World Health Organization. These are used in preference to the Interpol data on homicide, because they are based on a more consistent definition. Figure 9.1 shows a large rise in the total crime rate between 1951 and 1990 for all countries except Japan. The total crime rate is more subject to measurement error than the rates for more specific offences, since it is sensitive to the inclusion or exclusion of less serious offences. It is nevertheless useful as an indicator of the huge expansion for nearly all countries in the amount of crime that impinges on the criminal justice system. The highest increases in total crime rate recorded for

---

5. Wilson and Herrnstein (1985) draw together this evidence, particularly the work of Gurr (1977a & b), Monkkonen (1981), and Archer & Gartner (1981). Gurr (1981) covers violent crime in the USA, England and Wales, and some other Western societies over a much longer period.

the selected countries are for Spain (by a factor of 29) and Canada (by a factor of 27). There were also exceptionally steep increases for Sweden (factor of 14) and Norway (factor of 13). For the remaining countries except Japan, the crime rate increased over this period by a factor of between 2 and 6. Remarkably, in the context of the trends for other countries, the total crime rate in Japan declined slightly over the 40-year period. There are some differences between countries in the shape of the upward trend. Unfortunately, the Interpol figures recorded for the United States are incomplete, but the detailed statistics (available in the Uniform Crime Reports) show a decline in the total crime rate during the 1980s, following the earlier upward trend. Canada and Australia similarly registered a decline in the 1980s. In the remaining countries (always excepting Japan) the upward trend continued. A more short-lived reversal of the upward trend is evident in some countries, for example England and Wales, if year by year statistics are studied.

Figure 9.1   Total recorded offences, 1951-1990

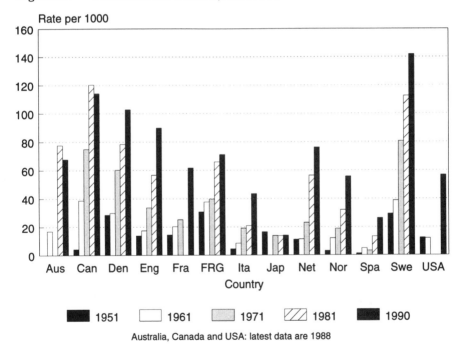

Australia, Canada and USA: latest data are 1988

Warning: Australian data show sharp rise at 1976/1977 junction.

Source: Interpol.

Figure 9.2   Aggravated theft, 1951-1990

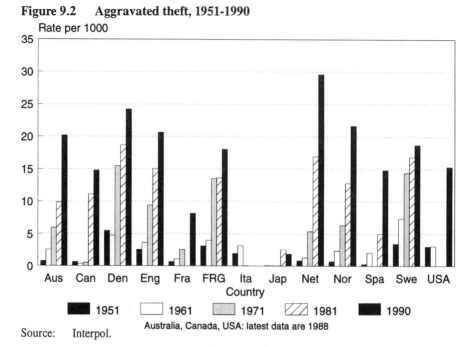

Source: Interpol.

Figure 9.3   Theft (excluding aggravated), 1951-1990

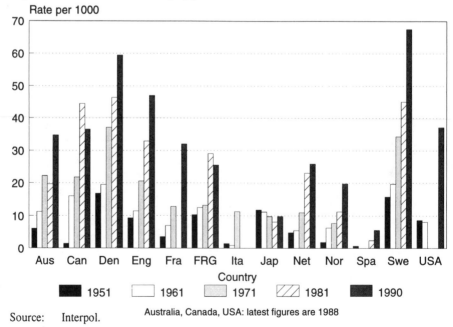

Source: Interpol.   Australia, Canada, USA: latest figures are 1988

The story of steeply rising crime rates is confirmed when more specific offences are considered rather than total crime. Over the full time series, property crimes are encompassed by the broadly interpreted categories of aggravated theft, and other theft. Although there are many detailed variations between countries, the trends for aggravated theft and other theft are comparable to those for total crime rates. In England and Wales, for example, the total crime rate increased by a factor of 5.5, aggravated theft by a factor of 7.5, and other theft by a factor of 4.5. The pattern of change for two more specific offences - theft of motor vehicles, and breaking and entering – can be traced for the more recent period starting in 1977. Substantial increases are again registered for many countries in the crime rates for these more specific offences over a much shorter time period.

Crimes of violence other than homicide cannot be identified in the Interpol statistics until 1977. Since then, there have been substantial increases in the rates of serious assault in Australia, Denmark, England and Wales, and the USA.

Figure 9.4a   Homicide, 1951-1990

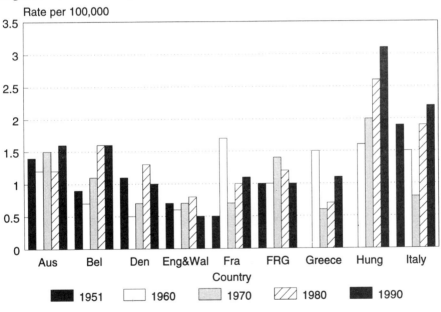

Source: World Health Organization.

Figure 9.4b   Homicide, 1951-1990

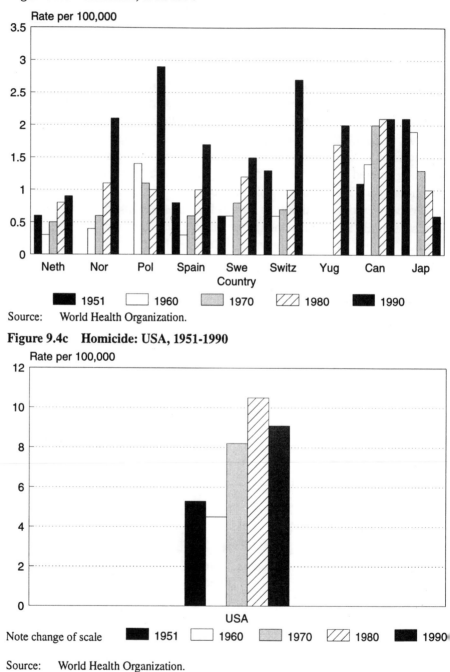

Source: World Health Organization.

Figure 9.4c   Homicide: USA, 1951-1990

Source: World Health Organization.

For all of the offences so far considered, the great majority of offenders are teenagers and young adults in their twenties. The same is not true of homicide, but homicide rates are of special interest because records are more complete than for other crimes. Although there were increases in homicide rates between 1951 and 1990 in a number of countries, these were generally less marked than the increases in other types of crime, and in some countries any increases in homicide rates were small or inconsistent. Countries that showed substantial increases in homicide rates over the period were Hungary, Norway, Poland, Spain, Sweden, Switzerland, Canada, and the United States. Lesser increases were shown by Belgium, France, and the Netherlands. Countries showing no increase, or a pattern of fluctuating change, were Austria, Denmark, England & Wales, West Germany, Greece, and Italy. Remarkably, in one country alone – Japan – there was a substantial and consistent decline in the homicide rate over the postwar period.

Figure 9.5   Breaking and entering, 1977-1990

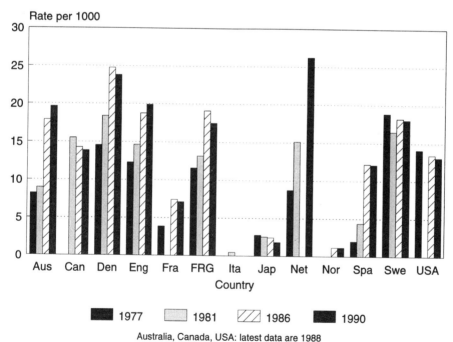

Australia, Canada, USA: latest data are 1988

Source: Interpol.

Figures 9.4a to c also illustrate the cross-national differences in homicide rates at any one time. The most striking feature is that the rate is far higher in the United States than elsewhere (note that Figure 9.4c has to be drawn to a different scale from the rest). In fact, the US homicide rate is more than 10 times as high as in England & Wales or the Netherlands, the two European countries having the lowest rates. These contrasts become even more stark when deaths by homicide of young people are considered. Aggregating the data for 1987-1990, the WHO statistics show that annual deaths by homicide of people aged 15 to 24 were 15.3 per 100,000 in the United States, compared with 0.9 in both the UK and the Netherlands, 0.7 in France, and 0.4 in Japan (UNICEF, 1993: 45).

Figure 9.6   Theft of motor cars, 1977-1988

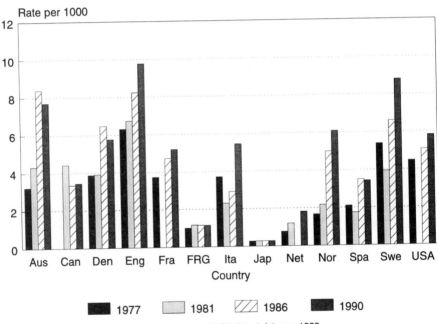

Australia, Canada, USA: latest data are 1988

Source: Interpol.

European countries with relatively high homicide rates in 1990 were Hungary, Poland and Switzerland. The recent increases in the homicide rates in both Poland and Switzerland are striking.

Figure 9.7　　**Serious assault, 1977-1990**

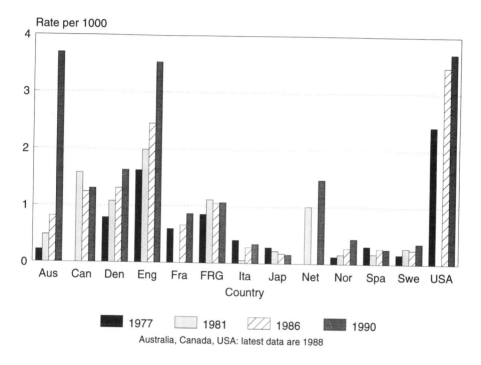

Source:　　Interpol.

Recent Trends in England and the United States

Information about trends over time can be provided from victim surveys for England and the United States from 1981 onwards. Figures 9.8 and 9.9 (based on data in Farrington & Langan, 1992) show the percentage change in crime rates for selected offences over the period 1981-87 (for England) and 1981-86 (for the USA). Figure 9.8 is based on victim survey data, while Figure 9.9 is based on offences recorded by the police. The victim survey data show substantial increases in England for burglary and motor vehicle theft, and small increases for robbery and assault; for all four of these offences, and also for rape, the victim survey data for the USA show decreases, and for three offences (burglary, robbery, and rape) these are substantial. In some ways, the crime rates based on recorded offences show a different pattern of change over time; in particular, the changes shown by official data are smaller for burglary and motor vehicle theft than shown by the victim survey data. However, the pattern of difference between England and the USA in change over time is for the most part maintained. In England there was an enormous increase in the number of officially recorded rapes, which coincided with a new police policy of encouraging rape victims to report these offences. Recorded homicide increased in England, but declined in the USA.

Figure 9.8   Increase in crime rates: from victim surveys

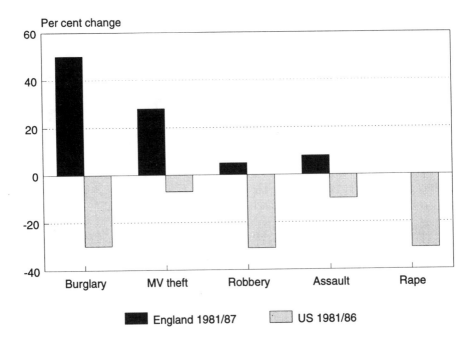

Source: Farrington & Langan (1992).

These comparisons illustrate an interesting contrast in crime trends between England and the United States. They also show a reasonable degree of consistency between the pattern of change shown by official data and victim surveys for four major offences.

Figure 9.9   Increase in crime rates: police recorded offences

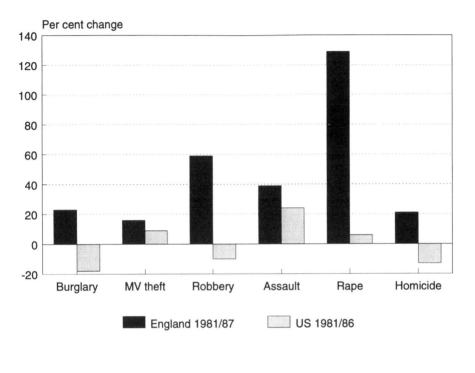

Source: Farrington & Langan (1992).

Research on Antisocial Personality as an Indicator of Trends

In general, self-reported offending has not been used as a method of tracking trends in crime. Nevertheless, useful confirmation of the sharp increase in crime in recent years is provided by the data on antisocial personality within the Epidemiological Catchment Area Study (ECA) in the United States (Robins & Regier, 1991). As explained in greater detail in a later section, antisocial personality is defined by reference to a cluster of symptoms in both childhood and adulthood, only a few of which are illegal behaviours. In the ECA, a cross-sectional survey in six US cities, antisocial personality was diagnosed on the basis of respondents' answers to questions about their own behaviour in a recent period, and throughout their lives from early childhood.

Answers to questions about their behaviour many years before are subject to unknown but possibly substantial recall errors. Although antisocial personality is far less prevalent than criminal activity, there is a strong correlation between the two (Robins et al., 1991).

The ECA found that lifetime prevalence of antisocial personality (for the aggregate of the six areas covered) was 3.8 per cent among those aged less than 30, 3.7 per cent among those aged 30-44, 1.4 per cent among those aged 45-64, and 0.3 per cent among those aged 65 and over (Robins et al., 1991: Table 11-3, 265). Setting aside any recall problems, these findings of course imply that antisocial personality has increased in recent cohorts, 'since young people had higher rates than their elders even though the older groups have had more years in which to carry out the behaviours that warrant the diagnosis' (Robins et al., 1991: 270). In fact, the difference between the two youngest cohorts is grossly understated by the raw statistics, and it can be shown that 'by the time the youngest cohort reaches 30 to 44 years of age, if the same proportion of those with three or more childhood symptoms meets adult criteria as among the current 30-44 year olds, their lifetime prevalence rate will be 6.4 per cent, compared with the rate of 3.7 per cent in the cohort now 30-44 years old' (Robins et al., 1991: 271).

The methodological problems in using cross-sectional ECA data as an indicator of change over time are discussed in some detail in relation to depression in Chapter 11. Although the recall problems are potentially serious, it seems most unlikely that they could explain the whole of the very large differences between cohorts in lifetime prevalence of antisocial behaviour. These findings therefore provide useful evidence on the basis of self-reports for an increase in conduct disturbances that underlies the increase in crime shown both by recorded crime statistics and by victim surveys.

Trends in Juvenile Crime

In England and Wales the official figures on juvenile offending show the numbers of convictions and cautions of persons aged 10-16 for indictable offences per 1,000 population in this age group. (Indictable offences are all except the least serious ones.) On this definition, offending by males 'increased to a peak from 1961 to the mid-1970s, then decreased somewhat in the late 1970s, then increased again to a greater peak in 1985, before decreasing again up to 1989.' Offending by females 'increased fairly steadily to a peak in 1985 before decreasing up to 1989. The changes are quite dramatic' (Farrington, 1992). However, it is most unlikely that juvenile behaviour changed in the direction shown by these statistics. Farrington (1992) explained the matter as follows:

> It is unfortunate that the official figures probably reflect reactions to delinquency more than juvenile misbehaviour. Between the mid-1960s and mid-1970s, there was increasing emphasis on diverting juveniles from court appearances to cautions, and many cautioning schemes were set up during this period. For example, before 1969, a juvenile arrested in London was almost always prosecuted in court in much the same way as an adult offender. During 1969, the London police introduced their juvenile cautioning scheme. Between 1968 and 1970 in London, Farrington and Bennett (1981) found that arrests of 10-13 year olds increased by 88 per cent, while arrests of 14-16 year olds increased by 44 per cent ... Hence, they concluded that the introduction of juvenile cautioning had caused a widening of the net of official processing, as juveniles who would previously have received an unrecorded warning now began to receive a recorded caution.
>
> Precisely the reverse process has been occurring since 1985, as some police forces have begun to use unrecorded warnings rather than recorded cautions (155-156).

Hence neither the earlier increases nor the recent decline in officially recorded juvenile offending is a true reflection of changes in juvenile behaviour. Rather, both reflect changes in policy for dealing with juvenile offenders (changes, that is, in the proportion of cases where the juvenile was formally charged with an offence). Similar patterns of change in officially recorded juvenile delinquency have been observed in many European countries. Kyvsgaard (1991) drew attention to the widespread recent decline in official juvenile offending and quoted the relevant statistics for a range of countries. Although she assumed that these statistics indicate a decline in juvenile misbehaviour, she quoted no convincing evidence in support of this view. Mayhew (1992b) wrote that 'after a period of increasing numbers of juveniles before the courts, in most countries the proportion of juvenile offenders prosecuted has decreased over time, reflecting both demographic change and a general increase in formal or informal cautioning. In a sample of thirteen countries[6], the number of juvenile offenders fell by 21 per cent between 1980 and 1989, the sharpest drops being in Greece, Northern Ireland and West Germany'.

---

6. The countries were Austria, Canada, England and Wales, Finland, France, Greece, Japan, Luxembourg, Netherlands, Northern Ireland, Norway, Scotland, and West Germany.

Differences in Time Trends Between Males and Females

As set out in a later section, although the rate of offending remains very much higher among males than among females in all countries, there is evidence that the difference narrowed in many countries over a 20-year period starting around 1960. This conclusion is based on recorded crime statistics. It follows that the rate of increase in crime was considerably greater among females than among males over that 20-year period. Nevertheless, because males account for the great preponderance of recorded crime, most of the postwar increase in crime is attributable to males rather than to females.

Cross-national Comparisons of Rates of Recorded Crime

So far it has been established that most recorded crime is committed by teenagers and adults in their twenties, and that in most developed countries, with the signal exception of Japan, there have been enormous increases in the rates of recorded crime in the postwar era.[7] In part these changes are due to changing perceptions, laws, institutions, and ways of dealing with offensive behaviour, but statistics of recorded crime, victim surveys, and surveys of self-reported conduct disorders converge in showing that there has clearly been a substantial increase in crime, in criminal behaviour, and in the prevalence of offending, on any appropriate definition. Although there have been declines during the 1980s in the prevalence of officially recorded juvenile offending in many countries, these probably reflect for the most part changes in the response of the criminal justice system. However, contrary to the trend in most countries, there has been a marked decrease in crime in the United States during the 1980s; the contrasting trends in England and the United States are confirmed by close comparisons of official and of victim survey data.

The Interpol statistics also show wide differences in rates of recorded crime between countries at any one time. For the period 1986-88, for example, the rate of burglary per 100,000 population was 2,776 in the Netherlands, 1,965 in West Germany, 1,769 in England and Wales, 1,010 in Switzerland, 828 in Austria, 697 in France, 588 in Belgium, 257 in Greece, and 228 in Japan. The rate of recorded burglary in the Netherlands was therefore 2.7 times the rate in Switzerland, and 12.2 times the rate in Japan.

---

7. Switzerland is probably a second exception, although it is not included in Figures 9.1-3 and 9.5-7 because Interpol data are not available for earlier years.

No very clear pattern has yet emerged from the various attempts to interpret these striking cross-national differences. One reason for this, no doubt, is that there is a large amount of 'noise' in the statistics compiled. Two articles have assessed the degree of correspondence between four series of cross-national crime statistics: the Interpol statistics, the United Nations Crime Surveys, homicide information from the World Health Organization, and the Comparative Crime Data File compiled by Archer and Gartner (1984). Both of these (see Huang & Wellford 1989; Bennett & Lynch 1989) concluded that for point or rank estimates the four datasets often give different results, although there is some correspondence between them.

However, even allowing for these data problems, it is clear that the most popular theories either do not fit the facts, or else are so vaguely specified that they will fit any facts. They tend to deal in broad-brush accounts of societal structures, because writers lack the detailed information about individual countries that would allow them to describe mechanisms that might link broad structure with the control of crime. Mayhew (1992a) has summed up most of these theories as relying on a broad notion of 'modernization'. The germ of the idea is that crime was low in earlier societies based mainly on agriculture and that rising crime is a product of the process of development to modern industrial or post-industrial society. Writers mention a number of features of the process of development or modernization as being important: for example, the move from agriculture to industry, the concentration of population in large towns, increasing social heterogeneity brought about by the mobility of the population, the destruction of small, tightly-knit village communities, the growth of individualism, a weakening of community controls associated with all of these developments, a decline in fatalistic acceptance of a low position in a preordained hierarchy, increasing affluence creating more goods to be stolen, increasing feelings of relative deprivation. The question that has not yet been answered is which specific aspects of development, or what specific pattern of interactions between different factors, accounts for the striking differences in recorded crime rates between developed nations. Any appeal to a general process of development that is assumed to be similar in all countries is bound to fail, since the most developed country, Japan, not only has very low crime rates, but has always had very low crime rates (at any rate since the Second World War). For the moment, cross-national comparisons do not seem to have got very far; in order to move towards explaining rising crime, we will have to look to more detailed studies of crime and the conditions that give rise to it in specific societies.

Cross-national Comparisons of Survey Data

One reason why cross-national studies of recorded crime rates have been inconclusive is that – for all the reasons already rehearsed – these crime rates mean different things in different countries. Comparisons based on the results of victim surveys have begun to suggest that cross-national differences on survey-based measures tend to be smaller. For example, rates of recorded crime are substantially higher in Scotland than in England and Wales for all offences except violence against the person. In 1982, the first British Crime Survey was carried out on a closely comparable basis in England and Wales and in Scotland. The results showed few differences in survey-based crime rates between the two countries, and where there were differences, some of them ran in the opposite direction (showed higher rates in England and Wales than in Scotland). Mayhew and Smith (1985) concluded that for the most part the differences in rates of recorded crime between the two countries were due to differences in counting practices, particularly where a single person is known to have committed a number of crimes. Specific arguments can be mounted against an explanation in terms of the incidence of criminal behaviour in the two countries: for example, the statistics of recorded crime do not show a higher level of violence in Scotland than in England and Wales (or *vice versa*) since although the rate for robbery is higher in Scotland than in England and Wales, the rate for violence against the person is higher in England and Wales than in Scotland..

A number of comparisons have also been made between the results of crime surveys carried out independently in Canada, England and Wales, Australia, the Netherlands, and the United States. There are important differences between the methods used in these surveys, and in particular the US National Crime Survey is substantially different from all the others, and uses more refined methods. A general feature of the results emerging from these comparisons is that they show similar rates of assault and other violent crime in the USA and in the other countries, whereas the statistics of recorded crime show much higher rates in the USA. For example, Hough (1986) found survey-based rates of robbery to be only slightly higher in the USA than in Canada, the Netherlands, or England; assault rates in the USA were lower, although particular difficulties of comparison were acknowledged here. On the other hand, the results of the limited comparisons so far possible do show a degree of fit between survey-based crime rates and recorded crime. For example, Killias (1989a) showed that survey-based rates of victimisation were

Table 9.2 **Rank order correlation between survey measures of victimization and offences recorded by the police: 1989 International Crime Survey[a]**

	Rank order correlations
Theft of vehicles[b]	
unadjusted	0.766
adjusted for 'own country'[c]	0.813
adjusted for reporting[d]	0.714
Burglary[e]	
burglary/entry, unadjusted	0.442
burglary/entry + attempts, unadjusted	0.490
burglary/entry, adjusted for reporting	0.473
Robbery	
unadjusted	0.371
adjusted for 'own country'	0.681
adjusted for reporting	0.666
Assaults[f]	
assaults/threats, unadjusted	0.037
assaults/force, unadjusted	0.178
assaults/threats, adjusted for reporting	0.653
Sexual offences[g]	
sexual incidents, unadjusted	0.247
sexual assaults, unadjusted	0.396
sexual incidents, adjusted for reporting	0.835

(a) Police figures are based on crimes per 100,000 population (all ages); survey figures are based on 5-year prevalence rates (those aged 16 or more). Annual returns are often not made to Interpol. Additional crime figures were collected from other sources where possible.
(b) Survey figures exclude motorbikes and bicycles. Interpol figures are often for undefined vehicles. Switzerland is excluded.
(c) Excluding from survey figures incidents which were said to have happened abroad, based on the 'last incident' of the offence type, which occurred over the 5-year period.
(d) Figures of percentage of incidents said to have been reported to the police are taken, based on the 'last incident' of the offence type which occurred over the 5-year period.
(e) Interpol figures include all burglaries (residential and commercial).
(f) Percentage of assaults with force based on 1988 data.
(g) USA excluded because of missing police data. Survey risks based on women only. Percentage of sexual assaults based on 1988 data.

Source: van Dijk et al. (1991), Table E11.

lower in Switzerland than in the Netherlands, England and Wales, Canada, Australia, or the USA; and rates of recorded crime are also lower in Switzerland than in those other countries.

These comparisons between independently organized crime surveys are useful in showing that there is some degree of fit between survey-based estimates and recorded crime, but that substantial differences in recorded crime between countries are in some cases not replicated in survey-based estimates, and may arise for example from differences in counting procedures. They cannot yet provide a basis for systematic comparison of crime rates between countries. The 1989 International Crime Survey for the first time made possible a more systematic comparison of this kind (see van Dijk et al., 1991). The survey had some fairly severe limitations. Sample sizes were fairly small (2,000 households in most countries) and for the most part the survey was carried out through computer-assisted telephone interviews. Where telephone interviewing was used, at least 70 per cent of households had telephones, and in most countries the figure was 90 per cent or higher. However, the response rates from the telephone interviews were variable and generally low: they ranged from 30 per cent to 71 per cent, and the average was 41 per cent. Response rates of this order leave substantial scope for biases that may be just as important as the reporting and recording problems underlying official statistics.

Despite these faults and limitations, there is a fairly high correlation between the ranking of countries on survey victimization measures and on recorded crime rates (see Table 9.2). This correlation was highest (around 0.8) for theft of vehicles, and correction for the proportion of incidents reported to the police in this case makes little difference, because most vehicle thefts are reported anyway. It was also very high (over 0.8) for sexual incidents that were said to have been reported to the police, but if all sexual incidents mentioned in the survey were counted, then the correlation was low. The correlation was again substantial (over 0.6) for assaults and for robbery, when only those reported to the police were counted. The lowest correlation (around 0.5) was found for burglary, and in this case adjustment for reporting makes little difference. These findings indicate that in time the survey method will produce data of great value for international comparative studies of crime. Second, they show that national statistics of recorded crime do provide a useful measure of incidents that are reported to the police; but that, to a considerable extent, variations in rates of recorded crime between countries reflect variations in the propensity of the public to report incidents to the police.

Table 9.3 presents the overall prevalence of victimization (for all offences) shown by the International Crime Survey, and the percentage of all incidents said to have been reported to the police. The pattern that emerges from comparing the rates of victimization between countries, as shown by the International Crime Survey, is similar in many respects to the pattern shown for the rates of recorded crime in Figure 9.1: for example, Canada, Australia and the USA have high rates on both measures, while Japan has a low rate on both. Spain is low on recorded crime but much higher on victimization rate, probably because the proportion of incidents reported to the police is low.

Table 9.3   Overall victimization and reporting rates: 1989 International Crime Survey

	Victimization[a]		% reported to
	1988	Past 5 years	the police[b]
England and Wales	19.4	46.0	58.8
Scotland	18.6	41.4	62.3
Northern Ireland	15.0	33.4	45.8
Netherlands	26.8	60.4	52.6
West Germany	21.9	51.3	47.9
Switzerland	15.6	47.1	58.7
Belgium	17.7	48.3	48.6
France	19.4	52.0	60.2
Spain	24.6	51.6	31.5
Norway	16.5	38.9	42.6
Finland	15.9	40.1	41.8
USA	28.8	57.6	52.1
Canada	28.1	53.0	48.3
Australia	27.8	57.2	46.9
Japan	9.3	.	.
Warsaw	34.4	59.4	.
Surabaja	20.0	44.5	.

(a) Prevalence victimization rates: percentage of people who have been subject to any of the types of incident covered: theft of car, theft from car, car vandalism, theft of motorcycle, theft of bicycle, burglary with entry, attempted burglary, robbery, personal theft (and within that, pickpocketing), sexual incidents (and within that, sexual assault), assault/threat (and within that, with force).

b) Percentage of incidents in 1988 which respondents said were reported to the police.

Source: van Dijk et al. (1991), Tables E.1, E.2 and E.4 (adapted).

One clear finding that emerges from the survey is an association between the proportion of the national population living in large cities of 100,000 inhabitants or more and the national risk of victimization. The relevant findings are shown in Table 9.4. The correlations between the national statistics shown in the two columns is $r = 0.64$. Major exceptions to the general pattern are Japan, where the rate of victimization is low in relation to the high proportion living in cities, and the United States and the Netherlands, where the rate of victimization is high in relation to the proportion living in cities. It has long been known that within countries the rate of crime (however measured) is much higher in large cities than elsewhere. In addition, the ECA found that in the two sites, St. Louis and Durham, that had sufficient rural populations to examine, the lifetime rate of antisocial personality was considerably higher in the urban than in the rural areas (Robins et al., 1991). Further to this, the findings of the International Crime Survey suggest that national differences in crime rates arise, to a considerable extent, because of national differences in the urban/rural mix. A similar result was obtained by Pease and Harvey (1988) from analysis of the UN surveys; they showed that at the national level population density is a strong predictor of overall crime rates.

These findings raise the question whether crime rates have increased more rapidly in urban than in rural areas in recent years. The topic has not yet been investigated in any depth, but some preliminary analyses of British data have been carried out by the Home Office in London (Mayhew, personal communication). Each of the 43 police force areas in England and Wales contains a mix of urban and rural areas, but there are only six 'metropolitan' forces that contain major conurbations. Between 1950 and 1990, the increase in recorded crime was greater in the non-metropolitan than in the metropolitan force areas. This pattern of change is partially confirmed by the results of the British Crime Survey. The number of household crimes per 100 households increased from 56 to 57 in inner city areas between 1983 and 1987, whereas in other areas it increased from 38 to 44, although in the case of personal crimes there was no difference in the pattern of change between the two types of area. Taken together, these findings suggest that although urban areas have higher crime rates than rural areas, their crime rates are tending to converge over time. In another type of analysis, small areas are classified into a number of types on the basis of a large number of socio-demographic variables. Preliminary analysis of the BCS has found that crime has risen more rapidly in types of area where rates are relatively low than in types where it is relatively high (Mayhew, personal communication).

Table 9.4 Overall national victimization rates (percentages victimized in 1988) and percentage of population living in cities of more than 100,000 residents: 1989 International Crime Survey

	Overall victimization risk 1988	% living in cities of 100,000 residents
Total	21.1	23.0
Japan	9.3	.
N. Ireland	15.0	1.6
Switzerland	15.6	10.1
Finland	15.9	22.1
Norway	16.5	16.3
Belgium	17.7	5.9
Scotland	18.6	23.4
England and Wales	19.4	32.2
France	19.4	20.4
W. Germany	21.9	26.3
Spain	24.6	44.7
Netherlands	26.8	18.5
Australia	27.8	34.8
Canada	28.1	45.4
USA	28.8	19.6

Source: van Dijk et al. (1991), Table E6 (adapted).

At present, these preliminary findings are hard to interpret. They may perhaps be explained by a pattern of demographic shift in which rural areas are becoming more urban, whereas conurbation areas are becoming less densely populated. Such a shift is occurring throughout Britain, but is particularly evident in the South East, where the total population is increasing, whereas the population of the London conurbation is declining. The period of formation and growth of the present cities was of course primarily the nineteenth century. It is reasonable to suppose that during that period the rate of crime rose more quickly in London, Liverpool, Manchester, and Birmingham than in the countryside, and that the present contrast in crime rates between the town and countryside is the result of that earlier pattern of change. However, since the Second World War the pattern of change in the spatial distribution of the population has been reversed, and it seems that this spreading out of the population has been accompanied by a blurring of the contrast in crime rates between town and countryside. However, this interpretation must remain speculative at present, and the topic is one that would repay further study.

Explaining the Low Crime Rate in Japan

In his book comparing the policing of Japan and the United States, Bayley (1991) discussed the reasons for Japan's remarkably low crime rate. He pointed out that Japan is just as modern, economically advanced, and democratic as the United States, just as urbanized, and far more densely populated. Distribution of income is more equal in Japan than in the United States, unemployment is lower, and there are few pockets of chronic poverty, unemployment, family pathology and high crime. There are no 'ghettoes' in Japan – areas occupied by minorities subject to discrimination; only 0.5 per cent of the population is ethnically not Japanese.

Sentences for similar crimes are more lenient in Japan than in the United States. However, offenders are far more likely to be caught and punished in Japan than in the United States. 'A suspect is charged and officially dealt with in some manner in more than one third of all crimes reported to the Japanese police. In the United States, the comparable figure is a meager 5 percent.' (172). Of course, low crime rates tend to be part of a virtuous spiral leading through high detection rates to still lower crime rates; whereas high crime rates tend to be part of the inverse vicious spiral.

Japan has tough and effective laws controlling firearms, whereas the United States, famously, does not. On the other hand, popular culture in Japan (as reflected, for example, in adult comics) is especially violent.

Recognizing that it is impossible to determine scientifically whether these differences in social circumstances can account for the difference in crime rate, Bayley went on to claim that 'crime, more generally the impulse to deviance, is inhibited by mechanisms that are peculiar to Japan in their strength and extensiveness'. First, 'Japanese are bound by an infinite number of rules about what is proper', and 'the pervading sense of propriety produces startling demonstrations of orderliness'. Second, 'Japanese are enmeshed in closely knit groups that inhibit behavior through informal social controls'. Third, 'discipline is maintained in Japan because people take enormous pride in performing well the roles demanded of them'.

Because countries are unique, inconceivably complex, and small in number, it seems inevitable that useful international comparisons, like Bayley's, will have to examine individual cases in depth. It is significant that Bayley's analysis of the Japanese example identified the strength of social controls through reciprocal social bonds as the main reason for the low crime rate. This tends to confirm the findings of research using entirely different methods, for example Sampson and Laub's (1993) reanalysis of longitudinal studies of offenders and others earlier carried out by Glueck and Glueck (1950).

CRIME AND INDIVIDUAL DEVELOPMENT

The next task is to review the extensive research on individual development, the characteristics of offenders, and pattern of offending, for the light that it throws on mechanisms that might explain the secular increase in youth crime.

Explaining the Age-crime Curve

Although the age-crime curve is the most basic fact of criminology, social scientists are very far from understanding its significance, or explaining the developmental processes that give rise to it. As Rutter (1989: 2) has argued, 'age as such cannot be used as an explanation for behavioural change; either physical maturation or experience may be operative'. Furthermore, either of these basic types of explanation requires a great deal of further elaboration.

Hirschi & Gottfredson have tried to resist the need to explain why age is related to crime (Hirschi & Gottfredson, 1983; Gottfredson & Hirschi, 1990). They have argued that age has a direct causal effect on criminal behaviour: it does not summarize or act as a proxy for biological or social processes that succeed in an orderly way as the individual develops. If the explanation did lie in processes of that kind, then the relationship between age and crime should vary between groups distinct in biology or social experience. Yet, according to Hirschi and Gottfredson, the age-crime curve is invariant for different social groups, offences, times and places.

Even though this statement incorporates an element of exaggeration, we have seen that the age-crime curve is surprisingly constant. Nevertheless, it is difficult to grasp what is meant by saying that age directly causes criminal behaviour. Although there is a reasonably regular relationship between age and crime, the mere statement that there is such a relationship cannot amount to a full explanation. Gottfredson and Hirschi (1990) quote the analogy of Boyle's law, which expresses the relationship (holding only within certain limits) between the temperature, volume and pressure of a gas: but the statement of that relationship in Boyle's law does not amount to a full explanation. Some of the underlying processes are described by molecular physics, which provides a deeper and more accurate account. In a similar way, there must be another level of explanation that will help to make the age-crime curve more intelligible, and provide a deeper and more accurate account of it. The constancy of the relationship suggests that it springs from some very basic features of human development. Particularly indicative is the evidence collected by Gottfredson and Hirschi on misbehaviour in prison, and motor vehicle accidents, which are related to age in much the same way as crime. Surprisingly, however, the evidence does not seem consistent with the idea that the age-crime curve reflects a changing disposition to offend as the individual moves through the life cycle. It is helpful at this point to make the distinction between prevalence (the proportion of people offending over a given period) and incidence (the number of offences per offender). Summarizing the evidence, Farrington (1986) has written:

> The limited amount of present knowledge, then, suggests that the peak in the crime rate in the teenage years reflects a peak in prevalence and that incidence does not vary consistently with age. This has the clear implication that individual curves relating age and crime will be very different from aggregate curves (219).

If the age-crime curve were the direct consequence of a continuously changing disposition to offend over the life cycle, then a gradual change would occur in the individual life course, so that incidence (the number of offences committed by each offender) as well as prevalence (the proportion of people offending) would vary with age. In fact, it seems that the individual life course is characterized not by smooth change in the disposition to offend, but by fairly abrupt changes. The rise in the rate of crime up to the peak age reflects entry into crime by a large number of individuals between the ages of 12 and 16, and the fall after the peak reflects, first, desistance from crime by a large proportion of the earlier entrants, and second, a sharp reduction in the number of new entrants after the peak age. This suggests that explaining the age-crime curve must involve explaining why individuals in their early teenage years start engaging in criminal activity, and in their late teenage years or in their twenties, abandon it. The following discussion considers, first, the earlier process of development leading to entry into crime, and second the later process of development leading to desistance from crime.

Continuity Between Crime and Childhood Conduct Disorders

The apparent rise in the prevalence of crime up to the age of 14 or 15 may in some respects be misleading. Rutter and Giller explained the matter as follows:

> Of course official statistics show that delinquency reaches a peak during the middle or late teens, with many individuals not receiving their first conviction until well into adolescence or even early adult life. But this simply reflects the fact that, by law, young children cannot be convicted, that the police are less likely to prosecute young first offenders and that it may take some time for delinquent activities to be detected. Certainly, both self-report data and behavioural ratings from teachers and others make clear that most delinquent individuals already show some form of antisocial behaviour during middle childhood or pre-adolescence. (Rutter & Giller, 1983: 51; their citations have been omitted.)

In most jurisdictions, young children cannot be convicted of a criminal offence, while special criminal justice procedures apply to teenagers (up to an age boundary between juveniles and adults which varies widely from one country to another). For that reason alone, there is a need for a wider and inevitably vaguer concept than crime, such as antisocial behaviour, conduct disorder, or delinquency, when discussing the behaviour of juveniles. Broader concepts of this kind can also be useful as a background to our understanding of adult criminal behaviour.

Among the conduct disorders that have been included in studies of antisocial behaviour and delinquency are disruptive aggression such as teasing, quarrelsomeness, lying, malicious mischief and fire-setting, stealing, truancy, staying out late at night, running away from home, and gang activities. There is some disagreement about the importance of distinguishing between different types of conduct disturbance in children. Robins and her colleagues (Robins, 1978; Robins & Ratcliff, 1979) have argued that there is a single syndrome of antisocial behaviours, citing the inter-correlations between different forms of childhood deviance, and between various forms of childhood deviance and total adult deviance.

Research on child development before the peak age of offending at 14 or 15 suggests that specific forms of antisocial behaviour peak at different ages; on one view, the peak in offending in the teenage years may reflect a shift, associated with the passage into the adult world, towards types of antisocial behaviour regarded as criminal, rather than an increase up to that age in the amount of antisocial behaviour. Thus, Farrington (1991a) has argued that different specific behaviours at different ages may be expressions of the same underlying antisocial tendency:

> For example, the antisocial child may be troublesome and disruptive at school, the antisocial teenager may steal cars and burgle houses, and the antisocial adult male may beat up his wife and neglect his children. These changing manifestations reflect changes both within the individual (e.g. maturation) and in his environment (258).

On another view, however, there is a genuine change in the prevalence of antisocial behaviour with age. Although an impressive body of evidence from longitudinal studies demonstrates the continuity between antisocial behaviour in childhood, adolescence and in adulthood, the results also reveal a substantial element of discontinuity. Summarizing the earlier findings, Robins (1978) claimed that while adult antisocial behaviour is nearly always preceded by childhood antisocial behaviour, most antisocial children do not become antisocial adults. This conclusion was strengthened more recently by the results of a large prospective study from birth to age 15 in Dunedin, New Zealand.

> Eighty-four per cent of children found to be 'uncontrolled' at age 11 met criteria for stable and pervasive antisocial disorder when reassessed at 13. Antisocial behavior at 13 was predicted by 'externalizing behavior' at age 3 and behavior problems at age 5, long before a diagnosis of conduct disorder could be made. Further, these early behaviors were stronger predictors than IQ, mothers' attitudes, language level, or any other variable tested (Robins, 1991: 202).

Robins also pointed out that aggressive behaviour in childhood is the most stable of all early detectable personality characteristics. A review of 18 follow-up studies estimated a 0.63 correlation between earlier and later measurements.

Further analysis of the Dunedin cohort (White et al., 1990) made use of reports from a number of sources: parent, teacher, self-report, psychiatric interview, and police data. A group of children were identified as showing persistent and pervasive antisocial disorder: persistent in that it was manifest at the ages of 9, 11 and 13, or at least at two of these three stages; pervasive in that the child was rated antisocial by at least two out of five possible raters (the child, the parent, or any of three teachers). It was found that children who had

had behavioural problems at the age of 5, particularly as rated by their parents, were considerably more likely to show persistent and pervasive antisocial disorder in middle childhood, on this definition, than those without behavioural problems at the age of 5. In turn, the children who showed persistent and pervasive antisocial behaviour at the age of 11 were considerably more likely than others to have committed several criminal offences involving contact with the police by the age of 15. However, behavioural problems in early childhood were more weakly predictive of criminality at the age of 15. Hence, although there was a considerable degree of continuity from one stage to the next, the predictive power of behaviour problems in early childhood had become diluted by other influences by the time the cohort reached adolescence.

The Epidemiological Catchment Area Study has measured antisocial personality within a large cross-sectional survey of Americans in both private households and institutions such as prisons and hospitals (Robins & Regier, 1991). In the broadest terms, 'antisocial personality is characterized by the violation of the rights of others and a general lack of conformity to social norms' (Robins et al., 1991). In more specific terms, the diagnosis requires three childhood problems out of a possible 12 before the age of 15, and four adult problems out of a possible ten, together with continuity of symptoms and occurrence. Among the childhood symptoms are five related to aggressiveness, including weapon use, cruelty to animals, cruelty to people, forcing sex on others, and stealing with confrontation. Other childhood symptoms are vandalism, truancy, other school problems, drug use, and early sexual activity. Among the adult symptoms are lack of remorse, work problems, marital problems, child neglect, violence, transiency, illegal behaviours, sexual behaviour, and lying.

All of the items are of course highly inter-correlated. Nevertheless, the findings show that while criminality is one of the symptoms of antisocial personality, it is neither a necessary nor a sufficient condition. Lifetime prevalence of antisocial personality among this general population sample was 2.6 per cent, which is far lower than the prevalence of arrests or criminal convictions. Of those with antisocial personality, 47 per cent had been arrested more than once for a non-traffic offence; of those with two or more such arrests, 37 per cent had antisocial personality.

As mentioned in an earlier section, for the adults covered by the survey the relationship between age and antisocial personality was broadly similar to the age-crime curve. Among those who had ever had antisocial personality, the proportion who had not had it over the past year (the rate of remission) increased from 39 per cent among those aged under 30, through 59 per cent among those aged 30-44 and 86 per cent among those aged 45-64 to 100 per cent for those aged 65 or more. Although antisocial personality eventually remits, just as offenders desist from crime, it nevertheless has a long duration. Among those with no symptoms in the past year, the average duration from first to last symptom was 19 years.

Most antisocial children recover without developing the diagnosis of antisocial personality in adulthood. Overall, only 26 per cent of individuals who had met the childhood criteria for antisocial personality also met the adult criteria. However, the ECA, like earlier longitudinal studies, confirmed that childhood problems are a strong predictor of adult antisocial personality. The more symptoms a child has shown, the more likely the adult is to be diagnosed as having antisocial personality. Also, early onset in childhood predicts adult antisocial personality, though not as strongly as the number of childhood symptoms.

Further insights into the continuity between conduct disorders in childhood and later antisocial behaviour is provided by a longitudinal study of young adults who had spent their childhood in children's homes, together with a comparison sample from an inner city deprived area (Zoccolillo et al., 1992). The study used the same definition of antisocial personality disorder as Robins et al. in their analysis of the ECA data. Forty per cent of males and 35 per cent of females with childhood conduct disorder went on to show antisocial personality disorder as adults, but many more showed persistent and pervasive social difficulties: 86 per cent of males and 73 per cent of females across at least two domains. These findings showed that the outcomes of conduct disorder in childhood are much more diverse than antisocial personality in adulthood. Conduct disorder in childhood is a much better predictor of pervasive and persistent adult dysfunction than of just one adult dysfunction, such as antisocial behaviour.

It should be clear from this review that there is an impressive body of research that demonstrates some degree of continuity between conduct disorders in childhood and adult behaviour problems including crime. However, in spite of the high level of continuity overall, West and Farrington (1977) showed that a minority of adult criminals were free of conduct disturbance during childhood, and that late onset was associated with low social status and criminality of the parents. Recent studies have tried to identify the more specific pathways from childhood to adult antisocial behaviour. Earlier onset is associated with more serious problems later, although this pattern is less clear for females than for males (Loeber & Hay, 1994). Analysis of the Pittsburgh Youth Study has identified three sequences of problem behaviours in boys (Loeber et al., 1993). The first, *authority conflict*, starts with stubborn behaviour, followed by defiance, and later by authority avoidance (e.g. running away). The second consists of an escalation in *covert acts*. The third consists of an escalation of *aggression*. Boys could follow a single pathway, or several, and later rates of offending were found to vary according to the combination of pathways followed.

It seems that early aggression is nearly always a precursor of violent offending in adulthood. Farrington (1978) found that 7 out of 10 males arrested for a violent offence by the age of 21 had been rated as highly aggressive between the ages of 12 and 14. Again, Magnusson et al. (1983) found that 9 out of 10 males who had committed violent offences by the age of 26 had been rated as highly aggressive between the ages of 10 and 13. However, Magnusson (1987) later found from the same longitudinal study in Stockholm that the apparent link between aggressiveness in childhood and later criminality arose because there was a group of boys having a combination of characteristics including both aggressiveness and hyperactivity (which was shown to be related to a low level of responsiveness by the autonomic nervous system). Boys who were hyperactive and aggressive were likely to become persistent offenders, whereas those who were aggressive but not hyperactive had no more than an average chance of offending later.

Although this body of research is successful in establishing a degree of continuity between childhood conduct disorders and criminal behaviour during adolescence, it is less successful in explaining the steep increase in criminal offending in the teenage years. The best shot at an explanation offered by the developmentalists is that antisocial behaviour is treated as mischief in children, but as crime in adolescents; or that, to the extent that the nature of the antisocial behaviour actually changes with ageing, adolescent law-breaking is a different expression of the same antisocial tendency that was already present in childhood. Although this kind of explanation may have some utility at the margins, it seems unconvincing as a general account of the relationship between age and antisocial behaviour, because a wide variety of antisocial behaviours, however measured, rise to a peak in adolescence or early adulthood, then sharply fall.

A different kind of explanation might be developed from the interpretation of social control theory elaborated by Sampson and Laub (1993). On that account, social control is the capacity of a group to regulate itself according to desired principles and values, and hence to make norms and rules effective. The most powerful controls do not emerge from the formal criminal justice process, but from reciprocal relationships and the resulting interpersonal bonds. It may be argued that adolescence is a period of transition from one set of reciprocal relationships to another, and that there is a period of instability when one set of bonds are being loosened, and before another set have been tied. Although, as set out in Chapter 4, most adolescents are not in conflict with their parents, parental ties tend to weaken during the teenage years. Again, as set out in Chapter 4, there is generally a period of instability before a young person settles into a job and forms a new family, and a growing proportion never do. During the transitional period, the young person is moving away from the restraining influence of his or her parents, and has not yet invested in reciprocal adult relationships that may in future be a restraining influence. On this account, adolescents are unruly because they slip between the mechanisms of informal social control that are effective for children and for adults. To the extent that the nature and length of adolescence has changed, this account might lead to an explanation of the increase in the crime rate.

Desistance from Crime

The vast majority of those who engage in crime in adolescence have given up by their early to mid-20s, although the few who continue are responsible for a substantial number of offences. Gottfredson and Hirschi (1990) have argued that existing theories fail to explain desistance. In their view, theories that explain crime in terms of power relationships between social classes, or labelling by the criminal justice system, or associating with others who are criminally minded, have nothing to say about why crime should decline with age – in fact, they ought to predict a continuous increase. Also, theories that emphasize social bonds cannot explain why these become more effective in adulthood than in childhood. They cited, in particular, an explanation by Trasler (1980) of desistance from crime in terms of social bonds and social situations:

> The simplest... explanation... is one which concentrates upon the satisfactions of delinquent conduct... which maintain such behaviour during adolescence, but cease to do so when the individual becomes an adult. I suggested earlier that much teenage crime is fun... But as they grow older most young men gain access to other sources of achievement and social satisfaction – a job, a girlfriend, a wife, a home, and eventually children – and in doing so become gradually less dependent upon peer-group support. What is more to the point, these new life-patterns are inconsistent with delinquent activities (11-12).

Gottfredson and Hirschi claimed that in spite of the plausibility of this kind of explanation, the evidence for the effect of these factors was relatively weak, especially in the light of the overwhelming strength of the age-crime relationship. Although those who have been delinquent from childhood were much more likely than non-delinquents to have frequent periods of unemployment (West & Farrington, 1977), the evidence that getting a job was associated with desistance from crime was far from clear-cut. A longitudinal study by Bachman et al. (1978) suggested that there might be some relationship of that kind, but it was not a powerful one. There was no evidence that having a girlfriend was associated with giving up crime. On the contrary, 'dating can be equated with smoking and drinking in terms of its connection with delinquency' (Gottfredson & Hirschi, 1990: 139). In their review of the effects of marriage, Rutter & Giller (1983), too, indicated that the findings were contradictory and inconclusive. They concluded that 'whether marriage increases or decreases delinquent tendencies may well be largely determined by what sort of change (if any) in social group and personal relationships it entails' (234). There was no evidence that having children was associated with a reduction in criminal activity.

Yet more recently, more powerful analytical methods applied to longitudinal data have begun to demonstrate that the formation of adult social bonds is a major cause of desistance from crime. Sampson and Laub (1993), in their reanalysis of the Gluecks' longitudinal data from the 1940s and 50s, found substantial support for the theory that 'social ties... create interdependent systems of obligation and restraint that impose significant costs for translating criminal propensities into action' (141). Within a sample of 500 convicted teenage offenders, they found a strong relationship between job stability, commitment to conventional educational and occupational roles, and marital attachment, on the one hand, and the chance of later criminality on the other. Because of the wealth of longitudinal data available, and through the forms of analysis used, the direction of the causal pathways was very firmly established. The same variables also predicted future criminality among a matched control sample of boys in the same area who had not been convicted of an offence when selected for inclusion in the sample.

The finding that job stability predicts desistance from crime is potentially of great importance in explaining secular change in the crime rate, as discussed in a later section. However, the Gluecks' data are historic, and there is a need for further studies of the effect of job stability during the more recent period when unemployment has been very much higher than in the immediate postwar era. Confirmation of the effect of marital attachment is provided by a recent analysis of a longitudinal study of young adults who had spent their childhood in children's homes, and a comparison sample from an inner city deprived area. Zoccolillo et al. (1992) found that a minority of those having conduct disorders in childhood did not show antisocial personality or other social difficulties as adults, but this transition was strongly associated with the presence of a supportive nondeviant spouse. Extending the analysis to two general population samples, Quinton et al. (1993) found that the positive effect of a supportive cohabiting relationship in early adulthood was replicated, but that people with conduct disorders were less likely than others to gain such support, because they were more likely to pair with those who provided less support.

This field of research is currently very active, but it now seems that the formation of social bonds may turn out to be the central explanation for desistance from crime after adolescence.

Explaining Continuity and Discontinuity

Sampson and Laub (1993) began their account of a reanalysis of the Gluecks' longitudinal data with some general reflections on the tradition of life-course research and the ideas associated with it. They made the point that the developmentalists, whose training was generally in psychology, have concentrated for the most part on micro processes, such as interactions within the family, and have tended to ignore the effect of macro-level or structural variables such as social class, ethnicity, or mobility. It may be added that Sampson and Laub themselves, although they were aware of the problem, did not get very far with analysing the relationship between the micro and macro levels. For example, they showed that a stable job history was an important factor restraining the individual from engaging in crime: but the number of individuals having stable job histories is powerfully determined by the aggregate level of unemployment, yet Sampson and Laub's analysis was still presented as though the individual's job history had largely been determined by that individual's characteristics and micro-level interactions.

Second, Sampson and Laub pointed out that the life-course tradition highlights both continuity and discontinuity in individual life histories. The term *trajectory* refers to long-term and relatively stable patterns of behaviour throughout the life course. The term *transition* refers to life events, such as first job or first marriage, that may be embedded in the trajectory and consolidate it, or may lead to a change of trajectory. From this it is clear that the developmentalists are concerned with explaining change as well as stability.

The preceding review has shown that there is considerable stability of antisocial and criminal behaviour throughout the life course, but also considerable change. The most striking evidence of change is the age-crime curve itself. Because the prevalence of antisocial or criminal behaviour varies very much between age groups, it must follow that a majority of those who are antisocial or criminal at one age are not so at another. The reasons for the rise and fall of criminal behaviour with age are likely to provide some insight into the causes of the rise in the aggregate level of crime since the Second World War.

A third general point made by Sampson and Laub was that the continuities in individual behaviour throughout the life course do not necessarily spring from unchanging individual dispositions. On the contrary, these continuities may arise from the way the individual interacts with others in the immediate social sphere, and with the wider social environment. A highly specific example is provided by Quinton et al. (1993), who found that people without a history of conduct disorder were more likely than those with such a history to get married to a supportive, nondeviant spouse; and that such a marriage protected against future conduct disorders. From these findings, Quinton et al. argued that continuity in personal behaviour may be created through the stability of the environments selected, created, or accepted by the individual.

Generalizing this third point, it is clear that the interactions between the individual and the environment will tend to be like a positive feedback system. For example, adopting Sampson and Laub's social bonds theory, weak social bonds will lead to delinquency, but in addition delinquency will lead to the choice of environments that cause a further weakening of social bonds. Alternatively, strong social bonds will lead to conformity, and also to the choice of environments (e.g. a supportive, nondeviant spouse) that strengthen social bonds further and reinforce conformity.

It is an important conclusion that the continuity in the life course arises as much from stability in the environment as from the stable dispositions of the individual. It implies that the macro structural factors, traditionally the province of sociologists and economists, may have great importance in explaining the developmentalists' findings.

PERSONAL CHARACTERISTICS OF OFFENDERS

IQ and Scholastic Attainment

There is a substantial body of research that shows a consistent association between lower IQ and an increased risk of delinquency (Hirschi & Hindelang, 1977). The association remains regardless of the way that delinquency is measured. There is also a similar relationship between delinquency and low educational attainment (which in turn is closely related to IQ). In a systematic review of 47 relevant studies, Moffitt (1993) found evidence for a specific link between a deficit in verbal intelligence and juvenile delinquency. Although this association was weak overall, there was a stronger association among a subset of young people, diluted by its absence among the majority. There was also evidence for a specific link between a deficit in self-control functions, such as planning and self-monitoring, and delinquency.

These relationships probably reflect rather complex underlying processes. It is not the case that delinquency causes lower IQ or school failure, because in many studies the lower IQ has been measured before delinquency became manifest. However, part of the explanation may lie in a link at an early age between lower IQ and troublesome behaviour, which is in turn a predictor of later delinquency.

There is some support for the theory that educational failure through lowered self-esteem and antagonism to school causes delinquency. For example, the longitudinal study by Elliott and Voss (1974) showed that the delinquency of school drop-outs (which was higher than for those who stayed on) markedly diminished at the time when they left school.

Another possibility is that both cognitive defects and conduct disorders are the result of a third factor, such as family functioning or temperament. Although there is ample evidence that family functioning is important as a direct influence on delinquency, there is less clear evidence that it is the factor linking cognitive defects and conduct disorders. There has been little investigation of the possibility that temperament might be the link.

Personality

A considerable body of research has failed to show convincingly that personality is a consistent or significant explanation of crime. One of the major problems with this line of research, as Gottfredson and Hirschi (1990) argued, is that there are important overlaps between supposedly distinct personality dimensions, and between each of these dimensions and delinquency: that is, the personality scales incorporate items that refer to conduct disorder or offending. The results of studies relating Eysenck's neuroticism scale (N) and extraversion scale (E) to delinquency have produced inconsistent results; where relationships are shown, they tend to be quite small; and for cross-sectional studies there is the problem that high E could be a consequence of imprisonment rather than a cause of offending.

Other Personal Characteristics

While a number of earlier studies found that mesomorphic (muscular) body build was associated with delinquency, this was probably because of limitations of method of the studies concerned (inadequate control groups, use of institutionalized populations). Studies of general population samples have found either no relationship of this kind (West & Farrington, 1973), or a contrary relationship between delinquency and light build or late puberty (Wadsworth, 1979), which however disappeared when social factors were taken into account.

In summarizing the research findings on a number of physiological and psychological characteristics as determinants of offending, Rutter and Giller (1983) concluded that those who persist in offending into adult life tend to show hyperactivity, attentional defects, low autonomic reactivity (for example, low pulse rate even when stressed), impaired avoidance learning in response to punishment (involving reduced anxiety and low response to pain), and a greater than normal need for stimulation. The longitudinal study in Stockholm directed by Magnusson and others provided support for the theory that low autonomic reactivity (as measured by adrenaline excretion) and hyperactivity (from teachers' ratings) is a predictor of later criminality among boys (Magnusson, 1987, 1988; Magnusson & Bergman, 1990). Also, the level of adrenaline excretion at the age of 10 or 13 predicted the level of criminal activity *after* the age of 20 better than the level *before* the age of 20 (Magnusson, 1988). This may indicate that boys with low adrenaline excretion are likely to become *persistent* offenders.

Genetic Factors

A fairly recent review of the evidence on the influence of genetic factors on antisocial and criminal behaviour (DiLalla & Gottesman, 1989) suggests that it is important to distinguish between antisocial behaviour during the adolescent years only and antisocial behaviour that continues into adult life. It would also, in theory, be important to distinguish late onset antisocial behaviour, although none of the genetic studies have done so. Rutter and Giller (1983) had earlier concluded that the weight of evidence from twin studies suggested that genetic factors probably play a significant role in antisocial personality disorders that continue into adult life, but not in transitory delinquency in adolescence. DiLalla and Gottesman's later assessment concurred. They listed six studies that established whether pairs of twins were concordant (both or neither officially delinquent in adolescence) or discordant (one officially delinquent, the other not). Taking the average of the six studies, among the identical (MZ) twins, 87 per cent were concordant, compared with 72 per cent among the fraternal same-sex (DZ) twins. This suggests a very small role, if any, for genetic factors as a determinant of officially recorded delinquency in adolescence. By contrast, one study (Rowe, 1983), which relied on an antisocial behaviour scale based on self-reports rather than official delinquency, and which included aggressiveness in the scale, found a considerable difference in concordance between MZ and DZ twins, suggesting a heritability of about 70 per cent. DiLalla and Gottesman suggested that this finding may be attributable to the use of self-reports, or to the inclusion of aggressiveness in the antisocial behaviour scale.

The same authors listed nine twin studies of adult criminality (as opposed to officially recorded juvenile delinquency). Across these studies, the average concordance rate was 51 per cent for MZ twins, compared with 22 per cent for DZ twins. These findings suggest a moderate degree of heritability for *adult* criminality. Although there is little information about heritability for different types of crime, a study of adult twins by Cloninger and Gottesman (1986) suggested that there was a moderate degree of heritability for both violent and non-violent crimes, but that heritability was higher for non-violent crimes. However, this does not fit well with the view that Rowe's (1983) finding of high heritability for self-reported antisocial behaviour in adolescence could be explained by the inclusion of aggressive behaviours in the antisocial scale. Thus, the evidence on which types of antisocial behaviour are most likely to be inherited is currently contradictory.

DiLalla and Gottesman also cited a number of adoption studies that suggested a considerable genetic influence on adult criminality. However, another review of the evidence in this field, Walters and White (1989) pointed to a number of weaknesses in these studies. Possible confounding factors are that the process of adoption may itself tend to cause criminality, and that the adoptees were more likely than others to have had criminal parents. Walters and White (1989), who were generally more critical of the published studies than DiLalla and Gottesman (1989), concluded that there is probably a moderate genetic influence on crime, but that alternative explanations of the results from twin and adoption studies had not been ruled out, and a causal relationship had not been firmly established. In their view there was some evidence from adoption and twin studies that the joint effect of heredity and (family) environment is greater than the sum of their separate effects, because of an interaction between them.

The bulk of crime is committed by adolescents, whereas the main genetic influence seems to be on antisocial behaviour that persists into adulthood. Therefore inherited characteristics probably have little influence on the bulk of crime.

SOCIOCULTURAL PATTERNS

Sex

Official statistics (of arrests, where available, or of persons convicted or cautioned), studies of self-reported offending, and studies of self-reported conduct disorders or antisocial personality all show much higher rates among males than among females. Wilson and Herrnstein (1985) showed female suspects as a percentage of total suspects for 25 countries in 1963-72. The proportion ranged from 2 per cent in Brunei to 21 per cent in the West Indies. The larger European countries lie around or above the midpoint of this range: Netherlands, 10 per cent; England and Wales, 14 per cent; France, 14 per cent; West Germany, 17 per cent.

Hindelang et al. (1981) summarized data from 13 self-report studies on the ratio of males to females who admitted to various offences and types of misconduct. These were all studies of children and young people, although the exact age groups varied. Because there were wide variations between the results of different studies, the authors calculated the median sex ratio across the studies considered. This ranged from 1 to nearly 4; among items with a high median sex ratio were steal $2-$50 (2.7), commit robbery (2.87), damage or destroy property (2.92), participate in gang fight (3.28), take a car (3.37), beat up or assault (3.61), and steal more than $50 (3.68). Items with lower sex ratios were generally lesser or non-criminal forms of misconduct. Reviews of both self-report studies and official statistics have concluded that 'Sex differences are larger in official data than in self-reports. They are greater for adults than for juveniles, for property offenses than for personal offenses, for more serious crimes than for less serious ones, and for whites than for nonwhites.' (Wilson & Herrnstein, 1985: 114). The last statement refers to comparisons between white and black people in the United States. For certain ethnic minorities – for example, people originating from the Indian sub-continent in Britain – the difference in rates of offending between males and females is exceptionally large, because offending among females is so rare. Also, the difference between official statistics and self-report studies noted by Wilson and Herrnstein and all other writers on this subject may not be genuine. Nearly all self-report studies cover children and young people only, and most cover non-criminal misconduct as well as criminal offences. The lower sex differences in the self-report studies may therefore arise because the findings (compared with those of official statistics) are weighted towards less serious kinds of misconduct and the younger age groups for which sex differences are known to be less marked.

The lifetime prevalence of antisocial personality found by the Epidemiological Catchment Area Study was 4.5 per cent for males compared with 0.8 per cent for females, a ratio of 5.5:1. This ratio rose steadily over the age groups from 3.7 for age 18-29, 6.3 for age 30-44, 10.3 for age 45-64, to 17.3 for age 65+. These differences presumably reflect both a period effect (a narrowing over historic time in the difference between males and females) and an ageing effect (a widening of the gap between males and females over the life course). The male-female ratio was twice as high for white as for black Americans, and among black (unlike white) Americans it varied little between age groups (Robins et al., 1991).

In many countries, the difference in the rate of offending between the sexes has narrowed over the past 40 years, although the male preponderance remains very great. In England and Wales, the sex ratio[8] dropped from around 11:1 in 1957 to around 5:1 in 1977. However, since 1977, the ratio has remained completely stable. The pattern of change in the United States was similar over the 1960s and 1970s. In both countries, the difference between the sexes has narrowed most markedly for petty property crimes (Wilson & Herrnstein, 1985); nevertheless, in Britain at least, the difference between the sexes in the prevalence of violent offences has narrowed as well.

In spite of these recent changes, the large difference in criminal behaviour and conduct disorders between the sexes is on the whole strikingly stable across

---

8. Persons cautioned or convicted for indictable offences per 100,000 population. The source for these statistics is Home Office (1978, 1992).

cultures and periods. Along with the age-crime curve, this is one of the two most basic facts of criminology. The difference in crime rates is clearly connected in some way with the substantial difference (on average) in overt aggression between males and females. Most personal as opposed to property offences are manifestly aggressive acts, but it is important to consider whether aggressive antisocial behaviour in the child is a predictor of aggressive criminal behaviour in the adult. In fact, many retrospective and prospective longitudinal studies suggest that it is (for example, Farrington, 1978). Also, aggressiveness itself is a relatively stable characteristic over the life course (Olweus, 1979). Further, there is a link between aggression and non-violent crime; this seems to be because there is a group of young boys who are both aggressive and steal, although there is also a group who steal but are not aggressive.[9] Hence there is evidence that a difference in aggressiveness between males and females would lead to a difference in the prevalence of criminal and antisocial behaviour.

There is a consistent body of evidence (reviewed by Maccoby & Jacklin 1980a & b) to show that males are more aggressive than females from an early age. Among the arguments for the view that the difference has a biological basis are that it starts from an early age, that it is reproduced across many cultures, and that alterations in male hormone levels have been shown through experiments to have an effect on aggressiveness.

Against this, Magnusson (1987) has argued from analyses of the Stockholm longitudinal study that the apparent relationship between childhood aggression and adult criminality only arises because there is a group of hyperactive boys who are also aggressive and often become persistent offenders. More generally, Magnusson and Bergman (1990) argued for a person-oriented as opposed to a variable-oriented approach to understanding these relationships. On this view, the difference in criminality between males and females arises because the two groups vary in terms of a complex cluster of characteristics, and follow widely divergent developmental paths in a variety of ways. Aggression on its own might be a relatively unimportant aspect of these differences.

---

9. Farrington (1978) showed that boys who were aggressive at the age of eight or ten had an increased risk of non-violent as well as violent crime, although the link with violent crime was stronger. However, the indications from other research (Moore et al., 1979), are that children who steal but do not show aggressive antisocial behaviour have no increased risk of committing violent offences later, although they do have an increased risk of committing property offences.

In fact, this view that differences influenced by heredity are the product of a complex gene-environment interaction is in line with the thinking of most contemporary researchers on genetic influences. One of the mechanisms through which inherited sex differences may lead to distinct paths of development is the formation of peer groups. In a review of recent research, Loeber and Hay (1994) pointed out that the peer group is a setting that encourages the consolidation of aggression and other conduct problems. Adolescents with conduct problems will tend to be rejected by their normal peers, and will tend to select their deviant peers, so that their peer groups will tend to reinforce aggressive behaviour. Adolescent peer groups are of the same sex, and boys' and girls' groups acquire highly distinct characteristics. Hence, adolescent peer groups will tend to consolidate differences between the behaviour of males and females that have biological origins. Loeber and Hay pointed out that social cognitive deficiencies may also be involved in the development of aggressive behaviour, and a genetic component of such deficiencies may vary between the sexes. It can be hypothesized that those who aggress are seen as likely to aggress (even when they are behaving neutrally) and to see others' actions as aggressive (even when neutral), and that this leads to the creation of a restricted environment of aggressive peers. This developmental sequence may be more likely to happen in males than in females because of a genetic difference at the beginning of the sequence, although interaction with the environment would subsequently have great importance.

Robins (1986) reported a factor analysis of data from St. Louis, Missouri, which showed that the intercorrelations between specific conduct problems were similar for boys and girls. There were three virtually identical factors: one including precocious sex, substance abuse, and fighting; a second covering school problems including discipline, expulsion, truancy, and under-achievement; and a third covering arrest and running away. Only the more covert activities of vandalism, lying, and cheating had different correlates for the two sexes. In general, therefore, the nature of conduct disorders in girls and boys is similar, although their prevalence is much lower in girls. However, the relatively small proportion of girls with conduct problems tend to grow up with a more varied range of problems than in the case of boys (Robins, 1986), and their adult problems may be more pervasive (Zoccolillo et al., 1992).

Findings from a study by Keane et al. (1989) suggest that criminality is more likely to develop among males than among females because males are more likely to have a taste for risk, so that police contacts are more likely to lead to deviance amplification in males than in females. Results from a self-report study among high-school students in the Toronto area showed that among both males and females, use of marijuana predicted contact with the police. Among females, contact with the police predicted lower use of marijuana, supporting the argument that police contact had been a deterrent. Among males, contact with the police predicted increased use of marijuana, supporting the argument that police contact amplified deviance. However, controlling for taste for risk largely removed the sex differences in the pattern of relationships. This suggested that police contact amplified deviance in males, but not in females, by satisfying a desire to experience the sensation of risk.

On the evidence so far available, it seems that the major differences in criminality and antisocial behaviour between the sexes arise from inherited differences, particularly in aggressiveness, in association with patterns of development that tend to be highly distinct for boys and girls; and that in this process of development, there is a complex interaction between heredity and the social environment which reinforces and amplifies the different emerging patterns of behaviour.

Another line of explanation is in terms of male and female roles, and the stresses and criminal opportunities attaching to them. It seems plausible that changes in the roles and usual activities of men and women will largely explain the narrowing of the male-female crime ratio of the past 40 years, yet explanations of this kind are not yet supported by detailed analysis. It has not been demonstrated that the changes in the male-female crime ratio, which occurred over a fairly limited period of 15 years or so, coincided with a period of exceptional change in female roles; but closer specification of the important dimensions of female roles is needed before the matter can be fully analysed. It is not clear, without detailed analysis, that the more traditional female roles offer fewer opportunities than the male ones for committing either property or personal offences. It is striking, for example, that men are more likely than women to be violent within the family, even though women spend much more time interacting with children and parents in the family setting than men do.

It has recently been argued (Zoccolillo, 1993) that a different definition of antisocial behaviour should be adopted for girls, because behaviour that is normal in boys is not normal in girls. The argument against that approach, well put by Zahn-Waxler (1993), is that the use of a sliding scale would obscure a real and important difference in behaviour between the sexes, and would make attempts to describe and explain the difference more difficult. As the main focus of this chapter is on crime as defined by the law, rather than antisocial behaviour as defined by psychologists, the use of a single definition is appropriate for the present purpose. It is clear that our understanding of the causes of the striking difference in criminality between the sexes is limited as yet, and that further research on this problem is likely to enlarge our understanding of criminality in general.

Ethnic Group

Wilson and Herrnstein (1985: 459) began their discussion of 'race and crime' by stating that 'in virtually every society, there are differences in crime rates between some racial and ethnic groups'. In fact, however, this statement is based, at best, on weak and anecdotal evidence. In virtually every society (to adopt the phrase) information about rates of crime among different ethnic groups is non-existent or inadequate. In practice, discussion of the issue has been dominated by the American agenda, first because of the dominance of American quantitative social science, and second because the position of the descendants of former African slaves in America is the central issue of American social policy. The result is that very good information is available about criminality among American blacks, and there is a high level of scholarly debate about the facts and their interpretation, especially in view of the high emotions raised by the subject. On the other hand, it is wrong to assume that essentially the same pattern applies 'in virtually every society'. There is good reason to believe, as argued above, that the age-crime curve and the massive difference in criminality between males and females are both fairly constant across different societies; by contrast, the cultural identity, history, and current circumstances of ethnic minority groups are highly specific to particular societies. The fairly recent migrants from former colonies and other less developed countries that are present in many European countries have a fundamentally different history and position in society from black Americans, who have been present for 200-300 years, and were formerly slaves.

The United States

In the present discussion, the main conclusions from American research will be set beside the much more meagre results available for certain European countries. In the USA:

> No matter how one adjusts for other demographic factors, blacks tend to be overrepresented by a factor of four to one among persons arrested for violent crimes, and by a factor of nearly three to one among those arrested for property crime. Stated another way, if blacks were arrested for robbery at the same rate as whites, there would be half as many robbers arrested in the United States (Wilson & Herrnstein, 1985: 461-62).

The disproportion is even greater in the prison population, showing that the various filters between arrest and imprisonment work to the disadvantage of black people. How far this is the result of discrimination, or of the fair application of legitimate criteria, will not be discussed here. However, most of the disproportionate imprisonment of black people – according to the analysis of Blumstein et al. (1978), about 80 per cent – is already manifest in the pattern of arrests. The central question is how far that pattern reflects a disproportionate level of criminality among black people as opposed to a bias in the pattern of law enforcement.

Self-report studies generally show much smaller differences in the prevalence of offending between white and black people. Although there is much evidence to support the proposition that self-reports have some validity, they are clearly incomplete and biased as a measure of all offending. There is evidence that young black Americans underreport their misconduct to a greater extent than their white counterparts; and a recent study (see below) has produced similar evidence for certain ethnic minorities in the Netherlands. Also, as Wilson and Herrnstein (1985) pointed out, self-report studies cannot provide good information about incidence as opposed to prevalence, and tend to concentrate on less serious offences. These arguments have led many writers to conclude that the evidence from self-report studies is not persuasive. This may be right, although it is notable that the same writers tend to rely on the results of self-report studies when analysing differences between other population groups (for example, single-parent versus two-parent families).

Striking findings that are relevant to this discussion have recently emerged from the Epidemiological Catchment Area Study, a cross-sectional survey of people in prisons and other institutions as well as private households. Most of the items used to define antisocial personality within this study relate to misconduct or disturbed behaviour rather than criminal offences, but, as noted earlier, there is a strong link between antisocial behaviour and having been arrested more than once. The ratio between the proportion of black and white males who reported having been convicted of a felony was 2.6; and the ratio between the proportion of the two groups who reported two or more arrests for non-traffic offences was 2.2. These findings might leave some room for differential under-reporting by black respondents, but they do show large differences between black and white people in line with the statistics of arrests and convictions. However, the study found that prevalence of antisocial personality was the same among black and white people. Among all respondents up to the age of 44, 1.8 per cent of the blacks compared with 0.3 per cent of the whites were in prison, a black/white ratio of 6. The proportion in prison was much higher among those with than those without antisocial personality (by a factor of 13). However, whether one considers those with antisocial personality, or those without, blacks were more likely to be in prison than whites by a factor of more than 5. For example, among those with antisocial personality, 14.6 per cent of blacks compared with 2.7 per cent of whites were in prison.

These findings are powerful, because they are based on a large sample and carefully designed instruments, and cannot be explained by a higher level of underreporting among black than among white respondents (given the result for convictions and arrests). They seem to show that black people are no more likely than white people to show a pattern of behaviour, called antisocial personality, which is often associated with crime; and that black people who do show that pattern of disturbed behaviour are far more likely than similar white people to end up in prison. However, these findings have only an indirect bearing on the debate about the prevalence of criminal behaviour among black people, because antisocial personality is distinct from criminal behaviour, and much less prevalent.

Evidence from American victim surveys shows that black people are substantially more likely than white people to be victims of robbery and burglary, and there is good reason to think that for these crimes victims and offenders tend to belong to the same ethnic group. These surveys also analyse victims' reports about offenders, where they saw or heard them. The ethnic profile of offenders as shown by these reports corresponds closely to arrest data. In the case of homicide, where the clear-up rate is over 70 per cent, there is strong evidence that black people are around six times as likely as white people to be both offenders and victims.

On the balance of the evidence, the prevalence of criminal behaviour is substantially higher among black than among white Americans, although it is probably true in addition that law enforcement is biased against black people. Because of conflicts of evidence, it is not possible to quantify the black/white offending ratio with any degree of confidence. Although this is less often mentioned, it is clear that rates of offending among Chinese and Japanese Americans are lower than among whites. The reasons for the high rate of offending among black Americans cannot be discussed here, but it is worth pointing out, following Wilson (1987), that the explanation may lie in 'social pathologies of the inner city' rather than present-day racial discrimination, or characteristics of black culture as such.

England and Wales

In Britain, the main ethnic minority groups originate from the Indian sub-continent (including African Asians, who had already resettled in an East African country before migrating again to Britain) and from the West Indies. The migration started around 1950. The inflow of West Indians reached its peak around 1960, whereas the peak of the South Asian migration came about ten years later. Currently, a substantial proportion of the older generation of Asians and West Indians in Britain were born abroad, while the great majority of the younger generation were born in Britain. The great majority have British nationality (in the fullest sense) and right of abode in Britain. Afro-Caribbeans are about 1.5 per cent of the population; South Asians about 3 per cent. These minorities are therefore much smaller than the ethnic minorities in the United States.

For the period up to about 1970, there is fragmentary evidence to suggest that the crime rate was lower than average among South Asians, and low to average among West Indians.[10] Since about 1970 there is increasing evidence of higher than average rates of arrest and imprisonment of people of West Indian origin, while the pattern of lower than average official criminality among South Asians probably continues (see Smith, 1994, for a review of all of the evidence on ethnic minorities and criminal justice in Britain). From 1986 onwards there are reliable statistics of the ethnic profile of the prison population. The results show a substantial overrepresentation of people of West Indian and African origin, by a factor of around 5. South Asians are represented about equally in the prison and general population (Home Office, 1991).

In London, police have published statistics showing the ethnic profile of persons arrested (utilized, for example, in the study by Stevens & Willis, 1979). Like the prison statistics, these show a large overrepresentation of 'black-skinned' people (mostly of West Indian origin) but they also show an underrepresentation of South Asians (Home Office, 1989). A number of studies have shown that Afro-Caribbeans are more likely to be stopped and searched by the police than whites or South Asians (Smith, 1983; Skogan, 1990; Crawford et al., 1990). The London survey by Smith also found, however, that the proportion of stops producing a 'result' (leading to a person

---

10. Wilson and Herrnstein (1985) quote a study by Ira Reid which showed that in the 1930s the rate of imprisonment of West Indian immigrants in New York was lower than average, while the rate for American blacks was three times the average.

being arrested and charged with an offence, or being reported for an offence) was the same (12 per cent) for Afro-Caribbeans and whites; given that the stopping was not a random procedure, this suggested that the police practice of stopping a higher proportion of Afro-Caribbeans than whites was justified by the results. The same survey also showed that, according to victims' reports, Afro-Caribbeans were overrepresented among offenders in cases where they had seen them.

Some (for example, Jefferson, 1988, 1991) seek to explain the overrepresentation of Afro-Caribbeans in terms of selective perceptions by white victims, selective reporting of incidents to the police by organizations and individuals (incidents involving black suspects more likely to be reported, those involving white suspects more likely to be ignored or informally resolved) and selective law enforcement practices. From a careful review of the available evidence, Smith (1994) has concluded that it is implausible to suggest that there is no difference in the rate of offending between white and Afro-Caribbean people. If the difference in rate of imprisonment between white and Afro-Caribbean people were substantively the result of bias at each stage of the criminal justice process, then the gap between rates for white and Afro-Caribbean people should increase at each stage of the process from victims' reports through prosecution to imprisonment, but in fact it does not. A further problem with Jefferson's (1993) interpretation is that racial discrimination has been shown to be directed equally at South Asians and Afro-Caribbeans in Britain (Smith, 1977; Brown & Lawton, 1986), while South Asians are more subject than Afro-Caribbeans to racial attacks and harassment (Home Office, 1981). The theory that Afro-Caribbeans but not South Asians are singled out for discriminatory treatment by crime victims and the police does not fit with the wider picture of racial discrimination and disadvantage in Britain.

In summary, it seems clear that in Britain the crime rate among Afro-Caribbeans is substantially higher than among whites. However, this is probably a recent phenomenon; in the 1960s, the crime rate was probably lower than average among all ethnic minority groups.

The Netherlands

The three main ethnic minority groups in the Netherlands are Surinamese, Turks, and Moroccans. The largest group, the Surinamese, account for about 1.5 per cent of the population, while each of the other two groups accounts for just over 1 per cent. The Surinamese are highly diverse; they include Creoles, the descendants of former slaves originating from Africa; Hindu originating from India, the descendants of former contract workers; and people from Indonesia and China. The migration from Surinam began in 1961, while the migration from Turkey and Morocco began slightly earlier.

In the Netherlands there are no routine statistics by ethnic group of arrests, convictions, or prison population, but some useful information is provided by a recent study of about 800 boys aged 12-17 (including about 200 from each of four ethnic groups), using both self-report and official data (Junger, 1990). From comparing the self-reports with police records, it was found that the proportion who had been arrested or in contact with the police but did not admit the fact was much higher for Moroccans and Turks than for Surinamese or Dutch respondents. It was concluded that the self-reports were not a valid basis for comparing crime rates between ethnic groups. There was a considerable difference in arrest rates (as shown by police records) by ethnic group: the proportion who had ever been arrested was 35 per cent for Moroccans, just over 20 per cent for Turks and Surinamese, and 15 per cent for Dutch boys from areas and social class groups comparable to those of the ethnic minority samples. Thus, for two of the minority groups – Turks and Surinamese – the arrest rate was only slightly higher than for Dutch boys.

An earlier study (Junger-Tas, 1985) analysed a representative sample of files for suspects aged 0-19 at police stations in Rotterdam and Eindhoven. Rates of crime were again found to be higher among young people belonging to ethnic minorities than among those originating from the Netherlands, although the results were somewhat different in detail. Expressed as a ratio of the crime rate for Dutch youth, the rate for Surinamese was 1.9 in Eindhoven, and 4.5 in Rotterdam; for Moroccan youths it was 2.9 in Eindhoven, and 2.6 in Rotterdam; and for Turkish youths it was 1.8 in Eindhoven, and 1.2 in Rotterdam.

France

In France, official statistics and other studies do not identify ethnic or racial groups, as this would conflict with the dominant assimilationist ideology. However, the French have no reservations about identifying foreigners (defined as those who do not have French nationality) in statistics and research. Statistics on the prison population according to nationality are available from 1968 onwards, and on persons suspected of an offence (similar to arrests) from 1973. These data have been analysed in a recent study by Tournier and Robert (1991). It has to be recognized, of course, that because of the inclusive attitude to French nationality implied by assimilationist policy in overseas possessions, there are many people in France who are visually identifiable as belonging to ethnic minorities, but who have French nationality. Equally, some foreigners do not belong to visually identifiable ethnic minorities. There is a major difference, therefore, between the French concept of foreigners, and the Anglo-Saxon concept of a racial or ethnic minority.

Foreigners in France account for about 7 per cent of the population. Among these the largest group is from the North African countries Algeria, Morocco and Tunisia, who together account for 2.5 per cent of the population. A further 1.2 per cent are from Spain and Italy. Apart from a small number from African countries not on the Mediterranean, most other foreigners are from various other countries in Europe. The migration from North Africa has happened almost entirely since the end of the Algerian War of Independence in 1962.

In 1990 a remarkable 30 per cent of the prison population were foreigners; the proportion of foreigners in prison was about 4.5 times the figure for French people. The latest year for which a more detailed breakdown is available is 1982. This shows that the ratio between the rate of imprisonment for the foreign group and French people was 7.5 for Algerians, 7.0 for Tunisians, 3.7 for Moroccans, and 9.1 for other Africans. For foreigners from Europe, the ratio was 2.1.

Of all those suspected of an offence (comparable to arrests) in 1987, 16.8 per cent were foreigners. However, about 5 per cent of these cases related to immigration offences. When these are excluded, the proportion of suspects who are foreigners is reduced to 12.9 per cent. Tournier and Robert calculated that the suspect rate in relation to population was about twice as high for foreigners as for French people (excluding the immigration offences).

According to Tournier and Robert's calculations, the overrepresentation of foreigners among prisoners and suspects was even more marked among the younger age groups. An earlier study (Lahalle, 1982) found among files submitted to juvenile court judges a much higher representation of immigrant than of French youths.

There seems to be no hard information to help evaluate how these police statistics relate to the prevalence of crime among the different communities. Tournier and Robert believed that foreigners are more likely than French people to be arrested at least partly because of an active drive by the police against immigration offences. Because of that policy, all foreigners, but especially the most visible groups, become the targets of police activity. While this is ostensibly directed at immigration offences, it often also results in the detection of other types of offence, particularly possession of drugs, and theft.

It seems less likely, however, that policing practices could account for the substantial overrepresentation of foreigners among those accused of violent crimes.

Germany

Killias (1989b) listed seven studies based on police statistics for various years between 1979 and 1985 which showed a considerably higher rate of official offending among young immigrants in West Germany than among those of German origin. Most of these immigrants are from Southern Europe. In all but one study, they belonged predominantly to the second generation (born in Germany of migrant parents). The disparities were greater for those aged 15 or over than for children. There is little or no evidence to show how far these differences result from law enforcement policies and practices.

Explaining Ethnic Differences

There is a considerable body of writing attempting to explain the high crime rate among US blacks. By contrast, discussion of the European data is at a much earlier stage; it has been mainly concerned, up to now, with how far apparent differences in crime rates between ethnic groups are a consequence of law enforcement practices and the operation of the criminal justice system. On that point, it seems likely from the available evidence that in Britain and the Netherlands, at least, there is a substantially higher than average rate of offending for certain minority groups, but not for others: a higher than average rate for Afro-Caribbeans in England, and for Moroccans in the Netherlands; a lower than average rate for South Asians in England; and perhaps slightly above average rates for Surinamers and Turks in the Netherlands. This at least shows that the causes of high crime rates are specific to particular ethnic groups, and are not a consequence of the process, largely shared by these groups, of migration and adaptation over the recent postwar period. The explanation for the high crime rate of black people in the United States is highly controversial, and there is not enough space to address the issues here. It is worth pointing out, however, that a number of different factors and processes are probably involved, including inadequate socialization connected with stressed family circumstances, a breakdown of social controls in largely black inner-city areas, and perceptions of a lack of legitimate opportunities.

Social Class

Many sociological theories have assumed that both youth and adult crime is much more common among the lower than among the higher social classes, but evidence to support the assumption has always been weak. This matter became the subject of academic controversy in the United States in the late 1970s and early 1980s. An enormous number of studies had collected relevant results. Braithwaite (1981) listed 31 studies in the period 1958 to 1969, and 40 studies from the 1970s. From a secondary analysis of 35 studies, Tittle et al. (1978) concluded that there was a slight negative relationship between class and criminality. Self-report studies produced lower associations than official statistics studies. One possible reason for this is that many of the behaviours covered by self-report studies are non-criminal and even trivial. Another is that the association with social class in studies of official statistics arises from selective law enforcement practices. In addition, Tittle et al. found a historic decline in the strength of the association so that by the 1970s no association appeared in either self-report or official statistics studies. From a review of a larger number of studies, Braithwaite (1981) challenged the conclusion of a decline; he found a modest association between class and criminality in a majority of studies of self-report and offical data. Axenroth (1983) found a strong association between class and criminality in Korea, using both official statistics and self-report data. He concluded that social class may be more strongly associated with criminality in less developed or developing societies than in advanced industrial societies.

Rutter and Giller (1983) summarized the British evidence on this question as follows:

> The evidence suggests that there is a modest (but not strong) association between low social status and delinquency, but that this association applies mainly at the extremes of the social scale, that it is due in part to social class differentials in detection and prosecution, and that in so far as it applies to real differences in delinquent activities, the association is largely confined to the more serious delinquencies. Moreover, even that association is more strongly evident with measures of parental unemployment or reliance on welfare than with indices of parental occupation or education (136-37).

They thought that at least some of the data suggested that the social class-delinquency association may be slightly stronger in Britain than in the United States. They also concluded that measures of poverty, unemployment and reliance on welfare showed stronger associations with delinquency than parental occupation or education.

As already pointed out, official offending is more strongly related to social class than self-reported offending. If people subject to serious sanctions by the criminal justice system are considered, the relationship with social class becomes much stronger. For example, a national survey of prisoners in England and Wales (Walmsley et al., 1992) found that members of lower social class groups were heavily overrepresented in the prison population. Groups that are strongly represented in the prison population are repeated offenders, unsuccessful or inadequate offenders, and serious offenders. On this last category, although many of those given prison sentences have committed relatively trivial offences, those that have committed more serious offences tend to be given longer sentences, so they form a relatively high proportion of the prison population at any one time.

Taken together these findings show that offending in itself is only weakly related to social class; being caught and going onto police records is related rather more strongly to social class; whereas being the type of serious, recidivist, or unsuccessful offender who is likely to be in prison is strongly associated with social class. This may imply that it is interactions with the criminal justice system, rather than offending in itself, that is related to social class: but further investigation is needed before firmly coming to that conclusion.

There is some evidence that the effect of social class on delinquency may be mediated by other factors associated with low social status. Farrington (1979) found that the association disappeared when the effect of parental supervision was taken into account. Also, West and Farrington (1973) found that while parental criminality and family income were associated with each other, and while each was associated with delinquency, the effect of parental criminality was more basic, for it tended to remain after controlling for family income, while the reverse was not the case.

Family Influences

Loeber and Stouthamer-Loeber (1986) have reported the results of a meta-analysis of a large number of American, British and Scandinavian studies on the relation of family factors to juvenile conduct problems and delinquency. They included both longitudinal and concurrent studies, ones using self-reports and official data on delinquency, and ones based on normal samples along with others comparing delinquents with non-delinquents, and aggressive with non-aggressive children. As a method of organizing the data, they distinguished four paradigms of family influences. First, there is the neglect paradigm, in which parents spend too little time interacting with their children and are often unaware of the mischief they are getting into. The pattern has two distinct aspects: a lack of supervision, and a lack of involvement. Second, there is the conflict paradigm, which refers to a pattern of escalating conflict between child and parents. Aspects of the pattern are inadequate, inappropriate or inconsistent disciplining, and rejection (of the child by the parents, or of the parents by the child). The third paradigm concerns deviant behaviours and values. Parents may be delinquent themselves, or they may hold attitudes that condone lawbreaking. Fourth, there is the disruption paradigm. Neglect and conflict may arise because of marital discord, breakup of the marriage with the subsequent absence of one parent, and parental illness.

Variables belonging to all four paradigms were found to be consistently related to conduct problems or delinquency. These relationships tended to be strongest for the neglect paradigm, intermediate for the deviant behaviours and attitudes and the conflict paradigms, and lowest for the disruption paradigm. Broadly speaking, socialization variables (such as parents' involvement with children) were more strongly related than familial background variables (such as the absence of a parent).

In more detail, the ranking of the familial variables varied to some extent according to the type of study. In concurrent studies comparing delinquent with non-delinquent samples, the variables most strongly related to delinquency were parent-child involvement, supervision, discipline, and parental rejection. Slightly lower, but still high, were children's rejection of parents and child-parent involvement. Still lower were variables that did not directly reflect parent-child interactions, such as parental criminality, marital discord, or parental absence. Concurrent studies of normal samples showed weaker relationships because the subjects reflect the full range of characteristics rather than the extremes of a distribution. The rank order of the variables in terms of their association with delinquency was also somewhat different. Among the variables with the strongest association were parents' rejection of children, children's rejection of parents, parental criminality, and marital discord. Parents' child-rearing variables were less strongly related to delinquency than shown by the studies with comparison samples. A possible reason for these differences is that the comparison sample studies generally used official data on delinquency, while the normal sample studies generally used self-report data. The child-rearing variables may be more strongly related to the serious forms of delinquency that tend to be officially reported than to the less serious forms that tend to be captured by self-reports.

Nearly all of the longitudinal studies used relatively normal samples. In these studies, the variables most strongly related to delinquency were parents' involvement with their children, parental rejection of their children, and supervision, all of which concern socialization. The only socialization variable that was less strongly related to delinquency was discipline. The familial background variables (parental criminality, marital discord, parental absence, and parental health) were all related less strongly to delinquency. The results suggest that the socialization variables have a sleeper effect: parental supervision and parental rejection have stronger relations to child conduct problems over time than concurrently.

The familial variables were related to the full range of child problems captured by self-reports of conduct and delinquency and by arrest or court records. The amount of supervision was related (inversely) to the seriousness or amount of delinquency, and the association was stronger for official than for self-reported delinquency. The same was true for several other familial variables.

Various findings suggest that different family problems interlock and jointly increase the chances that children will become delinquent. The risk of child antisocial behaviour increases rapidly as the number of family adversities increases. Child conduct problems can be divided into those that are overt and confrontational (arguing, fighting, etc.) and those that are covert (stealing, vandalism, truancy, drug use, etc.). There is some evidence that distinct patterns of familial impairments may be associated with the two kinds of problem behaviour.

Sampson and Laub (1993) argued that processes of informal social control are the mechanism through which the family has an important influence on prosocial versus antisocial behaviour, and that supervision, attachment, and discipline are the main parts of the mechanism. They argued that consistent discipline, using 'integrative shaming', has a positive influence, whereas stigmatizing or arbitrary discipline, implying rejection rather than integration, has a negative influence. In their reanalysis of the Gluecks' longitudinal data they were able to show that family factors had an important influence on whether the boy was delinquent in adolescence; the specific family variables found to be influential were whether a parent used erratic or threatening discipline, whether the child was rejected by a parent, and the extent of the mother's supervision. Other social processes having an important influence on delinquency in the logistic regression model were attachment to school, and to delinquent peers.

Sampson and Laub (1993) also found that the family process variables were related to adult criminality, but that this relationship was entirely mediated by adolescent delinquency (such that if adolescent delinquency was included in the model, family process variables no longer had a significant effect on adult criminality). On the basis of these findings, they suggested that much of the linkage between childhood family experiences and adult criminality may be due to interactional and cumulative continuity through the responses of other people and institutions, and not to stable dispositions formed in childhood as a result of family experiences.

Influence of Peer Groups

Sutherland's theory (Sutherland & Cressey, 1978) that people become criminal because of the company they keep was enormously influential for many years. As Sampson and Laub (1993) have explained, this idea, formally tagged 'the theory of differential association', was an attempt – for many years a successful one – to appropriate the study of crime for sociology. If true, the theory would show that crime flows from the structure of social groups, the province of sociologists, and not from biology, family influences, or psychological dysfunction, the provinces of other disciplines. There is indeed a large body of evidence, summarized by Sampson and Laub (1993), to show that relationships with criminal others are associated with criminal behaviour. However, identifying the direction of the causation tends to be very difficult. Sutherland's theory was that association with delinquent peers causes delinquency. The other possibility is that 'birds of a feather flock together'. A particularly strong reason for expecting the causation to run that way is that many crimes are committed by several people acting together.

Robins (1966) suggested a method of testing the direction of the causation. 'If "differential association" were a powerful determinant of sociopathy, the siblings' behavior ought to be an even more potent predictor than friends', since association with siblings is more constant and less avoidable' (1966: 180). Following Robins's logic, Sampson and Laub (1993) examined the joint and several effects of delinquent companions and siblings on delinquent behaviour. After controlling for structural background factors, they found that attachment to delinquent siblings was not predictive of delinquency, whereas attachment to delinquent peers was. They therefore concluded that the association arose because delinquent adolescents tended to become attached to delinquent peers. From a general review of the evidence, Rowe et al. (1994) concluded that there was some peer group influence after discounting the effect of peer selection, and that the main result was to reinforce the individual's existing predispositions.

Unemployment

There is a strong relationship, at the individual level, between unemployment and criminality. For example, Smith (1983) analysed the characteristics of those who said they had been arrested by the police among a large representative sample of the general population of London aged 15 and over. Confirming findings summarized above, he found a distinct but not very strong relationship with social class. There was, however, a much stronger relationship with unemployment. Among men aged 15-59, 52 per cent of the unemployed said they had ever been arrested, compared with 22 per cent of those in full-time work; and 32 per cent of the unemployed said they had been arrested in the previous five years, compared with 10 per cent of those in full-time work. According to the reports of men aged 15-59, the mean number of times they had been arrested in the previous five years was six times as high among the unemployed as among those in full-time work. Smith explained these findings by suggesting that there is an 'underclass' of people who, among other things, are often in trouble with the police.

> One likely characteristic of such a group would be that they are marginal to the labour market, do jobs that offer little security of employment and are therefore often in and out of work, so that a relatively high proportion of them are at any one time unemployed. The jobs that they do when in work would not necessarily be low paid or at a low level: for example, scaffolders, construction workers, some of those working in the hotel and restaurant trade and people working in scrap yards might fall into the group, as well as street sweepers and factory cleaners; some of these occupations are semi-skilled or even skilled. According to this view, it would not be low pay that was associated with being in trouble with the police so much as discontinuity, insecurity and rootlessness (1983: 125).

This concept is very close to the one of 'job instability' used by Sampson and Laub (1993) in their reanalysis of the Gluecks' data. As already set out, they found that job instability is a powerful predictor of adult criminality, and convincingly established that the direction of causation runs from job instability to criminality. Like Smith (1983) they assumed that the underlying mechanism was attachment to the social fabric (or detachment from it) rather than earnings, economic power, or economic needs.[11]

Use of Alcohol and Illicit Drugs

There is overwhelming evidence of a strong association between use of alcohol and aggression, including violent crime; and between use of various illicit drugs and a wide range of delinquent and criminal activity (Hore, 1990; Evans, 1990; Gordon, 1990; Fagan, 1990; Chaiken & Chaiken, 1990). The nature and meaning of this association is much more difficult to establish, but some fairly firm conclusions can now be drawn from the extensive research on the subject.

As Fagan (1990) has pointed out, one of the difficulties is that different disciplines have tended to define the questions differently: for example, experimental psychologists have studied the effect of drinking alcohol on aggressive behaviour induced in a laboratory situation, but sociologists have studied the kinds of social setting in which alcohol-related aggressive behaviour is more or less likely to take place. In more detail, Fagan distinguished four types of theory that attempt to explain the association between intoxication and aggression. First, 'pharmacological theories suggest that intoxicants have direct psychoactive effects on behaviour independent of intervening psychological processes. Behavioral change following intoxication results from changes in physiological response, intensified primary drives such as sex, food, or aggression, or activation of specific brain functions or dysfunctions. These theories view the intoxication-aggression relation as exclusively biological'. Second, psychopharmacological perspectives suggest that aggressive behaviours result from the effects of intoxicants on personality and affective states. Third, psychological and psychiatric perspectives suggest that intoxication and aggression are linked by a range of underlying psychological processes. For example, alcohol or drug use may be a 'defence' to excuse or justify behaviour, or to deny responsibility for aggression. In developmental terms, there may be no direct relation between substance use and aggression, but both may arise from family influences of the kind already discussed. Fourth, social and sub-cultural explanations draw attention to the fact that intoxication may be associated with entirely different kinds of behaviours according to the situation, the sub-culture, and the wider society.

---

11. For an extended analysis of the interrelationships between race, class, unemployment, family, and the inner cities of the USA, see Wilson (1987).

Fagan argued that these various types of explanation need to be integrated within a single explanatory model. There is little explanatory power to the intoxication-aggression association when the effects of culture and social interaction are removed. A satisfactory explanation has to describe the interactions between use of psychoactive substances and the way people perceive the social setting and their own and others' behaviour, the expectations they form, cultural beliefs about the effects of the substance, and the operation of social controls; it is only when these combine together in specific ways that they produce aggressive behaviours.

Although the link between alcohol and aggression is certainly not straightforward, there is good evidence from time series analyses of data for Scandinavian countries (Wiklund & Lidberg, 1990) and Australia (Smith, 1990) that changes in the total consumption of alcohol are associated with changes in the level of recorded violent crime.

According to Chaiken and Chaiken (1990) in a recent review of the results of American research on the relation between drugs and predatory crime, 'there is strong evidence that predatory offenders who persistently and frequently use large amounts of multiple types of drugs commit crimes at significantly higher rates over longer periods than do less drug-involved offenders, and predatory offenders commit fewer crimes during periods in which they use no heroin'. While these multiple heavy users probably account for a considerable proportion of predatory crime, they are a special group; the relation between drugs and crime for the majority of offenders and drug users is entirely different. Most adolescents and adults who use illicit drugs do not commit predatory crimes. About half of delinquent youngsters are delinquent before they start using drugs, while the remaining half start concurrently or after. This suggests that prevention of delinquency is likely to be a better approach than prevention of drug use among adolescents. 'Persistent use of drugs other than heroin (and perhaps also excluding cocaine) appears to be unrelated to persistence in committing predatory crimes. Amongst youngsters who use drugs and commit theft or other predatory crimes, most continue to use drugs as adults but stop committing crimes at the end of adolescence. Moreover, almost half of convicted offenders who are persistent offenders never used drugs' (Chaiken & Chaiken, 1990: 235).

Nevertheless, since there is an important group of persistent and frequent offenders who are also persistent multiple users of heroin and other drugs, it seems that use of drugs may be a cause of crime among a minority of offenders who account for a substantial proportion of all offences.

So far this discussion has concentrated on fairly direct links between alcohol or illicit drugs and crime. Sampson and Laub (1993) in their reanalysis of the Gluecks' longitudinal data uncovered a more indirect linkage. Offenders were far more likely to drink excessively, and to have done so before the age of 20, than non-offenders. However, this was not a direct causal relationship. Sampson and Laub found that unstable job history and weak marital attachment were the most important determinants of offending, and that men who had drunk excessively from an early age were far more likely than others to have an unstable job history and a weak attachment to a spouse. Their case histories illustrated how the breakdown of marital relationships and the failure to hold down a job were closely connected with excessive drinking in many cases. It seems likely that the use of illicit drugs will also lead to a style of life in which social bonds are loosened, so that crime becomes more likely.

Social Geography

A long tradition of British and American research documents variations in crime rates between areas, and analyses these differences in terms of social geography or ecology: that is, in terms of the social composition and physical layout of areas, rather than the characteristics of individuals. Large differences in crime rate can be demonstrated between different types of area. For example, an analysis of data from the British Crime Survey of 1984 (Hope & Hough, 1988) compared crime victimization rates within 11 types of area. The areas used in the analysis are census enumeration districts which contain on average 150 households, grouped into the 11 types on the basis of a cluster of socio-demographic characteristics.[12] The proportion of households that were victims of burglary varied from 1 per cent in 'agricultural areas' through 4 per cent in 'poor quality older terraced housing' to 12 per cent in 'poorest quality council estates'. The same analysis also showed that the risk of burglary was strongest for council tenants in areas consisting mostly or entirely of council housing. This demonstrates an ecological effect on top of the effect due to the tenure of the individual family.

Explaining such area differences is a more difficult matter. A great deal of attention and research effort has been devoted in recent years to the 'broken windows' hypothesis put forward by Wilson and Kelling (1982). They argued that minor disorder and incivility undermines the informal processes by which

---

12. The ACORN classification used for the analysis was derived from a principal components analysis of a range of enumeration-level census variables.

communities normally maintain order. In support of this idea, Hope and Hough (1988) have shown that types of area with high levels of perceived incivilities tend also to have high levels of crime as measured by total or burglary victimization. Also, the shape of the relationship suggests an accelerating process of decline associated with the positive feedback process envisaged by Wilson and Kelling (1982) (for example, rising crime increases fear and further discourages residents from trying to exert informal social controls).

A different approach to explaining area differences is to consider the opportunities for crime afforded by different types of area. These would be shaped by physical layout and routine activities of residents as well as by informal social controls. According to this approach, the tradition that explains criminal behaviour in terms of an assessment of perceived risks by a potential offender should be informed by the ecological tradition: in other words, the criminal's decision-making will be influenced by perceptions of risk associated with the perceived characteristics of areas (Gottfredson & Taylor, 1988). As yet, there is little systematic evidence supporting this idea.

Using data from the British Crime Survey of 1982, Sampson and Wooldredge (1987) have shown that as well as being associated with the characteristics of individuals or families, burglary risk was associated with characteristics of the local area: the proportion of single-person households, the rate of unemployment, and housing density. Personal theft was also related to area as well as individual characteristics.

Another recent line of research investigates the transformation of urban communities from low- to high-crime areas. In a study of areas in Los Angeles County, Schuerman and Kobrin (1986) distinguished between emerging high crime areas (changing from low to high crime between 1950 and 1970), transitional areas (showing a smaller increase in crime over the two decades) and enduring high-crime areas (showing high crime throughout the 20-year period). The enduring high-crime areas were undergoing a slow process of abandonment. The emerging high-crime areas were undergoing a shift from owner- to renter-occupied dwellings and from single to multiple dwelling units. Demographic changes included a reduction in size of household units and a rise in residential mobility and broken families. An increase in unrelated individuals and in the youth dependency ratio was prominent in the emerging high-crime areas. On the basis of these and other findings, the authors described a series of stages through which areas pass on changing from low crime to high crime; they end up more homogeneous in terms of socio-economic group and educational level than they began, which fits the thesis of white and black middle-class flight from declining areas. Speed of change seems to be the crucial factor that precipitates the move from low-crime to high-crime status.

Historically the ecological approach to analysis of crime developed independently of the study of individual behaviour. Studies integrating area-level and individual-level information about victimization are now beginning to show that both levels are important in shaping the individual's vulnerability to crime. Studies integrating area-level and individual-level information about offending are at an early stage (Gottfredson & Taylor, 1988). So far, they tend to show that individual characteristics overwhelm area characteristics as determinants of offending.

EXPLAINING TRENDS IN CRIME

As set out at the beginning of this chapter, psychology, sociology, and economics have each made contributions towards thinking about crime, although there has been little attempt to integrate the ideas arising from these different traditions. Both psychologists and sociologists have shown little interest in trying to explain trends in the aggregate level of crime; and economists have only just begun to address this issue. This final section cannot, therefore, review an established body of work. Instead, it is a preliminary attempt to consider the causes of the postwar increase in crime by making use of results from studies that had other objects in mind.

Although this can only be a preliminary survey, the ultimate objective must be to integrate ideas from psychology, sociology, and economics; to produce explanations at micro and macro levels that fit together; to take account of facts about individual differences, individual development, and aggregate trends; and to describe the mechanisms that link variables together. It is necessary to have this objective in view, even though little progress can yet be made towards reaching it.

It will be convenient to use the theory of Sampson and Laub (1993) as a heuristic – an aid to discovery – in thinking about the causes of the rise in crime. Like other contributions to the field, it does not acknowledge the need to explain time trends, but unlike most it does integrate a number of sociological and psychological elements. In essence, this is a social control theory, that starts from the need to explain why most people don't normally commit crimes, rather than why they sometimes do. It is assumed that criminal behaviour is inhibited by the painful, uncomfortable, or embarrassing consequences caused by formal and informal sanctions. The emphasis, in Sampson and Laub, is on informal sanctions, by family, school, and employer, rather than formal sanctions by the criminal justice system. They do not consider the possible interactions between the formal and informal domain (see Chapter 8). Social control is achieved through direct supervision and sanctions, at varying levels of formality, for example by the family, the school, peers, acquaintances in the neighbourhood, or strangers. Some of these (particularly family and school) may also be important as agents of socialization: the process whereby rules and values are internalized, become part of a person's outlook, and form the nucleus of a system of self-evaluation (Bandura, 1991).

In Sampson and Laub's words, 'our theory emphasizes the quality or strength of social ties more than the occurrence or timing of life events' (1993: 246). Such ties are reciprocal relationships in which the individual has invested and which generate benefits for both partners. They are ties in the sense that criminal or other deviant activity would weaken or break a relationship from which the individual has much to gain. It is assumed that the formation of social bonds with family and school is influenced by the social circumstances of the family, and by certain characteristics of the individual child (which may well be genetically influenced). Important social background factors are low family social class or income, family size, family disruption, residential mobility, parents' deviance, household crowding, immigrant origin, mother being in employment. The theory posits that factors such as these influence delinquency in the adolescent only indirectly, through the influence they exert on the social control processes of the family and school, and on the selection of the adolescent's peer group. Individual characteristics, such as difficult temperament or persistent tantrums, similarly influence social control processes, but do not influence adolescent delinquency directly.

From the period of adolescence, the theory proposes that all prior influences are mediated by juvenile delinquency, which leads directly to criminality in adulthood, but also tends to weaken social bonds, as evidenced by weak labour force attachment and weak marital attachment; weak social bonds in turn lead to adult criminality. A further causal path is created by the criminal justice system. Where adolescent delinquents are imprisoned, that imprisonment weakens their later attachment to the labour market and to a spouse, which in turn leads to adult criminality.

This theory draws attention to a number of aspects of economic and social structure and of social relations that might be examined as possible causes of the postwar rise in crime. Each of these is briefly reviewed below. Perhaps the main limitation of Sampson and Laub's theory, apart from the failure to address time trends, is that it ignores influences arising from the immediate situation. Those influences will be separately considered at the end.

Social Control and Self-regulation

There is no space here to review the large body of research supporting the theory that behaviour is regulated to a large extent by informal social controls. The question that does need to be addressed is whether the period since the Second World War has seen changes that might be expected to reduce the effectiveness of social controls, thereby explaining the rise in crime.

Urbanization and Social Control

As pointed out earlier, crime rates are higher in large cities than elsewhere, and there is a fairly high correlation between the ranking of countries by crime rate and by proportion of the population in towns of 100,000 or more inhabitants. Just what are the characteristics of large towns that lead to higher crime rates is a matter that would repay further study; but one possibility is lower social control and surveillance, arising from mobility and heterogeneity of the population, lack of consensus on social norms, and less interaction with neighbours.

Urbanization was certainly associated with the large rise in crime that probably occurred in England in the first half of the nineteenth century. However, urbanization continued, probably at an increasing pace, in the second half of the nineteenth century, when the rate of crime probably declined.

Increasing urbanization cannot account for rising crime in Britain during the postwar period, nor in a number of other European countries such as the Netherlands and Belgium, since the population was tending to spread out rather than to concentrate further into cities over this period. There has been little analysis of the comparative rise in crime in urban and rural areas, although in Britain it seems that the rate of increase has been greater in rural areas. However, this may be because rural areas are becoming more suburban, and inner city areas less densely populated.

Social Geography and Social Control

There is some evidence that crime rates are high in specific urban areas where social controls have tended to break down (Hope & Hough, 1988), and that speed of change in a local area is the crucial factor that precipitates the move from low-crime to high-crime status (Schuerman & Kobrin, 1986). Taken together, these findings suggest that rapid demographic change, and instability of the local population, may be the main ecological factors associated with the breakdown of social controls. It seems likely that social controls will be strongest in settled populations; so a postwar increase in mobility might be among the causes of the rise in crime. In Sampson and Laub's (1993) model, residential mobility was one of the factors, at the level of the individual family, that caused poor parenting, thus weakening social controls over the children; and this relationship is well supported, at the individual level, by the reanalysis of the Gluecks' data. This suggests the idea of a parallel link, at the aggregate level, between an increase in residential mobility and an increase in the crime rate, but this relationship has not been formally tested. It seems very likely that residential mobility has tended to increase during the postwar period when crime has risen. Also, there is some evidence already cited (Schuerman & Kobrin, 1986) that rapid demographic change in a neighbourhood may be associated with an increase in the crime rate. Finally, it may be easier to explain the probable crime trends in nineteenth-century England in terms of population movement, change, and instability, than in terms of urbanization. These are indications that residential mobility, and other indicators of instability, may be worth investigating as possible causes of change in aggregrate crime rates.

Internalization and Detachment

Although Sampson and Laub (1993) have little to say about it, social bonds presumably become most effective when they cause individuals to regulate themselves through internalized rules of conduct. Bandura's social cognitive theory (1991) attempts to give a completely general account of the causal relationships underlying all behaviour, placing considerable emphasis on self-reactive influences and self-regulatory mechanisms. Much popular thinking would ascribe the rise in crime to a decline in moral standards. Against that, Bandura argued that there is no invariant superego, and that self-reactive influences do not operate unless they are activated. There are four mechanisms through which moral standards can be disengaged: by reconstruing conduct, so that it appears not to transgress the code; by displacing or diffusing responsibility from oneself; by disregarding or misrepresenting the consequences of an act; and by blaming or devaluing the victim.

There is good experimental evidence to demonstrate that these mechanisms of moral disengagement do operate. If societal trends tend to strengthen some or all of these mechanisms, then the increase in crime could be explained not by a decline in personal or moral standards, but by an increasing tendency to disengage these standards in a selective and self-serving manner. Bandura argued, in particular, that many features of modern life are conducive to impersonalization and dehumanization. Presumably this means that there is a trend towards people entering into fewer relationships with other people or institutions, and thus forming fewer reciprocal social bonds. If Bandura is right, there should have been a decline in the number and quality of people's social attachments, and the pattern of that decline should be associated with the rise in crime. Future research should aim to test that prediction. It would also be worth trying to establish whether people in towns have fewer social attachments than people in rural areas, since a pattern of that kind would explain the difference between town and country in the rate of crime.

The Effect of Formal Sanctions

An assumption underlying Sampson and Laub's theory is that informal controls have an overwhelmingly greater effect than formal sanctions. It is hypothesized that the main effect of imprisonment is to weaken social bonds when the person leaves prison, thus increasing the likelihood of future offending. A problem with this analysis for our purposes is that it does not consider the aggregate level. The chance of detection and punishment may not be an important influence on the likelihood that this person rather than that will offend, or that this person will offend in youth rather than in maturity (the kind of prediction on which Sampson and Laub concentrate). Nevertheless, it could have an influence on the overall level of crime (on the likelihood that *anyone* will offend).

Such an influence seems more likely if we consider the possible interaction between the formal and informal systems of control. In Japan, where the level of crime is low, informal controls through social bonds seem to be particularly strong, as detailed in an earlier section (Bayley, 1991). At the same time, the chances that an offender will be caught and punished are high, and much higher than in the United States, where the crime rate is much higher, and informal controls much less effective. Knowledge that offenders are likely to be sanctioned by the formal system should strengthen the effectiveness of informal controls, because people must fear that their social bonds would be broken when a crime was detected and punished. Equally, effective informal controls strengthen the formal system, because they reduce the amount of crime, thus increasing the chances of detection and efficient processing for the small number of crimes that do occur. Furthermore, when both informal and formal systems are effective, they are likely to incorporate a single and coherent set of values and assumptions.

If this analysis is correct, then a high chance of detection and punishment by the formal system should tend, at the aggregate level, to maintain a low level of crime. It would achieve this effect by dissuading potential offenders from engaging in crime. At the same time, however, it would remain true (as suggested by Sampson and Laub, and strongly supported by their findings) that individual offenders who are imprisoned are more likely to reoffend as a result. Without much better quantification, it must remain entirely unclear whether the net effect, at the aggregate level, of increasing the chance of detection and punishment would be to increase or reduce the level of crime. One important problem is that potential offenders' knowledge of the actual chances of detection must be very limited, particularly since these chances vary widely between specific types of offence. Presumably increasing the chance of detection eventually has some influence on perceived chances of detection, but the relationship is probably indirect, and possibly tenuous. The problem is particularly complex because of the need to consider the effect of a *change* in the rate of detection and punishment, which is currently very low in most developed countries. For example, in England & Wales, it is only for about 2 per cent of recorded offences that someone is convicted or cautioned. The effect of *increasing* this chance of detection and punishment to the Japanese level over a period of, say, 20 years would probably be quite different from the effect in Japan of *maintaining* it at a high level over that period, and much less positive, because it would cause a huge increase in the prison population, whereas the prison population in Japan is and would remain low. Also, the positive and negative effects of increasing the chances of detection might operate over different time scales: for example, the negative effect of imprisoning more people, through their increased rate of reoffending, would only be felt after the end of their prison terms, when the flow of people out of prison began to increase.

One study has tried to address the critical question whether a change in the conviction rate can bring about a change in the crime rate. Farrington and Langan (1992) carried out a careful analysis of the contrasting trends in England and the United States between 1981 and 1986/7. 'Property crimes in England increased between 1981 and 1986-1987, while violent crimes stayed tolerably constant, and both types of crimes decreased in America.' (see Figures 9.8 & 9.9). After reviewing a large number of possible explanations of this difference, none of which seems satisfactory, Farrington and Langan concluded that:

Criminal justice processing was one obvious way in which England and America went in different directions in the 1980s. The probability of an offender being convicted and sentenced to custody in England decreased by more than half for property crimes and increased slightly for violent crimes, whereas this probability increased greatly in America for both property and violent crimes. To a considerable extent, changes in the risk of legal punishment mirrored changes in crime rates, suggesting that crime and risk might have been related during this period (1992:25).

However, they do not believe that any firm conclusion can be drawn. 'Changes in the risk of conviction or imprisonment emerged as one plausible explanation for our results, but we cannot be at all confident that this factor would have appeared plausible if we had studied more countries, more time points, or different periods' (Farrington & Langan, 1992:27).

Poverty and Inadequate Housing

Sampson and Laub (1993) hypothesized that social and economic conditions influence family life, which in turn influences the development of effective social bonds with children and adolescents. This fits with the popular assumption that crime is caused by adverse social and economic conditions, such as poverty and bad housing. Yet although poverty and overcrowding may have some influence, they cannot possibly explain trends in crime in the present century. As set out in Chapter 6, the postwar period between 1950 and 1973 was one of economic growth unprecedented in history, yet it coincided with major increases in crime rates. In general, as also detailed in Chapter 6, economic growth has historically been associated with a reduction in the level of inequality between the rich and the poor, and the less developed societies today tend to have much more unequal income distributions than the more developed ones. At the same time, of course, recorded crime rates are much higher in the developed than in the less developed countries, and it seems most unlikely that those substantial differences could be entirely due to better recording of crime in the richer countries. Contrary to expectation, therefore, it seems that at the national level high crime rates are associated with wealth, economic growth, and more even distribution of incomes. For example, the crime rate in Sweden increased particularly sharply during the postwar period of strong economic growth and reduction of income inequalities combined with the most comprehensive social welfare programmes in Europe.

Figure 9.10   Poverty and crime, West Germany, 1951-1990

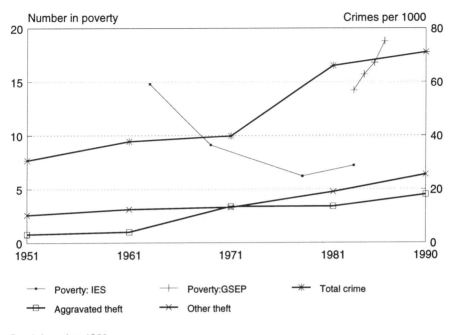

Break in series, 1983.

Source: (poverty) Hauser & Semerau (1990).
           (crime) Interpol.

On overcrowding specifically, housing conditions improved dramatically in all European countries between 1950 and 1980, and density of occupation was much reduced compared with the 1930s, as detailed in Chapter 6. Yet of course, the 1930s were a period of exceptionally low crime, whereas the crime rate rose rapidly during the period when housing conditions improved.

It is only recently that national statistics on the number and proportion of people in poverty have become established, and substantially different results are produced depending on whether a relative or an absolute standard of poverty is used (see Chapter 6). However, a series of statistics showing the proportion of the population in relative poverty can be established for West Germany between 1963 and 1986 (with a break in 1983). As shown in Figure 9.10, the proportion in poverty declined between 1963 and 1978, whereas the crime rate rose. After 1978, the proportion in poverty rose, whereas the total crime rate rose less sharply than before, although the rate of theft continued to rise at the same rate as before. These trends show, if anything, a *negative* association between changes in the rate of poverty and the rate of crime.

Family Structure and Functioning

In Sampson and Laub's (1993) theory, family functioning is a major cause of delinquency, whereas social conditions such as income and housing have an indirect effect through family functioning. In their theory, the family processes of informal social control are the dominant feature: in more detail, supervision, attachment, and discipline. They argued that families successfully achieve social control through discipline using 'integrative shaming', which strengthens social bonds, as opposed to stigmatizing and arbitrary discipline, which involve rejection and therefore the weakening of social bonds. Their analysis of the Gluecks' data showed that lack of supervision, threatening, harsh, or erratic discipline, and parental rejection all lead to delinquency in adolescence. This adds to a large body of data from other studies, summarized by Loeber and Stouthamer-Loeber (1986), showing strong links between family functioning and delinquency.

These findings raise the strong possibility that changes in the structure and functioning of families could be among the causes of the rise in crime at the aggregate level. As shown in Chapter 5, major changes in family structure have taken place in the postwar period, including large increases in the rate of divorce, the number of single parents, and cohabiting as an alternative to marriage. The largest category of single parents results from breakups of marriages and cohabiting relationships, but there is also a growing number of women having children without having had a stable marriage or cohabiting partner. Whether these changes in family structure are associated with a deterioration in family functioning remains entirely unclear. Separation and divorce certainly cause periods of turbulence, but it is possible that the quality of parenting in families that formerly remained intact was often low, that breakups occur because people are tending to expect more from relationships, and that the quality of parenting after a breakup may often be higher than it would have been within an unhappy marriage. Although inexperienced young women having children without a stable partner may often find it difficult to be good parents, particularly because of their weak economic position, it is possible that their opportunities to be good parents are no worse than in the kind of marriage that they would have entered twenty or thirty years before.

Perhaps surprisingly, there is no reliable information on trends over time in the quality of parenting, on dimensions that are relevant to the development of delinquency in the children. Whether the changes in family structure are associated with poorer parenting is an important subject for research in future. Because the changes in family structures are comparatively recent and swift-moving, up-to-date information is needed. For example, data on the behaviour of single parents twenty years ago would hardly be relevant.

As set out in Chapter 5, changes in family structure are much further advanced in Northern than in Southern Europe. It would be worth investigating, in future, whether there is a relationship at the national level between changes in crime rates and changes in family structure. However, such results cannot be interpreted without an answer to the more fundamental question about the relationship between family structure and family functioning.

Immigration

As set out in an earlier section, there is evidence that the crime rate is higher among certain ethnic minority groups (created by postwar immigration) in certain European countries than among the majority ethnic groups. On the other hand, crime rates are also lower than average among certain ethnic minority groups (notably those of Indian and African Asian origin in Britain). Also, crime rates among ethnic minority groups tend to be artificially inflated because of discrimination at various stages of the criminal justice process.

In simple statistical terms, any effect of relatively high crime rates among ethnic minorities would be trivial in the context of the postwar rise in crime in European countries. In the United States, it is true that a substantial part of the rise in crime is attributable to crimes committed by black people; but of course, the black population in the United States has been present for as long as the white population, so this has nothing to do with a change in the ethnic composition of the general population.

It might be argued that although in Europe ethnic minorities are responsible for a fairly small proportion of crimes (well under 10 per cent) immigration is an important contributor to instability and social change that has caused a weakening of community solidarity and hence social bonds. However, simple international comparisons tend to argue against that proposition. For example, Switzerland had a comparatively low rise in crime throughout most of the postwar period, even though it had a rather high level of immigration. However, it would be worthwhile to test this theory through more formal cross-national comparisons in future.

School

In Sampson and Laub's theory, school is an important arena for the formation of social bonds in adolescence. In their reanalysis of the Gluecks' data, they found that weak attachment to school and poor school performance led to adolescent delinquency. At the same time, there is evidence that rates of absenteeism vary widely between schools, and that an important part of this variation is due to school policies and practices (Rutter et al., 1979; Mortimore et al., 1988; Smith & Tomlinson, 1989). There is also evidence that schools vary in their effectiveness in preventing delinquency (Rutter et al., 1979). It is possible, therefore, that the effectiveness of schools in forming social bonds and activating social controls has tended to decline in the postwar years, and that this is among the causes of the rise in crime. However, this theory cannot be tested, since there is no relevant information on change over time in school effectiveness.

Peer Groups, Youth Culture and the Adolescent Stage

Although there is strong evidence against Sutherland's theory of 'differential association' (Sutherland & Cressey, 1978) as the main explanation of crime, Sampson and Laub (1993) ascribed an important influence to delinquent peer groups. There is evidence that delinquents tend to have delinquent associates to a large extent because they choose them; nevertheless, it is likely that delinquent groups also reinforce delinquent behaviour. It is possible, therefore, that the postwar growth in crime is associated with wider developments that have changed the nature of the adolescent stage of development (see Chapter 4) and created a more separately identifiable youth culture and youth market. The question is whether these developments have tended to create groups of young people who have an unstable attachment to people outside their own age group, or to societal institutions such as education and employment, and in which a self-reinforcing culture of delinquency might prosper. The long postponement of attachment to the labour market, associated with the recent high levels of youth unemployment, might well encourage that sort of development. It was earlier argued that a central explanation of the rise in crime in adolescence is that young people are at that stage shifting from one set of attachments to another, and are therefore unstable. Whether the length of this period of instability, or the extent of the instability, has increased in the postwar period remains unclear (see Chapter 4).

The growth of a specific youth culture and of youth markets in the postwar period has been striking. Although on the surface much of this culture is founded on opposition to established hierarchies and values, it is also closely associated with consumption, which involves joining the mainstream in order to earn and buy. It therefore seems unlikely that the growth of youth culture in general is associated with the growth in crime, but it is possible that specific youth subcultures have grown up in which criminality is common.

Alcohol and Drugs

In Sampson and Laub's (1993) theory, excessive drinking is closely bound up with the failure of marital relationships, and the failure to hold down a job, and these in turn are major causes of criminality. There is also a wealth of data showing a direct influence of drinking on specific acts of violence. In addition, there is persuasive evidence that among a relatively small group of persistent offenders, use of illicit drugs is among the causes of their offending. More generally, use of illicit drugs is probably associated with life styles that weaken social bonds.

As set out in Chapter 10, there has been a substantial rise in most countries in the postwar period in alcohol consumption and in use of illicit drugs. It is likely that this is among the causes of the rise in crime.

Imprisonment

On Sampson and Laub's (1993) theory, imprisonment increases the likelihood of reoffending, largely or entirely because it makes it more difficult for someone to hold down a job. It should follow that an increase in the prison population would cause an increase in crime, although of course the direction of causation would be extremely difficult to disentangle in practice.

This matter has not been formally analysed in this chapter, but the prison population has in fact declined in certain countries (most notably, West Germany) that have nevertheless experienced major increases in crime. It may indeed be true that, other things being equal, an increase in the use of imprisonment leads to an increase in the rate of crime, although as argued earlier, this depends also on the possible general deterrent effect of imprisonment on those not imprisoned. However, the large postwar increases in crime are certainly not due to an increased use of imprisonment, since prison populations in European countries have risen far more slowly than crime in the postwar period.

Economic Influences

Unemployment

On Sampson and Laub's (1993) theory, attachment to work is one of the most important social bonds, and weak labour force attachment leads to crime in adolescence and adulthood. Their reanalysis of the Gluecks' data provided strong support for this idea. This fits with other research showing that people are more likely to commit crimes during periods of unemployment than during periods of employment (Farrington, 1986), and that the unemployed are far more likely to be arrested than those in employment (Smith, 1983). The emphasis in Sampson and Laub's (1993) and in Smith's (1983) interpretation of their findings is on the implications of unemployment for social attachment. The other kind of argument, of course, is that people without a regular income from employment have more motivation to steal.

Whereas there is strong support for a link between unemployment and crime at the individual level, the evidence for a link at the aggregate level is unconvincing (see Orsagh & Witte, 1981, for a review of the earlier findings). Trends in unemployment in the twentieth century are discussed in Chapter 6. The main features of the long-term trends are very high levels in the late 1920s and 1930s, very low levels in the golden era of economic growth (1950-73), and very high levels since the late 1970s. It is immediately apparent that these do not fit the crime trends at all. Crime was very low in the late 1920s and 1930s when unemployment was high, whereas the largest rise in crime occurred during the postwar golden era when unemployment was very low. In the current period, youth unemployment is extremely high, and much higher than among older age groups, whereas in the interwar years unemployment did not affect young people disproportionately (see Chapter 6). Nevertheless, the long-term trends of *youth* unemployment have certainly run counter to the crime trends.

Figures 9.11 and 9.12 illustrate these trends for Sweden and Britain in the postwar period. They show total unemployment rate and crime rates (in total, and for aggregated theft and other theft). In order to emphasize long-term trends rather than short-term fluctuations, data points have been plotted at ten-year intervals. Sweden is chosen as a low unemployment country, and Britain as a high unemployment country. In Sweden, declining unemployment between 1951 and 1961 was accompanied by slowly rising crime rates. Between 1961 and 1971, a sharp rise in unemployment was accompanied by an increase in the rate of increase in crime, but between 1971 and 1981 unemployment was level and then fell sharply between 1981 and 1990, whereas over this twenty-year period crime continued to rise. In Britain (England & Wales for crime rates, UK for unemployment rates) the main features are the very steep rise in unemployment between 1971 and 1981, which was not accompanied by an accererated increase in the crime rate, and the reversal in the rate of unemployment, which fell sharply between 1981 and 1990, this fall being accompanied by an accelerating rise in the crime rate.

Figure 9.11   Crime and unemployment, Sweden 1951-1990

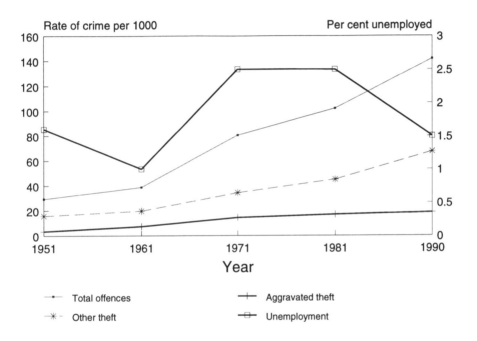

Source: Interpol; OECD.

In an econometric study of crime trends in England and Wales since the Second World War, Field (1990) constructed a regression model including growth in consumption and unemployment as explanatory variables, along with a considerable number of others. The results showed no effect of unemployment on the growth of crime, and this remained true whether unemployment in the current year, or one or two years previously, was considered. Dickinson (1993) has recently argued that since 1971 there has been a relationship in England and Wales between short-term fluctuations in rates of crime and rates of unemployment, but his rather simple analyses are not capable of rebutting Field's conclusions, which were based on far more powerful methods. However, Dickinson's data do suggest a more specific relationship between the rate of unemployment among males aged under 25 and the number of people convicted or cautioned for burglary offences between 1977 and 1990. Not much can be built on this result, however, in the context of the wider body of evidence, particularly since the measure of crime used in this case (convictions and cautions for a particular kind of offence) is a reflection of the level of police activity as much as the actual level of offending.

Figure 9.12   Crime and unemployment: England and Wales/UK, 1951-1990

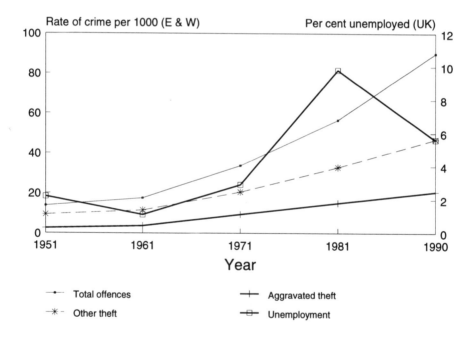

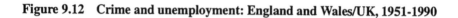

Source: Interpol; OECD.

Thus, unemployment is certainly an important factor in the individual histories leading to criminality, but has not been shown to be a cause of changes in the aggregate level of crime. If that seems puzzling, the explanation may be that the significance of unemployment for crime does lie in social bonds rather than economic motivations. At a time when the aggregate level of unemployment is low, weak attachment to the labour market may well be a cause or indicator of weak attachment to any relationships. At a time when the aggregate level of unemployment is high, being continuously or intermittently out of work becomes common, and even the norm in some social strata. In those conditions, the significance and the effects of unemployment may be different. Perhaps it does not generally lead to a weakening of all social bonds.

A different possibility is that after an extended period of high unemployment, an 'underclass' group begins to form, consisting of people having little or no relationship to the labour market over long periods. That particular development might lead to a rise in crime, but probably after a long time lag.

The conflict of evidence on the effects of unemployment at the individual and aggregate levels is a subject that ought to be targeted by future research. Pursuing the reasons for this conflict is likely to provide important insights into social processes.

Age Structure

Since most crime is committed by young men, an increase in the number of young males in the population can be expected to have a direct effect on the number of crimes committed. It is possible, in addition, that changes in the age structure could have indirect effects. Easterlin (1968) advanced the hypothesis that persons in large age cohorts will face greater competition combined with fewer social controls, so that crime rates in these cohorts will rise. Some econometric research (for example, Field, 1990) does show a relationship in the short term between growth in crime and growth in the number of young men in the population, consistent with the hypothesis of a direct effect. However, as set out in Chapter 6, in the longer term (over the past 100 years) there has been a substantial reduction in all developed countries in the proportion of the population accounted for by young people. Hence, Easterlin's hypothesis cannot possibly explain the long-term increase in crime, and nor is direct effect of the number of young men in the population an important explanatory factor.

Economic Growth

Long-term trends show a better fit between economic growth and crime than between negative economic indicators (such as unemployment) and crime. Most notably, the postwar growth in crime has broadly coincided with a period of economic growth. In more detail, however, the relationship between growth and crime has not been adequately analysed on a cross-national basis. It looks as though the sharpest increases in crime may have occurred later than the strongest period of growth in the postwar period.

In broad terms, the reason for expecting a relationship between economic growth and property crime is that increasing production means there are more things to steal. The weakness of this argument is that there were always things to steal in earlier societies (for example, sheep-stealing was one of the commonest crimes in eighteenth-century England), and that whatever possessions people have at any period of history they tend to be valuable to them in the context of the style of life at the time and therefore worth stealing. Nevertheless, the proliferation of consumer goods since the Second World War may well have produced increased opportunities for theft.

From his econometric analysis of crime trends in England and Wales since the Second World War, Field (1990) found an inverse relationship between growth in property crime and consumption growth in the short run, but no relationship in the long run. Growth in personal crime, including violence against the person and sexual offences, was found to be positively associated with growth in consumption both in the short and long run. Field explained these findings in terms of an economic theory of crime, in which increased consumption has three kinds of effect: it increases the opportunities for theft, it gives people the expectation of higher lifetime income from legitimate activity and therefore reduces the motivation to steal, and it increases the amount of time spent outside the home, and hence the opportunities for crime. The findings of this study suggest that increasing consumption is not the explanation for the long term rise in property crime, but may be part of the explanation for rising personal crime. As most crime is theft, this still leaves most of the increase in crime to be explained.

Opportunity and Limited Rationality

Like most researchers and writers in the field, Sampson and Laub (1993) concentrated on the relatively stable or predictable aspects of behaviour. Of course, they were concerned with changes as well as stabilities in the life course, and were particularly interested in explaining desistance from crime. However, they did not consider the influences on behaviour from the immediate situation. It is necessary to consider whether these situational influences may play a part in explaining the postwar rise in crime. These influences have been studied by the relatively recent tradition of research and theory on opportunity and limited rationality.

The broad theory of opportunity or limited rationality is that offending arises from an interaction between the individual and a constellation of competing risks and rewards. A large number of factors may influence the risks and rewards and the way they are perceived by the offender. These include the physical environment, social geography, the amount and nature of goods available to be stolen, how business is organized (for example, whether payments are made by cash, by cheque, or by credit card), and the lifestyles and routine activities of people in the neighbourhood. The opportunity theory therefore opens up many detailed possibilities for crime prevention, which may be tested individually, and some have been shown to work (Heal & Laycock, 1986; Clarke, 1992).

The emphasis on opportunity since the late 1970s was driven by policy imperatives rather than theoretical considerations. According to the account of Clarke (1992) it developed out of the failure of the policy of rehabilitation of offenders, which was the counterpart of dispositional theories. If criminal behaviour is seen as a consequence of relatively stable dispositions, then it may seem that the best policy is to change those dispositions. This runs up against two problems. First, the dispositions are, *ex hypothesi*, relatively stable, and hence hard to change. Second, the available institutions, such as prisons, are more likely to strengthen dispositions to crime (for example, through association with other criminals) than the opposite. If we go back further, and consider the factors (such as poor family functioning) which cause young people to become disposed to crime, then we are again faced with a problem in policy terms. It is easy to see that happy families do not produce criminals. It is very hard to see how public policy can decree that family relationships be constructive and positive.

It seems far more likely that public policy can reduce the opportunities for crime, and it was this perception that led to the increased emphasis on opportunity. It follows that opportunity theories do not deny the importance of dispositional factors. Crime is seen as the product of a motivated offender and his assessment on the basis of limited information of the risks and opportunities. The reason for emphasizing the risks and opportunities, rather than the offender's motivation, is that they can more easily be manipulated.

Situational prevention is the term used by Clarke (1992) to describe techniques that aim to manipulate the opportunities so as to reduce the level of crime. 'Situational prevention comprises opportunity-reducing measures that are (1) directed at highly specific forms of crime (2) that involve the management, design or manipulation of the immediate environment in as systematic and permanent way as possible (3) so as to increase the effort and risks of crime and reduce the rewards as perceived by a wide range of offenders.' (Clarke, 1992: 4). In more detail, Clarke distinguished three types of situational crime prevention.

1. *Increasing the effort.* Examples are target hardening (car steering locks, slug rejector devices in parking meters, toughened glass); access control (locked gates, entryphones, PIN numbers); deflecting offenders (bus stop placement, tavern location, litter bins, graffiti boards); controlling facilitators (controlling spray-can sales, gun control, credit card photos).
2. *Increasing the risks.* Examples are entry/exit screening (border searches, baggage screening, automatic ticket gates); formal surveillance (police patrols, security guards, burglar alarms); surveillance by employees (bus conductors, concierges, pay phone location); natural surveillance (pruning hedges, lighting bank interiors, defensible space).
3. *Reducing the rewards.* Examples are target removal (removable car radio, cash reduction, remove coin meters, phonecard); identifying property (cattle branding, property marking, vehicle licensing); removing inducements (graffiti cleaning, rapid repair); rule setting (drug-free school zone, public park regulation, library checkout). (Summarized from Clarke (1992):Table 1.)

While the need to find credible crime prevention policies was the spur to the development of situational crime prevention, this approach is increasingly grounded in a general theory connected with both economics and psychology. Economics provides the model of the reasoning criminal making choices on the basis of incomplete information. Interactionist psychology provides the model of the individual with a repertoire of different attitudes, perceptions, and predispositions that are selectively brought into play depending on the specific situation. Hence, the theory that behaviour is determined to a large extent by situations, rather than by fixed dispositions that operate equally in all situations, is one that fits well with some recent developments in psychology.

Much of the early opposition to opportunity theory and to situational prevention in particular was based on the assumption that dispositions to crime are relatively fixed, so that if one set of opportunities are closed, they will find another outlet. There is now a considerable body of well-designed studies that show that at least in some cases not all of the crime prevented by opportunity reduction is displaced to other targets. While there is evidence of displacement in some cases, there is also evidence of what Clarke calls diffusion in others: that is, crime prevention efforts focusing on one area or type of target also reduce crime in neighbouring areas or against related targets.

Thus, research in the tradition of situational crime prevention has demonstrated that opportunity is an important factor in specific cases, including some where motivation is extremely strong. However, researchers in this tradition have shown little interest in the question whether the general growth of crime is a consequence of a change in the structure of opportunities. It is feasible, though difficult, to consider how to reduce the opportunities for specific crimes. It is much more difficult to assess whether the whole 'constellation of risks and opportunities' has shifted in favour of the offender over the postwar period. That is because there are innumerable specific situations, and situational prevention insists on the need to analyse each one individually.

Research (for example, Sampson & Wooldredge, 1987) has shown that some aspects of social geography are associated with local crime rates, as predicted by the lifestyle/routine activities model: for example, burglary was associated with a high proportion of single-person households and with properties often left empty. These findings suggest that the general reduction in the size of households, and the increase in the proportion of single-person households, may be a cause of rising crime, through a change in the pattern of opportunity.

There is now a considerable body of research on ways in which the design of the built environment influences crime and other aspects of behaviour. Opportunity is only one of the mechanisms that are said to mediate the influence of architecture. In the postwar period there has been a growth of styles of architecture thought to be associated with opportunities for crime, particularly large high-rise or deck-access residential blocks. Research in this field has been highly localized. There has been no attempt to establish whether trends over time in the design of the built environment are among the causes of rising crime, but this is a possibility that might be examined in future research.

Other Sociological Theories

In general, the sociological theories of crime belong to a form of class analysis ultimately deriving from Marx. According to Merton's strain theory (1938, 1957), crime is caused by the strain or gap between cultural goals and the means available for achieving them. He thought that young people in the lower social strata experience frustration from the lack of opportunity to participate in the rewards of economic success. One type of reaction to this strain would be to adopt illegitimate means to achieve the goals, and this was the main explanation of the origin of crime. Thus, crime could be seen as a strategy used by the dispossessed to deal with class oppression.

The subcultural approach suggests that delinquency is 'normal' behaviour for a particular (working class) subculture and hence is learned like any other behaviour (Mays 1954; Willmott 1966; Downes 1966). This too springs from a class analysis. By adopting this strategy, sections of the working class succeed in denying or bypassing the demands of the dominant class, which are expressed in the morality and ideology which it seeks to impose on the whole society.

As set out in an earlier section, there is evidence that in the late 1960s in England and Wales the police began to arrest people they would previously have dealt with informally. Evidence of this kind gives rise to the more general theory that increases in crime are due to a 'widening of the net' – an enlargement of the scope of matters dealt with by formal process. This idea can be linked with labelling theory, which states that criminal process is a method of marking people as deviant, so that they can be controlled and dealt with in ways that would not be acceptable in the case of mainstream citizens. Putting these two ideas together, it might be suggested that crime increases because the criminal justice system widens the scope of the behaviour and people that it stigmatizes. Once a larger number of people have been labelled as deviant, there is a larger target for further police action leading to increasing 'offences' in the future. These ideas are less closely linked with class analysis than strain theory and subcultural theory; nevertheless, there may be the suggestion that net-widening and labelling are methods used by the ruling class to stigmatize and oppress increasingly large numbers of the working class.

The central problem for these three sociological theories is that the relationship between social class and delinquency is not strong. For some versions of the theories, it may also be a problem that it is implausible to see crime as an aspect of class conflict, if that means that crime is an attack by one class on another. Offenders and their victims tend to belong to the same social class, ethnic group, social networks, and geographical area.

Nevertheless, there is some association between social class (particularly parental unemployment and poverty) and crime, and each of these theories has some value and incorporates some important insights. The labelling theory can be taken as an example. Farrington (1977) set out evidence from the Cambridge cohort that boys convicted between the ages of 14 and 18 reported more delinquency at 18 than those not so convicted. A difference remained after controlling for early factors predictive of delinquency (criminality of parents, family income, family size, IQ, global index of parental behaviour).

There was some evidence to show that the order of causation was from labelling to deviance and not the opposite. Repeated labelling increased deviance amplification. Cautions (as opposed to convictions) did not lead to deviance amplification. Farrington was further able to show that some but not all of the deviance amplification effect was an increased tendency to admit offences. A more recent analysis of the Stockholm longitudinal study also supports the view that boys who become official offenders at an early age are thereby more likely to offend as adults (Magnusson & Bergman, 1990).

While ethnographic research adopting the sub-cultural perspective in England and America has provided valuable insights into the life and world view of delinquent boys, quantitative research has always disconfirmed the idea that these boys have value systems that are fundamentally different from the dominant ones. On the other hand, there may well be settings, in Southern Italy for example, where young boys are socialized into deviant life styles associated with organized crime, because the crime organizations are the main power base and source of employment and security.

The general conclusion on these three sociological theories is that although they provide interesting insights, they cannot explain any of the main sources of variation in observed patterns of crime.

CONCLUSIONS

In spite of the extensive body of research on crime and conduct disorders, this review has shown that it is extraordinarily difficult to explain why crime, most of it committed by young people, has increased so much in most developed countries in the postwar period. Informal social controls and social bonds must lie at the heart of any explanation of crime at the individual level and of crime trends at the aggregate level. It is likely that a range of social developments have tended to reduce informal controls and to weaken social bonding in reciprocal relationships. More specific factors that *may* be causes of the rise in crime are changes in family functioning, increasing mobility and associated declines in the cohesiveness of local communities, and changes in the pattern of crime opportunities and the associated risks.

It seems clear that poverty and inadequate housing are *not* among the causes of rising crime. Unstable attachment to employment is certainly an important cause of offending at the individual level, but at the aggregate level, rising unemployment was certainly *not* among the causes of the major rise in crime in the postwar period. It remains possible that a lengthy period of high unemployment will create new conditions in which an increasingly distinct section of the population has no attachment to the labour market or, more generally, to the social fabric, and that crime will rise rapidly among that group. Economic growth and the large increase in the quantity of consumer goods *may* be among the causes of the rise in crime, although econometric research has failed to demonstrate such a relationship in the long term.

There is no clear evidence that oppositional youth culture or changes in the usual sequence of life events in the adolescent period are among the causes of the rise in crime, although the subject has not been fully investigated. It has been shown that schools have an influence on delinquency, but there is no evidence of a decline in school effectiveness that would help to explain the rise in crime. Demographic changes certainly *cannot* explain the rise in crime: over the long term, the proportion of young men (who commit most of the offences) in the population has fallen; and although crime rates may be higher than average among some (but not all) groups of immigrant origin in European countries, this could have only a trivial effect on the overall crime rate. Although there is a substantial difference between the crime rate in town and countryside in most European countries, increasing urbanization is *not* among the causes of the rise in crime in the postwar period, because urbanization had already reached its height in a number of European countries by the time the major rise in crime occurred.

Findings on the effects of the criminal justice system on the rate of crime are complex. There is strong evidence that imprisonment increases the likelihood of reoffending among those who are imprisoned. In countries with high crime rates (most developed countries with the exception of Japan) only a small proportion of offences are detected and lead to a conviction. Presumably the actual chance of conviction has some influence (although possibly a tenuous one) with the decision-making of people who might be tempted to offend. However, it has not been demonstrated that increasing the rate of detection and conviction reduces the rate of crime. It is clear that the postwar rise in crime was *not* caused by an increase in the prison population, because it has occurred in countries where the prison population has declined. It is in principle possible that the rise in crime was caused by a decline in the rate of detection and conviction, but this has not been demonstrated, and it is likely that the causation is mostly in the opposite direction (a rise in crime causes a decline in the detection rate).

The implication for policy is that the effects of tougher law enforcement policies are likely to be mixed, and it will always be difficult to quantify them. The deterrent effect of an increased risk of conviction on those not convicted or imprisoned would have to be weighed against the amplification of delinquency among those convicted 'pour encourager les autres'. Mathematically and morally, that would be an equation with no solution. Punishment has to be justified (if at all) on grounds other than crime reduction.

Crime reduction policy must concentrate on pursuing objectives that are indubitably good in themselves. That means trying to improve family functioning and school socialization, improving the effectiveness of informal social controls, especially in local communities, and reducing the opportunities for crime.

REFERENCES

Archer, D. & Gartner, R. (1981). Homicide in 110 nations. In L. I. Shelley (ed.) *Readings in comparative criminology.* Carbondale, IL: Southern Illinois University Press.

Archer, D. & Gartner, R. (1984). *Violence and crime in cross-national perspective.* Yale: Yale University Press.

Axenroth, J. B. (1983). Social class and delinquency in cross-cultural perspective. *Journal of Research in Crime and Delinquency,* 164-182.

Bachman, J. G., O'Malley, P. M., & Johnston, J. (1978). *Adolescence to adulthood - Change and stability in the lives of young men, Vol. VI: Youth in transition.* Michigan: Institute for Social Research, University of Michigan.

Bandura, A. (1991). Social cognitive theory of moral thought and action. In W. M. Kurtines & J. L. Gewirtz (eds.) *Handbook of moral behaviour and development, Vol. I: Theory,* 45-103. Hillsdale, NJ: Lawrence Erlbaum.

Bayley, D. H. (1991). *Forces of order: Policing modern Japan* (2nd edition). Berkeley: University of California Press.

Bennett, R. R. & Lynch, J. P. (1989). Does a difference make a difference? Comparing cross-national crime indicators. *Criminology 28,* 153-181.

Blumstein, A., Cohen, J. & Nagin, D. (eds.) (1978). *Deterrence and incapacitation: Estimating the effects of criminal sanctions on crime rates.* Washington, DC: National Academy of Sciences.

Braithwaite, J. (1981). The myth of social class and criminality reconsidered. *American Sociological Review 46,* 36-57.

Brown, C. & Lawton, J. (1986). *Racial discrimination: 17 years after the Act.* London: Policy Studies Institute.

Chaiken, J. M. & Chaiken, M. R. (1990). Drugs and predatory crime. In M. Tonry & J. Q. Wilson (eds.) *Drugs and crime: Crime and justice, a review of research 13,* 203-40. Chicago: University of Chicago Press.

Clarke, R. V. (ed.) (1992). *Situational crime prevention: Successful case studies.* New York: Harrow & Heston.

Cline, H. F. (1980). Criminal behavior over the life span. In O. G. Brim & J. Kagan (eds.) *Constancy and change in human development*, 641-74. Cambridge, MA.: Harvard University Press.

Cloninger, C. R. & Gottesman, I. I. (1986). Genetic and childhood antecedents of antisocial behavior. In C. Shagass, R. C. Josiassen, W. H. Bridger, K. J. Weiss, D. Stoff & G. M. Simpson (eds.) Proceedings of the IV 'World Congress of Biological Psychiatry'. *Biological Psychiatry 1985*, 1448-51. New York: Elsevier.

Crawford, A., Jones, T., Woodhouse, T. & Young, J. (1990). *The Second Islington Crime Survey*. London: Middlesex Polytechnic.

Dickinson, D. (1993). *Crime and unemployment*. Cambridge: Department of Applied Statistics.

DiLalla L. F. & Gottesman, I. I. (1989). Heterogeneity of causes for delinquency and criminality: Lifespan perspectives. *Development and Psychopathology 1*, 339-349.

Downes, D. (1966). *The delinquent solution: A study of subcultural theory*. London: Routledge & Kegan Paul.

Easterlin, R. A. (1968). *Population, labor force and long swings in economic growth: The American experience*. New York: National Bureau of Economic Research.

Elliott, D. S. & Voss, H. L. (1974). *Delinquency and dropout*. Toronto: Lexington Books.

Evans, M. (1990). Unsocial and criminal activities and alcohol. In R. Bluglass & P. Bowden (eds.) *Principles and practice of forensic psychiatry*, 881-95. Edinburgh: Churchill Livingstone.

Fagan, J. (1990). Intoxication and aggression. In M. Tonry & J. Q. Wilson (eds.) *Drugs and crime: Crime and justice, a review of research 13*, 241-320. Chicago: University of Chicago Press.

Farrington, D. P. (1973). Self-reports of deviant behaviour: Predictive and stable? *Journal of Criminal Law and Criminology 64*, 99-110.

Farrington, D. P. (1977). The effects of public labelling. *British Journal of Criminology 17*, 112-125.

Farrington, D. P. (1978). The family backgrounds of aggressive youths. In L. A. Hersov, M. Berger & D. Shaffer (eds.) *Aggression and antisocial behaviour in childhood and adolescence*, 73-93. Oxford: Pergamon.

Farrington, D. P. (1979). Environmental stress, delinquent behavior, and convictions. In I. G. Sarason & C. D. Spielberger (eds.) *Stress and anxiety 6*, 93-107. Washington, DC: Hemisphere.

Farrington, D. P. (1986). Age and crime. In M. Tonry & N. Morris (eds.) *Crime and justice: An annual review of research, Vol. VII*, 189-250. Chicago: University of Chicago Press.

Farrington, D. P. (1989). Self-reported and official offending from adolescence to adulthood. In M. W. Klein (ed.) *Cross-national research in self-reported crime and delinquency*, 399-423. Boston, MA: Kluwer.

Farrington, D. P. (1990). Age, period, cohort and offending. In D. M. Gottfredson & R. V. Clarke (eds.) *Policy and theory in criminal justice: Contributions in honour of Leslie T. Wilkins*, 51-75. Aldershot, Hants: Avebury.

Farrington, D. P. (1992a). Explaining the beginning, progress, and ending of antisocial behavior from birth to adulthood. In J. McCord (ed.) *Advances in ciminological theory, Vol III: Facts, frameworks and forecasts*, 253-86. New Brunswick, NJ: Transaction.

Farrington, D. P. (1992b). Trends in English juvenile delinquency and their explanation. *International Journal of Comparative and Applied Criminal Justice 16*, 151-163.

Farrington, D. P. & Bennett, T. (1981). Police cautioning of juveniles in London. *British Journal of Criminology 21*, 123-35.

Farrington, D. P. & Dowds, E. A. (1985). Disentangling criminal behaviour and police reaction. In D. P. Farrington & J. Gunn (eds.) *Reactions to crime: The public, the police, courts and prisons*, 41-72. Chichester: Wiley.

Farrington, D. P. & Langan, P. A. (1992). Changes in crime and punishment in England and America in the 1980s. *Justice Quarterly 9*, 5-46.

Farrington, D. P. & West, D. J. (1990). The Cambridge Study in Delinquent Development: A long-term follow-up of 411 London males. In H. J. Kerner & G. Kaiser (eds.) *Criminality: Personality, behaviour and life history*, 115-38. Heidelberg: Springer-Verlag.

Field, S. (1990). *Trends in crime and their interpretation: A study of recorded crime in postwar England and Wales*. Home Office Research Study 119. London: HMSO.

Glueck, S. & Glueck, E. T. (1950). *Unraveling juvenile delinquency*. Cambridge, MA: Harvard University Press.

Gordon, A. (1990). Drugs and criminal behaviour. In R. Bluglass & P. Bowden (eds.) *Principles and practice of forensic psychiatry*, 897-901. Edinburgh: Churchill Livingstone.

Gottfredson, S. D. & Taylor, R. B. (1988). Community contexts and criminal offenders. In T. Hope & M. Shaw (eds.) *Communities and crime reduction*, 62-80. London: HMSO.

Gottfredson, M. R. & Hirschi, T. (1990). *A general theory of crime*. Stanford: Stanford University Press.

Gurr, T. R. (1977a). Contemporary crime in historical perspective: A comparative study of London, Stockholm and Sydney. *Annals 434*, 114-36.

Gurr, T. R. (1977b). Crime trends in modern democracies since 1945. *International Annals of Criminology 16*, 41-85.

Gurr, T. R. (1981). Historical trends in crime: A review of the evidence. In N. Morris & M. Tonry (eds.) *Crime and justice: An annual review of research, Vol.III*, 295-353. Chicago: University of Chicago Press.

Hauser, R. & Semerau, P. (1990). Trends in poverty and low income in the Federal Republic of Germany 1962/63-1987. In R. Teekens & B. M. S. van Praag (eds.) *Analysing Poverty in the European Community*, 313-333. Luxembourg: Eurostat.

Heal, K. & Laycock, G. (1986). *Situational crime prevention: From theory into practice*. London: HMSO.

Hindelang, M. J., Hirschi, T., & Weis, J. G. (1981). *Measuring delinquency*. Newbury Park, CA: Sage.

Hirschi, T. & Gottfredson, M. (1983). Age and the explanation of crime. *American Journal of Sociology 89*, 552-84.

Hirschi, T. & Hindelang, M. J. (1977). Intelligence and delinquency: A revisionist view. *American Sociological Review 42*, 571-87.

Home Office (1978). *Criminal statistics England and Wales 1977*. London: HMSO Cmnd 7289.

Home Office (1981). *Racial attacks: Report of a Home Office study*. London: Home Office.

Home Office Statistical Bulletin (1987). *Criminal careers of those born in 1953: Persistent offenders and desistance*. London: Home Office.

Home Office Statistical Bulletin (1989). *Criminal and custodial careers of those born in 1953, 1958 and 1963*. London: Home Office.

Home Office (1989). *Criminal Statistics England and Wales 1988*. London: HMSO, Cm 847.

Home Office (1991). *Statistical Bulletin*, 21 May 1991. London: Home Office.

Home Office (1992). *Criminal Statistics England and Wales 1990*. London: HMSO, Cm 1935.

Hope, T. & Hough, M. (1988). Area, crime and incivilities: A profile from the British Crime Survey. In T. Hope & M. Shaw (eds.) *Communities and crime reduction*, 30-47. London: HMSO.

Hore, B. (1990). Alcohol and crime. In R. Bluglass & P. Bowden (eds.) *Principles and practice of forensic psychiatry*, 873-80. Edinburgh: Churchill Livingstone.

Hough, J. M. (1986). Victims of violent crime: Findings from the British Crime Survey. In E. Fattah (ed.) *Re-orientating the justice system: From crime policy to victim policy*, 117-132. London: Macmillan.

Huang, W. S. W. & Wellford, C. F. (1989). Assessing indicators of crime among international crime data series. *Criminal Justice Policy Review 3*, 28-48.

Huizinga, D. & Elliot, D. S. (1986). Reassessing the reliability and validity of self-report delinquency measures. *Journal of Quantitative Criminology 2*, 293-327.

Interpol. *International Crime Statistics*, biennial. Lyon: Author.

Jefferson, T. (1988). Race, crime and policing: empirical, theoretical and methodological issues. *International Journal of the Sociology of Law 16*, 521-39.

Jefferson, T. (1991). Discrimination, disadvantage and policework. In E. Cashmore & E. McLaughlin (eds.) *Out of Order?*, 166-88. London: Routledge.

Jefferson, T. (1993). The racism of criminalization: Policing and the reproduction of the criminal other. In L. Gelsthorpe & W. McWilliam (eds.). *Minority ethnic groups and the criminal justice system*. Cambridge: Cambridge University Institute of Criminology.

Junger, M. (1990). *Delinquency and ethnicity: An investigation on social factors relating to delinquency among Moroccan, Turkish, Surinamese and Dutch boys*. Deventer/Boston: Kluwer.

Junger-Tas, J. (1985). *Jeunes allochtones aux Pays-Bas et leurs contacts avec la police*. The Hague: Research & Documentation Centre, Ministry of Justice.

Keane, C., Gillis, A. R. & Hagan, J. (1989). Deterrence and amplification of juvenile delinquency by police contact. *British Journal of Criminology 29*, 336-352.

Killias, M. (1989a). *Les Suisses face au crime*. Grusch, Switzerland: Ruegger.

Killias, M. (1989b). Criminality among second-generation immigrants in Western Europe: A review of the evidence. *Criminal Justice Review 14*, 13-42.

Kyvsgaard, B. (1991). The decline in child and youth criminality: Possible explanations of an international trend. In A. Snare (ed.) *Youth, crime and justice: Scandinavian studies in crime 12*, 26-41. Oslo: Norwegian University Press.

Lahalle, A. (1982). Délinquance des jeunes immigrés et politique institutionelle. In H. Malewska-Peyre (ed.) *Crise d'identité et déviance chez les jeunes immigrés*, 347-88. Paris: La documentation française.

Loeber, R. & Hay, D. F. (1994). Developmental approaches to aggression and conduct problems. In M. Rutter & D. H. Hay (eds.) *Development through life: A handbook for clinicians*. Oxford: Blackwell Scientific.

Loeber, R., Keenan, K., Green, S. M., Lahey, B. B. & Thomas, C. (1993). Evidence for developmentally based diagnoses of oppositional defiant disorder and conduct disorder. *Journal of Abnormal Child Psychology 21*, 377-410.

Loeber, R. & Stouthamer-Loeber, M. (1986). Family factors as correlates and predictors of juvenile conduct problems and delinquency. In M. Tonry & N. Morris (eds.) *Crime and justice: An annual review of research, Vol. VII, 7*, 29-149. Chicago: University of Chicago Press.

Maccoby, E. E., & Jacklin, C. N. (1980a). Psychological sex differences. In M. Rutter (ed.) *Scientific foundations of developmental psychiatry*, 92-100. London: Heinemann Medical Books.

Maccoby, E. E., & Jacklin, C. N. (1980b). Sex differences in aggression: A rejoinder and reprise. *Child Development 51*, 964-80.

Magnusson, D. (1987). Adult delinquency in the light of conduct and physiology at an early age: A longitudinal study. In D. Magnusson & A. Öhman (eds.) *Psychopathology*, 221-234. Orlando, FL: Academic Press.

Magnusson, D. (1988). Antisocial behaviour of boys and autonomic activity/reactivity. In T. E. Moffitt & S. A. Mednick (eds.) *Biological contributions to crime causation*, 135-146. Dordrecht: Martinus Nijhoff.

Magnusson, D. & Bergman, L. R. (1990). A pattern approach to the study of pathways from childhood to adulthood. In L. N. Robins & M. Rutter (eds.) *Straight and devious pathways from childhood to adulthood*, 101-115. Cambridge: Cambridge University Press.

Magnusson, D., Stattin, H., & Duner, A. (1983). Aggression and criminality in a longitudinal perspective. In K. T. Van Dusen & S. A. Mednick (eds.) *Antecedents of aggression and antisocial behaviour*. Boston, MA: Kluwer-Nijhoff.

Mayhew, P. (1992a). Cross-national comparisons of crime and victimisation, unpublished paper. London: Home Office.

Mayhew, P. (1992b). Law and justice system. *The Economist Atlas of the new Europe*, 246-49. London: Economist Books.

Mayhew, P., Elliot, D. & Dowds, L. (1989). *The 1988 British Crime Survey*. Home Office Research Study No. 111. London: HMSO.

Mayhew, P., Maung, N. A. & Mirrlees-Black, C. (1993). *The 1992 British Crime Survey*. London: HMSO.

Mayhew, P. & Smith, L. J. F. (1985). Crime in England and Wales and Scotland: A British Crime Survey comparison. *British Journal of Criminology 25*, 148-59.

Mays, J. B. (1954). *Growing up in the city*. Liverpool: University of Liverpool Press.

McCleary, R., Nienstadt, B. B. & Erven, J. M (1982). Interrupted time series analysis of uniform crime reports: The case of organisational reforms. In J. Hagan (ed.) *Quantitative Criminology*, 13-37. Beverly Hills, CA: Sage.

Merton, R. K. (1938). Social structure and anomie. *American Sociological Review 3*, 672-82.

Merton, R. K. (1957). *Social theory and social structure*. New York: Free Press.

Moffitt, T. E. (1993). The neuropsychology of conduct disorder. *Development and Psychopathology 5*, 135-181.

Monkkonen, E. H. (1981). A disorderly people? Urban order in the nineteenth and twentieth centuries. *Journal of American History 68*, 536-59.

Moore, D. R., Chamberlain, P. & Mukai, L. H. (1979). Children at risk for delinquency: A follow-up comparison of agressive children who steal. *Journal of Abnormal Child Psychology 7*, 345-355.

Mortimore, P., Sammons, P., Stoll, L., Lewis, D. & Ecob, R. (1988). *School matters: The junior years*. Wells, Somerset: Open Books.

Newman, G. R. (1976). *Comparative deviance: Perceptions and law in six cultures*. New York: Elsevier.

Normandeau, A. (1970). Crime indices for eight countries. *Journal of Criminal Law, Criminology and Police Science 15*, 234.

Olweus, D. (1979). Stability of aggressive reaction patterns in males: A review. *Psychological Bulletin 86*, 852-75.

Orsagh, T. & Witte, A. D. (1981). Economic status and crime: Implications for offender rehabilitation. *Journal of Criminal Law and Criminology 72*, 1055-71.

Pease, K. & Harvey, L. (1988). *Quantitative information from the Second UN Crime Survey: An overview*, mimeograph. Manchester: University of Manchester.

Quinton, D., Pickles, A., Maughan, B. & Rutter, M. (1993). Partners, peers and pathways: Assortative pairing and continuities in conduct disorder. *Development and Psychopathology 5*, 763-783.

Reynolds, D. A. & Blyth, P. D. (1975). Sources of variation affecting the relationship between police and survey-based estimates of crime rates. In I. Drapkin & E. Viano (eds.) *Victimology: A new focus, Vol. III*, 201-25. Lexington, MA: D. C. Heath.

Robins, L. N. (1966). *Deviant children grown up: A sociological and psychiatric study of sociopathic personality*. Baltimore: Williams & Wilkins.

Robins, L. N. (1978). Sturdy childhood predictors of adult antisocial behaviour: Replications from longitudinal studies. *Psychological Medicine 8*, 611-22.

Robins, L. N. (1986). The consequences of conduct disorder in girls. In D. Olweus, J. Block, & M. Radke-Yarrow (eds.) *Development of antisocial and prosocial behavior: Research, theories and issues*, 385-414. New York: Academic Press.

Robins, L. N. (1991). Conduct disorder. *Journal of Child Psychology and Psychiatry 32*, 193-212.

Robins, L. N. & Ratcliff, K. S. (1979). Risk factors in the continuation of childhood antisocial behaviours into adulthood. *International Journal of Mental Health 1*, 96-116.

Robins, L. N. & Regier, D. A. (eds.) (1991). *Psychiatric disorders in America: The Epidemiologic Catchment Area Study*. New York: Free Press.

Robins, L. N., Tipp, J., & Przybeck, T. (1991). Antisocial personality. In L. N. Robins & D. A. Regier (eds.) *Psychiatric disorders in America: The Epidemiologic Catchment Area Study*, 258-290. New York: Free Press.

Rowe, D. C. (1983). Biometrical genetic models of self-reported delinquent behavior: A twin study. *Behavior Genetics 13*, 473-389.

Rowe, D. C., Woulbroun, E. J. & Gulley, B. L. (1994). Peers and friends as nonshared environmental influences. In E. M. Hetherington, D. Reiss & R. Plomin (eds.) *Separate social worlds of siblings: The impact of nonshared environment on development*. Hillsdale, NJ/Hove & London: Lawrence Erlbaum.

Rutter, M. (1989). Age as an ambiguous variable in developmental research: Some epidemiological considerations from developmental psychopathology. *International Journal of Behavioural Development 12*, 1-24.

Rutter, M. & Giller, H. (1983). *Juvenile delinquency: Trends and perspectives*. Harmondsworth, Middx: Penguin.

Rutter, M., Maughan, B., Mortimore, P., Ouston, J. with Smith, A. (1979). *15000 hours: Secondary schools and their effects on children*. London: Open Books; Cambridge, MA: Harvard University Press.

Sampson, R. J. & Laub, J. H. (1993). *Crime in the making: Pathways and turning points through life*. Cambridge, MA/London: Harvard University Press.

Sampson, R. J. & Wooldredge J. D. (1987). Linking the micro- and macro-level dimensions of lifestyle-routine activity and opportunity models of predatory victimisation. *Journal of Quantitative Criminology 3*, 371-93.

Schuerman, L. & Kobrin, S. (1986). Community careers in crime. In A. J. Reiss Jr & M. Tonry (eds.) *Communities and crime: Crime and justice, an annual review of research*, 67-100. Chicago: University of Chicago Press.

Scott, J. E. & Al-Thakeb, F. (1980). Perceptions of deviance cross-culturally. In G. Newman (ed.) *Crime and deviance: A comparative perspective*, 42-67. London/Beverly Hills, CA: Sage.

Skogan, W. (1990). *The police and the public in England and Wales: A British Crime Survey report*. London: HMSO.

Smith, D. J. (1977). *Racial disadvantage in Britain*. Harmondsworth, Middx: Penguin.

Smith, D. J. (1983). *Police and people in London: Vol. I: A survey of Londoners.* London: Policy Studies Institute.

Smith, I. (1990). Alcohol and crime: The problem in Australia. In R. Bluglass & P. Bowden (eds.) *Principles and practice of forensic psychiatry*, 947-51. Edinburgh: Churchill Livingstone.

Smith, D. J. (1994). Race, crime and criminal justice. In M. Maguire, R. Morgan & R. Reiner (eds.). *The Oxford Handbook of Criminology*, 1041-1118.

Smith, D. J. & Tomlinson, S. (1989). *The school effect: A study of multi-racial comprehensives.* London: Policy Studies Institute.

Stevens, P. & Willis, C. (1979). *Race, crime and arrests.* Home Office Research Study No. 58. London: Home Office.

Sutherland, E. H. & Cressey, D. R. (1978). *Principles of criminology.* Philadelphia: J. B. Lippincott.

Tittle, C. R., Villemez, W. J. & Smith, D. A. (1978). The myth of social class and criminality: An empirical assessment of the empirical evidence. *American Sociological Review 43*, 643-56.

Tournier, P. & Robert, P. (1991). *Étrangers et délinquances: Les chiffres du débat.* Paris: Harmattan.

Trasler, G. B. (1980). *Aspects of causality, culture and crime.* Paper presented at the 4th International Seminar at the International Center of Sociological, Penal and Penitentiary Research and Studies, Messina, Italy.

UNICEF (1993). *The progress of nations 1993.* New York: Author.

van Dijk, J. J. M., Mayhew, P. & Killias, M. (1991). *Experiences of crime across the world* (2nd edition). Deventer/Boston: Kluwer.

Wadsworth, M. (1979). *Roots of delinquency: Infancy, adolescence and crime.* Oxford: Martin Robertson.

Walmsley, R., Howard, L. & White, S. (1992). *The National Prison Survey 1991 main findings.* Home Office Research Study No. 128. London: HMSO.

Walters, G. D. & White, T. W. (1989). Heredity and crime: Bad genes or bad research? *Criminology 27*, 455-85.

West, D. J. & Farrington, D. P. (1973). *Who becomes delinquent?* London: Heinemann.

West, D. J. & Farrington, D. P. (1977). *The delinquent way of life.* London: Heinemann Educational.

White, J. L., Moffitt, T. E., Earls, F., Robins, L. & Silva, P. A. (1990). How early can we tell? Predictors of childhood conduct disorder and adolescent delinquency. *Criminology 28*, 507-533.

Wiklund, N. & Lidberg, L. (1990). Alcohol as a causal criminogenic factor: The Scandinavian experience. In R. Bluglass & P. Bowden (eds.) *Principles and practice of forensic psychiatry*, 941-45. Edinburgh: Churchill Livingstone.

Wikström, P.-O. H. (1990). Age and crime in a Stockholm cohort. *Journal of Quantitative Criminology 6*, 61-83.

Willmott, P. (1966). *Adolescent boys in East London.* London: Routledge & Kegan Paul.

Wilson, J. Q. & Kelling, G. (1982). Broken windows. *The Atlantic Monthly*, March, 29-38.

Wilson, J. Q. & Herrnstein, R. (1985). *Crime and human nature.* New York: Simon & Schuster.

Wilson, W. J. (1987). *The truly disadvantaged: The inner city, the underclass, and public policy.* Chicago/London: University of Chicago Press.

World Health Organization. *World Health Statistics Annual.* Geneva: Author.

Zahn-Waxler, C. (1993). Warriors and worriers: Gender and psychopathology. *Development and Psychopathology 5*, 79-90.

Zoccolillo, M. (1993). Gender and the development of conduct disorder. *Development and Psychopathology 5*, 65-78.

Zoccolillo, M., Pickles, A., Quinton, D. & Rutter, M. (1992). The outcome of childhood conduct disorder: Implications for defining adult personality disorder and conduct disorder. *Psychological Medicine 22*, 971-986.

10

Secular Trends in Substance Use: Concepts and Data on the Impact of Social Change on Alcohol and Drug Abuse

RAINER K. SILBEREISEN, LEE ROBINS and MICHAEL RUTTER

During the Second World War alcohol was scarce and there was relatively little use of illicit drugs. Western nations had started to require prescriptions for psychoactive medicines that hitherto had been readily available over the counter, and doctors had begun to discover the risks involved in the wide-spread prescription of narcotics. On the whole, drug-taking in industrialized nations was limited to small enclaves of the musical and artistic population, and individuals associated with medicine. Although there was still consider-able overprescription of barbiturates, their use (mainly by women) was not at that time considered a major social issue.

With the end of the Second World War there was a dramatic increase in most Western countries. Amphetamines, used by soldiers during the war to stay alert and by women to lose weight, entered the illicit market. In the late 1950s, marijuana use became very common in the black inner cities of the USA, and some users progressed to amphetamine use and to various forms of narcotics, mainly in cough medicines still obtainable without prescription. In the late 1960s, the use of illicit drugs entered the middle class throughout the Western world, and continued to soar until the 1980s. Since 1980, there has been a decrease in the use of both alcohol and drugs among young people in the United States and some European countries, although the levels are still far from negligible, and seem to be growing in some areas.

The declines in some urbanized countries have not yet been seen in developing countries. In non-industrialized nations, the availability of alcohol (domestic production plus import/export) has increased dramatically. In all countries taken together, the growth since the sixties amounted to more than 140 per cent (Kortteinen, 1988). Between 1980 and 1990, the consumption of beverage alcohol increased 27 per cent in Latin America. Such remarkable changes in patterns are not unprecedented. Similar increases were observed during the period of industrialization in the second half of the nineteenth century, followed by relatively low levels of alcohol consumption between the two World Wars.

Nonetheless, Europe remains the continent with the highest alcohol consumption; in 1992, there were fifteen European countries in which consumption per annum in the general population was at least eight litres of pure alcohol per head. Although consumption figures declined or remained stable in two-thirds of Europe since the early 1980s, they are rising in the other third, particularly in some of the countries in Central and Eastern Europe (World Health Organization, 1992).

Excessive alcohol use results in a remarkable economic burden and implies far reaching consequences on public health in the European Community. The economic costs due to lost productivity and costs to the health, social welfare, traffic and criminal justice systems have been estimated at about five per cent of gross national product (Walsh, 1990). About six per cent of deaths among people under 75 years of age are related to alcohol use (Anderson, 1990).

DEFINITIONS AND MEASUREMENT ISSUES

Definitions

The substances on which this chapter concentrates are alcohol and the illicit drugs used for their effects on mood and behaviour and with undesirable psychological consequences when taken in excess. It does not discuss tobacco, because although one could argue that tobacco is the most dangerous of all substances used recreationally, its risks mainly apply to physical illness rather than behaviour.

The main focus of this chapter is on secular trends in substance *abuse*, but many of the relevant data concern levels of *use*, which have only an indirect association with drug problems. At one extreme, there is the experimental or recreational use of substances so occasional and so limited in the quantity taken that it is unlikely to cause any impairment no matter how long it continues. This may proceed to regular or heavy use, which in itself has not caused problems, but which puts the user at risk of developing problems. Problem use is defined as use that causes occasional difficulties, but over which the user still has control. Finally, there is dependence, where the difficulties in stopping use are severe enough that it may take a long period of experiencing physical, emotional, or social problems resulting from use before reduction or cessation of use occurs without treatment or forcible denial of access to the substance. Non-users and those at any of the lower levels of use are made up both of those who have never used at higher levels and those who have returned to this state after having progressed further in the hierarchy. Substance use disorders typically have periods of remission and relapse. Those in remission are at greater risk of problem use than are persons at the same current level of use who have never had problems. Thus, populations with the same proportions of abstainers and recreational substance users can be expected to have different future trajectories toward problem use, depending on their earlier history.

Trajectories for rates of future problem use also differ between countries with similar proportions of persons in the various levels of involvement with substances. A society's trajectory depends on that society's norms with respect to the acceptability of recreational use of substances, its definition of heavy use, and its tolerance for substance-related problem behaviour. These social norms may be expressed in popular attitudes; in laws governing hours during which legal substances can be sold, legal ages for drinking, production quotas for legal and prescription drugs, and taxes on substances; in the establishment of treatment facilities; and in legal action against sellers and users of illicit substances.

Measurement Issues

The issues involved in the measurement of secular trends in alcohol and drug misuse are not quite the same, the data on alcohol being perhaps rather more secure. The most direct measure of the overall alcohol consumption in any one country is provided by data on alcohol production, together with statistics on import and export available from national sources, Dutch Distiller's reports, and United Nations statistics (Moser, 1992; Walsh & Grant, 1985). Although these are imperfect in various ways, they provide a reasonable reflection of major trends over time within each country. However, they are insufficient for the appraisal of changes in drinking patterns (for example, whether the changes in total consumption reflect altering proportions of abstainers or of amounts consumed by heavy drinkers) and for the delineation of groups with a particularly high risk of alcohol problems. In particular, they cannot separate secular trends in young people from those in the population as a whole.

Statistics on reported deaths from cirrhosis of the liver provide a good guide to levels of alcohol abuse and, in most (but not all) countries, these correlate quite highly with the figures on overall alcohol consumption. However, because cirrhosis is a relatively late sequela of heavy alcohol consumption, there is likely to be a substantial time-lag between changes in the *initiation* of harmful drinking behaviour and its reflection in cirrhosis rates. The same applies to alcohol-related admissions to psychiatric units, for which the data are in any case less satisfactory. The statistics on convictions for driving under the influence of alcohol, and on car accidents and fatalities provide other indices of alcohol problems, as do arrests for drunkenness. However, these are much influenced by police practice (as well as by changes in the law).

In theory, repeated epidemiological surveys of the general population should provide the best assessment of secular trends in alcohol problems. Unfortunately, few countries have such data, and where available they are not always directly comparable in the measures used. Indeed many surveys have focused exclusively on levels of alcohol consumption rather than on alcohol problems.

Finally, cross-sectional surveys, with retrospective data on lifetime prevalence of alcohol problems (Robins & Regier, 1991) provide an indirect index of time trends through birth-cohort comparisons. Of course, they are open to the objection that lower rates in older people could be an artefact, caused by forgetting about problems manifest only in adolescence and early adult life. This issue is considered at great length in Chapter 11. There are three main reasons for concluding that errors in memory are unlikely to constitute a complete explanation, at least with respect to alcohol. First, the cohort differences vary markedly by gender and ethnicity. Thus, in the American Epidemiological Catchment Area (ECA) study (Helzer et al., 1991) the lifetime prevalence of alcoholism in white males fell with age (from 28 per cent in 18-29 year-olds to 13 per cent in those aged 65 or more), but rose with age in black males (13 per cent to 22 per cent respectively). Similarly, the cohort difference in rates was much greater in females (6.9 per cent to 1.5 per cent) than in males (26.6 per cent to 13.5 per cent). Second, the cohort differences are not the same for all problems. Thus, in the ECA study, those for illicit drug use were enormous (60.3 per cent for the 18-29 age group compared with 1.6 per cent for the 65+: Anthony & Helzer, 1991), whereas those for alcohol abuse (see above) were only moderate. Third, the trends evident from retrospective surveys agree well with the data from other sources.

There is no satisfactory equivalent of the alcohol production figures for drugs, if only because most of the drugs that give rise to concern are illicit (Institute for Study of Drug Dependence, 1993; Klingemann, 1992). The quantity of drugs seized by Customs provides an index of sorts, but it reflects only imported drugs (i.e. excluding those manufactured within the country) and trends over time may reflect changes in Customs' practices and efficiency as much as drug traffic. Moreover, the data refer only to controlled drugs. Thus, solvents, which provide an increasing cause for concern (see below) are excluded, as are over-the-counter medicines. In addition, controlled drugs such as tranquillizers rarely appear in the statistics because their use is not ordinarily treated as an offence. Similar problems attend the use of drug charges in number of convictions as an index because that varies with level of police activity as much as with the number of offences committed. In some countries, such as the UK, patients who are being treated for addiction to certain kinds of drugs (usually opiates and cocaine) have to be notified to the authorities. The numbers recorded probably provide a fair index of time trends for problems that lead to treatment but most do not. Surveys show that only about a fifth of regular opiate users in London are recorded in these statistics (Hartnoll et al., 1985). The figures are also influenced by the conscientiousness of doctors in their notifications. Of course, too, the data refer only to a very limited class of drugs.

Mortality statistics on drug-related deaths provide a useful reflection of serious drug problems but they are much influenced by the accuracy of diagnosis and reporting. Also, the time-lag between initiation of drug misuse and death makes them tardy indicators that change has occurred. The one clear exception concerns solvent-related deaths, most of which are in children, and which follow rapidly on use that affects liver function. The marked rise over time in the UK (from 82 in 1983 to 149 in 1990: Institute for the Study of Drug Dependence, 1993) almost certainly reflects a real rise in solvent misuse (predominantly in 12 to 16-year-old children) over that 7-year period.

Repeated epidemiological surveys have been available in the United States since the early 1970s (Johnston et al., 1991), but their use in Europe is both more recent and more patchy in coverage. Whereas surveys can overcome many of the problems of crime and mortality statistics, they have their own limitations and provide only limited information about the adverse effects of substance use. In the first place, those at highest risk for problem use are hardest to contact for interview, because they are often away from home and out of school and work. For example, until recently, the main American survey was of high school seniors – so omitting school drop-outs as well as truants.

Thus, the surveyed sample usually underrepresents those with problems resulting from use. In the second place, the proportion with serious substance use problems in most populations is so small that surveys find it inefficient to ask about problems in any detail. They leave it to the reader to guess what the likely risk of problems is among those meeting the study's definition of 'regular' or 'heavy' use. Even when problems resulting from use are pursued in surveys, one has to depend on respondents to make the correct attribution of their problems to substance use. This is fraught with difficulty because behaviours often blamed on substance use – aggression, spending extravagantly, irresponsibility, theft – can also be expressions of personality traits that predated first use of substances, and that appear to contribute to readiness to use substances heavily. The concern that subjects would falsely deny use, which was previously believed to be a major impediment to getting accurate survey results, has been fairly well laid to rest (Campanelli et al., 1987; Mensch & Kandel, 1988). In the few studies in which subjects did not know that their statements could be checked through records or urine screening, it appeared that privacy, guarantees of confidentiality, and a non-judgemental deportment on the part of the interviewer were sufficient to insure willingness to disclose substance use and abuse. However, these studies were in Western countries at a time when illicit drug use was commonplace; we cannot assume that the same would have been true in other places or other times.

Not only do we know little about problem use from surveys, but we also know little about those drugs considered by the general population to be especially dangerous, and therefore rarely used even experimentally. Thus it is difficult to learn much about trends in the use of heroin from general population surveys. Nor are surveys helpful in learning about the appearance of new drugs or the use of old drugs in new forms. To gather and analyse information from large numbers of persons requires a structured interview in which the topics are fixed ahead of time; it is impractical to ask large numbers of open-ended questions that must be coded by hand. The important changes that occurred with the availability of crack cocaine, for example, were signalled by following emergency room admissions, not general population surveys. Even now, the evidence on the extent of 'crack' usage mainly derives from drug seizures and studies of clinic population or high risk groups (Mott, 1992). The same applies to the indications that, in at least some European countries, the main recent rise in use of drugs concerns hallucinogens, Methylene Dioxy Metho Amphetamine (MDMA – 'ecstasy') and nitrates (Institute for the Study of Drug Dependence, 1993).

There are two main methodological conclusions that derive from these considerations. First, it is crucial to build up the picture of time trends from multiple sources and to do so in relation to data on a wide range of substances. Second, great caution is needed in the interpretation of apparent fluctuations over short periods of time; all the measures are much more satisfactory indicators of longer-term trends. The need for this caution is underlined by the fact that no sooner had the WHO Regional Office published its reports suggesting that the rate of substance abuse might have begun to fall in the late 1980s (Klingemann, 1992), than a more detailed analysis of the UK data suggested that the rate had begun to rise once more (Institute for the Study of Drug Dependence, 1993).

TRENDS IN ALCOHOL CONSUMPTION

The first point that derives from long-term data on alcohol consumption is that the first quarter of this century was characterized by a falling rate, the period between the two World Wars by a fairly stable (low) rate, and the period since

Figure 10.1　Per capita alcohol consumption in the United Kingdom, 1900-1989

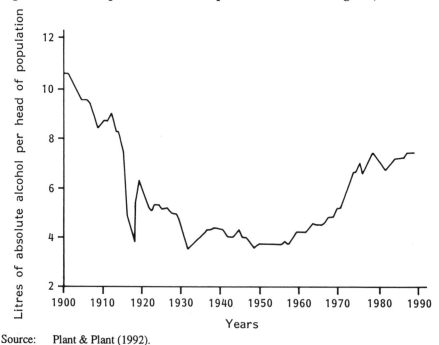

Source:　Plant & Plant (1992).

about 1950 by a marked increase, up to a plateau in the last decade or so. Figure 10.1 shows the per capita alcohol consumption in the UK from 1900 to 1989 (Plant & Plant, 1992), and Figure 10.2 the same for Norway between 1865 and 1982 (Skog, 1986b).

Room (1987) proposed a 'natural' periodicity in rates of substance use with intervals of about two generations (70 years). In his view, the troughs are the result of growing social concerns, after a period of increasing consumption (due to whatever reason). The resulting social problems and disruption of social life lead to a strengthening of social controls and legislation, ultimately contributing to a reversal of the trend. The trough ends as the absence of earlier problems leads to rising consumption. There may be some substance in this suggestion, but more detailed analyses of time trends suggest that multiple factors are operative (Skog, 1986a&b), as discussed further below.

Figure 10.2   Per capita alcohol consumption (A) and per capita private final consumption expenditures in fixed prices (B) in Norway, 1865-1982

Source: Skog (1986b).

If we concentrate on European trends in alcohol consumption since 1950, it is clear that almost all countries other than France (which had an unusually high rate initially) showed a very substantial increase up to about 1970 (Moser, 1992; Plant & Plant, 1992; Produktschaap voor Gedistilleerde Dranken, 1992). Between 1960 and 1980 the main tendency was towards a homogenization of levels across countries with rates rising in the majority of countries but falling in the few with very high levels at the beginning of this period (see Figure 10.3). The figures for deaths from cirrhosis of the liver follow a broadly similar pattern (see Figure 10.4) – the data coming from the statistics compiled by Moser (1992) for countries with measures on both indices for these two time points. The net effect for most countries has been a level of alcohol consumption in the last decade that is still far above that in the 1930s, but with less between-country variation than was the case in the earlier time period.

Figure 10.3   Annual per capita consumption of alcohol, 1960-1980

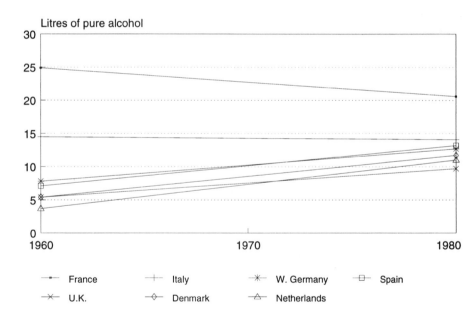

Population aged over 15

Source: Moser (1992).

Nevertheless, there are still important differences between countries in patterns of use that are not captured by per capita consumption. For example, frequency of total abstention varies widely – from half the women and one third of the men in Northern Ireland to only 10 per cent of women and 5 per cent of men in England, Wales, and Scotland (Plant & Plant, 1992).

Figure 10.4   Deaths from cirrhosis of the liver, 1960-80

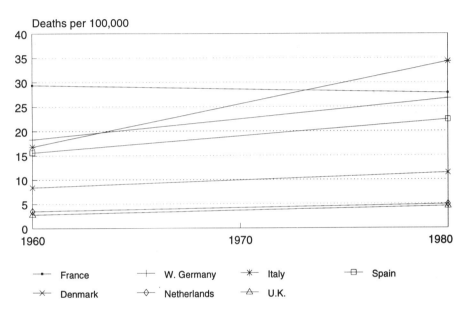

Source: Moser (1992).

The other trend has been the gradual coming together of beverage preferences. Even so, the countries in Europe can still be divided into groups according to their traditional preferences and drinking pattern. The Nordic group (Denmark, Finland, Iceland, Norway, Sweden) has a relatively low level of alcohol consumption, interspersed with binge drinking, and the beverages used are mainly beer and spirits. Latin-Hellenic countries (France, Greece, Italy, Portugal, San Marino, Spain) show the highest level of per capita consumption, dominated by wine. The Anglo-Germanic group vary somewhat in their levels of consumption, but are similar in their preference for beer. The mixed Germanic-Latin countries (Belgium, Luxembourg, Switzerland) mirror the drinking habits of their neighbours. Finally, the Eastern European group (previously composed of Bulgaria, Czechoslovakia, East Germany, Hungary, Poland, USSR) is known for very heavy sporadic drinking of spirits (Moser, 1992).

However, there is now more use of beer and spirits in traditional wine countries, and more wine drunk in traditional beer countries. Sulkunen (1989) characterized the 'modernization' of beverage preferences as a diffusion process, working its way from higher social strata and more urbanized regions to lower classes and rural areas. Sulkunen related the urban middle class's decrease in level of drinking and changes in beverage preferences to the growing awareness of health risk and a desire to appear 'cosmopolitan'.

According to a recent collection of data on substance use around the Baltic Sea, countries such as Estonia, Latvia, and Lithuania were characterized by a steep increase of alcohol consumption between the 1960s and the beginning of the 1980s. In Estonia, for instance, the per capita alcohol consumption rose from 5 litres of pure alcohol to almost 12 by 1984.

The anti-alcohol campaign launched throughout the former USSR in 1985 – implemented by raising prices for alcoholic beverages, reducing production, and restricting distribution – led to a drastic decrease in per capita consumption. In Estonia, the figures for 1987 fell close to levels of the early 1960s (Simpura & Tigerstedt, 1992). Similar control policies in Poland reduced consumption during the early 1980s. These changes may be reversed with the overthrow of the government whose policies caused them. A renewed increase seems likely (Moskalewicz & Swiatkiewicz, 1992).

Although the findings on overall per capita alcohol consumption and on cirrhosis of the liver are consistent in showing a major rise in most European countries since the Second World War (with the exception of the few countries with the highest initial levels), the evidence on the extent to which the increase applies to young people is less satisfactory. There is uncertainty as to whether the current trend constitutes a plateau or a slow decline in use, as suggested by surveys with young people.

British survey data (Duffy, 1991) covering annual assessments for 16 years since 1979, show stable rates of daily and weekly drinking for 15 to 19-year-old females. Among males of the same age, the percentages of daily drinkers declined slightly, as did the percentage of abstainers. Rates of heavy drinking (equivalent to 25 pints of beer per week for males) in other British studies (noted by May, 1992) ranged from 2 per cent to 7 per cent for adolescent males and half that for females. Although truly comparable data over time are not available, there is no indication of any substantial increase or decrease in the proportion of young people with alcohol problems during the past decade or so.

Yearly surveys of military conscripts in Sweden (Swedish Council for Information on Alcohol and Other Drugs, 1991) showed a decline between 1976 and 1985 in the proportion getting intoxicated. However, the decline among both high school students and military conscripts levelled off during the mid-1980s, and a slight new increase seems to have taken place.

The American 'Monitoring The Future' surveys (Johnston et al., 1991) are much quoted as indicating a slight fall in alcohol use among young people over recent years, but the data are of limited value as an index of alcohol problems. The rate of heavy drinking (defined as five or more drinks in a row at least once in the previous two weeks) is so very high (41 per cent in 1983 and 32 per cent in 1990) that the vast majority of 'heavy' drinkers must be problem-free, although there were no measures of alcohol problems. Further, the 15 to 20 per cent of high school drop-outs were omitted from the surveys, and this is probably the group that accounts for much of problem drinking in youths.

TRENDS IN DRUG MISUSE

American data first provided evidence of the massive increase in illicit use of drugs between the 1950s and 1970s. This was evident from the 1977 National Survey on Drug Abuse which involved interviews with 4,594 respondents aged 12 years or more (Parry, 1979). Figure 10.5 shows the finding that in 1977 the lifetime rate of drug use was very low in people born before 1940; was much higher in those born 1940-1949; and higher still in those born during the 1950s. The ECA data (Anthony & Helzer, 1991), gathered during the early 1980s, were closely similar, with the lifetime prevalence of illicit drug use ranging from 65 per cent in 18 to 29-year-old men, through to 44 per cent in 30 to 44-year-olds and 9 per cent in 45 to 64-year-olds to 3 per cent in those over 65. The comparable figures for females were 55 per cent, 28 per cent, 6 per cent and 1 per cent. The overall rates for drug abuse or dependency were much lower, but the age differences suggesting important trends over time were the same (the pooled figures for both sexes being 13.5 per cent, 6.7 per cent, 0.8 per cent and 0.11 per cent respectively for the same age groups).

The repeated surveys of the older adolescents and young adults in the USA (Johnston et al., 1991) indicated something of a decline in drug use in the 1980s (apart from cocaine use, which continued to increase until the late 1980s). However the data still showed a very high level of use; in the most recent survey over 60 per cent had tried some illicit drug other than (usually in

Figure 10.5   Lifetime experience with marijuana/hashish and stronger drugs* for selected birth cohorts**

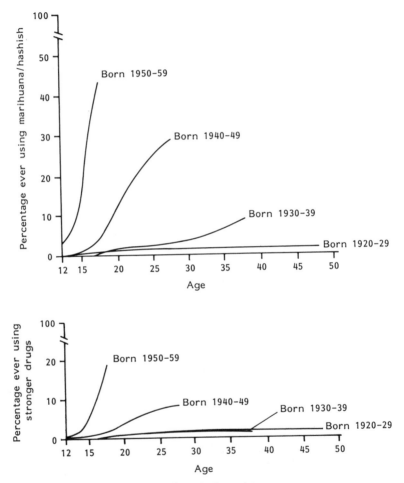

* Includes cocaine, hallucinogens, heroin and other opiates.

** Based on reconstructed data.

Source: Abelson et al. (1977).

addition to) marijuana and even among high school seniors the rate was 29 per cent. Moreover, by age 27, 40 per cent had tried cocaine and 5 per cent of young adults had used the particularly dangerous form of cocaine called 'crack'. The figures do not, however, provide much of an indication of serious and persisting drug problems. It should be remembered, too, that surveys tend to underestimate drug use when they are carried out in schools, because the more serious users truant more and more often leave school early. Nevertheless, data from drug shipment seizures, mortality statistics, and clinic attendance all confirm that the rise in occasional or regular recreational drug use was closely paralleled by a similar marked increase in substance abuse and dependency.

Although European countries lack both the retrospective lifetime prevalence data and the repeated epidemiological surveys available in the USA, it is clear that they have experienced a comparable (although slightly later) increase in both drug use and abuse (Klingemann, 1992; Institute for the Study of Drug Dependence, 1993; Plant & Plant, 1992). As in the USA, cannabis is much the commonest drug used but, in the UK, surveys suggest that amphetamines, hallucinogens, solvents and MDMA have all probably been used by some 5 to 10 per cent of young adults. By sharp contrast, less than 1 per cent have used heroin or cocaine (rates well below American figures). Both drug shipment seizure figures and the number of notified addicts in the UK suggest that there is likely to have been a modest increase in the use of cocaine and 'crack', but there is no evidence as yet of the epidemic that took place in the USA and which it was feared would take place in the UK (Mott, 1992).

European surveys of school age samples in the late 1980s (Klingemann, 1992) tended to show a slight decline in drug use, particularly with respect to cannabis. However, this decline did not occur in all countries. A recent report from the Netherlands is of particular interest because the questionnaire format and samples were comparable to Monitoring the Future (Plomp et al., 1991). Lifetime alcohol consumption was as high as in the US, but the use of most illicit drugs was much lower. Only heroin appeared to be used as frequently in Holland as in the USA. In contrast to the slightly declining trend of alcohol and drug use in the USA, however, Dutch high school seniors showed a slight increase in alcohol and cannabis use between 1984 and 1988. Surveys in Sweden among ninth-grade school students and military conscripts, however, showed a steep decline in lifetime prevalence from the beginning of the 1970s to the end of the 1980s (Swedish Council for Information on Alcohol and Other

Drugs, 1991). Since then, the level has remained stable. Monthly prevalences showed a similar trend.

Surveys are not very helpful in assessing trends in hard drug use (heroin, cocaine, etc.) because of the low rate at which these substances are used by high school students. We therefore use statistics on number of registered addicts, drug-related arrests, drug-related deaths, and amount of drugs seized by the police. Due to differences in the sources and assessment criteria, these data cannot be compared across countries. However, trends within countries should be reliable if policies and assessment criteria are stable.

Figure 10.6   Drug cases, seizures and legal offences

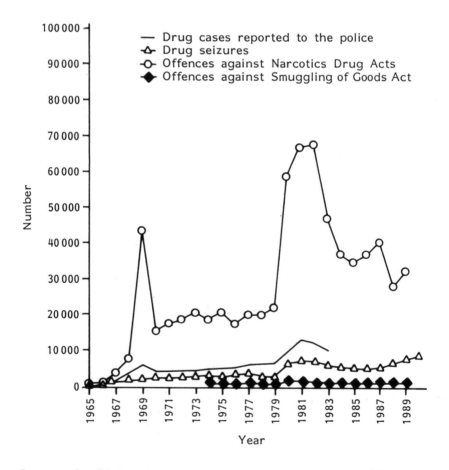

Source: Swedish Council for Information on Alcohol and other Drugs (1991).

Overall, official data support the picture of stability or slight decline in youthful drug use in many Western European countries, but data from Sweden illustrate the problem (Figure 10.6). Cases reported by police and drug seizures increased dramatically in the late 1960s and again at the end of the 1970s. The pronounced peaks shown in the figure, particularly for the number of offences against the law, reflect changes in law enforcement but not necessarily changes in use (Swedish Council for Information on Alcohol and other Drugs, 1991).

Figure 10.7   Drug addicts notified to the Home Office during the year and/or in treatment with notifiable drugs: England and Wales

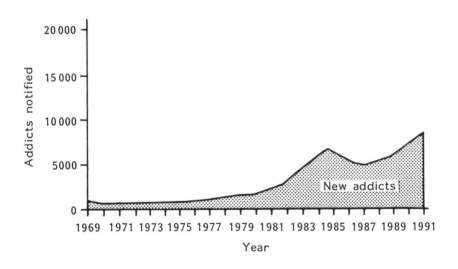

Source: Institute for the Study of Drug Dependence (1993).

The surveys of high school students asked age at first use of drugs. This age appeared to drop over time. It has been thought that this would cause a similar drop in the age of addicts. But, in fact, the opposite may have occurred. As reported by Hanel (1991), the trend has been toward addicts becoming older, with the mean age now between 25 and 30. It is not clear whether this ageing occurs because of a delay in the age of onset or is attributable to the large size of the 'baby boom' generation, whose addicts are now ageing, and pull the mean age higher.

With regard to the Norwegian situation in the early 1980s, Hauge (1985) showed that the shift in age groups is not due to older subjects beginning to use drugs. Rather, the mean age increased as new recruitment among teenagers leveled off, while users from earlier generations continued to use drugs. Klingemann (1992) noted that an increase in average age was reported by almost all European countries.

According to Interpol statistics (Bundeskriminalamt, 1992), various Western European countries – West Germany, Italy and Switzerland in particular – showed increases in deaths attributed to the consumption of hard drugs. Although the national data are not directly comparable due to differences in the assessment criteria, the similarity in within-country trends reveals a common pattern. In all eight countries for which complete information is available since 1980, the figures increased across the late eighties. The most recent changes show a remarkable increase in a single year. It would be important to know whether these changes could be due to changed criteria, for example a shift from main cause to contributory role as the criterion for assigning the cause of death to drugs. A first step would be to look for signs of reallocation of causes by finding corresponding declines in plausible alternative attributions, such as 'cause unknown'. The age distribution among victims of drug-related deaths showed a shift towards higher age groups, similar to the general trend (Klingemann, 1992).

British data similarly indicate that the rate of new opiate/cocaine addicts (as judged by official notifications) in 1991 is still at the same high level as in 1985, following a dip in 1986-1988, both being far higher than the comparable figures for the 1970s (see Figure 10.7). A more detailed breakdown by age shows that the main increase is among young adults, the rate being highest in 21 to 24-year-olds (see Figure 10.8). As already noted, however, the predominant drug usage among young people does not involve either opiates or cocaine. Rather, after cannabis, young people tend to use amphetamines, MDMA and nitrates as part of a dance and party culture. Surveys of young adults have also shown relatively high rates of LSD usage, with figures of 4 per cent to 10 per cent in surveys between 1985 and 1992 (Institute for the Study of Drug Dependence, 1993), with drug seizure figures also attesting to increased usage. Solvents stand out with respect to their predominant use by young teenagers rather than by older adolescents and young adults. Although there are uncertainties over the comparability of samples in most surveys that have been repeated over time, the British national surveys by Gallup in 1989 and 1992 showed a doubling in the proportion of 15 to 24-year-olds admitting drug use (15 per cent to 29 per cent), with particularly marked rises in the use of MDMA and LSD. These survey increases are consistent with the doubling of the mortality figures attributed to solvents between 1983 and 1990.

Figure 10.8   New addicts notified per million of the population of the same age: England and Wales

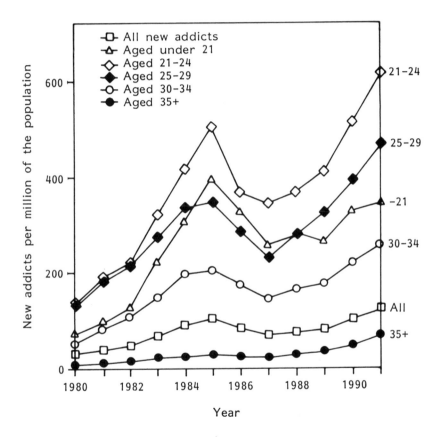

Source: Institute for the Study of Drug Dependence (1993).

Drug use has not received much attention in the past in most Eastern European countries. The substances used reflect the difficulties in importing caused by non-convertible currencies. Prior to the recent social and political changes, drug markets mainly provided supplies of opiates from domestic production (poppy straw) and chemical processing. In Poland, drug abuse was reported to spread rapidly during the early 1980s, but presumably declined since then (Moskalewicz & Swiatkiewicz, 1992). The death toll of about 100 per year is relatively small compared to the ten and more times higher figures in Germany, a country with only twice the population of Poland.

The problem seems to be even smaller in other Central and Eastern European countries. However, since the late 1980s an upward trend has been observed in terms of registered or treated cases of substance abuse. More importantly, in contrast to Western Europe, the age at onset seems to be decreasing, and the vast majority of known users are young adults (Jablensky, 1992).

While almost all males and females in Europe drink alcohol, males drink more and many more have alcohol problems. The gender gap also exists for illicit drugs, but is less pronounced, although perhaps it is greater in Europe than in the USA (Plomp et al., 1991). According to Hanel (1991), the male/female ratio of drug addicts is 3 or 4 to 1 across countries. Klingemann (1992) estimated a lower ratio (2:1). In some countries, however, the ratio is very large (19:1 in Turkey).

ETHNIC AND CULTURAL VARIATIONS

Substance use varies greatly by ethnicity, although the patterns are not the same in all countries. A general finding of general population studies in the United States and Canada is a higher prevalence of alcohol use among whites and Hispanics than among black and Asian high school students and young adults. Asians usually show the lowest figures of all (Newcomb & Bentler, 1986; Adlaf et al., 1989). However, it has also been found that the lifetime rate of alcoholism in elderly blacks exceeds that in elderly whites (although whites aged 65+ still have a higher rate of *current* drinking problems than blacks of the same age: Helzer et al., 1991). Illicit drug use data showed a somewhat similar pattern with respect to white-black differences; the rate in white males exceeded that in blacks in younger age groups but not in older men. In women, white rates were higher at all ages (Anthony & Helzer, 1991). Rates of illicit drug use in Hispanics were lower than those in whites in both sexes and in all age groups. Nevertheless, blacks and Hispanics are more likely than whites to be arrested for substance-related crimes and more likely to appear in treatment settings. The explanation for the difference between survey findings and official statistics is not clear. It could result from racially-biased police practices; or from the greater rate of arrests for non-drug crimes (so bringing drug-taking to notice); or because blacks and Hispanics play a greater role in drug dealing; or because they use heroin more than whites (and other drugs less often), heroin being more often a target of police interest.

Among 9 to 15-year-olds in England, the rates of alcohol use appear similar in whites and blacks: for instance, 65 per cent of white and 71 per cent of Afro-Caribbean adolescents ever tried alcohol in one survey. Among those of Asian background, however, lifetime prevalence was only 19 per cent (Health Education Authority, 1992).

Alcohol use is integrated into culture and life in the European countries. Nevertheless, there is substantial variation among the European nations in patterns of drinking, attitudes toward alcohol, social consequences, and health outcomes.

The European Omnibus Survey (Commission of the European Communities, 1991) assessed about 9,000 young people aged 11 to 15, living in twelve EC countries. Overall, 13 per cent reported heavy drinking (five or more drinks in a row in the past two weeks). The prevalence of heavy drinking varied between 7 per cent in France and 27 per cent in Denmark, a fourfold difference.

Moderate, socially-integrated drinking has been found to be characteristic among some ethnic/cultural groups, including the Greeks, the Jews, the Italians, and the Chinese. In these cultures, parents introduce the child to drinking in the family setting, and model acceptable amounts of drink and proper behaviour when drinking. Descriptions of ethnic groups that teach children how to drink and largely avoid alcohol problems began in the 1940s (Bales, 1946) and have continued since (Peele, 1984; Greeley et al., 1980; Vaillant, 1983). They are contrasted with groups such as the Irish, where drinking is done for individualistic reasons as part of a 'bachelor group ethic of hard drinking' (Stivers, 1985). As immigrant populations become acculturated, they accept local drinking patterns (Silbereisen et al., 1989). Their drinking may also increase because of strains in cultural adaptation itself (Cheung, 1991). However, according to Calahan & Room (1974), the customs and values of one's place of upbringing influence drinking patterns in adult life. Thus, for example, Feldman and Rosenthal (1990) found that, although Chinese immigrants in the United States quickly adopted American customs in behaviours such as TV watching, patterns of alcohol consumption in the children tended to follow Chinese norms.

Less is known about ethnic differences in illicit drug use. One would expect it to be peer-influenced rather than family-influenced because adolescents are only now beginning to have parents who were themselves exposed to the drug epidemic in adolescents or young adults. There are ethnic differences in choice of substances, at least in the USA: Mexican youngsters, for example, use inhalants more than US youngsters, and African Americans use heroin more and LSD less than their white contemporaries.

The Situation in Germany

German unification can be seen as a huge natural experiment. East and West Germany, before unification, had developed different beverage preferences (much less wine, more hard liquor in the East: Smart, 1989) and different patterns of use of illicit drugs.

Figure 10.9 shows comparative data for alcohol consumption in East and West Germany. Since the 1960s, per capita alcohol consumption steadily increased among the East German population, from about 4 litres of pure alcohol to almost 12 in 1990. In West Germany a similar increase took place from about 8 to about 12 litres in the mid-1970s. Since then a slight decrease could be observed in overall consumption. The effect of the open markets following unification is revealed in the twofold increase in wine consumption among East Germans from 1989 to 1990. However, they did not follow the West German trend away from the use of spirits, a trend that began about 1980 (Produktschaap voor Gedistilleerde Dranken, 1992: 52-55). Other data sources give slightly different figures; nevertheless, the pattern of trends is almost identical (Brewer's Society, 1992).

In West Germany, the Institut für Jugendforschung (1990) conducted repeated surveys with about 3,000 young people aged 12 to 25 from 1973 to 1990. The weekly alcohol consumption declined remarkably until 1986, after which it stabilized. In 1990, during the week preceding interview, 40 per cent had consumed beer, 15 per cent wine, and 6 per cent hard liquor. Gender differences were sizeable; among the 18 to 20-year-olds, about 60 per cent of the males but 20 per cent of the females had consumed beer in the past week. Although about one third believed alcohol had positive effects on sociability, most young people shared a rather sceptical attitude towards the benefits of alcohol.

Figure 10.9 Change in alcohol consumption in (a) East Germany and (b) West Germany

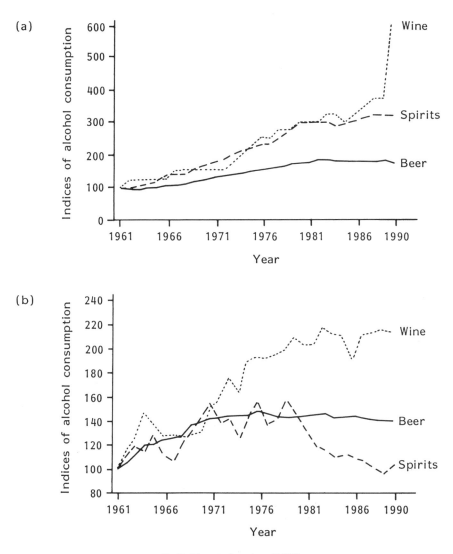

Source: Produktschaap voor Gedistilleerde Dranken (1992).

Simon et al. (1991) compared large samples of 12 to 39-year-olds (about 20,000 in all) from West and East Germany. They found a striking difference between the two parts of the country. In the East, about 14 per cent consumed beer daily compared to 8 per cent in the West; comparable figures for the 12 to 24-year-olds were 11 per cent and 4 per cent. Males drank much more than females, especially in the West. In the East twice as many males as females (19 per cent vs. 10 per cent) consumed beer daily; comparable figures for the West were 12 per cent of the males vs. 2 per cent of the females, a 6 to 1 ratio.

Those in the East were more favourably disposed towards alcohol. Whereas 20 per cent of the Eastern subjects agreed with the statement 'a party without beer is boring', only 10 per cent of the Western sample did so; the figures for 'it is necessary to have alcohol at home to cater for unexpected guests' were 35 per cent and 16 per cent respectively for East and West. Some years ago the attitudes in the West would have been similarly positive towards alcohol. The two parts of Germany did not differ in their negative evaluation of alcoholism.

A comparison of young people (ages 12 to 24) in East and West Berlin, conducted as part of the study reported by Simon et al. (1991), found virtually no differences in young people's regular drinking. This may well foreshadow increasing similarity in drinking patterns following unification. As with other survey data restricted to consumption, the findings shed little light on possible differences in alcohol abuse or dependence.

The two parts of the country also differed in their experience with illegal drugs. In 1990 the lifetime prevalence among 12 to 39-year-olds was about 16 per cent in the West, but only 2 per cent in the East. In East Berlin, however, only six months after unification much higher percentages were observed among young adults (Epidemiologische Forschung Berlin, 1991).

The stabilization or decline in the consumption of illegal drugs among high school students reported for the USA and some European countries was observed in West Germany as well. Reuband (1988) reported the results of secondary analyses on data gathered in the years 1972, 1981, and 1987 among high school students. In Figure 10.10, trends in lifetime prevalence for illegal drugs (including retrospective assessments) are shown for 15 to 18-year-olds. As can be seen, the peaks in drug use (mainly hashish) were in the early 1970s. Since then, the prevalence rates have declined remarkably.

According to the Institut für Jugendforschung (1990), only 5 per cent of young people aged 12 to 25 reported current use of any illegal drugs (mainly hashish) in 1990, less than half the figure at the beginning of the 1980s. The changes in attitudes were no less impressive. Whereas at the end of the seventies one in two young people shared a liberal-permissive attitude towards drugs, by the end of the eighties the figure had decreased to one in three.

Figure 10.10 Trends in lifetime prevalence of illegal drug use: high school students in West Germany

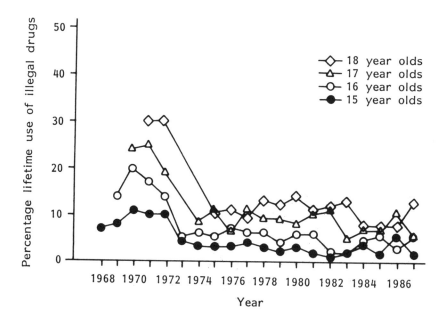

Source: Reuband (1988).

However, such survey data do not represent trends among the users of hard drugs. As depicted in Figure 10.11, after a gradual decline of 'registered consumers' ('Erstkonsumenten' – persons police registered the first time, irrespective of when they actually began consuming), during the early 1980s the figures increased again and reached an all-time high in 1991 (Bundeskriminalamt, 1992).

According to the most recent report (Bundeskriminalamt, 1992) 2,125 people died in 1991 from ingesting illegal drugs (1992: 2029, Tagesspiegel, 5.1.1993), making Germany with 2.4 deaths per 100,000 second only to Switzerland in Europe. The increase is dramatic: from 106 in 1973 the number of deaths climbed to 623 in 1979, declined gradually to 324 in 1985, and then increased anew year by year to the current figure, the highest ever. Females' share in these deaths decreased during the last few years, amounting to only 15 per cent of the total in 1991. The drug chiefly responsible for these deaths was previously heroin; cocaine and amphetamines are now gaining in importance.

Figure 10.11 Police-registered 'new' cases of users of hard drugs: West Germany, 1975-1991

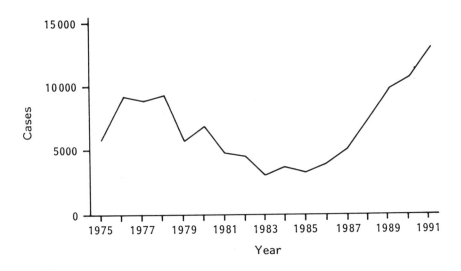

Source: Bundeskriminalamt (1992).

The contrast in findings from surveys and from other data sources underlines the point made earlier that data on use in general population surveys are not a good indicator of levels of abuse.

INDIVIDUAL-LEVEL EXPLANATIONS OF JUVENILE SUBSTANCE USE AND ABUSE

Age Trends

According to the European Omnibus Survey, 25 per cent of respondents aged 11 to 15 had their first drink (more than a drop in the bottom of a glass) before the age of 11. The smallest number of very young who drank was found in the Netherlands and Ireland (10 per cent) while 30 per cent or more drank in Denmark, Greece, Italy and the UK (Commission of the European Communities, 1991).

The frequency of drinking and the quantity of drinking per typical occasion vary across the life span. Adolescence and early adulthood represent periods of pronounced change. Utilizing data from more than 20 longitudinal studies from various European countries and from North America, Fillmore et al. (1991a) found a steep increase in drinking frequency during adolescence, followed by a comparably sharp decline in early adulthood. As the changes in both variables were much less in later phases of the life span, it appears that the maximum drinking level is typically established by young adulthood.

Although individual patterns of drinking that develop in the teenage years may influence later drinking behaviour in important ways, continuities in alcohol consumption between adolescence and adult life are only modest (Ghodsian & Power, 1987; Bagnall, 1991). Continuities may be particularly weak when heavy drinking in adolescence arises through circumstances, such as unusually early puberty, which become less relevant with increasing age (Stattin & Magnusson, 1990). This modest continuity in levels of alcohol consumption does not, of course, contradict the finding that early conduct disturbance is a predisposing factor for later alcoholism and drug abuse.

Changes in substance use over time may occur because changes are occurring in public attitudes toward use of substances, in availability of substances, in changes in mode of administration that may alter risks of transition from one stage to another, in opportunities for treatment, in vigour of law enforcement or in the demographic make-up of the society. These are the obvious immediate components of changes in a society's practices with regard to substance use.

For example, the post-Second World War 'baby boom' may help to explain the enormous increase in drug use during the 1970s, when the 'boom' generation was in the age bracket in which substance use typically begins. Not only were adolescents and young adults a larger proportion of the total population, but at that time there was no parallel increase in occupational opportunity. With a decline in job opportunities, there was postponement of marriage, which prolonged the period in which young people associated principally with their own age group. This set of social conditions tended to create a distinct 'youth culture', enhanced by the improvement in contraceptive methods, which allowed the postponement of parenthood. There have also been increases in access to the media, both of which enhance the speed at which social changes can spread (see Chapter 7). There have been changes in family and social structure (see Chapter 5) in terms of the proportion of one-parent families and of working mothers, which have reduced opportunities for parents to monitor teenagers' activities. An increase in marriages across cultures and religions, along with a decrease in religiosity, has reduced the influence of views of parents and older relatives, and thus presumably reduced the ability of the older generation to forbid or limit young people's substance use effectively.

The effect of these social changes on substance use are indirect as well as direct. They may foster in adolescents a general disrespect for adult authority and the law and, a lack of ability to visualize a future in which they will have career opportunities that could be jeopardized by substance use and its legal consequences. To understand secular trends in substance abuse in depth, it would be necessary to be able to chart these changes in the social structure that affect them. Such a charting presents its own problems in measurement.

It should be added that a robust research finding has been that early use of substances is associated with a worse outcome in terms of both likelihood of dependence and its persistence (Robins, 1992). It is not known whether this represents a direct biological effect (i.e. an effect of drugs on the immature nervous system) or rather an indirect reflection of people who are at higher risk (for whatever reason) being more likely to have an early onset.

Sex Differences

As already noted, boys use more of all substances (drugs and alcohol), with the sole exception of tobacco, and use them more heavily than girls (see Plant & Plant, 1992; Robins, 1992). The largest sex difference is in heavy drinking, where boys exceed girls by 5 to 1 or more, and least for marijuana use. Sex differences in the USA are particularly large among Hispanics (and are least among blacks). For most substances used by adolescents, there has been a trend towards convergence of female and male rates over the last two decades.

Socio-economic Status

There are few differences overall in use or abuse of substances by social class (Hawkins et al., 1992; Plant & Plant, 1992; Robins, 1992). Of course, different social subgroups have characteristic 'fashions' in drug usage, and it may be that abuse of opiates is particularly frequent among the socially disadvantaged. Nevertheless, drug problems are prevalent in all segments of society extending from the very poor to the extremely affluent.

Individual Characteristics

Numerous studies have shown that conduct problems are predictive of all forms of substance use and abuse (Berman & Noble, 1993; Robins & McEvoy, 1990; Robins, 1992). Not only do they predict use but they are associated with earlier use, heavier use, more frequent associated problems and a lesser tendency to remit. Poor school achievement, truancy and school drop-out are also highly associated with substance use. Precocious sexual activity is accompanied by a higher risk of use, and shyness with a lower risk.

Family Characteristics

Children who drink and use illicit drugs are more likely to have parents who drink heavily (Hawkins et al., 1992; Robins, 1992). The intergenerational transmission is especially strong with respect to serious drinking problems in the offspring. Offspring of alcoholics are approximately five times more likely to develop alcohol-related problems than offspring of non-alcoholics (Pickens et al., 1991). Substance abuse (alcohol and other drugs) is also more frequent in young people from families characterized by discord, erratic discipline and poor supervision.

Genetic findings (although somewhat contradictory) indicate that these features reflect both genetic and environmental transmission (Hodgkinson et al., 1991; Crabbe & Belknap, 1992; Goedde & Agarwal, 1989; Cloninger & Begleiter, 1990; Pickens et al., 1991). For example, in Pickens et al.'s (1991) study of clinic attenders, the heritability of alcohol abuse in males was 38 per cent and it was 31 per cent for the abuse of other substances. However, the heritability of alcoholic dependence in males was somewhat greater (60 per cent). The genetic component in females was lower in all cases. To date, it is not known how the genetic factors operate. However, it is quite likely that they include individual differences in response to alcohol and to other substances. Thus, many Asians show an unpleasant flushing response to alcohol, which appears to serve a protective function against alcohol abuse. It may be that, in other racial groups too, individual differences in the likelihood of experiencing negative side effects of alcohol may play a role. Differences in the rapidity with which tolerance develops, or efficiency with which substances are metabolized, constitute alternative modes of operation for genetic factors. Also, of course, at least some of the genetic influences may apply to behaviours, such as risk-taking, that predispose to drug-taking, rather than to the biological response to particular substances.

Other Risk Factors

In addition to these individual characteristics as risk factors for alcohol and drug use, the most important factors have been found to be attitudes towards substances, beliefs about one's peers use of them, religiosity, and attachment to school and conventional values with respect to academic and career achievement (Berman & Noble, 1993; Hawkins et al., 1992; Robins, 1992). At the beginning of the drug epidemic, political radicalism was also an important factor, but its importance has waned.

Although rare compared to the factors cited above, psychiatric disorder also appears to increase the affinity for substance abuse. Young manics and schizophrenics have particularly high rates of use.

These risk factors contribute more to understanding who will use drugs and alcohol heavily than to understanding shifts in overall levels of use in a society. However, to the extent that the importance of religion declines and the opportunities for occupational achievement by young people decrease in society as a whole, or in certain portions of that society, one can expect an increase in use of substances. Similarly, if the quality of parenting deteriorates, perhaps because both parents work long hours away from home or travel because of their work, or bear children in adolescence, one would expect the attachment to parents to be weaker, and thus the likelihood of substance use and abuse greater.

SOCIETY-WIDE INFLUENCES ON SUBSTANCE USE AND ABUSE

Because the abuse of alcohol and other drugs requires the availability of these substances, there has long been an interest in factors that influence the overall level of substance use in communities. Most research in this field has focused on alcohol consumption, with attention to features such as licensing, pricing, affluence, and minimum drinking age laws. The public health importance of research findings on this topic is underlined by the consistent evidence from correlations over time that the medical and social ill-effects of alcohol tend to increase and decrease in line with changes in overall levels of consumption (Royal College of Psychiatrists, 1986; Kendell, 1979; Mann & Anglin, 1988; World Health Organization, 1992). For example, Knibbe et al. (1985) related the 300 per cent increase in per capita consumption of alcohol in the

Netherlands between 1958 and 1981 to the proportion of heavy drinkers in the population (defined as drinking more than 22 glasses per week). As shown in Figure 10.12, the association between the two was very strong. Other data indicated that this, in turn, was accompanied by a parallel increase in cirrhosis of the liver.

With these well-demonstrated associations as a background, we need to turn to the evidence, first, on the consequences of planned changes designed to affect alcohol consumption and, second, on the effects on alcohol consumption of naturally occurring changes in the economy and in social conditions more generally. An example of the effects of an alteration in licensing laws is provided by the change in 1978 of the state law in North Carolina (USA) allowing liquor to be sold by the drink (as well as by the bottle) for the first time since Prohibition. A natural experiment arose because individual counties were given the option of allowing or not allowing sales of liquor-by-the-drink (LBD). Some took up the option and others did not, moreover those who did varied in their date of implementation. Holder and Blose (1987) used time-series analyses over the 1973 to 1982 time period, controlling for overall time trends, to determine whether the introduction of LBD affected overall alcohol consumption. The results showed that liberalization of the state law in 1978/79 resulted in a slight immediate increase of retail sales (about 7 per cent) in the counties allowing LBD and that increase persisted throughout the remaining four years. Thus the increase in availability led to an abrupt and lasting change.

This study necessarily relied on aggregate data and could not, therefore, examine possible differential effects in occasional versus heavy drinkers. Kendell et al. (1983), by contrast, were able to examine individual trends in alcohol consumption following an abrupt increase in the excise duty on alcoholic beverages in Scotland in 1981, a time that coincided with a general economic recession. The opportunity arose because a large general population survey of drinking habits had been undertaken in 1978/79; the same group was re-interviewed in 1981/82. Among those who had been heavy drinkers in 1978/1979, total alcohol consumption fell by 18 per cent, and associated adverse effects on health by 16 per cent. The reduction in alcohol consumption was even greater among the men who lost their jobs during the same period. Conversely, those in the top third of the income distribution did not show any reduction in alcohol consumption. The findings are important in showing that a marked and sudden economic change does have a real effect on problem drinkers. Lesser changes, or changes that are sufficiently gradual to allow adaptation, or changes in more favourable economic conditions are unlikely to make much difference. Also, the longer term sequelae are not known. It is possible that, in time, heavy drinkers might reallocate their spending to enable them to return to their previous level of consumption.

Figure 10.12 Relation between consumption per week and percentage drinking more than 22 glasses per week: the Netherlands,1958, 1970, 1981

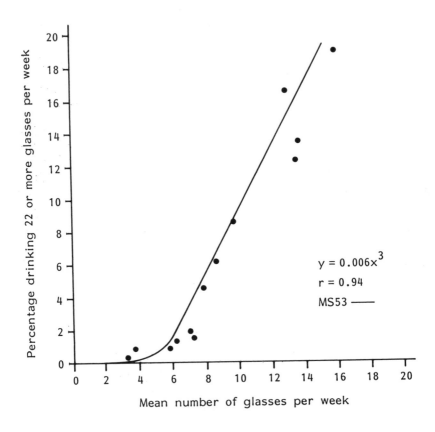

The findings relate to 18 subpopulations of men and women of protestant, Roman Catholic, or no religious denomination.

Source: Knibbe et al. (1985).

Less is known about the effects of advertising but such evidence as is available suggests that it does have some impact, although not a great one. According to Godfrey (1989), a 10 per cent reduction in advertising a particular alcoholic beverage in the UK would reduce its consumption by no more than 3 per cent. The existing data on advertising, however, do not allow an estimate of the effects of major policy changes, such as the banning of advertising or its rapid increase as occurred recently in East Germany and parts of Eastern Europe.

An interest in the effects of raising or lowering the minimum drinking age has been particularly strong in North America (Vingilis & De Genova, 1984). The research findings are informative but are limited by their reliance chiefly on alcohol-related traffic accidents. That is an important limitation because arrests for driving while intoxicated (DWI) are strongly influenced by cultural norms and police practice. Thus, Linsky et al. (1986), using aggregate data across the United States, showed that states with a prohibitive approach to alcohol (as indexed by sales restriction, religious views, and alcohol-free districts) had a low rate of both alcohol consumption and cirrhosis of the liver but a high rate of DWI arrests! Be that as it may, although the findings are not entirely consistent, raising the minimum drinking age has tended to reduce both consumption and alcohol-related accidents, whereas lowering the age has had the reverse effect.

Between 1970 and 1975, all provinces of Canada and 21 states of the USA reduced the drinking age; between 1976 and 1987, however, the pendulum swung back and 26 states raised their drinking age (Smart & Goodstadt, 1977; Vingilis & De Genova, 1984). Whereas the first wave of changes reflected the growing role of young adults in the society and was part of a trend towards defining the age of majority at 18, the second wave was dominated by a concern about drunk driving and traffic accidents.

The reductions of the drinking age in the early 1970s, was accompanied by substantial increases in youthful drinking, particularly in on-premise consumption. There was a greater increase in alcohol-related car accidents in areas where the legal age was lowered compared to other areas (Smart & Goodstadt, 1977). However, all these early studies were limited by their focus on very short-term effects.

When Douglass and Freeman (1977) compared two five-year periods, 1968-1973 before the new Michigan law raising the drinking age was introduced, and 1974-1977 after it was in place, the earlier-reported increases in traffic accidents proved to be part of a secular trend. Although the young drank less after the change in the law, alcohol-related accidents continued to increase.

Wagenaar and Maybee (1986) investigated change in single vehicle night-time crashes (seen as indicative of intoxicated drivers) after the drinking age was raised. Depending on the seriousness of the crash and the age group studied, the rates were reduced between 8 per cent and 15 per cent among those 18 and under. The results held up after controlling for changes in economic prosperity.

O'Malley and Wagenaar (1991) were able to demonstrate the effect of an increase in the legal drinking age from age 18 to 19, 20, or 21 years, utilizing data of their Monitoring the Future study. There was an average decrease in drinking of about one tenth of a standard deviation associated with raising the minimum drinking age. This effect seemed broadly comparable in subgroups varying by gender, race, religious commitments, and college plans. In order to better understand the mediating links, a number of other behaviours and attitudes were analysed. Most impressive was a reduction of about one third in the frequency of bar or tavern visits. There were also lower consumption levels and a decrease in fatal automobile crashes among drivers under 21 years of age.

Because an increase in the minimum drinking age would further remove teenagers from the legal age of purchase, proponents of higher drinking ages hoped to have an effect on the drinking of younger age groups as well. Comparing samples from states with (Massachusetts with a rise from 18 to 21) and without (New York State) changes in the law, Smith et al. (1984) found almost no effect on the amount and frequency of drinking. There were slightly fewer self-reported accidents and non-fatal crashes in Massachusetts. There, drinking at parties replaced drinking at bars and, unable to buy alcohol themselves, youngsters often asked others to purchase alcohol for them. Similarly, Mooney et al. (1992) compared Louisiana (where the minimum age was 18) and North Carolina (where it was 21). Questionnaires answered by college students showed that the higher legal drinking age was associated with a slightly lower alcohol consumption rate in *controlled* situations but a higher rate in *uncontrolled* situations. Also, in North Carolina, there was a lively trade in counterfeit age identification documents and a practice of drinking at home before going out.

On the whole, increases and decreases in the minimum age seem to be followed by parallel changes in consumption levels and traffic accidents, but the effects are not entirely consistent and seem to depend on community acceptance. According to a recent review of international policies on alcohol-impaired driving by Peacock (1992), a combination of random breath-testing, a high level of public awareness and support and measures to reduce overall alcohol consumption (through taxation or restrictions on the availability of alcohol) are the most promising, provided the policies fit the cultural context. This last qualification may well be important (see Mooney et al., 1992, above). Prohibition in the United States did not have the desired effect because it was not generally accepted as appropriate. Steps to limit the availability of alcohol to young adults may be more acceptable (and therefore effective) than legislation to outlaw their use of alcohol altogether.

One of the very few examples of an analysis of the effects of rapid social change in a restricted geographical area is provided by Caetano et al.'s (1983) study of the effects of the development of the oil industry in the Shetland Islands (Scotland). They compared changes in the frequency and quantity of alcohol consumption between 1975 and 1978, in an area directly affected by the industrialization and in a more remote comparison area. The development of the oil industry resulted in a remarkable increase in per capita income (from a bottom position to higher than the rest of the UK) and also in the number of alcohol outlets. Per capita consumption increased in both areas particularly among those younger than 30. However, this increase was about twice as great in the oil production area.

As Voorhees et al. (1989) noted, the Shetland Health Study cannot definitively answer questions concerning the mechanisms that brought about the increase in young men's drinking frequency. The unprecedented amount of disposable income probably led to the increased drinking of those already prone to alcohol consumption, but another factor may have been distress associated with industrialization. However, the finding that young men showed no increase in emotional symptomatology makes that a less likely explanation.

There are rather more studies of the associations between changes over time in economic prosperity and changes in alcohol consumption. Numerous methodological issues require attention in such time-series analyses (Godfrey, 1989; Plant et al., 1988). However, it has been a reasonably consistent finding that as unemployment goes down and disposable incomes go up, alcohol consumption increases. The reverse also applies. For example, Iversen and Klausen (1986) studied the effects of making Danish shipyard workers redundant following plant closure. Over the subsequent two years, unemployed workers were more likely than those in jobs to reduce their alcohol consumption. It was concluded that the loss of income was more influential than the stress of unemployment.

In the UK population as a whole over the time period 1970 to 1984, Plant et al. (1988) found a 0.64 differential correlation between per capita alcohol consumption and per capita disposable income. Hammer (1992), in a four-year prospective questionnaire survey of 17 to 20-year-olds in Norway, found that unemployed men had a higher than average alcohol consumption rate, but that heavy drinkers tended to drink somewhat less when out of work. By contrast, unemployment tended to lead to a slight increase in cannabis use. Plant et al. (1985; Peck & Plant, 1986) found much the same in Scotland. It was concluded that similar risk factors led to both unemployment and heavy drinking, that the loss of income constrained heavy drinking, but that unemployment possibly leads to an increased marginalization of young cannabis users and thus to an increased use of cannabis. If these inferences are correct, it would seem to follow that the effects of unemployment may differ according to economic and social conditions.

The finding that the loss of income consequent upon unemployment may constrain heavy drinking more than the stress of job loss instigates it, does not mean that stress is irrelevant to alcoholism. Cross-sectional comparisons of aggregate data by individual states in the USA showed significant associations between indices of stress (such as rates of business failure, divorce, welfare recipience and high school drop-out) and indices of alcoholism. However, such ecological correlations provide an extremely fallible guide to causal mechanisms (see Chapter 2) and the indices of stress reflect such a complex mixture of circumstances that it is bound to be unclear what is affecting what (even if causation could be inferred). Nevertheless, longitudinal data confirm that in school-leavers, failure to obtain work is associated with an increase in psychological symptoms and an increased abuse of alcohol and drugs (Hammarström et al., 1988). It may be inferred that, at least in part, the lack of employment increased substance abuse through its stressful impact (but perhaps also in making it more likely that the young people would form part of a deviant subculture). Note that because the school-leavers had not previously had an income, there was not the same contrasting effect of a loss of purchasing power.

Research on the role of social circumstances in influencing levels of illicit drug use has mainly focused on the effects of availability of drugs, perceptions of drug-users, friends' drug use and participation in street culture activities (for example, Clayton & Voss, 1981; Dembo et al., 1985; Hunt & Chambers, 1976; Jessor & Jessor, 1977; Jessor et al., 1991). There is some empirical support for the effects of each of these variables, but none of the research has provided a hard test of causal influences. Numerous longitudinal studies (see review by

Robins, 1992) have shown that the period of greatest risk for initiation into drug use is over by the age of 20 or 21 years and that there tends to be a progression from minor delinquencies and use of legal drugs (either alcohol or tobacco) to marijuana and more serious delinquent behaviour to other illicit drugs (for example, Hammersley et al., 1992; Raveis & Kandel, 1987; Elliot et al., 1985, 1989). Within illicit drugs, the main progression is from single drug to multiple drug use rather than a specific order of particular drugs. Of course, only some drug users progress in this way; the findings suggest that progression is most likely when drug use is heavy and starts at an early age (Kandel et al., 1992).

Robins' (1973, 1993) follow-up of Vietnam veterans is also informative in several key respects. First, the rate of use of narcotics (opium and heroin) among soldiers serving in Vietnam was extremely high (43 per cent) and about half of those became addicted. Second, this high rate was largely a function of market conditions rather than battle stress. The high availability of opiates (more than 80 per cent were offered them – usually within a week of arrival), their extreme cheapness, the lack of alternative recreational substances, and the absence of disapproving friends and family seemed crucial. Stress seemed less relevant as shown by the fact that use usually started soon after arrival in Vietnam before exposure to combat and by the men's reports that they took drugs for the pleasurable effects rather than to counter fear or stress. Third, a high proportion of heroin users in Vietnam gave up use of the drug on return to the very different social conditions of the USA and the great majority ceased to be addicted. Finally, although the high *levels* of drug use in Vietnam appeared to be largely a consequence of prevailing market conditions, *individual differences* were still associated with the same risk factors (antisocial behaviour, heavy drinking, poor school performance and inner city residence) as in other populations.

EXPLANATIONS FOR SECULAR TRENDS IN ALCOHOL AND DRUG USE AND ABUSE

The secular trends noted above are dramatic but their origins remain poorly understood. Two somewhat different features require explanation. First, since the Second World War there has been a major increase in the level of alcohol consumption in the population as a whole, and a relatively high proportion (up to about 25 per cent) of young people now engage in occasional recreational use of illicit drugs. This trend may well be undesirable because it exposes large numbers of persons to the possibility of abuse, although neither moderately heavy drinking nor recreational use of drugs in themselves can be regarded as indicative of any form of personal disorder. However, over the same time period, there *has* been a parallel increase in both alcohol and drug abuse/dependency, which do represent personal disorders. Accordingly, factors that may have led to increased levels of alcohol and drug *use*, as well as factors that may have increased the rates of psychosocial disorders including substance *abuse* among users are worth investigating.

In seeking to account for the secular trends, it may be instructive to focus on France, the one European country in which alcohol consumption has fallen since the Second World War. In 1960, the per capita annual consumption of pure alcohol in France was 17.5 litres, approximately 5 litres more than Italy, the second country in consumption at that time (Sulkunen, 1989). It might be supposed that the reason why consumption did not increase in France as in the rest of the Europe was that it had already reached saturation level. The finding that other high consumption countries in Europe (see above) also tended to remain at the same level or decrease consumption slightly, would seem to lead to an explanation in terms of homogenization of drinking patterns. However, a more detailed examination of the data shows that this was not the case.

As indicated by the graphs in Figure 10.13, all social groups in France showed a reduction in alcohol consumption over the period 1965 to 1979, including those with the lowest levels of consumption initially. Similarly, the trends were much the same in rural and urban populations in spite of the fact that the initial consumption level in agricultural workers was nearly twice as high as in other groups. Sulkunen (1989) argued that the main reason for the fall of alcohol consumption in France was an awareness of health risks. It is reasonable to suppose that such an awareness might have most impact in a very high consumption country, but evidence that this does in fact constitute the explanation is lacking. Also, it remains unclear why similar lesser trends have not been evident in other countries. Why, for example, did the alcohol consumption in Spain and Germany almost double over the same time period (see Figure 10.3). In short, we are not able to give a definitive explanation for the curious anomaly that France presents. This failure should make us cautious about accepting unquestioningly the explanations offered below for the trends in Europe as a whole.

Figure 10.13 Consumption of alcoholic beverages in French households, 1965-1979, by socio-professional categories (in pure alcohol)

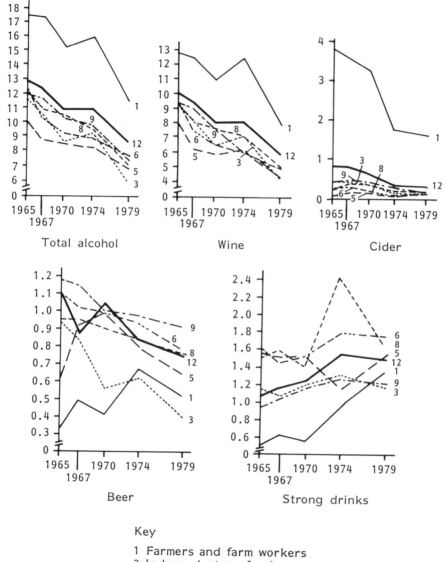

Key

1 Farmers and farm workers
3 Independent professions
5 Upper middle classes
6 Lower middle classes
8 Functionaries
9 Workers
12 France

Source: Sulkunen (1989).

Economic Factors

The post-Second World War increase in alcohol consumption in Western Europe came at a time of a general increase in economic growth and of personal prosperity, but comparisons across countries show that the correlation between the extent of economic growth and the extent of the rise in consumption is quite weak (Sulkunen, 1983). Nevertheless, the levelling-off of the trend towards increased consumption since the mid-1970s and the decline in consumption in some countries during the 1980s may be related to the economic recession (Österberg, 1986). The falling level of alcohol consumption in Sweden between 1976 and 1984 appears to be attributable in part to a decrease in disposable income during a period of stable prices for beverage alcohol (Swedish Council for Information of Alcohol and other Drugs, 1991).

However, examination of time trends over a longer time period makes it quite clear that economic factors alone cannot possibly account for the observed changes in alcohol consumption. As Figure 10.2 showed, alcohol consumption in Norway fell between 1880 and 1920 in spite of this being a period of rapid economic growth and increased buying power; consumption remained stable between 1920 and 1940 although economic prosperity continued to increase; but between 1950 and 1975 they rose in parallel; then in the late 1970s and early 1980s the economy remained static but alcohol consumption continued to increase (Skog, 1986b). As Skog (1986b) noted, it is clear that economic development during the first time period cannot possibly explain the concurrent decline in alcohol consumption. Probably, the explanation lies in the restrictive attitudes and control over alcohol that prevailed at the time. Nevertheless, equally, that does not mean that economic factors were irrelevant during that time period. Skog reanalysed the time-series cross-correlations after filtering out the major overall time trends. The results showed that during the first half of this century, as well as during the second half, the ups and downs in buying power were positively associated with similar ups and downs in alcohol consumption.

Structural changes in the economy probably played a crucial role in the increased availability of alcohol in the decades after the Second World War (Sulkunen, 1983) In highly industrialized countries the increases in worldwide trade, tourism, and monopolies made more beverage types available.

Sulkunen (1983), in an analysis of trends in Europe since 1950 with a particular focus on changes in Finland, argued that parallel social changes probably played a greater role. Prominent examples were the growing separateness of wage labour and self-controlled leisure spheres, the increase in work-related strains, the growth of the service sector in industries, and the disintegration of traditional neighbourhood networks in favour of socially isolated families and single households. Sulkunen placed greatest weight on the last two factors. The change in the ecology of life and work, he suggested, required new skills and competencies, particularly in the realm of social interaction. Drinking represented a way to demonstrate one's social status and prestige to others, and could be instrumental for integration into social groups. These needs arose as a consequence of the changes in the qualifications required for many kinds of jobs. The suggestions are plausible, but the causal inference lacks firm empirical support.

Beliefs, Attitudes and Values

As numerous studies have shown, having friends who use drugs and a positive attitude to drugs are important predictors of drug use (see Robins, 1992). Accordingly, it is necessary to consider whether changes in beliefs, attitudes and values played a part in the massive increase in the use of illicit drugs following the Second World War. No firm evidence is available to test the hypothesis. There have been changes in these features (see Chapter 8) and it is plausible that they played a role in the increased acceptability of drug-taking. However, it remains uncertain which is cause and which is effect. Furthermore, factors associated with *increases* in drug-taking need to be differentiated from those associated with decreases. Also, it is necessary to differentiate between general lifestyle measures (religious commitment, conventionality, etc.) and drug-specific attitudes and beliefs (about risks and acceptability). In that connection it is helpful that trends in usage have not been the same for different drugs.

Bachman et al. (1988, 1990), used the annual surveys of American high school seniors to tackle the issue. Over the time period 1976 to 1988, marijuana use rose for only two to three years and then fell progressively, but cocaine use continued to rise until the mid-1980s and only then began to fall. Analyses showed little change in overall life style measures over this period. Although they were important in relation to individual differences in drug-taking, changes in conventionality could not account for the diminution in drug-taking. Perceived availability of drugs may have played a role in the increase in drug-taking but did not seem crucial in the decrease. By contrast, changing attitudes (increased disapproval and an increased perception of risk) were related to the changes in drug use. In other words, the secular trends in drug use appeared to be an expression of changes in perceived risks and disapproval, which indeed increased remarkably during the 1980s. By contrast, the slight increase in conventionality was more likely to be a consequence of the decline in marijuana use.

Figure 10.14 Trends in annual marijuana and cocaine use, perceived availability, perceived risk and disapproval: high school seniors, USA, 1976-1988

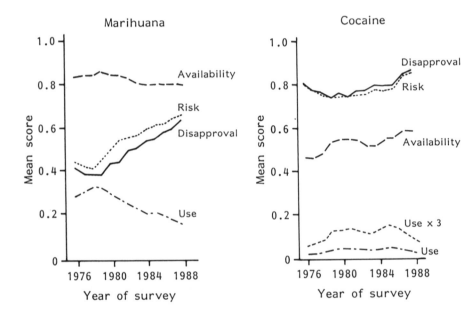

Source: Bachman et al. (1990).

According to Bachman et al., the change in the perceived risks 'got the ball rolling' by increasing the disapproval individuals felt and conveyed to their friends. Why, then, did risk perception work in this case, although experimental manipulations of normative information generally have not been successful (Leventhal & Keeshan, in press)?

The answer may lie in the quality of the information about risk gained from people's own experiences. After such a long period of extensive marijuana use among high school students, many more had had some personal experience with classmates who showed negative psychological consequences of extensive use (such as poor school performance, instability in interpersonal relations, etc.). Moreover, the media coverage on health consequences was more balanced and suited to the needs of the young. In short, youth received more information than before on the proximity of risks and negative short-term outcomes, and they also were confronted with realistic information on their own vulnerability.

Indirect evidence for the relevance of this theorizing comes from research on similar declines observed in Canadian surveys during the period 1977 to 1987. As Smart and Adlaf (1989) reported, decline in the prevalence of marijuana use corresponded to increases in law enforcement activities, but none of the associations were statistically significant. In their view, law enforcement activities at least in part reflected changes in public opinion, which may also have had an impact on the prevalence of use.

Age Cohort Size

Easterlin (1987) has argued that the size of an age cohort in relation to the population as a whole may have important psychological effects that could include delinquent behaviour and substance abuse (see Chapters 2 and 9). He contrasted a 'baby boom' generation, when the national birth rate was high, with a 'baby bust' generation, when the national birth rate was low. The former applied after the Second World War, whereas the latter applies in the 1990s. Kandel and Davies (1991) noted the parallel between the downward trend in illicit drug use during the 1980s in the USA and the decline in the proportion of young people (age 15-24) in the population; as well as the coincidence of the upward trend from 1960-80 with the 'baby boom' generation. Easterlin argued that the constraints involved in being part of a large generation size lead to increased difficulties in obtaining employment and to greater problems in establishing a position in society. The likely consequence, he suggested, of this anomic discrepancy between aims and means to attain them is damage to individuals' self-esteem, heightened feelings of inadequacy, lack of control, and alienation. The increase in the rates of crime, suicide, and violence, as well as in drinking and drug use, during the 1970s was interpreted as a response to the postulated increase in stress. As baby boomers passed out of the critical young adult years in the 1980s, the prediction was a decline in the proportion of young adults suffering mental stress, parallel to the smaller size of the subsequent generation, and consequently a decline in the prevalence of youthful problem behaviours.

The Easterlin hypothesis has been examined most critically with respect to delinquency (see Chapter 9) with somewhat contradictory findings that suggest only a rather small, inconsistent, effect. Menard and Huizinga (1989), using data from the American National Youth Survey, found a small, but significant, cohort effect on alcohol and marijuana use but not on polydrug use. However, although there may be some minor influence from being part of an unusually large birth cohort, it seems unlikely to constitute a major factor for secular trends in substance use and abuse in Europe, if only because there has been a continuing increase long after the 'baby boom' generation had passed the age of maximum risk (see Chapter 5). Thus, the birth rate started to fall in most countries during the late 1950s but teenagers born during the 1960s and 1970s (and therefore part of a smaller birth cohort) continued to show a high rate of substance use and abuse.

Family Structure

The last half-century has been associated with increasing divorce rates and growing numbers of single-parent households, which have seemed to imply a marked rise in family breakdown (see Chapter 5). Caution needs to be exercised with respect to their influence because at least part of the change reflects a shift in preferred patterns of living which may not carry the risks that have applied to similarly defined (but non-comparable) situations in the past (Bertram, 1992). Nevertheless, it is likely that there may have been an increase in family breakdown of a kind thought to carry an increased risk of substance abuse.

Fillmore et al. (1991b) used a meta-analytic combination of 19 longitudinal studies to study, at an aggregate level, the impact of divorce rates on drinking patterns. The findings were complex in that an elevated divorce rate in groups with an initially low rate of divorce was associated with an increase in heavy drinkers but, in groups with an initially high rate of divorce, the reverse was found.

Using American aggregate data on divorce rates and estimates of per capita expenditures for alcoholic beverages for the years 1933 to 1984, Magura and Shapiro (1988) analysed the direction of effects between the two variables. Their time-series model resulted in a clear support for the hypothesis that divorce rates affect alcohol consumption, not *vice versa*.

It is evident that firm conclusions cannot yet be drawn. It remains plausible that an increase in adverse family features (indexed by divorce) may have played a part in the postwar rise in substance use and abuse but the strength of its effects remains most uncertain.

Tensions in Status Transitions to Adulthood

An early approach to cultural differences in rates of alcoholism was provided by Bales (1946) who suggested that failed adjustments and inner tensions may play a role. Hurrelman (1989) has argued that the transition from childhood to adulthood may have become more difficult for recent generations because adolescence has become more prolonged and because there has been an increased lack of synchrony in the different aspects of adolescent transitions (see Chapter 4). The teenage years are increasingly dominated by schooling and training, and educational aspirations have increased, but the return achieved on educational qualifications appears to have declined. Increased schooling means that the transition to economic dependence is delayed compared with previous generations, and the time that young people live with their parents has extended. That there have been changes in the meaning of adolescence is not in doubt. It is also quite possible that the transitions have become more difficult, but if they have, whether this accounts for the changes in level of substance use and abuse is most uncertain.

Conduct Disorder

Up to this point, we have considered possible explanations for secular trends in terms of hypothesized direct effects on substance usage. It is important to add that indirect effects may be at least as important. Thus, for example, it is well demonstrated that antisocial behaviour is a common precursor of substance abuse and may well be a causal risk factor. As discussed in Chapter 9 there has been a major increase in conduct problems over the last 40 or 50 years and it is quite plausible that this has been important in increasing the propensity to use drugs and alcohol. However, there are no studies that have sought to assess the extent to which the rise in antisocial behaviour has actually led to an increase in heavy drinking or substance abuse.

Current Changes in Europe

Finally, we need to note that the discussion has necessarily focused on past trends in Europe. However, the massive social and political changes that have taken place (and which are continuing) in Eastern Europe are likely to have important implications for the future. The increased mobility across national borders, the increasing youth employment, the breakup of mechanisms of social control and increased racial and religious tensions may be particularly important (Jablensky, 1992). As already noted, German unification provides a natural experiment that should be informative, and on which there are relevant data. It is too early to draw conclusions about causal influences but it is pertinent to note the complex pattern of changes that are taking place. Thus, although the overall unemployment rate has risen in East Germany, this has not been the case for young people (although their overall rate is higher than that in older age groups). The younger generation is better off than their parents were at the same age and, from well before reunification, adolescents' value orientations have gradually come closer to those in the West and have been accompanied by a strong achievement orientation (Gensicke, 1992). Because of this, they may well adopt the health concerns that have associated with the recent decline in alcohol and drug use in West Germany. However, at least up to now, adolescents have placed a greater emphasis on the socializing role of alcohol (Silbereisen et al., 1992). This may remain the case as other leisure time experiences (such as provided by cinemas and sports facilities) continue in short supply. Perhaps the almost total breakdown of the state youth organization which occupied much free time, will have even greater consequences. It will be important to monitor trends and learn from their effects.

CONCLUSIONS

The findings on secular changes in alcohol and drug use and abuse are reasonably clear-cut in showing that, in both Europe and North America, there was a very substantial increase during the 1950s to 1980s. Overall levels of alcohol consumption rose and a substantial minority of young people came to engage in at least occasional recreational use of illicit drugs. There was also a parallel increase in the abuse of alcohol and other drugs. The last decade has seen some decline in the use of drugs in North America and this may also have occurred in some European countries, although there is uncertainty as to how general this reduction has been.

Evidence on the reasons for these changes is much less solid. It is not that we lack findings on possible causal factors, but rather that there have been few attempts to provide rigorous tests of competing causal hypotheses. As a consequence, only very tentative conclusions can be drawn. It seems most unlikely that any single factor has been responsible. Increased economic prosperity has probably played a role in making both alcohol and drugs more available. Nevertheless, this cannot be sufficient on its own as shown by the very different trends in the first third of this century. But, in conjunction with changing attitudes towards alcohol and drugs it may well have been part of the causal processes involved. Of course, that leaves open the question of why attitudes changed, and less is known on that issue. The increase in conduct problems may have been influential also, along with the increased rate of family breakdown and the increased problems associated with adolescent transitions to adulthood, with decreasing job opportunities and the ability to experience sex without parenthood.

Almost all research so far has concentrated on factors associated with the pronounced increase in alcohol and drug use. It is an open question, however, whether explanations addressing short-term increases can utilize the same concepts as explanations aimed at long-term periods of growth *and* decline, and to what degree the validity of explanations depends on the broader historical context. As Mäkelä et al. (1981) pointed out, the widespread growth in per capita alcohol consumption during the last century might seem to be easily explained by stressful circumstances, combined with increased purchasing power. But this does not explain the recent *decline* in use in North America.

In discussing the impact of social change on alcohol and drug consumption, it is important to bear in mind, too, that use and heavy use in particular are age-related phenomena, especially affecting youth and young adults. Consequently, the effect of social change on individuals' consumption is likely to affect only part of the population.

Another issue concerns possible differences in effects according to the particular circumstances of subgroups of the population. Kandel and Davies (1991) noted that the decline in drug use among young Americans during the late 1980s appeared to be sharpest in areas where rates were initially the highest. In these areas, the high prevalence of drug use may have attracted less deviant youth into use through peer influence. Less deviant youth are more likely to reduce their consumption or quit entirely when convinced that use is dangerous.

The theories advanced, as well as the empirical studies, focus on only a few facets of societal changes that might affect substance use. Because these changes have taken place simultaneously, it is difficult to disentangle which are responsible for the changes in substance use. In order to do that one must either contrast substance use in countries that have experienced some, but not all, of the same social changes, or in sub-populations within a country that have been differentially exposed to some of these changes.

None of the studies claiming links between the economy and substance use have specifically addressed substance use by young people. Nor have they spelled out the sequence of intermediary processes. A testable theory that does both is still needed.

Perhaps the most striking conclusion to be drawn is that the explanations for the growth and decline of substance use are not simply changes in direction of the same forces. The chief pressures toward increase seem to have been the secularization and urbanization of society, with consequent weakening of control over young people's behaviour by the family, church, and neighbourhood; increased disrespect for authority figures on the part of the young, linked to political radicalism early in the drug epidemic; postponement of or failure to form families of their own; increases in disposable income; and increased leisure time as educational expectations increased in response to declining opportunities for labouring jobs. Declines, in contrast, seem to be attributable mainly to changes in social policy with respect to pricing, laws, and taxation; a decline in the proportion of the population in vulnerable ages; and experience, both personal and through the media, of the adverse effects of substance use.

What is still uncertain is whether these remarkable changes in use of substances have had parallel effects on the relatively small group who have serious difficulty with substance dependence. It is possible that much of the decrease in use is accounted for by those whose low level of involvement with substances makes it easy for them to take on and act in accordance with the attitudes and behaviours of their peers and family members.

REFERENCES

Abelson, H. I., Fishburne, P. M. & Cisin, I. H. (1977). *National survey on drug abuse, 1977: A nationwide study-youth, young adults and older adults.* Princeton: Response Analysis Corporation.

Adlaf, E. M., Smart, R. C. & Tan, S. H. (1989). Ethnicity and drug use: A critical look. *International Journal of the Addictions 24*, 1-18.

Anderson, P. (1990). *Management of drinking problems.* (WHO Publications, European Series, No. 32; cited by WHO, 1992). Copenhagen: WHO Regional Office for Europe.

Anthony, J. C. & Helzer, J. E. (1991). Syndromes of drug abuse and dependence. In L. N. Robins & D. A. Regier (eds.) *Psychiatric disorders in America: The Epidemiologic Catchment Area Study*, 116-154. New York: Free Press.

Bachman, J. G., Johnston, L. D. & O'Malley, P. M. (1990). Explaining the recent decline in cocaine use among young adults: Further evidence that perceived risks and disapproval lead to reduced drug use. *Journal of Health and Social Behavior 31*, 173-184.

Bachman, J. G., Johnston, L. D., O'Malley, P. M. & Humphrey, R. H. (1988). Explaining the recent decline in marijuana use: Differentiating the effects of perceived risks, disapproval, and general lifestyle factors. *Journal of Health and Social Behavior 29*, 92-112.

Bagnall, G. (1991). Alcohol and drug use in a Scottish cohort: 10 years on. *British Journal of Addiction 86*, 895-904.

Bales, R. F. (1946). Cultural differences in rates of alcoholism. *Journal of Studies on Alcohol 6*, 480-499.

Berman, S. M. & Noble, E. P. (1993). Childhood antecedents of substance misuse. *Current Opinion in Psychiatry 6*, 382-387.

Bertram, H. (1992). *Die Familie in Westdeutschland*. Opladen: Leske & Buderich.

Brewers Society (1992). *Brewers Society statistical handbook*. London: Portman.

Bundeskriminalamt (ed.) (1992). *Rauschgift Jahresbericht 1991*. Wiesbaden: Bundeskriminalamt.

Caetano, R., Suzman, R. M., Rosen, D. H. & Voorhees-Rosen, D. J. (1983). The Shetland Islands: Longitudinal changes in alcohol consumption in a changing environment. *British Journal of Addiction 78*, 21-36.

Calahan, D. & Room, R. (1974). *Problem drinking among American men*. New Brunswick, NJ: Rutgers Center of Alcohol Studies.

Campanelli, P. C., Dielman, T. E. & Shope, J. T. (1987). Validity of adolescents' self-reports of alcohol use and misuse using a bogus pipeline procedure. *Adolescence 85*, 7-22.

Cheung, Y.W. (1991). Ethnicity and alcohol/drug use revisited: A framework for future research. *International Journal of the Addictions 25*, 581-605.

Clayton, R. R. & Voss, H. L. (1981). *Young men and drugs in Manhattan: A causal analysis*. Rockville, MA: National Institute on Drug Abuse.

Cloninger, C. R. & Begleiter, H. (1990). *The genetics and biology of alcoholism*. Plainview, NY: Cold Spring Harbour Laboratory Press.

Commission of the European Communities (eds.) (1991). *Young Europeans of 11 to 15 and alcohol. Survey conducted in the European Community by the European Omnibus Survey (Faits et Opinions)*. Luxembourg: Health and Safety Directorate of the Commission of the European Communities.

Crabbe, J. C. & Belknap, J. K. (1992). Genetic approaches to drug dependence. *Trends in Pharmacological Sciences 13*, 212-219.

Dembo, R., Allen, N., Farrow, D., Schmeidler, J. & Burgos, W. (1985). A causal analysis of early drug involvement in three inner-city neighborhood settings. *International Journal of the Addictions, 20*, 1213-1237.

Douglass, R. L. & Freeman, J. A. (1977). *A study of alcohol-related casualties and alcohol beverage market response to alcohol availability policies in Michigan.* Ann Arbor: Highway Safety Research Institute, (cited by Smart, 1979).

Duffy, J. C. (1991). *Trends in alcohol consumption patterns 1978-1989.* Henley-on-Thames: NTC Publications.

Easterlin, R. A. (1987). *Birth and fortune: The impact of numbers on personal welfare.* Chicago: The University of Chicago Press.

Elliott, D. S., Huizinga, D. & Ageton, S. S. (1985). *Explaining delinquency and drug use.* Beverly Hills, CA: Sage.

Elliott, D. S., Huizinga, D. & Menard, S. (1989). *Multiple problem youth: Delinquency, substance use, and mental health problems.* New York: Springer Verlag.

Epidemiologische Forschung Berlin (1991). *Konsum und Mißbrauch von Alkohol, illegalen Drogen und Tabakwaren durch junge Menschen in Ost-Berlin.* Munich: Infratest Gesundheitsforschung 3.

Feldman, S. S. & Rosenthal, D. A. (1990). The acculturation of autonomy expectations in Chinese high schoolers residing in two Western nations. *International Journal of Psychology 25*, 259-281.

Fillmore, K. M., Golding, J. M., Leino, E. V., Ager, C. R. & Ferrer, H. (1991b). *Proportions of chronic 'heavy drinking' among persons at risk and in the total population and postulated explanations from aggregate data accounting from cross-study differences: An analysis of multiple longitudinal studies from the ollaborative Alcohol-Related Longitudinal Project.* Paper presented at the 17th Annual Alcohol Epidemiology Symposium, Sigtuna, Sweden, 9-14 June, 1991.

Fillmore, K. M., Hartka, E., Johnstone, B. M., Leino, V., Motoyoshi, M. & Temple, M. T. (1991a). The collaborative alcohol-related longitudinal project. A meta-analysis of life course variation in drinking. *British Journal of Addiction 86*, 1221-1268.

Gensicke, T. (1992). *Mentalitätsentwicklungen im Osten Deutschland seit den 70er Jahren. Vorstellung und Erläuterung von Ergebnissen einiger empirischer Untersuchungen in der DDR und in den neuen Bundesländern von 1977 bis 1991* (Speyerer Forschungsberichte, 109). Speyer: Forschungsinstitut für Öffentliche Verwaltung.

Ghodsian, M. & Power, C. (1987). Alcohol consumption between the ages of 16 and 23 in Britain: A longitudinal study. *British Journal of Addiction 82*, 1-30.

Godfrey, C. (1989). Factors influencing the consumption of alcohol and tobacco: The use and abuse of economic models. *British Journal of Addiction 84*, 1123-1138.

Goedde, H. W. & Agarwal, D. P. (eds.) (1989). *Alcoholism: Biomedical and genetic aspects.* New York: Pergamon.

Greeley, A. M., McCready, W. C. & Theisen, G. (1980). *Ethnic drinking subcultures.* New York: Praeger.

Hammarström, A., Janlert, V. & Theorell, J. (1988). Youth and ill-health: Results from a 2-year follow-up study. *Social Science and Medicine 26*, 1029-1033.

Hammer, T. (1992). Unemployment and use of drugs and alcohol among young people: A longitudinal study in the general population. *British Journal of Addiction* 87, 1571-1581.

Hammersley, R., Lavelle, T. & Forsyth, A. (1992). Predicting initiation to and cessation of buprenorphine and temazepam use amongst adolescents. *British Journal of Addiction 87*, 1303-1311.

Hanel, E. (1991). *Literaturrecherche zu ausgewählten Fragestellungen aus dem Bereich der Drogenabhängigkeit.* Munich: IFT Institut für Therapieforschung.

Hartnoll, R., Lewis, R., Mitcheson, M. & Bryer, S. (1985). Estimating the prevalence of opiod dependence. *Lancet 26*, 203-205.

Hauge, R. (1985). Trends in drug use in Norway. *Journal of Drug Issues 15*, 321-331.

Hawkins, J. D., Catalano, R. F., & Miller, J. Y. (1992). Risk and protective factors for alcohol and other drug problems in adolescence and early adulthood: Implications for substance abuse prevention. *Psychological Bulletin112*, 64-105.

Health Education Authority (1992). *Tomorrows young adults: 9-15 year-olds look at alcohol, drugs, exercise and smoking.* London: Health Education Authority.

Helzer, J. E., Burnam, A. & McEvoy, L. (1991). Alcohol abuse and dependence. In L. N. Robins & D. A. Regier (eds.) *Psychiatric disorders in America: The Epidemiologic Catchment Area Study*, 81-115. New York: Free Press.

Hodgkinson, S., Mullan, M. & Murray, R. M. (1991). The genetic vulnerability to alcoholism. In P. McGuffin & R. Murray (eds.) *The new genetics of mental illness*, 182-197. Oxford: Butterworth-Heinemann.

Holder, H. D. & Blose, J. O. (1987). Impact of changes in distilled spirits availability on apparent consumption: A time series analysis of liquor-by-the-drink. *British Journal of Addiction 82*, 623-631.

Hunt, L. G. & Chambers, C. D. (1976). *The heroin epidemics: A study of heroin use in the United States, 1965-75.* New York: Spectrum.

Hurrelmann, K. (1989). The social world of adolescents: A sociological perspective. In K. Hurrelmann & U. Engel (eds.) *The social world of adolescents: International perspectives*, 3-260. Berlin/New York: Walter de Gruyter.

Institut für Jugendforschung (1990). *Die Entwicklung der Drogenaffinität Jugendlicher. Zusammenfassung der Ergebnisse einer Trendanalyse 1973/1976/1979/1982/1986/1990.* Munich: IFJ Institut für Jugendforschung.

Institute for the Study of Drug Dependence (1993). *National Audit of Drug Misuse in Britain 1992.* London: ISDD.

Iversen, L. & Klausen, H. (1986). Alcohol consumption among laid-off workers before and after closure of a Danish shipyard: A 2-year follow-up study. *Social Science and Medicine 22*, 107-109.

Jablensky, A. (1992). Characteristics of current substance abuse patterns in countries of central and Eastern Europe. In H. Klingemann, C. Goos, R. Hartnoll, A. Jablensky & J. Rehm (eds.) *European summary on drug abuse*, 27-31. Copenhagen: WHO Regional Office for Europe.

Jessor, R., Donovan, J. E., Costa, J. E. & Frances, M. (1991). *Beyond adolescence. Problem behavior and young adult development.* Cambridge: Cambridge University Press.

Jessor, R. & Jessor, S. L. (1977). *Problem behaviour and psycho-social development: A longitudinal study of youth.* New York: Academic Press.

Johnston, L. D., O'Malley, P. M. & Bachman, J. G. (1991). *Drug use among American high school seniors, college students and young adults, 1975-1990, Vol. I: High school seniors.* Rockville, MA: National Institute on Drug Abuse.

Kandel, D. B. & Davies, M. (1991). Decline in the use of illicit drugs by high school students in New York State: A comparison with national data. *American Journal of Public Health 81*, 1064-1067.

Kandel, D. B., Yamaguchi, K. & Chen, K. (1992). Stages of progression in drug involvement from adolescence to adulthood: Further evidence for gateway theory. *Journal of Studies on Alcohol 53*, 447-457.

Kendell, R. E. (1979). Alcoholism: a medical or a political problem? *British Medical Journal 1*, 367-371.

Kendell, R. E., de Roumanie, M. & Ritson, E. B. (1983). Effect of economic changes on Scottish drinking habits 1978-82. *British Journal of Addiction 78*, 365-379.

Klingemann, H. (1992). *Drug abuse in Europe from 1985 to 1990: An overview.* In WHO Regional Office for Europe (ed.) *European summary on drug abuse* (EUR/ICP/ADA 527/A). Copenhagen: WHO Regional Office for Europe.

Knibbe, R. A., Drop, M. J., Van Reek, J. & Saenger, G. (1985). The development of alcohol consumption in the Netherlands: 1958-1981. *British Journal of Addiction 80*, 411-419.

Kortteinen, T. (1988). International trade and availability of alcoholic beverages in developing countries. *British Journal of Addiction 83*, 669-676.

Leventhal, H. & Keeshan, P. (in press). *Promoting healthy alternatives to substance abuse.* Final draft prepared for the Carnegie Council on Adolescent Development. Health Promotion Volume. Washington, DC.

Linsky, A. S., Colby, J. P. & Straus, M. A. (1986). Drinking norms and alcohol-related problems in the United States. *Journal of Studies on Alcohol 47*, 384-393.

Magura, M. & Shapiro, E. (1988). Alcohol consumption and divorce: Which causes which? *Journal of Divorce 12*, 127-136.

Mäkelä, K., Room, R., Single, E., Sulkunen, P, & Walsh, B. (1981). *Alcohol, society and the state: A comparative study of alcohol* control. Toronto: Addictions Research Foundation.

Mann, R. E. & Anglin, L. (1988). The relationship between alcohol related traffic fatalities and per capita consumption of alcohol, Ontario, 1957-1983. *Accident Analysis and Prevention 20*, 441-446.

May, C. (1992). A burning issue? Adolescent alcohol use in Britain 1970-1991. *Alcohol and Alcoholism 27*, 109-115.

Menard, S. & Huizinga, D. (1989). Age, period, and cohort size effects on self-reported alcohol, marijuana, and polydrug use: Results from the National Youth Survey. *Social Science Research 18,* 174-194.

Mensch, B. S. & Kandel, D. B. (1988). Underreporting of substance use in a national longitudinal youth cohort. *Public Opinion Quarterly 52*, 100-124.

Mooney, L. A., Gramling, R. & Forsyth, C. (1992). Legal drinking age and alcohol consumption. *Deviant Behaviour: An Interdisciplinary Journal 13*, 59-71.

Moser, J. (1992). *Alcohol problems, policies and programmes in Europe*, Copenhagen: WHO Regional Offices for Europe.

Moskalewicz, J. & Swiatkiewicz, G. (1992). Social problems in the Polish political debate. In J. Simpura & C. Tigerstedt (eds.) *Social problems around the Baltic Sea. Report from the Baltic Study*, 85-107. Helsinki: Nordic Council for Alcohol.

Mott, J. (ed.) (1992). *Crack and cocaine in England and Wales*. Research and Planning Unit (Paper 70). London: Home Office

Newcomb, M. D. & Bentler, P. M. (1986). Substance use and ethnicity: Differential impact of peer and adult models. *Journal of Psychology 120*, 83-95.

O'Malley, P. M. & Wagenaar, A. C. (1991). Effects of minimum drinking age laws on alcohol use, related behaviors and traffic crash involvement among American youth: 1976-1987. *Journal of Studies on Alcohol 52*, 478-491

Österberg, E. (1986). Alcohol-related problems in cross-cultural perspective: Results of the ISACE-study. In T.F. Barbor (ed.) *Alcohol and culture: Comparative perspectives from Europe and America*, 10-20. New York: The New York Academy of Sciences.

Parry, H. J. (1979). Sample surveys of drug abuse. In R.I. Dupont, A. Goldstein & J. O'Donnell (eds.) *Handbook on drug abuse*, 381-394. Washington, DC: National Institute on Drug Abuse.

Peacock, C. (1992). International policies on alcohol-impaired driving: A review. *International Journal of the Addictions 27*, 187-208.

Peck, D. F. & Plant, M. (1986). Unemployment and illegal drug use: Concordant evidence from a prospective study and national trends. *British Medical Journal 293*, 929-932.

Peele, S. (1984). The cultural context of psychological approaches to alcoholism. Can we control the effects of alcohol? *American Psychologist 39*, 1337-1351.

Pickens, R. W., Svikis, D. S., McGue, M., Lykken, D. T., Heston, L. L. & Clayton, P. J. (1991). Heterogeneity in the inheritance of alcoholism: A study of male and female twins. *Archives of General Psychiatry 48*, 19-28.

Plant, M. A., Peck, D. R. & Sammuel, E. (1985). *Alcohol, drugs and school-leavers*. London: Tavistock.

Plant, M. A., Peck, D. F. & Duffy, J. C. (1988). Trends in the use and misuse of alcohol and other psychoactive drugs in the United Kingdom: Some perplexing connections. *British Journal of Addiction 83*, 943-947.

Plant, M. A. & Plant, M. (1992). *Risk-takers. Alcohol, drugs, sex and youth*. London/New York: Tavistock/Routledge.

Plomp, H. N., Kuipers, H. & van Oers, M. L. (1991). *Smoking and alcohol consumption and the use of drugs by school children from the age of 10. Results of the Fourth Dutch National Youth Health Care Survey in 1988/1989*. Amsterdam: VU University Press.

Produktschaap voor Gedistilleerde Dranken (eds.) (1992). *World drink trends.* Henley-on-Thames: NTC Publications.

Raveis, V. H. & Kandel, D. B. (1987). Changes in drug behavior from the middle to late twenties: Initiation, persistence and cessation of use. *American Journal of Public Health 46*, 109-116.

Reuband, K. H. (1988). Drogenkonsum im Wandel. Eine retrospektive Prävalenzmessung der Drogenerfahrung Jungendlicher in den Jahren 1967-1987. *Zeitschrift für Sozialisationsforschung und Erziehungssoziologie 8*, 54-68.

Robins, L. (1973). *A follow-up of Vietnam drug users.* Special Action Monograph, Series A, No. 1. Washington, DC: Special Action Office for Drug Abuse Prevention.

Robins, L. (1992). *Synthesis and analysis of longitudinal research on substance abuse.* A Report for the Robert Wood Johnson Foundation, US.

Robins, L. (1993). Vietnam veterans' rapid recovery from heroin addiction: A fluke or normal expectation? *Addiction 88*, 1041-1054.

Robins, L. N. & McEvoy, L. (1990). Conduct problems as predictors of substance abuse. In L. Robins & M. Rutter (eds.) *Straight and devious pathways from childhood to adulthood*, 182-204. Cambridge: Cambridge University Press.

Robins, L. N. & Regier, D. A. (eds.) (1991). *Psychiatric disorders in America: The Epidemiologic Catchment Area Study.* New York: Free Press.

Room, R. (1987). *Social dimensions of alcohol dependence.* Paper presented at an Invitational Conference on Alcohol Dependency honoring Robert Straus, 22 May, 1987, University of Kentucky, Lexington (cited by Hartka & Fillmore, 1989).

Royal College of Psychiatrists (1986). *Alcohol: Our favourite drug.* London: Tavistock.

Silbereisen, R. K., Kracke, B. & Nowak, M. (1992). Körperliches Entwicklungstempo und jugendtypische Übergänge. In J. Zinnecker (ed.) *Jugend '92: Lebenslagen, Orientierungen und Entwicklungsperspektiven im vereinigten Deutschland, Bd. 2: Im Spiegel der Wissenschaften*, 171-196. Opladen: Leske & Budrich.

Silbereisen, R.K., Schönpflug, U. & Otremba, H. (1989). Entwicklungsübergänge und Problemverhalten bei deutschen und türkischen Jugendlichen in Berlin. In G. Trommsdorff (ed.) *Sozialisation im Kulturvergleich*, 122-155. Stuttgart: Enke.

Simon, R., Bühringer, G. & Wiblishauser, P. M. (1991). *Repräsentativerhebung 1990 zum Konsum und Missbrauch von illegalen Drogen, alkoholischen Getränken, Medikamente und Tabakwaren. Bericht Nr. 3: Grundauswertung für die alten und die neuen Bundesländer.* Munich: IFT Institut für Therapieforschung (printed in Bundesministerium für Gesundheit, O.J.).

Simpura, J. & Tigerstedt, C. (1992). *Social problems around the Baltic Sea. Report from the Baltic Study.* Helsinki: Nordic Council for Alcohol.

Skog, O. J. (1986a). The long waves of alcohol consumption: A social network perspective on cultural change. *Social Networks 8*, 1-32.

Skog, O. J. (1986b). An analysis of divergent trends in alcohol consumption and economic development. *Journal of Studies on Alcohol 47*, 19-25.

Smart, R. G. (1989). Is the postwar drinking binge ending? Cross-national trends in per capita alcohol consumption. *British Journal of Addiction 84*, 743-748.

Smart, R. G. & Adlaf, E. (1989). Student cannabis use and enforcement activity in Canada: 1977-1987. *Drug and Alcohol Dependence 24*, 67-74.

Smart, R. G. & Goodstadt, M. (1977). *Alcohol and drug use among Ontario students in 1977: Preliminary findings.* Toronto: Addictions Research Foundation, (cited by Smart, 1979).

Smith, R. A., Hingson, R. W., Morelock, S., Heeren, T., Mucatel, M., Manione, T. & Scotch, N. (1984). Legislation raising the legal drinking age in Massachusetts from 18 to 20: Effect on 16 and 17 year-olds. *Journal of Studies on Alcohol 45*, 534-539.

Stattin, H. & Magnusson, D. (1990). *Pubertal maturation in female development.* Hillsdale, NJ: Lawrence Erlbaum.

Stivers, R. (1985). Historical meanings of Irish-American drinking. In L. A. Bennett & G. M. Ames (eds.) *The American experience with alcohol: Contrasting cultural perspectives.* New York: Plenum Press.

Sulkunen, P. (1983). Alcohol consumption and the transformation of living conditions: A comparative study. In R.G. Smart, F. B. Glassr, Y. Israel, H. Kalant, R. E. Popham & W. Schmidt (eds.) *Research advances in alcohol and drug problems,* vol. 7, 247-297. New York: Plenum Press.

Sulkunen, P. (1989). Drinking in France 1965-1979. An analysis of household consumption data. *British Journal of Addiction 84*, 61-72.

Swedish Council for Information on Alcohol and other Drugs (1991). *Report 91: Trends in alcohol and drug use in Sweden.* Stockholm: Centralförbundet för alkohol – och narkotikaaupplysning.

Vaillant, G. E. (1983). *The natural history of alcoholism: Causes, patterns, and paths of recovery.* Cambridge, MA: Harvard University Press.

Vingilis, E. R. & De Genova, K. (1984). Youth and the forbidden fruit: Experiences with changes in legal drinking age in North America. *Journal of Criminal Justice 12*, 161-172.

Voorhees, D. J., Rosen, D. H., Suzman, R. M. & Caetano, R. (1989). Shetland: Psychiatric symptoms and alcohol consumption in a community undergoing socioeconomic development. *Acta Psychiatrica Scandinavica 79*, 141-156.

Wagenaar, A. C. & Maybee, R. G. (1986). The legal minimum drinking age in Texas: Effects of an increase from 18 to 19. *Journal of Safety Research, 17*, 165-178.

Walsh, B. M. (1990). *Alcohol, the economy and public health.* Copenhagen: WHO Regional Office for Europe (unpublished document EUR/ICP/ADA 022; cited by WHO, 1992).

Walsh, B. & Grant, M. (1985). *Public health implications of alcohol production and trade.* Geneva: World Health Organization.

World Health Organization (1992). *A European alcohol action plan.* Copenhagen: WHO Regional Office for Europe (unpublished document EUR/RC42/8, ICP/GDP/110(6)/7 Rev. 1, 8941B/8942B).

11

Depressive Disorders: Time Trends and Possible Explanatory Mechanisms

ERIC FOMBONNE

The aim of this chapter is to establish whether there has been an increase over historical time in the incidence of depressive conditions in young people, and to consider possible explanations for such an increase in the light of the available evidence. The chapter begins by providing working definitions for the study of depressive phenomena. Next, it critically examines the evidence from a variety of sources for an increase in the rate of depressive conditions. The epidemiology of depression – its social and demographic patterns and other correlates – is then reviewed, with special reference to the period of adolescence. The next part analyses risk mechanisms that might explain time trends in depressive conditions among young people. The concluding section considers the implications of the findings and the priorities for future research.

DEFINITION AND MEASUREMENT

Definition

Feelings of sadness, unhappiness and misery are experienced by almost everyone; they are part of the human condition. Dysphoric mood may be a normal, healthy, reaction to stressful events (such as the loss of a loved person) and in those cases it is an aspect of the mechanisms for coping in the face of adversity. In other cases, sadness reaches extremes of intensity or duration, or possesses deviant features that significantly alter psychological functioning; in those circumstances, it is not an aspect of coping, but on the contrary impairs the individual's ability to adapt to the demands of normal life and to promote personal growth and achievement.

The term 'depression' therefore encompasses a huge array of psychological experiences; that heterogeneity is found both in the lay and in the professional literature (Angold, 1988a). To simplify the matter, three levels of depression have been distinguished (Kazdin, 1990), and the distinction between them will be observed throughout this chapter.

- *Depressed mood or affect* refers to a state of dysphoria that occurs frequently in the course of normal development, but is more than normal sadness, demoralization, or anxiety (Watson & Clark, 1984). It is distinguished from normal sadness by a lack of positive affect and a loss of emotional involvement with other persons, objects or activities. Depressed mood states tend also to be accompanied by a set of negative cognitions about oneself (guilt and self-depreciation), the external world (helplessness) and the future (hopelessness) (Beck, 1976; Rutter, 1988), and by an inability to cope efficiently with stressful events and normal life demands (Rutter, 1991).
- *Depressive syndrome* refers to a constellation of observable symptoms that tend to cluster together, including depressed mood, tearfulness, irritability, suicidal thoughts, loss of appetite, disturbances of sleep, and lack of energy. A depressive syndrome is recognized when the number of behavioural characteristics reaches a given threshold.
- *Depressive disorders* correspond to psychiatric diagnoses of depression. Most modern diagnostic schemes such as DSM-IV (American Psychiatric Association, 1994) and ICD-10 (World Health Organization, 1992) agree on a categorical definition of depression based on a pattern of typical symptoms (including sadness, irritability, loss of energy, loss of weight, sleep difficulties, hopelessness and helplessness, suicidal ideas) that are required to persist over time (at least several weeks) and to lead to significant impairment in major social roles. Persistence and impairment are crucial in the differentiation between depressive *syndrome* and depressive *disorder*. There is some variation between psychiatric classifications as to the duration and number of symptoms that set the threshold for the diagnosis of a depressive disorder, but agreement between clinicians using a particular scheme is generally very high.

These three definitions imply a gradient of severity from depressed mood to depressive disorder, and it is generally assumed that there is a path of development from the mild to the severe forms. Yet the evidence for this is slim, particularly during adolescence. Little is known on the antecedents of depressive disorders, on the rates and patterns of symptom recruitment from depressed mood to depressive disorder, or on the factors that precipitate (or, conversely, protect against) such transformations. These gaps in knowledge arise partly because each definition is closely connected with a different research tradition, each one using a distinct sampling and measurement approach. In reviewing the state of knowledge, it is not possible to impose a common definition on these diverse traditions. Instead, this chapter will refer to *depressive mood, depressive syndrome,* and *depressive disorders* as appropriate. The term depressive *phenomena* will be used to refer indiscriminately to the three levels of depressive behaviours.

Measurement

Broadly speaking, there are two methods of measuring depressive phenomena: questionnaires and diagnostic interviews.

Depressed mood and depressive syndromes are typically assessed by questionnaires consisting of items describing depressive symptoms. They are easy to use and may be self-administered or filled-in by observers – whether parents, teachers or professionals. Item scores are then summed to produce one or several scores. Some questionnaires have been calibrated with representative samples so as to produce standardized scores; the results obtained with any specific population can then be readily interpreted. Many questionnaires on general psychopathology include clusters of items that tap depressive features. Several measures, especially self-report measures, have also been specifically designed for the assessment of depressive phenomena, and are available for children, adolescents and adults. Rigorous methods (such as multivariate analysis) are available to gauge the psychometric properties of these instruments, and these have often been used to establish the construct validity of the syndrome, that is, to show that the specific components are highly inter-correlated. Typically, these instruments cover the past few days or weeks: they are not designed to collect retrospective information. When different questionnaire-based studies are compared, possible differences in the questionnaires used (such as differences in wording, scoring instructions, periods of reference, and item content) need to be borne in mind as potential threats to the validity of the comparisons across studies. Even when the same questionnaire has been used, differences may reflect variations in response styles between individuals, or, in cross-national studies, a lack of cultural equivalence. Despite these caveats, questionnaires provide an efficient method of measuring change over time and comparing rates of depressive symptomatology between different groups.

Diagnostic interviews are carried out face-to-face either with subjects or with key informants by trained interviewers. They collect systematic data on the occurrence, type, date of onset and remission, duration, sequence, and severity of several symptoms, which are investigated according to a standardized procedure. The information is processed by applying diagnostic decision procedures using strict criteria to generate psychiatric diagnoses. Unlike questionnaires, interviews may evaluate the occurrence of psychiatric problems during the entire lifetime, thereby providing assessment of both past and current psychiatric status. Age at first onset of a disorder may therefore be determined retrospectively, but reliance on memory for accounts of past episodes and their dating may be problematic. Psychiatric interviews vary in the levels of skill they demand from interviewers, and in their degree of structure. Highly structured interviews have been developed for large-scale surveys of the general population; in these studies, lay interviewers are trained to administer the interviews in a fixed format. By contrast, semi-structured interviews are designed for use by mental health professionals, usually on clinical samples. Here the style of questioning is more open and flexible, and the interviewer's judgement plays an important role. Both types of interview are used for the assessment of depressive disorders (along with other psychiatric conditions) among children, adolescents and adults. Rates of both current and lifetime prevalence can be calculated, where current prevalence covers the last six to twelve months, and lifetime prevalence the period from birth to the interview date.

Relationships between questionnaire scores and interview diagnoses are not always strong. Although questionnaire-based instruments possess good psychometric properties and are efficient at filtering out depressive symptoms in general population samples, they do have serious limitations as valid measures of depressive disorders (Costello & Angold, 1988). Both approaches on occasion use several informants (such as parents, teachers, peers, and children themselves); yet agreement between different informants is typically low, so there are problems in deciding on the weight to attach to the responses given by each informant, and the solution may vary between particular subsets of symptoms and between age groups. This problem occurs in particular when the subject is a child or adolescent: the agreement across informants about young subjects tends to be particularly low (Kazdin, 1990; Reynolds et al., 1985).

Another difference between these approaches is that between a score on some dimension of depression, which may vary continuously from zero to some upper limit, and a decision procedure that places subjects either in one category (with depressive disorder) or another (without). The scoring approach tends to be used in questionnaire-based studies (often longitudinal) of general population samples, focusing on normal development, whereas the categorical approach tends to be used in studies of clinical samples, focusing on people with severe disorders. These differences of method jeopardize efforts to understand continuities and discontinuities between normal and pathological depressive conditions. Thus, differences in the instruments used to measure depressive phenomena are superimposed on differences in the general aims of the inquiry, the type of design, and the type of sample. Bearing in mind these complications, we will need to make use of information about each of the three levels of depressive phenomena.

TIME TRENDS IN DEPRESSIVE CONDITIONS

The study of change over time in the incidence of diseases can give useful leads in the search of causal factors. Change occurring over a short period (a few decades) suggests that environmental causes are important, since the genetic pool can only alter at a much slower pace. Of course, even if there is rapid change in the incidence of a disease, genetic factors may still be important in determining which individuals are particularly susceptible to environmental influences.

Data Sources: Types, Strengths, and Limitations

There is no long time series of data on depression available in any country. In the few countries where longitudinal studies of birth cohorts or repeated surveys of adolescent health have been conducted, measures of depression were generally not included. This reflects the fairly recent recognition of depression as a problem among children and adolescents, and the equally recent development of appropriate measurement tools. The vast majority of the relevant datasets were generated after 1970, and most after 1980. The best design for examining secular trends is the *prospective follow-up study* of several birth cohorts, since this provides an unbiased estimate of incidence and age of onset. However, because most studies started recently, not much information has yet been generated by this method.

Instead, most of the available data come either from general population surveys of psychiatric disorders – *community surveys* – or from *family studies* of affective disorders. In both types of study, data are collected across all age groups at a single point in time. The present and past occurrence of depressive disorder and the age of each subject at the time of onset is established. Data are treated as if they were derived from a prospective study starting from birth, with the limitation that no further information is available beyond the date of interview. Problems inherent to this approximation of a true prospective design are discussed later on in the chapter.

Health statistics that are routinely collected in modern times may also be informative, although only indirectly. Hospital statistics may in principle provide evidence of the number of people hospitalized for psychiatric reasons who were suffering from depressive disorders. However, such data are sparse, and any increase would be difficult to interpret, since it would not be possible to estimate how much of the increase might reflect better detection or acknowledgement of depression, better access to hospital care, availability of new and more effective treatments, or changes in diagnostic practices.

Finally, although suicides are not for the most part a direct *consequence* of depressive conditions, suicide does occur *in combination with* a variety of depressive conditions. Therefore, if there is indeed a secular increase in rates of depression, then trends in *suicide rates* should at least not contradict that trend; perhaps more important, changes over time in the strength of the relationship between suicide and depression would need to be critically examined.

With few exceptions, there are no available data on changes over time in rates of depressed mood or depressive syndromes among young people; only changes in depressive disorders can be examined in detail.

The Evidence on Change Over Time

During the last ten years, a number of studies have provided evidence to support the hypothesis of a recent increase in the rates of depressive disorders. The following summary updates and expands previous reviews on the topic (Klerman, 1988; Klerman & Weissman, 1989).

Family Genetic Studies

Two large family genetic studies are an important source of evidence. In the first, 2,289 first-degree relatives of 523 persons diagnosed as suffering from depressive disorders were studied in five sites of the National Institute of

**Figure 11.1   Cumulative rates of major depressive disorders among seven birth
                 cohorts: a) in the USA; b) in Mainz, Germany**

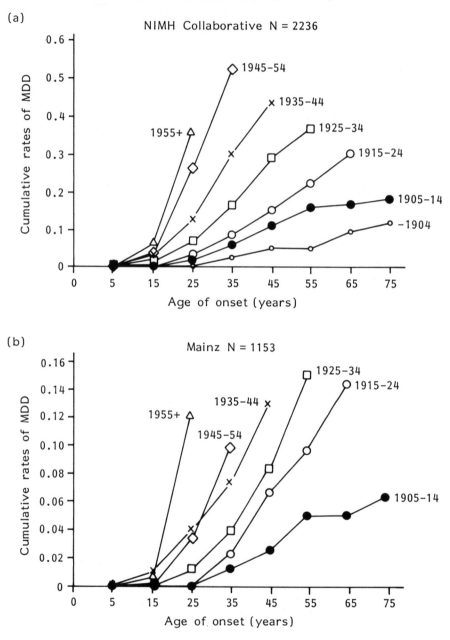

Source: Cross-National Collaborative Group (1992).

Mental Health (USA) research programme on the psychobiology of depression (Klerman et al., 1985). Findings suggested increasing rates of depressive disorders among successive birth cohorts throughout the century (see Figure 11.1a). The data also indicated an earlier age of onset in the most recent birth cohorts and a trend was noted towards a less pronounced sex differential in recent birth cohorts.

A second family genetic study examined 823 first-degree relatives of persons diagnosed as suffering from bipolar (manic-depressive) and schizoaffective conditions (Gershon et al., 1987). The likelihood that someone will already have experienced a disorder is partly a function of age. To get over this problem, the researchers used the data to estimate the proportion who would have experienced a disorder over their full lifetime. This 'age-corrected lifetime prevalence' of any affective disorder was 21.7 per cent for those born before 1940, compared with 40.6 per cent for those born after 1940. Actuarial life-table analysis was used to show that this difference could not have occurred by chance.

Three recent family studies yielded similar results. In one of these (Coryell et al., 1992), 965 adults who were relatives of persons diagnosed with affective disorders, but who were suffering from no such disorders themselves, were followed up after an interval of six years. The results showed an increased incidence of new onset depressive disorders among those aged under 40, who had rates three times as high as the oldest subjects. The prospective design of this study strengthens its findings. Finally, in a family study of prepubertal depressed children, the effect of date of birth on the cumulative risk of becoming depressed was examined amongst the 86 siblings of the children diagnosed as depressed and the 77 siblings of subjects not diagnosed as depressed (Ryan et al., 1992). Children and adolescents born later had significantly higher risks of depressive disorders than those born earlier. There were several indications that this increased risk among those born later was, to some extent, specific to depression rather than extending to all psychiatric disorders. Similar findings (see Figure 11.1b) arising from a German study (Maier et al., 1991) are discussed below.

Surveys of the General Population

Second, strikingly consistent evidence has come from the various studies of large samples of the general population conducted recently in various countries using precise sampling methods, comparable diagnostic definitions, and standardized diagnostic interviews of known reliability and validity. One of these large community surveys, the Epidemiological Catchment Area (ECA) study, was carried out in the USA in 5 sites among a total sample of over 18,000 adults (Robins et al., 1991a). The results are expressed as lifetime prevalence rates of selected disorders, a measure of disease occurrence that is not confounded with the duration of disorders. Lifetime prevalence is, of course, an underestimate of the eventual lifetime risk, because it does not take account of the years between the date of the interview and the subject's death. Assuming that psychiatric disorders are not strongly associated with increased mortality and that recall of past episodes remains constant throughout the life span, lifetime prevalence rates should increase with age, since the time at risk increases. One surprising finding was that the lifetime rate of any disorder declined with age, with lower rates being found among the elderly (Robins et al., 1991a). This pattern was particularly pronounced for affective disorders. For men and women respectively, the lifetime rates were 6.4 and 10.6 per cent for those aged 18-29; 6.6 and 15.3 per cent for those aged 30-44; and thereafter declined to 3.6 and 9.3 per cent in the 45-64 age group; and to 1.6 and 3.3 per cent among those aged over 64 (Weissman et al., 1991). These results were found at each of the five study sites, and reflected, at least in part, a younger mean age of onset. Figure 11.2 illustrates the results graphically. The curves for each birth cohort indicate that, at any age, the youngest birth cohorts that had completed the period at risk had higher rates of disorders than the older cohorts, and they also showed a progressively earlier age of onset.

Similar results were obtained in three other North American studies. Lifetime rates of major depression declined in the oldest age groups in a community sample of 3,258 adults studied in Canada, but no clear pattern in rates could be observed before age 55 (Bland et al., 1988). Another study of large community samples of adults using diagnostic interviews and criteria different from those of the ECA study led to similar results, thus ruling out the possibility that the finding was an artefact of the specific instrumentation used (Lewinsohn et al., 1993). In this carefully designed study, measures of current mood state, memory ability, social desirability and self-labelling were taken. The authors were therefore able to assess, and eventually partial out, the effect of these potential confounding factors on what they called the 'depression epidemic'. Significant differences were found between six birth cohorts for both sexes, the more recent ones experiencing a higher risk of a major depressive episode at a younger age. Amongst the four potentially confounding factors, three were significantly related to the number of past episodes of depressive disorders reported by the subjects, although the magnitude of these associations was quite small. Controlling for their effect either independently or in combination made little difference to the results for major depression. Moreover, whereas the oldest cohort (born 1968-1971) of their adolescent subsample had a higher lifetime rate than the youngest cohort (1972-1974) due to their increased time at risk, the cumulative probability of having developed a major depressive disorder by the age of 16 was already significantly higher in the youngest birth cohort; this shows that the trend towards an earlier age of onset can be detected even between two fairly recent birth cohorts. In a recent general population survey of over 8,000 Americans aged 15-54 (Kessler et al., 1993), lifetime rates of depression decreased again among older respondents. The particular strengths of this survey lie in the fact that the sample was selected to be nationally representative, that rates were adjusted to take into account higher levels of depression found among non-respondents, and that the data were collected with a new structured diagnostic interview (CIDI) especially modified to facilitate recall of past episodes of depression.

Figure 11.2   Lifetime prevalence of major depression at different ages among six synthetic birth cohorts

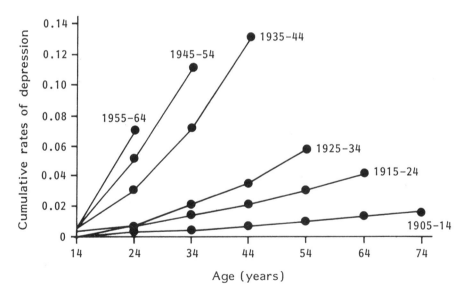

Data from ECA at five sites in the USA; date of interview, 1982; includes white people only of both sexes. Years shown are date of birth.

Source: Klerman & Weissman (1989).

Similar conclusions were reached in the long-term prospective study in Lundby, Sweden (Hagnell et al., 1982). Diagnostic assessments were based on a more classical clinical approach and, due to the true prospective design of the study, age-standardized incidence rates could be computed for each sex over a 25-year period, from 1947 to 1972. Rates increased in the most recent period for depressive disorders associated with mild or medium impairment, but *not* for the more severe psychotic type of depression. Again, an elevated rate was noticed among 20 to 39-year-old subjects, with a sharper rise for men than for women, thus reducing the difference between the sexes. The possibility of a progressive levelling off of sex differences was also suggested in a community study conducted in New Zealand on a sample of roughly 1,500 adults and calibrated by the ECA methods (Oakley-Browne et al., 1989; Wells et al., 1989; Joyce et al., 1990). Survival analyses showed a progressively increasing cumulative risk by birth cohort for major depression in both sexes, together with an earlier age of onset, and prevalence rates over a six-month period were found to be higher in men than in women for the youngest birth cohort (5.5 per cent vs. 3.5 per cent). Finally, using still another diagnostic procedure, a similar decline of lifetime rate of depression has been reported after the age of 50 in a community sample of 790 adults of South East London (Bebbington et al., 1989).

By contrast, three other major community surveys, using a similar method to the ECA, and two other datasets, failed to document an increase in the lifetime occurrence of affective disorder among the youngest birth cohorts. In a nationwide survey of mental disorders conducted in Korea in both a rural and an urban sample of 5,100 adults aged 18 to 65 years (Lee et al., 1987), no significant association of age group with lifetime rates of major depression was found. However, by contrast with the rural sample, the highest rate for affective disorders was indeed found in the 18-24 age group in the urban sample, and failure to reach a significant age trend may simply reflect the lack of power of the study due to the relatively limited subsample sizes and to the low base rate of the disorder (3.3 per cent averaged across age groups). Similarly, in the Mexican-American subsample of the Los Angeles site of the ECA study, the lifetime prevalence of major depressive episode was roughly equal in the younger and the older age groups in both sexes (Karno et al., 1987). By contrast, the lifetime rate in the youngest non-Hispanic whites was more than twice as much as that of the young Hispanic subsample, and their rate was also two to three times higher than that of the oldest white age group. Another community study, again drawing upon the ECA methods, was conducted in Puerto Rico among a representative sample of 1,513 adults (Canino et al.,

1987). Contrary to the majority of the other ECA-like studies where a decline in lifetime rates is found after age 45 (Robins et al., 1984), a continuous increase with age in the lifetime rates of major depressive episodes, and of affective disorders in general, was unexpectedly found in that study. In the fourth study also conducted in North America but using different methods, prevalence rates for depression were not found to vary between birth cohorts, but this negative finding in a sample of older adults could reflect the absence of recent birth cohorts in the study (Murphy et al., 1984). However, these data from Stirling County also suggested that sex differences in rates of depression may have diminished, especially in middle age. Finally, in the longitudinal analysis of the Alameda County study (Roberts et al., 1991), rates of depression remained higher in the oldest cohorts though some evidence was provided that overall prevalence rates of depression increased during the 1970s.

A cross-national collaborative group recently reevaluated the temporal trends in nine community samples and three family studies that used very similar diagnostic criteria and psychiatric interviews (Cross-National Collaborative Group, 1992). In addition to the already cited databases, new datasets were included from one German family study (Maier et al., 1991) and from recent community surveys conducted in Italy (Faravelli et al., 1990), Germany (Wittchen et al., 1992), France (Lépine et al., 1989), Lebanon (Karam et al., 1991) and Taiwan (Hwu et al., 1989) (for a summary, see Cross-National Collaborative Group, 1992). The total sample comprised over 43,000 subjects. Using a refined statistical modelling technique, the authors found in *every* dataset a significant 'drift'[1] in rates of depression over time, that is, a regular linear increase in the incidence of depressive disorders cutting across generations, historical periods and cultural boundaries. They further identified specific short-term cohort and period effects in some, but not all, sites but little attempt was made to relate these effects to other explanatory factors. The size of the temporal increase in rates of depression was the same in family studies and community studies, but none of the family datasets exhibited period or cohort effects. According to the authors, this finding could suggest either that depressive disorders occurring in genetically-loaded families are less sensitive to environmental factors, or that differences of instrumentation are having an influence (since the psychiatric interview (SADS) used in these three studies

---

1. The average relative risk of depression between two consecutive cohorts ranged between 1.3 and 2.6 (median=1.65). The term 'drift' was introduced to describe a regular trend over time without ascribing this to any particular period or cohort influence (see Clayton & Schifflers, 1987a & b).

differed from that (DIS) used in the community surveys). In spite of the statistical power provided by such a large sample, results are not provided separately for each gender, and there is no explanation of the failure in this analysis to find a period effect where prior analyses of the same family dataset had found one (Klerman, 1988; Lavori et al., 1987; Warshaw et al., 1991b). Moreover, the existence of a significant 'drift' in the Puerto Rican and Mexican-American samples contradicts prior findings from these datasets (see above) and this unnoticed discrepancy casts additional doubts on the meaning of the statistic and detracts somewhat from the persuasiveness of the overall findings.

Statistical modelling

As mentioned above, there was a suggestion in a few studies that gender differences had levelled off in the youngest cohorts (Hagnell et al., 1982; Joyce et al., 1990; Klerman et al., 1985; Murphy et al., 1984). This issue was taken further in a recent reanalysis of the NIMH data on the psychobiology of depression (Leon et al., 1993). The findings indicated a continuing twofold increase of risk of depression for women, together with increased rates for the 16 to 25-year-olds and for the 1960-1980 period applying uniformly to both genders. Some weight should be accorded to this study where formal statistical procedures were used to assess the significance of trends. However, it should be borne in mind that this dataset was a family study and that genetically-loaded families may not be as informative as other samples to examine this question. In this respect, it is noteworthy that trends towards a closing of the gender differential in rates were reported in the two studies where community samples were investigated prospectively (Hagnell et al., 1982; Murphy et al., 1984).

Weissman et al. (1993) have brought together the evidence on secular trends in rates of depression from epidemiology surveys using the same standardized interview schedule (the Diagnostic Interview Schedule – DIS). Figures 11.3a and 11.3b illustrate the findings, using the data from Canada and Germany respectively. The key comparison concerns the differences between the later age cohorts born in 1935, 1945, and 1955. It is evident that these show marked differences for males but much smaller ones for females. It is concluded that the rates for males seem to be still rising whereas they appear to be stabilizing in females for cohorts born after 1945.

Figure 11.3 **Cumulative lifetime rates of major depression by birth cohort and age of onset: a) Edmonton, Canada; b) Munich, Germany**

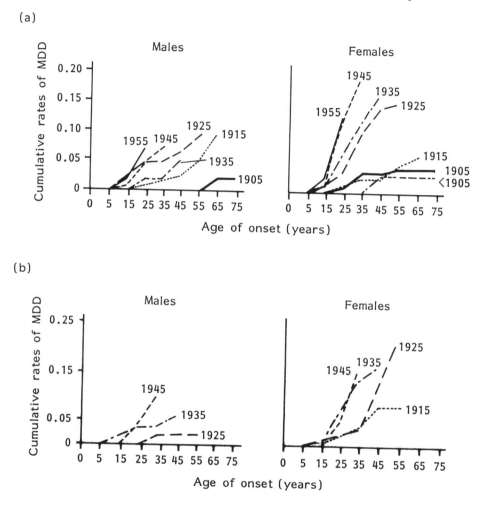

(a)

(b)

Source: Weismann et al. (1993).

The Link with Increasing Suicide Rates

Suicide rates have been rising in the youngest birth cohorts in several countries, especially in males, with a pronounced trend for a marked increase of suicides among adolescents and young adults but possibly not among children in their preadolescent years (see Chapter 13, this volume; see also Brent et al., 1987;

Holinger & Offer, 1991; Lester, 1991; Murphy & Wetzel, 1980; McIntosh, 1991; McClure, 1984; Shaffer & Fisher, 1981; Shaffer, 1988; Solomon & Hellon, 1980). These data are relevant for the study of depressive disorders for several reasons.

Retrospective studies of adult suicides have shown a high rate of depression preceding the suicidal act (Barraclough et al., 1974). Depressive conditions are elevated among suicidal adolescents too, although to a lesser extent (Shaffer, 1974, 1988). In the New York study of completed suicides (Shaffer, 1988), major depression was found to be the second strongest predictor of suicide (the strongest was a prior attempt). Similarly, in five recent psychological autopsies of adolescent suicides (Brent et al., 1988; Marttunen et al., 1991; Shafii et al., 1985; Rich et al., 1986; Runeson, 1989), the median rates of major depression and affective disorders were 24 and 52 per cent respectively. In the most recent study, conducted in Finland (Marttunen et al., 1991), 64 per cent of the 53 adolescent suicides were found to have had depressive syndromes, while among these were 40 per cent for whom the *principal* diagnosis was a depressive disorder. Two decades ago, Shaffer (1974) found about the same proportion (43 per cent) of suicides with depressed *mood*. At first sight, this seems to imply that there has been an increase in the proportion of suicides having depressive conditions, but for various reasons no conclusion can be drawn on that point.

Adolescents with general psychological dysfunction and with specific affective disorders who consult psychiatrists have a higher than normal risk of suicide (Kovacs & Puig-Antich, 1991; Rao et al., 1993). This is in line with the excess suicide risk found among adults with affective disorders (Miles, 1977; Sainsbury, 1986a & b).

Comparison of psychological autopsies in two series of adult male suicides studied 25 years apart, suggests that depressive disorders, especially in conjunction with other psychiatric diagnoses, are found in higher proportions among the young subjects of the most recent sample (Carlson et al., 1991). Further research is needed to assess how far secular trends in suicide rates can be explained by similar trends in depressive conditions. On present evidence, the link between depression and suicide is strong, so that rising suicide rates provide indirect evidence of rising rates of depression, and therefore support the findings from family and community studies of depression. However, it should be appreciated that there are other risk factors for suicide (see Chapter 13), especially drug abuse, so that the inference is necessarily uncertain.

Repeated Cross-sectional Surveys

Two surveys of large representative samples of American 7 to 16-year-old children were conducted at an interval of 13 years with identical instruments, providing the basis for a fine-tuned analysis of trends in problem behaviours (Achenbach & Howell, 1993). The results show that parents and teachers reported more depressed mood among children and adolescents recently than 13 years before, although the size of the increase was modest. Increases in scores were also found for depressive syndromes. However, these findings were paralleled by increased reports of many other behaviour problems and syndromes, especially antisocial conduct.

Also relevant are repeat cross-sectional surveys of mental health carried out in 1957 and 1976 on representative samples of over 2,200 American adults (Gurin et al., 1960; Veroff et al., 1981a & b). The strength of these two household surveys lies in the rigour of sampling and in the close comparability of the interview schedules used 19 years apart. In the more recent survey, young adult respondents reported fewer feelings of happiness, less high morale, increased worries and readiness to admit having problems, and increased anxiety. Though the focus was on general feelings of well-being and not on depression, results suggested that these changes reflected cultural shifts associated with new orientations towards work, family life and self-definition among the youngest generation (Veroff et al., 1981a). Similar findings arose from an analysis of time trends in levels of reported happiness in 15 American surveys of representative samples (total N=28,622) of adults conducted between 1957 and 1978 (Rodgers, 1982). Declines were found from 1957 up to the early 1970s, with subsequent increases thereafter. The declines applied mostly to the younger people, and to those with higher income or educational status. While these studies do not assess trends in depressive phenomenon as such, their results run parallel to the other studies both in terms of the direction and the timing of changes over time.

Hospital Data

Finally, two hospital datasets may be used to examine time trends on depressive conditions. The first study provides a long run of diagnostic data (1920-1982) on over 62,000 admissions to a university hospital in Zürich (Angst, 1985); before 1950, the proportion of cases diagnosed as depressive was always below two per cent, but it rose to five per cent or more subsequently. These data have been cited as evidence of an increased proportion of depressed patients in treatment settings (Klerman & Weissman, 1989), but they need to be examined critically. Inevitably, hospital record data of this kind are open to biases in referral, admissions policy, and diagnostic practice. The finding that the proportion of cases of affective disorder rose over time for all varieties, and did so equally for depression and mania, makes it unlikely that changing diagnostic practices constitutes the explanation; nevertheless there has to be uncertainty on this point because there was no independent check on diagnoses and no recoding according to standard criteria. A more serious concern is that the proportion of readmissions rose dramatically over the same time period, with the consequence that the *same* individuals contributed to the figures several times over. It is unfortunate that the data were not analyzed separately for first admissions.

The second dataset provides information on 6,357 children and adolescents (8 to 16-year-olds) attending the child psychiatry department of the Maudsley Hospital in London during the period 1968-1990 (Fombonne & Rutter, unpublished). While suicidal ideas, threats, or attempts increased during that period, no consistent trend was found for other depressive phenomena, whether defined as depressive symptoms or disorders. Again, because these data derive from routinely completed item sheets, and because the time-span is somewhat limited, these negative findings are not conclusive. However, the lack of an increase over time in the *proportion* of psychiatric disorders presenting as a depressive syndrome suggests that any increase in depression is likely to have been part of a broader increase in a wider range of disorders.

Methodological and Analytical Problems

Recall

In the ECA study, the finding of higher lifetime prevalence rates of psychiatric disorders among the younger groups led to the systematic search for ways of explaining this pattern without concluding that the prevalence of these disorders had actually increased. However, it was shown that the findings could not be explained, for example, by a tendency for older people to attribute psychiatric symptoms to physical illness or to dismiss symptoms causing little impairment, or by mild cognitive impairment among older people (Robins et al., 1991a). One obvious possibility to account for lower rates in older people is that they could have forgotten past episodes of disorder that happened a long time ago. Small but constant rates of forgetting with the passage of each year could create a pattern similar to that actually obtained with many datasets. Studies have shown that the test-retest reliability of lifetime rates decreases with time, and that recent episodes of depression increase recall of past episodes (Aneshensel et al., 1987; Prusoff et al., 1988). Since current rates of depressive disorders are low among older compared with younger respondents, they are less likely to have recently suffered a depressive episode and therefore to recall past episodes. This hypothesis receives some support from the analysis of Simon and VonKorff (1992) who showed that, at all ages, age of onset clustered in the 10 years prior to interview.

One feature of the ECA results, however, makes it much more difficult to sustain an explanation in terms of recall or any other systematic bias. Among black subjects, the proportion who had suffered any kind of psychiatric disorder during their lifetime did not decline with age, whereas among white subjects it did (Robins et al., 1991a). Yet lifetime rates of *affective* disorders among black Americans did decline with age, as in the case of white people, although rates of psychiatric disorders grouped together did not. Whatever is happening here, it is difficult to explain it by a recall effect, because it varies between specific psychiatric disorders.

Warshaw et al. (1991a) used a more direct method of establishing whether age differences could be the result of age-related forgetting of earlier episodes. Lifetime diagnoses of 1,684 first-degree relatives of subjects in a family study were re-evaluated after a six-year interval by interviewers blind to the original assessments. A high proportion (37 per cent) of diagnoses of depression 'disappeared' at the second interview, but age was not related to the amount of change; the most recent episodes were more likely to be forgotten than older ones, and age of first onset showed high stability. In another test-retest study, older respondents were even found to report an earlier age of first onset at the second interview (Farrer et al., 1989). These results make it unlikely that the decline in prevalence with age could arise through forgetting or through faulty memories moving incidents forward in time. Similarly, if memory effects were major artefacts, they should have applied to rates of affective disorders equally for each dataset, but results from a Puerto-Rican study ran in the opposite direction (Canino et al., 1987). Furthermore, the decline with age of lifetime rates of depression was perceptible in studies where analyses were restricted to relatively recent birth cohorts (Bland et al., 1988; Joyce et al., 1990; Lavori et al., 1987), and the findings from the prospective Lundby study (Hagnell et al., 1982) and the prospective follow-up sample of Coryell et al. (1992) could not possibly be due to artefacts of recall. In the same vein, convergent results from samples of adolescents and children (Lewinsohn et al., 1993; Ryan et al., 1992) argue against forgetting as the main explanation. However, the magnitude of the effect is much smaller in prospective studies than in cross-sectional surveys, and this may suggest that a part of the effect found in cross-sectional surveys is due to forgetting.

Validity and Reliability

Going beyond the specific question of recall, the validity and reliability of results obtained with psychiatric diagnostic interviews such as the Diagnostic Interview Schedule (DIS) in ECA-type studies has been questioned (Parker, 1987). As already mentioned, the test-retest stability of lifetime rates is far from satisfactory (Warshaw et al., 1991a) and, when the same subjects are re-interviewed, relatively low agreement has been found for depressive disorders (Anthony et al., 1985; Bromet et al., 1986; Helzer et al., 1985). Detailed examination of the sources of disagreement (for example, samples of patients vs. samples of the general population, questioning by lay persons vs. questioning by clinicians) falls outside the scope of this chapter. The central point is that even though measurement error may well affect the accuracy of the results as estimates of *absolute* lifetime prevalence rates, it is highly implausible that *age trends* in these rates could be the result of faulty instrumentation. To account for these trends by measurement errors, we would need to postulate that these vary in a regular way with the age of respondents. There is no evidence to suggest that instruments like the DIS would produce systematically different results for different age groups, and no one has suggested a plausible reason why they should operate in that way. Thus, in the recent National Comorbidity Survey conducted in America between 1990 and 1992 (Kessler et al., 1993) a structured diagnostic instrument similar to the DIS was used but special modifications in its structure were introduced to facilitate recall of past episodes among respondents. The lifetime rates of depression were much higher than in the ECA study but this finding applied to all age groups and decreased lifetime rates among respondents over the age of 45 were still reported. Furthermore, the increase in rates for recent birth cohorts has been found in studies that used other research instruments (Bebbington et al., 1989; Gershon et al., 1987; Klerman et al., 1985; Lavori et al., 1987; Lewinsohn et al., 1993; Maier et al., 1991; Ryan et al., 1992) or clinical diagnosis (Hagnell et al., 1982). The increases in levels of depressed mood as assessed by several informants in Achenbach & Howell (1993) support the convergent validity of the results and argue against the view that they are caused by instrumentation errors in self-report measures.

Differences in the psychological mindedness of younger and older subjects and in the way they label depressive descriptions have also been examined.

One study indicated that, presented with case vignettes portraying major depression, older subjects were less likely to recognize these descriptions as an emotional or psychological problem (Hasin & Link, 1988). Similarly, the work of Veroff et al. (1981b) suggested that the youngest generation relied less on classical role standards and more on self-expression as a basis of self-definition; these changes were paralleled by an increased tendency to think of problems as being psychological or emotional, and to seek help from mental health experts. These results were interpreted as showing that younger people are less likely to deny that they have psychological problems. In other studies, however, no association was found between age and labelling problems as psychological (Robins et al., 1991a; Lewinsohn et al., 1993). Also, the decrease in lifetime rates of depression is manifest during middle age, whereas any increase in labelling problems as psychological is among the youngest respondents only; hence, any change in labelling is unlikely to account entirely for the findings. Nevertheless, the findings as a whole do show that differences between generations in psychological orientation may well be a significant confounder.

Institutionalization, Mortality

Institutionalization is unlikely to be a plausible explanation of the findings since depressive disorders rarely lead to long-term hospitalization in psychiatric institutions. In addition, the last two decades have seen the development of more effective treatment methods, and a general trend in Western countries towards closing down psychiatric beds in favour of outpatient care (see Chapter 6). These changes will have reduced the impact of institutionalization. The ECA covered people in institutions as well as in private households, and found no significant difference between the rate of major depression among those in psychiatric institutions and those in private households (Weissman et al., 1991). Simon and VonKorff (1992) computed that rates of institutionalization would have to be 16 times higher than the average for 70-year-old women with a history of depression to explain age trends in the ECA data. Similarly, selective mortality can be ruled out as the main explanation. The difference in mortality between those with and without a history of depression would have to be so enormous that this hypothesis is not tenable. Some studies have reported a modest increase in mortality rates among people with affective disorders, with relative risks not in excess of two (Murphy et al., 1987). By contrast, Simon and VonKorff (1992) have estimated that, even with conservative assumptions, aggregate mortality rates for

40-year-old women with a history of depression would have to be eight times higher than in the general population in order to account for their findings.

Whether the Trends are Specific to Depression

It is an important question how far any increase in rates of psychiatric disorders is confined to depressive conditions. The alternative is that the increase in depression is part of a general increase in mental illness. Analyses of ECA data have shown the same pattern for manic disorders as for depression (Lasch et al., 1990), suggesting that the whole range of affective disorders is concerned, as already found in one family study (Gershon et al., 1987). Examination of the same ECA data also showed that rates of non-affective psychiatric disorders, in particular antisocial personality, were higher in the youngest than in the oldest cohorts (Robins et al., 1991b). Few studies have reported simultaneously on trends for several psychiatric disorders. The recent reanalysis of ECA data by Simon and VonKorff (1992) shed light on that issue. These authors showed that prevalence rates of depression, panic disorder and schizophrenia exhibited a six to eightfold increase among subjects aged 36-45 as compared to those over 65 years, while similar but less dramatic findings applied to alcohol use and phobia. These trends in non-affective disorders were not attributable to comorbidity with depression since the patterns remained unchanged after exclusion of comorbid cases (Simon & VonKorff, 1992). These authors further reported analyses of lifetime rates for individual psychiatric symptoms and found that lifetime rates again peaked among the youngest cohorts for almost all of them, with roughly a twofold increase in rates of reported symptoms of depression, schizophrenia and alcohol use among youngest respondents compared to oldest subjects, and nearly a threefold increment for symptoms of mania. This uniform pattern applying both to psychiatric symptoms and to disorders of a different kind shows that any increase in prevalence is not specific to depression. It suggests either a general increase in mental illness over the last 40 years or, alternatively, pervasive measurement errors. For the reasons already discussed, measurement errors are unlikely to be the whole explanation in the case of depression. Also, recent evidence of an increase in a *range* of behavioural problems comes from two repeat cross-sectional surveys of American children and adolescents using different measurement approaches (Achenbach & Howell, 1993).

Age-specific Effects

Interpretation of time trends is far from easy. As set out in Chapter 2, *secular change* is used interchangeably in this book with *period effect* to refer to a change over time that tends to affect all individuals regardless of age. It is contrasted with *age effect*, which is a change in some condition or risk as a function of the age of the individual; and with *cohort effect*, which is a variation in some condition or risk that applies to all individuals sharing a common experience, typically an experience associated with having been born at about the same time. Implicit in the discussion up to now has been the attempt to establish whether there has been a secular increase in the prevalence of depressive disorders. This section focuses more closely on the problem of distinguishing between a secular change of that kind and an age effect or cohort effect.

Although they are conceptually different, these three effects incorporate time as a common scale, and, as discussed in Chapter 2, they may be difficult or impossible to distinguish from any given set of data. One difficulty in disentangling them lies in their interdependence: one effect may be expressed as a function of the two others (for example, age=period – cohort). The fundamental statistical problem is to obtain independent estimates of the three effects, for which there exists no unique solution; several combinations of parameter estimates will provide comparable fitted rates in modelling techniques. Attempts have been made to solve this problem but extreme caution is needed on the underlying mathematical assumptions that are made and they often lack any biological or psychological plausibility (Clayton & Schifflers, 1987b; Holford, 1992). For example, whereas time-dependent variables ought to be treated as continuous variables for statistical purposes, a common practice is to create time *intervals* and age *groupings*: then the exact relationship between the variables no longer holds true (Clayton & Hills, 1993). Thus, it has been shown that changes in birth rates may mimic cohort effects and lead to spurious increases in rates of disorder (see Clayton & Schifflers, 1987b). The problem can be further complicated when groupings of unequal width are used, as is usually done for the extreme of the age distributions to compensate for lower sample sizes.

While these potential statistical artefacts have long been recognized, surprisingly little attention has been paid to them in the psychiatric literature. For example, it would be easy to examine the robustness of the findings within and across datasets for different age and time groupings, but no attempt has been made to do so. One study used year of birth as a continuous variable to test for 'cohort' effects (Ryan et al., 1992). However, as recognized by the authors, cohort and period effects were indistinguishable and the statistical analysis was based on another strong, and indeed unrealistic, mathematical assumption of a constant multiplicative annual increment of the risk across the study period. Moreover, the high statistical significance of findings derived from such a small sample (26 cases of depression out of a sample of 163 siblings), calls for prudence in the use and interpretation of statistical models.

As far as temporal trends in depression are concerned, the findings are sparse and contradictory. Analysis of a large dataset by Wickramaratne et al. (1989) suggested that a sharp increase in the risk of depression applies to the cohort of women born between 1935 and 1945, and to that of men born between 1935 and 1954. In addition, the authors identified a secular increase between 1960 and 1980 for both sexes, as was also found by Leon et al. (1993). These results were established on the white only subsample of the ECA study, and they are somewhat at variance with the age and period effects only described by Lavori et al. (1987), with those of Gershon et al. (1987) who suggested a single cohort effect applying to those born from 1950 onwards, and with those of Warshaw et al. (1991b) who described a period effect starting in the mid-sixties and an age-period interaction for both sexes. In a recent reanalysis of some of these data but with different statistical approaches (Cross-National Collaborative Group, 1992), the period effects found by Lavori et al. (1987) and Warshaw et al. (1991b) were not replicated. Period and cohort effects, and in general a combination of these, were found in six datasets (USA-ECA, France, Lebanon, Taiwan, Italy, Los Angeles non-Hispanic subjects) whereas in the other community samples (Canada, Germany, New Zealand, Los Angeles Hispanics, Puerto Rico) no such effects were reported. In the follow-up of unaffected relatives from a family study (Coryell et al., 1992), the design ruled out a period effect, at least for these particular years, but age and cohort effects could not be distinguished. One interesting finding of the study of Lewinsohn et al. (1993) was that the relapse rate was significantly higher for the more recent birth cohorts. In so far as relapse is independent of the particular time period, this result argues for a true cohort effect.

Altogether, there is no emerging pattern in the available analyses. The most consistent findings were that the increase in depression impinges mainly on young people with depression occurring at an earlier age, and perhaps too that of increased rates of depression in the period from 1950 to 1980. Further research is needed to follow up the early findings from US research. The findings of the recent international collaborative study (Cross-National

Collaborative Group, 1992) appear to support the theory that secular increases have occurred in rates of depressive disorders. However, as argued earlier, there are good reasons for thinking that statistical artefacts are at least partially responsible for these results. A harsher test could have been performed using the large ECA sample to replicate the results across five US sites; this natural experiment where homogeneity of instrumentation, sampling and background characteristics would have been high, would provide a more robust test of the validity of the model.

In any case, the pursuit of a purely statistical solution to the age-period-cohort analysis seems pointless. All these variables have time as a common scale, and time as such cannot be an explanatory variable. Time only acts as a proxy indicator for unmeasured causal influences which may be pinpointed using natural experiments, where one variable is allowed to fluctuate with the others fixed. There also seems to be an assumption that rising rates of depression reflect a single underlying mechanism, whereas it is more likely that a mixture of processes operate. The aim of research should be to establish what these causal mechanisms are, and this cannot be done by using statistical models on their own.

Conclusion

The evidence strongly suggests that there has been a true increase in depressive conditions in the most recent birth cohorts. Convergent findings from a wide array of studies conducted in various countries, using a variety of designs and measures, support this conclusion. However, the actual magnitude of this secular change is unknown and probably small, since there is also evidence that a sizeable portion of the apparent increase is in fact due to biases arising from the research methods used. The main reason for these biases is that intensive research on this subject began only within the past 15 years, so that little information is yet available from prospective longitudinal studies or repeated cross-sectional surveys, and heavy reliance must be placed on retrospective studies, which have inevitable weaknesses.

How far this increased prevalence applies specifically to depressive phenomena remains to be established; whereas one study provided some evidence of specificity (Ryan et al., 1992), other findings suggest that a wider range of other psychiatric disorders, be they affective (Lasch et al., 1990) or not (Robins et al., 1991a & b), exhibited similar time trends. Studies that simultaneously assess trends of a range of problem behaviours (Achenbach &

Howell, 1993) or of psychiatric disorders (Simon & VonKorff, 1992) do not support a high degree of specificity.

The evidence suggests that while females are considerably more likely to be depressed than males, there has been a possible shift towards unity in the sex ratio, and an earlier age of onset in the most recent birth cohorts. If confirmed, these findings would have important implications. First, they may act as pointers towards the risk mechanisms underlying the temporal changes. Second, they may imply a reconsideration of the analyses, interpretation and planning of family and genetic studies, both in children and in adults. Third, there are potential implications for public health policy if, indeed, more and more youth become depressed, and at a younger age.

DEPRESSION AND INDIVIDUAL DEVELOPMENT IN THE ADOLESCENT PHASE

Suicide statistics and findings from clinical and community studies of depressive conditions show that the incidence of depressive phenomena sharply increases during adolescence, and that prepubertal depressive conditions are rare and equally common in each sex, whereas large differences between the sexes appear during adolescence. These robust findings on the relationship between depressive phenomena and the developmental process during adolescence need therefore to be taken into account in any explanatory model.

Age and Sex Trends

Studies of Clinical Samples

Current estimates of prevalence rates of depressive disorders in clinically-referred children and adolescents range from 5 per cent to 55 per cent with an average estimate of 40 per cent across studies (Angold, 1988b; Kolvin et al., 1991; see review in Petersen et al., 1992). These samples were assessed by a variety of instruments, and variations of prevalence rates with age were rarely reported or subjected to systematic examination. However, evidence of an increase with age in the number and frequency of depressive syndromes has been provided by several studies conducted at the Maudsley Hospital in London. In a first study (Pearce, 1978), the rate rose from 10 per cent in prepubertal children to 25 per cent in postpubertal children. This increase in frequency was accompanied by a change in sex ratio: the male preponderance found in the prepubertal children was transformed among postpubertal adolescents into the 2:1 female to male ratio typically found in adult samples (Weissman & Klerman, 1977; Weissman et al., 1984). In other studies based on interviews and clinical records (Rutter, 1991; Angold & Rutter, 1992), the same pattern was confirmed with the additional finding that increase in depressive symptoms was not found for other psychopathological conditions such as anxiety or conduct disorders.

Large samples of clinically-referred children and adolescents have also been studied in different countries with the Child Behaviour Checklist, a parent rating scale of children's behaviour problems. The original American data (Achenbach & Edelbrock, 1981) showed that item scores related to depressed mood ('unhappy, sad or depressed') increased with age, a rise which was more pronounced in referred children than in the non-referred. Furthermore, this item had one of the strongest effects in predicting whether a child would be referred, a finding which has been replicated in other datasets and with youth self-report questionnaires as well (Achenbach, 1991; Fombonne, 1992; Verhulst et al., 1985).

These data point to the importance of depressed feelings and negative emotions as major correlates of child and adolescent psychopathology.

Community Surveys

On the basis of psychiatric interviews, the Isle of Wight study found a threefold increase in depressive *feelings* between age 10-11 (13 per cent) and age 14-15 (40 per cent) (Rutter, 1986). Among boys who expressed such feelings, the vast majority were either pubescent or postpubertal, irrespective of their chronological age, thus suggesting that negative mood was associated, at least for boys, with the onset of puberty. Over the same four-year period of adolescent development there was a more than tenfold increase in the prevalence of depressive *disorders*, with a much greater increase among females than among males, so that by the age of 14-15 there was a striking female preponderance (Rutter et al., 1976). Since then, many other studies of community samples have shown a rise in the prevalence of depressive disorders from childhood to adolescence (see Fleming & Offord, 1990). In fourteen studies, the point prevalence rate for children fluctuated around 1 per cent with a sex ratio around unity, while among adolescents, the rate was typically three to four times higher, ranging from 1.2 per cent (McGee et al., 1990) to 9.0 per cent (Garrison et al., 1992) for current-prevalence estimates. Since community surveys encompass diverse age groups and yield relatively small numbers of psychiatric 'cases', the precise developmental pattern of gender differences is rather difficult to portray. Nevertheless, the shift in sex ratio toward a female preponderance is established around mid-adolescence (14-15 years), as indicated in a recent follow-up study of a community sample that documented a change of sex ratio towards female preponderance between age 12 and 15 (McGee et al., 1992) and in a recent survey of American adults where the gender difference of cumulative onset risks was established by age 10 (Kessler et al., 1993). Most other community samples find that by mid-adolescence the risk of depressive disorders is twice as high among girls as among boys (Whitaker et al., 1990). Similar findings were obtained in a family study (Weissman et al., 1987) where rates for boys and girls were similar before age 10 whereas, by age 20, the gender differential typical from adult samples was reached. The incidence of depressive disorders remains high in adult life as shown by a mean age of onset of 27 years reported in the ECA study (Weissman et al., 1991) and of 24 years in the National Comorbidity Survey (Kessler et al., 1993). The latter study showed steady hazard rates in both sexes from age 15 to age 45.

Questionnaire surveys of depressive *syndromes* and depressed *mood* have also been conducted with diverse community samples of children and adolescents (see Achenbach et al., 1991; Angold, 1988a; Petersen et al., 1992, 1993; Radloff, 1991). In general, rates for individual items tapping depressed affect increase with adolescence. Throughout the adolescent phase, marked gender effects are found, and girls score consistently higher than boys on measures of depressed mood and depressive syndromes (Petersen et al., 1992). By contrast with developmental trends for depressive disorders, depressed mood does not exhibit similar age effects. Most studies do not indicate variations in rates of depressed mood with age; however, it ought to be noted that the vast majority of these data stem from cross-sectional studies of adolescents from different age groups rather than from true longitudinal studies. In other studies, rates have been found to decline from middle to late teens (Radloff, 1991; Wells et al., 1987), a finding that was interpreted by Wells et al. (1987) either as a manifestation of transient symptoms during adolescent turmoil, or as a cohort effect; however, their data did not allow for a precise test of either hypothesis. Yet, the latter possibility is unlikely since the same developmental trend was equally noticed in more recent longitudinal investigations (Petersen et al., 1991b), which found a sharp increase in levels of depressed affect in middle adolescence, with the emergence of a significant gender difference that was somewhat attenuated in late adolescence, along with declines in overall rates. Compared to adult rates, adolescent reports of depressive symptoms have been found to be higher in several studies (Allgood-Merten et al., 1990; Radloff, 1991). Trends established from questionnaire-based studies should be interpreted with caution. The measures used are self-report instruments where thresholds have been established to define excess levels of depressive symptomatology. These cut-offs are known to be imperfect and to be associated with significant misclassification rates (Fombonne, 1991). Such measurement limitations in themselves should not interfere with the interpretation of age and gender trends assuming that measurement properties are unaffected by these two variables. This assumption has indeed received little attention with many of these measures. When attention has been drawn to these issues, age- and gender-specific cut-offs have often been proposed to ensure that equivalence of measurement would be obtained across different subgroups. Thus, the gender differences and the relative absence of an age effect found with questionnaire surveys should be interpreted with these caveats in mind.

Suicide and Suicidal Behaviour

As discussed earlier, there are fairly close links between suicide and depressive disorders. Suicide, like depressive disorders, becomes much more common during adolescence, although in the case of suicide, the relationship with age is even stronger. Suicide is extremely rare in childhood before puberty (Shaffer, 1974; McClure, 1984; McIntosh, 1991; Sainsbury, 1986a & b); there is a tenfold increase in the suicide rate between preadolescent years and young adulthood (see Chapter 13, this volume; also, Lester, 1991). The rate increases most rapidly between the ages of 15 and 19, although there are further increases from the age of 20 onwards. Males outnumber females in completed suicides in every age group. Shaffer (1974) found that suicides tended to be taller than average for their age, which suggests a link with early onset of puberty.

By contrast, suicidal behaviour (short of completed suicide) peaks in the late adolescent years and declines thereafter, and rates are much higher in girls than in boys (Hawton & Goldacre, 1982). These age and sex differences in the patterns of adolescent suicides and attempted suicides suggest that somewhat different mechanisms are involved (Rutter, 1986). Similar rises in the frequency of suicidal behaviours and of suicidal ideation in adolescence have been described in samples of psychiatric inpatients (Borst et al., 1991; Carlson & Cantwell, 1982; Carlson et al., 1987).

In broad terms, the findings show that there are links between suicide, suicidal behaviours, and depression. All become much more common during the adolescent years, but in detail each is related in a different way to the process of individual development, as shown by the different timing and by the contrasting patterns for males and females, and each is probably caused by different but related mechanisms.

Risk Factors and Comorbidity

Most of the community surveys have failed to detect any consistent association of depressive disorders with variables such as IQ, physical health, socio-economic status, ethnicity, and, to a lesser extent with school performance. Because the absolute number of cases identified in these surveys is typically small, power to detect associations is limited. However, parental psychopathology, adverse psychosocial, and familial circumstances and stressful life events do appear to be associated with depression among young people, a finding that derives from both community and clinical samples (Berney et al., 1991; Fleming & Offord, 1990; Goodyer, 1990; Puckering, 1989). However, these variables are also associated with a range of different psychopathological outcomes.

Little is known on the protective factors or mechanisms that protect against depression among children and adolescents; however, high self-esteem and good coping skills, school achievement, involvement in extra-curricular activities and positive relationships with parents, peers and adults outside the family context all appear to exert protective influences against depressive outcomes (see Compas, 1994; Merikangas & Angst, 1994; Petersen et al., 1992, 1993).

In the majority of cases, depression in young people co-occurs with other forms of psychopathology such as eating disorders or alcohol and drug abuse (Rohde et al., 1991). In an exhaustive review of comorbidity in depression, Merikangas and Angst (1994) noted that anxiety frequently coexists with depressed mood and depressive syndromes, and also with depressive disorders, which are rarely found in a 'pure' form. Thus, depressed children have a rate of concomitant anxiety disorders ranging from 20 to 75 per cent which is much higher than that expected under the hypothesis of no association, a result which derives from community samples (Fleming & Offord, 1990) and is confirmed in clinical samples as well. There is evidence that comorbid depressive disorders have a more severe presentation and course, and longitudinal studies of epidemiological and clinical samples suggest that anxiety disorders are often antecedents of depressive conditions (Angst et al., 1990; Kovacs et al., 1988; Reinherz et al., 1989; Rohde et al., 1991).

Depressive conditions also overlap quite significantly with conduct disorders (Zoccolillo & Rogers, 1991), and the developmental interrelations between these two psychopathological dimensions are still poorly understood. From the limited evidence available, conduct disordered children with depression have a similar outcome to those without depression (Harrington et al., 1991; Kovacs et al., 1988) and their family history does not exhibit a high incidence of affective disorders. Longitudinal studies also suggest that depressive conditions occur as an adjunct to conduct disorders on which they are superimposed as transient conditions indexing a worsened functioning.

In contrast to the state of knowledge on adult depression, research on the efficacy of treatments for depression among young people is still very limited (see reviews in Harrington, 1993; Kazdin, 1990; Petersen et al., 1992, 1993; Mufson et al., 1993). Psychopharmacological treatments are not as effective as with depressed adults. Psychotherapeutic treatments, which take various forms, are widely used. From comparisons between experimental and control groups, psychological interventions appear to reduce the levels of depressive symptoms to a significant extent. However, these gains are unrelated to the particular form of intervention and they are not confined to depressive symptoms. While these treatment effects are substantial and maintained over time, nothing is known about the mechanisms underlying them.

Individual and Social Consequences

In view of the prevalence of depressive conditions during adolescence, their short- and long-term consequences at the individual and societal levels are important concerns.

Research has begun to address the question of how far depressive conditions that occur for the first time in adolescence tend to persist or recur, and tend to predict future disorders of other kinds. First, follow-up studies of depressed children and adolescents suggest a strong risk of recurrence in the short term, for cases identified both in clinical settings (Kovacs et al., 1984a & b) and in community samples (McGee & Williams, 1988). Second, longer-term follow-ups show that depressive symptoms in adolescence tend to predict the recurrence of depressive symptoms in adulthood, as assessed by questionnaires or record summaries (Kandel & Davies, 1986; Zeitlin, 1986). The best evidence on the continuity between childhood and adult depressive disorders comes from a long-term follow-up study of depressed children who, in adult life, had a sevenfold increase of risk of experiencing a major depression as compared to psychiatric controls (Harrington et al., 1990). The key findings of that study were that the design ruled out comorbid disorders as a possible explanatory factor for adult psychopathology and that the increased risk of adult psychiatric disorders was shown to be confined to affective disorders. Nevertheless, this study provided no clues on the intervening mechanisms of this strong and specific continuity over 18 years. Third, studies of adult drug addicts have consistently shown an association with major depressive episodes; some of these studies show that the onset of depression preceded drug abuse rather than the opposite (Christie et al., 1988). Similar findings arose from a questionnaire-based survey of a sample of adolescents followed-up until their early adulthood (Kandel & Davies, 1986). Thus, depression with adolescent onset apparently leads to a substantially increased risk of subsequent development of psychiatric conditions other than depression.

The second question concerns the magnitude of the direct and indirect costs of adolescent depressive disorders, once it is recognized that they do have a high rate of persistence into adult life. It is beyond the scope of this chapter to cover this fully, but some brief indications can be put forward. First, several studies showed a very high risk of rehospitalization during adolescence after a first index depressive episode (Asarnow et al., 1988; Garber et al., 1988). Second, there is also evidence that, in adult life, the relative risk of attending medical facilities and psychiatric services, and of using medication prescribed for psychiatric dysfunction, is two to three times higher for (ex)depressed children as compared to other psychiatric controls (Harrington et al., 1990). Given that adolescent depression is very likely to recur in adult life and will therefore contribute to the formation of the pool of depressed adults, recent findings from the ECA study are also relevant. Adults who had experienced a major depression during the last year were found to have a more than twofold increase in their use of outpatient and inpatient medical services, and an eight to elevenfold increase in the use of psychiatric services (Weissman et al., 1991). There are similar findings on the increased use of services amongst children and adolescents (Fleming et al., 1989).

Another implication derives from the relations between suicide and affective disorders. Thus, follow-up studies of samples of depressed children and adolescents have shown high rates of suicide in adult life (Rao et al., 1993). Suicide is the third most common cause of death among American youth; in England, it has become the second most common cause of death (after accidents) among young 15 to 24-year-old men, and the pattern is similar for other European countries (see Chapter 13). There is also evidence that 15 per cent of subjects with a depressive illness will ultimately die from suicide. On the basis of these findings, and assuming a 2 per cent prevalence rate of depressive illness among the general population, Sainsbury (1986a & b) estimated that the proportion of suicides attributable to depression in England and Wales is about 60 per cent. Caution is needed in reviewing these estimates, but they do point to the significant public health implications of adolescent depressive conditions.

These considerations also suggest that research into the mechanisms leading to a first onset of a depressive disorder, to its successful treatment and to the prevention of subsequent relapses, should focus on adolescence as a key developmental phase; and they underline the need to explore those processes that protect against negative developmental trajectories and promote healthy psychological outcomes in late adolescence.

MECHANISMS, PROCESSES, AND SOCIETAL INFLUENCES

This section selectively reviews risk factors that might explain secular change in the prevalence of depressive conditions among young people. The first part suggests that the importance of genetic factors varies depending on the specific type of depressive disorder, and that the various depressive disorders are determined by a range of factors in addition to genetic ones. The second part considers the influence of puberty and the third psychosocial aspects of adolescence such as family life and school life; these have changed over time, and contribute to pathways leading to depressive conditions, so that they may help to explain secular change in rates of depressive disorders. The final part discusses ways in which broader economic and social changes may impinge on the psychological health of young people.

Genetic Factors

Three rather separate issues need to be considered in relation to the possibility that genetic factors may play a role in the increase in rate of depressive disorders. First, it is possible that migration patterns have led to a net increase in high risk individuals. This is highly implausible both because the secular trend seems to apply to white groups within the USA (data are lacking for Europe) and because the level of migration is too low to account for the time trends.

Second, the trend could be a consequence of changes in the genetic pool within indigenous groups. That explanation can be ruled out because the rise has taken place over such a relatively short time period. Third, genetic factors may be indirectly relevant through their role in influencing susceptibility to environmental hazards (Rutter, 1994). This is thought to be the case, for example, with respect to obesity, insulin-resistant diabetes and gallstones (Weatherall, 1992). Thus, examination of the role of genetic factors in depression needs to be undertaken as part of investigation of multifactorial causation.

Family and twin studies of adult samples have demonstrated that genetic factors play a major role in some depressive disorders, particularly bipolar conditions (alternation between manic and depressive episodes) and severe major depressive disorders. For these clinical forms, heritability estimates are much higher (about 80 per cent) than for milder forms of unipolar depression (roughly 10 to 50 per cent), the latter forms representing the bulk of depressive conditions (McGuffin & Katz, 1989). The role of genetic factors in child and adolescent depression has not yet been investigated using twin or adoptee designs. However, their probable role had been suggested in a series of more recent family studies (for reviews, see Merikangas & Angst, 1994; Rutter et al., 1990a & b). First, the offspring of parents with an affective disorder have higher rates of psychiatric disorders than controls. The increased risk is relatively diagnosis-specific in the offspring of bipolar parents but the disorders seen in the offspring of unipolar parents are quite mixed. Second, an early age of onset appears to be associated with a higher familial loading, and the offspring of parents with early onset depression tend also to have an elevated risk of early onset major depression, and tend to have an equally earlier age of onset (Weissman et al., 1984, 1986, 1987). Third, family studies of children or adolescents diagnosed as depressed have shown a higher rate of depressive disorders in their first degree relatives as compared to normal or psychiatric control groups (Harrington et al., 1993; Puig-Antich et al., 1989; Strober et al., 1988). The last study also found that an earlier age of onset among those with bipolar disorders was related to a stronger familial loading, in keeping with the view that an early age of onset is an index of genetic vulnerability (see Strober, 1992). Fourth, more recent family and twin studies of adults have taken into account the high rates of comorbidity associated with depression as well as the role of assortative mating (for a review, see Merikangas & Angst, 1994). Studies of adult twins suggested that concordance was equally high for symptoms of depression and anxiety. In addition, familial transmission was stronger when parents had both anxiety and depression and was low for depression alone, suggesting a relative lack of specificity of the familial transmission of depression (Merikangas et al., 1988). Fifth, adoption studies have also been instrumental in showing the strong environmental determinants in the development of depressive conditions (Cadoret et al., 1985).

As part of the Swedish Adoption/Twin Study of Ageing (SATSA), a recent twin study was designed to assess genetic influences on self-reported depressive symptoms among adults, as measured by a widely-used scale (assessing depressive symptomatology) (Gatz et al., 1992). This rare design provided a natural experiment to compare identical and fraternal twins reared apart or reared together, which made it possible to disentangle variance due to genetic influences and to shared and non-shared environmental influences. Heritability, estimated by the intraclass correlation coefficient between MZ twins reared apart, was rather low and explained 16 per cent of the variance in total score. Interestingly, there was some suggestion of stronger effects for symptoms indicative of psychomotor retardation and somatic complaints. Shared environments had a greater effect but non-shared experiences (i.e. those that impinge on the individual rather than the family as a whole) accounted for the highest proportion of population variance.

In sum, family, twin and adoption studies have shown that a family history of affective disorder is a strong predictor of depression. Although they were suggestive of *some* genetic component in the pathogenesis of *some* cases of juvenile depression, the magnitude of genetic influences varies across the spectrum of depressive phenomena, with environmental influences playing a substantial role in the most common forms of depressive disorder.

Two recent longitudinal studies of children of depressed parents suggest that a significant proportion of the aggregate familial influence may be due to environmentally mediated risk mechanisms (Radke-Yarrow et al., 1992; Hammen et al., 1990). These findings derive from small samples and, although more prolonged follow-up periods (through adolescence and early adult life) might alter the pattern of results, they are in line with the literature showing that various kinds of severe parental psychopathology increase the risk of negative outcomes in their children, including affective disturbances among many others (Rutter, 1989; Rutter & Quinton, 1984). Recent research also indicates that measures of psychopathology of both parents, and not only that of the mother, should be included in family studies (Phares & Compas, 1992).

Of particular relevance to our purpose are the findings of a recent family study where first-degree relatives of persons diagnosed with unipolar depression exhibited different patterns of familial incidence according to biological characteristics (Giles et al., 1989). Specifically, rates of unipolar depression were similar in parents and siblings with reduced REM (rapid eye movement) latency, while, for those with normal laboratory measures, rates increased from the parental generation to the next one, providing a biological support to the delineation of clinical subtypes to which secular trends might or not apply. However, no biological measures were available in larger datasets demonstrating secular increases of depressive disorders, thus limiting the opportunity to confirm the validity of this biological distinction.

On balance, current knowledge of the genetic factors involved in the causation of depressive conditions remains largely inconclusive. While genetic transmission is likely to play a substantial role in bipolar disorders, the elevated risk of depression with a positive family history lacks specificity and the evidence for genetic mechanisms is weak for the bulk of depressive disorders. Moreover, depressive phenomena form a heterogeneous group for which possible modes of genetic mediation are likely to be both heterogeneous and complex. Secular changes in the incidence of depressive disorders are more likely to apply to less genetically determined forms of depressive conditions, although, the more severe forms of depression could also exhibit temporal variations over time. Further studies, combining genetic designs based on twin or adopted samples with prospective longitudinal studies, are clearly needed to understand for whom and according to what developmental circumstances genetic and environmental risk factors interact to create a liability for depressive conditions.

Pubertal Development

Data from various sources point to the onset of puberty as a potentially important factor. This is worth noting, since there has been a regular decline over the last century in the mean age of menarche, from 16.5 years in 1860 to 13.5 years in 1960 (Rubin, 1990). However, the fall seems to have reached a plateau now (Tanner, 1989). It might be thought that the decline in the age of puberty parallels the rise in depression but it is pertinent that the pubertal secular trend began many years before there was any evidence of a rise in depressive disorders.

Because the timing and nature of puberty are different for boys and girls, differential patterns in each sex for the development of depressive conditions would be predicted under the assumption of a direct causal influence of puberty. Indeed, age and sex trends in epidemiological data on suicide and depressive conditions, as well as the establishment of the female preponderance in depressive conditions in middle adolescence, argue indirectly in that direction (Weissman & Klerman, 1977; Nolen-Hoeksema,

1987). However, these data are not sufficient because most of these studies are cross-sectional and do not allow for a separation of the effects of puberty from those of other changes that accompany it. In addition, puberty itself is not a discrete event, and endocrinological changes occur progressively over a four- to five-year period. Major changes in the psychological and social context of the adolescent happen at the same time as the biological changes (see Chapter 4). Moreover, there are huge individual variations in the timing, length and sequencing of pubertal changes. Thus, longitudinal studies focusing on intra-individual changes during this period are crucial for the understanding of the effects of pubertal onset.

Findings from the adult literature have provided only limited support for a relationship between hormones and depressed mood. This relationship has been investigated in women during periods of hormonal changes, such as the menstrual cycle, pregnancy and the post-partum, or menopause. To summarize their results, low levels of oestrogens and irregular hormonal cycles have been inconsistently associated with increased depressed affect, with progesterone having a modifying effect in some instances. Furthermore, this association is confined to depressed mood rather than disorder, and evidence of a hormonal involvement in serious forms of psychopathology is very questionable (for example, see Cooper et al., 1988). Moreover, the causal nature of this association remains somewhat elusive (Nottelman et al., 1990) and few studies have been designed to assess the direct impact of hormones on mood after controlling for stereotypes, expectations and other relevant psychological confounders.

There is some evidence to suggest that an increased mood intensity and a higher frequency of mood swings are found among adolescents as compared to younger children. However, it is unclear to what extent these possible mood changes reflect hormonal effects rather than other aspects of pubertal development (Buchanan et al., 1992). In other studies of adolescent samples, attempts have also been made to measure hormonal levels directly and to relate them to levels of depressed affect (for a general review of hormonal effects on adolescent behaviour, see Buchanan et al., 1992). Brooks-Gunn and Warren (1989) found concurrent relationships between levels of testosterone and of oestradiol and depression indices, and Susman et al. (1991) reported a positive relationship between depressed affect and high concentrations of testosterone and cortisol in girls. Rapid increases in oestrogens in early stages of puberty for girls were also found to correlate with depressive symptoms but the magnitude of the effect was small, especially compared to that of concurrent psychosocial stressors (Brooks-Gunn & Warren, 1989; Paikoff et al., 1991).

Yet, hormonal levels predicted depressive symptomatology at one year follow-up, controlling for the level at baseline (Paikoff et al., 1991). Similar relations between hormonal levels at baseline and negative affect one year later were shown by another study that used both self-report and interview measures, but negative affect at baseline was a much stronger predictor of the persistence of negative affect (Susman et al., 1991). In general, the relationship between hormonal levels and depressive symptoms seems weak and inconsistent, and often disappears when other developmental markers such as chronological age and pubertal status are controlled for (Nottelman et al., 1990).

Results from a study of a large clinical sample have failed to demonstrate an independent contribution of pubertal status in explaining the rise of depressive phenomena during adolescence, after controlling for age (Angold & Rutter, 1992), and most studies of non-clinical samples of girls have not found a relationship between pubertal status and depressed mood (Brooks-Gunn & Warren, 1989; Paikoff et al., 1991; Simmons & Blyth, 1987). The endocrinological changes of puberty seem to exert only slight direct effects on depressed mood and feelings and these may well be part of a more general activation of emotionality.

In her review on pubertal development, Alsaker (1994) emphasized the need to adopt an interactionist point of view that simultaneously considers biological and psychological changes in the individual and the social context. There is strong evidence that girls do not welcome the body transformations (increase in weight and body fat) and the potential for reproduction brought by puberty, whereas boys see their increased height and strength as new positive attributes, associated with feelings of self-attractiveness and confidence (Tobin-Richards et al., 1983). Changes in cultural values over the last decades have also promoted an ideal of feminine beauty that closely matches prepubertal body shapes of girls, while secular trends towards an increasing relative weight have been noted for women (see Chapter 12). For such reasons, the psychological experience of puberty may have become more stressful and difficult to negotiate nowadays for girls. Of particular interest for secular changes is the finding that this gender difference in the experience of puberty is exacerbated among early maturers (Duncan et al., 1985; see Chapter 4, this volume). Longitudinal data have confirmed this association between depressed affect and early puberty in girls, particularly when it occurs in conjunction with transition from primary to secondary school (Simmons et al., 1979; Simmons et al., 1987; Petersen et al., 1991a). Simultaneous changes (as opposed to sequential changes) appear to carry an elevated risk for adolescent development (Petersen et al., 1991a). Girls, but also boys, who have reached puberty before this transition, express more depressed affect, a difference that is maintained four years later in girls (Petersen et al., 1991b). Girls who mature early have more disturbed body image and lowered self-esteem. In addition, as pubertal children become more interested in dating and heterosexual relationships (Petersen, 1987), they are more likely to socialize with older peers. As a result of this, early maturing girls were found to be at increased risk of alcohol and drug use in the Stockholm longitudinal study (Magnusson et al., 1985). Young pubertal girls were found to socialize preferentially with older girls, this change in peer relationships being responsible for a temporary higher frequency of deviant behaviours.

The onset of puberty, on-time or off-time, is also accompanied by changes in physical appearance (growth spurt, secondary sexual characteristics) that trigger new responses from both parents and peers (Brooks-Gunn & Warren, 1989; Simmons & Blyth, 1987; Steinberg, 1987). Attitudes and expectations in relation to puberty play a major role in psychological reactions to it (Alsaker, 1994). Interactions between biological and social factors have been found to account for larger amounts of variance in depressed affect than those variables considered independently in most studies (Alsaker, 1994; Brooks-Gunn & Warren, 1989). On average, puberty and its social correlates occur at an earlier age for today's youth, and changing sex roles in Western countries make the formation of their identity and self-concept a more complex and difficult task.

Current knowledge also suggests that cognitive maturation is related to chronological age rather than pubertal changes or timing. Hypotheses of a cognitive advantage for early maturers, or conversely of a disruptive impact of puberty on cognitive development, have received little empirical support. Rather, adolescents show linear increases in their cognitive abilities throughout early adolescence (see review in Graber & Petersen, 1991). A consequence is that today's pubertal adolescents may possess less developed cognitive maturity and skills to cope with the challenges of puberty. Yet, research data are very much needed both to describe and understand the social responses that a pubescent adolescent experiences in modern societies where sex roles have been redefined and are still changing. The cognitive skills and processes involved in successfully integrating these transformations of early adolescence need to be further understood.

To summarize, research findings indicate that puberty, which occurs at a much earlier age than a century ago, may impose greater challenges on those girls whose 'developmental readiness' is yet unattained. Girls are also more likely than in the past to face pubertal transformations at the same time as other important transitions, such as that from primary school to secondary school. The number of simultaneous developmental challenges has been shown to increase vulnerability in girls. The precise mechanisms of heightened risk of depressed affect for pubertal girls need to be further elucidated. It does not appear that endocrinological changes exert a major direct influence on depressed mood; rather, biological modifications need to be considered within a broader context of psychological and social individual transformations. Changes in some cultural values may have helped to augment the discomfort of puberty (by increasing body dissatisfaction). However, while depressed mood may increase as a result of this developmental phase, there are no data linking these developmental challenges to the onset of depressive disorders.

On the one hand, therefore, pubertal changes are associated with increased depressed mood; and on the other, secular trends in the timing of puberty, and its psychosocial context, may have tended over time to increase the vulnerability of pubertal adolescents to depressed affect. It is possible that the biological change in the timing of puberty, combined with changes in its social significance and context, have jointly predisposed to an increase in depressive conditions.

Family Life

There have been considerable changes in patterns of family life over the postwar decades (see Chapter 5). At the same time, many aspects of family functioning have been shown to be related to the process of development leading to psychosocial well-being or disorder among adolescents. The possibility that changes in patterns of family life are a cause of increases in psychosocial disorders in general, and depressive disorders in particular, therefore has some plausibility and needs to be examined carefully. Although some of the evidence relates to depressive disorders specifically, this review considers the role of family relationships in the developmental processes in a more general way.

With the approach of adolescence, family *functioning* changes. Parent-child relationships may become more conflictual and distant, at least in the early phases of adolescence (Steinberg, 1981, 1987, 1988); the amount of time spent with family declines considerably throughout adolescence, and young adolescents express negative emotions when in family company (Larson et al., 1990; Larson & Richards, 1991). As the adolescent's autonomy and independence grows, parent-child conflicts diminish; in late adolescence, time spent with parents is reduced, and relationships are no longer permeated by negative mood. Petersen et al. (1991b) found that maintaining closeness with the parents, especially with the father, tends to protect adolescents from periods of negative mood; this supports the idea that emotional distancing from parents might increase the risk of depressed mood. Friendships did not have the same protective effect. This study adds to a vast literature showing that parental support provides an effective protection against depression.

Adolescence is also a period when *structural* changes in the family system become increasingly likely. As the child grows older, parents are more likely to become seriously ill, to die, or to become handicapped. Separation or divorce of the parents, and remarriage or cohabitation, introducing step-parent, step-siblings, and half-siblings, have become quite common. The likelihood of divorce appears to be greater for parents of girls, while the presence of sons in a family seems to increase father's engagement in parental roles and, hence, to reduce the chance of marital breakdown (Morgan et al., 1988; Petersen et al., 1991a). The relation between divorce of the parents and long-term depressive phenomena has been established among preschool children (Hetherington et al., 1978) and adolescents as well. However, longitudinal data have provided evidence that children who were disturbed in the aftermath of divorce had behaviour problems *before* the divorce (Block et al., 1986), suggesting that marital discord rather than separation was the intervening mechanism. These findings have been recently replicated with two large longitudinal datasets from the USA and the UK, where increased post-divorce rates of behavioural disturbances almost disappeared when they were adjusted on pre-divorce levels of disturbance (Cherlin et al., 1991). Trends across genders suggested nonetheless that girls may react negatively to divorce, even when their prior level of functioning is taken into account. However, whereas behaviour problems in children at home and school recede with time, the current wisdom is that mother-son relations become persistently more difficult, whereas adolescent daughters and their mothers tend to develop close and intimate companionships.

The recomposition of family following parental breakup also has effects on the adolescent well-being. The effects of family structure on school achievement indicate that adolescents living in single-parent or stepfamilies lag behind their peers from intact families on achievement test scores (Zimiles & Lee, 1991). Furthermore, the same data showed a threefold increase in drop-out from school in non-intact families, and further analyses suggested that school drop-out in single-parent families was more likely to occur when the parent and the adolescent were of different gender, whereas a reverse pattern was found in step-parent families. There is now strong evidence that girls have more difficulties in adapting to stepfamilies than do boys (Hetherington et al., 1985; Vuchinich et al., 1991), whether assessed by self-reports, parent reports or observational measures. Adolescent girls have more conflicts with their stepfathers whom they see as intruders whereas stepfathers may have a more positive role for their stepsons.

Adolescents in single-parent households have been comparatively little studied. Because of financial hardship, these families are likely to provide fewer opportunities for the developing adolescent; children of single parents may have less time for interacting with their parents and for receiving emotional support, less access to male and female role models, and fewer opportunities for leisure and positive experiences outside the home. Since single-parent families have become much more common, there is a great need for research that aims to understand the experiences and particular needs of these adolescents in these families. For example, the intimate and close relationship that an adolescent girl is likely to develop with her divorced mother may place a burden on the girl if she becomes a major source of emotional support for the single parent.

On the whole, secular changes in patterns of family life expose children and adolescents to more frequent and earlier challenges: marital discord, parental breakdown and divorce, remarriage or cohabitation, and single-parent families have all been shown to be associated with negative outcomes in young people, with boys and girls being affected in rather different ways. These are solid research findings, but most of the studies have so far adopted a focus limited to the study of the child, the parent, and the step-parent. Recent research suggests that other adults in the family such as grandparents can play important roles in support of the adolescents (Clingempeel et al., 1992). Similarly, studies of relationships with full- and half-siblings have been relatively neglected. In general, little is yet known on the effects of unstable patterns of family life on the ability to develop satisfactory interpersonal relationships with peers. Above all, long-term longitudinal research is needed to determine the consequences in adult life of these earlier experiences. There are theoretical and empirical grounds to hypothesize that losses or disruption of significant relationships in childhood and adolescence increase the risk of depressive disorders in adult life (Brown & Harris, 1978, 1989). However, data are still needed to elucidate the processes leading from experiences carrying that kind of threat to actual negative outcomes. Perhaps the most important issue on this research agenda consists in the identification of protective mechanisms that build up resilience and promote healthy developmental pathways into adulthood after these, now extremely prevalent, experiences of broken or disturbed relationships.

In short, there is strong evidence that family conflict, broken family relationships, and lack of parental support and involvement, play a part in the developmental pathways leading to depression in adolescents. It is possible that secular changes in patterns of family life have led to an increase in the conditions of family functioning that lead to depression, and therefore explain, at least in part, the secular increase in depressive disorders among adolescents.

Other Psychological and Social Aspects of Adolescent Development

In conjunction with biological transformations, adolescence is accompanied by important changes in psychological development. Thus, cognitive abilities develop with access to formal thinking and abstract reasoning (Graber & Petersen, 1991). With maturation over the course of adolescence, self-esteem and self-image increase. Major changes in the social context of adolescent development take place at the same time, and the term 'embeddedness' has been coined to designate the intricacy of transitions occurring simultaneously in different spheres of individual development (Petersen, 1987). In the meantime, support systems that were commonly used by families and society to celebrate and facilitate developmental transitions, as they are exemplified in various rites of passage such as religious ceremonies or school graduations, tend to be abandoned. The extent to which such traditions did facilitate the successful integration of adolescent challenges has unfortunately been little researched; the study of groups that have maintained such practices would certainly help to gain an understanding of what key ingredients in these social and cultural traditions are developmentally appropriate and supportive.

School Factors

The educational system is at the core of adolescents' lives. Transition from primary to secondary school is an important move which places greater emphasis on evaluation and comparisons between students, increases grading standards, and disrupts the children's social networks. The demands of the school system are also likely to increase over the course of adolescence as the student progresses towards higher education; paradoxically, the increased cognitive abilities of the adolescent are, on average, paralleled by decreased grades at school due to more stringent grading practices (Petersen, 1987). Meanwhile, the social structure of secondary school is much less protective and supportive, and adolescents relate to several and more distant adults.

Research findings indicate that most secondary school teachers are not a strong source of social and emotional support for adolescents. Several studies have shown that transition to secondary school is accompanied by declines in self-esteem and perceptions of abilities in academic matters, with girls having decreased self-perceptions of maths abilities and boys decreased self-perceptions in language (Wigfield et al., 1991), but these changes are temporary and can be negotiated successfully by most young adolescents (Nottelman, 1987). Late adolescence is then marked by more demanding examinations which have been shown to augment psychological tension (Cairns et al., 1991); and, in a competitive environment, many adolescents will have to give up personal wishes and readjust their educational and vocational pursuits toward more readily attainable goals. The effects of these adjustments are likely to be unnoticed for most adolescents. However, for those adolescents who did not negotiate successfully challenges of early and mid-adolescence and for those who experience serious academic failures, it may represent a phase of heightened vulnerability for a range of negative outcomes, including depressive conditions. Thus, recent results from a prospective study of early adolescents showed that school performance predicted levels of stress at follow-up, and that, once started, a self-perpetuating reciprocal process linked school performance and psychological distress to stress and support and *vice versa* (DuBois et al., 1992). Studies assessing the impact on the psychological well-being of adolescents who fail to meet their academic goals would be important, as it would be useful to establish whether the provision of alternative educational or vocational tracks exerts a beneficial influence. In this regard, the preceding investigation (DuBois et al., 1992) provided preliminary evidence that school-based support was indeed effective, especially for adolescents from more problematic backgrounds. However, this study used self-report measures and replication is clearly needed.

Stressful Events

Adult literature has shown that stressful life events, such as the death of a close relative, play a role in the onset of a variety of psychiatric disorders (Brown & Harris, 1989). Recent research on child and adolescent psychiatric disorders has shown similar results (Goodyer, 1990), but so far there is a paucity of evidence on the specific role of life events in the causation of depressive disorders in children and adolescents (Berney et al., 1991; Goodyer, 1990). Interpretation of the available data in life events research is somewhat limited by methodological drawbacks in many studies; for example, reliance on parental reports, failure to differentiate the events from the outcomes under study, lack of consideration for the social context within which stress factors operate, and the failure to assess long-term change attributable to stressors, are only a few challenges in this field (Compas & Wagner, 1991; Rutter & Sandberg, 1992). Furthermore, knowledge is scarce on the distribution of specific life events in large normative samples of children and adolescents, and on ways age and gender alter the perception and significance of these events (Compas, 1987; Garrison et al., 1987; Rutter, 1991). Finally, few investigations of life events among children and adolescent samples have employed longitudinal designs, so that the results are difficult to interpret.

However, exceptional life events are likely to be influential on adolescents' psychological well-being in view of the many challenges that they already face. Events such as 'breaking up of a relationship' or 'unemployment of a family member' have been found to be associated with elevated levels of depressed mood among adolescents (Adams & Adams, 1991). Similarly, as children grow, there is an increased likelihood that their parents will become seriously ill. Thus, adolescents showed higher levels of distress than younger children when cancer was diagnosed in their parents, with a more pronounced effect on symptoms of depression in the case of mothers and daughters (Compas, 1994). As suggested by Compas et al. (1986), the transactions between life events, social support and psychological dysfunction need to be examined, particularly in the periods of transition that adolescents experience (from elementary school to high school, from high school to university, leaving the parental home). During these transitions, which involve dynamic changes in social networks and coping resources, vulnerability to negative events may be heightened, particularly when the effects are cumulative (Simmons et al., 1987).

Besides the impact of major, discrete events, attention has been focused on the important role of daily chronic stressors and strains, which seem to constitute the link between major stresses and psychological dysfunction (Compas & Wagner, 1991). Two recent prospective studies have shown that daily hassles were predictive of subsequent adolescent emotional distress over a one-year (Compas et al., 1989) and a two-year interval (DuBois et al., 1992). The latter study also indicated a negative impact on school performance. Interestingly, a reciprocal effect of initial levels of psychological distress and school performance was found on subsequent levels of daily hassles and support, suggesting an interactive linkage between stress and distress (DuBois et al., 1992).

As for adults (Kessler & McLeod, 1984), the impact of life events appears to be somewhat stronger in girls than in boys. Several studies have shown that adolescent girls report more negative life events and that the relationships between stress and psychological symptoms is stronger in girls than in boys. Adolescent girls report more 'network' events, that is, negative events that happen to others, a finding consistent with adult research and which underlines an orientation of girls to care for the needs and well-being of others (Compas & Wagner, 1991). Gender differences could also be explained by the use of different coping responses. Coping can be broadly divided into problem-focused coping and emotion-focused coping (see review in Compas, 1994). Unlike problem-focused coping, the emotion-focused strategy shows marked developmental differences and is more frequently used with increased age and maturity. Although we lack data on possible gender differences in the use of coping strategies by adolescents, adult literature on depression suggests that women tend to be more ruminating and men to engage in distractive behaviours (Nolen-Hoeksema, 1987). Indirect evidence supporting an association between coping strategy and depression comes from the study of resilient adolescents in families with a depressed parent (Beardslee & Podorefsky, 1988). These authors found that these adolescents realistically appraised their situation in recognizing that they could not cure their parents and thus obtained a good match between their coping response and their perceived control of the situation.

To summarize a recently burgeoning area of research, stressful events predict psychological distress, and especially depression, among adolescents. This vulnerability appears to increase with age and is higher in girls. Secular changes in patterns of adolescent life suggest that both major negative events (family breakdown) and chronic stressors (increased educational demands) may have become more frequent, and emotional and social support rarer. This set of findings provides possible psychosocial explanations that need further investigation for the increase in depressive conditions.

Out-of-school Time

Owing to the prolonged years spent in education and to delayed transition to adult status (see Chapter 6), part-time participation in the labour force during the secondary school years has become very common. Whereas these experiences may undoubtedly help to foster autonomy and a sense of achievement, attention has nevertheless been drawn to the negative effects on schooling and self-esteem of part-time employment among adolescents

(Steinberg & Dornbusch, 1991). Moreover, adolescents who are already facing many other challenges are the most likely to have jobs.

With women taking an increasing role in the labour force (see Chapter 6), the amount of daily contact of adolescents with their parents is likely to have decreased, and adolescents tend to be left alone more frequently after school. Several studies comparing adolescents in adult care with those in self-care ('latchkey children') have been conducted that failed to find differences on several indices such as academic achievement, self-esteem, peer relations and personality adjustment. Others suggested more negative consequences of self-care, especially for adolescents in urban environments. In an attempt to recognize the diversity of self-care arrangements (self-care at home, friend's house, hanging around outside), further research has shown that adolescents hanging around were more prone to conform to antisocial pressure (Steinberg, 1986), whereas adolescents in self-care at home appeared consistently comparable to those in adult care. For those adolescents in self-care, parental attitudes (permissiveness or demandingness) interacted with the conformity to peer pressure, suggesting that qualities of the parent-adolescent relationship are important determinants of peer relationships. Lack of adult out-of-school supervision has also been shown to be associated with poorer self-image, more deviant peers and increased risk of problem behaviour, in early adolescent girls with more distant parental control (Galambos & Maggs, 1991). This study also gave indications that these relationships between out-of-school supervision and peer experiences were stronger during summer time, when adult supervision becomes even less available. Further research is needed to examine the long-term impacts of after school or holiday arrangements and to study the particular experiences of adolescents in single-parent families, and of those attending various post-school programmes. Few efforts have been directed towards structuring the school environment and providing extra-curricular activities and leisure opportunities in developmentally appropriate ways; when these are available, their effects have not been systematically evaluated (see review by Quinn, 1994).

Community Influences

Few data exist on the impact of the local area on adolescent development. One comparative longitudinal study between a resource-poor rural area and a resource-rich area has been conducted in North America (Sarigiani et al., 1990). In a series of analyses, these authors drew attention to the differences in developmental trajectories that were found between the two samples. Thus, rural adolescents, and particularly girls, had lower academic expectations and poorer self-image, expected to have their transitions to adult roles at an earlier age, had their first sexual experience earlier, and so on. While there was some attempt to control for social class and parental education, differences between the two areas may still be attributable to individual and family characteristics, such as poverty. However, these data do raise issues that might be relevant to socio-economic groups that have been declining in size, fortune and importance. The shifts in economic activity (see Chapter 6) experienced by most Western countries have changed the patterns of life and expectations that adolescents living in traditional rural areas experience.

Conclusion

Young people spend most of their adolescence in the educational system, and academic demands are high, with many school environments not providing much emotional support. Extra-curricular activities are not equally accessible and adult supervision may be lacking. During these years, and besides the biological changes of puberty, adolescents are more likely to experience family dissolution, parental diseases or death, economic strains, and other negative events. The broad social context in which adolescents develop has therefore become more challenging while traditional support systems have possibly become weaker. Increases in depressed affect are found in response to these pressures, particularly in girls. Altogether, these changes in adolescent life provide a suggestion of explanatory pointers for the increase over time in depressive conditions.

Living Conditions

Generation Size

Since several reports converge in identifying the increased prevalence of depressive conditions in the postwar birth cohorts (the 'baby boom' generation), we need to examine the possible causal influence of the size of a generation in the development of negative psychological outcomes. Easterlin (1980) proposed that young people belonging to large generations have reduced opportunities. Because of increased competition with members of their generation, members of large birth cohorts supposedly will delay family formation, and difficulties in achieving personal goals will generate feelings of inadequacy and hopelessness. Consequently, it is argued, rates of problem behaviours will increase (crimes, suicide, alcoholism and drugs, divorce, accident, and so on). Easterlin indicated that national rates of a range of problem behaviours were correlated to generation size in the recent decades. As far as psychological distress and depressive conditions are concerned, the surveys reviewed in the section on time trends seem to provide support for Easterlin's theory, in that the apparent increase in depressive conditions most affected the 'baby boom' generation. Furthermore, the theory predicts that post-baby boom ('baby-bust') generations should exhibit a reverse pattern, and some studies have indeed indicated an attenuation of rates of depressive disorders in the very youngest cohorts (Wickramaratne et al., 1989). Similarly, recent increases in fertility rates among some European countries such as Sweden (see Chapter 5) are in line with this theory. However, other evidence does not support this argument. For example, one would expect an oscillating pattern of rates of depressive disorders across the century, which is not found; rather, data suggest a progressive increase in rates from the oldest generation to the youngest ones. Second, it is assumed by the theory that there is a close negative relationship between degree of wealth, success and achievement and rates of problem behaviours. The data do not support this prediction strongly either at the individual level (social class and poverty are not strong correlates of depression) or at a broader level of analysis (higher rates of depressive disorders are found in the most affluent Western countries). Regardless of its validity, an important limit of Easterlin's theory is that it leaves unexplained the intervening social and psychological mechanisms that would link generation size to individual problem behaviour.

Unemployment

Changes in rates of unemployment have been considerable over the last decades, and recently rates of unemployment have been reaching alarming levels, particularly among young people (see Chapter 6). The lack of comparative data on depressive conditions across countries and over time makes it hazardous to examine relationships between rates of unemployment and depression at a broad level of analysis. Furthermore, careful attention needs to be paid to the social context of unemployment which is likely to differ from one country to another, and also to carry different implications over time. Jahoda (1979) has underscored both similarities and divergences in the status of the unemployed in the 1970s and that during the recession of the 1930s. For example, unemployment in the Great Depression of the 1930s hit entire communities at one time, and its impact on the whole reference group could have lessened the psychological consequences on individuals mostly preoccupied by the financial and economic consequences. Conversely, current educational attainments and work aspirations of youth could lead employment issues to have more detrimental effects on self-esteem while survival issues have in general become less prominent. Jahoda (1981) has further proposed a theoretical model to account for the links between psychological well-being and employment. She posited that, beyond its manifest function of making a living, work has several latent functions: to impose a time structure on the waking day, to foster regularly shared experiences and contacts with people outside the nuclear family, to link the individual with collective goals and purposes, to define aspects of personal status and identity, and to enforce the daily exercise of competence and skill. This model therefore predicts that unemployment would favour the development of depressive conditions by removing the main source of self-esteem, social networks, practice of competence, and so on.

Unemployment can impinge on the psychological well-being of young people in at least two ways. Their parents may become unemployed, which almost always results in economic hardship and parental stress. Alternatively, they may experience unemployment themselves. Several studies suggest a connection between unemployment and depressive conditions. Thus, in the ECA study, subjects who had been unemployed for six months or more in the last five years had a threefold increase of major depression (Weissman et al., 1991); and a host of other correlational studies indicate that unemployed youth, compared to their employed counterparts, have higher levels of depressed mood, hopelessness and lower self-esteem (see brief review in Winefield et al., 1991). Longitudinal studies of the transitions from school to work and from employment to unemployment and *vice versa*, have been more informative since they permit a more precise analysis of the chain of events leading from school to employment status. In general, transition from school to employment has been associated with increased well-being, whereas unemployed youth fail to make these gains or even exhibit psychological deterioration. Thus, Banks and Jackson (1982), in a 20 month follow-up study of two cohorts of school leavers in the city of Leeds, showed higher levels of minor psychiatric morbidity among unemployed youth, controlling for the effects of sex, educational level and ethnicity. Furthermore, taking into account the effect of psychological variables before the end of school allowed for a clearer demonstration that unemployment, rather than prior between-group differences, was indeed the explanatory factor. Identical results were obtained in another British study (Donovan et al., 1986); in this study, a third group of young people within a government training scheme fell, for all outcome measures, between the fully employed and the unemployed. This provided additional validity to the main findings that unemployment causes distress, and it also suggested that intervention programmes may alleviate the negative psychological effects of unemployment. In both studies, the trends were in fact for youth in employment to improve on indices of psychological functioning rather than for the unemployed to show a deterioration.

Findings suggest that the experience of being unemployed after school is different from that of mature workers who lose their jobs; the mechanisms and consequences of the failure to find a job and of a job loss appear to be different as they impinge on subjects at different life stages (Warr & Jackson, 1984). Also, these results underline current life characteristics of late adolescence since most of these unemployed young people were still living with their families, therefore still benefiting from this 'arena of comfort' viewed by Simmons et al. (1987) as a crucial concept for promoting healthy adolescent outcomes.

Job satisfaction seems an important protective attribute of employment, and, in one study (Winefield et al., 1991), employed young women who were dissatisfied with their job expressed higher levels of depressed affect than the unemployed, a finding that did not apply to men. The meaning of this result is unclear since, rather than indicating a true gender difference, it could merely reflect unequal opportunities for men and women in the labour force. Similar findings were reported in a study of school leavers who had rates of depressed mood comparable to those of the unemployed when occupying jobs with no opportunity to express their skills and knowledge (O'Brien & Feather, 1990). Similarly, features of the social relationships within the work environment (with co-workers and supervisors) and enduring characteristics of the job (work overload, role ambiguity and conflict, level of participation, underutilization) have been shown to relate to mental health indices in complex ways, but data are still scarce on this issue (Winnubst et al., 1988).

The detrimental effect of unemployment varies also according to the degree of employment commitment, that is, the intensity with which the individual wants to be engaged in paid employment. Thus, the amount of change in psychological distress associated with transitions from employment to unemployment, and from unemployment to employment, was found to be proportional to the degree of commitment in two cohorts of young English males (Jackson et al., 1983). Results were obtained both in cross-sectional and in longitudinal analyses, and the effects were found for both transitions. Identical results were obtained in a study of 1,150 English 17-year-old unemployed where black respondents, perhaps as a result of a more realistic appraisal of their social disadvantage, had lower employment commitment and lower levels of distress and depression (Warr et al., 1985); in this ethnic Caribbean subgroup though, girls remained much more committed to work than boys. Similarly, depressed affect was lowered by high levels of self-esteem among unemployed Israelis with high educational degrees (Shamir, 1986), but generalization from this particular sample to other social contexts is not easy. The main conclusion, though, is that the relation between employment and psychological status is not a mechanical one; individual and sub-cultural characteristics are likely to exert either protective or exacerbating effects.

Studies thus far have been rather limited in the length of follow-up of unemployed samples of young people, though there is evidence that those who remained unemployed for prolonged periods of time showed in the long run increased depressed affect and lower self-esteem (Winefield & Tiggemann, 1990) and that job search attitudes were less positive as time in unemployment increased (Warr et al., 1985); more research is therefore needed on those young people who stay unemployed for long periods of time.

The implications for the current youth situation are important: prolonged years in the education system and transformations in work are likely to produce growing expectations from youth, in terms of employment commitment, job satisfaction and career development opportunities. Indeed, data from the European Values Survey show that young people have become increasingly demanding and expect their work to be rewarding in every sense (see Chapter 8). The available data suggest that the psychological impacts of unemployment and quality of employment, relative to their sole economic importance, are growing for younger generations. Nevertheless, it is most unlikely that unemployment has played any significant role in the increase in depressive disorders since the Second World War. The key point is that the main rise in depression occurred during the 1950s, 1960s and early 1970s when unemployment levels were particularly low. Moreover, if anything, the very marked rise in unemployment during the last dozen years or so has been accompanied by something of a reduction in the rise in depression.

Economic Hardship, Social Class, and Poverty

It is well established that unemployed adults fare worse than employed subjects on a range of measures of psychological functioning. The effects of economic hardship on adolescent development have been far less studied. Nevertheless, one sample of 167 children who grew up during the Great Economic Recession was followed up (Elder et al., 1985). The degree of economic depression was positively correlated with negative parental attitudes (rejection, lack of support, indifference) for fathers but not for mothers. Among boys, increased moodiness and oversensitivity were related to economic hardship; by contrast, economic deprivation had little direct effect on girls' behaviours, but an indirect effect on their psychological well-being was found to be mediated by father's rejecting behaviour. Moreover, the negative father-daughter interactions as a function of loss of income appeared to be restricted to the less physically attractive daughters. Attractive girls were protected from this chain of effects, whereas physical attributes of sons had no effect. In a more recent cross-sectional study of 622 adolescents living in a Midwestern community struck by the agricultural crisis of the 1980s, adverse effects of economic hardship on adolescent psychological health were also found (Lempers et al., 1989). However, economic hardship exerted direct and indirect effects (through changes in parental nurturance and inconsistent parental discipline). A specific effect was again found for girls whose distress was indirectly associated to economic stress through lowered paternal support (Lempers & Clark-Lempers, 1990). The magnitude of direct effects was stronger, but it is likely that this relationship is accounted for by a series of unmeasured contextual variables. It is noteworthy that a six-year prospective study of an adult sample selected in the same geographical area showed that, among women living in farms at the same time, there were high rates of new onsets of major depression reported (Coryell et al., 1992).

In an attempt to elucidate the causal processes that link economic pressures to adjustment difficulties among adolescents, Conger et al. (1992) studied cross-sectionally a sample of 205 12 to 14-year-old boys in the rural Midwest. Figure 11.4 illustrates the model that was tested in this study; it was postulated that the joint effect of four economic stressors creates a sense of pressure which provokes depressed mood in each parent. This, in turn, leads to marital dysfunction and to less effective parenting practices. The lack of skilled and involved parenting is then the crucial link which establishes a connection with adolescent well-being. In Figure 11.4, the theoretical model portrays relationships between constructs, that is unobserved, latent variables. Using modern statistical modelling techniques, the model was shown to fit the data. From a conceptual perspective, these findings illustrate the causal chain that might connect external stressors to psychological dysfunction, and emphasizes the key mediating role of depressed mood in the parents. The heuristic value of the model in Figure 11.4 is obvious: for example, other external stressors and intrafamily relationships or the moderating role of individual adolescent characteristics (physical attractiveness, positive involvement with peers and in extra-curricular activities, and so on) could be examined in the same way.

Figure 11.4   Conceptual model of the causal processes that link economic pressures to adjustment difficulties in adolescents

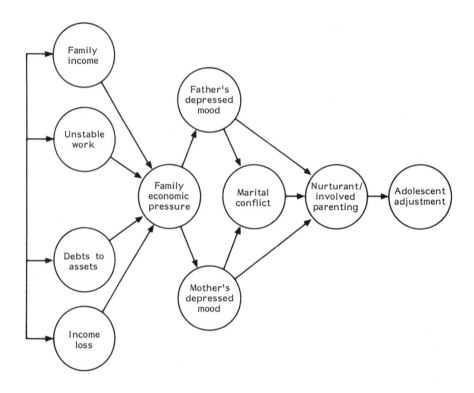

Source: Conger et al. (1992).

On the whole, these studies suggest that familial economic difficulties may indirectly predispose to adolescent distress and that altered parenting behaviours are one key mediating mechanism. Mutual support of husband and wife has also been found to promote a warm, supportive and involved parenting role for both fathers and mothers under economic strain, and to moderate the impact of economic hardship for mothers (Simons et al., 1992). These findings, if confirmed, carry implications for adolescents living in single-parent families where lack of support and economic strain might interact negatively. Children's individual characteristics, such as gender and attractiveness, are also important intervening factors. There is little evidence, however, for a direct effect of economic strain on adolescents. It is worth noting that, with few exceptions, research has mostly been conducted among rural and deprived North American samples. It could be that adolescents from different countries and social milieux would show different patterns of vulnerability to economic deprivation of their family. It is also conceivable that financial constraints *relative* to prior levels of wealth and comfort are equally or more important than absolute levels of family income. However, research in this area is just emerging and more data are needed on adaptive patterns of families undergoing economic pressure that take into account individual characteristics, family structure and relationships, and the broader social context and subculture of the adolescent.

The association between social adversities and a range of psychiatric disorders is a well-replicated finding. In the case of depressive disorders, convincing results have been produced that they constitute a risk factor for the onset of depressive disorders in adult life (Brown & Harris, 1978). High rates of depression among women in lower social groups have been taken as evidence that low social status causes depression (the alternatives are that social status reflects some other risk variable or that depressed people tend to drift into lower social classes) (Dohrenwend et al., 1992). However, the social causation theory remains very controversial. Indeed, cross-sectional examinations of the ECA data found virtually no relationship between affective disorders and low education, low income and low occupational status (Weissman et al., 1991). Only recently have adult studies addressed the question of poverty as a risk factor for the onset of diverse psychiatric outcomes, including depressive disorders. In one subsample of the ECA project, subjects below the Federal guidelines for poverty and free from a recent psychiatric disorder were followed up on a six-month interval (Bruce et al., 1991). Poverty appeared to increase the odds of developing a psychiatric disorder. However, the significant findings reported for major depression appeared rather non-specific, and applied to other disorders as well. Using an index of material possessions in the household as an indicator of socio-economic status (SES), Murphy et al. (1991) reanalysed the 16-year follow-up of the Stirling County study. Again, the incidence of depression was much higher in the low SES group while patterns for anxiety were different. Over this long time-span, social changes occurred in the county, with typical transformations of the economy (industrialization, development of services) and a rising standard of living. Unfortunately, there were no data in these studies to link individual psychological experiences to their social trajectories.

It should also be borne in mind that secular increases in the incidence of depressive disorders have been documented in the most industrialized countries, during a period of increasing wealth. That does not necessarily rule out a role of poverty in predisposing to the rise in depression. The key question is whether, during a period of generally increasing affluence, young people were disproportionately likely to experience economic privation. That may have been the case in the United States and probably, too, it has applied in parts of Europe during the past dozen years or so (see Chapter 6), but there is no indication that this was so during the 1950s to 1970s when the rise in depression was most apparent. We may conclude that an increase in the experience of poverty did not play any substantial role in the increase over time in depression in young people.

SUMMARY AND RESEARCH IMPLICATIONS

The research evidence suggests that rates of depressive conditions in adolescents and young adults have probably increased in the recent decades, that the rise in recent years may have been greater in males than females, and that such disorders may be having an onset earlier in life. However, due to an almost exclusive reliance on retrospective designs, the extent of this phenomenon is difficult to gauge. Repeated cross-sectional surveys of youth and true prospective studies have yielded trends in the same direction as cross-sectional studies, albeit of a much smaller magnitude. The extent to which this increase is specific to depressive conditions remains unclear.

Clinical and hospital data have not been informative in assessing time trends in rates of depressive disorders. Accordingly, monitoring trends in the future will imply repeated epidemiological studies. Because short-term trends are not easy to detect or to interpret, these studies would need to be repeated about every decade.

Cross-sectional studies of a kind of those reviewed in this chapter have been helpful but they have limitations, both in terms of measurement (that is, retrospective assessment summarized in lifetime prevalence rates) and in their inability to differentiate statistical associations from causal mechanisms (because of an inability to assess changes over time on individual psychopathology in relation to changing life circumstances). Thus, future epidemiological studies should use designs and measures that aim to generate not only information on rates of disorders and associations with risk indicators but also on causal processes. Thus, these studies should rely on methodologies that will allow both the comparison of rates over time *and* the linkage or changes in rates to changes in hypothesized risk factors.

Because young people appear to be at increased risk nowadays and because depressive disorders are strongly recurrent over the life span, the focus of such studies should be on young subjects in the age range of 15 to 30. Yet, it would be crucial that risk factors be assessed differentially in relation to the first onset of depressive disorder as compared to their potential role in the recurrence of depression. Another aim of these future studies should be to assess to what extent increases in rates of depression reflect, or are a consequence of, other forms of psychopathology.

Among several hypothesized risk mechanisms, genetic factors might be implicated in secular changes in rates of depression through an increased vulnerability to environmental stressors. The extent to which time trends apply similarly to genetically predisposed subjects is yet unknown. Future studies might therefore address this question by using a combination of research strategies based on high-risk samples and longitudinal designs. This would allow the identification of psychosocial circumstances that have changed over time and that are more or less likely to impinge on vulnerable individuals. By contrast, such studies might also shed an important light on the protective mechanisms and positive developmental trajectories that are found among resilient individuals in these high-risk samples. The identification of these protective influences are likely to be of considerable importance in the planning of interventions, at both the individual and community levels.

The role of depressed affect during adolescent development and the rising incidence of depressive disorders during that life stage have been established. However, the mechanisms of this developmental process are not well known. Research findings indicate that a range of biological, psychological, interpersonal and social factors operate. Studies have been notoriously restricted in their ability to integrate measures across these various domains and it remains an important task for future investigations to address these different processes simultaneously. Research findings so far suggest that changes in the psychological and familial context of adolescence are key candidate mechanisms to explain changes over time in rates of depression. It is also likely that the other risk factors, be they biological or macrosocial, act only indirectly in the development of depression, and that their influence is mediated by the preceding variables. Thus, future research should focus on adolescent development using an interactionist perspective in which the focus of the study is on person-environment interactions. An understanding of the mechanisms involved in time trends will probably come from several investigations designed to test the causal influence of risk factors known to have changed over time, rather than from one megastudy. Such interlinked studies might involve contrasting subgroups within populations known to differ in patterns of family life, life style, or cultural experiences. For example, comparative studies of adolescents from various ethnic backgrounds, or subcultures could be useful. Another route would be to make cross-national comparisons between samples studied with rigorously comparable procedures and selected from countries known to differ in the levels of the hypothesized risk factors.

REFERENCES

Achenbach, T. M. (1991). *Manual for the Child Behaviour Checklist/4-18 and 1991 profile.* Burlington, VT: University of Vermont, Department of Psychiatry.

Achenbach, T. M. & Edelbrock, C. S. (1981). Behaviour problems and competencies reported by parents of normal and disturbed children aged 4 through 16. *Monographs of the Society for Research in Child Development 46*, No. 188.

Achenbach, T. M. & Howell C. T. (1993). Are American children's problems getting worse? A 13-year comparison. *Journal of the American Academy of Child and Adolescent Psychiatry 32*, 1145-1154.

Achenbach, T. M., Howell, C. T., Quay, H. C. & Conners, C. K. (1991). National survey of competencies and problems among 4- to 16-year-olds: Parents' reports for normative and clinical samples. *Monographs of the Society for Research in Child Development*, Serial No. 225.

Adams, M. & Adams, J. (1991). Life events, depression, and perceived problem solving alternatives in adolescents. *Journal of Child Psychology and Psychiatry 32*, 811-820.

Allgood-Merten, B., Lewinsohn, P. M. & Hops H. (1990). Sex differences and adolescent depression. *Journal of Abnormal Psychology 99*, 55-63.

Alsaker, F. D. (1994). Timing of puberty and reactions to pubertal changes. In M. Rutter (ed.) *Psychosocial disturbances in young people: Challenges for prevention.* New York/Cambridge: Cambridge University Press.

American Psychiatric Association (1994). *Diagnostic and statistical manual of mental disorders - DSM-IV* (4th edition). Washington, DC: American Psychiatric Association.

Aneshensel, C. S., Estrada, A. L., Hansell, M. J. & Clark, V. A. (1987). Social psychological aspects of reporting behaviour: Lifetime depressive episode reports. *Journal of Health and Social Behaviour 28*, 232-246.

Angold, A. (1988a). Childhood and adolescent depression: I. Epidemiological aspects. *British Journal of Psychiatry 152*, 601-617.

Angold, A. (1988b). Childhood and adolescent depression: II. Research in clinical populations. *British Journal of Psychiatry 153*, 476-492.

Angold, A. & Rutter M. (1992). Effects of age and pubertal status on depression in a large clinical sample. *Developmental Psychopathology 4*, 5-28.

Angst, J. (1985). Switch from depression to mania – a record study over decades between 1920-1982. *Psychopathology 18*, 140-154.

Angst, J., Vollrath, M., Merikangas, K. R. & Ernst, C. (1990). Comorbidity of anxiety and depression in the Zürich cohort study of young adults. In J. D. Maser & C. R. Cloninger (eds.) *Comorbidity of mood and anxiety disorders*, 123-138. Washington, DC: American Psychiatric Press.

Anthony, J. C., Folstein, M., Romanoski, A. J., Von Korff, M. R., Nestadt, G. R., Chahal, R., Merchant, R., Brown, C. H., Shapiro, S., Kramer, M. & Gruenberg, E. M. (1985). Comparison of the lay Diagnostic Interview Schedule and a standardized psychiatric diagnosis. *Archives of General Psychiatry 42*, 667-675.

Asarnow, J. R., Goldstein, M. J., Carlson, G.A., Perdue, S., Bates, S. & Keller J. (1988). Childhood-onset depressive disorders. A follow-up study of rates of rehospitalization and out-of-home placement among child psychiatric inpatients. *Journal of Affective Disorders 15*, 245-253.

Banks, M. H. & Jackson, P. R. (1982). Unemployment and risk of minor psychiatric disorder in young people: Cross-sectional and longitudinal evidence. *Psychological Medicine 12*, 789-798.

Barraclough, B. M., Bunch, J., Nelson, B. & Sainsbury, P. (1974). A hundred cases of suicide: Clinical aspects. *British Journal of Psychiatry 125*, 355-373.

Beardslee, W. R. & Podorefsky, D. (1988). Resilient adolescents whose parents have serious affective and other psychiatric disorder: The importance of self-understanding and relationships. *American Journal of Psychiatry 145*, 67-69.

Bebbington, P., Katz, R., McGuffin, P., Tennant, C. & Hurry, J. (1989). The risk of minor depression before age 65: Results from a community survey. *Psychological Medicine 19*, 393-400.

Beck, A. T. (1976). *Cognitive therapy and the emotional disorders.* New York: International Universities Press.

Berney, T. P., Bhate, S. R., Kolvin, I., Famuyiwa, O. O., Barrett, M. L., Fundudis, T. & Tyrer, S. P. (1991). The context of childhood depression – The Newcastle childhood depression project. *The British Journal of Psychiatry, Supplement 11, 159*, 28-35.

Bland, R. C., Orn, H. & Newman, S. C. (1988). Lifetime prevalence of psychiatric disorders in Edmonton. *Acta Psychiatrica Scandinavica, Supplement 338, 77*, 24-32.

Block, J. H., Block, J. & Gjerde, P. F. (1986). The personality of children prior to divorce: A prospective study. *Child Development 57*, 827-840.

Borst, S. R., Noam, G. G. & Bartok J. A. (1991). Adolescent suicidality: A clinical-developmental approach. *Journal of the American Academy of Child and Adolescent Psychiatry 30*, 796-803.

Brent, D. A., Perper, J. A. & Allman C. J. (1987). Alcohol, firearms, and suicide among youth: Temporal trends in Allegheny County, Pennsylvania, 1960 to 1983. *Journal of the American Medical Association 257*, 3369-3372.

Brent, D. A., Perper, J. A., Goldstein, C. E., Kolko, D. J., Allan, M. J., Allman, C. J. & Zelenak J. P. (1988). Risk factors for adolescent suicide: A comparison of adolescent suicide victims with suicidal inpatients. *Archives of General Psychiatry 45*, 581-588.

Bromet, E. J., Dunn, L. O., Connell, M. M., Dew, M. A. & Schulberg, H. C. (1986). Long-term reliability of diagnosing lifetime major depression in a community sample. *Archives of General Psychiatry 43*, 435-440.

Brooks-Gunn, J. & Warren M. P. (1989). Biological and social contributions to negative affect in young adolescent girls. *Child Development 60*, 40-55.

Brown, G. W. & Harris T. O. (1978). *Social origins of depression. A study of psychiatric disorder in women*. London: Tavistock Publications.

Brown, G. W. & Harris, T. O. (1989). *Life events and illness*. New York: Guilford Press.

Bruce, M. L., Takeuchi, D. T. & Leaf, P. J. (1991). Poverty and psychiatric status: Longitudinal evidence from the New Haven Epidemiologic Catchment Area study. *Archives of General Psychiatry 48*, 470-474.

Buchanan, C. M., Eccles, J. S. & Becker, J. B. (1992). Are adolescents the victims of raging hormones: Evidence for activational effects of hormones on moods and behavior at adolescence. *Psychological Bulletin 111*, 62-107.

Cadoret, R. J., O'Gorman, T. W., Heywood, E. & Troughton, E. (1985). Genetic and environmental factors in major depression. *Journal of Affective Disorders 9*, 155-164.

Cairns, E., McWhirter, L., Barry, R. & Duffy U. (1991). The development of psychological well-being in late adolescence. *Journal of Child Psychology and Psychiatry 32*, 635-643.

Canino, G. J., Bird, H. R., Shrout, P. E., Rubio-Stipec, M., Bravo, M., Martinez, R., Sesman, M. & Guevara, L. M. (1987). The prevalence of specific psychiatric disorders in Puerto Rico. *Archives of General Psychiatry 44*, 727-735.

Carlson, G. A., Asarnow, J. R. & Orbach I. (1987). Developmental aspects of suicidal behavior in children. *Journal of the American Academy of Child and Adolescent Psychiatry 2*, 186-192.

Carlson, G. A. & Cantwell, D. P. (1982). Suicidal behavior and depression in children and adolescents. *Journal of the American Academy of Child Psychiatry 21*, 361-368.

Carlson, G. A., Rich, C. L., Grayson, P. & Fowler, R. C. (1991). Secular trends in psychiatric diagnoses of suicide victims. *Journal of Affective Disorders 21*, 127-132.

Cherlin, A. J., Furstenberg Jr., F. F., Chase-Lansdale, P. L., Kiernan, K. E., Robins, P. K., Morrison, D. R. & Teitler, J. O. (1991). Longitudinal studies of effects of divorce on children in Great Britain and the United States. *Science 252*, 1386-1389.

Christie, K. A., Burke, Jr. J. D., Regier, D. A., Rae, D. S., Boyd, J. H. & Locke B. Z. (1988). Epidemiologic evidence for early onset of mental disorders and higher risk of drug abuse in young adults. *American Journal of Psychiatry 145*, 971-975.

Clayton, D. & Hills, M. (1993). *Statistical models in epidemiology*. Oxford: Oxford University Press.

Clayton, D. & Schifflers, E. (1987a). Models for temporal variation in cancer rates. I: Age-period and age-cohort models. *Statistics in Medicine 6*, 449-467.

Clayton, D. & Schifflers, E. (1987b). Models for temporal variation in cancer rates. II: Age-period-cohort models. *Statistics in Medicine 6*, 469-481.

Clingempeel, W. G., Colyar, J. J., Brand, E. & Hetherington, E. M. (1992). Children's relationships with maternal grandparents: A longitudinal study of family structure and pubertal status effects. *Child Development 63*, 1404-1422.

Compas, B. E. (1987). Stress and life events during childhood and adolescence. *Clinical Psychological Review 7*, 275-302.

Compas, B. E. (1994). Promoting successful coping during adolescence. In M. Rutter (ed.) *Psychosocial disturbances in young people: Challenges for prevention*. New York/Cambridge: Cambridge University Press.

Compas, B. E., Howell, D. C., Phares, V., Williams, R. A. & Giunta, C. T. (1989). Risk factors for emotional/behavioral problems in young adolescents: A prospective analysis of adolescent and parental stress and symptoms. *Journal of Consulting and Clinical Psychology 57*, 732-740.

Compas, B. E. & Wagner, B. M. (1991). Psychosocial stress during adolescence: Intrapersonal and interpersonal processes. In M. E. Colten & S. Gore (eds.) *Adolescent stress: Causes and consequences*, 67-85. New York: Aldine de Gruyter.

Compas, B. E., Wagner, B. M., Slavin, L. A. & Vanatta, K. (1986). A prospective study of life events, social support, and psychological symptomatology during the transition from high school to college. *American Journal of Community Psychology 14*, 241-257.

Conger, R. D., Conger, K. J., Elder Jr., G. H., Lorenz, F. O., Simons, R. L. & Whitbeck, L. B. (1992). A family process model of economic hardship and adjustment of early adolescent boys. *Child Development 63*, 526-541.

Cooper, P. J., Campbell, E. A., Day, A., Kennerley, H. & Bond, A. (1988). Non-psychotic psychiatric disorder after childbirth: A prospective study of prevalence, incidence, course and nature. *British Journal of Psychiatry 152*, 799-806.

Coryell, W., Endicott, J. & Keller, M. (1992). Major depression in a nonclinical sample: Demographic and clinical risk factors for first onset. *Archives of General Psychiatry 49*, 117-125.

Costello, E. J. & Angold, A. (1988). Scales to assess child and adolescent depression: Checklists, screens and nets. *Journal of the American Academy of Child and Adolescent Psychiatry 27*, 726-737.

Cross-National Collaborative Group (1992). The changing rate of major depression: Cross-national comparisons. *Journal of the American Medical Association 268*, 3098-3105.

Dohrenwend, B. P., Levav, I., Shrout, P. E., Schwartz, S., Naveh, G., Link, B. G., Skodol, A. E. & Stueve, A. (1992). Socio-economic status and psychiatric disorders: The causation-selection issue. *Science 255*, 946-952.

Donovan, A., Oddy, M., Pardoe, R. & Ades, A. (1986). Employment status and psychological well-being: A longitudinal study of 16-year-old school leavers. *Journal of Child Psychology and Psychiatry 27*, 65-76.

DuBois, D., Felner, R. D., Brand, S., Adan, A. M. & Evans, E. G. (1992). A prospective study of life stress, social support, and adaptation in early adolescence. *Child Development 63*, 542-557.

Duncan, P. D., Ritter, P. L., Dornbusch, S. M., Gross, R. T. & Carlsmith, J. M. (1985). The effects of pubertal timing on body image, school behavior, and deviance. *Journal of Youth and Adolescence 14*, 227-235.

Easterlin, R. A. (1980). *Birth and fortune. The impact of numbers on personal welfare.* London: Grant McIntyre.

Elder Jr., G. H., Nguyen, T. V. & Caspi, A. (1985). Linking family hardship to children's lives. *Child Development 56*, 361-375.

Faravelli, C., Guerrini-Degl'Innocenti, B., Aiazzi, L., Incerpi, G. & Pallanti, S. (1990). Epidemiology of mood disorders: A community survey in Florence. *Journal of Affective Disorders 20*, 135-141.

Farrer, L. A., Florio, L. P., Bruce, M. L., Leaf, P. J. & Weissman, M. M. (1989). Reliability of self-reported age at onset of major depression. *Journal of Psychiatric Research 23*, 35-47.

Fleming, J. E. & Offord, D. R. (1990). Epidemiology of childhood depressive disorders: A critical review. *Journal of the American Academy of Child and Adolescent Psychiatry 29*, 571-580.

Fleming, J. E., Offord, D. R. & Boyle, M. H. (1989). Prevalence of childhood and adolescent depression in the community, Ontario Child Health Study. *British Journal of Psychiatry 155*, 647-654.

Fombonne, E. (1991). The use of questionnaires in psychiatry research: Measuring their performance and choosing an optimal cut-off. *Journal of Child Psychology and Psychiatry 32*, 677-693.

Fombonne, E. (1992). Parent reports on behavior and competencies among 6 to 11-year-old French children. *European Child and Adolescent Psychiatry 1*, 233-243.

Galambos, N. L. & Maggs, J. L. (1991). Out-of-school care of young adolescents and self-reported behavior. *Developmental Psychology 27*, 644-655.

Garber, J., Kriss, M., Koch, M. & Lindholm, L. (1988). Recurrent depression in adolescents: A follow-up study. *Journal of the American Academy of Child and Adolescent Psychiatry 25*, 49-54.

Garrison, C. Z., Addy, C. L., Jackson, K. L., McKeown, R. E. & Waller, J. L. (1992). Major depressive disorder and dysthymia in young adolescents. *Journal of Epidemiology 135*, 792-802.

Garrison, C. Z., Schoenbach, V. J., Schluchter, M. D. & Kaplan, B. H. (1987). Life events in early adolescence. *Journal of the American Academy of Child and Adolescent Psychiatry 26*, 865-872.

Gatz, M., Pedersen, N. L., Plomin, R., Nesselroade, J. R. & McClearn, G. E. (1992). Importance of shared genes and shared environments for symptoms of depression in older adults. *Journal of Abnormal Psychology 101*, 701-708.

Gershon, E. S., Hamovit, J. H., Guroff, J. J. & Nurnberger, J. I. (1987). Birth-cohort changes in manic and depressive disorders in relatives of bipolar and schizoaffective affective patients. *Archives of General Psychiatry 44*, 314-319.

Giles, D. E., Roffwarg, H. P., Kupfer, D. J., Rush, A. J., Biggs, M. M. & Etzel, B. A. (1989). Secular trend in unipolar depression: A hypothesis. *Journal of Affective Disorders 16*, 71-75.

Goodyer, I. M. (1990). *Life experiences, development and childhood psychopathology.* Chichester: Wiley.

Graber, J. A. & Petersen, A. C. (1991). Cognitive changes at adolescence: Biological perspectives. In K. R. Gibson & A. C. Petersen (eds.) *Brain maturation and cognitive development: Comparative and cross-cultural perspectives*, 253-279. New York: Aldine de Gruyter.

Gurin, G., Veroff, J. & Feld, S. C. (1960). *Americans view their mental health.* New York: Basic Books.

Hagnell, O., Lanke, J., Rorsman, B. & Ojesjö, L. (1982). Are we entering an age of melancholy? Depressive illnesses in a prospective epidemiological study over 25 years: The Lundby study, Sweden. *Psychological Medicine 12*, 279-289.

Hammen, C., Burge, D., Burney, E. & Adrian, C. (1990). Longitudinal study of diagnoses in children of women with unipolar and bipolar affective disorder. *Archives of General Psychiatry 47*, 1112-1117.

Harrington. R. (1993). *Depressive disorder in childhood and adolescence.* Chichester: Wiley.

Harrington, R., Fudge, J., Rutter, M., Bredenkamp, D., Groothues, C. & Pridham, J. (1993). Child and adult depression: A test of continuities with data from a family study. *British Journal of Psychiatry 162*, 627-633.

Harrington, R., Fudge, H., Rutter, M., Pickles, A. & Hill, J. (1990). Adult outcomes of childhood and adolescent depression: I. Psychiatric status. *Archives of General Psychiatry 47*, 465-473.

Harrington, R. C., Fudge, H., Rutter, M., Pickles, A. & Hill, J. (1991). Adult outcomes of childhood and adolescent depression: II. Risk for antisocial disorders. *Journal of the American Academy of Child and Adolescent Psychiatry 30*, 434-439.

Hasin, D. & Link, B. (1988). Age and recognition of depression: Implications for a cohort effect in major depression. *Psychological Medicine 18*, 683-688.

Hawton, K. & Goldacre, M. (1982). Hospital admissions for adverse effects of medicinal agents (mainly self-poisoning) among adolescents in the Oxford region. *British Journal of Psychiatry 141*, 166-170.

Helzer, J. E., Robins, L. N., McEvoy, L. T., Spitznagel, E. L., Stoltzman, R. K., Farmer, A. & Brockington, I. F. (1985). A comparison of clinical and diagnostic interview schedule diagnoses. *Archives of General Psychiatry 42*, 657-666.

Hetherington, E. M., Cox, M. & Cox, R. (1978). The aftermath of divorce. In J. H. Stevens Jr. & M. Matthews (eds.) *Mother-child, father-child relations.* Washington, DC: NAEYC.

Hetherington, E. M., Cox, M. & Cox, R. (1985). Long-term effects of divorce and remarriage on the adjustment of children. *Journal of the American Academy of Child Psychiatry 24*, 518-530.

Holford, T. R. (1992). Analysing the temporal effects of age, period and cohort. *Statistical Methods in Medical Research 1*, 317-337.

Holinger, P. C. & Offer, D. (1991). Sociodemographic, epidemiologic, and individual attributes. In L. Davidson & M. Linnoila (eds.) *Risk factors for youth suicide*, 3-17. New York: Hemisphere Publishing Corporation.

Hwu, H.-G., Yeh, E.-K. & Chang, L.-Y. (1989). Prevalence of psychiatric disorders in Taiwan defined by the Chinese Diagnostic Interview Schedule. *Acta Psychiatrica Scandinavica 79*, 136-147.

Jackson, P. R., Stafford, E. M., Banks, M. H. & Warr, P. B. (1983). Unemployment and psychological distress in young people: The moderating role of employment commitment. *Journal of Applied Psychology 68*, 525-535.

Jahoda, M. (1979). The impact of unemployment in the 1930s and the 1970s. *Bulletin of the British Psychological Society 32*, 309-314.

Jahoda, M. (1981). Work, employment and unemployment: Values, theories and approaches in social research. *American Psychologist 36*, 184-191.

Joyce, P. R., Oakley-Browne, M. A., Wells, J. E., Bushnell, J. A. & Hornblow, A. R. (1990). Birth cohort trends in major depression: Increasing rates and earlier onset in New Zealand. *Journal of Affective Disorders 18*, 83-89.

Kandel, D. B. & Davies, M. (1986). Adult sequelae of adolescent depressive symptoms. *Archives of General Psychiatry 43*, 255-264.

Karam, E. G., Barakeh, M. & Karam, A. N. (1991). The Arabic Diagnostic Interview Schedule. *Revue Médicale Libanaise 3*, 28-30.

Karno, M., Hough, R. L., Burnam, M. A., Escobar, J. I., Timbers, D. M., Santana, F. & Boyd, J. H. (1987). Lifetime prevalence of specific psychiatric disorders among Mexican Americans and non-Hispanic whites in Los Angeles. *Archives of General Psychiatry 44*, 695-701.

Kazdin, A. (1990). Childhood depression. *Journal of Child Psychology and Psychiatry 31*, 121-160

Kessler, R. C., McGonagle, K. A., Swartz, M., Blazer, D. G. & Nelson, C. B. (1993). Sex and depression in the National Comorbidity Survey: I. Lifetime prevalence, chronicity and recurrence. *Journal of Affective Disorders 29*, 85-96.

Kessler, R. C. & McLeod, J. D. (1984). Sex differences in vulnerability to undesirable events. *American Sociological Review 49*, 620-631.

Klerman, G. L. (1988). The current age of youthful melancholia: Evidence for increase in depression among adolescents and young adults. *British Journal of Psychiatry 152*, 4-14.

Klerman, G. L., Lavori, P. W., Rice, J., Reich, T., Endicott, J., Andreasen, N. C., Keller, M. B. & Hirschfield, R. M. A. (1985). Birth-cohort trends in rates of major depressive disorder among relatives of patients with affective disorder. *Archives of General Psychiatry 42*, 689-693.

Klerman, G. L. & Weissman, M. M. (1989). Increasing rates of depression. *Journal of American Medical Association 261*, 2229-2235.

Kolvin, I., Barrett, M. L., Bhate, S. R., Berney, T. P., Famuyiwa, O. O., Fundudis, T. & Tyref, S. (1991). The Newcastle childhood depression project: Diagnosis and classification of depression. *British Journal of Psychiatry 159*, (supplement 11), 9-12.

Kovacs, M., Feinberg, T. L., Crouse-Novak, M. A., Paulauskas, S. L. & Finkelstein, R. (1984a). Depressive disorders in childhood: I. A longitudinal prospective study of characteristics and recovery. *Archives of General Psychiatry 41*, 229-237.

Kovacs, M., Feinberg, T. L., Crouse-Novak, M. A., Paulauskas, S. L., Pollock, M. & Finkelstein, R. (1984b). Depressive disorders in childhood: II. A longitudinal study of the risk for a subsequent major depression. *Archives of General Psychiatry 41*, 643-649.

Kovacs, M., Paulauskas, S., Gatsonis, C. & Richards, C. (1988). Depressive disorders in childhood: III. A longitudinal study of comorbidity with and risk for conduct disorders. *Journal of Affective Disorders 15*, 205-217.

Kovacs, M. & Puig-Antich, J. (1991). 'Major psychiatric disorders' as risk factors in youth suicide. In L. Davidson, & M. Linnoila (eds.) *Risk factors in youth suicide*, 127-143. New York: Hemisphere Publishing Corporation.

Larson, R. W., Raffaelli, M., Richards, M. H., Ham, M. & Jewell, L. (1990). Ecology of depression in late childhood and early adolescence: A profile of daily states and activities. *Developmental Psychology 99*, 92-102.

Larson, R. & Richards, M. H. (1991). Daily companionship in late childhood and early adolescence: Changing developmental contexts. *Child Development 62*, 284-300.

Lasch, K., Weissman, M., Wickramaratne, P. & Bruce, M. L. (1990). Birth-cohort changes in the rates of mania. *Psychiatry Research 33*, 31-37.

Lavori, P. W., Klerman, G. L., Keller, M. B., Reich, T., Rice, J. & Endicott, J. (1987). Age-period-cohort analysis of secular trends in onset of major depression: Findings in siblings of patients with major affective disorder. *Journal of Psychiatric Research 21* , 23-35.

Lee, C. K., Kwak, Y. S., Rhee, H., Kim, Y. S., Han, J. H., Choi, J. O. & Lee, Y. H. (1987). The nationwide epidemiological study of mental disorders in Korea. *Journal of Korean Medical Sciences 2*, 19-34.

Lempers, J. D. & Clark-Lempers, D. (1990). Family economic stress, maternal and paternal support and adolescent distress. *Journal of Adolescence 13*, 217-229.

Lempers, J. D., Clark-Lempers D. & Simons, R. L. (1989). Economic hardship, parenting, and distress in adolescence. *Child Development 60*, 25-39.

Leon, A. C., Klerman, G. L. & Wickramaratne, P. (1993). Continuing female predominance in depressive illness. *American Journal of Public Health 83*, 754-767.

Lépine, J.-P., Lellouch, J., Lovell, A., Teherani, M., Ha, C., Verdier-Taillefer, M.-H., Rambourg, N. & Lempérière, T. (1989). Anxiety and depressive disorders in a French population: Methodology and preliminary results. *Psychiatrie et Psychobiologie 4*, 267-274.

Lester, D. (1991). Suicide across the life span. A look at international trends. In A. A. Leenaars (ed.) *Life span perspectives of suicide: Time-lines in the suicide process*, 71-88. New York: Plenum Press.

Lewinsohn, P., Rohde, P., Seeley, J. R. & Fischer, S. A. (1993). Age-cohort changes in the lifetime occurrence of depression and other mental disorders. *Journal of Abnormal Psychology 102*, 110-120.

Magnusson, D., Stattin, H. & Allen, V. (1985). Biological maturation and social development: A longitudinal study of some adjustment processes from mid-adolescence to adulthood. *Journal of Youth and Adolescence 14*, 267-284.

Maier, W., Hallmayer, J., Lichtermann, D., Philipp, M. & Klingler, T. (1991). The impact of the endogenous subtype on the familial aggregation of unipolar depression. *European Archives of Psychiatry and Clinical Neurosciences 240*, 355-362.

Marttunen, M. J., Aro, H. M., Henriksson, M. M. & Lönnqvist, J. K. (1991). Mental disorders in adolescent suicide: DSM-III-R axes I and II diagnoses in suicides among 13- to 19-year-olds in Finland. *Archives of General Psychiatry 48*, 834-839.

McClure, G. M. G. (1984). Recent trends in suicide amongst the young. *British Journal of Psychiatry 144*, 134-138.

McGee, R., Feehan, M., Williams, S. & Anderson, J. (1992). DSM-III disorders from age 11 to age 15 years. *Journal of the American Academy of Child and Adolescent Psychiatry 31*, 50-59.

McGee, R., Feehan, M., Williams, S., Partridge, F., Silva, P. A. & Kelly, J. (1990). DSM-III disorders in a large sample of adolescents. *Journal of the American Academy of Child and Adolescent Psychiatry 29*, 611-619.

McGee, R. & Williams, S. (1988). A longitudinal study of depression in nine-year-old children. *Journal of the American Academy of Child and Adolescent Psychiatry 29*, 611-619.

McGuffin, P. & Katz, R. (1989). The genetics of depression and manic-depressive disorder. *British Journal of Psychiatry 155*, 294-304.

McIntosh, J. (1991). Epidemiology of suicide in the United States. In A. A. Leenaars (ed.) *Life span perspectives of suicide: Time-lines in the suicide process*, 55-69. New York: Plenum Press.

Merikangas, K. R. & Angst, J. (1994). The challenge of depressive disorders in adolescence. In M. Rutter (ed.) *Psychosocial disturbances in young people: Challenges for prevention.* New York/Cambridge: Cambridge University Press.

Merikangas, K. R., Prusoff, B. A. & Weissman, M. M. (1988). Parental concordance for affective disorders: Psychopathology in offspring. *Journal of Affective Disorders 15*, 279-290.

Miles, C. P. (1977). Conditions predisposing to suicide: A review. *Journal of Nervous and Mental Diseases 16*, 231-246.

Morgan, S. P., Lye, D. N. & Condran, G. A. (1988). Sons, daughters, and the risk of marital disruption. *American Journal of Sociology 94*, 110-129.

Mufson, L., Moreau, D., Weissman, M. M. & Klerman, G. L. (1993). *Interpersonal psychotherapy for depressed adolescents.* New York: Guilford Press.

Murphy, J. M., Monson, R. R., Olivier, D. C., Sobol, A. M. & Leighton, A. H. (1987). Mortality risk and psychiatric disorders: Results of a general population survey. *Archives of General Psychiatry 44*, 473-480.

Murphy, J. M., Olivier, D. C., Monson, R. R., Sobol, A. M., Federman, E. B. & Leighton, A. H. (1991). Depression and anxiety in relation to social status. *Archives of General Psychiatry 48*, 223-229.

Murphy, J. M., Sobol, A. M., Neff, R. K., Olivier, D. C. & Leighton, A. H. (1984). Stability of prevalence: Depression and anxiety disorders. *Archives of General Psychiatry 41*, 990-997.

Murphy, G. E. & Wetzel, R. (1980). Suicide risk by birth cohort in the United States, 1949 to 1974. *Archives of General Psychiatry 37*, 519-523.

Nolen-Hoeksema, S. (1987). Sex differences in unipolar depression: Evidence and theory. *Psychological Bulletin 101*, 259-282.

Nottelmann, E. D. (1987). Competence and self-esteem during transition from childhood to adolescence. *Developmental Psychology 23*, 441-450.

Nottelman, E. D., Inoff-Germain, G., Susman, E. J. & Chrousos, G. P. (1990). Hormones and behavior at puberty. In J. Bancroft & J. Machover Reinisch (eds.) *Adolescence and puberty*, 88-123. Oxford: Oxford University Press.

Oakley-Browne, M. A., Joyce, P. R., Wells, J. E., Bushnell, J. A. & Hornblow, A. R. (1989). Christchurch psychiatric epidemiology study: II. Six month and other period prevalences of specific psychiatric disorders. *Australian and New Zealand Journal of Psychiatry 23*, 327-340.

O'Brien, G. E. & Feather, N. T. (1990). The relative effects of unemployment and quality of employment on the affect, work values and personal control of adolescents. *Journal of Occupational Psychology 63*, 151-165.

Paikoff, R. L., Brooks-Gunn, J. & Warren, M. P. (1991). Effects of girls' hormonal status on depressive and aggressive symptoms over the course of one year. *Journal of Youth and Adolescence 20*, 191-215.

Parker, G. (1987). Are the lifetime prevalence estimates in the ECA study accurate?. *Psychological Medicine 17*, 275-282.

Pearce, J. B. (1978). The recognition of depressive disorder in children. *Journal of the Royal Society of Medicine 71*, 494-500.

Petersen, A. C. (1987). The nature of biological-psychosocial interactions: The sample case of early adolescence. In R. M. Lerner & T. T. Foch (eds.) *Biological-psychosocial interactions in early adolescence: A life-span perspective,* 35-61. Hillsdale, NJ: Lawrence Erlbaum.

Petersen, A. C., Compas, B. & Brooks-Gunn, J. (1992). *Depression in adolescence: Current knowledge, research directions and implications for programs and policy.* Report to the Carnegie Council on Adolescent Development.

Petersen, A. C., Compas, B., Brooks-Gunn, J., Stemmler, M., Ey, S. & Grant, K. (1993). Depression in adolescence. *American Psychologist 48,* 155-168.

Petersen, A. C., Kennedy, R. E. & Sullivan, P. (1991a). Coping with adolescence. In M. E. Colten & S. Gore (eds.) *Adolescent stress: Causes and consequences,* 93-110. New York: Aldine de Gruyter.

Petersen, A. C., Sarigiani, P. A. & Kennedy, R. E. (1991b). Adolescent depression: Why more girls? *Journal of Youth and Adolescence 20,* 247-271.

Phares, V. & Compas, B. E. (1992). The role of fathers in child and adolescent psychopathology: Make a room for daddy. *Psychological Bulletin 111,* 387-412.

Prusoff, B. A., Merikangas, K. R. & Weissman, M. M. (1988). Lifetime prevalence and age of onset: Recall 4 years later. *Journal of Psychiatric Research 22,* 107-117.

Puckering, C. (1989). Maternal depression. *Journal of Child Psychology and Psychiatry 30,* 807-817.

Puig-Antich, J., Goetz, D., Davies, M., Kaplan, T., Davies, S., Ostrow, L., Asnis, L., Twomey, J., Iyengar, S. & Ryan, N. D. (1989). A controlled family history study of prepubertal major depressive disorder. *Archives of General Psychiatry 46,* 406-418.

Quinn, J. (1994). Positive effects of participation in youth organizations. In M. Rutter (ed.) *Psychosocial disturbances in young people: Challenges for prevention.* New York/Cambridge: Cambridge University Press.

Radke-Yarrow, M., Nottelmann, E., Martinez, P., Fox, M. B. & Belmont, B. (1992). Young children of affectively ill parents: A longitudinal study of psychosocial development. *Journal of the American Academy of Child and Adolescent Psychiatry 31,* 68-77.

Radloff, L. S. (1991). The use of the Center for Epidemiological Studies Depression Scale in adolescents and young adults. *Journal of Youth and Adolescence 20,* 149-166.

Rao, U., Weissman, M. M., Martin, J. A. & Hammond, R. W. (1993). Childhood depression and risk of suicide: A preliminary report of a longitudinal study. *Journal of the American Academy of Child and Adolescent Psychiatry 32,* 21-27.

Reinherz, H. Z., Stewart-Berghauer, G., Pakiz, B., Frost, A. K. & Moeykens, B. A. (1989). The relationship of early risk and current mediators to depressive symptomatology in adolescence. *Journal of the American Academy of Child and Adolescent Psychiatry 28,* 942-947.

Reynolds, W. M., Anderson, G. & Bartell, N. (1985). Measuring depression in children: A multi-method assessment investigation. *Journal of Abnormal Child Psychology 13,* 513-526.

Rich, C. L., Young, D. & Fowler, R. C. (1986). San Diego suicide study: I. Young vs. old subjects. *Archives of General Psychiatry 43*, 577-582.

Roberts, R. E., Lee, E. S. & Roberts, C. R. (1991). Changes in prevalence of depressive symptoms in Alameda County. *Journal of Aging and Health 3*, 66-86.

Robins, L. N., Helzer, J. E., Weissman, M. M., Orvaschel, H., Gruenberg, E., Burke, J. D. & Regier, D. A. (1984). Lifetime prevalence of specific psychiatric disorders in three sites. *Archives of General Psychiatry 41*, 949-958.

Robins, L. N., Locke, B. Z. & Regier D. A. (1991a). An overview of psychiatric disorders in America. In L. N. Robins & D. A. Regier (eds.) *Psychiatric disorders in America: The Epidemiologic Catchment Area study*, 328-366. New York: Free Press.

Robins, L. N., Tipp, J. & Przybeck, T. (1991b). Antisocial personality. In L. N. Robins & D. A. Regier (eds.) *Psychiatric disorders in America: The Epidemiologic Catchment Area Study*, 258-290. New York: Free Press.

Rodgers, W. (1982). Trends in reported happiness within demographically defined subgroups, 1957-78. *Social Forces 60*, 826-842.

Rohde, P., Lewinsohn, P. M. & Seeley, J. R. (1991). Comorbidity of unipolar depression: II. Comorbidity with other mental disorders in adolescents and adults. *Journal of Affective Disorders 100*, 214-222.

Rubin, R. T. (1990). Mood changes during adolescence. In J. Bancroft & J. Machover (eds.) *Adolescence and puberty*, 146-153. Oxford: Oxford University Press.

Runeson, B. (1989). Mental disorders in youth suicide: DSM-III-R axes I and II. *Acta Psychiatrica Scandinavica 79*, 490-497.

Rutter, M. (1986). The developmental psychopathology of depression: Issues and perspectives. In M. Rutter, C. Izard & B. Read (eds.) *Depression in young people: Developmental and clinical perspectives*, 3-30. New York: Guilford Press.

Rutter, M. (1988). Depressive disorders. In M. Rutter, A. H. Tuma & I. S. Lann (eds.) *Assessment and diagnosis in child psychopathology*, 347-376. London: David Fulton Publishers.

Rutter, M. (1989). Psychiatric disorder in parents as a risk factor for children. In D. Shaffer, J. Philips & N. B. Enzer (associate eds.) *Prevention of mental disorders, alcohol and other drug use in children and adolescents*, 157-189. OSAP Prevention Monograph 2. Rockville, Maryland: Office for Substance Abuse Prevention, US Department of Health and Human Services.

Rutter, M. (1991). Age changes in depressive disorders: Some developmental considerations. In J. Garber & K. A. Dodge (eds.) *The development of emotion regulation and dysregulation*, 273-300. Cambridge: Cambridge University Press.

Rutter, M. (1994) Genetic knowledge and prevention of mental disorders. Background paper for P. J. Mrazek & R. J. Haggerty (eds.) *Reducing risk factors for mental disorders: Frontiers for preventive intervention research.* Washington, DC: Committee on Prevention of Mental Disorders, Institute of Medicine.

Rutter, M., Bolton, P., Harrington, R., Le Couteur, A., MacDonald, H. & Simonoff, E. (1990a). Genetic factors in child psychiatric disorders: I. A review of research strategies. *Journal of Child Psychology and Psychiatry 31*, 3-37.

Rutter, M., MacDonald, H., Le Couteur, A., Harrington, R., Bolton, P. & Bailey, A. (1990b). Genetic factors in child psychiatric disorders: II. Empirical findings. *Journal of Child Psychology and Psychiatry 31*, 39-83.

Rutter, M. & Quinton, D. (1984). Parental psychiatric disorder: Effects on children. *Psychological Medicine 14*, 853-880.

Rutter, M. & Sandberg S. (1992). Psychosocial stressors: Concepts, causes and effects. *European Child and Adolescent Psychiatry 1*, 3-13.

Rutter, M., Tizard, J., Yule, W., Graham, P. & Whitmore, K. (1976). Research report: Isle of Wight studies, 1964-1974. *Psychological Medicine 6*, 313-332.

Ryan, N. D., Williamson, D. E., Iyengar, S., Orvaschel, H., Reich, T., Dahl, R. E. & Puig-Antich J. (1992). A secular increase in child and adolescent onset affective disorder. *Journal of the American Academy of Child and Adolescent Psychiatry 31*, 600-605.

Sainsbury, P. (1986a). The epidemiology of suicide. In A. Roy (ed.) *Suicide*, 17-40. Baltimore: Williams & Wilkins.

Sainsbury, P. (1986b). Depression, suicide, and suicide prevention. In A. Roy (ed.) *Suicide*, 73-88. Baltimore: Williams & Wilkins.

Sarigiani, P. A., Wilson, J. L., Petersen, A. C. & Vicary, J. R. (1990). Self-image and educational plans of adolescents from two contrasting communities. *Journal of Early Adolescence 10*, 37-55.

Shaffer, D. (1974). Suicide of childhood and early adolescence. *Journal of Child Psychology and Psychiatry 15*, 275-291.

Shaffer, D. (1988). The epidemiology of teen suicide: An examination of risk factors. *Journal of Clinical Psychiatry Supplement 9, 49*, 36-41.

Shaffer, D. & Fisher, P. (1981). The epidemiology of suicide in children and young adolescents. *Journal of the American Academy of Child Psychiatry 20*, 545-565.

Shafii, M., Carrigan, S., Whittinghill, J. R. & Derrick, A. (1985). Psychological autopsy of completed suicide in children and adolescents. *American Journal of Psychiatry 142*, 1061-1064.

Shamir, B. (1986). Self-esteem and the psychological impact of unemployment. *Social Psychology Quarterly 49*, 61-72.

Simmons, R. G. & Blyth, D. A. (1987). *Moving into adolescence: The impact of pubertal change and school context.* New York: Aldine de Gruyter.

Simmons, R. G., Blyth, D. A., Van Cleave, E. F. & Mitsch Bush, D. (1979). Entry into early adolescence: The impact of school structure, puberty, and early dating on self-esteem. *American Sociological Review 44*, 948-967.

Simmons, R. G., Burgeson, R., Carlton-Ford, S. & Blyth, D. A. (1987). The impact of cumulative change in early adolescence. *Child Development 58*, 1220-1234.

Simon, G. E. & VonKorff, M. (1992). Reevaluation of secular trends in depression rates. *American Journal of Epidemiology 135*, 1411-1422.

Simons, R. L., Lorenz, F. O., Conger, R. D. & Wu, C.-I. (1992). Support from spouse as mediator and moderator of the disruptive influence of economic strain on parenting. *Child Development 63*, 1282-1301.

Solomon, M. I. & Hellon, C. P. (1980). Suicide and age in Alberta, Canada: 1951 to 1977. *Archives of General Psychiatry 37*, 511-513.

Steinberg, L. D. (1981). Transformations in family relations at puberty. *Developmental Psychology 17*, 833-840.

Steinberg, L. D. (1986). Latchkey children and susceptibility to peer pressure: An ecological analysis. *Developmental Psychology 22*, 433-439.

Steinberg, L. (1987). Impact of puberty on family relations: Effects on pubertal status and pubertal timing. *Developmental Psychology 23*, 451-460.

Steinberg L. (1988). Reciprocal relation between parent-child distance and pubertal maturation. *Developmental Psychology 24*, 122-128.

Steinberg, L. & Dornbusch, S. M. (1991). Negative correlates of part-time employment during adolescence: Replication and elaboration. *Developmental Psychology 27*, 304-313.

Strober, M. (1992). Relevance of early age-of-onset in genetic studies of bipolar affective disorder. *Journal of the American Academy of Child and Adolescent Psychiatry 31*, 606-610.

Strober, M., Morrell, W., Burroughs, J., Lampert, C., Danforth, H. & Freeman, R. (1988). A family study of bipolar I disorder in adolescence: Early onset of symptoms linked to increased familial loading and lithium resistance. *Journal of Affective Disorders 15*, 255-268.

Susman, E. J., Dorn, L. D. & Chrousos, G. P. (1991). Negative affect and hormone levels in young adolescents: Concurrent and predictive perspectives. *Journal of Youth and Adolescence 20*, 167-190.

Tanner, J. M. (1989). *Foetus into man: Physical growth from conception to maturity* (2nd edition). Ware: Castlemead Publications.

Tobin-Richards, M. H., Boxer, A. M. & Petersen, A. C. (1983). The psychological significance of pubertal change: Sex differences in perceptions of self during early adolescence, 127-154. In J. Brooks-Gunn & A. C. Petersen (eds.) *Girls at puberty: Biological and psychosocial perspectives*, 127-154. New York: Plenum Press.

Verhulst, F. C., Akkerhuis, G. W. & Althaus, M. (1985). Mental health in Dutch children: I. A cross-cultural comparison. *Acta Psychiatrica Scandinavica, Supplement 323*.

Veroff, J., Douvan, E. & Kulka, R. (1981a). *The inner American*. New York: Basic Books.

Veroff, J., Kulka, R. A. & Douvan, E. (1981b). *Mental health in America. Patterns of help-seeking from 1957 to 1976*. New York: Basic Books.

Vuchinich, S., Hetherington, E. M., Vuchinich, R. A. & Clingempeel, W. G. (1991). Parent-child interaction and gender differences in early adolescents' adaptation to stepfamilies. *Developmental Psychology 27*, 618-626.

Warr, P., Banks, M. & Ullah, P. (1985). The experience of unemployment among black and white urban teenagers. *British Journal of Psychology 76*, 75-87.

Warr, P. B. & Jackson, P. R. (1984). Men without jobs: Some correlates of age and length in unemployment. *Journal of Occupational Psychology 57*, 77-85.

Warshaw, M. G., Klerman, G. L. & Lavori, P. W. (1991a). Are secular trends in major depression an artifact of recall? *Journal of Psychiatric Research 25*, 141-151.

Warshaw, M. G., Klerman, G. L. & Lavori, P. W. (1991b). The use of conditional probabilities to examine age-period-cohort data: Further evidence for a period effect in major depressive disorder. *Journal of Affective Disorders 23*, 119-129.

Watson, D. & Clark L. (1984). Negative affectivity: The disposition to experience aversive emotional states. *Psychological Bulletin 96*, 465-490.

Weatherall, D. (1992). The Harveian Oration. *The role of nature and nurture in common diseases: Garrod's legacy.* London: The Royal College of Physicians.

Weissman, M. M., Bland, R., Joyce, P. R., Newman, S., Wells, J. E. & Wittchen, H-E. (1993). Sex differences in rates of depression: Cross-national perspectives. *Journal of Affective Disorders 29*, 77-84.

Weissman, M. M., Gammon, D., John, K., Merikangas, K.R., Warner, V., Prusoff, B.A. & Sholomskas, D. (1987). Children of depressed parents: Increased psychopathology and early onset of major depression. *Archives of General Psychiatry 44*, 847-853.

Weissman, M. M. & Klerman, G. L. (1977). Sex differences in the epidemiology of depression. *Archives of General Psychiatry 34*, 98-111.

Weissman, M. M., Leaf, P. J., Holzer III, C. E., Myers, J. K. & Tischler, G. L. (1984). The epidemiology of depression. An update on sex differences in rates. *Journal of Affective Disorders 7*, 179-188.

Weissman, M. M., Livingston Bruce, M., Leaf, P. J., Florio, L. P. & Holzer III, C. (1991). Affective disorders. In L. N. Robins & D. A. Regier (eds.) *Psychiatric disorders in America: The Epidemiologic Catchment Area study*, 53-80. New York: Free Press.

Weissman, M. M., Merikangas, K. R., Wickramaratne, P., Kidd, K. K., Prusoff, B. A., Leckman, J. F. & Pauls, D. L. (1986). Understanding the clinical heterogeneity of major depression using family data. *Archives of General Psychiatry 43*, 430-434.

Wells, J. E., Bushnell, J. A., Hornblow, A. R., Joyce, P. R. & Oakley-Browne, M. A. (1989). Christchurch psychiatric epidemiology study: I. Methodology and lifetime prevalence for specific psychiatric disorders. *Australian and New Zealand Journal of Psychiatry 23*, 315-326.

Wells, V. E., Klerman, G. L. & Deykin, E. Y. (1987). The prevalence of depressive symptoms in college students. *Social Psychiatry 22*, 20-28.

Whitaker, A., Johnson, J., Shaffer, D., Rapoport, J., Kalikow, K., Walsh, B. T., Davies, M., Braiman, S. & Dolinsky, A. (1990). Uncommon troubles in young people: Prevalence estimates of selected psychiatric disorders in a nonreferred adolescent population. *Archives of General Psychiatry 47*, 487-496.

Wickramaratne, P. J., Weissman, M. M., Leaf, P. J. & Holford, T. R. (1989). Age, period and cohort effects on the risk of major depression: Results from five United States communities. *Journal of Clinical Epidemiology 42*, 333-343.

Wigfield, A., Eccles, J. S., Mac Iver, D., Reuman, D. A. & Midgley, C. (1991). Transitions during early adolescence: Changes in children's domain-specific self-perceptions and general self-esteem across the transition to junior high school. *Developmental Psychology 27*, 552-565.

Winefield, A. H. & Tiggemann, M. (1990). Employment status and psychological well-being: A longitudinal study. *Journal of Applied Psychology 75*, 455-459.

Winefield, A. H., Tiggemann, M. & Winefield, H. R. (1991). The psychological impact of unemployment and unsatisfactory employment in young men and women: Longitudinal and cross-sectional data. *British Journal of Psychology 82*, 473-486.

Winnubst, J. A. M., Buunk, B. P. & Marcelissen, F. H. G. (1988). Social support and stress: Perspectives and processes. In S. Fisher & J. Reason (eds.) *Handbook of life stress, cognition and health*, 511-528. New York: Wiley.

Wittchen, H. U., Essau, C. A., von Zerssen, D., Krieg, J. D. & Zaudig, M. (1992). Lifetime and six-month prevalence of mental disorders in the Munich follow-up study. *European Archives of Psychiatry Clinical Neurosciences 241*, 247-258.

World Health Organization (1992). *The ICD-10 classification of mental and behavioural disorders: Clinical descriptions and diagnostic guidelines*. Geneva: Author.

Zeitlin, H. (1986). *The natural history of psychiatric disorder in children*. Maudsley Monographs No 29. New York: Oxford University Press.

Zimiles, H. & Lee, V. E. (1991). Adolescent family structure and educational progress. *Developmental Psychology 27*, 314-320.

Zoccolillo, M. & Rogers, K. (1991). Characteristics and outcome of hospitalized adolescent girls with conduct disorder. *Journal of the American Academy of Child and Adolescent Psychiatry 30*, 973-981.

12

Eating Disorders: Time Trends and Possible Explanatory Mechanisms

ERIC FOMBONNE

This chapter examines the evidence that eating disorders and disturbances (anorexia nervosa and bulimia nervosa) have increased in recent decades among young people, and evaluates possible causal explanations for any such increase. Issues of definition and measurement are considered first. The second section examines the main sources of data and reviews the available evidence on change over time. The third section summarizes results from epidemiological studies on the pattern of risk, with particular reference to age, sex, the role of genetic factors, and a possible tendency for eating disorders to occur in conjunction with other psychological or psychosocial disorders. In the light of these findings on the pattern of risk, the fourth section then discusses the causal mechanisms that might explain an increase in eating disorders or in more broadly defined eating disturbances. The final section summarizes the findings and draws out the implications for future research on this topic.

DEFINITION AND MEASUREMENT

Although they were first described many years ago, eating disorders became a subject of major systematic study only in the 1970s. There is now a growing body of literature and a number of journals devoted to the topic.

Two types of definition have been used by researchers in the field. The first, which is categorical (classifies each subject as having or not having the condition), grows out of the medical tradition; it is analogous to the approach used by clinicians to diagnose a disease. The second regards eating behaviours as a continuum that may vary from normality to extreme deviance; on this approach, which grows out of the tradition of psychological research using behavioural dimensions, each subject is assigned a score to indicate the degree of disturbance shown. Eating *disorder* will be used to describe conditions identified by a diagnostic approach using categorical definitions, whereas eating *disturbance* will be used to describe conditions identified by a scalar approach, generally on the basis of responses to self-completion questionnaires.

Because eating disorders involve clear-cut behavioural symptoms, measurable physical signs, and manifestations of abnormal psychological functioning, it is fairly easy to agree on a definition that treats them as psychiatric disorders. Current classification schemes such as DSM-IV (American Psychiatric Association, 1994) and ICD-10 (World Health Organization, 1992) distinguish two main categories. *Anorexia nervosa* (AN) is defined by weight loss, fear of gaining weight or becoming fat despite the fact that the subject is excessively thin, disturbed perception of body image and shape, and, in females, a stop to menstruation. *Bulimia nervosa* (BN) shares with AN the core features of excessive concern with body shape and weight and use of extreme strategies of weight control. It is characterized by recurrent episodes of binge eating accompanied by a distressful sense of loss of control, and the use of drastic means of weight reduction such as overdoses of diuretics and laxatives, and excessive dieting or physical exercise, while body weight remains roughly in the normal range. The two disorders overlap in many features, but the most distinctive difference is that anorectics become excessively thin, whereas bulimics have a normal body weight. Published series vary in the extent of co-occurrence. However, bulimia tends to begin at a somewhat later age (early adult life rather than late adolescence) and a substantial minority arise following earlier anorexia.

Diagnostic criteria for AN changed in the 1980s. DSM-III (American Psychiatric Association, 1980) required a weight loss of 25 per cent, whereas DSM-III-R (American Psychiatric Association, 1987) reduced this to 15 per cent, but added the condition that three consecutive menstrual cycles should have been absent. Similar changes have been made to the diagnostic criteria for BN such as the frequency of binge eating episodes (at least two per week during the last three months in DSM-III-R whereas DSM-III imposed no frequency criterion). On the other hand, DSM-III required depressed mood and self-depreciation following the binges, whereas these were no longer required in DSM-III-R. In general, the diagnostic criteria in DSM-III were broader than those used in DSM-III-R. BN meeting the requirements of the earlier definition will be called bulimia or DSM-III bulimia, whereas BN meeting the requirements of the DSM-III-R definition will be called bulimia nervosa.

These variations in diagnostic definitions could jeopardize attempts to compare rates over time. A further problem affecting cross-national comparisons is that the cross-cultural validity of these definitions has not been demonstrated, especially in non-Western countries. For example, there is some evidence that 'morbid fear of fatness' and 'disturbed body image' are not appropriate diagnostic criteria for Chinese girls with anorexia (Lee, 1991). Similarly, the lack of cross-cultural equivalence of measurement of self-report measures has been shown in studies of non-Western adolescent girls, such as in India where religious and cultural factors created artificially high rates of deviant answers on a widely used self-report measure on eating habits (King & Bhugra, 1989). In addition, various investigators have used sub-clinical categorizations of both disorders, frequently called 'partial syndromes', to describe symptoms falling short of current diagnostic criteria. This causes further difficulties when comparisons are made between various studies.

In keeping with the view that eating disturbances may be thought of as falling along a continuum, many studies have used the second approach to definition, which quantifies the degree of deviation from normal eating behaviour. Studies that treat these conditions as a continuous variable generally rely on self-report measures; cases are defined as those having elevated scores above a given threshold. The Eating Attitude Test or EAT (Garner & Garfinkel, 1979) is a widely-used measure of this kind. However, as a basis for estimates of rates of prevalence, this kind of measure is particularly problematic in the case of disorders with very low base rates, since it produces high false positive rates and low positive predictive value (in other words, there is a low probability that a subject with a score surpassing the threshold actually has the disorder). Similar limitations apply to more recently developed questionnaires, such as the Eating Disorder Inventory (EDI) (Garner et al., 1983), the Bulimia Test (BULIT) (Smith & Thelen, 1984), and the BITE (Henderson & Freeman, 1987). These self-report questionnaires are nevertheless a relatively low-cost method of obtaining quantitative measures of the frequency of anorectic and bulimic disturbances, and of the characteristics of those affected by them.

EVIDENCE OF AN EPIDEMIC OF EATING DISORDERS

Sources

Three main sources of data may be used to examine time trends in eating disorders: records kept by those responsible for treatment, including psychiatric case registers and hospitals' admissions records; community surveys; and family studies.

The advantage of using records of cases is that in some areas long runs of data are available, going back to the 1930s in a few instances. The drawbacks are that the records can only cover cases that came to the attention of the relevant health services; and that diagnostic criteria are not always precisely defined, vary between sites or between clinicians at the same sites, and change over time. The first limitation means that the records understate the number of cases. Cases will be missed either because they were not notified at all (it is reasonable to assume that the mild forms will be more likely than the severe forms to remain unnotified) or because they were treated by non-specialist facilities. Although these records understate the actual number of cases, they may be used to study trends over time, assuming that the proportion of cases missed remains constant. However, it is difficult to establish whether that assumption is tenable. The proportion of cases that come to the attention of specialists could change with the growth and increasing accessibility of services, with change in health-seeking behaviours (for example, a lowering of the threshold for seeking help), and with increasing recognition of the disorder by health professionals and the general population.

The second problem can be tackled by limiting variation in diagnostic practice: for example, the records can be processed afresh, using fixed diagnostic procedures. However, the quality of the records may be uneven, and information may be missing on core symptoms, especially those that have become important diagnostic criteria since the time when the records were compiled.

General population surveys, usually called community surveys in this field, have been carried out among both adolescents and adults to estimate the prevalence of eating disorders. Prevalence rates are reported either for a recent period or for the entire lifetime. In detail, these surveys use a range of different methods. Some are based on probability samples, others on convenience samples; some identify eating disorders, others eating disturbances; some identify cases through a short 'screening' interview, then carry out more detailed interviews with the small sub-sample so identified, whereas others are straightforward single-phase surveys; some use diagnostic interviews, whereas others use self-report measures only. The results of community surveys can be examined to detect secular trends in two ways. First, repeat surveys yield rates that can be compared at various points in time. Second, lifetime rates of disorders measured at a single point in time may be compared across successive birth cohorts, using life-table analysis methods. If the incidence of a disorder (the number of cases occurring over a given period of time as a proportion of the population at risk) has remained constant, then lifetime prevalence (the proportion of people who have suffered from the disorder at any time in their lives) should normally be expected to increase with age, since each year of life is an additional year at risk. Hence, if lifetime prevalence is actually *higher* among younger than among older people, this may be taken as evidence that the incidence of the disorder has increased. However, as discussed in detail in Chapter 11, a range of possible measurement artefacts must first be ruled out before such a conclusion can be drawn. In particular, careful attention must be paid to response rates, since concealment and secrecy are central characteristics of eating disorders and disturbances, so that the girls and young women who suffer from them may well tend to avoid taking part in the surveys. There is, in fact, evidence that this is so (King, 1989; Johnson-Sabine et al., 1988; Beglin & Fairburn, 1992). Information about response rates and the characteristics of non-respondents, where available, may be used to adjust the raw survey results and to derive better estimates of prevalence rates, but not all studies have made such adjustments. Sampling problems are particularly important when interpreting survey results on prevalence of AN. Because AN has a low base rate, even large surveys identify only a small number of cases, so that any response bias (and any change in response bias) can have a major effect on the results. A different problem is that rising and falling tides of public concern about these fashionable diseases may influence people's willingness to participate in surveys, and the detailed answers they give. If, among people who have experienced the disorders, willingness to participate in surveys, or to acknowledge their symptoms in the answers they give, varies over time or between age groups, then the results could indeed show spurious changes in rates, or conceal true ones.

Finally, the same methods as in community surveys can be used in family and twin studies. Lifetime prevalence of eating disorders among relatives of people identified as suffering from the disorders can be compared across successive birth cohorts. This is a way of defining a group having a much higher prevalence rate than the general population. As in the case of a general population survey, lifetime prevalence would be expected to rise with age if incidence has remained constant over time. If, instead, prevalence is *higher* among younger than among older respondents, then this is evidence that incidence of the disorder has increased over time: but many of the same problems of interpretation arise as in the case of general population surveys.

Anorexia nervosa

Psychiatric case registers have been particularly helpful in estimating the rates of incidence of AN. Table 12.1 summarizes the results of these studies and provides age- and sex-specific incidence rates when available. There is wide variation in crude incidence estimates, which range from 0.08 a year per 100,000 population in Sweden for the pre-war era (Theander, 1970) to 14.6 in Rochester, USA (Lucas et al., 1991). To a large extent, these variations reflect differences in the proportion of actual cases recorded or identified both between periods and between registers.

Studies Showing an Upward Trend

An increase over time has been detected for various periods between 1930 and 1990 at five different sites: Monroe County (Jones et al., 1980; Kendell et al., 1973), North-East Scotland (Kendell et al., 1973; Szmukler et al., 1986), Sweden (Theander, 1970), Switzerland (Willi & Grossmann, 1983; Willi et al., 1990) and Rochester, USA (Lucas et al., 1988, 1991). In fact, an upward trend was shown in every study based on case registers in which incidence could be estimated at more than one point in time. However, most of these register data relied on hospitalized cases and, with few exceptions (Szmukler et al., 1986; Lucas et al., 1988, 1991), no attempts were made to assess the validity and reliability of diagnoses or to ensure that consistent diagnostic criteria had been used throughout the study periods. Accordingly, trends in rates may reflect only changes in diagnostic practice. For example, anorectic patients were recorded as 'hysterical neuroses' prior to 1966 in the North-East Scottish register, making it impossible to derive incidence estimates for AN in the first years of operation of the register (Kendell et al., 1973). Also, these trends may be caused by an increase in the use of services. For example, there is some evidence that the increased frequency of AN reported in Monroe County (Jones et al., 1980) could have reflected, at least in part, an increase in the availablity and use of mental health services by children and adolescents in the region for a range of psychiatric disorders (Roghmann et al., 1982). Similarly, evidence

Table 12.1 Anorexia nervosa: incidence rates from studies on medical records for women (unless otherwise indicated)

Place	Author	Year of publication	Period	Diagnostic criteria	Age group	Annual rate per 100,000 per year	Total number of female cases
1 Denmark Nationwide register	Nielsen[+] (see figure 12.2)	1990	1973-87	ICD-8	All	1.90	744
Denmark (Fyn County)	Joergensen[+]	1992	1977-86	DSM-III-R	All	3.25	87
Denmark (First psychiatric admissions National Register)	Moller-Madsen & Nystrup	1992	1970-89	ICD-8	All ages[++]		844
					1970	0.42*	
					1988	1.36*	
					1989	1.17*	
					15-24 (women)		536
					1970	3.37	
					1987	11.96	
					1989	8.97	

contd.../

Table 12.1 continued

	Place	Author	Year of publication	Period	Diagnostic criteria	Age group	Annual rate per 100,000 per year	Total number of female cases
2	Netherlands local psychiatric case register	Hoek & Brook	1985	1974-82	ICD-9	All*	5.00*	20
	Netherlands (58 general practices)	Hoek	1991	1985-86	DSM-III	All*	6.30*	19
3	Sweden	Theander	1970	1931-40 1941-50 1951-60	Clinical	All	0.08 0.19 0.45	94
	Sweden (South East Stockholm)	Cullberg & Engström-Lindberg	1988	1984-85	DSM-III modified	All	2.60	16

contd.../

Table 12.1 continued

	Place	Author	Year of publication	Period	Diagnostic criteria	Age group	Annual rate per 100,000 per year	Total number of female cases
4	Switzerland Zurich	Willi & Grossmann Willi et al.	1983 1990	1956-58 1963-65 1973-75 1983-85 1956-58 1963-65 1973-75 1983-85	Clinical	All 12-25	0.38 0.55 1.12 1.43 3.98 6.79 16.76 ?	10 17 38 48
5	UK Scotland (psychiatric register)	Kendell et al. Szmukler et al.	1973 1986	1966-69 1978-82	Clinical Russell	All All	1.60* 4.68*	28 120 (approx)
6	USA Monroe County New York**	Jones et al.***	1980	1960-69 1970-76	Clinical	All* All women 15-24 All* All women 15-24	0.35* 0.49 0.55 0.64* 1.16 3.26	16 29

contd..../

Table 12.1 continued

Place	Author	Year of publication	Period	Diagnostic criteria	Age group	Annual rate per 100,000 per year	Total number of female cases
7 USA Rochester Minnesota	Lucas et al.	1988	1935-49 1950-64 1965-79	DSM-III-R/ Russell	10-19	52.40 21.60 48.60	128
	Lucas et al. (see Figure 12.1)	1991	1935-84 1950-54 1980-84	DSM-III-R/ Russell	Age adjusted rates for all women	14.60 7.00 26.30	166

* incidence rate for total population (both sexes combined).

** rates are for the white population only of Monroe County (the estimated average annual incidence rate for the non-white female population was 0.42 for the period 1970-1976).

*** slightly different rates and numbers have been published by Kendell et al. (1973) but the pattern of results is broadly similar.

+ these two studies do not provide separate incidence rates across the study period but graphical displays of yearly incidence rates of number of cases identified were produced by the authors and showed no evidence of an increase. Nielsen (1990) obtained a non-significant result for a statistical test for time trends.

++ for the diagnosis of anorexia nervosa *and* other eating disorders.

has been produced that the proportion of cases of AN identified as psychiatric cases had increased over time, thereby suggesting that upward trends in rates might partially reflect better case identification methods. Thus, in the Aberdeen region, 63 per cent of the total number of cases were known to the psychiatric case register in 1970-1974, a proportion that rose to 87 per cent in 1978-82 (Szmukler et al., 1986).

These crude rates may be misleading because they relate the number of cases to the total population, whereas most sections of the population have virtually zero risk of eating disorders or disturbances. Yet incidence rates for the section of the population mainly at risk (girls and young women) have not consistently been reported. Also, formal tests of the statistical significance of the recorded increases have scarcely been used. The study by Lucas et al. (1988, 1991) deserves more attention because it avoided many of these pitfalls. The incidence rates reported in this study in Rochester were higher than in other studies, probably because a more comprehensive method of recording cases was used. Cases were identified through medical records, regardless of whether the subject had been hospitalized or in contact with a psychiatrist: in fact, there had been no such contact in most cases. Since this comparatively effective case-finding procedure was used from the beginning of the period under study, the results are unlikely to reflect an improvement over time in case-finding methods. This study, which spans a longer period than any other, supports fine-tuned analyses of short-term trends over five decades. It was conducted in a circumscribed geographical area, and the sample of cases is large (N=166) compared with other studies. Cases were diagnosed by applying consistent criteria to all records screened. Finally, rates were adjusted and standardized in relation to the main population at risk, and appropriate analyses of trends were provided.

The Rochester study showed that for girls aged 10-19 there were high rates of AN in 1935-1939, a regular decline over the next 20 years until the 1950s, then an increase up to 1980-1984, the last quinquennium for which there are published data (Lucas et al., 1991). In mathematical terms, a curve of this type can be described by a quadratic equation (see Figure 12.1). The increase in AN over the 1950s to 1980s showed a statistically significant linear increase. The authors speculated that the number of more severe cases may have remained steady, whereas the fluctuations may have been in the number of less severe cases. They suggested that these fluctuations may have been a response to changes in women's fashion, which emphasized thinness in the 1920s, then more curvaceous forms after the Second World War, then thinness again in the 1960s.

Figure 12.1 Age-specific incidence rates[a] for anorexia nervosa, by 5-year periods, in two age groups of female residents of Rochester, Minn[b]

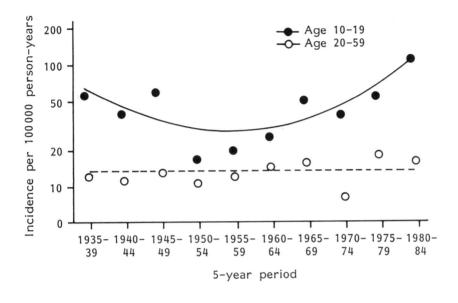

a. Plotted on a log scale.
b. Observed = circles, predicted = lines.

Source: Lucas et al (1991)

Although the basic design of the Rochester study is more robust than that of the others showing an upward trend since the 1950s, there are some limitations in the analysis and interpretation of the data as presented in the published papers. These fall into four groups.

1. *Analysis of trends.* The increase in rate of AN since the 1950s seems reasonably definite, although it should be noted that the significance of the linear trend is strongly dependent on the last data point (accounting for 23 per cent of cases). What is much less certain is the claim in the 1991 paper (Lucas et al., 1991) that for the differently selected age group of 15 to 24-year-olds there has been a significant linear increase in AN starting in the 1930s. It is not clear why these overlapping age groups (females aged 10-19 and 15-24) should show an opposite pattern of change over time (a

fall between the 1930s and 1950s for those aged 10-19, and a linear increase for those aged 15-24). If confirmed, these findings would imply that in the early quinquennial periods rates went in opposite directions for different age groups; this would be a surprising result needing careful interpretation. However, the overlap between the age categories used in the two analyses makes the results particularly hard to interpret, and more work needs to be done on the original data to describe the patterns more fully. Assessment of statistical significance is particularly important here, not only because AN is rare, so that the number of cases is inevitably small, but also because of the danger that some tests of statistical significance will produce an apparently positive result simply because many tests have been carried out on groups defined in various different ways.

2. *Migration into and out of the area.* Lucas and colleagues recognized the possibility that a spurious increase in the rate of AN could occur because people who expect to have or actually have health problems (or specifically anorexia) in the family may tend to move into a region having exceptionally good health facilities and a world-famous hospital. To control for this possibility, they excluded cases where the patient had moved into the Rochester area during the 12 months prior to the consultation. Whether this is an adequate control is uncertain. Eating disorders tend to be chronic. As shown by Hsu (1990), Willi et al. (1990), and Garfinkel & Garner (1982), the first symptoms generally appear several years before the first medical consultation. Hence it is possible that concern about eating disorders specifically, or about health problems more generally, could influence decisions to move into a well-resourced region more than one year before a first consultation in connection with AN. In their first report, Lucas et al. (1988) stated that 11 per cent of the original body of cases had been rejected because the patients had recently migrated into the area; unfortunately, no corresponding figures were quoted in the later report for the more recent period. Also, Lucas and colleagues had not investigated this matter thoroughly, for example by considering whether in-migrants are a higher proportion of patients treated for eating disorders than of the general population. There is also the possibility that people already resident in the area will be less likely to move out if a member of their family has anorexia than otherwise.

3. *Change in social class composition.* Lucas et al. (1988, 1991) noted that, over the time period studied, there had been a shift in the local economy from farming and light industry to employment based on the Mayo Medical

Center and IBM (computers). This may well have led to an upward trend in social class. This may be relevant because rates of AN are known to be greater among higher social classes. Yet, although Lucas and colleagues standardized the rates of AN for age and sex, they did not standardize for social class. It is possible, therefore, that the upward trend in AN could partly result from the upward shift in social class composition.

4. *Reliability of diagnosis.* Those who carried out the diagnostic review knew the date of the consultation, so with respect to period, the diagnosis was not carried out blind. The reliability of the diagnoses was not assessed for the whole series of cases nor compared between periods.

Overall, the findings from the Rochester study are potentially an important indication of time trends in AN, but further work is needed to test alternative interpretations, to allow for the influence of possible confounding factors, and to check the reliability of the diagnoses. Interpretation will also become easier as new data points are added for later years.

Studies Showing no Upward Trend

Three investigations have suggested that the apparent increase in the incidence of AN could be explained by demographic changes in the general population (Williams & King, 1987; Willi et al., 1990) and by higher re-admission rates (Nielsen, 1990; Williams & King, 1987). The Zurich study found an increase from the mid-1950s to the 1970s, but no difference between the 1970s and the 1980s (Willi et al., 1990). More specifically, the difference in the crude incidence rates for the 1970s and the 1980s (see Table 12.1) was not statistically significant and disappeared entirely after standardization for age and sex (Willi et al., 1990). Similarly, Williams and King's (1987) analysis of psychiatric first admissions and re-admissions with the diagnosis of AN concluded that the increase shown by English hospital statistics for the period 1972-1981 was accounted for by changes in the age structure of the general population in the case of first admissions, and by changes in patterns of treatment in the case of re-admissions. Identical conclusions were reached by Nielsen (1990) in a nationwide study of psychiatric registers conducted in Denmark for the period 1973-1987. Analysing the 807 first psychiatric admissions for AN thus identified, Nielsen found that rates of first admissions remained stable during this period (see Figure 12.2). A reduction by over one third in the number of psychiatric beds, combined with increasing re-admission rates for AN could have contributed, according to the author, to the false impression of an

epidemic of AN. Another Danish register study was performed by
Moller-Madsen and Nystrup (1992), who, unlike Nielsen, found a significant
increase in rates between 1970 and 1988. Their study, however, used a broader
case definition (including anorexia nervosa *and* other eating disorders) and
also a different case identification method. Since most of the reported increase
was found after 1982, it is clear that these results might have been confounded
by the newly recognized bulimic disorders. In addition, the rates were not
standardized and the authors provided only weak evidence that their results
were not a reflection of a differential pattern of health services use for eating

**Figure 12.2   Anorexia nervosa in Denmark, 1973-87: first admission rates per
100,000 population per year**

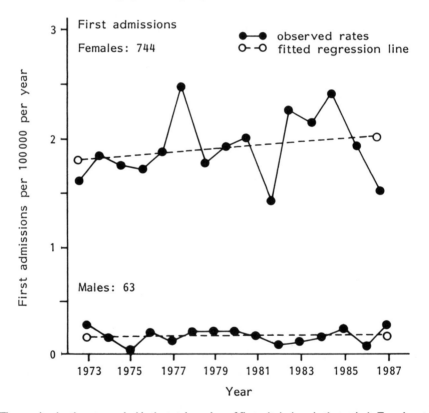

The number by the sex symbol is the total number of first admissions in the period. Female rates
were about 10 times higher than male rates. In neither sex did first-admission rates significantly
increase.

Source: Nielsen (1990).

disorders, with more eating disordered subjects being admitted in psychiatric rather than somatic hospitals in the more recent period. The conflicting results between studies derived from the same nationwide psychiatric register point to the methodological vulnerabilities of studies based on registers and on the need to replicate findings across studies that do not share the same methodological limitations.

Two studies of referrals to treatment centres have provided additional data on recent trends for AN. Referral rates for AN in an urban area of New Zealand remained fairly stable over a ten-year period (Hall & Hay, 1991), as they were in two Canadian specialized treatment centers for eating disorders from 1972 to 1986 (Garner et al., 1985; Garner & Fairburn, 1988).

However, it could be that power to detect time trends was limited in these five investigations because the period of investigation (ranging from 10 to 15 years) was too short. Furthermore, Williams and King's (1987) national study relied solely on data on the number of psychiatric admissions where AN was diagnosed: yet there is evidence that clinical features of anorectic patients and treatment approaches have changed (Willi et al., 1990). These results nevertheless rightly emphasized that changes in the demographic composition of the population need to be taken into account, if possible by calculating age- and sex-specific incidence rates.

Prevalence Rate

The prevalence rate of AN as shown by surveys (see Table 12.2) varies from a low of 0 per 1,000 among schoolgirls in Japan (Suzuki et al., 1990) to 1 per cent among girls in English private schools (Crisp et al., 1976; Szmukler, 1983), and even 1.08 per cent among Swedish adolescent girls below the age of 18 (Rastam & Gillberg, 1992). On average, the prevalence rate fluctuates around 1 to 2 per 1,000 women or girls. Once again it is difficult to make close comparisons between studies because of differences in the methods used. In particular, there were special features of the study that yielded the highest rate of 1.08 per cent among schoolgirls within the high risk age band up to 18. This finding was based on a small sample of 25 subjects (Rastam & Gillberg, 1992). Three cases were 'partial' syndromes that did not meet strict diagnostic criteria. If DSM-III-R criteria were used, the rate would become 0.94 per cent; if the more stringent DSM-III criteria were used, the rate would be 0.70 per cent. Since considerably different results can be obtained by applying different definitions to the same set of data, it is likely that substantial difficulties are

Table 12.2   Anorexia nervosa: prevalence rates shown by population surveys and psychiatric case registers

	Authors	Year of publication	Period	Place	Age group	Sample size	Diagnostic criteria	Rate per 100
1	Crisp et al.	1976	1967-74	UK (7 girls schools)	All ages 16+	? (private schools) 2,786 (state schools)	Clinical Clinical	F 0.2150[5] F 0.0360[1]
2	Nielsen	1990	1973-87	Denmark	All 15-19 10-24	300,000	ICD-8	F 0.0067 F 0.0347 F 0.0237
3	Lucas et al.	1988	1980	USA Rochester Minnesota	All ages 15-19	F 30,628 F 2,654	DSM-III-R	F 0.204[6] F 0.330
4	Whitehouse & Button	1988	1980	UK (Chichester)	16-19	F 446	Feighner/ Russell DSM-III	F 0.220 F 0.450
5a 5b 5c	Robins et al.	1984	1981-82	USA, New Heaven USA, Baltimore USA, St. Louis	18-65 18-65 18-65	3,058 3,481 3,004	DSM-III DSM-III DSM-III	0.030 0.100 0.100

contd.../

Table 12.2 continued

	Authors	Year of publication	Period	Place	Age group	Sample size	Diagnostic criteria	Rate per 100
6	Mann et al.	1983	1982	UK (2 London schools)	15	F 262	Clinical	F 0.000
7	Szmukler	1983	1982	UK (6 private girls schools)	14-19 16-18	F 1,331	Clinical Clinical	F 0.830 F 1.110
				(state schools)	16+		Clinical	F 0.140
8	Joergensen	1992	1977-86	Denmark (Fyn County)	All 10-14 15-19 20-24	450,000	DSM-III-R	F 0.026 F 0.070 F 0.120 F 0.060
9	Cullberg & Engström-Lindberg	1988	1984-85	Sweden (South East Stockholm)	16-24	F 4,651	DSM-III modified	F 0.258
10	Whitaker et al.	1990	1984	USA New Jersey	14-17	F 2,544	DSM-III	F 0.200
11	Lee et al.	1987	1984	Korea (Seoul and rural area)	18-65	5,100	DSM-III	F 0.038[1]

contd.../

Table 12.2 continued

	Authors	Year of publication	Period	Place	Age group	Sample size	Diagnostic criteria	Rate per 100
12	Hwu et al.	1989	1982-86	Taiwan (nationwide)	18+	11,004	DSM-III	0.000
13a	Rastam et al.	1989	1985	Sweden (Göteborg)	15	F 2,136	DSM-III and DSM-III-R modified	F 0.70[2] F 0.84[2,7]
13b	Rastam & Gillberg	1992	1987	Sweden (Göteborg)	17		DSM-III-R	F 0.94[2] F 1.08[2,7]
14	Bland et al.	1988	1983-86	Canada (Edmonton)	18+	3,258	DSM-III	0.100
15	Lucas et al.	1991	1985	USA Rochester, Minn	All 15-19	F 32,353	DSM-III-R	F 0.270[6] F 0.480
16	Hoek	1991	1985-86	Netherlands (58 general practices)	All	151,781	DSM-III	0.0184
17	Suzuki et al.	1990	1986-87	Japan (5 junior high schools, Gunma prefecture)	12-15	1,992	Clinical	0.000

contd..../

Table 12.2 continued

	Authors	Year of publication	Period	Place	Age group	Sample size	Diagnostic criteria	Rate per 100
18	Wells et al.	1989	1986	New Zealand (Christchurch)	18-64 25-44	1,498	DSM-III	0.100[4] F 0.300[4]
19	Ben-Tovim & Morton	1990	1987	Australia (South Australia)	12-18	F 5,705	DSM-III	F 0.105
20a	Johnson-Sabine et al.	1988		UK (8 London schools)	14-16	F 1,010	Clinical	F 0.000
20b	Patton et al.	1990		UK (8 London schools)	15-17	F 176	Russell	F 0.21[1,2] 0.000
21	Lewinsohn et al.	1993	1987-89	USA (Oregon)	15-18	1,710 F 891	DSM-III-R	0.000[3] F 0.450[4]
22	Scheinberg et al.	1992	1989	Israel (Female army recruits)	18	F 1,112	DSM-III-R	F 0.180
23	Beglin & Fairburn	1992		UK (2 family practices)	16-35	F 285	DSM-III-R	F 0.23[2,3] F 1.40[2,4]

contd.../

Table 12.2 continued

1. Rates computed by the author.
2. Rates computed after taking into account information on non-respondents.
3. Current prevalence.
4. Lifetime prevalence.
5. Much higher rates (1 per cent) are often reported for this study. These estimates were, however, wrongly calculated by the authors since they were confounded with the period of observation (3 to 6 year rates) and by the duration of the disease (the contribution of each case to the numerator was weighed by the number of years of the disease). The rate reported in this table was compiled by the author from the original data (Table II, p. 552) and corresponds to the rates found in table I (p.551) of the original paper under the heading 'presenting cases per 1000 girl-years'.
6. Age adjusted rate to the 1970 US female white population.
7. This rate takes into account 'partial' syndromes (see text).

F Rate for females
M Rate for males
Neither **F** nor **M** means males and females combined.

The median prevalence rate obtained from the 25 studies appearing in this table was 0.12/100 and did not vary across time periods (see text). In order to compute this median rate, we selected for each study the rate that was specific to the age group 15-20 years old (or an approximation of that age band), when they were available. Studies that were only follow-up studies of prior samples were not included (i.e. study 20b and 13b). In those studies where separate rates were produced in high risk samples (i.e. studies 1 and 7), only the rates available for the more representative samples were included. Although they were part of the same nationwide survey of psychiatric disorders, studies 5a, 5b, and 5c were treated as 3 different studies as they were conducted in 3 different sites, each with a large sample size.

involved in comparing rates between studies that used different definitions and instrumentation.

It can be shown that non-response bias has a major influence on the results of survey-based studies of AN. In two such studies, the prevalence of AN among survey respondents was nil (Johnson-Sabine et al., 1988; Beglin & Fairburn, 1992). However, in one of these surveys 39 women failed to take part out of 385 originally selected, and further research showed that 3 of the 39 had met clear-cut diagnostic criteria for AN in the past, and that one met them currently (Beglin & Fairburn, 1992). From this information, true prevalence rates can be calculated for this study (see Table 12.2). Similarly, a best estimate can be derived from another study (Johnson-Sabine et al., 1988) which had originally generated a null prevalence rate (see Table 12.2). These two estimates are in close agreement once age differences between the two samples are taken into consideration. However, other surveys have not found a similar association between participation and morbidity, at least as estimated by the Body Mass Index (Whitaker et al., 1990).[1]

In spite of these caveats, the consistency of the results is striking. As shown by general population surveys, prevalence rates are low for AN, fluctuating around 1 to 2 per 1,000 women. In Table 12.2, the median rate of anorexia nervosa computed from 25 studies was 1.2 per thousand. That computed for a sub-set of 21 studies, excluding 3 studies conducted in Asia (studies 11, 12 and 17) and a study in New Zealand where only lifetime rates were available (study 18), was 1.4 per 1,000. Time trends in rates were gauged in computing the median rate of 7 studies conducted before the year 1982, of 10 other studies conducted between the years 1982 to 1985, and from 8 studies conducted since 1986. The corresponding median rates for the three periods were respectively 1.0, 1.3 and 1.4 per thousand suggesting therefore that no clear trend could be found in surveys conducted at different time periods (although it ought to be borne in mind that the time interval encompassed by these surveys, i.e. 1973 up to 1991, is relatively short).

Both clinic and survey data show that rates are consistently higher for late adolescent girls. It should also be noted that, in the recently completed Epidemiological Catchment Area study designed to assess with precision rates of psychiatric disorders in a huge sample of American adults (Robins & Regier, 1991), only 11 cases of AN were detected in a sample of nearly 20,000 persons; accordingly, prevalence rates could barely be estimated on three sites (see

---

1. The Body Mass Index is the ratio of weight to height squared (kg/m^2). Values above 25 kg/m^2 define overweight or mild obesity, while moderate and severe obesity are defined by values over 30 and 40 kg/m^2, respectively.

Table 12.2; and Robins et al., 1984). Because this was a very large general population survey that is judged to have provided good data on most psychiatric disorders, its finding of a very low rate of prevalence of AN must be given considerable weight, and this finding is not consistent with the theory that the incidence or prevalence of AN has markedly increased.

However, the findings summarized in Table 12.2 do show a clear difference between the rates of prevalence found in Asian countries in contrast to Europe, North America, Australia and New Zealand. The three Asian countries have much lower prevalence rates (Hwu et al., 1989; Lee et al., 1987; Suzuki et al., 1990), which supports the notion that AN is more common in affluent, Western societies than elsewhere. Further, a study conducted in Malaysia found that AN was rare among people born in Malaysia, and that the few cases identified were mostly of immigrant women (Buhrich, 1981).

Summary

AN is a rare condition, so that secular changes in its incidence or prevalence are difficult to detect. Since most surveys yield prevalence rates around 1 to 2 per 1,000 women, sample sizes are too small to support the comparisons between rates for different birth cohorts which might otherwise provide evidence on time trends. Comparisons between surveys carried out at different times, although weakened by differences in the methods used, suggest that prevalence rates probably remained stable over the 1970s and 1980s.

Studies based on records kept by health services are a richer source of information on time trends than surveys. Wherever incidence rates have been derived from the same registers at different periods, all studies have shown an apparent increase over time. However, over the period covered by these studies, knowledge and recognition of the disorder have considerably improved, and diagnostic definitions, the availability of services, and patterns of care have also changed substantially. It is not possible to assess how far changes in rates derived from health service records reflect changes in the response to the condition as opposed to changes in its incidence. Several studies have shown that the effect of such artefacts may indeed have been great enough to create a false impression of an epidemic of AN.

The most robust data are those from a study in Rochester, Minnesota, which was based on a range of health service records. The findings show a linear increase in rates of AN from 1950 to 1984 among 15 to 24-year-old women, although the apparent increase was very small in magnitude. However, because of some weaknesses in the analysis of the results, these findings must be interpreted with caution. Furthermore, this whole time series consisted of only about 100 cases. If the results from studies based on health service records were to be weighted by the number of cases recorded, the evidence from studies showing no increase over time would be overwhelming.

The finding from a single site is not sufficient to support the conclusion that there was a true increase in the incidence of AN in the modern era, particularly in view of the limitations that have been identified in this study. The apparent increase in Rochester (Minnesota) would have to be confirmed by data for more recent periods in the same area, and the study would have to be replicated in other areas with similar results, before it could be concluded with confidence that an actual increase in the incidence of AN had occurred. In any case, current data suggest that any increase over time could not have been large, and, although the Rochester study begins to address these problems, there remains a need to demonstrate more firmly that an apparent increase does not merely reflect better recognition or different diagnostic and treatment practices or health-seeking behaviours.

Bulimia Nervosa

BN was first formally described in the late 1970s (Russell, 1979). It was introduced in systematic descriptions of psychiatric disorders only in 1980 (American Psychiatric Association, 1980). In 1981, the *International Journal of Eating Disorders* was founded. One year later, the magazine *Newsweek* (January 1982) referred to 1981 as the 'year of the binge purge syndrome'. Because BN is less visible than AN, it is likely that a smaller proportion of bulimics than of anorectics have contacts with mental health professions and that a substantial proportion of bulimic cases are never seen in psychiatric or primary care settings (Fairburn & Cooper, 1984; Fairburn et al., 1993; Joergensen, 1992). Consequently, case registers have severe limitations as a source of information about rates of incidence or prevalence or about time trends.

Studies Based on the Records of Health Services

There have been only five studies based on the records kept by health services that have estimated the incidence of BN (Cullberg & Engström-Lindberg, 1988; Hall & Hay, 1991; Hoek, 1991; Joergensen, 1992; Soundy et al., submitted). Three of these yielded roughly comparable unadjusted incidence rates of 3.9, 3.7 and 9.9 per 100,000 per year (Cullberg & Engström-Lindberg, 1988; Hall & Hay, 1991; Hoek, 1991), whereas higher rates of 65 and

44.3/100,000/year were reported for young women in the two former studies. From a search of national and local registers of hospital admissions and outpatient psychiatric services for 1977-1986, together with a general practice survey, Joergensen (1992) estimated that the incidence of BN among 10 to 24-year-old women was 5.5 per 100,000 per annum in a region of Denmark. Although the number of cases identified increased in later years, this increase was not statistically significant.

The most recent study (Soundy et al., submitted) provided a more refined analysis of trends over time. This study of the Mayo Clinic register (Rochester, Minnesota) identified all cases of BN (N = 103) over a ten-year period. The rate of incidence was 26.5 per 100,000 per year for women only; the age- and sex-adjusted rate was 13.5 per 100,000 per year. Interestingly, rates were very low at the beginning of the period, when BN had just been described as a psychiatric disorder. They then rose sharply to a peak in 1983, the year in which a pharmacological clinical trial was conducted on BN at the Mayo Clinic; thereafter, rates declined and remained steady throughout the second half of the decade. This pattern of change seems to correspond to the history of recognition and attention given to the condition, and is therefore consistent with a stable incidence of BN in the community at large. In order to mask a true increase in rates since 1983, the ratio of untreated to treated cases would have had to go up, whereas all data suggest trends in the opposite direction over the 1980s.

Several studies of the number of contacts with specialized services have suggested that there were substantial increases in the 1980s, but these studies provide relatively weak evidence of an increase in the actual rate of BN. Hall and Hay (1991) reported a sevenfold increase in service attendance in two consecutive 5-year periods, but changes in the health service organization at the beginning of the study, and the abrupt rise, within one year, of incidence based on treated cases cast serious doubts on the meaning of these results. There are similar difficulties in interpreting the report of an increased proportion of bulimic patients among referrals to two specialized treatment centres for eating disorders in Toronto between 1972 and 1986 (Garner et al., 1985; Garner & Fairburn, 1988). Because the increase started in 1981, immediately after BN became formally recognized by psychiatrists as a disease, it can probably be explained by changes in diagnostic and referral practices. In England too, increases in absolute numbers of bulimic women attending a bulimic clinic have been reported for the 1980-1989 period (Lacey, 1992). However, it is unclear if the population in the catchment area remained stable during the period, and different diagnostic criteria (DSM-III and

DSM-III-R) were used during the study period. Furthermore, the proportion of patients referred to the clinic by psychiatrists declined over the period, whereas the proportion referred by general practitioners increased. This suggests that there may have been changes in recognition of the disorder and in referral practices rather than an increase in the actual rate.

These reported increases in the number of bulimic patients treated have all come from clinical centres specializing in the treatment of eating disorders. By contrast, no increases were shown at the same centres for AN, a more severe form of eating disorder for which contact with treatment facilities is more systematic. At the same time, several surveys have drawn attention to the low rate of treatment contact for BN both in community samples (Fairburn & Cooper, 1982, 1984; Whitaker et al., 1990) and in general practice samples (King, 1989; Whitehouse et al., 1992). Any increase in referral rates of bulimic women is therefore most likely to reflect an increased flow of cases from community reservoirs to clinics rather than an increased population incidence. An increase in the number of cases of AN presenting at clinics would be much more difficult to explain in this way, so it is very pertinent that no such increase has been found.

Studies Based on Survey Methods

Only a few community surveys using diagnostic interviews have been carried out. They yield an average lifetime prevalence around 1 per cent for BN (for a review and update, see Fairburn & Beglin, 1990, and Fairburn et al., 1993). Most of these studies have aimed at providing a single prevalence estimate for a narrow age band of young adolescents or women; they do not support comparison of rates between different age groups or birth cohorts. For example, Lewinsohn et al. (1993) found a one-year incidence rate of 0.75 per cent for BN among a sample of 810 16-year-old high school girls. However, a few surveys have been more general and provide comparisons between age groups. One of these is a general population survey in New Zealand using the ECA methodology (Bushnell et al., 1990; Oakley-Browne et al., 1989; Wells et al., 1989). The *lifetime* prevalence rate for DSM-III bulimia among adults aged 18 to 64 was estimated at 1 per cent, with a corresponding lifetime rate of 1.9 per cent for women and 0.2 per cent for men (Wells et al., 1989). Lifetime rates were much higher among younger than among older women: they were 4.5 per cent among women aged 16-24, 2.0 per cent among those aged 25-44, and 0.4 per cent among those aged 45-64 (Bushnell et al., 1990). This sharp decline of lifetime rates among older respondents suggests that the disorder has become more frequent in the recent birth cohorts. It could be that older respondents are more forgetful, but the decline is already evident from the age of 25, which tends to argue against memory effects as the explanation. Prevalence rates over a recent period could not be compared across age groups because they were so low (from 0 per cent to 0.5 per cent according to length of the period considered). However, this study also showed that the reliability of the measure of lifetime occurrence of bulimia using structured diagnostic interviews was poor, since only about one third of women aged 18-44 who had met the diagnostic criteria at the first interview also met them at the second interview (Bushnell et al., 1990). Data on the effect of the respondent's age on test-retest reliability would have helped to interpret the differences in rates between age groups, but unfortunately no information on this point was published. In any case, these results certainly demonstrate that recall of bulimic symptoms was far from satisfactory, which seriously weakens the authors' confident conclusion that the difference between age groups reflects a true difference in the incidence of bulimia between birth cohorts. Moreover, it ought to be borne in mind that these age group differences derived from a handful of 20 cases, and that biases may have been caused for example by the oversampling of young women (although compensated for in the analyses) and non-response (the response rate was 70 per cent).

Similar birth cohort differences have emerged from the Virginia twin study (Kendler et al., 1991) which found significantly higher rates of BN among younger than among older members of a sample of 2,163 female twins. Kendler et al. (1991) regarded these findings as consistent with a period or cohort effect, but they also speculated that older subjects could have forgotten episodes or else been simply unaware of BN as a disorder. One difficulty of interpretation lies in the fact that most of those showing symptoms of bulimia also suffered from other disorders. Only 22.8 per cent of the cases of bulimia had no other lifetime history of psychiatric disorder, while over half had a history of depressive disorder. The authors did not, unfortunately, try to assess how far the differences between age groups in risk of BN was associated with differences in risk of depression in conjunction with BN. Higher rates among younger than older age groups of other psychiatric disorders such as phobias, generalized anxiety disorders, panic disorders and alcoholism were also reported; this emphasizes the need to show whether any increase in the incidence of BN is specific, or alternatively associated with an increase in the incidence of a range of psychiatric disorders (see Chapter 11). Anecdotal evidence is provided by a family study which established rates of BN and AN for 195 female first-degree relatives of 95 persons diagnosed as anorectic

(Strober et al., 1990). Rates of AN were three times higher in mothers than in sisters (6.2 per cent compared with 2.0 per cent) whereas, for BN, the difference, although not statistically significant, was in the opposite direction (1.0 per cent compared with 4.1 per cent). While the authors were rightly cautious in their interpretation of these findings, they suggested that there might have been a secular change from AN to BN in the form in which eating disorders are expressed among vulnerable subjects (Strober et al., 1990). However, no further studies have yet tested this hypothesis.

Eating Disturbances

The studies of BN so far reviewed have been concerned with bulimia as an eating *disorder*, that is, a condition identified by a diagnostic approach using categorical definitions. Many other studies have been concerned with eating *disturbances* related to bulimia, that is, conditions assessed by a scalar approach, generally on the basis of self-completion questionnaires. (The relevant studies are reviewed in Crowther et al., 1992, and in Fairburn & Beglin, 1990). In their review, Fairburn and Beglin (1990) pointed out that most research had been conducted with samples of convenience (generally college students at selected universities) and with self-report measures of doubtful diagnostic validity. The mean prevalence rates in studies using self-report questionnaires were 9 per cent for DSM-III bulimia and 2.6 per cent for BN, as opposed to 1.7 per cent and 1 per cent for diagnostic interview studies respectively (Fairburn & Beglin, 1990). Perhaps one of the most striking results of self-report questionnaire studies is the high prevalence rates of symptomatic features of eating pathology. Thus, retaining a strict frequency criterion of 'at least weekly', the mean prevalence rates across studies of binge eating, self-induced vomiting and laxative misuse were respectively 15.7 per cent, 2.4 per cent and 2.7 per cent, whereas 29 per cent of subjects on average said they were currently following a strict diet or fasting (Fairburn & Beglin, 1990). If these studies are to demonstrate changes over time in rates of disturbed behaviours, then they need to repeat the same measures on comparable samples.

One group has conducted three repeat surveys in North America on large samples of first-year college students at two mid-western universities. Comparison between the 1980 and 1983 surveys showed an increase among female students from 1 per cent to 3.2 per cent in the proportion who had a history at any time in their lives of DSM-III bulimia with weekly binge or purging behaviour, as established from answers to a self-completion questionnaire (Pyle et al., 1986). However, a further repeat survey among the same group in 1986 (Pyle et al., 1991) produced an estimate of 2.2 per cent, which invalidated prior claims of an alarming epidemic trend.[2] In the meantime, a replication study was conducted in Cambridge, UK; in this case, the repeat survey was five years after a baseline survey; no increase was found over this period (Cooper et al., 1987). Another study investigated changes in the prevalence of binge eating and DSM-III bulimia, using a similar self report measure, among two large comparable samples of 14 to 18-year-old adolescent girls surveyed in 1981 and 1986 (Johnson et al., 1989). The results indicated a significant decrease in the prevalence of DSM-III bulimia (from 4.1 per cent to 2 per cent). Significant reductions were reported in rates of dieting behaviours, both currently and for prior attempts, in binge eating behaviours, and in excessive exercise. Changes in attitudes were also noticeable with a significant decline in concern about weight among respondents (and also among their friends and family) and a lower drive towards thinness. Since average body weight and body dissatisfaction remained constant across the two samples, it seemed likely that attitudinal and behavioural changes had reflected changes in the socio-cultural context. The authors speculated that a mixture of factors, including the AIDS epidemic, the emergence of an anti-dieting literature, and increased knowledge of the detrimental effects of eating disorders, could have played a role. Also relevant to this review is a recent report of a baseline and follow-up survey of national samples of American children and adolescents studied in 1976 and 1989 (Achenbach & Howell, 1993). Two items (*Does not eat well*; and *Overeats*) of the survey instrument (the Child Behaviour Checklist) tap eating behaviours (albeit very crudely); of these, only one (*Does not eat well*) showed moderate increases in scores in the follow-up survey. However, no differences were found according to age or sex, which suggests that this modest increase was unrelated to the more specific disorder of bulimia. In addition, since the study was based on parental reports only, and focused on adolescents aged 16 or under, little weight can be placed on the findings.

Recent surveys show that concerns about weight and attempts to lose weight are common among adolescents; yet 25 years ago, surveys of high school students already showed that over two-thirds of the girls were dissatisfied with

---

2. This decrease was not statistically significant (computed by the present author). Furthermore, point prevalence rates for current DSM-III bulimia did not differ between the three surveys, and a lifetime history of bulimia meant that each of the various symptoms were reported by the respondent at some point in her life, but not necessarily *simultaneously*.

their bodies and wished to lose weight (Huenemann et al., 1966), and a study of high school seniors found that 30 per cent of the young women were currently dieting, and 60 per cent had dieted at some time in their lives (Dwyer et al., 1969). At around the same time, similar findings were reported in European studies of adolescent girls. Nylander (1971) found in a survey of 2,000 teenagers that the proportion of girls who were dieting increased from 10 per cent among the 14-year-olds to 40 per cent among the 18-year-olds.

A number of studies of eating disturbances, using self-completion questionnaires, have apparently found differences between age groups that suggest there has been a secular increase, but on closer examination the evidence they provide for such an increase is very weak. In one of these studies, 39 per cent of women originally enrolled in a college in the mid-1960s participated in a postal survey covering current and past bulimic behaviours (Rosenzweig & Spruill, 1987). The rate of bulimic behaviours for the current period was found to be higher than for the college years. In what seems a mistaken conclusion due to a confusion between age and time, the authors inferred from this that 'more women today are engaging in bulimic-like behaviors' (64). Pope et al. (1984) surveyed 300 women in a suburban shopping mall. The lifetime incidence of DSM-III bulimia decreased with age from 17.7 per cent among those aged 13-20 to 10.3 per cent, 6.3 per cent and 5.3 per cent among those aged 21-30, 31-40 and 41-64 respectively. Similar results were found for current bulimia but *not* for a lifetime history of 'narrow' bulimia. These significant age trends[3] were presented as evidence of a time trend, but there must be strong reservations about the definition and measurement techniques used in this study. Among the youngest respondents, there was an unexpectedly large discrepancy between lifetime and active 'bulimia', and psychometric properties of the survey instrument were not properly assessed. Furthermore, these figures derived from a convenience sample, and no data were provided on the level of acceptance of the survey by women shoppers.

Age trends in eating disturbances were also incidentally reported from a survey of a probability sample of 2,075 adults in Florida, USA (Langer et al., 1991). The proportion who had engaged in binge eating at any time in their lives decreased significantly with age, but no similar age trend was found for vomiting after a binge, for use of laxatives or diuretics to lose or control weight,

---

3. Since appropriate statistical analyses were not provided, the linear trends in proportions were computed by the present author, and were significant for lifetime history of bulimia (p=0.011) and active bulimia (p=0.006), but not for lifetime history of 'narrow' bulimia (p=0.11) The data are shown in Table 1, Pope et al. (1984), 293.

for dieting within the past 2 months, for eating less in public and more later, or for conflicts about eating. Although three other symptoms were significantly associated with age, the findings were largely due to a drop in rates among the oldest respondents (aged over 65) and not to a progressive decrease. This pattern of results suggests that the difference between age groups in binge eating, while genuine, applies only to this specific behaviour. However, the relevance of this item to eating disorders is dubious; in particular, the difference between the sexes on the item is very moderate, whereas both BN and AN are of course far more common among females than among males. Fairburn and Beglin (Fairburn et al., 1993) found poor agreement between self-report measures and interviews in assessing binges, perhaps because there are differences between the professional and everyday use of the term.

Summary

Solid evidence for a rising incidence of BN is so far lacking. Two studies, one of over 2,000 female twins (Kendler et al., 1991), the other of a large general population sample (Bushnell et al., 1990) suggested increased rates among the youngest birth cohorts. However, the number of cases identified was small (123 in the twin study; 20 in the community survey). The differences between the age groups in these two studies could reflect either a secular increase in the incidence of BN or a cohort effect arising from shared experiences of specific cohorts. Since eating disorders are for the most part confined to a narrow age band, it is particularly hard to interpret the limited findings available.

Studies of people in contact with health services showed increased referrals for BN during the 1980s in centres specializing in eating disturbances. While such findings are consistent with an actual increase in BN, they could well be explained in other ways, for example by a much increased tendency to recognize BN since the disorder was formally described in 1980. It is unclear whether any increase in the rate of BN would denote changes in eating disturbances specifically, or would be an aspect of a more general increase in psychological dysfunction.

Several repeat cross-sectional surveys of comparable samples of young people have failed to find increases in rates of bulimic disturbances over the 1980s (Achenbach & Howell, 1993; Cooper et al., 1987; Johnson et al., 1989; Pyle et al., 1991).

Yet precisely because the first description of BN as a distinct psychopathological syndrome was so recent, there is as yet a lack of data to test the hypothesis of an actual increase. Frequent changes over the 1980s in the definitions of BN and in its operationalization in survey research have made interpretation of epidemiological studies extremely difficult[4]. It is because there are few datasets allowing an examination of time trends that the results are so far inconclusive. The overall conclusion must be that no increase in bulimia has yet been demonstrated, but that conclusion is based on a critical and conservative examination of limited evidence, and not on a wealth of well-designed and replicated studies that have failed to support the hypothesis of an increase.

Conclusion

Definite conclusions cannot yet be drawn on time trends for eating disorders. Time series data on AN over long periods are scarce. Where trends have been found, they are of small magnitude, and explanations other than an actual increase cannot be ruled out. In the case of BN, data are even more rare, and present the same problems of interpretation. Also, data on BN cover only the very recent period from around 1980 when the disorder was first officially recognized. Retrospective estimates of its incidence before that time are bound to be imprecise.

Whereas no data firmly support the notion of an epidemic increase of either disorder, it remains entirely possible that the professional and public interest recently devoted to eating disturbances (especially symptoms of bulimia) may be a response to actual changes in the incidence of eating disturbances of some kind. AN and BN have in common psychological features, such as fear of being fat and a drive towards thinness, and behavioural features, such as weight control measures. There is evidence that these features, which both define eating disorders and constitute risk factors for them, are highly prevalent among populations of young girls and women, although it remains difficult to assess how far they have become *more* prevalent, or whether their form has become more severe. In any case, a 'normative discontent' with weight is now part of the day-to-day psychological life of most young women accompanied, at least temporarily, by some alteration of their behaviour. The next section, which summarizes the results from epidemiological studies on the pattern of risk, sticks to a strict definition of eating disorders, but the fourth section, which considers the mechanisms underlying a possible increase in these conditions, ranges more widely so as to include discussion of the reasons for an increase

---

4. Unfortunately, these difficulties will persist, as new diagnostic schemes will most likely introduce further changes in the diagnostic criteria for BN (Fairburn et al., 1993), and possibly new related diagnostic categories (Spitzer et al.,1992; Thompson, 1992).

in 'normative discontent' with weight as well as for a possible increase in eating disorders.

PATTERNS OF RISK

This section reviews the epidemiological evidence on patterns of risk for eating disorders, in preparation for an analysis, in the following section, of explanatory models that might account for possible change over time.

Age and Sex

The mean age of recognized onset for AN is about 17 years (Hsu, 1990). Nearly all relevant studies show that the rate of AN peaks between the ages of 15 and 19, and that the peak rate is much higher than for other age groups. However, the studies record the age of recognition rather than the age of onset, since precise determination of onset is virtually impossible. One study (Halmi et al., 1979) found two peaks in the age of onset, one at 14 and the other at 18, in a clinical sample. However, this bimodal distribution has not been found in other, larger, clinical samples (for example, Nielsen, 1990) or general population samples (for example, Hoek, 1991; Lucas et al., 1991).

The rate of AN is about ten times as high among females as among males. AN seldom starts before puberty, but boys form a higher proportion of pre-pubertal than of other cases. The exact prevalence and correlates of eating disorders in childhood are, however, unknown (for a review, see Thelen et al., 1992).

Most studies of BN show a later age of onset than for AN. Typically, BN starts at the age of 19 or 20. The contrast in rates between females and males is identical for BN and AN (about 10:1) in both community and clinical samples. No information is available on the incidence of BN among prepubertal children (Thelen et al., 1992).

Thus, eating disorders coincide with two key transitions that adolescent girls have to negotiate (Attie et al., 1990; Attie & Brooks-Gunn, 1992). The first, in early adolescence, corresponds to the development of self-concept and the establishment of autonomy and sexual maturity. The second is the passage from late adolescence to young adulthood, a time when girls are faced with challenges involving relationships with intimate partners, achievement of educational and career goals, and development of a personal identity outside the family.

The Role of Genetic Factors

A number of family studies of eating disorders have been flawed by methodological weaknesses such as the lack of control groups, biases in the identification of subjects who suffer from eating disorders, for example through treatment centres, reliance on the family history method only, or a failure to report separate results for males and females. Nevertheless, there are now enough well-designed studies to show that genetic factors have considerable importance in the causation of anorexia.

The first evidence suggesting a genetic influence came from reports that among relatives of patients with eating disorders there was an elevated prevalence of such disorders ranging from 6 per cent to 14 per cent (Theander, 1970; Crisp et al., 1980; Hudson et al., 1983). Then, in one of the first controlled studies (Gershon et al., 1984), the age-corrected prevalence rate of eating disorders was estimated at 4 per cent and 8 per cent for relatives of anorectics and bulimics respectively, compared with 1 per cent among the control group. Another study compared the first- and second-degree relatives of patients diagnosed as anorectic with a control group of female patients diagnosed as having other psychiatric conditions. The female relatives had a five times greater risk of eating disorders than the controls, a finding that did not apply to male relatives (Strober et al., 1985).

Two well-designed family studies have recently been reported among people diagnosed as suffering from BN and AN. In the first, which used direct interviews of relatives, the prevalence of BN among first-degree relatives of hospitalized people diagnosed as suffering from BN was nearly three times as high as among the normal control group (Kassett et al., 1989). The second study extended the findings from an earlier one (Strober et al., 1985) by increasing the sample size. Rates of eating disorders were compared between first-degree relatives of three groups: 97 people diagnosed as suffering from AN, 66 from affective disorders, and 117 from other psychiatric conditions (Strober et al., 1990). A five- to tenfold increase in rates of eating disorders was found in first-degree female relatives of AN patients as compared to the two control groups, the difference being significant for AN. In addition, the rate of eating disorders was found to be five times as high among second-degree relatives (aunts) as among the control group. Contrary to a preliminary report (Strober et al., 1985), the risk of BN was not found to be significantly elevated among relatives of anorectics.

A number of studies have also investigated the prevalence of other psychiatric conditions among the relatives of people diagnosed as suffering from eating disorders. Such studies have found that the risk of depression was two to three times as high among the relatives of people diagnosed as suffering from AN or BN as among the control groups (Hsu, 1990; Hudson et al., 1983; Gershon et al., 1984; Swift et al., 1986; Winokur et al., 1980); and one study suggested that this association between eating disorders and depression in relatives was stronger in the case of BN than in the case of AN (Strober et al., 1982). However, it is likely that these associations arise because the same individuals often suffer both from eating disorders and from depression, and that the mechanisms of familial transmission of these two conditions are independent. Two further findings support that interpretation. First, in many of these studies it was only when the individual suffered from both depression and eating disorders that her relatives showed an elevated risk of depression; and, second, no study has yet shown an elevated risk of eating disorders among the relatives of people diagnosed as suffering from depression. This matter has been more thoroughly investigated by Strober et al. (1990). They compared rates of eating and affective disorders among the relatives of three groups: people diagnosed as suffering from AN but not depression, from depression but not AN, and from both conditions. The results showed that where the subject suffered from anorexia without depression, or depression without anorexia, her relatives showed an elevated rate of the same disorder as the subject, but did not show an elevated rate of the other one. Where the subject suffered from both disorders, her relatives also showed an elevated rate of both. This pattern applied both to first- and to second-degree relatives. Of course, these studies merely show that to some extent eating disorders are transmitted through the family. No attempt was made to measure features of the family environment in order to differentiate between transmission through genetic as opposed to environmental mechanisms.

Several twin studies have been conducted with anorectic patients. Despite uneven rigour in the methods used to determine whether the twins were monozygotic (MZ, meaning identical) or dizygotic (DZ) and to diagnose eating disorders, the results are in agreement in showing that the proportion of cases in which an anorectic's twin is also anorectic is much higher for MZ (about 50 per cent) than for DZ twins (about 10 per cent). For example, Treasure & Holland (1991) studied 68 sets of female twins using direct interview methods, where one of the twins had been diagnosed as suffering from AN on a strict definition. The proportion of subjects whose co-twin was also anorectic was 51 per cent for MZ and 8 per cent for DZ twins, yielding an estimate of 76 per cent for the proportion of the variance accounted for by genetic influences (heritability). By contrast, data from the same study on the twins of subjects who had been diagnosed as suffering from BN showed no difference between MZ and DZ pairs in the proportion whose twin was also suffering from BN. The near-zero heritability estimate for BN suggested that environmental factors are far more important in the causation of BN than of AN.

The largest twin study of bulimia nervosa derives from the Virginia Twin Register (Kendler et al., 1991). The MZ concordance rate for BN was 23 per cent for the diagnosis as narrowly defined and 26 per cent when broadly defined, as compared with 9 per cent and 16 per cent respectively in DZ pairs. These figures gave rise to a heritability estimate of about 50 per cent, suggesting that the near-zero figure in the Treasure and Holland (1991) study is likely to have been an underestimate resulting from the small sample size or from selective sampling. However, the two studies are agreed in showing a substantial environmental influence on BN.

Overall, the findings from family and twin studies suggest an important genetic influence for AN. There is still much uncertainty as to the influence of genetic factors in BN, although for that disorder environmental influences appear to play a more important role. Much has still to be learned about the genetic and environmental risk mechanisms.

Other Risk Factors

The most consistent risk factor associated with eating disorders is the weight gain that accompanies puberty in females. This is considered in more detail when dealing with possible causes of an increase over time in eating disorders (see below). Other factors are noted in this section.

Although anorectic patients have often been portrayed as of above average intelligence with particular strength in verbal skills, empirical evidence does not support this hypothesis (Ranseen & Humphries, 1992). Because body dissatisfaction and pursuit of thinness are at the core of eating disorders, it has been postulated that eating disordered subjects suffer from a body image disturbance. However, studies comparing body size estimation by anorectics, bulimics, and control groups have failed to find consistent differences, although eating disordered patients displayed consistently more negative attitudes toward their bodies (Hsu & Sobkiewicz, 1991). Studies of body dissatisfaction, especially when construed as a discrepancy between perception of the ideal and of one's own body, have found a higher level of body dissatisfaction among those who suffer from eating disturbances than among those who do not, and that those who are dissatisfied with their bodies tend to develop eating disturbances later (Rosen, 1992; Thompson, 1992).

In clinical studies, patients with eating disorders have been reported as having a range of personality characteristics: they have been described as perfect children, overcontrolled, obsessive, perfectionist, and having a sense of personal ineffectiveness. Bulimic patients have been described as extraverted, high achievers, sensitive to rejection, and having poor impulse control (Hsu, 1990; Yates, 1989). However, these findings have not been consistently replicated, due to variations between studies in terms of age of subjects, mean duration of disorders, type of treatment, and measures of personality dimensions. In addition, the results of studies investigating personality profiles of eating disordered patients tend to be contaminated by the effects of psychological illness that accompanies the eating disorders; these behavioural, emotional and cognitive changes can be mistakenly described as personality traits. Similarly, mood states, especially depression, can influence personality measures. For example, one study showed that the introversion of a group of anorectic adolescents reduced over time in parallel with improvements in their mood and eating symptoms (Strober, 1980). Some studies have controlled for the confounding effects of concurrent symptoms of mental illness (i.e. Casper et al., 1992); however, their conclusions are limited by the cross-sectional nature of the data.

Families of patients have been described as having covert psychopathology and distorted interaction patterns. Enmeshment, rigidity, overprotectiveness, and lack of conflict resolution are descriptive terms coined by family therapists; once again, very few studies have used proper measurement instruments and several information sources together with follow-up designs. Taken together, the findings suggest that disturbed interactions are likely to be found in families of eating disordered patients, but it is not known whether these are causes or consequences; the types of interactions associated with the disorder are likely to differ between specific eating disorders, with the bulimic group being more consistently associated than the anorectic group with dysfunctional family environments (Humphrey, 1987; Rastam & Gillberg, 1991).

A number of studies have shown that eating disorders were more prevalent amongst white people, and among the higher social classes, than among ethnic minorities and the working class (Hsu, 1990; Jones et al., 1980; Szmukler et al., 1986). In the British studies (Crisp et al., 1976; Mann et al., 1983; Szmukler, 1983), rates of eating disorders were found to be higher in fee-paying than in state schools. From a large national sample of 12 to

17-year-old adolescents, Dornbusch et al. (1984) showed that, at each level of actual fatness, girls from upper-class families desired to be slimmer as compared to their peers from lower social class backgrounds; this did not apply to boys. Conversely, obesity is more prevalent and less stigmatized among lower social classes.

Some studies have attempted to establish a connection between the onset of eating disorders and precipitating events or stressors. However, few studies were carefully designed, so that where eating disordered patients have reported more stressful events than controls, this could have arisen because later events, such as the eating disorder itself, influenced recall. In any case, the stressors appeared to be associated with a range of other conditions in addition to eating disorders (Hsu, 1990).

Claims have been made that childhood sexual abuse was much more common among eating disordered patients than among others. However, most studies were based on a small number of cases, accounts of child abuse were obtained retrospectively with limited control for recall biases, and control groups were often lacking. When all these methodological shortcomings are taken into consideration, the frequency of childhood sexual abuse does not appear to exceed that found in adequate control groups nor in the general population (see review in Pope & Hudson, 1992). Several reports have suggested that the incidence of eating disorders was elevated among young people with diabetes mellitus, especially girls (Steel et al., 1989). However, three independent investigations, using standardized diagnostic instruments tailored to obtain measures of eating disturbances uncontaminated by treatment effects or medical diet, have not confirmed the earlier reports (Fairburn et al., 1993).

Finally, above average rates of eating disorders have consistently been found among young people training for certain specific careers, such as ballet dancing and modelling (Garner & Garfinkel, 1980; Garner et al., 1987; Hamilton et al., 1985; Szmukler et al., 1985), and also among swimmers, skaters, wrestlers, marathon runners, gymnasts, jockeys, and others pursuing activities that impose weight constraints on the performers (Attie et al., 1990; Brooks-Gunn et al., 1988). Eating disorders increase to the extent that the activities impose higher demands in terms of weight control and thinness (Attie & Brooks-Gunn, 1992). Colleges and campuses have also been depicted as 'breeding grounds' for eating disorders, and there is evidence that social and peer influences are important in the development of bulimic behaviours among young women (Crandall, 1988).

Cultural and Ethnic Differences

In less developed countries, prevalence rates of AN are lower than in advanced industrial economies (Buhrich, 1981; Hwu et al., 1989; Lee et al., 1987; Suzuki et al., 1990). Adolescents who have migrated from less industrialized to more industrialized countries have higher frequencies of eating disorders than those who have stayed in the country of origin, as shown by comparisons between girls living in Greece and girls of Greek origin living in Germany (Fichter et al., 1988), and by similar contrasts between Egyptian girls living in Cairo and those who have emigrated to the UK (Nasser, 1986). Clinical reports have also suggested that rates increased among Asian children who had migrated to the UK (Bryant-Waugh & Lask, 1991); and among schoolgirls of Pakistani origin living in England the prevalence of eating disorders has been found to be thirteen times as high as among schoolgirls in Pakistan (Mumford et al., 1991, 1992). That the degree of acculturation to the values of Western societies is associated with increased levels of eating disturbances has been further demonstrated in a study comparing white, black and mixed race schoolgirls in Zimbabwe (Hooper & Garner, 1986) where eating symptoms were found to be common among white adolescents, rare among black girls, and at intermediate levels among the mixed race group. Similarly, a positive relationship was found between acculturation and eating symptom scores for Hispanic girls aged 16 to 18 living in North America (Pumariega, 1986). Again, a study of Kenyan Asian women living in the UK showed that they rated large figures negatively and were more comparable to white British women in their evaluations of body shapes than Asian women in Kenya, who were more likely to prefer large figures (Furnham & Alibhai, 1983). In most non-Western societies, thinness is not considered to be attractive, so these findings probably indicate that as migrants adapt to Western societies, their body ideal shifts towards thinness.

Among ethnic minority groups living in the USA, eating disorders have typically been found to be rare. Black people were extremely rare among anorectic patients reported in the literature but, at least in part, this may reflect the middle-class areas that are mainly served by the clinics reporting series of cases. The prevalence of bulimic syndromes has generally been found to be lower among black than among white college students (Nevo, 1985; Gray et al., 1987) but not always (Johnson et al., 1989; Langer et al., 1991). Anecdotal evidence suggests that, within Western societies, adolescents from ethnic minority groups who develop eating disorders tend to come from upwardly mobile families (Garfinkel & Garner, 1982; Silber, 1986). Recent reports of eating disorders among ethnic minority groups (reviewed in Pate et al., 1992) have not always controlled for social class, making the results difficult to interpret. The bulk of the evidence suggests thus far that eating disorders are less prevalent among ethnic minority groups than among white people belonging to the same social classes.

Some differences in rates of eating disturbances have been found between countries in Western Europe and North America. In a comparison between large samples of Spanish and American adolescents aged 14 to 17, Raich et al. (1992) found significantly higher rates of bulimic symptoms in North America. However, most studies of eating disturbances have been carried out in English-speaking countries, and it is unclear whether this is because the disorders are more common in English-speaking countries than elsewhere.

Association Between Eating Disorders and Other Conditions

High rates of personality disorders, considered as categorically defined psychiatric conditions, have been found among samples of anorectic and bulimic patients (see review by Johnson & Wonderlich, 1992). As already mentioned above, personality research is permeated by measurement problems that largely account for the inconsistency of the findings, particularly when, as in studies relying on single, self-report measures, contamination by concurrent psychopathological states cannot be avoided. However, Johnson and Wonderlich (1992) found in their review that histrionic personality was found with an elevated frequency (range:25-53 per cent) among bulimic patients, but not anorectic subjects. By contrast, anorexia was found to be associated with anxious and fearful personality disorders (in particular avoidant and obsessive-compulsive personalities). These authors argued that these personality differences between anorexic and bulimic subjects could explain differences in age of onset and in symptom profiles, as well as gender differences. Specifically, they posited that, facing the challenges of puberty and adolescent development, girls with anxious and fearful personality traits would starve themselves to control and avoid pubertal transformations and to maintain prepubertal status, whereas boys with similar traits, with such a response less part of their repertoire, would be more likely to show other (or different) types of psychiatric symptoms. On the other hand, girls with unstable affect, poor impulse control, and high social sensitivity would develop symptoms typical of bulimia. However, the empirical findings of personality research and their theoretical implications have yet to be firmly established.

The interest of personality research lies in its potential for providing clues to the early precursors of eating disorders.

High lifetime rates of depressive disorders (over 50 per cent) have consistently been reported among people with either anorectic or bulimic symptoms. Rates of anxiety disorders among those with eating disorders are also substantial, ranging from 10 to 20 per cent (Kendler et al., 1991; Herzog et al., 1992). Other disorders resembling each of the main types of eating disorder have also been found to be linked with them: such as obsessive compulsive disorders with AN, and disorders of impulse control such as kleptomania, alcoholism or substance abuse, with BN. However, these links are less consistent than in the case of depression. Moreover, studies of comorbidity have essentially been performed on treatment-seeking subjects, which could lead to over-estimation of the amount of comorbidity and distortion of its patterns. Furthermore, the key issue of the temporal sequence in which the various disorders occurred cannot be satisfactorily addressed by these studies, which must rely on retrospective reports.

Finally, it is important to investigate the relationships between AN and BN within the developmental process. A substantial minority of anorectic patients go on to develop bulimic symptoms, either concurrently or subsequently, whereas follow-up studies have been consistent in showing that AN is not an outcome of BN (Johnson-Sabine et al., 1992). Bulimic anorectic subjects appear to have a more chronic course and higher levels of comorbid disorders (Herzog et al., 1992). The significance of these relationships is not well understood.

Outcome Studies

Follow-up studies of anorectic patients (see Steinhausen et al., 1991) show that over half of them return to normal weight and menstruation. Whereas careers and employment return to normal in two-thirds of former patients, there may be persistent interpersonal difficulties, especially with establishing stable partnerships. About 20 per cent of anorectic patients have a generally poor outcome, with chronic symptoms of eating disorder and poor psychosocial adaptation.

Formerly anorectic women also have reduced fertility rates, and when pregnancy occurs, there may be a reactivation of fears of losing control of weight and of the associated eating disturbances (Fahy & O'Donoghue, 1991). Low weight in the mother is a known risk factor for low birth weight in the infant; not surprisingly, therefore, currently anorectic or bulimic mothers have been shown to give birth to babies with significantly lower birth weights than recovered anorectic mothers (Stewart et al., 1987). Among currently anorectic or bulimic mothers, the risk that the infant's birth weight will be below 2500g has been estimated to be twice as high as among mothers generally (Brinch et al., 1988). Furthermore, obstetric complications are more frequent than average for both anorectic and bulimic women; this leads to a higher rate of perinatal mortality and perhaps of congenital abnormalities. Studies have also indicated that both bulimic and anorectic mothers may be impaired in their performance of parental functions, especially in feeding; the mother's preoccupation with body shape and image may lead in some instances to severe malnutrition (Brinch et al., 1988; Stein & Fairburn, 1989).

Death is an outcome of eating disorders in a substantial minority of cases. Crude mortality rates vary from 2 per cent to 18 per cent according to the characteristics of the samples and the durations of follow-up. The best estimate comes from a study of 460 anorectic and bulimic patients followed up on average seven years after the first consultation (Patton, 1988). The standardized mortality ratio (SMR) was estimated at 6 for the anorectic subjects, which means that the mortality rate among subjects with eating disorders was six times as high as among the general population with the same demographic characteristics. This substantial elevation in mortality rate was mainly due to complications arising from starvation, and to suicide. The SMR remained high during the first eight years from onset, and then declined but remained higher than 1. Very low body weight when first coming to medical attention, and repeated admissions to hospital, were predictors of mortality.

With the exception of two reports (Hsu & Sobkiewicz, 1989; Johnson-Sabine et al., 1992), few follow-up studies of samples of bulimic women with adequate sample sizes and duration of follow-up are available. These two outcome studies showed a slightly better outcome for bulimic than anorectic patients. Between 20 per cent to 25 per cent of the patients still fulfilled diagnostic criteria for BN at follow-up, whereas about one third no longer showed any symptoms. As in the case of AN, severity when first coming to medical attention and longer duration of illness were the strongest predictors of a poor outcome in some studies, but these findings were not replicated in other investigations (Hsu, 1990; Johnson-Sabine et al., 1992).

Conclusion

Eating disorders and disturbances occur specifically among young women during adolescent development. Genetic factors probably play an important role in the development of AN but a lesser role in BN. The risk of eating disorders is found to be greater among the higher social classes, among those in highly industrialized Western countries than among those in less developed countries, among the white majority than among ethnic minorities both in the USA and in Europe, and among young people training for certain specific careers in which low body weight is a requirement than among young people on other career paths. A number of psychological and family characteristics have also been found to be associated with eating disorders. The part played by these correlates in the causation of eating disorders remains to be established in most cases; and little understanding has yet been gained of the mechanisms through which genetic, biological and psychosocial factors operate to heighten the risk that an individual will develop eating disorders. Eating disturbances often coexist with other psychosocial disorders, but the developmental relationships between these psychopathological states are not well understood. Outcome studies have shown that eating disorders, and especially AN, are associated with a substantial increase in the risk that the person will later develop other medical and psychiatric conditions.

POSSIBLE CAUSES OF AN INCREASE IN EATING DISTURBANCES

The purpose of this section is to investigate mechanisms that might explain secular changes in eating disturbances. The previous sections, which have been principally concerned with anorexia nervosa and bulimia nervosa, have found that an increase over time in these narrowly-defined conditions may have occurred, but that is not certain. The present section is concerned with a wider range of behaviours and attitudes that are part of a continuum of eating problems from normality to pathology. While some of these are found in isolation among normally developing individuals, they also represent developmental pathways leading toward full-blown eating disorders, and constitute symptoms of those disorders. Although an increase in these more widely-defined eating disturbances has also not been demonstrated, some have been shown to be very prevalent. Evaluation of the causal mechanisms leading to a possible increase over time is likely to be more fruitful if the full range of eating disturbances is considered, because the disturbances are constituents of the more narrowly defined disorders, and because this strategy makes the best use of the limited evidence available.

As possible explanations of an increase in eating disturbances, the following sections consider changes in the biological context, in the immediate social environment (family, school, friends), and in the wider society.

Changes in the Context of Adolescence

Two major changes have occurred in the relation to adolescence. First, as discussed in Chapters 4 and 11, the onset of puberty has occurred at an increasingly early age over the past 200 years. It is unlikely that this has played any role in the possible increase in eating disorders, because although the weight changes associated with puberty serve as a trigger for eating disturbances, there is no evidence that the absolute age of puberty is relevant. Second, running counter to changes in body ideal, the average weight of young women has tended to increase regularly. To establish the links between these trends and increased rates of eating disturbances, it would be necessary to show that puberty itself and increased body weight both heighten the risk of eating disturbances.

With the onset of puberty, girls experience a weight spurt due to a substantial increase in their body fat. On average, their weight increases by 10 kilograms. The pattern of increased body fat then persists across the life span. At puberty, this increase is accompanied by negative psychological states, particularly among early maturers (see Chapters 4 and 11). By contrast, boys experience at puberty an increase in weight and muscularity that enhances their self-esteem. Boys perceive thinness rather negatively; they would generally prefer to be tall and muscular (Paxton et al., 1991). Surveys consistently show that adolescent girls, but not boys, report high levels of body dissatisfaction despite actual normal weights (Attie & Brooks-Gunn, 1989; Huenemann et al., 1966; Paxton et al., 1991; Richards et al., 1990a). The desire to be thinner also increases among girls proportionately to the development of body fat (Dornbusch et al., 1984). The timing of puberty also appears to play a role in levels of body dissatisfaction, a finding that is only partially explained by the fact that early maturers tend to be heavier (Alsaker, 1992). Late maturers are much less driven by the desire to be thinner than early maturers (Dornbusch et al., 1984), while early maturing girls express more dissatisfaction with their appearance and their body (Petersen, 1987). In addition, Alsaker (1992) has shown that the negative effects on self-evaluation and body image were more pronounced among girls who reached puberty when still in elementary school, where they were more 'deviant' than if they had transferred to secondary school.

The role of body dissatisfaction in the development of eating disturbances has been well established in longitudinal investigations of adolescent girls. Thus, Striegel-Moore et al. (1989) showed that body dissatisfaction, along with measures of perceived attractiveness, predicted levels of dieting and changes in eating disturbances one year later. Similarly, Attie and Brooks-Gunn (1989) found in a sample of 193 adolescent girls that negative body image was the variable most strongly correlated with eating problems in two cross-sectional analyses of girls in their early and mid-adolescent years, and that it was the only independent predictor of a high score for eating problems two years later. The same study showed that actual and perceived early puberty was associated in early adolescence with a range of psychological and family variables that increased the risk of eating disturbances at that time, but that in mid-adolescence, these psychological and family variables assumed greater importance, independently of pubertal timing, in determining the risk of eating disturbances continuing. These prospective data suggest therefore that eating problems may be triggered by pubertal changes but that their persistence over time depends upon other variables.

As it is common for adolescent girls to be dissatisfied with their body shape, so it is common for them to try to reduce their weight, most often by dieting. Weight reduction behaviours, which increase in frequency during the adolescent years, were already common in the 1960s (Dwyer et al., 1969; Huenemann et al., 1966; Nylander,1971). Many studies show only a limited association between dieting and overweight; for example, only half of the girls studied by Dwyer et al. (1969) were actually overweight.

Dieting as a risk factor for the development of eating disorders has been established in studies of ballet dancers, student fashion models, and certain groups of young athletes (Attie & Brooks-Gunn, 1992; Garner & Garfinkel, 1980; Garner et al., 1987; Hamilton et al., 1985; Szmukler et al., 1985). All of these groups had higher scores on self-report measures of eating disturbances than the general population, and developed clinically defined eating disorders at much higher frequencies. Thus, AN was found in 7 per cent of ballet dancers and student fashion models (Garner & Garfinkel, 1980). The eating disorders had developed during their training as a consequence of excessive dieting to meet high standards of thinness. Self-selection biases could not account for these findings since the disorders developed after enrolment on the courses; an additional argument against self-selection as the explanation was that the level of competitiveness of the school was found to be directly related to the incidence of eating disorders (Garfinkel & Garner, 1982).

Studies that have followed up general population samples of school-age girls for a period of one year have also found that dieters at the first interview were seven times as likely as non-dieters to develop an eating disorder by the time of the second interview (Johnson-Sabine et al., 1988; Patton et al., 1990). High levels of physical exercise and activity have also been shown to alter the secretion of neurochemical elements in a way that could set the stage for the development of eating disorders (Yates, 1989). In addition, there is evidence that among people volunteering to take part in an experiment, strict diet regimens can induce eating disorders (Hsu, 1990).

Time Trends in Body Weight

Recent studies conducted in the United Kingdom (Gulliford et al., 1992), the USA (Harlan et al., 1988; Shah et al., 1991), and in several other countries (Garfinkel & Garner, 1982) have provided strong evidence that historical changes in actual body weight have run counter to the trend towards the ideal of slimness shared by most women and eating disordered young people. Thus, the English study of a sample of over 8,000 adults shows that among women the body mass index (BMI: see footnote 1) increased by 0.10 per year between 1973 and 1988, after controlling for the effects of age, social class, and family size. This trend was more pronounced among women married to manual workers, and it was not found for men. The most recent US sample (Shah et al., 1991) showed an annual increase of 0.19 among women over a seven-year period, after controlling for age and education, an increase almost twice as high as that shown by the British study. A smaller, but still significant, increase was also shown for US men (0.08 per year). These increases in BMI in the US study correspond to yearly gains in average weight of 0.50 kg among women and 0.25 kg among men. The US surveys also indicated secular increases in the prevalence of obesity among women and more pronounced increases in BMI for overweight subjects (Harlan et al., 1988; Shah et al., 1991), although secular changes in BMI in women were not entirely accounted for by overweight people (Shah et al., 1991). There also was an increase in the prevalence of obesity over the ten years from 1970 among US children and adolescents, particularly among blacks and adolescent girls (Dietz, 1990).

The relationship between weight or BMI and social class runs in the opposite direction in developed as compared with developing countries. In affluent societies, higher social class and education are associated with lower weight and BMI, particularly among women (Leigh et al., 1992). By contrast, among developing countries, average weight increases as a function of economic growth, and in such societies high body weight is a well-accepted sign of wealth.

There are reasons for thinking that the actual increase in body weight in developed countries is among the causes of a possible increase in eating disorders. There is some evidence that bulimic patients tend to have been slightly overweight before they became bulimic (Hsu, 1990) and that being overweight is a risk factor for the development of BN (Striegel-Moore et al., 1986). Actual overweight appeared to exert a powerful negative independent effect on body image and self-evaluation among Norwegian adolescent girls over and above pubertal timing and development (Alsaker, 1992). As shown earlier, weight gains triggered by pubertal development among girls are associated with body dissatisfaction and thereby lead to eating disturbances.

Conclusion

The following conclusions are well established by the existing research findings. Puberty is associated with increasing rates of body dissatisfaction among adolescent girls, at least partly because they gain weight at that time, and early maturers exhibit even more pronounced reactions. The recent trend towards increasing body weight may be expected to heighten the discomfort of pubertal girls, especially early maturers. These changes have quite different implications for boys, because they tend to value height and bulk rather than thinness. The impact of time trends in body weight is likely to vary between social classes and to be radically different in developing countries, where ideals of body shape are sometimes opposite to those in the developed countries in which most of the research has been carried out. Adolescent girls frequently engage in weight reduction behaviours which, in turn, increase the risk of eating disorders.

Accordingly, secular changes in body weight, in conjunction with changing concepts of ideal body shape, may have increased vulnerability to eating disturbances.

Family, School and Peer Influences

Parental attitudes toward weight may interact with other factors to increase the risk of eating disturbances among girls. In support of this view, a number of authors have underscored the fact that bulimia has spread among the daughters of the first generation of women of the Weight Watchers Program (Striegel-Moore et al., 1986; Rodin et al., 1990). However, although the idea that parents' attitudes and comments have an impact is plausible, these and other data do not demonstrate that they are a cause of eating disturbances in their daughters.

Infant feeding practices have changed since 1945; babies are now given more food and at more frequent intervals. Some authors have speculated that there may be a connection between changed feeding practices and later onset of AN (Duddle, 1973), but a study of series of eating disordered patients argues against this relationship (Hsu, 1990), even though there is some evidence of a relationship between early feeding practices and prepubertal anorexia (Jacobs & Isaacs, 1986). Among recent changes in eating patterns reported in Western societies are decreases in sit-down and family meals. Whether or not an association exists between more individualistic or disorganized patterns of family eating and higher levels of eating disturbances among adolescents remains to be established. Parent-daughter relationships in the development of disordered eating have been essentially studied through analyses of clinical samples, and the limits of such studies have already been emphasized. Fewer studies have prospectively assessed these relationships among general population samples. In one such study of a socially advantaged sample (Attie & Brooks-Gunn, 1989), puberty was associated with eating disturbances but not in their persistence two years later. However, throughout adolescence, a negative body image was quite strongly associated with eating problems. Emotional features (especially depression) also showed associations with eating difficulties, but not with changes in eating problems between early and middle adolescence. According to maternal ratings, but not ratings by the young people themselves, eating difficulties in mid-adolescence were associated with lower levels of family cohesion and organisational expressiveness. It is unclear whether these were causes or consequences of eating problems in the girls. It should be added that none of the associations found were particularly strong, and generalization to other samples has still to be established.

As set out in Chapter 5, women's roles in society have changed dramatically. It has been postulated that young women are confronted with the demands of the pursuit of excellence in multiple roles that combine and surpass traditional views of both feminity and masculinity (Levine & Smolak, 1992). The need to become a 'superwoman' might increase vulnerability to eating disturbances in girls who have high and multiple ambitions that would be extremely difficult to realize in combination. However, this construct has not yet been properly validated, and more empirical research is needed to examine its utility.

The behaviour of adolescent girls is also likely to be influenced by the peer group. Campuses, boarding schools, theatre and dance companies, have been described as 'breeding grounds' for eating disorders. Women who have friends who purge or diet are more likely to engage in similar behaviours than those who do not (Gibbs, 1986; Schwartz et al., 1981). Studying two sororities at different times in the school year, Crandall (1988) showed that bulimic behaviours could be acquired through social influences. Over the school year, young women became more and more like their friends in terms of their binge-eating levels, a finding that could not be explained by the way they chose their friends. To what extent some other environments provide an opposite protective effect has been little studied. Richards et al. (1990b) studied 284 adolescents living in two adjacent suburban white communities. Higher levels of body dissatisfaction were found in one community than in the other among girls, but not among boys, which suggests that body satisfaction reflects an interaction of gender with social environment. In the community where girls were more dissatisfied, they were involved in fewer after-school activities, especially sports, and this was associated with a lower level of satisfaction with athletic strength and performance. Also in the community where girls were more dissatisfied, there was a lower level of peer acceptance (indexed by the level of perceived cliquishness in schools). Using rather different measures, Richards et al. (1990a) also found that in girls a high body weight and a high level of concern about eating were associated with a low level of involvement in social activities and little time spent with friends. Both studies are limited by the cross-sectional nature of the data and by the measures available. Their findings need to be confirmed and the underlying mechanisms explored further. However, they do show the importance of studying the social context in the development of adolescents.

Other changes that affect the context of adolescent development are prolonged years in education (see Chapters 4 and 6), higher career expectations (see Chapter 8), and changes in patterns of family life (see Chapter 5). While there is some evidence that such changes may have implications for the development of eating disturbances among adolescents, only limited data are available. There is a need for more prospective investigations to develop and test causal models on the development of eating problems, and also a need to bring together information about the individual and about the wider social context within the same framework of analysis.

Cultural Changes

Brumberg (1988) proposed that anorexia emerged as a modern disease among the Victorian bourgeois family as a result of economic wealth and changes in adolescent development. Increased dependency and intimacy with parents characterized middle-class adolescents; in particular, mother-daughter relationships became more emotionally charged. Brumberg argued that, in a context of material privilege, food became a social and emotional tool. Food privation had replaced corporal punishment as a means of parental control. Food and feminity were also closely linked; showing appetite was perceived as a sign of abandon, sexuality, and physical ugliness. To eat in public was to show a lack of refinement, whereas to control the body was to show strength of the soul. As reflected in the nineteenth-century Romantic cliché of the sensitive tubercular look (Garfinkel & Garner, 1982) and reinforced by the middle-aged female saints who refused food (Brumberg, 1988), the ideal image of the Victorian adolescent girl associated fragility, illness, asceticism, thinness, and spirituality. Thinness was already fashionable at the turn of the century, and the mass production of clothing and standard-size dresses acted as important forces to promote the thin ideal. Brumberg also argued that weight and eating concerns declined during the Great Depression and the Second World War. The popularization of adolescent female weight control in the late 1940s set the scene for modern compulsive dieting and exercise. Brumberg also emphasized the profits made from the dieting and cosmetics industries. Brumberg accepted that this account of changes in the cultural context that accompanied changes in eating disturbances necessarily described only one of the many groups of causes leading to such disturbances: in particular, social history cannot explain why the proportion of women who have developed eating disorders in all classes and social contexts has always remained fairly low.

Central to Brumberg's argument is the role played by physical appearance and attractiveness in female development. Research (reviewed in Striegel-Moore et al., 1986) showed that little girls learn very early that neatness and attractiveness are important female attributes and that thinness is associated with feminity and popularity. Attractive women are thought to be more feminine, unattractive ones more masculine. The particular ways chosen to achieve physical attractiveness depend on societal norms. Many practices involving unhealthy manipulations of women's bodies have existed throughout history. The wearing of corsets in the nineteenth century, footbinding in China, tattooing, and scarification are a few examples (Garfinkel & Garner, 1982) but today's emphasis is placed on more internal means of control (Rodin et al., 1990). Although the body ideal has changed since the Second World War, the persistent standard of a thin body ideal has been established since the mid-1960s. Thus, repeated surveys in a London wax museum have shown that

Elizabeth Taylor had been replaced by the emaciated model Twiggy in the course of the 1970s as the most beautiful female figure (Garfinkel & Garner, 1982). There is also evidence of a link between feminity (as culturally perceived) and eating behaviours. In one experiment, women who ate small meals were rated as more feminine than women who ate large meals by raters of both sexes, whereas men who ate small meals were not rated more masculine (Chaiken & Pliner, 1987). In another experiment, women appeared to restrict their food intake in order to enhance their feminine characteristics and influence the perceptions of men eating with them (Mori et al., 1987). Women also ate significantly less in an experimental condition where their feminity was threatened. Thus, sexual stereotyping plays an important part in girls' development, and feminine attractiveness is associated both with a thin body ideal and with distinctive eating styles.

The Role of the Media

It has been suggested that the mass media have been active in promoting a slim body ideal for women in recent years and hence have contributed to the rise in eating disorders. From an analysis of media content, several empirical studies have demonstrated that, in Western cultures, there has been during the three decades from 1960 a gradual shift towards an unrealistic ideal of thinness for women, which compares well with prepubertal shapes (slimness, tubular shape, and lack of fat deposits). Thus, data on various parts of the body (height, bust size, hip size, waist size and weight) and on diet articles were obtained from series of Miss America contestants, Playboy centrefolds, Ladies Home Journal and other magazines over two decades from 1960 (Garner et al., 1980; Silverstein et al., 1986a). The results showed a progressive decline in average weight for age and height, while bust and hip measurements became smaller and waist measurements larger (Garner et al., 1980). Miss America contestants had an average decline in weight of 0.13kg per year; this decline was more steep for winners and, since 1970, winners have weighed significantly less than other contestants. Over the same period, an increase in the number of articles devoted to dieting was found in popular magazines. These findings on diet articles and weight of contestants have been replicated for the period up to 1990 (Wiseman et al., 1992).

As Silverstein et al. (1986b) rightly argued, in order to demonstrate that the media had played a part in an increase in eating disturbances, it was necessary to establish that:

- standards of attractiveness are slimmer for women than for men;
- standards for women are slimmer now than in the past; and
- these findings apply to different types of media.

These authors conducted four studies to test these hypotheses. In the first study, the slimness of 221 characters of selected television shows was evaluated by pairs of independent raters. The results showed that, controlling for estimated age, female were consistently rated as slimmer than male characters. In the second study, the editorial and publicity content of eight popular women's and men's magazines were analysed. Articles dealing with diet foods, body shape or size and ads for figure-enhancing products were almost exclusively found in women's magazines. At the same time, and with the exception of alcoholic beverages, women received many more messages than men about eating and cooking as judged by the elevated number of articles and advertisements related to food topics. Next, Silverstein et al. (1986b) assessed changes since the turn of the century in standards of bodily attractiveness by sampling photographs in two popular women's magazines (*Vogue* and *Ladies Home Journal*) and measuring their bust-to-waist or hip-to-waist ratios (see Figure 12.3). In both journals, these indices of bodily attractiveness dropped steadily from a high at the beginning of the century to its lowest value in the mid-1920s, it then climbed back up by the late 1940s to reach a secondary peak that was lower than the high in 1900, and then declined again regularly. From 1965, it remained constantly at a low level, and the authors emphasized that young girls and women have been consistently exposed since then to a very noncurvaceous standard. Similar trends were found in body configurations of 38 famous actresses from 1932 to 1979.

This set of studies provided strong evidence for changes in media messages of a kind that could explain increased pressures to conform to a thin body ideal. The gender discrepancies and the time trends were striking, and the general conclusion was strengthened by the replication of the results across a variety of media. However, these studies were mostly confined to US materials, although similar findings were found in a study of Spanish magazines targeted at female youth, albeit over a smaller period and with a somewhat less extreme standard of slimness (Toro et al., 1988). Some data produced by Silverstein et al. (1986a) also suggest that the short-term trends found toward a thin body ideal in the mid-1920s (Silverstein et al. 1986b) were accompanied by more frequent eating disorders at that time. Data from the Mayo Clinic register (Lucas et al., 1988) appear to support the view that eating disorders declined in the 1930s but increased again after the Second World War, although some discrepancies between trends in different age groups have been noted in the detailed analysis of this study in an earlier section in the light of a later report (Lucas et al., 1991). The fact that the decrease in bust-to-waist ratios mainly occurred between 1950 and 1965 whereas the postulated rise in eating problems was detected somewhat later remains intriguing.

Figure 12.3 Mean bust-to-waist ratios of models appearing in Vogue and Ladies Home Journal at four-year intervals during this century

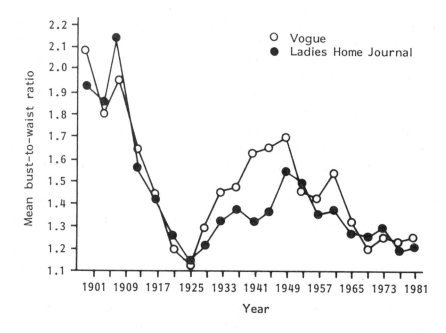

Source: Silverstein et al. (1986b).

The findings on changes in media content are, however, not sufficient to establish that the media were a cause of change. The findings certainly suggest that the media can play an important role in the diffusion of a standard of thinness across all strata of society, as illustrated by the fact that different media showed the same trend. However, these data do not indicate that the thin body ideal actually *originated* in the media. Indeed, the very rapid changes observed in media messages around the mid-1920s, contrasted with the lasting message delivered since 1965 (Silverstein et al., 1986b), suggest that the media are guided by, or respond to, some external factor or factors in the cultural ambience. Since the media aim to communicate up-to-date information about the social milieu, it should be no surprise that they rapidly reflect new fashions and lifestyles.

Media, in particular television, also convey important messages about food and eating behaviours. In his study of US television programmes and commercials, Kaufman (1980) showed that foods of low nutritional value were presented by characters who mostly snacked between meals, ate primarily when engaged in other behaviours, and used food to fulfil social and psychological needs. In addition, characters were rarely depicted as obese and overweight, and teenagers never. Thin body shapes of characters were often associated with female gender and with positive personal and social characteristics (intelligence, popularity and attractiveness) whereas disproportionate numbers of ethnic minority characters, especially of blacks, were represented as obese. Kaufman (1980) concluded that television messages provided the viewer with simultaneous conflicting messages: that he or she eats food that would lead to fatness, yet should strive for thinness.

Kaufman's findings were replicated more recently in another content analysis of TV programme content and commercials (Story & Faulkner, 1990). Food references occurred roughly once every 6 minutes, over half dealt with low nutrient beverages and sweets, and snacking rather than meals was the dominant way of eating. Fast food restaurants were heavily promoted in commercials. According to Story and Faulkner (1990), these data were consistent with national surveys showing that American adults and children snack increasingly often, and that a declining proportion of families take their meals together. Taking the analysis a step further, Myers and Biocca (1992) attempted to demonstrate the direct effects of television viewing on self-perception of body image among young women. In an experimental design, 76 female university students were randomly exposed to four videotapes combining neutral or body-image programmes or commercials, and to a control condition. Results showed that exposure to 30 minutes of tapes oriented to body images changed the subjects' perceptions of their own body shapes, thereby supporting the hypothesis that body image reflects a dynamic compromise between a socially represented body image, an internalized body image, and the objective body shape, a compromise that can be significantly altered by a short exposure to television material. However, contrary to the prediction, women exposed to commercial advertisements felt thinner and had lessened depressed mood compared either to women exposed to regular programmes or to the control group. The authors interpreted these findings by postulating that women viewing the advertisements had seen the body ideal as more attainable, and had internalized the marketed body image. They further speculated that the changes in women's self-perceptions were greater in response to the advertisements than to the programmes because the advertisements spoke directly to the viewer and were tied to an agenda of personal change. These findings are limited due to the highly selected nature of the experimental subjects, and because only short-term effects were assessed. However, they caution against taking too simple a view of the effect of exposure to media influences, and suggest that it is important to study in detail the cognitive changes that take place in individuals exposed to the media, to take account of the probable diversity of these changes, and to trace any links with more long-lasting behavioural effects.

Television has also been shown to propagate messages about attractiveness in much the same way that it propagates messages about the character and roles of women and black people (see Downs & Harrison, 1985). The importance of television in the diffusion of messages about attractiveness has been demonstrated by an analysis of 4,294 commercials broadcast on three major US networks (Downs & Harrison, 1985). The audience was exposed to some form of attractiveness message in over one quarter of commercials, and direct messages on the importance and value of beauty were found in one out of eleven commercials. Beauty and attractiveness were used to sell all kinds of products, not only those connected with appearance. Downs and Harrison (1985) calculated that over a 12-month period viewers were exposed to 5,260 attractiveness messages and 1,850 messages directly dealing with beauty. Commercials most commonly showed female performers with authoritative male voice-overs, and such commercials contained the highest proportion of attractiveness messages. The commercials therefore act out a male demand that females should be attractive, and they much less frequently emphasize male attractiveness. Another analysis of 160 television commercials shown between children's programmes found that a high proportion were for food products, and that almost all of those concerned with enhancing personal appearance were aimed at females (Ogletree et al., 1990).

On the basis of analysis at one point in time, a significant correlation has been found between time spent watching television and obesity among children and adolescents, with an increase of 2 per cent in the prevalence of obesity for each additional hour of viewing (Dietz, 1990). This relationship held true when all variables known to be associated with obesity were controlled for, and obese children did not differ from others on a wide range of characteristics except time spent watching television. Moreover, a longitudinal analysis found that viewing time among children who were not obese was the strongest predictor of later obesity in adolescence, after adjusting for other correlates of obesity at baseline. Dietz (1990) hypothesized several mechanisms to explain the association between obesity and television viewing: that increased viewing leads to a reduction in the amount of exercise, a reduction in the metabolic rate, and an increase in food intake. All of these have received some empirical support. In particular, Dietz (1990) found that levels of viewing were related to the kinds of food consumed, and to the amount of snacks consumed.

Taken together, these findings suggest that heavy viewing may contribute to the development of eating disturbances through several distinct mechanisms. Viewing may lead to increased body weight among children and adolescents, because it reduces their level of physical activity, reduces the likelihood of family meals and thereby increases the likelihood of snacking, while at the same time exposing young people to commercials for snack foods (to which they can respond instantly, if snack foods are available). The resulting increase in body weight may, in itself, be among the causes of eating disturbances. Quite separately, however, television widely propagates messages about female attractiveness while also propagating messages about the desirability of fattening (frequently snack) foods, often in the same commercials; in fact, slim female models are routinely used to sell the fattening foods. These conflicting messages are obviously a possible contributor to the risk of eating disturbances. Because viewing has increased and become widespread since the early 1960s (see Chapters 6 and 7) the theory that television is among the causes of an increase in eating disturbances has some plausibility, but no study has yet firmly demonstrated such a causal relationship.

CONCLUSIONS

The review of available data has left us without any definite conclusion as to whether or not the incidence of eating disorders has increased over time. In the case of AN, much weight has hitherto been placed on studies that appeared to show an increased incidence over time, when alternative explanations for these findings had not been systematically ruled out, and studies showing no increase have not been given their due weight. In the case of BN, it is difficult to test the hypothesis of an increased incidence, because the condition was first systematically described in psychiatry only 15 years ago, and the description was widely diffused among the general public soon after. Whether this was the recognition of a true increase in disordered eating or a new label for an old phenomenon remains debatable.

In some respects, epidemiological studies have shown very clear patterns of risk. Eating disorders, and the more widely defined disturbances, occur mostly among young women during adolescent development, AN at an earlier age than BN. There is evidence that genetic factors have some influence in the development of AN. A range of findings concur in showing that these are disorders of affluence, plenty, and economic development: they are more common among the higher than among the lower social classes, much more common in advanced industrial nations than in developing countries, and also among the white majority in the USA and Europe than among ethnic minority groups. Although a number of psychological and family characteristics have been found to be associated with eating disorders, the mechanisms through which these psychosocial factors exert an influence on the developmental process remain unclear. Eating disorders are often associated with other psychosocial disorders, and lead on to other medical and psychiatric conditions.

Although it has not yet been established that an increase in eating disorders or disturbances has occurred, a number of factors can be identified that might well have led to such an increase. The recent trend towards increasing body weight, in conjunction with the increasing emphasis on slimness, may be expected to have increased the level of dissatisfaction that girls feel with their appearance at puberty and for some time thereafter. Because boys do not value thinness, these changes should not affect rates of disorder in boys. Lower rates of eating disorders in less developed countries may be explained by the contrasting ideals of feminine beauty that are current there. However, the problem with explanations in terms of biological changes is that these have been gradual and very long-term, compared with the much more recent and sudden increase in eating disturbances that has been posited. It remains plausible that the biological changes have increased vulnerability to eating disturbances, without constituting a sufficient cause.

A number of changes in the family sphere might be linked with an increase in eating disturbances: an increased number of dieting mothers, the practice of feeding infants more frequently, the decrease in the number of sit-down family meals, and a possible decline in family cohesiveness and expressiveness. The change in women's roles could also have had an effect. However, there is limited research evidence, as yet, to show that any of these have had an important influence on eating disturbances. There is relatively good evidence to show that peer groups have an important influence, but it is not clear why this should have led to an increase over time.

An increase in eating disturbances has been linked with broad social and cultural changes that have taken place since around 1850. It has been suggested, for example, that in an increasingly affluent society, and especially for the upper classes, food became much less a necessity, and more a social and emotional tool. The thin body ideal of feminine beauty, established continuously since around 1960, seems an important predisposing condition for the development of eating disorders. It has been shown that the media have widely disseminated the messages that beauty and attractiveness are important for women (though much less so for men), and that only thin women are attractive; and that they have used female glamour to sell every kind of product, including fattening foods. In view of the great increase in exposure to the media (especially television) since the 1950s, it is plausible that these messages may have caused an increase in eating disorders, but no research as yet has demonstrated a causal relationship of that kind.

Further Research

Most epidemiological investigations in this field have been plagued by confusion in definitions and inadequacy in sampling and measurement methods. Future research should use designs that overcome these problems to generate new data that test for secular changes in eating disturbances. Longitudinal studies of multiple birth cohorts should be carried out, using well-defined measures and procedures that remain constant over time and for different cohorts. Recognizing that current psychiatric definitions of eating disorders are only working hypotheses, future studies should focus on description of individual symptoms, and should investigate the whole continuum of eating-related disturbances. Only an approach of that kind will allow researchers to examine the continuities and discontinuities between normal eating difficulties and pathological syndromes.

Future research should capitalize on cross-national differences in order to shed light on possible underlying mechanisms. Explorations of differences within countries in rates of eating disturbances according to social class or ethnicity might help to pinpoint important risk or protective factors. An efficient strategy could be to focus research efforts on immigrant groups. More specifically, multigenerational studies of immigrant families in Western countries would help researchers to identify the factors associated with the development of eating disturbances, or with protection against them, as those factors are modified by the processes of acculturation.

A striking feature of eating disturbances is the extremely high rates of isolated symptoms that are found among girls compared with the small proportion who develop clinically defined eating disorders. Systematic assessment of risk factors for conditions along the continuum of eating behaviours would shed light on the modes of transition from normative symptoms to sustained disturbed eating behaviours.

There is still some remaining potential for research on groups that are known to have a high risk of developing eating disturbances, such as girls on training programmes that place stringent demands on body weight or shape. There have so far been no long-term longitudinal studies of such groups, where extensive data were collected before sustained exposure to the training and at repeated intervals thereafter. There may also be a case for research on groups in which eating disorders are known to be rare, such as boys and pre-pubertal children, concentrating for the most part on the few cases that do occur.

Although it is generally accepted that eating disturbances are caused by a multitude of factors, few studies have taken account of constructs from several domains of measurement in order to assess simultaneously the causal relationships and interactions between a number of diverse risk factors.

Research should also aim to elucidate the early developmental precursors of eating disturbances, and the contextual experiences, in family life and peer relationships, that heighten the risk of the development of disordered eating. Little is currently known about the childhood antecedents of eating disturbances. Changes have occurred in feeding practices, and the limited evidence suggests that disturbed feeding patterns may be connected with prepubertal onset of AN. Whether or not particular feeding patterns in early childhood are linked to the later onset of disordered eating remains to be established.

There should also be research on the wider social context of eating and food-related experiences. Eating pathology appears to be more common in societies where snacking has replaced sit-down meals, and among individuals who are under high pressure for achievement. Modern lifestyles may have reduced children's opportunities to observe and comment on the eating habits of their parents. In this field, research will need to look at opportunities for social learning from people outside as well as within the immediate family circle.

More research is needed on the causal impact of the media, and especially that of television, in the diffusion of ideals of beauty and attractiveness, and of food-related messages. These influences are likely to differ between age groups and social strata. There is a need for fundamental research on cognitive processes to form the basis of a model describing the responses of individuals to media exposure. It is important to assess both the short-term and the long-term effects of exposure to audiovisual and printed materials, and to trace the links between repeated exposure to specific media content and long-term behavioural changes. In particular, research should examine whether children and young adolescents are more susceptible than adults to media influences, and, if so, why.

REFERENCES

Achenbach, T. M. & Howell, C. T. (1993). Are American children's problems getting worse? A 13-year comparison. *Journal of the American Academy of Child and Adolescent Psychiatry 32*, 1145-1154 .

Alsaker, F. D. (1992). Pubertal timing, overweight, and psychological adjustment. *Journal of Early Adolescence 12*, 396-419.

American Psychiatric Association (1980). *Diagnostic and statistical manual of mental disorders – DSM-III* (3rd edition). Washington, DC: American Psychiatric Association.

American Psychiatric Association (1987). *Diagnostic and statistical manual of mental disorders – DSM-III-R* (3rd revised edition). Washington, DC: American Psychiatric Association.

American Psychiatric Association (1994). *Diagnostic and Statistical Manual of Mental Disorders (DSM-IV)* (4th edition). Washington, DC: American Psychiatric Association.

Attie, I. & Brooks-Gunn, J. (1989). Development of eating problems in adolescent girls: A longitudinal study. *Developmental Psychology 25*, 70-79.

Attie, I. & Brooks-Gunn, J. (1992). Developmental issues in the study of eating problems and disorders. In J. H. Crowther, D. L. Tennenbaum, S. E. Hoboll & M. A. Parris Stephens (eds.) *The etiology of bulimia nervosa: The individual and familial context*, 35-58. Washington, DC: Hemisphere Publishing Corporation.

Attie, I., Brooks-Gunn, J. & Petersen, A. C. (1990). A developmental perspective on eating disorders and eating problems. In M. Lewis & S. M. Miller (eds.) *Handbook of developmental psychopathology*, 409-420. New York: Plenum Press.

Beglin, S. J. & Fairburn, C. G. (1992). Women who choose not to participate in surveys on eating disorders. *International Journal of Eating Disorders 12*, 113-116.

Ben-Tovim, D. I. & Morton, J. (1990). The epidemiology of anorexia nervosa in South Australia. *Australian and New Zealand Journal of Psychiatry 24*, 182-186.

Bland, R. C., Orn, H. & Newman, S. C. (1988). Lifetime prevalence of psychiatric disorders in Edmonton. *Acta Psychiatrica Scandinavica Supplement 338, 77,* 24-32.

Brinch, M., Isager, T. & Tolstrup, K. (1988). Anorexia nervosa and motherhood: Reproductional pattern and mothering behaviour of 50 women. *Acta Psychiatrica Scandinavica 77,* 98-104.

Brooks-Gunn, J., Burrow, C. & Warren, M. P. (1988). Attitudes toward eating and body weight in different groups of female adolescent athletes. *International Journal of Eating Disorders 7,* 749-758.

Brumberg, J. J. (1988). *Fasting girls: The history of anorexia nervosa.* Cambridge, MA: Harvard University Press.

Bryant-Waugh, R. & Lask, B. (1991). Anorexia nervosa in a group of Asian children living in Britain. *British Journal of Psychiatry 158,* 229-233.

Buhrich, N. (1981). Frequency of presentation of anorexia nervosa in Malaysia. *Australian and New Zealand Journal of Psychiatry 15,* 153-155.

Bushnell, J. A., Wells, J. E., Hornblow, A. R., Oakley-Browne, M. A. & Joyce, P. (1990). Prevalence of three bulimia syndromes in the general population. *Psychological Medicine 20,* 671-680.

Casper, R. C., Hedeker, D. & McClough, J. F. (1992). Personality dimensions in eating disorders and their relevance for subtyping. *Journal of the American Academy of Child and Adolescent Psychiatry 31,* 830-840.

Chaiken, S. & Pliner, P. (1987). Women, but not men, are what they eat: The effect of meal size and gender on perceived feminity and masculinity. *Personality and Social Psychology Bulletin 13,* 166-176.

Cooper, P.J., Charnock, D.J. & Taylor, M.J. (1987). The prevalence of bulimia nervosa: A replication study. *British Journal of Psychiatry 151,* 684-686.

Crandall, C. S. (1988). Social contagion of binge eating. *Journal of Personality and Social Psychology 55,* 588-598.

Crisp, A. H., Hsu, L. K. G., Harding, B. & Hartshome, J. (1980). Clinical features of anorexia nervosa: A study of consecutive series of 102 female patients. *Journal of Psychosomatic Research 24,* 179-191.

Crisp, A.H., Palmer, R.L. & Kalucy, R.S. (1976). How common is anorexia nervosa? A prevalence study. *British Journal of Psychiatry 128,* 549-554.

Crowther, J. H., Wolf, E. M. & Sherwood, N. E. (1992). Epidemiology of bulimia nervosa. In J. H. Crowther, D. L. Tennenbaum, S. E. Hobfoll & M. A. Parris Stephens (eds.) *The etiology of bulimia nervosa: The individual and familial context,* 1-26. Washington, DC: Hemisphere Publishing Corporation.

Cullberg, J. & Engström-Lindberg, M. (1988). Prevalence and incidence of eating disorders in a suburban area. *Acta Psychiatrica Scandinavica 78,* 314-319.

Dietz, W. H. (1990). You are what you eat – What you eat is what you are. *Journal of Adolescent Health Care 11,* 76-81.

Dornbusch, S. M., Carlsmith, J. M., Duncan, P. D., Gross, R. T., Martin, J. A., Ritter, P. L. & Siegel-Gorelick, B. (1984). Sexual maturation, social class, and the desire to be thin among adolescent females. *Developmental and Behavior Pediatrics 5*, 308-314.

Downs, A. C. & Harrison, S. K. (1985). Embarrassing age spots or just plain ugly? Physical attractiveness stereotyping as an instrument of sexism on American television commercials. *Sex Roles 13*, 9-19.

Duddle, M. (1973). An increase of anorexia nervosa in a university population. *British Journal of Psychiatry 123*, 711-712.

Dwyer, J. T., Feldman, J. J., Seltzer, C. C. & Mayer, J. (1969). Body image in adolescents: Attitudes toward weight and perception of appearance. *American Journal of Clinical Nutrition 20*, 1045-1056.

Fahy, T. A. & O'Donoghue, G. (1991). Eating disorders in pregnancy. *Psychological Medicine 21*, 577-580.

Fairburn, C.G. & Beglin, S.J. (1990). Studies of the epidemiology of bulimia nervosa. *American Journal of Psychiatry 147*, 401-408.

Fairburn, C.G. & Cooper, P. J. (1982). Self-induced vomiting and bulimia nervosa: An undetected problem. *British Medical Journal 284*, 1153-1155.

Fairburn, C. G. & Cooper, P. J. (1984). Binge-eating, self-induced vomiting and laxative abuse: A community study. *Psychological Medicine 14*, 401-410.

Fairburn, C. G., Hay, P. J. & Welch, S. L. (1993). Binge eating and bulimia nervosa: Distribution and determinants. In C. G. Fairburn & G. T. Wilson (eds.) *Binge eating: Nature, assessment and determinants* (in press). New York: Guilford Press.

Fichter, M.M., Elton, M., Sourdi, L., Weyerer, S. & Koptagel-Ilal, G. (1988). Anorexia nervosa in Greek and Turkish adolescents. *European Archives of Psychiatry and Neurological Sciences 237*, 200-208.

Furnham, A. & Alibhai, M. (1983). Cross-cultural differences in the perception of female body shape. *Psychological Medicine 13*, 829-837.

Garfinkel, P. E. & Garner, D. M. (1982). *Anorexia nervosa: A multidimensional perspective*. New York: Brunner-Mazel.

Garner, D. M. & Fairburn, C. G. (1988). Relationship between anorexia nervosa and bulimia nervosa: Diagnostic implications. In D. M. Garner & P. E. Garfinkel (eds.) *Diagnostic issues in anorexia nervosa and bulimia nervosa*, 56-79. New York: Brunner-Mazel.

Garner, D. M. & Garfinkel, P. E. (1979). The eating attitude test: An index of symptoms of anorexia nervosa. *Pychological Medicine 9*, 273-279.

Garner, D. M. & Garfinkel, P. E. (1980). Socio-cultural factors in the development of anorexia nervosa. *Psychological Medicine 10*, 647-656.

Garner, D. M., Garfinkel, P. E., Rockert, W. & Olmsted, M. P. (1987). A prospective study of eating disturbances in the ballet. *Psychotherapy and Psychosomatics 48*, 170-175.

Garner, D. M., Garfinkel, P. E., Schwartz, D. & Thompson, M. (1980). Cultural expectations of thinness in women. *Psychological Reports 47*, 483-491.

Garner, D. M., Olmsted, M. P. & Garfinkel, P. E. (1985). Similarities among bulimic groups selected by different weights and weight histories. *Journal of Psychiatric Research 19*, 129-134.

Garner, D. M., Olmsted, M. P. & Polivy, J. (1983). Development and validation of a multidimensional Eating Disorder Inventory for anorexia nervosa and bulimia. *International Journal of Eating Disorders 2*, 15-34.

Gershon, E. S., Schreiber, J. L., Hamovit, J. R., Dibble, E. D., Kaye, W., Nurnberger, J. I., Andersen, A. E. & Ebert, M. (1984). Clinical findings in patients with anorexia nervosa and affective illness in their relatives. *American Journal of Psychiatry 141*, 1419-1422.

Gibbs, R. (1986). Social factors in exaggerated eating behavior among high school students. *International Journal of Eating Disorders 5*, 1103-1107.

Gray, J. J., Ford, K. & Kelly, L. M. (1987). The prevalence of bulimia in a black college population. *International Journal of Eating Disorders 6*, 733-740.

Gulliford, M. C., Rona, R. J. & Chinn, S. (1992). Trends in body mass index in young adults in England and Scotland from 1973 to 1988. *Journal of Epidemiology and Community Health 46*, 187-190.

Hall, A. & Hay, P. J. (1991). Eating disorder patient referrals from a population region, 1977-1986. *Psychological Medicine 21*, 697-701.

Halmi, K. A., Casper, R., Eckert, E., Goldberg, S. C. & Davis, J. M. (1979). Unique features associated with age of onset of anorexia nervosa. *Psychiatry Research 1*, 209-215.

Hamilton, L. H., Brooks-Gunn, J. & Warren, M. P. (1985). Sociocultural influences on eating disorders in female professional dancers. *International Journal of Eating Disorders 4*, 465-477.

Harlan, W. R., Landis, R., Flegal, K. M., Davis, C. S. & Miller, M. E. (1988). Secular trends in body mass in the United States, 1960-1980. *American Journal of Epidemiology 128*, 1065-1074.

Henderson, M. & Freeman, C. P. L. (1987). A self-rating scale for bulimia, the 'BITE'. *British Journal of Psychiatry 150*, 18-24.

Herzog, D. B., Keller, M. B., Sacks, N. R., Yeh, C. J. & Lavori, P. W. (1992). Psychiatric comorbidity in treatment-seeking anorexics and bulimics. *Journal of the American Academy of Child and Adolescent Psychiatry 31*, 810-818.

Hoek, H. W. (1991). The incidence and prevalence of anorexia nervosa and bulimia nervosa in primary care. *Psychological Medicine 21*, 455-460.

Hoek, H. W. & Brook, F. G. (1985). Patterns of care of anorexia nervosa. *Journal of Psychiatric Research 19*, 155-160.

Hooper, M. S. H. & Garner, D. M. (1986). Application of the eating disorders inventory to a sample of black, white, and mixed race schoolgirls in Zimbabwe. *International Journal of Eating Disorders 5*, 161-168.

Hsu, L. K. G. (1990). *Eating disorders*. New York: Guilford Press.

Hsu, L. K. G. & Sobkiewicz, T. A. (1989). Bulimia nervosa: A four- to six-year follow-up study. *Psychological Medicine 19*, 1035-1038.

Hsu, L. K. G. & Sobkiewicz, T. A. (1991). Body image disturbance: Time to abandon the concept for eating disorders? *International Journal of Eating Disorders 10*, 15-30.

Hudson, J. I., Pope, H. G., Jonas, J. M. & Yorgelun-Todd, D. (1983). A family history study of anorexia nervosa and bulimia. *British Journal of Psychiatry 142*, 133-138.

Huenemann, R. L., Shapiro, L. R., Hampton, M. C. & Mitchell B. W. (1966). A longitudinal study of gross body composition and body conformation and their association with food and activity in a teenage population. *American Journal of Clinical Nutrition 18*, 325-338.

Humphrey, L. L. (1987). Comparison of bulimic-anorexic and nondistressed families using structural analysis of social behavior. *Journal of the American Academy of Child and Adolescent Psychiatry 26*, 248-255.

Hwu, H.-G., Yeh, E.-K. & Chang, L.-Y. (1989). Prevalence of psychiatric disorders in Taiwan defined by the Chinese Diagnostic Interview Schedule. *Acta Psychiatrica Scandinavica 79*, 136-147.

Jacobs, B. W. & Isaacs, S. (1986). Pre-pubertal anorexia nervosa: A retrospective controlled study. *Journal of Child Psychology and Psychiatry 27*, 237-250.

Joergensen, J. (1992). The epidemiology of eating disorders in Fyn County, Denmark, 1977-1986. *Acta Psychiatrica Scandinavica 85*, 30-34.

Johnson, C. L., Tobin, D. L. & Lipkin, J. (1989). Epidemiologic changes in bulimia behavior among female adolescents over a five-year period. *International Journal of Eating Disorders 8*, 647-656.

Johnson, C. & Wonderlich, S. (1992). Personality characteristics as a risk factor in the development of eating disorders. In J. H. Crowther, D. L. Tennenbaum, S. E. Hobfoll & M. A. Parris Stephens (eds.) *The etiology of bulimia nervosa: The individual and familial context*, 179-196. Washington, DC: Hemisphere Publishing Corporation.

Johnson-Sabine, E., Reiss, D. & Dayson, D. (1992). Bulimia nervosa: A 5-year follow-up study. *Psychological Medicine 22*, 951-959.

Johnson-Sabine, E., Wood, K., Patton, G., Mann, A. & Wakeling, A. (1988). Abnormal eating attitudes in London schoolgirls – a prospective epidemiological study: Factors associated with abnormal response on screening questionnaires. *Psychological Medicine 18*, 615-622.

Jones, D. J., Fox, M. M., Babigian, H. M. & Hutton, H. E. (1980). Epidemiology of anorexia nervosa in Monroe County, New York: 1960-1976. *Psychosomatic Medicine 42*, 551-558.

Kassett, J. A., Gershon, E. S., Maxwell, M. E., Guroff, J. J., Kazuba, D. M., Smith, A. L., Brandt, H. A. & Jimerson, D. C. (1989). Psychiatric disorders in the first-degree relatives of probands with bulimia nervosa. *American Journal of Psychiatry 146*, 1468-1471.

Kaufman, L. (1980). Prime-time nutrition. *Journal of Communication* (Summer), 37-46.

Kendell, R. E., Hall, D. J., Hailey, A. & Babigian, H. M. (1973). The epidemiology of anorexia nervosa. *Psychological Medicine 3*, 200-203.

Kendler, K. S., MacLean, C., Neale, M., Kessler, R., Heath, A. & Eaves, L. (1991). The genetic epidemiology of bulimia nervosa. *American Journal of Psychiatry 148*, 1627-1637.

King, M. B. (1989). Eating disorders in a general practice population: Prevalence, characteristics and follow-up at 12 to 18 months. *Psychological Medicine, Supplement 14.*

King, M. B. & Bhugra D. (1989). Eating disorders: Lessons from a cross-cultural study. *Psychological Medicine 19*, 955-958.

Lacey, J. H. (1992). The treatment demand for bulimia: A catchment area report of referral rates and demography. *Psychiatric Bulletin 16*, 203-205.

Langer, L. M., Warheit, G. J. & Zimmerman, R. S. (1991). Epidemiological study of problem eating behaviors and related attitudes in the general population. *Addictive Behaviors 16*, 176-173.

Lee, S. (1991). Anorexia nervosa in Hong Kong: A Chinese perspective. *Psychological Medicine 21*, 703-711.

Lee, C.K., Kwak, Y.S., Rhee, H., Kim, Y. S., Han, J. H., Choi, J. O. & Lee, Y. H. (1987). The nationwide epidemiological study of mental disorders in Korea. *Journal of Korean Medical Sciences 2*, 19-34.

Leigh, J. P., Fries, J. F. & Hubert, H. B. (1992). Gender and race differences in the correlation between body mass and education in the 1971-1975 NHANES I. *Journal of Epidemiology and Community Health 46*, 191-196.

Levine, M. P. & Smolak, L. (1992). Toward a model of the developmental psychopathology of eating disorders: The example of early adolescence. In J. H. Crowther, D. L. Tennenbaum, S. E. Hobfoll & M. A. Parris Stephens (eds.) *The etiology of bulimia nervosa: The individual and familial context*, 59-80. Washington, DC: Hemisphere Publishing Corporation.

Lewinsohn, P. M., Hops, H., Roberts, R. E., Seeley, J. R. & Andrews, J. A. (1993). Adolescent psychopathology: I. Prevalence and incidence of depression and other DSM-III-R disorders in high school students. *Journal of Abnormal Psychology 102*, 133-144.

Lucas, A. R., Beard, C. M., O'Fallon, W. M. & Kurland, L. T. (1988). Anorexia nervosa in Rochester, Minnesota: A 45-year study. *Mayo Clinic Proceedings 63*, 433-442.

Lucas, A. R., Beard, C. M., O'Fallon, W. M. & Kurland, L. T. (1991). 50-year trends in the incidence of anorexia nervosa in Rochester, Minnesota: A population-based study. *American Journal of Psychiatry 148*, 917-922.

Mann, A. H., Wakeling, A., Wood, K., Monck, E., Dobbs, R. & Szmukler, G. (1983). Screening for abnormal eating attitudes and psychiatric morbidity in an unselected population of 15-year-old schoolgirls. *Psychological Medicine 13*, 573-580.

Moller-Madsen, S. & Nystrup, J. (1992). Incidence of anorexia nervosa in Denmark. *Acta Psychiatrica Scandinavica 86*, 197-200.

Mori, D., Chaiken, S. & Pliner, P. (1987). 'Eating slightly' and the self-presentation of femininity. *Journal of Personality and Social Psychology 53*, 693-702.

Mumford, D. B., Whitehouse, A. M. & Platts, M. (1991). Sociocultural correlates of eating disorders among Asian schoolgirls in Bradford. *British Journal of Psychiatry 158*, 222-228.

Mumford, D. B., Whitehouse, A. M. & Choudry, I. Y. (1992). Survey of eating disorders in English-medium schools in Lahore, Pakistan. *International Journal of Eating Disorders 11*, 173-184.

Myers, P. N. & Biocca, F. A. (1992). The elastic body image: The effect of television advertising and programming on body image distortions in young women. *Journal of Communication 42*, 110-133.

Nasser, M. (1986). Comparative study of the prevalence of abnormal eating attitudes among Arab female students of both London and Cairo universities. *Psychological Medicine 16*, 621-625.

Nevo, S. (1985). Bulimic symptoms: Prevalence and ethnic differences among women. *International Journal of Eating Disorders 4*, 151-168.

Nielsen, S. (1990). The epidemiology of anorexia nervosa in Denmark from 1973 to 1987: A nationwide register study of psychiatric admission. *Acta Psychiatrica Scandinavica 81*, 507-514.

Nylander, I. (1971). The feeling of being fat and dieting in a school population: Epidemiologic interview investigation. *Acta Sociomedica Scandinavica 3*, 17-26.

Oakley-Browne, M. A., Joyce, P. R., Wells, J. E., Bushnell, J. A. & Hornblow, A. R. (1989). Christchurch psychiatric epidemiology study, Part II: Six month and other period prevalences of specific psychiatric disorders. *Australian and New Zealand Journal of Psychiatry 23*, 327-340.

Ogletree, S. M., Williams, S. W., Raffeld, P., Mason, B. & Fricke, K. (1990). Female attractiveness and eating disorders: Do children's television commercials play a role? *Sex Roles 22*, 791-797.

Pate, J. E., Pumariega, A. J., Hester, C. & Garner, D. M. (1992). Cross-cultural patterns in eating disorders: A review. *Journal of the American Academy of Child and Adolescent Psychiatry 31*, 802-809.

Patton, G. C. (1988). Mortality in eating disorders. *Psychological Medicine 18*, 947-951.

Patton, G. C., Johnson-Sabine, E., Wood, K., Mann, A. H. & Wakeling, A. (1990). Abnormal eating attitudes in London schoolgirls – a prospective epidemiological study: Outcome at twelve month follow-up. *Psychological Medicine 20*, 383-394.

Paxton, S. J., Wertheim, E. H., Gibbons, K., Szmukler, G. I., Hillier, L. & Petrovich, J. (1991). Body image satisfaction, dieting beliefs, and weight loss behaviors in adolescent girls and boys. *Journal of Youth and Adolescence 20*, 361-379.

Petersen, A. C. (1987). The nature of biological-psychosocial interactions: The sample case of early adolescence. In R. M. Lerner & T. T. Foch (eds.) *Biological-psychosocial interactions in early adolescence: A life-span perspective*, 35-61. Hillsdale, NJ: Lawrence Erlbaum.

Pope, H. G. & Hudson, J. I. (1992). Is childhood sexual abuse a risk factor for bulimia nervosa? *American Journal of Psychiatry 149*, 455-463.

Pope, H. G., Hudson, J. I. & Yurgelun-Todd, D. (1984). Anorexia nervosa and bulimia among 300 suburban women shoppers. *American Journal of Psychiatry 141*, 292-294.

Pumariega, A. J. (1986). Acculturation and eating attitudes in adolescent girls: A comparative and correlational study. *Journal of the American Academy of Child and Adolescent Psychiatry 25*, 276-279.

Pyle, R. L., Halvorson, P. A., Newman, P. A. & Mitchell, J. E. (1986). The increasing prevalence of bulimia in freshman college students. *International Journal of Eating Disorders 5*, 631-647.

Pyle, R. L., Neuman, P. A., Halvorson, P. A. & Mitchell, J. E. (1991). An ongoing cross-sectional study of the prevalence of eating disorders in freshman college students. *International Journal of Eating Disorders 10*, 667-677.

Raich, R. M., Rosen, J. C., Deus, J., Perez, O., Requena, A. & Gross, J. (1992). Eating disorder symptoms among adolescents in United States and Spain: A comparative study. *International Journal of Eating Disorders 11*, 63-72.

Ranseen, J. D. & Humphries, L. L. (1992). The intellectual functioning of eating disorder patients. *Journal of the American Academy of Child and Adolescent Psychiatry 31*, 844-846.

Rastam, M. & Gillberg, C. (1991). The family background in anorexia nervosa: A population-based study. *Journal of the American Academy of Child and Adolescent Psychiatry 30*, 283-289.

Rastam, M. & Gillberg, C. (1992). Background factors in anorexia nervosa: A controlled study of 51 teenage cases including a population sample. *European Child and Adolescent Psychiatry 1*, 54-65.

Rastam, M., Gillberg, C. & Garton, M. (1989). Anorexia nervosa in a Swedish urban region: A population-based study. *British Journal of Psychiatry 155*, 642-646.

Richards, M. H., Casper, R. C. & Larson, R. (1990a). Weight and eating concerns among pre- and young adolescent boys and girls. *Journal of Adolescent Health Care 11*, 203-209.

Richards, M. H., Boxer, A. M., Petersen, A. C. & Albrecht, R. (1990b). Relation of weights to body image in pubertal girls and boys from two communities. *Developmental Psychology 26*, 313-321.

Robins, L. N., Helzer, J. E., Weissman, M. M., Orvaschel, H., Gruenberg, E., Burke, J. D. & Regier, D. A. (1984). Lifetime prevalence of specific psychiatric disorders in three sites. *Archives of General Psychiatry 41*, 949-958.

Robins, L. N. & Regier, D. A. (eds.) (1991). *Psychiatric disorders in America: The Epidemiologic Catchment Area Study*. New York: Free Press.

Rodin, J., Striegel-Moore, R. H. & Silberstein, L. R. (1990). Vulnerability and resilience in the age of eating disorders: Risk and protective factors for bulimia nervosa. In J. Rolf, A. S. Masten, D. Cicchetti, K. H. Nuechterlein & S. Weintraub (eds.) *Risk and protective factors in the development of psychopathology*. London: Cambridge University Press.

Roghmann, K. J., Babigian, H. M., Goldberg, I. D. & Zastowny, T. R. (1982). The increasing number of children using psychiatric services: Analysis of a cumulative psychiatric case register. *Pediatrics 70*, 790-801.

Rosen, J. C. (1992). Body-image disorder: Definition, development, and contribution to eating disorders. In J. H. Crowther, D. L. Tennenbaum, S. E. Hobfoll & M. A.

Parris Stephens (eds.) *The etiology of bulimia nervosa: The individual and familial context*, 157-177. Washington, DC: Hemisphere Publishing Corporation.

Rosenzweig, M. & Spruill, J. (1987). Twenty years after Twiggy: A retrospective investigation of bulimic-like behaviors. *International Journal of Eating Disorders 6*, 59-65.

Russell, G. (1979). Bulimia nervosa: An ominous variant of anorexia nervosa. *Psychological Medicine 9*, 429-448.

Scheinberg, Z., Bleich, A., Koslovsky, M., Apter, A., Mark, M., Kotler, B. M. & Danon, Y. L. (1992). Prevalence of eating disorders among female Israel defence force recruits. *Harefuah 123*, 73-78.

Schwartz, D. M., Thompson, M. G. & Johnson, C. L. (1981). Anorexia nervosa and bulimia: The socio-cultural context. *International Journal of Eating Disorders 1*, 20-36.

Shah, M., Hannan, P. J. & Jeffery, R. W. (1991). Secular trend in body mass index in the adult population of three communities from the upper mid-western part of the USA: The Minnesota Heart Health Program. *International Journal of Obesity 15*, 499-503.

Silber, T. J. (1986). Anorexia nervosa in blacks and Hispanics. *International Journal of Eating Disorders 5*, 121-128.

Silverstein, B., Peterson, B. & Perdue, L. (1986a). Some correlates of the thin standard of bodily attractiveness for women. *International Journal of Eating Disorders 5*, 895-905.

Silverstein, B., Perdue, L., Peterson, B. & Kelly, E. (1986b). The role of mass media in promoting a thin standard of bodily attractiveness for women. *Sex Roles 14*, 519-532.

Smith, M. C. & Thelen, M. H. (1984). Development and validation of a test for bulimia. *Journal of Consulting and Clinical Psychology 52*, 863-872.

Soundy, T. J., Lucas, A. R., Suman, V. J. & Melton III, L. J. (submitted). Bulimia nervosa in Rochester, Minnesota, 1980 through 1990.

Spitzer, R. L., Devlin, M., Walsh, B. T., Hasin, D., Wing, R., Marcus, M., Stunkard, A., Wadden, T., Yanovski, S., Agras, S., Mitchell, J. & Nonas, C. (1992). Binge eating disorder: A multisite field trial of the diagnostic criteria. *International Journal of Eating Disorders 11*, 191-203.

Steel, J. M., Young, R. J., Lloyd, G. G. & Macintyre, C. C. A. (1989). Abnormal eating attitudes in young insulin-dependent diabetics. *British Journal of Psychiatry 155*, 515-521.

Stein, A. & Fairburn, C. (1989). Children of mothers with bulimia nervosa. *British Medical Journal 299*, 777-778.

Steinhausen, H.-Ch., Rauss-Mason, C. & Seidel, R. (1991). Follow-up studies of anorexia nervosa: A review of four decades of outcome research. *Psychological Medicine 21*, 447-454.

Stewart, D., Raskin, J., Garfinkel, P. E., McDonald, O. & Robinson, G. E. (1987). Anorexia nervosa, bulimia, and pregnancy. *American Journal of Obstetrics and Gynecology 157*, 1194-1198.

Story, M. & Faulkner, P. (1990). The prime time diet: A content analysis of eating behavior and food messages in television program content and commercials. *American Journal of Public Health 80*, 738-740.

Striegel-Moore, R. H., Silberstein, L. R., Frensch, P. & Rodin, J. (1989). A prospective study of disordered eating among college students. *International Journal of Eating Disorders 8*, 499-509.

Striegel-Moore, R. H., Silberstein, L. R. & Rodin, J. (1986). Toward an understanding of risk factors for bulimia. *American Psychologist 41*, 246-263.

Strober, M. (1980). Personality and symptomatological features in young, nonchronic anorexia nervosa patients. *Journal of Psychosomatic Research 24*, 353-359.

Strober, M., Lampert, C., Morrell, W., Burroughs, J. & Jacobs, C. (1990). A controlled family study of anorexia nervosa: Evidence of familial aggregation and lack of shared transmission with affective disorders. *International Journal of Eating Disorders 9*, 239-253.

Strober, M., Morrell, W., Burroughs, J., Salkin, B. & Jacobs, C. (1985).A controlled family study of anorexia nervosa. *Journal of Psychiatric Research 19*, 239-246.

Strober, M., Salkin, B., Burroughs, J. & Morrell, W. (1982). Validity of the bulimia-restricter distinction in anorexia nervosa. Parental personality characteristics and family psychiatric morbidity. *Journal of Nervous and Mental Disease 170*, 345-351.

Suzuki, M., Morita, H. & Kamoshita, S. (1990). Epidemiological survey of psychiatric disorders in Japanese school children, Part III: Prevalence of psychiatric disorders in junior high school children. *Nippon Koshu Eisei Zasshi 37*, 991-1000.

Swift, W. J., Andrews, D. & Barklage, N. E. (1986). The relationship between affective disorder and eating disorders: A review of the literature. *American Journal of Psychiatry 143*, 290-299.

Szmukler, G. I. (1983). Weight and food preoccupation in a population of English schoolgirls. In G. J. Bargman (ed.) *Understanding anorexia nervosa and bulimia*, 21-27. Columbus, Ohio: Ross Laboratories.

Szmukler, G. I., Eisler, I., Gillies, C. & Hayward, M. E. (1985). The implications of anorexia nervosa in a ballet school. *Journal of Psychiatric Research 19*, 177-181.

Szmukler, G., McCance, C., McCrone, L. & Hunter, D. (1986). Anorexia nervosa: A psychiatric case register study from Aberdeen. *Psychological Medicine 16*, 49-58.

Theander, S. (1970). Anorexia nervosa: A psychiatric investigation of 94 female patients. *Acta Psychiatrica Scandinavica Supplement 214*, 1-194.

Thelen, M. H., Lawrence, C. M. & Powell, A. L. (1992). Body image, weight control, and eating disorders among children. In J. H. Crowther, D. L. Tennenbaum, S. E. Hobfoll & M. A. Parris Stephens (eds.) *The etiology of bulimia nervosa: The individual and familial context*, 81-101. Washington, DC: Hemisphere Publishing Corporation.

Thompson, J. K. (1992). Body image: Extent of disturbance, associated features, theoretical models,assessment methodologies, intervention strategies, and a proposal for a new DSM-IV diagnostic category – Body Image Disorder. In M.

Hersen, R. M. Eisler & P. M. Miller (eds.) *Progress in behavior modification*, 3-54. Sycamore, IL: Sycamore Publishing Inc.

Toro, J., Cervera, M. & Perez, P. (1988). Body shape, publicity and anorexia nervosa. *Social Psychiatry and Psychiatric Epidemiology 23*, 132-136.

Treasure, J. L. & Holland, A. J. (1991). Genes and the aetiology of eating disorders. In P. McGuffin & R. Murray (eds.) *The new genetics of mental illness*, 198-211. Oxford: Butterworth-Heinemann.

Wells, J. E., Bushnell, J. A., Hornblow, A. R., Joyce, P. R. & Oakley-Browne, M. A. (1989). Christchurch psychiatric epidemiology study, Part I: Methodology and lifetime prevalence for specific psychiatric disorders. *Australian and New Zealand Journal of Psychiatry 23*, 315-326.

Whitaker, A., Johnson, J., Shaffer, D., Rapoport, J., Kalikow, K., Walsh, B. T., Davies, M., Braiman, S. & Dolinsky, A. (1990). Uncommon troubles in young people: Prevalence estimates of selected psychiatric disorders in a nonreferred adolescent population. *Archives of General Psychiatry 47*, 487-496.

Whitehouse, A. M. & Button, E. J. (1988). The prevalence of eating disorders in a U.K. college population: A reclassification of an earlier study. *International Journal of Eating Disorders 7*, 393-397.

Whitehouse, A. M., Cooper, P. J., Vize, C. V., Hill, C. & Vogel, L. (1992). Prevalence of eating disorders in three Cambridge general practices: Hidden and conspicuous morbidity. *British Journal of Medical Practice 42*, 57-60.

Willi, J., Giacometti, G. & Limacher, B. (1990). Update on the epidemiology of anorexia nervosa in a defined region of Switzerland. *American Journal of Psychiatry 147*, 1514-1517.

Willi, J. & Grossmann, S. (1983). Epidemiology of anorexia nervosa in a defined region of Switzerland. *American Journal of Psychiatry 140*, 564-567.

Williams, P. & King, M. (1987). The 'epidemic' of anorexia nervosa: Another medical myth? *The Lancet*, January 24, 205-207.

Winokur, A., March, V. & Mendels, J. (1980). Primary affective disorder in relatives of patients with anorexia nervosa. *American Journal of Psychiatry 137*, 695-698.

Wiseman, C. V., Gray, J. J., Mosimann, J. E. & Ahrens, A. H. (1992). Cultural expectations of thinness in women: An update. *International Journal of Eating Disorders 11*, 85-89.

World Health Organization (1992). *The ICD-10 classification of mental and behavioural disorders: Clinical descriptions and diagnostic guidelines*. Geneva: Author.

Yates, A. (1989). Current perspectives on the eating disorders: I. History, psychological and biological aspects. *Journal of the American Academy of Child and Adolescent Psychiatry 28*, 813-828.

13

Suicide and Suicidal Behaviour Among Adolescents

RENÉ F. W. DIEKSTRA, C. W. M. KIENHORST & E. J. de WILDE

In many countries, official statistics show that suicide ranks among the top ten causes of death overall, and among the two or three leading causes for those aged 15-34 years. Yet these statistics clearly provide a disturbingly incomplete picture of the magnitude of the phenomenon at the global level. In the 1991 World Health Statistics Annual (World Health Organization, 1992), only 36 of the 166 member states of the United Nations are listed as reporting data on mortality by suicide. In total, these 36 countries reported almost 160,000 suicidal deaths in one year. Of these, 17,414 (or 11 per cent) were amongst children and adolescents aged 5 to 24 years.

Of course, suicide also occurs in the non-reporting countries, and there is more than suggestive evidence that in some of these countries the suicide rate at times equals or even surpasses the highest national rates shown by official statistics in the reporting countries. Well-documented reports on Western Samoa, for example, indicate that in the first half of the last decade this country had one of the world's highest suicide rates, if not the highest rate of all (Bowles, in press). In addition, even in the reporting countries a considerable proportion of suicidal deaths (estimates vary from 30 to 200 per cent) are not recorded as such.

It follows that mortality by suicide is an extremely important public health problem. It is, however, a problem that is painfully neglected. This becomes apparent, for example, from a comparison with motor traffic accidents. Today in many industrialized countries the number of people dying through suicide is higher than the number dying on the road. Over the last two decades motor traffic fatality rates have decreased, while at the same time suicide rates, particularly among adolescents and young adults, appear to have increased considerably. Yet, throughout the world, resources devoted to prevention of suicide are only a tiny fraction of those devoted to prevention of road traffic accidents.

Of course, in addition to deaths, road traffic accidents cause a much larger number of injuries, including a considerable number of serious ones. However, this cannot explain why much larger resources are devoted to road accident prevention than to suicide prevention. For non-fatal suicidal behaviours have to be considered along with completed suicides, just as non-fatal accidents have to be considered along with fatal ones. In addition to the number of suicidal deaths, at least ten times as many persons make non-fatal attempts to harm themselves, often seriously enough to require medical attention and not infrequently resulting in irreversible disability.

Our knowledge of the true magnitude of this phenomenon of non-fatal suicidal behaviours (called 'parasuicide' in specialist writings, following Kreitman, 1977) is very limited. National records on parasuicide are kept nowhere in the world. Health care institutions that treat people who have behaved suicidally may or may not record such cases. Those that do use a wide variety of definitions. Nevertheless, the available data from special area studies in some (but not all) countries suggest that rates of parasuicide have been rising since the late fifties or early sixties, and that among young people suicidal actions have become one of the most important reasons for hospital emergency admissions and treatment. The majority of parasuicides are by adolescents and young adults, who form a pool from which many future suicides are drawn.

This chapter is divided into seven main parts. The first discusses the difficult problems of definition and measurement in this field of research. The second reviews the evidence on time trends, in order to assess whether today's adolescents are indeed at a greater risk of suicide or parasuicide than previous generations. The main emphasis will be on countries in the European region, although comparisons with non-European countries will be made where relevant. The third part reviews the evidence on the causal pathways leading to suicide in individual cases. The fourth part reviews the evidence on the effectiveness of various prevention strategies, for the light that this throws on the causes of suicide. The sixth part considers possible causal explanations for time trends in rates of suicide. A final section draws out the main conclusions.

CONCEPTS AND MEASURES

There are three main lines of research and writing in the field, which concentrate respectively on

- the formation of suicidal ideas ('suicidal ideation');
- suicidal behaviours short of completed suicide ('parasuicide'); and
- suicide.

Within each of these lines of research there is, to some extent, a different theoretical and empirical tradition. The separate study of parasuicide, for example, has emerged from the theory, backed up by research findings, that suicidal behaviours are, to an important extent, different from suicide in the form that they take, in their function, in their likely causes, and in the demographic characteristics of those affected.

Definitions

In everyday life, the terms 'suicide' and 'suicidal behaviour' are used to refer to voluntary actions intended to bring about one's own immediate death. However, among the behaviours and experiences commonly described as suicidal, many are not motivated by a wish to die. Often people who act suicidally do not even mean to harm themselves, but only to express or communicate feelings such as despair, hopelessness and anger. Contemporary writings therefore distinguish between three classes of phenomena.

1. *Suicidal ideation* is commonly used to describe cognitions that can vary from fleeting thoughts that life is not worth living, through concrete, well thought-out plans for killing oneself, to an intense, delusional preoccupation with self-destruction (Goldney et al., 1989). Strictly speaking, however, the term should not be used for vague death wishes or isolated thoughts that life is not worth living, but only for thoughts implying a desire, intention, or plan to end life by one's own hand. Because this distinction is not made in many, perhaps most, studies, it is difficult to draw any conclusions about the prevalence or incidence of suicidal ideation, or about its causes.

2. *Parasuicide* is the term originally proposed by Kreitman (1977) to cover behaviours that can vary from what are sometimes called 'suicidal gestures'

or 'manipulative attempts' to serious but unsuccessful attempts to kill oneself. It refers to any deliberate act with non-fatal outcome that appears to cause, or actually causes, self-harm, or, without intervention from others, would have done so; this includes taking a drug in excess of its prescribed therapeutic dose (Kreitman, 1977). Because it makes no reference to intention, more and more authors on the subject prefer the term 'parasuicide' to 'attempted suicide'. As Kreitman (1977) has pointed out, intention cannot be used as a criterion since the person's motive may be too uncertain or complex to be readily ascertained. When asked 'Why did you do it?' most will deny (afterwards) that they wanted to kill themselves. Many will reply 'I just don't know'. Since parasuicide, particularly during adolescence and early adulthood, is usually carried out at the height of an interpersonal crisis by an individual feeling desperate and confused, such obscurity of intent is not surprising. Moreover, approximately two-thirds of the men and nearly half of the women who present as parasuicides have taken alcohol within a few hours of the act (Kreitman, 1977).

This points to another important aspect of the definition of parasuicide: the act should be non-habitual. A habitual user of excessive quantities of alcohol or a habitual user of dangerous quantities of (hard) drugs is not considered a case of parasuicide if found unconscious as a result of an overdose (assuming that other information indicating suicidal intent, such as a suicide note, is not present). Also, habitual self-mutilation (cutting, piercing, head banging) is not described as parasuicide.

However, it is important to note that there is as yet no international agreement on the precise definition of parasuicide. In contrast to the majority of European researchers, most North American authors (for example, Spirito et al., 1989) continue to use the term 'attempted suicide', and often require the presence of a suicidal intention for an act to be recorded as such. Comparison of the results of studies from the two continents, for example with regard to lifetime prevalence of parasuicide, therefore remains hazardous.

3. *Suicide* commonly refers to any death that is the direct or indirect result of an act accomplished by a victim who knows or believes that this will be the result (see Maris, 1991). This definition implies that the term 'suicide' should only be applied in the case of a death. Risk-taking that leads to death, if the indirect causal sequence can be specified and was intentional, is suicide. This can be conceptualized by regarding the failure to take action

to prevent or avoid death as a negative act. 'Indirect suicide' of this kind is a common but neglected form. Some authors (see Farberow, 1980) believe that it is particularly common in adolescence and young adulthood and that a considerable number of road traffic fatalities in young males are suicides. Self-neglecting behaviours, sometimes referred to as suicidal 'erosion', such as hunger strike or refusal to take life-preserving medication, should also be considered as suicide where they result in death.

Those who are officially involved in the certification of deaths may diverge in the extent to which they apply this definition of suicide, both within and between countries. Such differences would influence recorded rates and their international comparability, an issue that will be considered in more detail later.

It is apparent from these definitions that there must be considerable overlap between the three classes of suicidal behaviour, and this is confirmed by research. There is also some evidence of developmental pathways running from suicidal ideation through parasuicide to suicide. Follow-up studies of people admitted to hospital for self-poisoning have shown a markedly increased risk of suicide in the years afterwards. Thus, in a 10 year follow-up in Denmark (Nordentoft et al., 1993), 103 out of 974 patients aged 15 years and over committed suicide – a 30 times greater risk than in the general population. The increased risk is most evident in the first two or three years following the parasuicide. More than two previous parasuicides, increasing age, living alone and manic-depressive illness were all high risk factors for a completed suicide. The risk of suicide following parasuicide is probably less in teenagers than adults but the increase in risk is still substantial (Hawton et al., 1993). The two factors most strongly associated with completed suicide following parasuicide seem to be previous in-patient psychiatric treatment and substance misuse (alcohol or drugs). However, we still know relatively little about the causal mechanisms in the patterns of recruitment from suicidal ideation to parasuicide and from parasuicide to suicide, or about the factors that precipitate or protect against these transformations.

Measurement

The quality and quantity of information available on suicidal ideation, parasuicide and suicide are variable. Differences of definition and method, and deficiencies of quality, are major obstacles to establishing a reliable account of cross-national secular trends. National statistics are available for suicide, but not for the other two categories. In a very few countries, records are kept at the regional or local level that allow the incidence of parasuicide to be monitored: examples are the former Medical Research Council Unit associated with the Royal Infirmary at Edinburgh, Scotland, and the Department of Clinical and Health Psychology at the University of Leiden, the Netherlands. However, these records only cover cases of parasuicide treated by hospitals. Also, the lower age limit for case identification in these centres is commonly 15 years, so that no data are available on early adolescence.

In the few countries, such as the USA and the Netherlands, where repeated national surveys of adolescent mental and behavioural health are carried out, either measures of suicidal ideation or parasuicide are not included (Bachman et al., 1986) or the studies have not been in place long enough to allow any solid conclusions on secular trends (Centers of Disease Control, 1991; Diekstra et al., 1991). Longitudinal studies could in principle provide information on the incidence of parasuicide at each stage of the life course, but such results are not yet available.

There is still some confusion over measurement tools for each of the categories, but some progress has been made during the last decade or so. There are three principal methods of measurement: self-completion questionnaires, personal interviews, and administrative records.

For the assessment of *suicidal ideation* a number of psychometrically sound questionnaires exist (Goldney et al., 1989), but they do not appear to have been widely used as yet. The same is true of 'suicide attitude scales', which measure, among other things, affective, cognitive and instrumental attitudes towards one's own suicide (Diekstra & Kerkhof, 1989). Most studies have tended to use their own questions or ones included in commonly-used instruments for assessing (mental) health status such as the General Health Questionnaire (GHQ, see Goldney et al., 1989). Consequently, it is difficult to compare results between studies, especially since the period covered by the questioning varies substantially, from 'over the past weeks', through 'over the last year', to 'ever'.

Most studies of *parasuicide* have used hospital admission data for case identification. Since criteria for treating a case, for administrative purposes, as a suicide attempt are often obscure, and, where not obscure, have been shown to vary considerably both within and between countries, there are limited opportunities for making comparisons between studies. Furthermore, there is evidence of a relationship between method (not just medical seriousness) and probability of hospital referral of parasuicide cases. In addition, there are substantial differences between countries and regions in customs or procedures for referral to hospitals. Consequently, hospital-based data provide a much more valid estimate of the incidence of parasuicide in one place than in another, but in general hospital-based rates underestimate 'true' rates, as community surveys have shown (Kerkhof, 1985). This seems to be especially the case amongst adolescents and young adults. The magnitude of the underestimation remains obscure, however, because of differences between surveys in identifying parasuicide, even within the same country. One problem is that most surveys, with a few exceptions (Kienhorst et al., 1990a; Diekstra et al., 1991; Centers of Disease Control, 1991) do not cover the whole adolescent age spectrum (the lower age limit is usually 15 years). More important are the differences in questioning methods. In the Epidemiological Catchment Area Studies organized by the National Institute of Mental Health in the United States, respondents were asked 'Have you ever attempted suicide?' (Moscicki et al., 1989: 117). Surveys in other countries (Diekstra, 1989a) have sometimes used 'self-destructive behaviour' questionnaires, in which the term 'attempted suicide' is deliberately avoided. Instead respondents are asked questions like: 'Have you ever because of social, emotional or other problems, tried to hang yourself? Taken an overdose of ...?' etc. Whenever respondents tick one or more of these (potentially) self-harming behaviours, they are asked to provide further details about each episode. Only episodes that meet a certain number of informational criteria are then classified as parasuicides. A slightly adapted version of this method is being used in the Parasuicide Monitoring Study of the World Health Organization's Regional Office for Europe. This study is currently in progress at 16 centres in 11 European countries. Most of these centres collect cases of parasuicide from a variety of sources: hospitals, general practitioners, out-patient clinics, mental health centres, social work agencies, and so on. So far only a preliminary report of this study has been published (see Platt et al., 1992) and although it is expected soon to provide the first internationally comparable data on 12-month period prevalence and life-time prevalence (from retrospective questioning) such data are not yet available.

By far the largest quantity of data on secular trends is available for *suicide*. In many European countries as well as in the USA, Australia, and Japan, suicide rates have been recorded for at least a century. This seems to offer an opportunity to establish whether suicide mortality among the young has increased during the twentieth century. But whether or not that question can indeed be answered must depend on the quality of national suicide statistics. Before discussing secular trends, it is therefore necessary to consider how valid and reliable these data are.

The Validity and Reliability of National Suicide Statistics

The salient question here is whether methods and criteria in identifying suicides vary so much among different populations that they may account for the differences in national rates. Several authors have argued that attitudes within specific cultures towards suicide so affect certification that official suicide statistics are virtually valueless (see, for example, Douglas, 1967). However, a WHO working group, on the basis of a careful examination of the available evidence, expressed 'confidence in the use of official suicide statistics from European countries for trend analysis' (World Health Organization, 1982). The 1982 review clearly indicated that differences in ascertainment procedures do not explain differences in suicide rates between populations. In a now classical study, Sainsbury and Barraclough (1968) compared the suicide rates of immigrants to the USA from 11 countries with those reported by their countries of origin. Cases of suicide in the various immigrant groups were identified by US procedures, whereas suicides in the home countries were identified by the methods used in each particular country. The rank order of the two sets of suicide rates (see Table 13.1) was nearly identical (r=0.90). A study of suicide mortality statistics of immigrants to Australia confirmed this finding, and also showed that it held for both sexes (Whitlock, 1971; Lester, 1972). The correlation between the suicide rates of male immigrants from 16 countries and the rates in their countries of birth was 0.79; for females it was 0.76. Given the small number of suicides in some immigrant groups and hence the large standard error of their rates, the correlations are surprisingly high.

There is another aspect of the problem that needs to be mentioned. Suicide is certainly underreported to a greater or lesser extent everywhere (see, for example, McCarthy & Walsh, 1975, for Ireland, and Jobes et al., 1986, for the United States). Where the officials responsible for certifying deaths in any country have doubts about recording a death as suicide, they probably record it either as a death from unknown causes or as an accidental death. The report of the 1968 WHO working group (WHO Chronicle, 1975) found that there was indeed wide variation in the extent to which officials opt for these alternatives. It is therefore of considerable interest to examine the variations between countries in the use of these two categories alongside the variations in suicide rates. Barraclough (1973), who was the first to look into this matter, found a high rank order correlation (r = 0.89) between the officially recorded suicide rates for 22 countries and the rates of suicide plus death from unknown causes. Sainsbury and co-workers (1981) reported a study showing that variations in the use of the categories 'accidental' and 'undetermined' causes of death contribute little towards explaining differences among the suicide rates of European countries.

Table 13.1   Suicide rates in 1959 of immigrants to the USA from eleven countries

Rates per 100,000

	A	B	C	D
	Foreign-born in USA	In country of origin	Rank order of A	Rank order of B
Country of origin				
Sweden	34.2	18.1	1	4
Austria	32.5	24.8	2	2
Czechoslovakia	31.5	24.9	3	1
Germany (FR)	25.7	18.7	4	3
Poland	25.2	8.0	5	6
Norway	23.7	7.8	6	7
England and Wales	19.2	11.5	7	5
Italy	18.2	6.2	8	9
Canada	17.5	7.4	9	8
Ireland	9.8	2.5	10	10
Mexico	7.9	2.1	11	11
USA-born in USA	10.4			

Rank order correlation of columns C and D = r=0.90, p<0.001.

Source: Sainsbury & Barraclough (1968).

Taken together, these findings show that national suicide statistics are a valuable source of data on which to base comparative epidemiological studies. This conclusion is further supported by the fact that consistent differences in rates between national, demographic, and social groups have been recorded over very long periods, in several instances for more than a century; and these differences persist despite political changes that have altered ascertainment procedures in many countries. To ignore the implications of such conspicuous regularities as the higher suicide rates of males, of those living alone or divorced, and of the mentally ill, would surely be a failure of vision.

In summary, then, suicide is underreported for a number of reasons, and the rates are subject to many errors of a kind encountered in mortality statistics in general. Nevertheless, the evidence from studies designed to settle this point clearly indicate that these errors are more or less random, at least to an extent that allows useful comparisons to be made between countries, between socio-demographic groups, and over time.

A note of caution should be struck, however, about extending this general conclusion to all age groups. Most work on the reliability and validity of suicide statistics has limited itself to the analysis of data from those aged 15 and above. There are two reasons for this limitation. First, not all countries that keep suicide statistics extend these records to those below 15 years of age, but where such records are kept, death by suicide appears to be so rare among children under the age of 15 that neither studies of reliability and validity nor analysis of trends seems to be feasible. Secondly, many researchers believe that if cultural, religious and political attitudes play a role in the certification of deaths as suicide, this is particularly so in the case of children and young adolescents. Consequently, the analysis in this chapter will be largely confined to suicide in middle and late adolescence and in young adulthood (the age groups from 15 to 29) although the epidemiology of suicide in early adolescence will be addressed as far as empirically defensible.

PREVALENCE OF SUICIDAL BEHAVIOURS IN ADOLESCENCE

For the reasons stated in the last section, our 'maps' of suicidal behaviours in adolescence are still incomplete, particularly if comparisons between different countries are needed. In addition to the discrepancies and deficiencies in data sources and in methods of recording and classification, there are also inconsistencies in methods of collecting information, in the size and characteristics of samples, and in methods of data analysis, that make comparison between studies hazardous. For such reasons, the following conclusions on the point prevalence and lifetime prevalence of suicidal behaviours in adolescence must be tentative.

Suicidal Ideation

What percentage of young people exhibit suicidal tendencies or 'suicidal mood' episodes during adolescence? This question could only be answered definitively by means of prospective longitudinal studies that would tap experiences of suicidal mood from early childhood to young adulthood. On that basis, an accurate estimate of lifetime prevalence, based on contemporaneous questioning, could be obtained for people up to the age of, say, 25. However, studies of that kind have not so far been reported. This leaves an important question unanswered: whether the occurrence of 'suicidal mood' episodes belongs to 'normal' developmental trajectories in adolescence. There is, however, evidence suggesting that, to a large extent, this may be the case.

Community surveys of suicidal ideation in adolescent populations (defined here as high-school student populations) published since 1985 have produced widely varying estimates of the prevalence of suicidal thoughts: ranging from 4 per cent (Kienhorst et al., 1990b), through 15 (Pronovost et al., 1990), to 19 per cent (Diekstra et al., 1991), to over 50 per cent (Smith & Crawford, 1986; Harkavy Friedman et al., 1987). To a large extent, these variations in reported rates can be explained by differences in the definition of suicidal ideation and in the reference period used. Some studies have asked about the 'recent' period (Kienhorst et al., 1990b), others about the past year (Diekstra et al., 1991; Dubow et al., 1989) and yet others have asked whether the subject has 'ever' or 'at least once' had suicidal thoughts (Pronovost et al., 1990; Smith & Crawford, 1986, Harkavy Friedman et al., 1987). Not surprisingly, the longer the reference period, the higher the rate tends to be. On the assumption that retrospective questioning about suicidal ideation 'ever' or 'at least once' provides some kind of estimate of lifetime prevalence rate, this rate is estimated to fall within the range between 15 per cent to 53 per cent among adolescents, which suggests that suicidal thoughts are indeed a common phenomenon among young people.

Most of the studies reviewed show a clear preponderance of girls among those having suicidal thoughts. There is also some evidence of an increase in point prevalence with age, at least over the period from 12 to 17 years of age, and more prominently in girls than in boys (Diekstra et al., 1991). No data are available to test whether this rise is a function of puberty, of some other function of age, or of changing experiences.

Parasuicide

Estimates of the rate of parasuicide in the population as a whole, or specifically in young people, vary considerably depending on whether the data come from records kept by hospitals and other services, or from community surveys.

Studies based on patient records

There are so far two international studies based on patient records, one completed and one in progress, that shed some light on this issue. The first (Diekstra, 1982) was carried out in 1976 in seven of the nine countries that constituted the European Economic Community (EEC) at that time. Extrapolating from data provided by centres with well-defined catchment areas, it was estimated that for the whole of the EEC (which had a population of about 200 million at the time) approximately 430,000 episodes of deliberate self-harm were treated during 1976 by either in-patient or out-patient facilities. This implied an average annual rate of 215 cases per 100,000 persons aged 15 years and older (162 for males and 265 for females). Between countries and centres, rates varied considerably: for males, the range was from 26 to 353, for females from 82 to 527. This finding can be explained at least partially by differences in referral and data recording procedures.

The other study in this category, which is still in progress, is being carried out under the auspices of the World Health Organization (WHO Multicentre Study on Monitoring Trends in Parasuicide, see Platt et al., 1992). The first progress report, comprising data from 15 centres in 10 countries (Finland, France, Hungary, Italy, the Netherlands, Norway, Spain, Sweden, Germany, Denmark) indicates that parasuicide rates (based on admission to health facilities for the year 1989) vary widely between centres. Among males, the highest rate of parasuicide (414 per 100,000) was found in Helsinki, Finland, and the lowest (61) in Leiden, the Netherlands, a ratio in excess of 7:1. Among females, the rate was highest (595) in Pontoise, France, and lowest (95) in Guipuzcoa, Spain. Although in most centres parasuicide rates were higher among females than among males, there were exceptions, such as Helsinki, Finland, where rates for males appeared to be remarkably high, and were higher than among females.

From both studies it appears that peak ages for parasuicide, whether in absolute numbers or relative to the population in the relevant age group, fall somewhere within the first half of the life cycle, (that is, between 15 and 44 years of age), although between countries and sexes there is considerable and unexplained variation in the age category (15-24, 25-34, 35-44) with the highest rate.

The results of community surveys (see below) suggest that patient records substantially underestimate the scale of the phenomenon of parasuicide. Estimates of the overall crude annual rate of incidence based on patient records range from 300 to 800 per 100,000 population aged 15 and over (Diekstra, 1985). On the one hand, these differences may be a valid reflection of differences between countries or regions in parasuicide rates. On the other hand, however, differences in methods of data collection between studies have certainly had an impact on their findings.

Community Surveys

A review of 10 community surveys of samples of adolescents (high school students), published after 1985, shows that estimates of one-year prevalence of parasuicidal acts vary between 2.4 per cent and 20 per cent (Dubow et al., 1989; Pronovost et al., 1990; Rubinstein et al., 1989; Nagy & Adcock, 1990; Centres of Disease Control, 1991), whereas estimates of lifetime prevalence rates range from 2.2 per cent to 20 per cent (Diekstra et al., 1991; Kienhorst et al., 1990b; Smith & Crawford, 1986; Rubinstein et al., 1989; Andrews & Lewinsohn, 1990; Harkavy Friedman et al., 1987). These differences in rates must be interpreted in the light of differences in case definition.

All community studies report a strong preponderance of girls. Clearly parasuicide increases with age over the adolescent period (because it is very much less frequent in children than young adults). However, there is uncertainty on just when the main rise occurs. Clinical studies, too, are not decisive in the assessment of the role of puberty in the rise (see Diekstra, 1992; Rey & Bird, 1991; Andrus et al., 1991).

Both community surveys and studies of clinical samples show that a considerable proportion of parasuicidal adolescents repeatedly engage in these behaviours: between 14 per cent (Hawton et al., 1982) and 51 per cent (Mehr et al., 1981, 1982), depending partially on the length of the follow-up period.

Suicide

Generally speaking suicide is a relatively rare event, although there is large variation in death rates from suicide between countries in the European region (see Table 13.2). Among the countries whose suicide rates were published in the 1991 World Health Statistics Annual (WHO, 1992), suicide rates spanned the range from a low of almost zero suicides per million females in Malta, to a high of over 600 per million males in Hungary. In all the countries taken together there were around 120,000 suicidal deaths reported in a one-year period.

Table 13.2   Age-standardized suicide mortality rates for European countries c. 1989

Rate per 100,000 population

	Year	Males	Females
Austria	1990	33.8	11.5
Belgium	1986	30.1	13.3
Bulgaria	1990	20.9	7.9
Czechoslovakia	1990	30.0	8.5
Denmark	1990	30.7	14.8
Finland	1989	45.7	11.1
France	1989	29.9	10.8
Germany	1989	22.0	8.2
Greece	1989	5.5	1.9
Hungary	1990	61.4	18.8
Iceland	1990	27.2	4.9
Ireland	1989	13.4	4.2
Israel	1988	12.2	4.9
Italy	1988	10.9	3.8
Luxembourg	1989	28.0	9.2
Malta	1990	5.0	0.0
Netherlands	1989	12.9	7.4
Norway	1989	22.5	8.1
Poland	1990	23.7	4.7
Portugal	1990	13.9	4.1
Spain	1987	11.0	3.7
Sweden	1988	25.1	10.9
Switzerland	1990	29.9	11.5
USSR	1990	39.3	9.1
–Byelorussia	1990	37.2	7.8
–Ukraine	1990	36.5	7.8
UK	1990	12.2	3.5
–England and Wales	1990	11.7	3.4
–Northern Ireland	1990	15.9	5.9
–Scotland	1990	16.3	4.4
Yugoslavia	1989	26.0	10.0

Source: WHO (1992), *World Health Statistics Annual*, Table 11.

Table 13.2 shows that Southern European countries have the lowest suicide rates, followed by the countries in the North-West region (United Kingdom, the Netherlands) with somewhat higher rates. The Scandinavian countries form a third group with again higher rates, while a fourth group of countries, also with relatively high rates is located in Europe's 'midriff' – starting with Belgium and France in the West, running through Switzerland, Austria and Hungary, and ending in the East with Russia. The main lines of this geographical 'suicide-chart' have remained more or less constant for the European region over the course of the present century.

Age, Gender and Suicide

According to a multitude of authors (see Vaillant & Blumenthal, 1990) one of the most basic facts about suicide is that its risk increases with age. In fact, completed suicide is extremely rare in children under the age of twelve; it becomes more common after puberty, and its incidence increases in each of the adolescent years (Moens, 1990). From late adolescence or young adulthood onwards, however, the relationship between age and suicide varies between countries and between males and females in the same countries (see Figures 13.1-3).

Figure 13.1   Suicide and age: females in selected countries

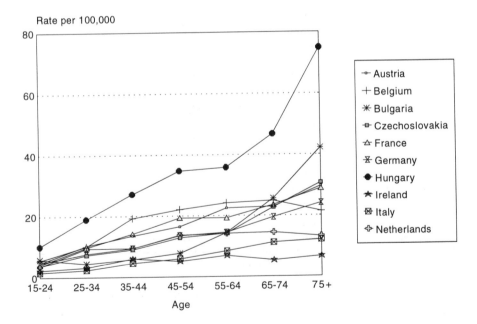

Source: WHO Statistics Annual (1989).

Figure 13.2   Suicide and age: females in selected countries

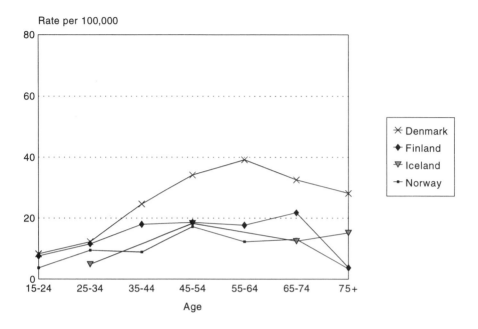

Source: WHO Statistics Annual (1989).

In some countries a first peak in the suicide rate comes between the ages of 24 and 35: this applies, for example, to males in Iceland, to females in Norway, to females in Bulgaria, and to both sexes in the USA. By contrast, in other countries suicide rates continue to rise up to mid-life (between the ages of 45 and 54, or sometimes 64), after which stage a dip occurs: this applies, for example, to both sexes in Hungary and Denmark. In almost all countries the highest suicide rates are among elderly men (age category 75+), but in many countries the highest suicide rates among females are found at a considerably younger age. This applies particularly to women in Scandinavian countries: the peak age for women in Norway and Iceland is between the ages of 45 and 54, and for Finnish women between the ages of 55 and 64.

Although the pattern is complex in detail, there is a high correlation between suicide and age in most countries. In 12 of the 14 European countries shown in Figures 13.1-3, the correlation between the suicide rate and age among males lay within the range from 0.78 to 0.91: the exceptions are Iceland (0.51) and Ireland (0.26). In 11 of these countries this correlation among females lay

Figure 13.3   Suicide and age: males in selected countries

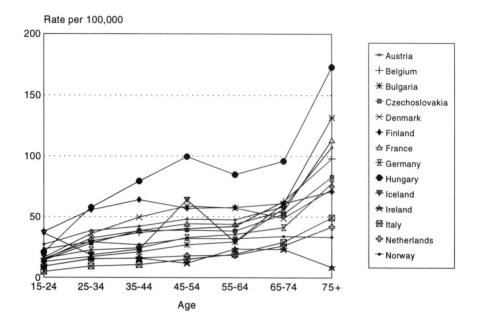

Source: WHO Statistics Annual (1989).

within the range from 0.77 and 0.98: the exceptions are Iceland (0.59), Norway (0.15) and Finland (0.10).

However, caution must be exercised in drawing conclusions about mechanisms. Kreitman (1988) showed that, at least in the UK, the rise in later life is largely a function of changing life circumstances with age. Figure 13.4 shows the age trends separated out according to whether people were single, married, widowed or divorced and Figure 13.5 shows the age trends after standardization for these family circumstances. The rise in suicide in early adult life remained after standardization, but that in later life was almost entirely removed.

Another way of considering age trends is to consider the proportion of deaths attributable to suicide within each age group. Among both males and females, suicides account for a substantial proportion of deaths among adolescents and young adults, but from the age of about 30 onwards, they account for a declining proportion, as the incidence of deaths from other causes increases with age.

Over the period between 1980 and 1990, the suicide risk among adolescents (11 to 18 years) varied from about 0.04 per cent to 0.2 per cent among countries that report statistics to the World Health Organization. The proportion of adolescents who have engaged in acts of parasuicide is between 40 and 100 times as high as the proportion who have actually ended their own lives.

Figure 13.4   Males: suicide rates by marital status, Scotland, 1973-83

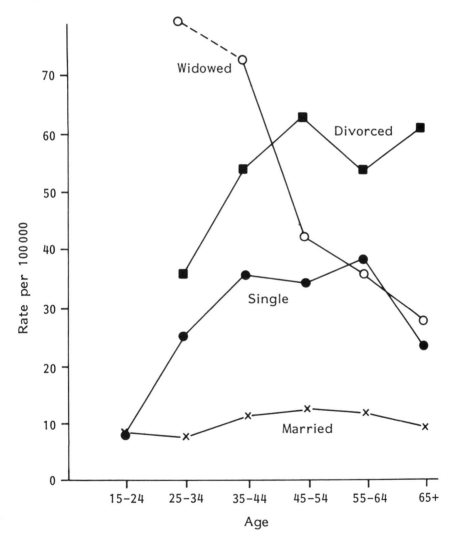

Source: WHO Statistics Annual (1989).

Figure 13.5   Male suicide rates: effects of marital status standardization, Scotland, 1973-83

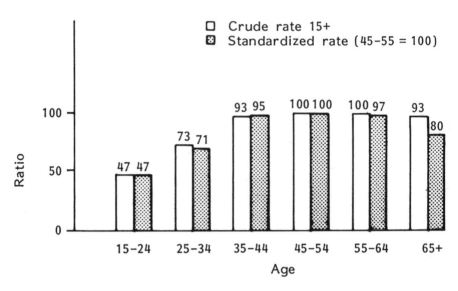

Source: Kreitman (1988).

TIME TRENDS IN SUICIDAL BEHAVIOUR

Suicide

For 16 of the countries listed in Table 13.2, suicide rates have been recorded for at least one hundred years, so there is a considerable body of data available about long-term trends (see Table 13.3). In nine of the 16 countries the national suicide rate reached an all-time high during the 1980s, whereas in seven countries the peak came earlier, in most instances in the first part of the twentieth century. Table 13.3 shows only European countries, but the USA is another country where the peak suicide rate was reached before the Second World War: the US rate at the beginning of the century was 10.2 per 100,000; it increased to 16.2 by 1915, then decreased sharply to reach 10.2 again in 1920. From 1925 it climbed to a maximum of 17.4 in 1932, but has since stayed below that level, reaching 13.3 in 1977, and 12.7 in 1987.

Table 13.3 Rates of suicide in Europe, 1881-1988

Rate per 100,000 population

	1881-90	1921-25	1951-54	1961-67	1972-74	1982-84	1987-88
Austria	16.1	28.3	23.0	21.9	23.6	28.0	25.0
Belgium	11.4	13.4	13.6	14.1	15.5	23.0	22.5
Denmark	22.5	13.8	23.5	18.3	24.6	28.9	28.0
Finland	3.9	12.7	17.4	20.7	24.2	24.6	27.6
France	20.7	19.5	15.5	15.5	15.8	21.8	22.1
Germany	20.9	22.1	18.6	18.9	20.6	21.4	17.9
Ireland	2.3	2.8	2.3	12.5	3.4	7.5	6.9
Italy	4.9	8.8	6.5	5.4	5.6	5.3	8.3
Netherlands	5.5	6.2	6.3	6.5	8.7	11.6	11.0
Norway	6.8	5.8	7.1	7.5	9.4	14.4	15.5
Portugal	.	6.9	10.2	.	8.7	10.2	8.1
Spain	2.4	5.6	5.9	6.0	4.3	7.2	7.8
Sweden	10.7	14.4	17.2	18.0	20.4	19.4	18.5
Switzerland	22.7	23.1	21.8	18.1	19.6	24.7	22.7
England and Wales	7.7	10.1	10.6	11.8	7.8	8.7	8.5
Scotland	5.5	6.6	5.6	8.5	8.3	10.7	11.9

'1987/88' refers to the last year reported in the World Health Statistics Annual (1989); the latest year is 1986 for some countries.

Source: Cavan (1928); Moens (1990); WHO databank.

Although the time trends vary considerably between countries, the averaged rate for the 16 European countries has risen substantially over the 100-year period (see Figure 13.6). Over the same period, the variation of the 16 countries around the European mean, and also the rank order of the countries, have remained fairly constant. This shows that cross-national differences in the prevalence of suicide are fairly stable, probably because they are determined by other persisting cross-national differences, for example, in traditions, customs, religious convictions, social attitudes, and climate. Nevertheless, there is some tendency for cross-national differences in suicide rates to diminish over time, since the standard deviation has remained more or less constant, while the mean has risen.

Figure 13.6   Suicide rates in European countries, 1881-1988

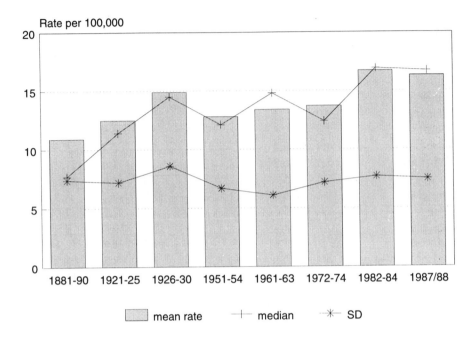

Averaged rates for 16 countries taken together, see Table 13.3;
Median rates and standard deviation (SD).

Source: Cavan (1928); Moens (1990); WHO databank.

Secular Trends Among Adolescents and Young Adults

Analysis of trends in suicide among young people is hampered by deficiencies
in the available statistics for those under the age of 15. Figure 13.7 shows
suicide rates as published by the World Health Organization (WHO 1972,
1981, 1992) in three selected years (1970, 1980, and 1988) for the 15 to 24
year age group. The crude suicide rates reported for children and early
adolescents (5-14 years of age) both within and outside Europe were very low.
Those authors (see Moens et al., 1988) who nevertheless have tried to analyse
the data for this age group have concluded that there appears to have been a

Figure 13.7a Suicide rates, 1970-1988

a) Males aged 15-24

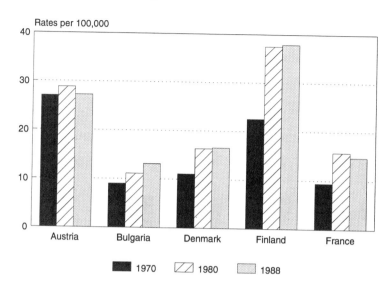

b) Females aged 15-24

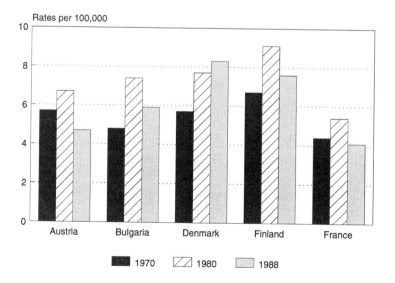

Austria: 1988 data.
Bulgaria, Denmark, Finland, France: 1987 data.

Figure 13.7b Suicide rates, 1970-1988

a) Males aged 15-24

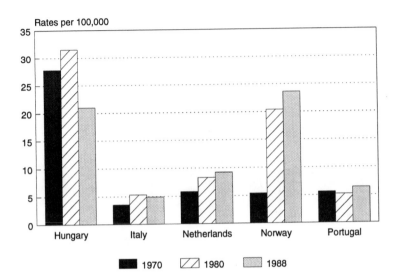

b) Females aged 15-24

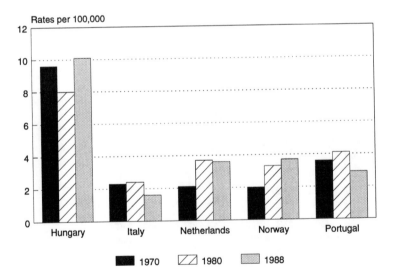

Portugal: 1988 data. Hungary, Netherlands, Norway: 1987 data.
Italy: 1986 data.

Figure 13.7c Suicide rates, 1970-1988

a) Males aged 15-24

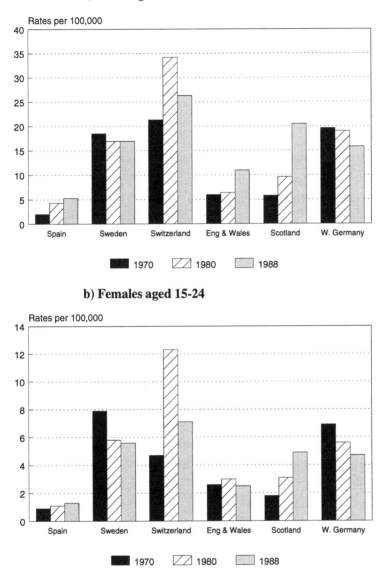

b) Females aged 15-24

Spain: 1985 data. Switzerland: 1986 data.
England & Wales, Scotland, West Germany: 1987 data. Sweden: 1988 data.

Source: World Health Organization.

trend towards an increase of suicides among boys, at least up to 1984, in most European countries.

However, since the value of the statistics for children aged 5-14 is unclear, it is best to confine the analysis to the 15-24 age groups. There are substantial differences between the time trends shown for males as compared with females in these two age groups. In the case of males, there has been a considerable increase in most of the 17 European countries over the past two decades or so. The only notable exception is West Germany. In most countries, the increase in rates was greatest in the period from 1970 to the early 1980s. In the period 1983-1986 the earlier upward trend levelled off or even reversed in a number of countries, although rates remained significantly above the level of 1970.

For young females the picture is different. Although about half of European countries showed an upward trend between 1970 and 1980, there is a substantial minority (7 countries) where no upward trend was shown. By 1987 or 1988, the suicide rate for young females in most countries was at around its 1970 level, or even lower.

The pattern of increasing rates among young males and stable or decreasing rates among young females also applies to countries outside Europe with a population predominantly of European descent, such as Canada and the USA; it also applies partially to Australia, but in that case not to females aged 15-24. It does not seem to apply, however, to Asian countries like Japan, or to Latin-American countries like Chile.

The second feature of the trends over time in suicide rates is the marked difference in pattern between age groups. The increase seen in younger males is not at all evident in older age groups of either sex in most countries. Figure 13.8 shows the UK figures for males aged 15-24 and those age 45+ (Murphy et al., 1986). In sharp contrast to the rising rate of suicide in young males, the rate has *fallen* over the same period of time in men (and women) age 45 or older. The data from other countries are broadly similar.

Thus, Figure 13.9 portrays the trends over time for Sweden between 1952 and 1981 (Asgård et al., 1987) in terms of the change in suicide risk over this time period for different age groups of men. The risk more than doubled over the 30-year period for those aged 15 to 19, and it more than trebled for those aged 20 to 24. By sharp contrast, the risk remained virtually unchanged (with a marginal overall decrease) for those aged 50 or more. In females, the age contrast was much less marked, with a variable trend for an increase in risk for all age groups.

Figure 13.8   **Male suicides per 100,000 population for alternate five-year age groups: UK, 1921-1925 to 1976-1980**

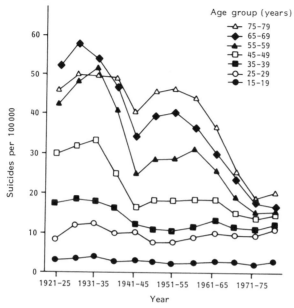

Source: Murphy et al. (1986).

Figure 13.9   **Relative male suicide risk change (RR) by age with 95 per cent confidence interval: Sweden, 1952-1981**

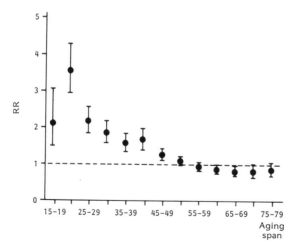

An RR-value = 1 signifies no change.

Source: Asgärd et al. (1987).

One consequence of the age difference in secular trends in risk of suicide is that young people today account for a considerably higher proportion of suicides than they did some years ago. Figures 13.10 and 13.11 illustrate this with data from the Netherlands and from the USA for 1970 and 1987.

Figure 13.10 Suicides in each age group as a percentage of all suicides: the Netherlands, 1965-87

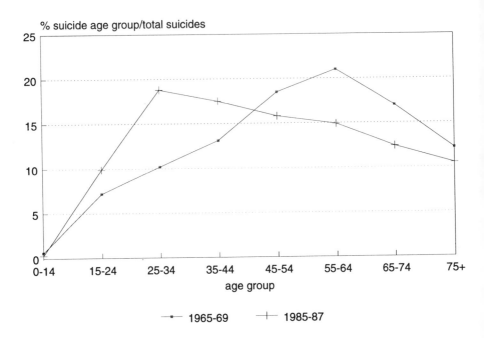

10 year age groups.

Source: WHO databank (data for the Netherlands).

A number of studies using birth cohort methods have confirmed this pattern of a shift in the balance of risk towards younger age groups, and towards young males, over the past two to three decades (up to about 1982-83), not only for the USA (Murphy & Wetzel, 1980; Lester, 1984) and the Benelux countries (Belgium and the Netherlands, Moens, 1990), but also for other countries such as Canada (Solomon & Hellon, 1980; Reed et al., 1985; Barnes et al., 1986), Australia (Goldney & Katsikitis, 1983), West Germany (Häfner & Schmidtke,

Figure 13.11 Suicides in each age group as a percentage of all suicides: USA 1970-87

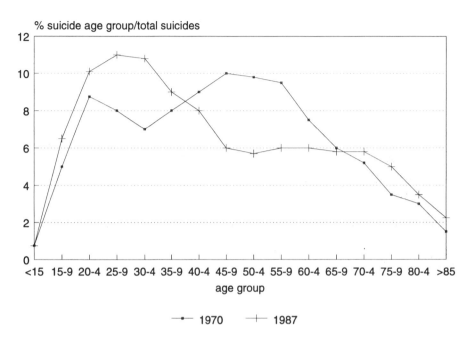

% suicide age group/total suicides

age group

—•— 1970   —+— 1987

5-year age groups.

Source: Tsuang & Buda (1990) data for USA.

1985), England & Wales (Murphy et al., 1986), Italy (La Vecchia et al., 1986), and Sweden (Asgård et al., 1987).

A result of these changes is that suicide rates for adolescents and young adults in most of the European countries listed in Table 13.3 reached an all-time high in the period between 1980 and 1987. The same is true for the USA. Figures 13.12 and 13.13 illustrate this point by presenting the suicide rates for young people over the period 1900 through 1987 in the Netherlands and the USA. In both countries there were two conspicuous peaks in youth suicide mortality over the course of the present century: one around 1910, and another, higher one around 1980. This pattern has been observed in other European countries as well. It is worth recalling that the first scientific meeting on suicide ever held took place in Vienna in 1910. The meeting was organized by the

Viennese Psychoanalytic Society and chaired by Alfred Adler, while Sigmund Freud was one of the discussants. The special topic of the meeting was suicide among adolescents. Increased rates of youth suicide in Austria and other European countries, and several so-called 'school epidemics' at that time had aroused public and professional concerns.

Figure 13.12 Suicide rates, 1900-87: the Netherlands

Rate per 100,000

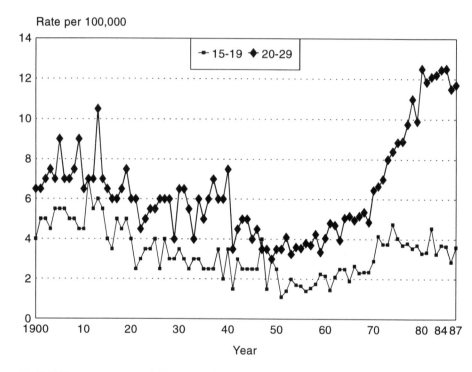

Until 1950 age groups are 16-20 and 21-29 years.

Source: Central Bureau of Statistics.

The graphs for the Netherlands and the USA show both similarities and differences. After an all-time low around 1950, the rates rose rapidly in both countries until around 1980, when they reached the level of the 1910 period and then rose still higher to all-time highs. However, in the Netherlands, in contrast to the USA, this pattern was shown only for the 20-29 age group, in males as well as in females. For the 15-19 age group, suicide rates after 1950 rose much more slowly, and, although they increased substantially, they remained below the level reached at the beginning of the century.

Figure 13.13 Suicide rates, 1900-87: USA

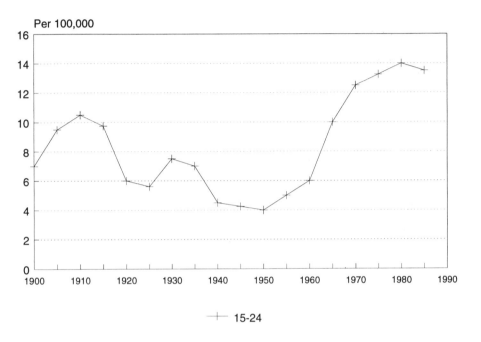

Source: Tsuang & Buda (1990).

In summary, the rate of suicide among male adolescents and young men increased markedly in the postwar period up to the early or mid-1980s, when an all-time high was reached in many European countries. The time trends for young females have been much less consistent; in about half the countries there was some rise, but in the other half rates tended to fall or remained fairly stable. Most strikingly, the rise in suicide rate in young men has been paralleled by a fall in rate in older men. Since the early to mid-1980s, the suicide rates in young people have levelled off cr even decreased, first in women and then in men, in some but certainly not in all countries. One of the exceptions is Great Britain, where rates among males 15-24 years old were still climbing in the late 1980s, although this was not the case for young females, whose suicide rate fell over the same time period (Hawton, 1992).

Parasuicide

Local studies of records kept by centres that treat people who have harmed themselves provide the only available data on time trends in parasuicide. Only a few countries have centres that have monitored episodes of parasuicide within defined populations for one decade or more. The records of such centres in the United Kingdom (see Kreitman, 1977; Hawton & Fagg, 1992; Hawton et al., 1982; Gibbons et al., 1979; Jones, 1977; Platt et al., 1988), the Netherlands (Diekstra, 1989a), West Germany (Schmidtke, 1992), Italy (Crepet, 1986) and Spain (Noguera, 1986) indicate that the incidence of parasuicide increased markedly in the period from the early 1950s to the mid-1970s or early 1980s. Figure 13.14 shows the data for males in Edinburgh, Scotland for the 1968 to 1982 time period (Platt & Kreitman, 1984). Over this 14-year time-span the rate rose by well over 60 per cent. A similar development was noted in the USA (Weissman, 1974).

Figure 13.14 Unemployment and incidence of parasuicide in men in Edinburgh, 1968-82

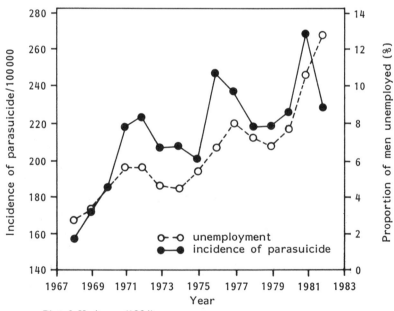

Source: Platt & Kreitman (1984).

Since the late 1970s or early 1980s, a decrease in parasuicide rates has been noted in the following European countries: the United Kingdom (Hawton & Fagg, 1992; Platt et al., 1988), Italy (Crepet, 1986), the Netherlands (Diekstra, 1989a), Spain (Noguera, 1986) and West Germany (Schmidtke, 1992). This decline, however, was observed earlier in some countries (such as Great Britain from 1981 onwards) than in others (such as the Netherlands from 1983 onwards, see Platt, 1986) and also earlier in women (for example, Great Britain from 1977 onwards, see Hawton & Fagg, 1992 and Platt, 1988) than in men. The decline in parasuicide rates also seems to be more marked among women then among men (all age groups) – see Figure 13.15 for trends in Oxford, England.

Figure 13.15 Rates of attempted suicide by adolescents in Oxford City 1976-89, shown as three-year moving averages, by sex and age group

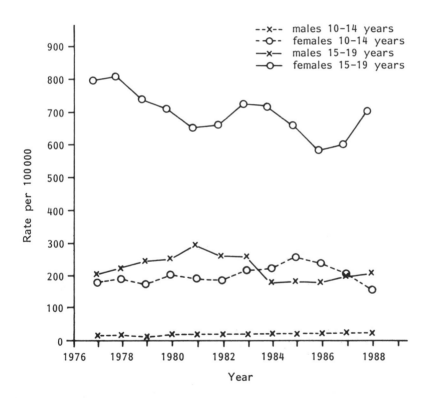

Source: Hawton & Fagg (1992).

Among adolescents and young adults (approximately aged 20-34) these time trends were exaggerated: there was a steeper rise over the 20 years up to 1975, and then a steeper decline. The rates for this age group in 1988 were about the same as in 1970, although they were just above the 1970 level for males, and just below it for females. Among those aged 15-19, the rates in 1988 were still clearly above the 1970 level, but considerably more so for males than for females. Consequently, the female preponderance in parasuicides among adolescents and young adults has reduced over the past 20 years.

Conclusions on Time Trends

It may be concluded that a true increase in suicide and parasuicide occurred between the early 1950s and the early 1980s among the adolescent and young adult (but not older adult) populations of Europe and North America. The data on suicide and parasuicide converge in showing a particularly sharp increase among young males. In the last dozen years, however, there has been some divergence, with suicide rates in young males continuing to rise, those in young females remaining more stable, and parasuicide rates falling in many (but by no means all) countries.

It may seem reasonable to assume that an increase in parasuicide will lead to an increase in suicide, and therefore, that there is likely to be a close relationship between the two trends. In fact, however, the exact nature of any such relationship remains unclear. One reason for this is the lack of comparable information. Data on parasuicide rates come from local studies of the records of treatment centres, whereas data on suicide rates come from national statistics on the causes of all recorded deaths. It is necessary to exercise extreme caution in drawing definite conclusions from comparisons between such disparate sources of data. Furthermore, data on parasuicide are available in only a few European countries for the period beginning in the mid-1950s when suicide rates among the young began to rise.

The complexity of the relationship between suicide and parasuicide is underlined by the finding that in a number of countries the recent decline in parasuicide rate was not accompanied by a similar decline in suicide rate. This may be because the decline in parasuicide is mainly a decline in certain specific types of parasuicidal act. Preliminary results of the WHO Parasuicide Monitoring Study (Schmidtke, 1992) suggest that while the proportion of the general population who have engaged in a parasuicidal act may be decreasing, the proportion of 'repeaters' among those who have ever engaged in a parasuicidal act may be increasing. Since the risk of a fatal outcome is higher among repeaters than among first-timers, a decrease in either the prevalence or the incidence of parasuicide might not automatically lead to a decrease in the suicide rate.

In addition, there is a current debate as to whether or not the observed decline in parasuicide rate is an artefact (Platt et al., 1988). On that hypothesis, the 'true' population rate may have remained unchanged or even increased; it is only that parasuicides or their families have become less willing to consult medical agencies, or that general practitioners have become more likely to treat these patients themselves and less likely to refer them to hospitals or specialist centres. The great majority of parasuicidal acts do not lead to contact with medical agencies, according to the few studies that provide information on this point. For example a community survey study in the Netherlands (Diekstra & van de Loo, 1978) found that only about 25 per cent of cases of parasuicide were seen by medical agencies. A recent study in the United States (CDC, 1991) among students in grades 9-12 in 50 states found that 8.3 per cent of students had engaged in a parasuicidal act, and 24 per cent of these (almost the same proportion as found in the earlier Dutch study) had been in contact with medical agencies following such an act.

Because the parasuicides recorded by centres are only the tip of the iceberg, as has also been observed for a large variety of other mental disorders, it may well be argued that the observed decline in recorded instances of parasuicide reflects a decline in the proportion that are recorded. The iceberg may be sinking further under water.

Although the interpretation of the limited data on parasuicide, and the relationship between parasuicide and suicide, are both debatable, the conclusion that the rate of suicide among young people increased in the three decades from around 1955 is well established. The purpose of the rest of this chapter is to evaluate the possible causes of this increase in the light of the available evidence. This is a very complex problem, which can only be tackled in a preliminary way from the existing research. On the one hand, it would clearly be insufficient to point to changes in social conditions that accompanied the increase in rates of suicide, for any causal explanation must be rooted in an account of the mechanisms involved. On the other hand, studies of the causal pathways leading to suicide may well tend to overlook predisposing conditions within the wider society that are not among the central causes of any particular suicide, but tend to increase the likelihood that suicides will occur. Similarly, weather conditions may constitute predisposing conditions for traffic accidents, but yet not rank among the main causes of most accidents. Given that a complex behaviour like suicide is determined by a multitude of causes, studies of causal pathways may tend not to focus on those causes that are most significant in explaining change over time.

In seeking to explain time trends, we need to find variables that are both known to play a part in the causal mechanism leading to some form of suicidal behaviour, and whose changes over a specified period are related to changes in the prevalence or incidence of suicidal behaviours. In practice, there are so far no research programmes that address these two issues in conjunction. By default, it is necessary to piece together information from a variety of studies that did not aim to explain secular trends. Inevitably, only preliminary conclusions can be drawn from an analysis of that kind. The next step is to review the findings on risk factors for suicidal behaviours in adolescence, so as to identify a number of causal factors that are candidates for explanation of observed time trends.

CAUSAL PATHWAYS LEADING TO SUICIDAL BEHAVIOUR IN ADOLESCENTS

There are no clear-cut, generally accepted answers to the question why adolescents commit suicidal acts. Suicide and parasuicide are behaviours and not in themselves diseases, although they may be, and often are, symptoms or expressions of psychological disorders. There are many different pathways to this kind of behaviour. Usually, suicidal behaviour results from the convergence of multiple predisposing and immediate risk factors, and these risk factors must come together in the absence of multiple protective factors (see Vaillant & Blumenthal, 1990). People move in and out of suicidal crises at different points over their life cycle as a result of changes in the balance between these risk and protective factors. We know little, however, about whether suicide and parasuicide are the same phenomena in adolescence as in adulthood, or about whether they have different meanings and sets of risk factors within the different phases of adolescence.

In part, our lack of understanding can be attributed to the relative dearth of prospective longitudinal research in this field. In part, it can also be attributed to the fact that opportunities for collection of valid data are often very limited. In most cases, data can only be collected after the suicide or parasuicide has taken place. Once a suicide has occurred, the subject can no longer be a source of information. The investigator has to rely on personal documents or other materials that the victim has left behind, or on information from persons such as relatives, friends, doctors or therapists who had contact with the deceased.

Their awareness that the person later committed suicide may strongly influence their testimonies about what happened before (the so-called 'effort after meaning' phenomenon). Nevertheless, well-conducted case-control studies can be highly informative (Gould et al., 1990). Also, during the last few years valuable data on the predictors of completed suicide have been provided by several long-term studies of children and adolescents with psychiatric disorders (see below).

It has sometimes been suggested that suicide researchers can resort to the 'method of substitutes', that is, can use parasuicides or people expressing suicidal ideas to represent suicides. But the problems with doing so are substantial. First, there is the problem that those who kill themselves are in a number of ways a different population from those who threaten or attempt to do so without fatal outcome. Second, a parasuicidal act and its psychological and practical effects may influence the accounts given by the subjects themselves and by their friends and relatives of what happened before the act. Such retrospective colouring will be greater for some types of information than for others. Demographic data or information on social conditions will be less affected than information about psychological and interpersonal states or conditions preceding or eliciting the suicidal act. For that reason, many researchers have confined themselves to studying social and demographic characteristics of suicidal persons, and the majority of scales designed to predict suicidal behaviour mainly consist of variables of this kind.

A third difficulty is that measurement of personality characteristics, such as cognitive styles, and reliable diagnosis of psychiatric conditions, is complex and time consuming. It is often difficult to get large enough samples to permit adequate statistical analyses. In addition, the choice of appropriate control groups with which to compare suicidal persons, so as to draw valid conclusions about their distinctive characteristics, is difficult.

Where characteristics have been identified that distinguish suicidal from non-suicidal adolescents, these descriptive distinctions do not necessarily imply causal mechanisms. Usually, such characteristics have been identified one at a time. Although some studies have looked into sets of interrelated characteristics at different levels of aggregation, most have studied single variables or variables only at either the individual or the total population level (for example, Herjanic & Welner, 1980; Petzel & Riddle, 1981; Spirito et al., 1989; Blumenthal, 1990; Kienhorst et al., 1990b, 1991; de Wilde et al., 1992, 1993).

The following review considers four main categories of variables: characteristics directly related to the suicidal act, such as method, intent, and motives expressed by adolescents; characteristics of the social environment (ecological variables); characteristics of individual psychology or psychopathology; and behavioural correlates of suicide and parasuicide.

Method, Intent and Reasons Given for Suicidal Acts

Although there are large international variations, the following is a broad description of methods of parasuicide and suicide in European countries. Most parasuicidal acts by adolescents involve poisoning, such as drug overdose (Hawton, 1986; Hawton & Goldacre, 1982; Kienhorst et al., 1991). Other, less common parasuicidal acts are cutting, piercing, jumping from high places, jumping in front of a moving vehicle, hanging and drowning. In the case of completed suicide by adolescents, poisoning is again a relatively common method, but so is hanging, jumping, drowning, shooting a firearm, and car exhaust fumes. Generally, males are more likely than females to use 'harder' or more aggressive methods, which at least partially explains the higher degree of fatality of suicidal acts among males. There is also a relationship between availability of means and methods commonly employed in a given community or population. It has, for example, been shown that in some parts of the United States restrictive licensing of handguns was associated with a prompt decline in suicide by firearms (Garland & Zigler, 1993). Restriction of availability of other methods such as certain types of poison (see Bowles, in press) and toxic gas (see World Health Organization, 1982) has been shown to have a similar effect. Little is known, however, about the causal mechanisms of such effects, their duration and the mechanisms of change towards other means or methods. It is also important to note that in many suicidal acts, multiple methods, such as the combination of psychotropic drugs and alcohol, are used (see Kreitman, 1977).

As to suicide intent, a number of studies, all with regard to parasuicide, that employed the Suicide Intent Scale as developed by Beck and co-workers (Beck et al., 1974) found that on a scale of 0 to 13, parasuicidal adolescents scored an average of about 7 (standard deviation ranges between 3 and 4); this shows that elements of an intention to end their lives were present in many cases, and that the majority of these behaviours cannot be dismissed as manipulative or attention-getting devices (Hawton et al., 1982; Kienhorst et al., 1991). Perhaps surprisingly, comparison between the mean intent scores of adolescent and adult parasuicides showed no difference (see Kerkhof, 1985).

A few studies have looked (after the event) into the parasuicidal persons' self-reported motives for their acts. Bancroft and colleagues (Bancroft,

Skrimshire & Simkin, 1976; Bancroft, Hawton, Simkin & Kingston, 1979) formulated a number of possible motives for parasuicide. The endorsements by 50 British (Hawton et al., 1982) and 48 Dutch adolescents (Kienhorst et al., in revision) of these motives are strikingly congruent: the ones most frequently endorsed were the wish to stop a certain state of mind or to escape from a painful situation. All formulations of the appeal motive ('drawing attention') and revenge motive were endorsed by only a minority of the adolescents. Interestingly, clinicians gave far more weight to the appeal motive (Hawton et al., 1982).

Characteristics of the Social Environment

A large number of studies have looked into the associations between adolescent suicidal behaviours and possible causative factors such as early parental loss through death or divorce, parental disharmony, parental unemployment, family deprivation and poverty, parental (chronic) mental or physical illness, physical and sexual abuse of the child or adolescent by parents, victimization by peers, unemployment in the adolescent, unwanted pregnancy, and exposure to suicidal models at home, in peers, or in the media.

The overall conclusion from these studies is that, at the aggregate level (town or nation), the presence of these conditions, separately or concurrently, is usually accompanied by an increase in the risk of both suicide and parasuicide, but the causal mechanisms involved remain obscure. In addition, many of those conditions are also accompanied by an increase in other deviant behaviours or disorders, implying that they are not specifically 'suicidogenic'. For example, most studies comparing suicidal adolescents with depressed non-suicidal adolescents (without a history of parasuicidal acts or suicidal ideation) have found that the two groups are not clearly distinguished on the basis of these conditions, with the exception of physical and sexual abuse, quality of parental support and exposure to suicidal models.

A number of recent studies have shown that suicidal adolescents are somewhat more likely to have a history of physical and sexual abuse than both normal adolescents, and those who are depressed or otherwise psychiatrically disturbed but not suicidal (Bayatpour et al., 1992; de Wilde et al., 1992; Garnefski et al., 1992; Riggs et al., 1990). However, the differences between suicide attempts and depressed adolescents tend to be much less than those between these two groups and normal samples. Phares and Compas (1992) examined suicidal and non-suicidal pre-adolescent psychiatric in-patients and found that the suicidal children were significantly more likely to have a physically abusive biological father and a physically abusive mother than the non-suicidal children. There was no difference between the two groups in family history of alcoholism, depression, antisocial activities, personality disorders or psychotic disorders, a finding that has been confirmed in a study by Pfeffer and colleagues (1989) with suicidal and non-suicidal adolescent in-patients.

A number of studies have found differences in perceived parental support between suicidal and non-suicidal adolescents. Jacobs (1971) reported an accumulation of stressful events from the onset of puberty among adolescent parasuicides that was not found among normal adolescents. De Wilde et al. (1992) reported a similar difference between parasuicidal and depressed non-suicidal adolescents. Particularly during the 12 months preceding the parasuicidal act, the differences found in both studies were substantial. Among the stressful events that preceded parasuicide, there was a preponderance of ones that resulted in breakdown of social and emotional support and family relations.

D'Attilio and colleagues (1992) investigated the relationship between quantity and perceived quality of social support on the one hand and risk of suicide on the other hand in a number of adolescent populations. They concluded that perceived quality of social support was the single variable that explained the greatest proportion of variance in risk of suicide. It seems that it is particularly the absence or breakdown of parental support that is important. Kienhorst et al. (1992) found that adolescents who had performed a parasuicidal act reported less perceived support and understanding from their parents than depressed non-suicidal adolescents, but there was no similar difference in perceived support from persons other than their parents.

Against this background it comes as no surprise that problems with their parents are most frequently given by parasuicidal adolescents as the main reason for their parasuicidal acts (Mansmann & Schenck, 1983; Kienhorst et al., 1987). Miller et al. (1992) found that suicidal adolescents (n=15), in comparison with psychiatric (n=14) and normal (n=14) controls rated their families as the least cohesive and most rigid.

Exposure to Suicidal Models

Although no study has yet clearly demonstrated a causal relation between exposure to suicide or suicidal behaviour and the risk of suicidal behaviour among adolescents, there is enough evidence to suggest that this is a promising line of research. Attention has focused on exposure to models within the family and immediate circle, and through the media. As to the first, it appears that parasuicidal adolescents report more people in their immediate family and intimate circle who attempted or committed suicide than do non-suicidal 'normal' adolescents, depressed non-suicidal adolescents, or adolescents who have at one time or another harboured suicidal thoughts but have never performed a parasuicidal act (Jacobs, 1971; Smith & Crawford, 1986; Conrad, 1992; Kienhorst et al., 1992). Social modelling is not, however, the only possible explanation of these findings. An alternative possibility is that the cause of the elevated risk of parasuicide is increased stress associated with living with a suicidal person.

Modelling might also occur within the context of a peer group or school community. Several studies (for example, Robbins & Conroy, 1983; Gould & Shaffer, 1986; Brent et al., 1989; Philips & Carstensen, 1986; Davidson et al., 1989) have described clustering of teenage suicides or parasuicides in specific groups or schools. Although Robbins & Conroy suggested 'contagion' as a possible cause for parasuicide, Davidson et al. (1989) reported that adolescents who had committed suicide (n=14) were no more likely than non-suicidal control subjects (n=42) to have been exposed to suicide as measured by their acquaintance with a person who committed suicide.

As to media exposure, there is some evidence of an effect on adolescent suicidal behaviour, but it is rather unclear what mechanisms are involved. Although Kessler et al. (1988) could find no relationship between exposure to fictional films or television newscasts about suicide on the one hand and adolescent suicidal behaviour, a number of studies do support the hypothesis of such a relationship (Philips & Carstensen 1986; Ostroff et al., 1987). Not only is an increase in adolescent suicidal behaviour observed, but the effect is specific in that the increase is in the use of a suicide method identical to the one shown in the film or newscast (Schmidtke & Häfner, 1988; Ostroff et al., 1987). Moreover, there is some evidence that the effect of media exposure is greater on adolescents than on adults (Schmidtke & Häfner, 1988), even if the 'model' was not an adolescent (Philips & Carstensen, 1986).

However, since all of these studies are correlational in nature, one cannot automatically conclude that an increase in suicides after (media) exposure of suicide demonstrates the existence of imitation. Imitation effects have to be established in controlled experiments, and thus far there are only two studies that have used such an experimental design. From their study exposing 116 high school students to different video-simulated conditions, Steede and Range (1989) concluded that adolescents may not be influenced by news about suicide or may just deny such influence. In another experimental study, Range et al. (1988) reported that their 142 subjects were influenced by exposure to material on suicide and there was evidence that their behaviour would be affected.

Chapter 7 summarizes the results of a number of studies that show relationships between short-term fluctuations in rates of suicide and dramatic examples of suicide that were widely disseminated by the media.

Individual Characteristics of People Committing Suicide

The data on the characteristics of individuals completing suicide derive from both case-control and follow-up studies, the findings from these two very different research strategies being closely similar. Gould et al. (1990) compared 173 young people (under age 20) who committed suicide with a matched group of parasuicides and a random general population sample. Approximately a quarter of those who committed suicide had attempted suicide previously and about half had previously consulted a mental health professional. In both sexes, suicide was very strongly associated with a prior attempt and with major depression. In males, but not females, substance abuse and, to a lesser extent, antisocial behaviour were associated with suicide. A family history of suicide or parasuicide was also about twice as common in the suicide group as in the general population control sample.

Hawton et al. (1993) compared parasuicide subjects who committed suicide during a long-term follow-up with those who did not. The two variables that best discriminated the groups were substance abuse and a previous in-patient psychiatric admission. Rao et al. (1993) found that 4.4 per cent of children (7 out of 159) with a major depressive disorder committed suicide during the subsequent 10 years compared with zero per cent in subjects with anxiety disorders and normal controls (all figures are so far based on an incomplete follow-up).

Individual Psychopathology and Parasuicide

Follow-up studies also provide the best data on the risk factors for parasuicide among individuals who have been referred for some form of psychiatric disorder. The findings are consistent in showing that the main risk stems from affective disorder (rather than from any other type of psychiatric condition), and that the risk is particularly great in the case of severe depressive disorders, being least for adjustment disorders with depressed mood (Brent et al., 1993; Kovacs et al., 1993; Strober et al., 1993). Harrington et al.'s (in press) long-term follow-up (a mean of 18 years) of children and adolescents treated for a psychiatric disorder also showed that depression in childhood was a strong predictor of parasuicide in early adult life. However, the risk seemed to come about largely because childhood depression was associated with a much increased risk for major depressive disorder in adult life. Conduct disorder increased the risk for parasuicide in the absence of childhood depression, but not in its presence.

As is further discussed in Chapter 11, depressive mood and depressive disorder are among the strongest correlates of suicidal behaviour (Chabrol & Moron, 1988; Crumley, 1982; Friedman et al., 1984; Kienhorst et al., 1990b). Also, they are related to several of the most salient psychological and behavioural characteristics of suicidal adolescents, such as low self-esteem, and drug abuse.

A number of recent studies have shown that many of the generally observed differences between adolescent parasuicides and other groups of adolescents arise because most of the parasuicidal adolescents are also subject to affective disorders or depressed mood (Kienhorst et al., 1992; de Wilde et al., 1993; Lewinsohn et al., 1993). For example, many adolescent suicides or parasuicides share characteristics such as low self-esteem or a tendency towards social withdrawal and isolation (Yanish & Battle, 1985; Kienhorst et al., 1990b) with non-suicidal depressed adolescents.

According to a number of authors, however, one feature that distinguishes suicidal from non-suicidal depressed persons is hopelessness. Indeed the correlation between suicidal intent and depression is influenced by hopelessness, both among adults (Minkoff et al., 1973; Salter & Platt, 1990; Wetzel et al., 1980) and among children (Kazdin et al., 1983), and hopelessness appears to be a predictor of completed suicide in (psychiatric) adults (Beck et al., 1985).

For adolescents, however, the picture is less clear. On the one hand, Topol and Reznikoff (1982) found a significant difference in hopelessness between hospitalized suicidal adolescents and hospitalized non-suicidal adolescents. On the other hand, Asarnow et al. (1987) observed that the correlation in children and young adolescents between hopelessness and suicidality decreased considerably after controlling for depression. Rotherham-Borus and Trautman (1988) found no significant difference in hopelessness between adolescent female parasuicides and a matched group of psychiatrically disturbed adolescents.

In conclusion, although suicidal behaviour and depressive disturbances are very closely related, nevertheless the majority of depressed adolescents do not attempt or commit suicide, and not all adolescents who commit suicide or perform parasuicidal acts suffer from diagnosable depressive disorders. Hence, depression and the propensity to suicide or parasuicide are by no means the same thing.

Given the comorbidity of anxiety and depression, it is surprising how little research is done on the relation between anxiety disturbances and suicidal behaviour in adolescents. In the case of adults, some studies have indicated that suicidal persons have a higher level of anxiety than non-suicidal controls (Kreitman, 1977; Diekstra, 1973, 1981), but others (Schmidtke & Schaller, 1992) were unable to find any difference on either state or trait anxiety between suicidal and non-suicidal psychiatric patients, although differences on these dimensions were reported between their patient groups and normal controls. As to adolescents, de Wilde et al. (1993) found no differences in trait or state anxiety between adolescent parasuicides and depressed adolescents who had not engaged in any parasuicidal act. However, both these groups reported more state and trait anxiety than a group of 'normal' adolescents. Very few suicidal adolescents reported strong feelings of anxiety in the last days and hours before their parasuicidal act (Kienhorst et al., in revision).

Individual Psychology and Suicidal Behaviour

Two broad categories of psychological characteristics of suicidal adolescents have been investigated: perceptual-cognitive styles, and personality traits such as neuroticism or impulsivity.

Cognitive Styles and Suicidal Behaviour

The hypothesis that the cognitive organization of self-destructive people is a critical variable in suicidal behaviour has a great attraction for those interested in its nature and causes (Weishaar & Beck, 1990; Schmidtke & Schaller, 1992). Neuringer (1976) stated that the way life experiences are perceived, coded, organized and understood is the basic clue to the explanation why a person acts to end his existence. He and a number of more recent authors on the subject (Arffa, 1983; Weishaar & Beck, 1990) believe that cognitive variables directly related to suicidal behaviour have been identified. According to these authors the research (mainly on adults) has convincingly demonstrated that suicidal persons compared to non-suicidal persons (Neuringer & Lettieri, 1982; Weishaar & Beck, 1990):

* have impoverished internal judgemental processes;

- have a stronger tendency towards polarized (dichotomous or 'black-and-white') thinking;
- are more rigid and constricted in their thinking and problem solving;
- are much more present-oriented and have an inability to project or imagine themselves into the future.

However, there are several reasons to hesitate before drawing these conclusions. First, most of the research has been done on parasuicidal persons and ideators who did not later commit suicide. Second, most of the suicidal subjects were psychiatric patients tested at some time fairly soon after the suicidal act. The question here is whether the patterns of thought that are characteristic of suicidal patients at that time are indeed associated with propensity to suicide rather than the high level of stress during the period following a suicidal act. These patterns of thought might be shared with persons under high levels of stress in general instead of being specific to persons with a propensity to suicide.

Research by Neuringer and Lettieri (1982), however, seems to point in the opposite direction. They took daily measures of dichotomous thinking from high-risk, medium-risk, low-risk and zero-risk suicidal persons over a three-week period following a suicidal crisis. They reported that the high-risk suicidal subjects were far more extreme in their dichotomizations than the others. They also reported that this extreme dichotomous thinking did not diminish over time. The authors drew the conclusion that extreme polarization of thinking found in suicidal individuals is not a temporary state produced by stress but a dispositional characteristic of the individual. But this conclusion has been contested by other researchers (see Diekstra, 1973; Schmidtke & Schaller, 1992) who indicated that severely depressed patients are also characterized by an extreme level of polarized thinking, so that depression and not suicidality *per se* might be the crucial correlate. But, more importantly, in the recent study by Schmidtke & Schaller (1992) comparing parasuicides, non-suicidal psychiatric patients, and normal controls, it was demonstrated that cognitive rigidity is a common feature of persons in crises and depressive states and that dichotomous thinking is probably a state rather than a trait variable.

This conclusion also seems to be valid for adolescents. A few studies have investigated the role of inflexibility or rigidity in thinking and problem solving in suicidal behaviour among prepubertal children (Cohen-Sandler,1982; Orbach et al., 1987) and adolescents. Puskar et al. (1992) found that adolescent parasuicides, contrary to a non-suicidal group, used only affect-oriented coping methods, whereas the others used problem-oriented methods as well.

However, it remains questionable if this difference was specifically related to the propensity to suicide, since there were so many other differences between the control and experimental groups besides the experience of parasuicide. The same applies, in essence, to the studies by Hart et al. (1988) who found that adolescent parasuicides displayed more attributional errors as compared to psychiatric controls, and by Kahn (1987), who found that suicidal adolescents, compared to non-suicidal adolescents, experienced difficulties in coping with their emotions and could not think through the consequences of their actions.

Topol & Reznikoff (1982) reported a significantly more external locus of control in hospitalized adolescent parasuicides than normal adolescents. De Wilde et al. (1993) confirmed these results, but added that the locus of control was no more external among suicidal adolescents than among a comparable group of depressed non-suicidal adolescents.

Kienhorst et al. (1992) found that adolescents who had performed a parasuicidal act evaluated comparable life events as more negative than non-suicidal depressed adolescents. They suggested that one possible explanation for this difference could be that compared with non-suicidal depressed adolescents, parasuicidal adolescents more often show a tendency towards a negative evaluation of comparable events, or are more outspoken in expressing such evaluations; but these authors added that it remains unclear whether such a tendency is state- or trait-dependent (Perrah & Wichman, 1987).

The overall conclusion then is that the evidence for a core cognitive organization that is related to fatal or non-fatal suicidal behaviour among adolescents is still weak. It may be that certain subgroups of suicidal adolescents are characterized by a particular and more or less stable cognitive organization that makes them more prone to suicidal behaviour. Among other subgroups, suicidality might be the outcome of a similar but transient cognitive organization produced by specific events or stimuli. Present knowledge, however, is not capable of making a valid distinction between these categories.

Personality Traits

A number of authors (see Schmidtke, 1988) in their search for a suicidal personality, have tried to link specific personality traits with suicidality. For the most part, standard psychological tests such as the Minnesota Multiphasic Personality Inventory (MMPI) have been used to measure such traits, but there are also numerous studies that used less well-known instruments.

Neuroticism

Lester (1972) found that students who had attempted or threatened suicide had higher neuroticism scores than non-suicidal students. Koller and Castanos (1968) found that alcoholics who had a history of parasuicide had significantly higher neuroticism scores than non-suicidal alcoholics. Similar results were reported by McCulloch and Philip (1972) from a comparison of attempted suicides with normals on the neuroticism scale of Scheier and Cattell. Diekstra (1973, 1981) found no significant differences, either in the case of adolescents or in the case of adults, between non-suicidal psychiatric patients and psychiatric patients who had attempted or threatened suicide, although the latter two groups had a tendency to score higher on neuroticism. Schmidtke (1988) in his study of young suicidal ideators and attempters also found that they had higher scores on neuroticism (emotional instability) than controls.

Introversion-Extraversion

Koller and Castanos (1968), who used the Maudsley Personality Inventory (MPI) found no differences between suicidal and non-suicidal alcoholics on the extraversion scale. Diekstra (1973) too, found no differences between suicidal and non-suicidal psychiatric patients on the extraversion-scale of the Dutch version of MMPI. On the other hand Philip (reported by Kreitman, 1977) found that parasuicides had higher scores on social extraversion measured by the 16PF of Cattell than non-suicidal psychiatric patients had. Schmidtke (1988) on the other hand found that suicidal youngsters were generally more introverted.

Internal-external orientation

Equally contradictory are the results of studies regarding the relationship between internal-external orientation (I/E) and suicidality. Doroff (1968) compared adolescent parasuicidal girls with delinquent girls matched for age, social class and intelligence. The parasuicides showed a high degree of internalization of conflict contrasted with the acting out and externalization of conflict of the delinquent girls. Doroff, however, did not use the I/E scale by Rotter as did Williams and Nickels (1969). They found that both suicidal and accident-prone individuals were characterized by an external orientation: they viewed others or fate, rather than themselves, as responsible for the things that happened to them. Similar findings were reported by Neuringer & Lettieri

(1982) on the basis of a study comparing the I/E scores of hospitalized serious parasuicidal patients with non-suicidal patients.

Field dependency

From the studies of Williams and Nickels (1969) and Levenson (1974), Neuringer and Lettieri (1982) drew the conclusion that, especially in the case of young people, suicidal individuals tend to be controlled to a greater extent than others by outer stimuli rather than by inner promptings. This seems to suggest that suicidal persons in their behaviour as well as in their perceptions are dependent on environmental stimuli or cues. The best-known measure of field dependency in the perceptual sense is the Rod-and-Frame Test developed by Witkin. The subject is asked to make estimations of the upright in the absence of visual cues. He is seated in a dark room with a tiltable luminous rod placed before him first at one angle, then at another. The subject can manipulate the rod by instruments into a position which he feels is upright, while visual cues are not available. Levenson (1974, see Neuringer & Lettieri, 1982) found that suicidal individuals had greater difficulties in finding the true upright than other subjects.

Levenson and Neuringer (1974, see Neuringer & Lettieri, 1982) compared the scores of 84 male suicidal and 84 non-suicidal patients on subtests of the Wechsler Adult Intelligence Scale (WAIS) that are known for their high correlation with field dependency measures such as the Rod-and-Frame Test and the Embedded Figure Test (EFT). They found that the scores of the suicidal patients were significantly more in the direction of field dependency than those of the comparison group. On the other hand Diekstra (1973, 1981) compared adolescent and adult non-suicidal psychiatric patients with a group of psychiatric parasuicides and suicidal ideators and found no differences in EFT scores. Schmidtke and Schaller (1992) comparing suicidal and non-suicidal patients and normal controls also were unable to find evidence for a relationship between propensity to suicide and field dependence as measured by the EFT.

Impulsivity

Social extraversion, external orientation, and field dependency have often been associated with impulsivity. A number of authors (for example, Kessel, 1965) have argued that many suicidal acts, especially in younger people, are characterized by impulsivity. Leonard (1967) using a scale of impulsiveness found that students who had performed a parasuicidal act or had threatened to commit suicide scored higher than non-suicidal students. Iga and Ohara (1967) reported data collected by Kenshiro Ohara in Japan, who administered two temperament tests, of which one was the Thurstone Temperament Schedule, to parasuicidal young males and females and to control groups of female nurses and male applicants to the Japan Air Academy. On the Thurstone Test, the parasuicides proved to be less impulsive but also more insecure and sub-assertive.

Equally unclear or contradictory are the results of more recent studies. Hawton and Catalan (1987) found that two-thirds of their subjects in two studies (n=48; n=50) only thought about attempting suicide within one hour before their parasuicide. But the authors cast doubts on their own findings by suggesting that at some time in the development of the suicidal crisis there must have been earlier thoughts about suicide or parasuicide. Stiffman (1989) reported that 80 per cent of parasuicides of 291 adolescent runaway youths were not planned even a day in advance, but in the same publication made the contradictory statement that one in every five had thought of a suicide plan within the last two days, and one in every three had considered such a plan within the last week (whereas just three had planned the act more than one week ahead). Hoberman and Garfinkel (1988) reported that in their sample of 229 adolescent suicides it appeared that 'in only 28 per cent of the cases there was credible evidence of a plan to commit suicide and this typically appeared of brief duration' (691).

As Spirito et al. (1989) stated, given the frequent reference to teenage suicidal behaviour as impulsive, it is surprising how few adequately designed studies have been conducted on the relation between impulsivity and adolescent suicidal behaviour. Schmidtke's (1988) conclusion from his review of the literature on this issue seems sound: although there appears to be a correlation between impulsivity and suicidal behaviour, this association is moderate, implying that only a subgroup of suicidal adolescents is characterized by a high level of impulsivity.

Behavioural Correlates of Suicide and Parasuicide

It is clear from the findings so far reviewed that much the strongest predictor of suicidal behaviour is the presence of a serious depressive disorder. However, previous parasuicidal acts, the misuse of alcohol and drugs, and a family history of suicidal behaviour all add to the risk. Cognitive styles and personality traits probably play at most a minor role once these main factors have been taken into account. However, both models of suicidal behaviour and acute negative stress experiences may also serve as important precipitants. The relationship between suicidal behaviour and alcohol or drug abuse or addiction also suggest that suicidal adolescents may have a preference for palliative coping reactions. There is indeed evidence that suicidal behaviour in adolescents is part of a more general, unsuccessful, strategy for coping with stressful circumstances, including the use of mind-changing chemical substances (Kienhorst, 1988; Kienhorst et al., 1992).

THE PREVENTION OF SUICIDAL BEHAVIOUR IN ADOLESCENCE

The evidence on the efficacy of programmes to prevent suicidal behaviour, or to prevent the recurrence of parasuicide or to reduce the likelihood that it will lead to completed suicide, is largely outside the scope of this chapter, although very important from a public health perspective. Nevertheless, findings on prevention programmes may be relevant to the consideration of secular trends in suicidal behaviour in so far as they cast light on factors that increase or decrease the risk of suicide or parasuicide.

Curriculum-based Programmes

The approach to suicide prevention that has received most attention in recent years has been that implicit in curriculum-based or educational interventions (see critical review by Garland & Zigler, 1993). There has been a substantial recent growth of such programmes in the USA (Garland et al., 1989) but there are only a few other countries, such as the Netherlands (Mulder et al., 1989) and Canada (Dyck, 1994), where that has occurred. The main goals of most of these programmes (see Diekstra & Hawton, 1987; Garland & Shaffer, 1990; Garland & Zigler, 1993; Ross, 1980; Shaffer et al., 1988) are to raise awareness of the problem of adolescent suicide; to train participants to identify adolescents at risk for suicide; and to educate participants about community mental health resources and referral techniques. The programmes are presented by mental health professionals or educators and are most commonly aimed at secondary school students, their parents, and teachers. The contents of a typical suicide prevention programme for students include a review of the epidemiology of (adolescent) suicide; a list of 'warning signs' of suicide, usually emphasizing symptoms of depression; a list of community mental health resources and how to access them; a discussion of skills for referring a student or peer to counselling, stressing concerns about confidentiality; training in contact-making and referral skills. A number of programmes also include a training in communication skills, problem solving skills and/or stress management.

Although specific methods and contents vary across programmes, the theoretical model guiding them is consistent. Virtually all of the suicide prevention programmes employ a stress model of suicide, as opposed to a mental illness model (Garland et al., 1989). Suicide is presented as a reaction to extreme psychosocial or interpersonal stress and the link to mental illness is markedly de-emphasized. The curricula often explicitly state that people who commit suicide are not mentally ill and that everyone is vulnerable to suicidal behaviour. The rationale behind this approach is that the destigmatization of suicide will encourage students who are feeling suicidal to identify themselves and to seek help.

In reviewing over 300 prevention programmes of various types (not just suicide prevention), Price et al. (1989) concluded that the most effective programmes are those based on a sound foundation of empirical knowledge. That knowledge should include a clear understanding of the risks and problems confronting the target population. Another essential element is the collection of evaluative data to inform planners how well the programme achieves its goals or how it can be modified to do so.

Unfortunately, many suicide prevention programmes have fallen short on one or both of these requirements. Thus, by greatly underplaying the role of serious depressive disorder, the facts are misrepresented. A considerable proportion of youth suicides have or have had diagnosable psychiatric conditions (see Pardes & Blumenthal, 1990). In their attempt to 'destigmatize' suicide some school-based suicide prevention programmes may be normalizing the behaviour and reducing potentially protective taboos. Suicide is sometimes portrayed as a reaction to common stresses of adolescence, namely problems with parents and teachers, problems with relationships, performance anxiety, and peer pressure. The emphasis on the role of stressful experiences however, is more appropriate with regard to parasuicide than to suicide. Also, the incidence of adolescent suicide is sometimes exaggerated in suicide prevention programmes in order to increase awareness and concern about the problem. This exaggeration seems unnecessary in that surveys of teenagers indicate that they are well aware of the problem (Gallup Organization Inc., 1991; Kalafat & Elias, 1992). The danger of exaggeration is that students may perceive suicide as a more common, and therefore more acceptable act.

They may also become unnecessarily anxious about the possibility of suicide in their immediate peer group.

Another problem is the common use of the media to present case histories of adolescents who have attempted or committed suicide. The purpose is to teach students how to identify friends who may be at risk for suicidal behaviour. However, this may have a paradoxical effect. Students may closely identify with the problems portrayed by the case examples and may come to see suicide as the logical solution to their own problems. A documentary on the suicide of an adolescent broadcast twice (1981 and 1982) in Germany on television that was meant to educate about suicide was followed by more suicides (Schmidtke & Häfner, 1988). The model behaviour, jumping in front of a train, was imitated in excess of what might be expected on the basis of control periods, in the period following the broadcasting (especially in young viewers). This study that provides the best empirical evidence regarding the imitation effect, shows the importance of restraint in using fictional models. Mulder (in press) suggested that if programmes encourage more permissive attitudes towards suicide, this might lower 'suicidal thresholds'.

Finally, suicide prevention programmes may never reach adolescents who are most at risk for suicide (Garland & Zigler, 1993) – such as those who are runaways or regular truants.

Although many curriculum-based suicide prevention programmes have been operating since 1981 (Garland et al., 1989), there are only a few published evaluation studies using a control group (Garland & Zigler, 1993; Nelson, 1987; Ross, 1980). Spirito and colleagues' (1988) evaluation of a suicide awareness programme for ninth graders is one of the exceptions. Approximately 300 students who attended the programme were compared with about 200 students in a geographically matched control group. All students completed a battery of exercises covering suicide, hopelessness, helping behaviours, and coping skills prior to, and ten weeks after the implementation of a six-week curriculum in their health classes. The results indicated that the programme was minimally effective in imparting knowledge, and was ineffective in changing attitudes. In another similar study of boys by the same research group (Overholser et al., 1989) there was a change for the worse: an increase in hopelessness and maladaptive coping responses. In a large, well-controlled study in New Jersey, Shaffer et al. (1991) found few positive effects of three suicide prevention curriculum programmes and some possible negative effects. Programme attendance did not effect a significant change in maladaptive attitudes (such as a view that suicide can be a good solution or that suicidal confidences from friends should never be disclosed).

Programme attendance was associated with a small, but significant, increase in the number of students who responded that suicide could be a possible solution to problems, a finding that converges with that from Mulder's study (Mulder, in press). Most importantly, however, there was no significant increase or reduction in self-reported suicidal ideation or suicide attempts following programme implementation.

Crisis Intervention Centres

Virtually all metropolitan areas in Europe and North America now have at least one crisis intervention or suicide prevention centre. These centres typically provide a 24-hour hotline plus referrals to other mental health or social work agencies.

Shneidman and Farberow (1957, 1965) outlined the rationale for suicide crisis centres as follows: suicidal behaviour is often associated with a crisis situation; the victim often experiences ambivalence about living and dying; and people have a basic need for interpersonal communication, which will often be expressed in a last minute 'cry for help'.

Although crisis or suicide hotlines were already present before the Second World War, the spread of such services really began in the early sixties, stimulated by the establishment of the Samaritans in London and the first Suicide Prevention Center in Los Angeles. Generally such centres do not have an active outreach; they do not systematically seek out and try to establish contact with groups in the community who can be considered high risk. It is the suicidal person who has to contact the centre.

It is for that reason that evaluation studies have addressed two major facets of their functioning: whether centres attract persons with an elevated risk for suicidal behaviour; and whether they prevent these individuals' suicide or suicide attempt (Lester, 1974; Bridge et al., 1977; Dew et al., 1987).

In meta-analysis of studies addressing these two questions Dew et al. (1987) drew two main conclusions. First, centres do attract a high-risk population; centre clients were much more likely to commit suicide than were members of the general population. Second, the evidence on whether the suicide rate decreases more in communities with a suicide prevention centre than in those without such a centre is contradictory and inconclusive. Nevertheless, there is no indication of any marked effect, either positive or negative. Given the fact that centres are somewhat successful in attracting the population they are designed to help, it may be that effectiveness should be tested within specific cohorts rather than across the population as a whole. Miller et al. (1984)

compared 28 centre communities with 48 control communities over the period 1968-1973 and found no significant difference between them in the overall suicide rate change over time. However, the suicide rate for white females under the age of 25 showed a large and significant decrease in communities with a centre as compared to control communities. This finding, if replicated, is potentially important because young white women are the most frequent users of prevention centres and telephone emergency services.

Aftercare Programmes for Parasuicides Treated in Hospitals

In the past 30 years, the number of people treated in hospitals following an act of parasuicide has increased substantially in most countries. Follow-up studies have shown that such patients have a much raised risk of both further parasuicide and completed suicide. The question arises, therefore, of whether appropriate treatment following the initial parasuicide act can diminish the subsequent risk. Unfortunately, most studies lack both suitable controls and adequate follow-up (Streiner & Adams, 1987) and few firm conclusions are warranted.

The most recent study, using a methodologically sound design, found no effect of treatment (Allard et al., 1992). 150 subjects were randomly allocated to an experimental group or to a comparison group. The intensive intervention programme was multifaceted, including both an explicit treatment plan for each patient and free use of outside resources such as Alcoholics Anonymous. Results showed that 22 subjects (35 per cent) in the experimental group and 19 subjects (30 per cent) in the comparison group performed at least one parasuicidal act in the two years following randomization. Three completed suicides occurred among experimental subjects and one among the comparison subjects. Clearly the intensive intervention did not have the intended effect.

It is possible that appropriate treatment following a parasuicidal act might reduce subsequent risks, but, with the treatments evaluated so far, there is no convincing evidence of efficacy.

Therapies for Affective Disorders

Because major depressive disorder constitutes such an important risk factor for both parasuicide and suicide (see above), its effective treatment ought to carry the potential for reducing suicidal behaviours. Unfortunately, it is not known whether it does in fact have this desirable effect. Much less is known about the efficacy of treatments for depressive disorders in adolescents than for those used with adults. However, even in adults, although there is much evidence on the short-term efficacy of both pharmacological and psychological treatments, few studies have examined effects on recurrence or on the long-term suicidal risks. This constitutes a research priority.

Restriction of Easy Access to Lethal Methods

The oldest method of preventing suicide is the reduction of means to commit suicide. This plays a crucial role, of course, in the case of suicidal patients in hospital. However, it could well be an important way of reducing risks in the community. Because many suicides, especially in the young, are carried out impulsively, there have been claims that the removal of easily accessible means should reduce the number of impulsive suicidal or parasuicidal acts (Lester, 1988, 1992) The best known example of this kind is the switch in the United

Figure 13.16 Suicide rates per 100,000, by method and percentage concentration of carbon monoxide (CO) in domestic gas, England & Wales, 1960-1973

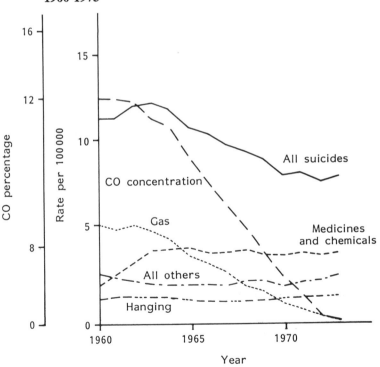

Source: World Health Organization (1981).

Kingdom in the 1960s from lethal coal gas to natural gas containing no carbon monoxide (Kreitman, 1976). This was immediately followed by a highly dramatic drop in the suicidal deaths due to coal gas poisoning (see Figure 13.16), which had fallen to zero by the mid-1970s. The drop closely paralleled the reduction in the carbon monoxide content of the gas and obviously it represented a causal relationship. The key question, however, is whether there was a concomitant increase in the use of *other* suicidal methods, and what effect there was on the overall suicide rate as a result of removing the most common means of attempting suicide. The figures for England and Wales showed that there was a substantial overall drop, albeit one that mainly applied to old people, there being little, if any, effect on the young. There was a similar overall drop in Scotland for older men, but not women, who showed a marginal

Figure 13.17 Suicide rates in the Netherlands per 100,000, aged 15 years and over, by method and percentage concentration of carbon monoxide (CO) in domestic gas, 1960-1972

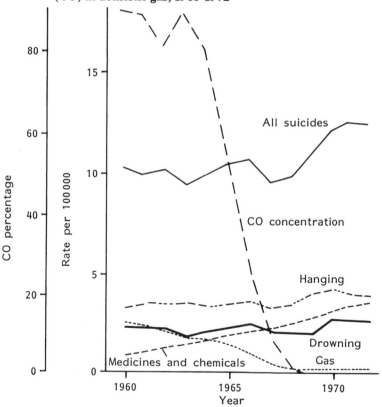

Source: World Health Organization (1981).

increase in suicide rate over the same time period. Since the early 1970s the suicide rates in older men have risen again whereas they have not in England and Wales (Crombie, 1990). In the Netherlands, by contrast with the UK, although there was a similar drop in deaths due to gas as the carbon monoxide content was reduced to zero, this was more than compensated for by an increase in other methods of suicide, most notably in self-poisoning and overdoses (World Health Organization, 1982) - see Figure 13.17. Car emission control may have an incidental impact on suicide (Lester, 1992). The shift to safer hypnotics and anxiolytics should also carry benefits (although strikingly it has not made any impact on suicide as yet), and given control legislation seems to be associated with differences in regional suicide, as well as homicide, rates (Lester, 1988).

It may be concluded that, in the right circumstances, a very marked reduction in the means to commit suicide might make an impact on suicide rates. However, where there is a wide range of means available, the elimination of any one means, even a common one, is not likely to make a long-term difference.

CAUSAL EXPLANATIONS OF SECULAR TRENDS IN SUICIDAL BEHAVIOUR

The Role of Depression

As set out in more detail in Chapter 11, many studies point to an increasing risk for depressive disorders among successive birth cohorts over the course of this century (Hagnell et al., 1982; Klerman, et al., 1985; Weissman et al., 1991; Robins & Regier, 1991). To express this in a slightly different way, the lifetime prevalence rates for depression appear to be higher for adolescents and young adults today than they were for their parents at that age, who in turn had higher rates during their adolescence and young adulthood than their parents had.

One of the features of this increase seems to be the lowering of the age of onset. There is, however, reason to believe that the increase is mainly restricted to white populations living in the industrialized urban areas of North America and Northern Europe, since studies of other populations using identical designs have not been able to confirm it (Canino et al., 1987; Karno et al., 1987). It is not known whether the rise in suicidal behaviour since the Second World War applies to ethnic minorities in Europe as well as to the indigenous white population. The same studies that showed an increase in risk for depression in younger birth cohorts also suggest a possible closing of the gap between higher rates in females than males, in that the rise seems to be greater for young men than for young women (see Chapter 11).

The hypothesis that the observed secular increase in depressive disorder might help to explain the secular increase in suicidal behaviours is corroborated by a number of findings. First, both the increase in depressive disorders and in suicide is particularly conspicuous among young males. Second, the rise in depressive disorders applies only to younger age groups and not to old people; the same applies to suicide and parasuicide. Third, there is evidence suggesting that the percentage of adolescent male suicides who suffered from a depressive disorder at the time of their death may have increased over the past decades. A comparison of the psychological autopsies of two sets of male suicides separated by a gap of 25 years found that the prevalence of depressive disorders was higher among young males in the recent set (Carlson et al., 1991). Third, there is indirect evidence that the earlier age of onset observed for depressive disorders is paralleled by an increase in suicide mortality at an early age, although it is difficult to establish this definitely because of the defects of suicide statistics for early adolescence. A number of studies have assembled retrospective data on lifetime prevalence of parasuicide both among the general population and among high school student populations. On the expectation that lifetime prevalence rates should increase with age (since cumulative risk increases with time) it is surprising that the lifetime rates of parasuicide in general population studies do not exceed and sometimes even remain below the rates for high school students (see Diekstra, 1992). As in the case of depression, interpretation of this finding depends on whether and to what extent recall of earlier episodes is thought to decline with age, a question that is under heavy debate (see Chapter 11), but a part of the explanation may be that 'first-ever' parasuicidal acts have tended to take place at an earlier age in recent decades. Since parasuicide is an important precursor of suicide, and probably the most important one, a lowering of the age of first-ever parasuicide can be expected to cause a lowering of the age of suicide as well.

The Role of Antisocial Disorders and Substance Misuse

As discussed above, suicidal acts are also associated with antisocial disorders and substance misuse – associations that are evident both cross-sectionally and longitudinally. Accordingly the rise over time in these two sets of psychosocial problems (see Chapters 9 and 10) might well play a role in the somewhat parallel rise in suicide and parasuicide (Miles, 1977; Kreitman, 1977; Fremouw et al., 1990; Diekstra, 1989a). Both are predominantly found in younger age groups so that this would be consistent with the suicidal findings. However, although adequate data are lacking, there is no reason to suppose that the increase in alcohol and drug misuse applies only to males. On the other hand, the association between substance misuse and suicide seems to be largely confined to males (Gould et al., 1990), so it could be relevant to the rise in male, but not female, suicide.

It is known that the increase in crime is by no means restricted to males. To the contrary, there is some evidence that the increase has been greater in females than males (with a diminution in the male preponderance that contrasts with its accentuation in the case of suicide). Moreover, it is probable that the association between antisocial behaviour and suicide or parasuicide mainly applies to persistent conduct and personality disorders and not to the much commoner transient delinquency. It remains uncertain whether the rise in crime rate applies equally to both (see Chapter 9).

The mechanisms involved in the association between substance misuse and suicidal behaviour remain ill-understood. It could be that both reflect similar types of underlying psychopathology. Alternatively, the use of alcohol or drugs might play a role at the time of the suicidal act through their actions in reducing inhibitions (and hence in increasing the propensity to take life-threatening risks). Or, yet again, the key feature might be that people who use drugs on a regular basis are more likely to have at their disposal a ready means of ending their life. Some light on these last two possibilities is shed by the findings on suicides in prisons, where prisoners constitute a particularly high risk group (Kerkhof & Bernasco, 1989). Data for England and Wales indicate that there has been a substantial rise over the last 20 years; Dooley (1990) found an increase of 81 per cent between 1972-5 and 1984-7. Such few data as are available from other countries suggest increases in many, but not all, nations (Liebling, 1992). Although it is difficult to be sure about the changes in rate of suicide in prison, the evidence points to the likelihood of an appreciable rise. Most suicides take place within a month of entering prison and over 90 per cent are by hanging, so clearly it is not that drugs provide the means. As alcohol is not freely available in prisons, intoxication is unlikely to have played a disinhibitory role. However, the same does not apply to drugs and that mechanism cannot be firmly ruled out. Nevertheless, on the whole, the figures suggest that either the prison population is sharing in an increase in the individual predisposition to suicide, or that there are situational influences in prison that, although different from those in the community, have shown parallel changes over time.

The Lowering of the Age of Puberty

As set out in Chapter 4, a remarkable change in the timing of individual development has taken place in the highly industrialized countries of Europe and North America over the past 150 years. The average age of first menstruation in girls has shifted from about 16 years in the middle of the 19th century to about 13 years in most industrialized countries today. A similar trend seems to have taken place in boys, but it is harder to document. There have been attempts to attribute secular changes in emotional disturbances in adolescence to this shift in timing (Hamburg, 1989). Whether puberty contributes to the risk of depressive conditions or suicidal behaviours is an issue that is not yet settled (Angold & Rutter, 1992). However, even if it does, a reduction in the age at which puberty occurs cannot readily explain higher prevalence rates of these disorders, although it might explain their earlier onset.

Another possibility is that the lowering of the age of puberty has caused an increased disjunction between biological, psychological, and social development. In spite of the shift in the age of puberty, the brain does not reach a fully adult state of development until the end of the teenage years (Hamburg, 1989); also, social changes particularly during this century, have led to a continuation of social dependence until a much later age than before. This phenomenon of *bio-psycho-social dysbalance* may cause stresses and strains that overtax the coping repertoires of young people and their families. In addition, as discussed in Chapter 4, the present average age of puberty in girls (but not boys) coincides in most countries with another important developmental task for the early adolescent, namely the transition from elementary to secondary or high school. This might seem to suggest that negative effects should impinge more on girls. If that is the case, clearly it can account for the rise in suicide in young females, but not males. However, to date, there is no good evidence that there has been an increase over time in the postulated dysbalance, or that the effects are necessarily negative. It is a phenomenon worth investigating further but it lacks explanatory power on the basis of existing data.

The Influence of Suicidal Models

The study by Gould et al. (1990) showed that over one third of adolescent suicides (41 per cent in males and 33 per cent in females) had a first- or second-degree relative who had previously performed a parasuicidal act or committed suicide. This suggests either that genetic factors play a role or that the probability of suicidal behaviour is influenced by the availability of suicidal 'models' in the social environment of the adolescent, or both. Earlier studies (for example, Kreitman et al., 1969) demonstrated the same relationship for parasuicides: suicidal behaviour was significantly more frequent among intimates (not necessarily kin) of parasuicidal persons than in representative samples of the general population. An 'imitation' effect has also been observed where the models do not belong to family or other immediate social networks, but to the peer group at school. Broadcasts portraying celebrities or other young people (either fictional or non-fictional) who committed suicide are often followed by an increase in suicides, particularly among youth (Diekstra, 1992; see also Chapter 7).

From these findings it seems plausible that availability of suicidal models may have had an enhancing effect on suicidal behaviour among young people. Although there are no studies available that have measured increases in, for example, media coverage of (fictional or non-fictional) suicide cases over the course of this century, it seems safe to assume that such an increase has occurred, if only because of the massive increase in exposure to media, and the increased population coverage achieved through television.

Changes in Social Conditions

It has been shown at an individual level that both depression and suicidal behaviours among young people are associated with parental discord and family conflicts, loss of a parent through death or divorce, parental mental disorders, substance abuse by parents, and physical and sexual abuse during childhood or adolescence (see Chapters 4 and 11). There are also both cross-sectional and longitudinal studies indicating that the experience of unemployment is associated with an increase in psychological disturbance. As shown elsewhere in this book (Chapters 5, 6 and 10), there is much evidence that the proportion of adolescents who experience these conditions has increased during the postwar period. If the prevalence of such risk factors in the community in general has been rising (see also Rutter, 1980), then the increasing rates of depression and suicidal behaviour may be due in part to the rise in the incidence of these social stressors.

However, there are considerable difficulties in undertaking rigorous tests of hypotheses of this kind. The problems may be illustrated by taking the example of unemployment. There is abundant evidence of a very strong association between being unemployed and attempting suicide (Platt, 1984). Thus, for example, Platt and Kreitman (1984) found that the rate of parasuicide among the unemployed was over 10 times that in the employed. Also, during the 1970s the rate of unemployment and the rate of parasuicide in the same geographical sample rose in parallel, leading to the inference that the former may have led to the latter (see Figure 13.14). However, a closer inspection of the data casts some doubt on the causal inference.

Table 13.4 shows that during the 1970s the rate of parasuicide in men who were *in* jobs rose by nearly 50 per cent, whereas the rate in the unemployed *fell* by about the same amount. One possible explanation is that the association reflected the personal factors underlying both unemployment and parasuicide at a time when few people were out of work; as unemployment affected higher proportions of the population, the role of personal vulnerability factors became less important.

Table 13.4 Incidence of parasuicide among employed and unemployed men in Edinburgh 1968-82

Incidence of parasuicide per 100,000

	Among unemployed	Among employed
Year		
1986-71	2341	113
1972-75	2232	141
1976-79	1750	159
1980-82	1584	137

Source: Platt & Kreitman (1984).

Another way of testing the causal hypothesis is to take a longer time period in which the trends in rates of one or other variable have altered direction. Figure 13.18 illustrates the point by extending the data for the population used in Figure 13.14. During the first half of the 1980s, the unemployment rate *rose* very sharply in males but the parasuicide rate in males *fell* equally precipitously. The two rates diverged even more in females. The parasuicide rate rose greatly between 1968 and 1975 at a time when there was little change in unemployment; from 1976 to 1986 the unemployment rate in females went up over sixfold, an almost unprecedented rise, but the parasuicide rate fell by a third.

A further strategy is provided by cross-national comparisons of time trends in the two variables (unemployment and suicide behaviour – in this case

Figure 13.18 Relationship between unemployment and parasuicide in Scotland, 1968-1986: a) males; b) females

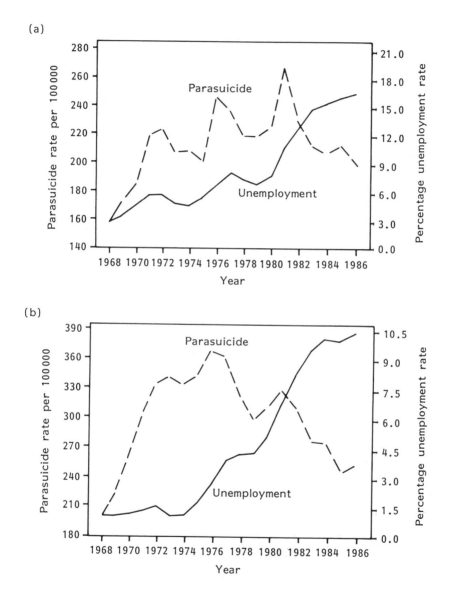

Source: Platt & Kreitman (1984).

indexed by completed suicide). The WHO report in 1982 reported a set of analyses by Sainsbury relating the social characteristics of countries in 1961-3 to the change in their suicide rate over the next few years. The key predictors were: a) a high divorce rate; b) a low proportion of the population aged under 15; c) a high unemployment rate; d) a high murder rate; and e) a high proportion of women in employment. An alternative approach was then adopted, relating *changes* in social conditions in the 1960s to *changes* in national suicide rates over the same time period. This produced a somewhat different set of variables: i) percentage of population under 15 (as before); ii) percentage over 65; iii) room occupancy; and iv) women in tertiary education. Some years later, Diekstra (1989b) undertook a similar analysis for WHO, this time focusing on changes in suicide rate for the 15 to 29-year age group. The findings only partially paralleled Sainsbury's analyses. Thus, unemployment for men and employment for women reappeared as predictors, as did divorce and homicide rate. However, the effect found for the proportion of children in the population actually reversed direction and change in alcohol use and change in church affiliation appeared as new predictors. The lack of replication across analyses is more striking than the consistencies. Clearly much depends on the particular time period chosen for study and rigorous testing requires analyses that span both time periods in which trends have changed direction and a range of countries that differ in their patterns of either social characteristics or their secular trends in suicide rates or both. Such analyses would be possible but have yet to be undertaken.

Altogether there are very few cross-national studies that shed any light on this issue (World Health Organization, 1982). They have focused on the relationship between changes in some of these social conditions and changes in rates of suicide: no relevant studies are available for depression or parasuicide.

A limitation of all these studies is that the social conditions used as explanatory variables are in many cases only loosely related to the causal mechanisms identified by more detailed research. For example, while family conflict and lack of parental care and involvement are risk factors for suicide, parasuicide, depression, and also crime, the relationship between these impairments in family functioning and the divorce rate or the proportion of women in employment has not been clearly established. Hence, whereas these models demonstrate a pattern of relationships at the macro level, it is not yet clear how the findings can be used to infer the causal mechanisms.

A further difficulty in interpreting these results is that, as shown in Chapter 6, many distinct changes in living conditions have occurred over the same period. Correlational studies at the macro (national) level of analysis cannot establish with any degree of certainty which particular societal changes play a specific role in the causation of secular trends in suicide or in the other problem behaviours.

The results from these studies nevertheless are consistent with the view that the social conditions prevailing in a country may play a role in risk of suicide and that changing social conditions may contribute to changes over time in rates of suicide and parasuicide in young people. The exact nature of these processes, however, remains obscure.

CONCLUSION

The main findings on trends in suicide stand out quite clearly from this review. Since the Second World War, the suicide rate in young males aged 15-34 has risen greatly in most European countries. To some extent there have been similar lesser trends in young females but the trends have been much less consistent, and the pattern in the two sexes has diverged markedly in the last decade or so. Before the last 40 years or so the rate of suicide was typically some three times as high among young males as among young females, and an effect of recent trends has been to increase still further this difference in risk. A further prominent feature of the secular trends in suicide has been the tendency for rates to fall in old people at the same time as rates were rising in the young. The data on trends in parasuicide are much less reliable, but there seems to have been a marked increase between around 1955 and 1980, and probably a decline since then.

Information about the reasons for these trends is much less satisfactory. Studies that rigorously test causal explanations of adolescent suicide are extremely rare, and even correlational studies are highly unusual. Knowledge of the correlates of parasuicidal behaviour is also limited, and sometimes contradictory. Soundly-based information on the effectiveness of intervention and prevention activities is limited. All this is partly due to fundamental problems inherent in carrying out research in the field, but also to avoidable defects in the studies so far undertaken. There is an almost complete lack of studies using prospective designs.

In short, despite the considerable volume of research and clinical work on adolescent suicidal behaviour, there is still a long way to go in explaining the upward secular trend and in finding effective methods of prevention. In setting out the possible explanations that are worthy of further study, this chapter has drawn particular attention to the role of depression in suicide; the increase in use of alcohol and psychoactive drugs; the possible role of antisocial behaviour; the influence of suicidal models either within the family and intimate circle, or in the mass media; the possible increase in family conflict and decline in parental support associated with changes in family structures; the possible effect of an extended period of social dependency during adolescence; and the likely role of changing circumstances in society as a whole.

REFERENCES

Allard, R., Marshall, M. & Plante, M.C. (1992). Intensive follow-up does not decrease the risk of repeat suicide attempts. *Suicide and Life Threatening Behavior 22*, 303-314.

Andrews, J.A. & Lewinsohn, P.M., (1990). *The prevalence, lethality and intent of suicide attempts among adolescents.* Paper presented at the 98th Annual Convention of the American Psychological Association, Boston.

Andrus, J.K., Fleming, D.W., Heumann, M.A., Wassel, J.T., Hopkins, D.D. & Gordon, J. (1991). Surveillance of attempted suicide among adolescents in Oregon. *American Journal of Public Health 81*, 1067-1069.

Angold, A. & Rutter, M. (1992). The effects of age and pubertal status on depression in a large clinical sample. *Developmental Psychopathology 4*, 5-28.

Arffa, S. (1983). Cognition and suicide: A methodological review. *Suicide and Life Threatening Behavior 13*, 109-122.

Asarnow, J., Carlson, G. & Guthrie, D. (1987). Coping strategies, self-perceptions, hopelessness, and perceived family environments in depressed and suicidal children. *Journal of Consulting and Clinical Psychology 55*, 361-366.

Asgård, U., Nordström, P. & Rabåck, G. (1987). Birth cohort analysis of changing suicide risk by sex and age in Sweden, 1952 to 1981. *Acta Psychiatrica Scandinavica 76*, 456-463.

Bachman, J.G., Johnston, L.D. & O'Malley, P.M. (1986). *Monitoring the future.* Questionnaire responses from the nation's high-school seniors. Michigan: Institute for Social Research, University of Michigan, Ann Arbor.

Bancroft, J., Hawton, K., Simkin, S. & Kingston, B. (1979). The reasons people give for taking overdoses: A further inquiry. *British Journal of Medical Psychiatry 52*, 353-365.

Bancroft, J. H. J., Skrimshire, A. M. & Simkin, S. (1976). The reasons people give for taking overdoses. *British Journal of Psychiatry 128*, 538-548.

Barnes, R.A., Ennis, J. & Schober, R. (1986). Cohort analysis of Ontario suicide 1877-1976. *Canadian Journal of Psychiatry 31*, 208-213.

Barraclough, B. (1973). Differences between national suicide rates. *British Journal of Psychiatry 122*, 95-96.

Bayatpour, M., Wells, R. D. & Holford, S. (1992). Physical and sexual abuse as predictors of substance use and suicide among pregnant teenagers. *Journal of Adolescent Health 13*, 128-132.

Beck, A., Steer, R., Kovacs, M. & Garrison, B. (1985). Hopelessness and eventual suicide: A 10-year prospective study of patients hospitalized with suicidal ideation. *American Journal of Psychiatry 142*, 559-563.

Beck, A. T., Weissman, A., Lester, D. & Trexler, L. (1974). The measurement of pessimism: The hopelessness scale. *Journal of Consulting and Clinical Psychology 42*, 861-865.

Blumenthal, S. J. (1990). Youth suicide: Risk factors, assessment, and treatment of adolescent and young adult suicidal patients. Adolescence: Psychopathology, normality, and creativity. *Psychiatric Clinics of North America 13*, 511-556.

Bowles, J.R. (in press). Suicide in Western Samoa. In R. F. W. Diekstra & W. Gulbinat (eds.) *Preventive strategies for suicide.* Leiden/Canberra: Brill Publishers; Geneva: World Health Organization.

Brent, D. A., Kerr, M. M., Goldstein, C., Bozigar, J., Wartella, M. & Allan, M. J. (1989). An outbreak of suicide and suicidal behavior in a high school. *Journal of the American Academy of Child and Adolescent Psychiatry 28*, 918-924.

Brent, D. A., Kolko, D. J., Wartella, M. E., Boylan, M. B., Moritz, G, Baugher M. & Zelenak, J. P. (1993). Adolescent psychiatric in-patients' risk of suicide attempt on six-month follow-up. *Journal of the American Academy of Child and Adolescent Psychiatry 32*, 95-105.

Bridge, T.P., Potkin, S.G., Zung, W.W.K., & Soldo, B.J. (1977). Suicide prevention centers: Ecological study of effectiveness. *The Journal of Nervous and Mental Diseases 164*, 18-24.

Canino, G.J., Bird, H.R., Shrout, P.E., Rubio-Stipec, M., Bravo, M. Martinez, R., Sesman, M. & Guevara, L.M. (1987). The prevalence of specific psychiatric disorders in Puerto Rico. *Archives of General Psychiatry 44*, 727-735.

Carlson, G.A., Rich, C.L., Grayson, P. & Fowler, R.C. (1991). Secular trends in psychiatric diagnoses of suicide victims. *Journal of Affective Disorders 21*, 127-132.

Cavan, P. S. (1928). *Suicide.* New York: Russel & Russel.

CDC-Centers of Disease Control (1991). Attempted suicide among high school students – United States 1990, leads from the Morbidity and Mortality Weekly Report. *Journal of the American Medical Association 266*, 14, 911.

Chabrol, H. & Moron, P. (1988). Depressive disorders in 100 adolescents who attempted suicide [letter]. *American Journal of Psychiatry 145*, 379.

Cohen-Sandler, R. (1982). Interpersonal problem-solving skills of suicidal and non-suicidal children: Assessment and treatment. *Dissertation Abstracts International 43*, 17.

Conrad, N. (1992). Stress and knowledge of suicidal others as factors in suicidal behavior of high school adolescents. *Issues in Mental Health Nursing 13*, 95-104.

Crepet, P. (1986). *Suicide and attempted suicide: New trends and correlations in Italy.* Background paper presented to WHO (EURO) Working group on Preventive Practices in Suicide and Attempted Suicide, 22-26 September, York.

Crombie, I.K. (1990). Suicide in England and Wales and in Scotland: An examination of divergent trends. *British Journal of Psychiatry 157*, 529-532.

Crumley, F. E. (1982). Adolescent suicide attempts and melancholia. *Texas Medicine 78*, 62-65.

D'Attilio, J. P., Campbell, B. M., Lubold, P., Jacobson, T. & Richard, J. A. (1992). Social support and suicide potential: Preliminary findings for adolescent populations. *Psychological Reports 70*, 76-78.

Davidson, L. E., Rosenberg, M. L., Mercy, J. A., Franklin, J. & Simmons, J. T. (1989). An epidemiologic study of risk factors in two teenage suicide clusters. *Journal of the American Medical Association 262*, 2687-2692.

Dew, M.A., Bromet, E.J., Brent, D. & Greenhouse, J.B. (1987). A quantitative literature review of the effectiveness of suicide prevention centers. *Journal of Consulting and Clinical Psychology 55*, 239-244.

de Wilde, E. J., Kienhorst, C. W. M., Diekstra, R. F. W. & Wolters, W. H. G. (1992). The relationship between adolescent suicidal behavior and life events in childhood and adolescence. *American Journal of Psychiatry 1*, 45-51.

de Wilde, E. J., Kienhorst, C. M. W., Diekstra, R. F. W. & Wolters, W. H. G. (1993). The specificity of psychological characteristics of adolescent suicide attempters. *Journal of the American Academy of Child and Adolescent Psychiatry 32*, 51-59.

Diekstra, R.F.W. (1973). *Crisis en Gedragskeuze.* Amsterdam: Swets & Zeitlinger.

Diekstra, R.F.W. (1981). *Over suïcide (About suicide).* Alphen aan den Rijn: Samsom.

Diekstra, R.F.W. (1982). Epidemiology of attempted suicide in the EEC. In J. Wilmotte & J. Mendlewicz (eds.) *New trends in suicide prevention*, 1-16. Basle: Bibliotheca Psychiatrica Karger.

Diekstra, R.F.W. (1985). Suicide and suicide attempts in the European Economic Community: An analysis of trends with special emphasis on trends among the young. *Suicide Life Threatening Behaviour 15*, 402-421.

Diekstra, R.F.W. (1989a). Suicidal behavior and depressive disorders in adolescents and young adults. *Neuropsychobiology 22*, 194-207.

Diekstra, R. F. W. (1989b). Suicidal behavior in adolescents and young adults: The international picture. *Crisis 10*, 16-35.

Diekstra, R.F.W. (1992). Suicide and parasuicide: A global perspective. *Archives of Public Health 48* (1990/1992), 141-166.

Diekstra, R.F.W. & Hawton, K (1987). *Suicide in adolescence.* Dordrecht/New York: Kluwer Academic Publishers.

Diekstra, R.F.W., de Heus, P., Garnefski, N., de Zwart, R., van Praag, B.M.S. (1991). *Monitoring the future: Behavior and health among high school students.* The Hague: NIBUD.

Diekstra, R.F.W. & Kerkhof, A.J.R.M. (1989). Attitudes towards suicide: The development of a suicide-attitude questionnaire (SUIATT). In R. F. W. Diekstra, R. Maris, S. Platt, A. Schmidtke, & G. Sonneck (eds). *Suicide and its prevention:*

The role of attitude and imitation, 91-107. Leiden/New York: Brill Publishers (World Health Organization's co-publication).

Diekstra, R.F.W. & van de Loo, K.J.M. (1978). Attitudes towards suicide and incidence of suicidal behaviour in a general population. In H. Z. Winnik & L. Miller (eds.) *Aspects of suicide in modern civilization*, 79-85. Jerusalem: Academic Press.

Dooley, E. (1990). Prison suicide in England and Wales 1972-1987. *British Journal of Psychiatry 156*, 40-45.

Doroff, D. R. (1968). *Attempted suicide and gestured suicide in adolescent girls.* Rutgers University (DAI, 29/7B, 2631).

Douglas, J.D. (1967). *The social meanings of suicide.* Princeton, NJ: Princeton University Press.

Dubow, E.F., Kausch, D.F., Blum, M.C., Reed, J. et al. (1989). Correlates of suicidal ideation and attempts in a community sample of junior high and high school students. *Journal of Clinical Child Psychology 18* , 158-166.

Dyck, R. (1994). Guidelines for the development and organisation of suicide prevention programs. In R. F. W. Diekstra & W. Gulbinat (eds.) *Preventive strategies on suicide.* Canberra/Leiden: Brill Publishers (World Health Organization's co-publication).

Farberow, N.L. (ed.) (1980). *The many faces of suicide: Indirect self-destructive behaviour.* New York: McGraw-Hill.

Fremouw, W.J., De Perczel, M. & Ellis, Th.E. (1990). *Suicide risk: Assessment and response guidelines.* New York: Pergamon Press.

Friedman R.C., Corn, R., Hurt, S. W., Fibel, B., Schulick, J. & Swirsky, S. (1984). Family history of illness in the seriously suicidal adolescent. *American Journal of Orthopsychiatry 54*, 390-397.

Gallup Organization Inc. (1991). *Teenage suicide study: Executive summary.* (Available from the Gallup Organization Inc.).

Garland, A. & Shaffer, D. (1990). School-based adolescent suicide prevention programs. In M. J. Rotheram, J. Bradley & N. Obolensky (eds.) *Planning to live. Evaluating and treating suicidal teens in community settings.* Tulsa, OK: University of Oklahoma Press.

Garland, A., Shaffer, D. & Whittle, B. (1989). A national survey of school-based, adolescent suicide prevention programs. *Journal of the American Academy of Child and Adolescent Psychiatry 28*, 931-934.

Garland, A. & Zigler, E. (1993). Adolescent suicide prevention: Current research and social policy implications. *American Psychologist 48*, 169-182

Garnefski, N., Diekstra, R.F.W. & de Heus, P. (1992). A population-based survey of the characteristics of high school students with and without a history of suicidal behavior. *Acta Psychiatrica Scandinavica 86*, 189-196.

Gibbons, J. S., Elliot, J., Urwin, P. & Gibbons, J. L. (1979). The urban environment and deliberate self-poisoning: Trends in Southampton (1972-1977). *Social Psychiatry. 13*, 159-166.

Goldney, R.D. & Katsikitis, M. (1983). Cohort analysis of suicide rates in Australia. *Archives of General Psychiatry 40*, 71-74.

Goldney, R.D., Winefield, A.H., Tiggeman, M., Winefield, H.R. & Smith, S. (1989). Suicidal ideation in a young adult population. *Acta Psychiatrica Scandinavica 79*, 481-489.

Gould, M. & Shaffer, D. (1986). The impact of suicide in television movies. Evidence of imitation. *New England Journal of Medicine 315*, 690-694.

Gould, M.S., Shaffer, D. & Davies M. (1990). Truncated pathways from childhood to adulthood: Attrition in follow-up studies due to death. In L. Robins & M. Rutter (eds.) *Straight and devious pathways from childhood to adulthood*, 3-9. Cambridge: Cambridge University Press.

Häfner, H. & Schmidtke, A. (1985). Do cohort effects influence suicide rates? *Archives of General Psychiatry 42*, 926-927.

Hagnell, O., Lanke, J., Rorsman, B. & Ojesjö, L. (1982). Are we entering an age of melancholy? Depressive illness in a prospective epidemiological study over 25 years: The Lundby study, Sweden. *Psychological Medicine 12*, 279-289.

Hamburg, D. (1989). Preparing for life: The critical transition of adolescence. In R.F.W. Diekstra (ed.) *Preventive interventions in adolescence*, 4-15. Toronto/Bern: Hogrefe & Huber.

Harkavy Friedman, J. M., Asnis, G. M., Boeck, M. & DiFiore, J. (1987). Prevalence of specific suicidal behaviors in a high school sample. *American Journal of Psychiatry 144*, 1203-1206.

Harrington, R., Bredenkamp D., Groothues, C., Rutter, M. & Fudge, H. (in press). Adult outcomes of childhood and adolescent depression. III. Links with suicidal behaviour. *Journal of Child Psychology & Psychiatry*.

Hart, E. E., Williams, C. L. & Davidson, J. A. (1988). Suicidal behavior, social networks and psychiatric diagnosis. *Social Psychiatry and Psychiatric Epidemiology 23*, 222-228.

Hawton, K. (1986). *Suicide and attempted suicide among children and adolescents*. Beverly Hills, CA: Sage Publications.

Hawton, K. (1992). By their own young hand. *British Medical Journal 304*, 1000.

Hawton, K. & Catalan, J. (1987). *Attempted suicide: A practical guide to its nature and management*. Oxford: Oxford University Press.

Hawton, K., Cole, D., O'Grady, J. & Osborn, M. (1982). Motivational aspects of deliberate self-poisoning in adolescents. *British Journal of Psychiatry 141*, 286-291.

Hawton, K. & Fagg, J. (1992). Deliberate self-poisoning and self-injury in adolescents: A study of characteristics and trends in Oxford, 1976-89. *British Journal of Psychiatry 161*, 816-823.

Hawton, K., Fagg, J., Platt, S. & Hawkins, M. (1993). Factors associated with suicide following parasuicide in young people. *British Medical Journal 306*, 1641-1644.

Hawton, K. & Goldacre, M. (1982). Hospital admissions for adverse effects of medicinal agents (mainly self-poisoning) among adolescents in the Oxford Region. *British Journal of Psychiatry 141*, 166-170.

Herjanic, B. & Welner, Z. (1980). Adolescent suicide. *Advances in Behavioral Pediatrics 1*, 195-223.

Hoberman, H. & Garfinkel, B. (1988). Completed suicide in children and adolescents. *Journal of the American Academy of Child and Adolescent Psychiatry 27*, 689-95.

Iga, M. & Ohara, K. (1967). Suicide attempts of Japanese youth and Durkheim's concept of anomie. *Human Organization 26*, 59-68.

Jacobs, J. (1971). *Adolescent suicide*. London: Wiley Interscience.

Jobes, D. A., Berman, A. L. & Josselsen, A. R. (1986). The impact of psychosocial autopsies on medical examiner's determination of manner of death. *Journal of Forensic Science 31*, 177-189.

Jones, D.I.R. (1977). Self-poisoning with drugs: The past 20 years in Sheffield. *British Medical Journal 1*, 28-29.

Kahn, A. U. (1987). Heterogenity of suicidal adolescents. *Journal of the American Academy of Child and Adolescent Psychiatry 1*, 92-96.

Kalafat, J., & Elias, M. (1992). Adolescents' experience with and response to suicidal peers. *Suicide and Life Threatening Behavior 22*, 315-321.

Karno, M., Hough, R.L., Burnam, M.A., Escobar, J.I., Timbers, D.M., Santana, F. & Boyd, J.H. (1987). Lifetime prevalence of specific psychiatric disorders among Mexican Americans and non-Hispanic whites in Los Angeles. *Archives of General Psychiatry 44*, 695-701.

Kazdin, A., Esveldt, D. K., Unis, A. & Rancurello, M. (1983). Child and parent evaluations of depression and aggression in psychiatric in-patient children. *Journal of Abnormal Child Psychology 11*, 401-413.

Kerkhof, A.J.F.M. (1985). *Suicide en de geestelijke gezondheidszorg*. Amsterdam: Swets & Zeitlinger.

Kerkhof, A.J.F.M. & Bernasco, W. (1990). Suicidal behavior in jails and prisons in the Netherlands. *Suicide and Life Threatening Behavior 20*, 123-137.

Kessel, N. (1965). 'Self poisoning'. *British Medical Journal 2*, 1265-1270, 1336-1340.

Kessler, R., Downey, G., Milavsky, J. & Stipp, H. (1988). Clustering of teenage suicides after television news stories about suicides: A reconsideration. *American Journal of Psychiatry 145*, 1379-1383.

Kienhorst, C. W. M. (1988). *Suicidaal gedrag bij jongeren. Onderzoek naar omvang en kenmerken.* (Suicidal behaviour among adolescents. A study of the frequency and characteristics. Thesis). Baarn: Ambo.

Kienhorst, C. W. M., de Wilde, E. J., Diekstra, R. F. W. & Wolters, W. H. G. (in revision). *The adolescents' image of their suicide attempt.* British Journal of Psychiatry.

Kienhorst, C. W. M., de Wilde, E. J., Diekstra, R.F.W. & Wolters, W. H. G. (1990b). Characteristics of suicide attempters in a population-based sample of Dutch adolescents. *British Journal of Psychiatry 156*, 243-248.

Kienhorst, C. W. M., de Wilde, E. J., Diekstra, R. F. W. & Wolters, W. H. G. (1991). Construction of an index for predicting suicide attempts in depressed adolescents. *British Journal of Psychiatry 159*, 676-682.

Kienhorst, C. W. M., de Wilde, E. J., Diekstra, R. F. W. & Wolters, W. H. G. (1992). Differences between adolescent suicide attempters and depressed adolescents. *Acta Psychiatrica Scandinavica 85*, 222-228.

Kienhorst, C. W. M., de Wilde, E. J., Van den Bout, J., Broese van Groenou, M. I., Diekstra, R. F. W. & Wolters, W. H. G. (1990a). Self-reported suicidal behavior in Dutch secondary education students. *Suicide and Life-Threatening Behavior 20*, 101-112.

Kienhorst, C. W. M., Wolters, W. H. G., Diekstra, R. F. W. & Otte, E. (1987). A study of the frequency of suicidal behaviour in children aged 5 to 14. *Journal of Child Psychology and Psychiatry 28*, 153-165.

Klerman, G.L., Lavori P.W. & Price J. (1985). Birth-cohort trends in rates in major depressive disorders among relatives of patients with affective disorders. *Archives of General Psychiatry 42*, 689-699.

Koller, K. M. & Castanos, B. E. (1968). Attempted suicide and alcoholism. *Medical Journal of Australia 2*, 835-37.

Kovacs, M., Goldston, D. & Gatsonis, C. (1993). Suicidal behaviors and childhood onset depressive disorders: A longitudinal investigation. *Journal of the American Academy of Child and Adolescent Psychiatry 32*, 8-20.

Kreitman, N. (1976). The coal gas story: United Kingdom suicide rates 1960-1971. *British Journal of Preventative Social Medicine 30*, 86-93.

Kreitman, N. (1977). *Parasuicide*. London: Wiley & Sons.

Kreitman, N. (1988). Suicide, age and marital status. *Psychological Medicine 18*, 121-128.

Kreitman, N., Smith, P. & Tan, E. (1969). Attempted suicide in social networks. *British Journal of Preventative & Social Medicine 23*, 116-123..

La Vecchia, C., Bollini, P. & Imazio, C. (1986). Age period of death and birth cohort effects on suicide mortality in Italy, 1955-1979. *Acta Psychiatrica Scandinavica 74*, 137-143.

Leonard, C. (1967). *Understanding and preventing suicide*. Springfield, IL: Thomas.

Lester, D. (1972). *Why people kill themselves: A summary of research findings on suicidal behaviour.* Springfield, IL: Thomas.

Lester, D. (1974). Effect of suicide prevention centers on suicide rates in the United States. *Health Services Reports 89*, 37-39.

Lester, D. (1984). Suicide risk by birth cohort. *Suicide and Life-Threatening Behaviour 14*, 132-136.

Lester, D. (1988). Gun control, gun ownership and suicide prevention. *Suicide and Life-Threatening Behavior 18*, 176-180.

Lester, D. (1992). Is there a need for suicide prevention? *Crisis, The Journal of Crisis Intervention and Suicide Prevention 2*, 94.

Levenson, M. (1974). Cognitive correlates of suicidal risk. In C. Neuringer (ed.) *Psychological assessment of suicidal risk*. Springfield, IL: Thomas.

Levenson M., & Neuringer C. (1974). Problem solving behavior in suicidal adolescents. *Journal of Consulting and Clinical Psychology 37*, 433-436.

Lewinsohn, P. M., Rohde, P. & Seeley, J.R. (1993). Psychosocial characteristics of adolescents with a history of suicide attempt. *Journal of the American Academy of Child and Adolescent Psychiatry 32*, 60-68.

Liebling, A. (1992). *Suicide in prison*. London: Routledge.

Mansmann, V. & Schenck, K. (1983). Vordergrundige Motive und langfristige Tendenzen zum Suizid bei Kindern und Jugendlichen. In I. Jochmus & E. Forster (eds.) *Suizid bei Kindern und Jugendlichen*, 38-44. Stuttgart: Enke.

Maris, R.W. (1991). Suicide: In *Encyclopedia of Human Biology,* Vol. VII, 372-335. New York: Academic Press.

McCarthy, P.D. & Walsh, D. (1975). Suicide in Dublin: The underreporting of suicide and the consequences for national suicide statistics. *British Journal of Psychiatry 126*, 301-308.

McCulloch, J. W. & Philip, A. E. (1972). *Suicidal behaviour.* New York: Pergamon Press.

Mehr, M., Zeltzer, L.K. & Robinson, R. (1981). Continued self-destructive behaviours in adolescent suicide attempters: Part I. *Journal of Adolescent Health Care 1*, 269-274.

Mehr, M., Zeltzer, L.K. & Robinson, R. (1982). Continued self-destructive behaviours in adolescent suicide attempters: Part II. *Journal of Adolescent Health Care 2*, 182-187.

Miles, C.P. (1977). Conditions predisposing to suicide: A review. *Journal of Nervous and Mental Diseases 16*, 231-246.

Miller, H.L., Coombs, D.W. & Leeper, J.D. (1984). An analysis of the effects of suicide prevention facilities on suicide rates in the United States. *American Journal of Public Health 74*, 340-343.

Miller, K. E., King, C. A., Shain, B. N. & Naylor, M. W. (1992). Suicidal adolescents' perceptions of their family environment. *Suicide and Life-Threatening Behavior 22*, 226-239.

Minkoff, K., Bergman, E., Beck, A. T. & Beck, R. (1973). Hopelessness, depression and attempted suicide. *American Journal of Psychiatry 130*, 455-459.

Moens, G.F.G. (1990). *Aspects of the epidemiology and prevention of suicide.* Leuven: Leuven University Press.

Moens G.F.G., Haenen, W. & Voorde H.v.d. (1988). Suicide bij jongeren in Belgie. *Tijdschrift voor sociale gezondheidszorg 66*, 239-244.

Moscicki, E.K., O'Caroll, P.W., Rae, D.S., Roy, A.G., Locke, B.Z. & Regier, D.A. (1989). *Suicidal ideation and attempts: The Epidemiological Catchment Area Study.* In *Report of the Secretary's Task Force on Youth Suicide,* 4-115/4-128. Rockville, US: Department of Health and Human Services Publication, no. (ADM) 89-1264.

Mulder, A., Methorst, G. & Diekstra, R.F.W. (1989). Prevention of suicidal behavior in adolescents: The role and training of teachers. *Crisis 10*, 36-51.

Mulder, A. (in press). *Prevention of suicidal behaviour in adolescents: The development and evaluation of a teachers education programme.* Doctoral dissertation. Leiden: University of Leiden.

Murphy, G.E., Lindesay, J., Grundy, E. (1986). 60 years of suicide in England and Wales. A cohort study. *Archives of General Psychiatry 43*, 969-976.

Murphy, G.E. & Wetzel, R.D. (1980). Suicide risk by birth cohort in the United States, 1949 to 1974. *Archives of General Psychiatry 37*, 519-523.

Nagy, S. & Adcock, A. (1990). *The Alabama Adolescent Health Survey: Health knowledge and behaviours.* Summary Report II. Alabama: The University of Alabama and Troy State University.

Nelson, F. (1987). Evaluation of a youth suicide prevention school program. *Adolescence 22*, 813-825.

Neuringer, C. (1976). Current developments in the study of suicidal thinking. In E.S. Schneidman (ed.) *Suicidology: Contemporary developments*, 229-252. New York: Grune & Stratton.

Neuringer, C. & Lettieri, D. (1982). *Suicidal women. Their thinking and feeling patterns.* New York: Gardner Press.

Noguera, R. (1986). *Suicide and trends in deliberate self-harm in Spain.* Background paper presented to WHO (EURO) Working Group on Preventive Practices in Suicide and Attempted Suicide, 22-26 September, York.

Nordentoft, M., Breum, L., Munck, L. K., Nordestgaard, A. G., Hunding, A. & Laursen Bjældager P. A. (1993). High mortality by natural and unnatural causes: A 10 year follow up study of patients admitted to a poisoning treatment centre after suicide attempts. *British Medical Journal 306*, 1637-1641.

Orbach, I., Rosenheim, E. & Hary, E. (1987). Some aspects of cognitive functioning in suicidal children. *Journal of the American Academy of Child and Adolescent Psychiatry 26*, 181-185.

Ostroff, R. B., Boyd & Jeffrey H. (1987). Television and suicide. *The New England Journal of Medicine 316*, 877-879.

Overholser, J., Hemstreet, A.H., Spirito, A. & Vyse, S. (1989). Suicide awareness programmes in the schools: Effects of gender and personal experience. *Journal of the American Academy of Child and Adolescent Psychiatry 28*, 925-930.

Pardes, H., & Blumenthal, S.J. (1990). Youth suicide: Public policy and research issues. In S.J. Blumenthal & D.J. Kupfer (eds.) *Suicide over the lifecycle*, 665-684. Washington, DC: American Psychiatric Press.

Perrah, M. & Wichman, H. (1987). Cognitive rigidity in suicide attempters. *Suicide and Life-Threatening Behavior 17*, 251-255.

Petzel, S. V. & Riddle, M. (1981). Adolescent suicide: Psychological and cognitive aspects. *Adolescent Psychiatry 9*, 343-398.

Pfeffer, C., Newcorn, J., Kaplan, G., Mizruchi, M. & Plutchik, R.(1989). Subtypes of suicidal and assaultive behaviors in adolescent psychiatric inpatients: A research note. *Journal of Child Psychology and Psychiatry 30*, 151-163.

Phares, V. & Compas, B.E. (1992). The role of fathers in child and adolescent psychopathology: Make room for daddy. *Psychological Bulletin 11*, 387-412.

Philips, D. P. & Carstensen, L. L. (1986). Clustering of teenage suicides after television news. Stories about suicide. *The New England Journal of Medicine 315*, 685-689.

Platt, S. (1984). Unemployment and suicidal behavior: A review of the literature. *Social Science & Medicine 19*, 93-115.

Platt, S. (1986). Suicide and parasuicide among further education students in Edinburgh. *British Journal of Psychiatry 150*, 183-188.

Platt, S. (1988). *Data from the Royal Infirmary Edinburgh,* Scotland.

Platt, S., Bille-Brahe, U. & Kerkhof, A.J.F.M. (1992). Parasuicide in Europe: The WHO/EURO multicentre study on parasuicide, I: Introduction and preliminary analysis for 1989. *Acta Psychiatrica Scandinavica 85*, 97-104.

Platt, S., Hawton, K., Kreitman, N., Fagg, J. & Foster, J. (1988). Recent clinical and epidemiological trends in parasuicide in Edinburgh and Oxford: A tale of two cities. *Psychological Medicine 18*, 405-418.

Platt, S. & Kreitman, N. (1984). Trends in parasuicide and unemployment among men in Edinburgh, 1968-82. *British Medical Journal 289*, 1029-1032.

Price, R. H., Cowen, E. L., Lorion, R. P. & Ramos-McKay, J. (1989). The search for effective prevention programs: What we learned along the way. *American Journal of Orthopsychiatry 59*, 49-58.

Pronovost, J., Cote, L. & Ross, C. (1990). Epidemiological study of suicidal behaviour among secondary-school students. *Canada's Mental Health 38*, 9-14.

Puskar, K., Hoover, C. & Miewald, C. (1992). Suicidal and nonsuicidal coping methods of adolescents. *Perspectives in Psychiatric Care 28*, 15-20.

Range, L., Coggin, W. & Steede, K. (1988). Perception of behavioral contagion of adolescent suicide. *Suicide and Life-Threatening Behavior 18*, 334-341.

Rao, U., Weissman M. M., Martin, J. A. & Hammond, R. W. (1993). Childhood depression and risk of suicide: A preliminary report of a longitudinal study. *Journal of the American Academy of Child and Adolescent Psychiatry 32*, 21-27.

Reed, J., Camus, J. & Last, J.M. (1985). Suicide in Canada: Birth-cohort analysis. *Canadian Journal of Public Health 76*, 43-47.

Rey, J.M. & Bird, K.D. (1991). Sex differences in suicidal behaviour of referred adolescents. *British Journal of Psychiatry 158*, 776-781.

Riggs, S., Alario, A. & McHorney, C.(1990). Health risk behaviors and attempted suicide in adolescents who report prior maltreatment. *Journal of Pediatrics 116*, 815-821

Robbins, D. & Conroy, R. C. (1983). A cluster of adolescent suicide attempts: Is suicide contagious? *Journal of Adolescent Health Care 3*, 253-255.

Robins, L.N. & Regier, D.A. (eds.) (1991). *Psychiatric disorders in America: The Epidemiologic Catchment Area Study.* New York: Free Press.

Ross, C. P. (1980). Mobilizing schools for suicide prevention. *Suicide and Life Threatening Behavior 10*, 239-243.

Rotheram-Borus, M. & Trautman, P. (1988). Hopelessness, depression, and suicidal intent among adolescent suicide attempters. *Journal of the American Academy of Child and Adolescent Psychiatry 27*, 700-704.

Rubinstein, J.L., Heeren, T., Housman, D., Rubin, C. & Stechler, G. (1989). Suicidal behaviour in 'normal' adolescents: Risk and protective factors. *American Journal of Orthopsychiatry 59*, 59-71.

Rutter, M. (1980). *Changing youth in a changing society. Patterns of adolescent development and disorder.* Cambridge, MA: Harvard University Press.

Sainsbury, P. & Barraclough, B.M. (1968). Differences between suicide rates. *Nature 220*, 1252.

Sainsbury, P., Jenkins, J. & Baert, A.E. (1981). *Suicide trends in Europe.* Copenhagen: WHO Regional Office for Europe (ICP/MNH 036).

Salter, D. & Platt, S. (1990). Suicidal intent, hopelessness and depression in a parasuicide population: The influence of social desirability and elapsed time. *British Journal of Clinical Child Psychology 29*, 361-371.

Schmidtke, A. (1988). *Verhaltenstheoretisches Erklärungsmodell suizidalen Verhalten.* Regenburg: Roderer.

Schmidtke, A. (1992). *The influence of mood factors on cognitive styles.* Paper presented on the Silver Anniversary Conference of the American Association of Suicidology, Chicago.

Schmidtke, A. & Häfner, H. (1988). The Werther effect after television films: New evidence for an old hypothesis. *Psychological Medicine 18*, 665-676.

Schmidtke, A. & Schaller, S. (1992). Covariation of cognitive styles and mood factors during crises. In P. Crepet, G. Ferrari, S. Platt & M. Bellini (eds.) *Suicidal behavior in Europe*, 225-232. Rome/New York: Libley.

Shaffer, D., Garland, A., Gould, M., Fisher, P. & Trautman, P. (1988). Preventing teenage suicide: A critical review. *Journal of the American Academy of Child and Adolescent Psychiatry 27*, 675-687.

Shaffer, D., Garland, A., Vieland, V., Underwood, M. & Busner, C. (1991). The impact of curriculum-based suicide prevention programmes for teenagers. *Journal of the American Academy of Child and Adolescent Psychiatry 30*, 588-596.

Shneidman, E.S. & Farberow, N.L. (1957). *Clues to suicide.* New York: McGraw-Hill.

Shneidman, E.S. & Farberow, N.L. (1965). The Los Angeles suicide prevention center: A demonstration of public health feasibilities. *American Journal of Public Health 55*, 21-26.

Smith, K. & Crawford, S. (1986). Suicidal behavior among 'normal' high school students. *Suicide and Life-Threatening Behavior 16*, 313-325.

Solomon, M.I. & Hellon, C.P. (1980). Suicide and age in Alberta, Canada: 1951 to 1977. *Archives of General Psychiatry 37*, 511-513.

Spirito, A., Brown, L., Overholser, J. & Fritz, G. (1989). Attempted suicide in adolescence: A review and critique of the literature. *Clinical Psychology Review 9*, 335-363.

Spirito, A., Overholser, J., Ashworth, S., Morgan, J. & Benedict, D. C. (1988). Evaluation of a suicide awareness curriculum for high school students. *Journal of the American Academy of Child and Adolescent Psychiatry 27*, 705-711.

Steede, K. K. & Range, L. K. (1989). Does television induce suicidal contagion with adolescents? *Journal of Community Psychology 17*, 166-172.

Stiffman, A. (1989).Suicide attempts in runaway youths. *Suicide and Life-Threatening Behavior 19*, 147-159.

Streiner, D.L. & Adams, K.S. (1987). Evaluation of the effectiveness of suicide prevention programmes: A methodological perspective. *Suicide and Life Threatening Behavior 17*, 93-106.

Strober, M., Lampert, C., Schmidt, S. & Morrell, W. (1993). The course of major depressive disorder in adolescents, I: Recovery and risk of manic switching in a follow-up of psychotic and nonpsychotic subtypes. *Journal of the American Academy of Child and Adolescent Psychiatry 32*, 34-43.

Topol, P. & Reznikoff, M. (1982). Perceived peer and family relationships, hopelessness and locus of control as factors in adolescent suicide attempts. *Suicide and Life-Threatening Behavior 12*, 141-150.

Tsuang, M. T. & Buda, M. (1990). The epidemiology of suicide: Implications for clinical practice. In S. J. Blumenthal & D. J. Kupfer (eds.) *Suicide over the lifecycle*, 17-38. Washington, DC: American Psychiatric Press.

Vaillant, G. E. & Blumenthal, S. J. (1990). *Suicide over the life cycle: Risk factors and life span development.* Washington, DC: American Psychiatric Press.

Weishaar, M.E. & Beck, A.T. (1990). Cognitive approaches to understanding and treating suicidal behavior. In S. Blumenthal & D. Kupfer (eds.) *Suicide over the lifecycle*, 469-498. Washington, DC: American Psychiatric Press.

Weissman, M. M., Livingston Bruce, M., Leaf, P.J., Florio, L.P. & Hozer III, C. (1991). Affective disorders. In L. N. Robins & D. A. Regier (eds). *Psychiatric disorders in America: The Epidemiologic Catchment Area Study*, 53-80. New York: Free Press.

Weissman, M.M. (1974). The epidemiology of suicide attempts. *Archives of General Psychiatry 30*, 737-746.

Wetzel, R. D., Margulies, T., Davies, R. & Karam, E. (1980). Hopelessness, depression, and suicide intent. *Journal of Clinical Psychiatry 41*, 159-167.

Whitlock, F.A. (1971) Migration and suicide. *Medical Journal of Australia 2*, 840-848.

Williams, C. B. & Nickels, J. B. (1969). Internal-external control dimensions as related to accident and suicide proneness. *Journal of Consulting and Clinical Psychology 3*, 485-494..

World Health Organization (1972). *World Health Statistics Annual.* Geneva: Author.

World Health Organization (1981). *World Health Statistics Annual.* Geneva: Author.

World Health Organization (1989). *World Health Statistics Annual.* Geneva: Author.

World Health Organization (1992). *World Health Statistics Annual.* Geneva: Author.

World Health Organization (1975). Suicide statistics: The problem of comparability. *Chronicle 29*, 188-193.

World Health Organization (1982). *Changing patterns in suicide behaviour.* Copenhagen, Denmark: WHO/Euro reports and studies.

Yanish, D. & Battle, J. (1985). Relationship between self-esteem, depression and alcohol consumption among adolescents. Psychological Reports, *Annals de Pediatriae (Paris), 1966, 33*: 503-506.

PART IV

Conclusions

14

Time Trends in Psychosocial Disorders of Youth

DAVID J. SMITH and MICHAEL RUTTER

The purpose of this study was to consider the scientific evidence on whether psychosocial disorders in young people have become more, or less, frequent over the last 50 years, to determine how possible explanations for any changes found might be tested, and to make a preliminary assessment of possible causal explanations in the light of the evidence. The psychosocial disorders considered are ones that are common but involve a serious malfunctioning of individuals in their social setting. The study is therefore concerned both with individual factors (including the process of individual development) and with social structures and conditions. The disorders that we have examined are those that tend to rise or peak in frequency during the teenage years: namely crime, suicide and suicidal behaviours, depression, eating disorders (anorexia nervosa and bulimia), and abuse of alcohol and psychoactive drugs. However, we have not studied those less common conditions that also increase in frequency during adolescence but which seem to represent qualitatively distinct disorders apparently less open to broader social influences. Thus, schizophrenia was excluded from our remit.

This concluding part of the report is divided into two chapters. The first presents the main conclusions on time trends in the psychosocial disorders, but also highlights major gaps in knowledge and weaknesses in the methods underpinning present knowledge. The second sets out our conclusions on possible causal explanations of the time trends and suggests priorities for future research.

Since several of the target disorders are ones that have been associated with social disadvantage, it might be expected that, as living conditions have improved over the course of this century, they would have become progressively less frequent. The evidence from our study firmly contradicts that commonly held assumption. Physical health has improved in step with better living conditions, as shown by the steadily falling infantile mortality and a steadily increasing life expectancy. However, against expectation, psychosocial disorders have shown no such fall in frequency, and indeed the evidence reviewed in earlier chapters indicates that many have become substantially more prevalent. This study is a first attempt to bring together information from a wide range of sources and to develop a new framework of analysis in order to tackle this puzzling problem.

DISTINCTIVE FEATURES OF THIS STUDY

This study is distinctive in several key respects. It is unusual in considering a diverse range of psychosocial disorders and the ways in which they may be interrelated. It is also unusual in bringing together several normally separate traditions of research: the psychological tradition, which concentrates on explaining why one individual behaves differently from another; the sociological tradition, which concentrates on change in social conditions and institutions; and the tradition of epidemiology, which concentrates on patterns of disease as they are distributed in the community. For the first time, this report brings together separate bodies of data on secular trends, on differences between nations, on risk and protective factors for individuals, and on how disorders relate to the developmental processes linking childhood with adult life.

A central element of the research strategy was the decision to make certain specific and serious psychosocial disorders the main object of study. Naturally, the background to an understanding of malfunction is an explanation of how, under favourable circumstances, the individual grows and develops so as to function well. However, a crucial advantage of focusing on disorders is that these can be defined – even though definitional problems remain substantial – whereas well-being and happiness are extremely vague concepts, open to marked attitudinal biases. Candidates for inclusion in the study were psychosocial disorders that are serious, yet affect a substantial minority of the population; that are capable of reasonably tight definition and measurement; and that are a threat to individual and social well-being. We are alert to the possibility that there is increasing polarization – an increasing risk of disorders for certain groups along with increasing protection for others – just as rising unemployment has in recent years been accompanied by increasing prosperity among those in employment. Nevertheless, the research strategy was based on the assumption that changes in the prevalence of psychosocial disorders might constitute indicators of wider changes affecting most people.

A possible objection is that behaviour may be functional for the individual or group, but dysfunctional for society at large. For example, it could be true that for some people, at least, crime does pay. Thus, in some areas, it may be that organized crime provides the best available opportunity for some young people to earn a living and establish a stable pattern of relationships (see Chapter 9). Nevertheless, this kind of example is highly exceptional. Crime is generally an unsuccessful way of life both in terms of standard of living and in terms of personal fulfilment; moreover, there is ample evidence that persistent criminal offenders tend to suffer from a range of other problems and difficulties. Crime is correctly seen as both an individual and a social failure. Similarly, depression, anorexia and bulimia, suicide and suicidal behaviours, and abuse of psychoactive drugs, are rightly called disorders.

The second element of the research strategy was the decision to focus on secular trends: that is, change over historic time. This contrasts with the main research tradition, which has concentrated on individual differences and developmental pathways. Of course, the study also aims to make use of the findings on individual differences and developmental processes in testing causal explanations of secular trends. However, it is important to be aware, as argued in Chapter 2, that explanations of individual differences may not generalize to the aggregate level. For example, individual differences in height are largely determined by genetic inheritance, while the secular trend of increase in average height is probably a result of improved diet.

Having defined psychosocial disorders in a fairly restrictive way, the final element of the research strategy was to cast the net more widely when looking for societal changes that may help to explain trends in the disorders. Among the changes reviewed are the lengthening period of adolescence, the increase in life expectancy, the postwar baby boom superimposed on the long-term reduction in the proportion of young people within the population, the dramatic economic growth and improvement in the standard of living, the substantial improvements in health, housing and other living conditions, the lengthening of education, the increase in leisure, fluctuations in the level of unemployment, the increasing instability of family units, the widespread changes in family structure and functioning, the increase in female employment, and in particular employment of mothers with young children, the growth of the mass media, and the complex changes in moral concepts and values. Not much progress has yet been made towards identifying the separate effect of each of these variables. As set out in Chapter 2, the methods for doing this are in principle available, although cross-national comparisons have their limitations, as well as providing opportunities. The main problem is that many of the social and economic changes of the past 50 or 100 years tended to occur at the same time, so that natural experiments that test the separate effect of particular changes are rare. Also, the number of countries for which useful information is available is fairly small, and each has a unique combination of complex characteristics. In spite of these limitations, the study of cross-national trends has great potential, and this report aims to open up the field.

MEASURING THE TARGET DISORDERS

Substantial difficulties arise in finding measures for each of the target disorders, and in establishing reliable time series data. Problems of method have been discussed in a systematic way in each of the preceding chapters, but a few general points stand out.

None of the target disorders constitutes a uniform set of behaviours; each is heterogeneous. With the exception of suicide, all of the target disorders vary widely in severity. The variation is perhaps widest in the case of crime, which covers everything from stealing a ball of string to murder. Depression varies from a passing mood to long-lasting feelings of despair that severely limit a person's capacities and activities. The problems caused by alcohol range from occasional rowdiness and a hangover to chronic ill-health, inability to hold down a job, and frequent and serious violence. There is a similar range of problems caused by other psychoactive drugs, depending, among other things, on the specific drugs and their level of use. Finally, suicidal behaviours encompass a wide range, some coming much closer to actual suicide than others. Whereas many suicides are recruited from people who had earlier shown suicidal behaviour, the majority of those who engage in suicidal behaviour never complete suicide (and some never intended to do so). Hence, the measurement of suicidal behaviours, as opposed to suicide, is an important goal, and the wide range of severity among these behaviours becomes an important issue.

Because the target disorders are heterogeneous, it can be misleading to rely on a single, composite measure. For example, it is more fruitful to study trends in homicide or theft than in all recorded crimes. An important limitation of data currently available is that they often lump together disorders that ideally would be counted separately.

In studying cross-national time trends there is also the conceptual problem that disorders must be defined in relation to a particular society at a particular time. A simple example is theft, which varies in seriousness according to the value of what is stolen. Hence, theft of a pound of tea was far more serious in eighteenth-century England than now, because tea at that time was a relatively expensive item. Similarly, contemporary comparison of theft between different countries has to take account of values. This looks like a simple problem at first sight, because modern economic systems make it possible to value every item, and researchers have established 'purchasing power parities' between currencies, which allow comparisons to be made between countries. However, calculation of purchasing power parities raises difficult questions, and can only begin to make sense when the economies under consideration are broadly similar.

Other kinds of crime are defined in relation to shifting norms that are still harder to quantify. For example, what used to count as parental discipline has become criminal child abuse, and more sympathetic investigation has led to large increases in the incidence of reported rapes. These problems apply to other psychosocial disorders too. For example, all the elements of the definition of depression (such as sadness, irritability, loss of energy, loss of weight, sleep difficulties, hopelessness, helplessness, and suicidal ideas) involve an implicit appeal to a cultural norm. If people come to expect a fuller or more serene existence they will presumably become more likely to report symptoms of these kinds. A parallel argument has led to the development of relative definitions of poverty (by reference to normal living standards within a particular society). The problem is a very difficult one, which may eventually enforce a new approach towards definition. At present we can only be alert to shifting values that underlie available measures of the target disorders.

For most types of disorder, several measures are available, and much can be learnt from systematically comparing the results produced by each one. In the case of crime, for example, three types of measure are available: self-reported offending; official records of offences, arrests, and prosecutions; and victim surveys. Both self-reports and victim surveys reveal far more offences than appear in official statistics, but cross-checks show that both self-reports and victim surveys have high validity. Detailed research on the inter-relationships between these measures has improved understanding of the filters between a crime occurring and its being recorded in some way or other.

In the field of alcohol use, there are measures of consumption, and measures of various specific harms associated with alcohol, such as traffic accidents, cirrhosis of the liver, and violent crime. The evidence suggests that total consumption tends to be associated with an increase in problem drinking, and in alcohol-related disorders, but the relationship is mediated by the patterns of consumption within a particular society. A wide range of measures have been used to capture use and abuse of illicit psychoactive drugs, all of them indirect (there are no reliable statistics on the amounts sold or consumed, and general population surveys are of very limited use). There is not much systematic knowledge about the relationships between these various measures (such as seizures by customs, addicts notified to the authorities, drug-related deaths, studies of clinic populations, and recorded drug offences).

In the case of suicide, the central core of evidence comes from the officially recorded cause of death. It is generally accepted that while nearly all deaths are recorded in developed countries, there is a systematic bias against recording the cause as suicide, because suicide was for a long time condemned by the church, considered to be shameful, and in most countries illegal. To a degree that is perhaps surprising, the decision to classify a death as suicide does depend on judgement and perception, as well as fact. However, there is powerful evidence to show that rates of recorded suicide are a good indicator of actual rates, even though suicides are under-recorded (see Chapter 13). In particular, the recorded rates of suicide of immigrants to the United States have been shown to reflect the rates recorded in their countries of origin. However, evidence about suicidal behaviours is far more fragmentary; it mainly derives from hospital admissions data, but there is little or no standardization of the definitions and recording procedures used.

In short, for all of these disorders the measurement problems are formidable. In some cases, there is a considerable body of work that systematically compares the results of different measures; in other cases, this research effort has hardly begun. These measurement problems set limits on what can be said at present about cross-national trends, although some important conclusions can already be drawn. However, many of the problems can in principle be overcome by future research, as set out at the end of the next chapter.

PSYCHOSOCIAL DISORDERS AND INDIVIDUAL DEVELOPMENT

All of the psychosocial disorders considered in this study tend to increase during adolescence, although the exact relationship with the process of individual development varies substantially from one disorder to another. The link between age and crime is particularly close. The rate of crime, whether measured by convictions, arrests, or self-reports, rises from a very low level before adolescence to reach a peak around the age of 17, and thereafter declines rapidly to reach a very low level again by the age of 30. The decline after the peak is so steep that there are few new recruits to criminal activity after the end of adolescence. Crime, therefore, is mostly committed by adolescents and young adults.

The decline after the peak at 17 is real enough, but the rise before the age of 14 or 15 is probably misleading: to a large extent, it reflects the fact that misbehaviour by children and young adolescents is not normally dealt with by the criminal justice system. Crime in adolescents and adults is nearly always preceded by conduct disorders of some kind in childhood, although most antisocial children do not become criminal adults. Adolescence coincides not so much with an increase in antisocial behaviour as with a change in the form of such behaviour and in the way it is dealt with.

The crime rate is much higher among males than among females, although the contrast is greater among official offenders (typically around 8:1) than among self-reported offenders (typically around 3:1), partly because surveys tend to emphasize the less serious offences to a greater extent than official statistics. Nevertheless, the shape of the age-crime curve is closely similar for the two sexes. It is also very similar in different countries and at different times. Furthermore, it has been shown that certain other life events, such as misbehaviour in prisons and motor vehicle accidents, are related to age in much the same way as crime. All of this suggests that the age-crime curve springs from certain basic and general features of human development. Perhaps surprisingly, researchers have not so far been successful in establishing what these features are. In particular, theories that seek to explain why people tend to desist from crime after a certain age have not stood up well to the evidence.

Use of alcohol (as reflected in both frequency of drinking, and the quantity consumed per occasion) increases steeply during adolescence, then declines sharply in early adulthood. These age trends are broadly similar in a range of European countries and in North America, although the rise in adolescence and the subsequent fall are particularly marked in countries with a high overall level of consumption. Use of other psychoactive drugs also increases sharply during adolescence. In the case of marijuana, this is followed by a rapid decline in use after the age of 20. Although the data are inadequate, it is likely that use of heroin, cocaine, and certain other drugs, tends to persist to a later age, but declines after the age of 30. There is evidence of a trend during the 1980s for the average age of drug users to increase, probably because new recruitment of teenage users levelled off after increasing in an earlier period.

A large number of studies agree in showing that the rate of depressive disorders increases sharply during adolescence. The rates for girls and boys are about the same up to the age of 11, but thereafter the rate rises much more quickly among girls. As a result, adult rates of depressive disorders are about twice as high among females as among males. This broad pattern is found both among clinical samples and among samples of the general population. However, unlike the crime rate and the use of psychoactive drugs, the rate of depressive disorders does not decline after adolescence, but remains high in adult life.

As mentioned earlier, both of the eating disorders considered in this report – anorexia nervosa, and bulimia nervosa – occur almost exclusively during adolescence or early adulthood. Also, both are far more common among females than among males.

The risk of suicide tends to increase with age. It is very low among children, increases substantially around mid-adolescence, then increases more steadily throughout the later teenage years. Thereafter the relationship with age varies according to family circumstances and between the sexes and between countries, but there is a general tendency for the risk to increase further with age in most countries. However, suicide accounts for a far higher proportion of all deaths among younger than among older people.

The data on suicidal behaviour (short of completed suicide) derive from two main sources: records kept by centres where suicidal patients are treated, and general population surveys. Both are agreed in showing a much higher risk among females than among males (in contrast to the higher rate of completed suicide among males than among females). Studies of records kept by centres show higher rates of suicidal behaviour among those aged 15 to 44 than among older people (whereas rates of completed suicide continue to increase with age in the second half of the life cycle). Surveys of the general population similarly show a rise in suicidal behaviours during the teenage period.

These results show striking contrasts between the sexes in the development of psychosocial disorders. Eating disorders are far more common among females than among males. Crime, alcohol and drug abuse, and suicide are all more common among males than among females (the male excess being greatest for crime), whereas depressive disorders and suicidal behaviour (short of completed suicide) are considerably more frequent among females than among males. In the case of depressive disorders, and possibly also in the case of suicidal behaviour, the difference between the sexes emerges during adolescence. This may also be true of suicide, but this is hard to establish, because of the very low rate of suicide in childhood (and uncertainty over its recording). By the age of 15 there is a large difference in suicide rates between males and females. Crime and conduct disorders are more common among males than females even in childhood. A possible explanation of the pattern is that aggression and impulsivity – more characteristic of males than females – are common factors in crime and completed suicide; whereas expressed or acknowledged emotion – more characteristic of females than males – is the common factor in depression and suicidal behaviour.

Although all of the psychosocial disorders increase during adolescence, the reasons for this increase are not well understood and are unlikely to be the same for all disorders. Adolescence is a period of multiple transitions (puberty, first sexual relationship, distancing from parents, leaving school, starting work, forming a new family) and it may be that the stresses associated with these transitions cause an elevated risk of psychosocial disorder. However, a broad and general explanation of this kind cannot account for the relationships with age after adolescence: for example, the continued increase with age in the rate of completed suicide, compared with the sharp decline in crime after the peak at the age of 17.

TIME TRENDS IN PSYCHOSOCIAL DISORDERS

Overview

It is clear that there have been substantial increases in psychosocial disorders of youth since the Second World War in nearly all developed countries. Information on longer-term trends, going back to the beginning of the twentieth century and beyond, is limited and completely absent for certain disorders such as depression. However, the limited information available shows that the increases in psychosocial disorders of the past 40 to 50 years were sudden, and were not the continuation of trends established earlier in the century. In the case of eating disorders, the evidence is too weak to justify the conclusion that there has clearly been an increase, although it does not contradict the hypothesis that one may have occurred. For all of the other disorders, there is unmistakable evidence of a postwar increase.

Findings for Specific Disorders

Crime

Increases in crime during the past 40 years have been particularly striking, and most of this crime is committed by young people up to the age of 29. The long run of statistics on which this conclusion is based are those of recorded crime for the period 1951 to 1990. These show considerable variations between countries, but a typical increase in the rate of crime per head of population was by a factor of around 5. The USA, Australia, and Canada registered a decline in the 1980s following the earlier upward trend. In the remaining countries, except Japan, the upward trend continued.

Unfortunately, crime classification systems vary so much between countries that detailed comparisons cannot be made for highly specific types of crime. However, if broad categories of crime are considered, such as aggravated theft, and other theft, the strong upward trend in crime rates is confirmed. Some more specific offences can be compared over a more recent period (1977-1990). Substantial increases are registered for theft of motor vehicles and for breaking and entering in most countries. Also, there have been substantial increases over the same period in the rates of serious assault (other than homicide) in Australia, Denmark, England and Wales, and the USA. Homicide is of particular interest because few homicides remain unrecorded, at least in developed countries. While there have been substantial increases in rates of homicide in most of these countries since 1951, these increases are considerably smaller in most countries than increases in the rates of other crimes. In France and Japan the homicide rate has declined, and in Japan the decline has been substantial (to 40 per cent of the 1951 figure).

Information about trends over time in crime rates can be provided from victim surveys for England and the United States from 1981 onwards. There is a reasonable degree of consistency between the pattern of change shown by official data and victim surveys. This suggests that the long-run increases in crime rates shown by statistics of recorded crime reflect an increase in criminal behaviour on any appropriate definition. Further confirmation is provided by an international victim survey carried out in 1989. There is a reasonably good fit between cross-national differences in crime rates shown by this survey and cross-national differences shown by statistics of recorded crime.

Evidence on trends in the nineteenth and twentieth centuries suggests that there is a U-shaped curve, with high rates of crime and disorder in the early part of the nineteenth century, especially in larger cities, falling rates in the latter half of the nineteenth century and the early part of the twentieth century, followed by a large increase after the Second World War.

Because antisocial behaviour almost always begins in childhood or adolescence, and falls off in early adolescence, the rise in crime is something that applies to young people. Over the last 50 years the sex difference in crime has narrowed somewhat indicating that if anything, the rise has been more marked in females than males. The rise began after the Second World War and has continued up to the present time, although possibly at a slower pace in the last decade or so.

Alcohol and Drugs

There was a falling rate of alcohol consumption in the first quarter of the twentieth century, a stable rate between the two World Wars, then a marked increase between about 1950 and 1980, when a plateau was reached. The net effect for most countries is a level of alcohol consumption in the 1980s that is still far above that in the 1930s, but with less between-country variation than was the case in the earlier time period. Of course, consumption of alcohol and psychosocial disorders related to alcohol are not the same thing, but there is a considerable body of evidence to show that drink-related problems tend to increase in line with total consumption. The figures for deaths from cirrhosis of the liver follow broadly the same pattern as the consumption figures.

Evidence on use of psychoactive drugs (other than alcohol) before the Second World War is sparse, although opiates were probably quite commonly used in Victorian England, and were freely available until the early part of the twentieth century. There is clear evidence from large-scale epidemiological surveys in the USA of a massive increase in use of illicit drugs in the 30-year period starting in 1950. The 1977 National Survey on Drug Abuse showed that the lifetime rate of drug use was very low among those born before 1940, but increased substantially for each successive cohort after that. The ECA (Epidemiological Catchment Area) data gathered in six US cities in the early 1980s were closely similar. The ECA produced findings on drug abuse or dependency as well as use, and these also indicated a massive increase starting in the 1950s.

The large-scale survey data available in the USA are lacking for European countries, but for certain countries information is available on number of registered addicts, drug-related arrests, drug-related deaths, and amount of drugs seized by the customs and police. From such sources it is clear that Western European countries, like the USA, have experienced a massive increase in drug use and abuse, although this may have occurred slightly later in Europe.

A wide range of illicit drugs are in use. Each has specific effects, and some are more harmful than others. In both North America and Europe, cannabis is much the commonest drug used, but, in the UK, surveys suggest that amphetamines, hallucinogens, solvents and 'ecstasy' have all probably been used by some 5 to 10 per cent of young adults. A much smaller proportion (less than 1 per cent in the UK) have used heroin or cocaine.

There is conflicting evidence about trends in use of illicit drugs since 1980. Survey evidence both for the USA and for European countries suggests that there has been a decline or levelling off in the use of cannabis since around 1980, but this is not necessarily paralleled by changes in the use or abuse of other drugs. Thus, Interpol statistics for eight European countries show substantial increases in drug-related deaths since 1980. A range of British data suggest a continuing increase in drug use in the 1980s (official notifications of new opiate and cocaine addicts, seizures, drug-related deaths, national surveys).

Depression

There are, of course, no official statistics on depressive disorders, and it is only in recent years that general population surveys have been carried out that provide estimates of their prevalence. Nothing is known about time trends before the Second World War, but a range of studies show that there has been an increase in depressive disorders during the postwar period. There are five kinds of relevant evidence. The first is from US studies of the relatives of people diagnosed as suffering from some kind of mental illness together with control groups ('family studies'). These have tended to use diagnostic interviews and a categorical method of assignment to depressive or non-depressive groups, rather than psychometric scaling. They show that the risk of depression and other affective disorders tends to be greater for younger cohorts. One relevant study is prospective and longitudinal.

The second source is cross-sectional general population surveys ('community surveys'). The most important is the US Epidemiological Catchment Area Study (ECA) carried out in 1981. This used fully structured personal interviews in six areas within the USA, conducted by trained, non-specialist interviewers, from which a categorical diagnosis of a range of psychiatric disorders was made according to rigorous decision procedures. The study covered both the residential and the institutional population. A number of other studies subsequently used closely similar methods. The survey results can be used to calculate lifetime prevalence rates for depression and other disorders (the proportion of respondents who have suffered from a depressive disorder at any time in their lives). If the risk of depression is equal for successive age cohorts, then the lifetime prevalence rate should increase with age. In fact, the study found the opposite pattern, suggesting that the risk of depression is substantially higher for younger than for older respondents. Another similar study in the USA, one in Canada, one in New Zealand, and one in south-east London have also shown a decline in lifetime prevalence for later age groups, although in two cases the decline started at a later age (50 or 55) than in the case of the ECA. A prospective community study in Lundby, Sweden, also showed an increasing risk of depression for later age cohorts, this time based on contemporaneous assessments by trained clinicians. However, several other cross-sectional surveys have failed to find a decline in lifetime prevalence with age: one in Korea, one in Puerto Rico, and two local studies in the USA.

The third type of evidence comes from the link between depression and suicide. Rates of suicide among young people (aged 15-24) have increased, while at the same time there has been an increase in the proportion of suicides diagnosed (for example, from psychological 'autopsies') as having suffered from depressive disorders.

Fourth, in two American studies, repeat surveys were carried out using closely similar questioning methods. The first, which covered children aged 7 to 16, showed an increase in the prevalence of depressive disorders after an interval of 13 years. The second showed a decline in psychological well-being among cross-sectional samples of adults after a 19-year interval.

Fifth, two studies, one in Zurich, the other in London, have used hospital admissions data to assess change in the proportion of patients who were suffering from depressive disorders. However, because of substantial problems of interpretation, no firm conclusions can be drawn from the results (diagnosis from hospital records is difficult, and changes in the characteristics of patients admitted may reflect changes in the treatment available).

On balance the evidence from these five types of study supports the view that there has been an increase in depressive conditions in the most recent birth cohorts. A considerable effort has been made to establish whether the results of the cross-sectional research, which are crucial to the overall balance of evidence, could be the result of recall effects. These effects will arise if respondents are less likely to remember earlier than more recent episodes of depression. Particularly if these episodes are more likely to occur early than late in life, then lifetime prevalence will appear to decline with age because older respondents will have tended to forget about episodes of depression that are now in the distant past. The detailed discussion of this issue (see Chapter 11) concludes that recall effects are unlikely to be the main explanation for the pattern of results. Perhaps the two most important points are that the decline in lifetime prevalence with age did not apply to black respondents (nor to

Hispanics in the Los Angeles area); and that the results of studies in which respondents are questioned again after an interval are wholly inconsistent with the theory that earlier incidents tend to be forgotten.

Although the evidence supports the view that there has been an increase in depressive disorders in young people, it provides an extremely limited description of the pattern of increase (apart from the suggestion that the increase may have been slightly greater in males than in females). The size of the change cannot be estimated, especially because of the reliance on recall in many studies (there *are* recall effects, even if they cannot account for the whole pattern of the results). It is not clear, as yet, whether the observed increase in prevalence is confined to depression, or whether it also applies to other psychiatric disorders: the evidence from the ECA suggests that there has been a general increase in psychological dysfunction, but this would need to be confirmed by further research.

Eating Disorders

Two types of eating disorder are covered by this study: anorexia nervosa, and bulimia nervosa. Anorexia is characterized by weight loss and an exaggerated fear of gaining weight, an unrealistic perception of body shape (the subject believes she is fat when she is in fact thin), and (in girls) a stop to menstruation. Bulimia is characterized by episodes of binge eating along with use of extreme methods for losing weight, while body weight remains roughly normal. Females are far more at risk of both disorders than males (by a factor of 10:1). Anorexia peaks in the adolescent years, somewhere between 14 and 19. The age of onset of bulimia is later, at around 19 or 20 years of age. Because both conditions are rare, it is difficult to obtain good information about time trends, and it is not clear whether the incidence of either disorder has increased.

In the case of anorexia, the longest run of data (from clinic records) goes back 60 years. Although it has been interpreted as showing an upward trend, other interpretations are also possible, and there is not enough agreement between different studies to conclude that the trend is, indeed, upward.

Bulimia was first formally described in the late 1970s, and although a number of studies have shown increased referrals for the condition over the last decade, this could result from 'recognition bias' due to the extreme modernity of the disease. Community surveys have shown higher lifetime prevalence rates for younger birth cohorts, which suggests that prevalence may have increased over time, but there is evidence of substantial recall problems. Also, because bulimia is rare, differences between age groups in community surveys reflect a small number of identified cases, and are sensitive to sampling biases and errors. Hence, an increase in bulimia has not yet been demonstrated conclusively by the limited research so far carried out.

Suicide and Suicidal Behaviours

Information on time trends in suicide is far more complete, and extends over a longer period, than for the other target disorders. Although not all suicides are officially recorded as such (perhaps particularly where the dead person was a child) there is strong evidence to show that the official statistics are a good indicator. In Europe as a whole, the pattern of change in the present century is an increase in overall rates of suicide (all age groups); there are considerable variations in trends between individual countries, which have reduced cross-national differences. However, in the last 30 years or so, the increase in suicide has been confined to adolescents and young adults: in many countries rates in old people have fallen over the same time period.

Rates of suicide are substantially higher among males than among females, typically by a factor of 2.5 to 3.0. The male to female ratio tends to be higher in the case of young people.

In most European countries, with the notable exception of West Germany, there has been a considerable increase in the rate of suicide among young males aged 15-24 and 25-34 over the period between 1970 and 1990. This trend was particularly strong during the 10 years from 1970, whereas in the period 1983-86 the increase levelled off or in some countries reversed. Among young females, there were increasing rates in a majority of European countries, but no such increases in seven of them; in the period after 1980, there were declines in the rates of suicide among young females in most countries, so that the female rate had by the end of the period returned to its 1970 level, or had gone down below it. One effect of these trends is to increase still further the difference in risk of suicide between young males and females.

Information on suicidal behaviours short of suicide is, of course, much less reliable. Data are, however, available from certain centres that keep records of treatment of patients following suicidal behaviour. These show a marked increase in suicidal behaviours from the early 1950s to the mid 1970s or early 1980s, followed by a decline, the latter having been possibly more marked among women than among men. In contrast to suicide, the rate of suicidal behaviours is much higher among females than among males, but the effect of recent changes has been to bring the male and female rates closer together.

Time Trends by Age and Sex

The earlier section on individual development summarized changes in incidence of the disorders throughout the life course. This section considers the evidence on time trends in the disorders among young people specifically, and briefly reviews the differences between males and females.

Crime is so much more common among young males than among other groups that the upward trend in crime overall since around 1950 largely reflects an upward trend in offending by young males. The proportion of offences committed by females varies between countries, but typically, the rate of offending is between five and ten times as high among males as among females. In many countries, the difference in the rate of offending between the sexes has narrowed over the past 40 years, although the male preponderance remains very great. These findings imply that the crime rate among young females has risen very substantially from a low base over the postwar period.

Although it is known that consumption of alcohol and illicit drugs peaks in youth and young adulthood, there is little detailed evidence on time trends for consumption by particular age groups. However, it is certain that the postwar rise in overall alcohol consumption implies a considerable rise in consumption among young people. In the case of illicit drugs, the picture is dominated by young people, so that overall rises in consumption are largely rises in consumption among young people. Boys use more of all substances, with the exception of tobacco, than girls, but there is some evidence of a trend towards convergence in levels of use between the sexes.

The most impressive evidence for an increase in rates of depression comes from comparing different birth cohorts in cross-sectional community surveys. These comparisons suggest that rates of depression are higher among people who are young now than they were among young people 20 or 30 years ago. It is not yet known whether rates of depression among people in later age groups have also increased, but it seems probable that they have not. After the age of 11, rates of depression are higher among females than among males by a factor of about 2:1. However, the difference in rates between the sexes is possibly gradually reducing over time, with the rise in depressive disorders probably more marked in young men.

Both anorexia and bulimia occur mainly among girls and young women. As already discussed, evidence on time trends for these disorders is uncertain, but if there are any trends they will apply to girls and young women.

There were substantial increases in rates of suicide among young males aged 15-34 between 1970 and 1990 but in many countries rates in old people have tended to fall over the same time period. Among young females, there was a much less marked upward trend up to 1980, but a slight decline after that. The suicide rate is 2 to 3 times as high among young males as among young females, and the effect of recent trends is to increase the gap. Since 1970, there has been a relative increase in the risk of suicide among younger as compared with older age groups, so that young people have come to form an increasing proportion of a generally increasing number of suicides. Going back to 1900 and beyond, where records are available, suicide rates for the 15-24 and 25-34 age groups reached an all-time high in most European countries in the period 1980-87.

The rate of suicidal behaviours, unlike suicide, is much higher among females than among males. The increase in suicidal behaviours in the 25-year period from 1950 applied to all age groups. The decline since the early 1980s has been more marked among females than among males, so that the rates for the sexes have tended to converge.

Two broad conclusions emerge from this analysis. First, the prevalence of all of the disorders among young people has increased in the postwar period, except that there is insufficient evidence to come to a firm decision on eating disorders. This broad conclusion is qualified by the decline in rates of suicide among young females since 1980, and the possible declines in use of certain illicit drugs over that same recent period. Second, while there are striking differences in the prevalence of disorders between males and females (crime, suicide, and substance use are high for males, whereas depression, eating disorders, and suicidal behaviours are high for females), there has been a trend towards convergence between rates for males and females in several cases (crime, substance use, depression, suicidal behaviours) contrasting with a trend towards divergence in one case (suicide). However, the convergence has come about through contrasting secular trends in some instances. Thus, the rise in crime has been more marked in females but that in depression more so in males.

Cross-national Differences

Some researchers on crime, alcohol consumption, and suicide, have carried out formal, quantitative analyses that assess the relationships between national rates, or trends in national rates, and demographic, social, and economic factors at the national level. In this style of research, which has not so far been very successful, cross-national differences are taken as the starting point, and are what the analysis seeks to explain. The results of research of that kind will be summarized in the next chapter on causal explanations. This section briefly notes the known differences between countries in rates of the disorders and in trends over time.

There are some considerable differences between countries in the slope of the increase in rate of crime per head of population since around 1950. While the steepest increases between 1951 and 1990 were by a factor of 29 in Spain and 27 in Canada, a more typical increase was by a factor of around 5. Remarkably, in the context of the trends for other countries, the total crime rate in Japan started at a low level, and declined slightly over the 40-year period. The major exception of Japan will be a good starting point for any attempt to explain increasing crime rates. The USA, Australia, and Canada registered a decline in the 1980s following the earlier upward trend. In the remaining countries, except Japan, the upward trend continued. These general findings are confirmed when major categories of crime are considered separately, although, as mentioned earlier, increases in homicide were smaller in most countries than increases in other crimes. In France and Japan the homicide rate has declined, and in Japan the decline has been substantial (to 40 per cent of the 1951 figure).

While consumption of alcohol increased substantially from 1950 to around 1970 in most countries, there have been recent declines in some developed countries; however, in developing countries consumption continues to increase. The postwar increases in consumption occurred in all Western European countries except France, which already had the highest level of consumption at the beginning of the period. Between 1960 and 1980, the effect of cross-national trends was to bring levels of consumption in European countries closer together. The countries in Europe can be divided into groups according to their beverage preferences. There is a high level of consumption in the southern wine-drinking countries, where consumption tends to be frequent, a low level in the northern countries where beer and spirits were traditionally preferred, and tended to be consumed on infrequent binges, and several other less obviously distinct groups. There is a trend towards convergence of beverage preferences in different countries, associated with increased trade and cultural diffusion. In countries around the Baltic there was a steep increase in alcohol consumption between 1960 and 1980, then a steep decline associated with public anti-alcohol campaigns.

Cross-national data on use of illicit drugs are rather fragmentary. The postwar increase occurred rather sooner in the USA than in Europe, and absolute levels of use are considerably higher in the USA than in European countries.

The evidence on depression is not sufficient for detailed cross-national comparisons, especially since definitions and methods vary considerably between the various studies. The same applies to eating disorders.

There are large and consistent cross-national differences in suicide rates among European countries (the lowest rates in southern Europe, the highest in a belt stretching from Belgium and France through Switzerland, Austria and Hungary, to Russia). Trends in the present century have led to some convergence among national suicide rates in Europe. The considerable increase in rate of suicide among males aged 15-34 occurred in most European countries, but West Germany was a notable exception. Data on suicidal behaviours are more localized, and have not been analysed in terms of national differences.

More and Less Severe Varieties

With the exception of suicide, all of the target disorders are heterogeneous, and all encompass a wide range of severity. Where information is available about the more severe varieties, it tends to confirm the conclusion that these have substantially increased during the postwar period. The statistics for the more serious crimes show a strong upward trend, although the rising trend in homicide is less pronounced than for other crimes. Statistics on serious harm caused by alcohol and drug abuse (for example, cirrhosis of the liver, and drug-related deaths) show large increases in the postwar period. Most of the studies showing an increase in depression refer to depressive disorders and not to the less serious depressive syndrome or mood. Although the evidence is less clear-cut for suicidal behaviours, there is no indication that the increase in these behaviours has been accompanied by a decline in their severity.

CONCLUSION

This report has provided a careful analysis of problems of definition and method that could have created a misleading impression of an increase in psychosocial disorders. These are indeed important, and the information currently available is incomplete in many ways. Yet, after taking account of the problems and limitations, it must still be concluded that there has been a real rise in psychosocial disorders of youth in the postwar period.

15

Towards Causal Explanations of Time Trends in Psychosocial Disorders of Young People

MICHAEL RUTTER and DAVID J. SMITH

OVERVIEW

Inevitably, there are immense problems in testing hypotheses about the causes of the surprising and troubling rise over time in the rate of psychosocial disorders in young people. Also, the enterprise of formulating and testing hypotheses has scarcely begun. Little of the research reported in this volume was designed to test alternative explanations of time trends in a systematic way, using the strategies described in Chapter 2. Detailed and rigorous research has tended to concentrate on individual differences and on developmental processes. The analyses of cross-national trends in rates of suicide reported in Chapter 13 constitute something of an exception, as do some analyses of cross-national trends in rates of recorded crime mentioned in Chapter 9. Even so, such analyses have had little success in identifying the specific societal changes that have an influence.

To a large extent, therefore, finding causal explanations of the increases in psychosocial disorders remains a project for the future. Nevertheless, this report shows that substantial research leverage may be obtained by comparing trends across countries that differ in circumstances connected with postulated risk factors, and by doing so in a way that spans a period of time when rates have gone down, as well as up. From existing evidence, this study can rule out certain widely held causal assumptions and can point to those that remain plausible and worth further study.

What has to be explained is a rise in a wide range of psychosocial disorders in young people that began shortly after the end of the Second World War, that has continued up to the present time but which, at least for some disorders, may have decelerated somewhat in the last decade or so. The rise is one that applies largely to common disorders in adolescents and young adults and not to similar conditions in old people and not to major mental illnesses such as schizophrenia and organic brain disorders (Sartorius et al., 1989). With some disorders in young people, the rise seems to apply about equally to both sexes but with suicide and possibly depression it has affected males more than females and with crime it has affected females somewhat more than males. Ten main conclusions stand out.

1. Although social disadvantage is associated with many psychosocial disorders at any one point in time, worsening living conditions do not account for the rising levels of disorder. At a time when disorders were increasing in frequency, living conditions were improving. Moreover, in those countries where social inequities have increased over the last decade, this has not been associated with an acceleration in the rise in rate of psychosocial disorders in young people. The evidence as a whole indicates that, although poor social circumstances may increase other risk factors (such as family disorganization and breakup), the effects on disorder are indirect.

2. Conversely, increasing affluence in itself also probably does *not* account for the overall increase in psychosocial disorders, although it is likely to play a role in increasing opportunities for crime, and for alcohol and drug abuse. Living conditions in the first half of this century were improving (with concomitant benefits for physical health), but it seems that this was *not* accompanied by any marked increase in psychosocial disorder.

3. Unemployment does create psychosocial risks for individuals but a high level of unemployment does not explain the rise in disorder since the Second World War. Unemployment rates in most countries were rather low in the 1950s and 1960s when disorders were becoming more frequent. Furthermore, the marked rise in unemployment in the late 1970s and 1980s was not associated with any increase in the gradient of rise in disorder.

4. Although poor physical health creates mental hazards, worsening health does not account for the increase in psychosocial disorders. As physical health was improving, psychosocial disorders were becoming more frequent.

5. Increasing levels of family discord and breakup may well have played a role in the rise in psychosocial disorders; the association has been confirmed at both individual and community (or other aggregate) levels. However, there is some uncertainty over this conclusion because the evidence indicates that the main risk stems from discord, and from lack of parental support and involvement, rather than breakup as such. It is clear that divorce rates have risen substantially in most countries in the last 50 years, but the extent to which this reflects an increase in family discord and lack of parental involvement and support, rather than an increasing tendency to resort to divorce when there are marital difficulties, is uncertain.

6. Although the meaning of adolescence has clearly changed over time, it is not known how far this has led to an increase in psychosocial risks. The mere lengthening of the adolescent age period (through a falling age of puberty and a rising age of finishing education) cannot itself account for the rise in disorder because this lengthening was already well advanced before the rise in disorder. Nevertheless, the changing pattern of transitions in adolescence and early adult life may cause risks associated, for example, with a growth of youth culture, a possible increasing isolation of adolescents from adults, a greater financial dependence on parents that coincides with greater autonomy in other respects, earlier engagement in sexual relationships, a possible increase in psychosocial stressors, an increase in peer group influence and a greater number of breakdowns in cohabiting love relationships. This is an issue requiring further research.

7. It is most unlikely that adverse effects of mass media (for example, increasing violence in films and television) largely account for the rise in psychosocial disorders. However, the media do reflect changing attitudes in society and, thus, they may augment the effects of societal change. There is good experimental evidence that people are, to some extent, influenced in their behaviour by what they see and hear in film or television dramas, but the effects depend heavily on the detailed characteristics of the narrative and on individual susceptibilities. Some cross-national longitudinal studies have shown that exposure to television has an influence on later behaviour.

8. There have been important changes in moral values over the last half century, but there is no evidence of a general moral decline, despite the popular assumption that it has occurred. The actual changes in moral concepts and priorities, such as the growth in respect for individual beliefs,

may be connected with the increase in psychosocial disorder, but that must be a subject for future research.

9. Although increasing affluence on its own does not explain the rise in psychosocial disorder, it is possible that the associated increase in people's expectations, together with a parallel difficulty in meeting them, has played some role, and this possibility warrants further investigation.

10. Finally, despite the fact that most psychosocial disorders have increased over much the same period, the evidence suggests that, to some extent, the explanations are different for different specific disorders. For example, it seems that the increased availability of drugs has played a key role in the rise in misuse of drugs, and also perhaps in suicide, and the increased opportunity for crime has had a part in the rise in rates of delinquency.

The rest of this chapter develops these conclusions in greater detail.

LINKS BETWEEN PSYCHOSOCIAL DISORDERS

The detailed results set out in earlier chapters have shown that there are important links between certain of the target disorders. The following are the more important links so far established.

1. *Alcohol and crime.* There is good evidence that changes in the total consumption of alcohol are associated with changes in the level of recorded violent crime (see Chapter 9). The direct psychoactive effect of alcohol is probably only a small part of the explanation of this association. A range of psychological and sociological processes are probably also involved.

2. *Other psychoactive drugs leading to crime.* The connection between use of drugs and crime is much less close than is often assumed: for example, whereas a substantial proportion of young offenders use drugs, most go on using drugs after they have stopped offending. Such findings suggest that use of drugs is more an aspect, than a cause, of delinquency. However, there is a group of persistent and frequent offenders who are also persistent multiple users of heroin and other drugs, and for this important group, the link between drugs and offending may be much stronger. For example, they commit crimes to get money to buy drugs, and their multiple drug use makes it difficult or impossible for them to adopt a conventional style of life.

3. *Conduct disorders leading to use of drugs.* Looking at the matter the other way round, many studies have shown that antisocial behaviour is a common

precursor of all forms of substance use and abuse (see Chapter 10). It is plausible, therefore, that the rise in crime and conduct disorders has been important in increasing the propensity to use drugs and alcohol.

4. *Depression and suicide.* Depression is one of the strongest correlates of suicidal behaviour (see Chapter 13), and is also linked to the *other* correlates of suicidal behaviour. However, depressive disorders are far more prevalent than suicide or suicidal behaviour. A range of other risk factors, and a number of protective mechanisms, are involved in determining whether a depressed person engages in suicidal behaviour. Nevertheless, it is notable that, with both suicide and depression, the rise in frequency has been more evident in males than females.

5. *Alcohol and drugs, and suicide.* Abuse of alcohol and psychoactive drugs is the strongest predictor of suicidal behaviour (among survivors) except for major depressive disorder and previous suicidal behaviour or threats (see Chapter 13). Part of the explanation for this link is that most suicidal acts consist of taking an overdose of drugs and are, therefore, a form of drug abuse. Drug abusers are more likely than others to have available the means of suicide, and more likely, through habit and familiarity, to make use of drugs for this purpose. Similarly, alcohol abusers are already used to seeking to solve their problems through reliance on a psychoactive substance; a suicide attempt is one further step along the same road. In addition, once under the influence of alcohol or other drugs, people are more likely to make a mistake over dosage.

While these and other links between the target disorders are important, it is clear that some other important causal factors are specific to particular disorders. For example, opportunity may well be the most important factor leading to the rise in crime (see Chapter 9). Opportunity is also important in the case of suicide: it has been shown that the rate of suicide in older adults (although not to the same extent in the young) declined in England when domestic gas was changed from lethal town gas to harmless natural gas. But the specific opportunities involved in each case are completely unrelated. To take another example, one factor influencing the level of crime is the effectiveness of informal social controls (for example, through the family or school) and of formal controls (for example, through the criminal justice system). Legal regulation is also relevant to abuse of alcohol and drugs. But social and legal controls have no relevance in the case of depression or suicide.

While, therefore, there are many links between the psychosocial disorders considered in this study, the specific disorders remain relatively distinct, they vary widely in prevalence, and the causal pathways leading to them are only partly intertwined. Although each of these disorders has increased in prevalence, the explanations of these increases will be somewhat different in each case, even if they have certain elements in common.

STANDARD OF LIVING

The economies of the developed (OECD) countries grew by a factor of six between 1900 and 1987, but the pattern of growth was highly uneven. There was, first, a phase of steady growth up to 1913; second, a phase of conflict and low growth from 1913 to 1950; third, the 'golden era' of 1950-73 when economies grew at an unprecedented rate; and, fourth, a phase of slower growth and accelerated inflation from 1973. Rates of growth varied widely between countries, the explosive growth of the Japanese economy between 1950 and 1973 being the most remarkable feature. Throughout the developed world, the 'golden era' saw rapid growth in key consumer products such as cars, telephones and television sets. Improvement in housing conditions was also dramatic.

It is striking that the period during which psychosocial disorders are known to have increased broadly coincides with the 'golden era' of rapid economic growth. This certainly disproves the hypothesis that the observed rising levels of psychosocial disorders during the last half-century were caused by worsening living conditions (although, of course, it does not necessarily rule out increased risks for disorder stemming from seriously impaired living conditions in other societies or in Western societies at other times or even now in subgroups). Before assuming that poverty can be ruled out as an explanation, even during a period of increasing affluence, it is necessary to ask whether young people have been relatively disadvantaged during the period of economic growth (see Chapter 9). There is some evidence that they have during the 1980s in some countries (most notably the UK and the USA), but that was not the case during the 1950s and 1960s when psychosocial disorders showed a major rise in frequency. We can firmly rule out the hypothesis that worsening living conditions accounted for that rise. A more difficult question to answer is whether economic growth (through mechanisms as yet unspecified) causes an increase in psychosocial disorders. Potentially the best way of testing this hypothesis is by comparing rates of increase in psychosocial disorders during the 'golden era' of 1950-73 and during the period of much slower growth from 1973 onwards. A detailed cross-national analysis using econometric techniques would be needed, since rates of economic growth and rates of increase in psychosocial disorders varied substantially between countries. In addition, it would be necessary to consider economic conditions as they applied to young people, because changes in prosperity have had a disproportionate impact on different age groups during different time periods. Few such data are available. Unfortunately, too, the data for the psychosocial disorders would be highly incomplete. All that can be said at present is that some of the psychosocial disorders have shown a reduced rate of increase during the period of reduced economic growth (alcohol abuse, suicide and parasuicide in some countries; drug abuse and crime in North America, all after some time lag), whereas others have not (most notably, crime in European countries, and perhaps also drug abuse in Europe).

Against the hypothesis that economic growth causes increasing psychosocial disorders, there was economic growth during the first half of the century, with benefits for physical health, whereas there were rather small and inconsistent increases in psychosocial disorders during that period. The strength of that argument is hard to evaluate, because the data available on psychosocial disorders in the first half of the century are highly incomplete. The argument is less than clear-cut because the rate of economic growth was much slower before 1950 than after, so that correspondingly small increases in psychosocial disorders would be expected.

However, the main difficulty in testing the hypothesis that economic growth causes increases in psychosocial disorders is that the causal mechanisms have not been specified. At the individual level there is no evidence that a high standard of living (indexed by income or social class) is associated with high risk of disorder. Presumably any link would have to be indirect. For example, most crime is theft, and economic growth produces more goods to be stolen. Again, economic growth is associated with changes in routine activities affecting, for example, the proportion of the time that homes are left unattended and therefore vulnerable to burglary. At the same time, growth puts money into the pockets of young men, who may tend to spend it on getting drunk, with a consequent increase in the number of fights. Finally, growth increases the opportunities for earning money legitimately, thus *reducing* the motivation to steal. As outlined in Chapter 9, a more detailed analysis from the viewpoint of economics therefore suggests that a model of the relationship between economic growth and crime might well be highly complex. Possible mechanisms linking growth with the other disorders might well be complex, too. Until the hypothesized mechanisms are specified in some detail, it will not be possible to set up a good test of whether there is a link of any kind.

Econometric analysis of crime statistics for England (reported in Chapter 9) based on a fairly specific model has been carried out. It suggests that there may be links between the pattern of crime and the pattern of economic growth and recession, but that the long-term growth in crime cannot be explained by the long-term growth in the economy. However, there is scope for much more research of this kind in the future, and it should make use of cross-national data. It is, of course, striking that the period of explosive growth in the Japanese economy between 1950 and 1973 was not a period of growth in crime.

PHYSICAL HEALTH

In broad terms, the increase in the prevalence of psychosocial disorders over the past 40 years stands in contrast with a continuing improvement in the physical health of the population. Certainly the growth in psychosocial disorders cannot be explained by trends in physical health.

At a more detailed level of analysis, the timing of the improving trend in physical health, as shown by mortality statistics, and the deteriorating trend of psychosocial disorders, does not coincide. In most European countries, there was a sharp and persistent decline in death rates between around 1915 and 1955: further declines after 1955 were slight for all age groups aggregated, although there has been a dramatic reduction in *infant* mortality since then. The period of the greatest improvement in physical health (1915-55) therefore came before the period during which psychosocial disorders are known to have increased substantially.[1]

---

1. A recurring problem is that information about trends in the psychosocial disorders in the earlier part of the century is limited. Statistics of recorded crime (where available) show some increases between 1900 and 1950, but the sharp and persistent increases have come since 1950. Long runs of statistics are available on suicide for many countries. In a number of European countries, there was a substantial increase in rates of suicide (all age groups aggregated) in the earlier part of the century (up to 1930), as well as an increase since 1960, although a number of countries show no increase in the earlier period. The averaged suicide rates for 16 European countries show a substantial increase from 1880 to 1930, a drop from 1931 to 1954, and a rise thereafter, becoming particularly sharp during the ten years starting in 1972. The long-term data on alcohol consumption show that the first quarter of this century was characterized by a falling rate, the period between the two world wars by a fairly stable (low) rate, and the period since by a marked increase, up to a plateau from around 1980. Little or no information is available about long-term trends in depression or in the use of psychoactive drugs, although it is likely that use of drugs was at a very low level around 1950.

These findings warn against drawing an analogy between physical and psychosocial disorders. Nevertheless, the extensive research on patterns of mortality may be used as a source of ideas. Improvements in health and life expectancy are strongly correlated with economic growth. Thus, for example, life expectancy began to rise much earlier in Britain than in Japan, because economic growth and industrialization happened much earlier in Britain. Improvements in health and life expectancy were brought about mainly by environmental change, public health measures and changes in life styles rather than by improvements in medical treatment. Systematic research has confirmed that there is a close relationship between economic development (as measured by gross domestic product per head of population) and life expectancy, until a threshold is reached at a gross domestic product of $5,000 per head of population at 1984 values. Beyond that threshold further economic growth bears little or no relationship to improvements in life expectancy.

At the same time, cross-sectional evidence shows that life expectancy increases with income, but that these increases level off once a certain income threshold is reached. Among developed countries, moreover, high life expectancy is correlated with a relatively even income distribution rather than with high average incomes. At earlier stages of economic development, the standard of living of a large part of the population tends to rise, and has not yet reached the threshold beyond which there is no further increase in life expectancy. At later stages, further growth mostly enriches people already above that threshold, and therefore has little effect on life expectancy. There are still people below the threshold, but they can best be raised above it by redistribution of income.

While there is no direct analogy between physical ill-health and psychosocial disorders, psychosocial disorders may also be related to economic growth in different ways during different phases of economic development.

Another contrast between physical ill-health and psychosocial disorders lies in their relationship with social class. There is a strong relationship between social class and life expectancy, largely because of differences between the living conditions of social classes, which in turn are related to mortality. The key factor accounting for differences found even between grades of affluent employees may be the level of autonomy both at work and in other social contexts. By contrast, differences between social classes in the prevalence of psychosocial disorders are less striking and consistent. Most studies in developed countries show only a weak relationship between crime or conduct disorders and social class. There is no clear relationship between abuse of alcohol and social class. Whereas persistent users of hard drugs tend to descend into lower social classes as a consequence of their style of life, there is no relationship between parents' social class and drug abuse among their children. A number of studies have shown a higher rate of depression among lower than among higher social classes, but this is not a consistent finding: in particular, the largest and most recent general population survey (the Epidemiological Catchment Area Study in the USA) found no relationship between affective disorders and low education, low income, or low occupational status (see Chapter 11). There is no consistent relationship between social class and the risk of suicide. All of this suggests that the causal mechanisms involved in physical ill-health and psychosocial disorders may be widely different.

Finally, caution needs to be exercised before assuming that, just because infantile mortality has fallen and life expectancy increased, that means that all aspects of physical health in young people have improved. Thus, as discussed in Chapter 5, the major gains in the survival of very small babies has probably made no appreciable difference to the proportion left with brain damage.

AGE STRUCTURE OF THE POPULATION

There are two kinds of theory that make a link between age structure and psychosocial disorders. First, social learning theory predicts that deviant behaviour will be more easily controlled where the younger age groups are a small minority, so that the older majority are more likely to prevail. Second, Easterlin's economic theory (referred to in most earlier chapters) predicts that competition will be greater among members of larger as compared with smaller age cohorts, so that members of 'baby boom' generations will tend to be at a disadvantage in a variety of ways. These disadvantages might, in turn, lead to an increase in psychosocial disorders.

In the longer term, young people have come to form an increasingly *small* proportion of the population over the present century. Either of the two theories should, therefore, predict a *decline* in rates of psychosocial disorders over the present century, instead of the actual increase. Consequently, changes in age structure can be rejected as an explanation of long-term secular change.

Superimposed on the long-term trend towards an ageing population, there has been a short-term 'bulge' of children born in the years immediately following the Second World War. In the United States the large cohorts were aged 5-19 in 1970 and 25-39 by 1990. Most countries in Western Europe also experienced a postwar bulge in birth rate, but the timing and extent of these short-term changes varied considerably between countries. Although changes in age structure cannot explain long-term secular change in psychosocial disorders of youth, it is an interesting question whether the short-term changes have had some effect. Very few studies have analysed these effects with respect to psychosocial disorders, although a considerable number have found a relationship between age structure and economic variables such as unemployment. One study (Diekstra, 1989: see Chapter 13, this volume) found that an increase between 1960 and 1985 in the proportion of the population aged under 15 was associated with an increase in the national suicide rate among those aged 15 to 29. Another (Field, 1990: see Chapter 9, this volume) found a relationship between growth in crime and growth in the number of men aged 10-29 in England and Wales during the years since the Second World War.

Nevertheless, the general conclusion is that age structure cannot explain the major and long-term changes in rates of psychosocial disorders.

STRUCTURE OF EMPLOYMENT

A major structural change associated with economic growth is a decline in the proportion employed in agriculture, and an increase in the proportion employed in industry, and, later, in services. These changes, and particularly the decline of employment in agriculture, signals fundamental social change, including migration from villages to towns and cities. In many European countries, much of the change occurred before the beginning of the present century, although the timing varied substantially between countries; some still had substantial employment in agriculture as late as 1950.

A hypothesis worth considering is that these structural changes are connected (through intervening mechanisms not yet specified) with the increase in psychosocial disorders. The main problem for such a theory is that in many countries the greatest structural changes associated with industrialization happened long before the known increase in psychosocial disorders. It would be necessary to postulate a delayed reaction: for example, it might be supposed that industrialization after several generations brings about a change in family structures which in turn causes a change in psychosocial disorders.

Such a theory could be tested by considering whether there is a consistent difference in rates of disorders now, or in rates of increase over a recent period, between early- and late-industrializing countries. The theory would predict high rates of disorders in the UK, the USA, Belgium, and the Netherlands, and low rates in Japan, Italy, and Austria. Results set out earlier in this report are in some respects consistent with this prediction. Future research should analyse the evidence in more detail.

URBANIZATION

The move of population from villages to towns and cities is closely related to the change in the structure of employment. Again the major part of this change occurred in Western European countries well before the period of known increase in psychosocial disorders. Nevertheless, there is evidence that crime, at least, is strongly related to urbanization. Within countries, the rate of crime is much higher in large cities than elsewhere. Also, analysis of victim survey results shows (in spite of some important exceptions) a clear relationship at the national level between the proportion of the population living in large cities and the overall risk of victimization. Analysis of recorded crime statistics has also produced a similar result (see Chapter 9). Nevertheless, although the data are inadequate for any decisive test, the *changes* over time in crime within individual countries have not been closely linked with trends in urbanization. Also, crime rates have risen as much in rural, as urban, areas. It has been demonstrated that the development of the oil industry between 1975 and 1978 in a remote rural area (the Shetlands, Scotland) resulted in a remarkable increase in consumption of alcohol (see Chapter 10). The mechanism may have been connected with industrialization or urbanization, although many other explanations are possible (for example, increased disposable income or increased stress).

A useful project for future research is to establish how far the other psychosocial disorders are related to urbanization.

EDUCATION

In advanced economies, there has been a steady increase throughout the century in the level of education of the population as a whole. The growth of education is, of course, closely linked with economic growth and industrialization. It is linked, in particular, with the expansion of higher occupations (managerial, administrative, technical, scientific, and professional).

There are two ways in which rising levels of education might be linked with increasing psychosocial disorders. The first suggestion is that increasing education may lead to widening horizons, increasing awareness of possibilities, and increasing expectations that are difficult to fulfil. It can be argued that in the earlier half of the century, the main part of the education system was designed to prepare young people for manual or simple clerical jobs and acted to limit their vision and ambitions. In the later stages of industrialization, there is a steeply declining demand for manual workers, and an increasing need for people with specialist training and with flexible skills and problem-solving ability. The type of education required to produce those skills inevitably increases vision, awareness, and therefore, expectations. Psychosocial disorders could be seen as the result of expectations running ahead of actual conditions, such as job satisfaction, even where those are also increasing.

The second point, which is entirely separate, is that increasing education has brought about a transformation in the phasing of adolescent development. Even over a short period starting in 1975, changes in the proportion of young people aged 19 or 21 who were enrolled in educational establishments were radical. Consequently, the transition to adult status has been pushed to a later and later age. This change in the patterning of transitions may, in turn, be associated with an increase in disorders.

Both of these possible effects of increasing education are indirect. They will be discussed in later sections on adolescent transitions and rising expectations.

UNEMPLOYMENT

The theory that rising unemployment has caused the secular increase in psychosocial disorders can be decisively rejected. There is no evidence of a sudden and substantial rise in psychosocial disorders in the 1930s, when there was a massive and sustained rise in unemployment.[2] Still more important, the period during which the known rise in psychosocial disorders was greatest – the 1960s and early 1970s – was a period of unusually *low* unemployment.

---

2. As explained in Chapter 6, unemployment in the 1930s did not affect young people as severely as older people. Even so, young people, like the rest of the population, experienced a sharp rise in the risk of unemployment.

A multivariate model of crime trends in England and Wales since the Second World War (Field, 1990: see Chapter 9, this volume) showed no effect of unemployment on the growth of crime. A multivariate model of changes in suicide rates in a range of European countries (Diekstra, 1989: see Chapter 13, this volume) showed that between 1960 and 1985 increases in unemployment in men were associated with increases in rates of suicide among young people aged 15 to 29. However, there was a parallel association with an increase in the proportion of women in paid work and the findings were inconsistent across analyses (see Chapter 13). The associations between levels of unemployment and rates of parasuicide have been similarly inconsistent.

Although unemployment cannot explain long-term secular trends in disorder, there is substantial evidence of a link between unemployment and psychosocial disorders at the individual level. For example, many studies have shown that young people who are unemployed after leaving school are more likely to suffer from depression than those who find jobs (see Chapter 11). Also, individuals who are unemployed, or have a history of unemployment, are more likely to commit crimes than those with a history of regular employment (see Chapter 9).

POVERTY AND THE DISTRIBUTION OF INCOME

As set out in an earlier section, improvements in health and life expectancy are associated with both economic growth and equality of income distribution, although equality becomes a far more important determinant than growth in the late phase of economic development. These findings can be understood on the assumption that gains in life expectancy are achieved by improving living conditions, but that, beyond a certain point, further improvements produce rapidly diminishing gains.

The theoretical basis for expecting a relationship between inequality and psychosocial disorders is much less clear. On the one hand, there is evidence that poverty causes stresses, for example in family life, that are among the causes of disorders. On the other hand, some causes of psychosocial disorders (for example, increased opportunity, rising expectations) may derive from increasing affluence.

Over the long term, income disparities tend to be reduced as economic development progresses, at least during the phases involving a switch from agriculture to industry and services and the introduction of mass education. In line with this historic trend, income disparities are currently greatest in countries at an early stage of economic development. At the same time, there are substantial differences both in income dispersion and in the incidence of poverty among countries now at an advanced stage of economic development (see Chapter 6). Some of the most successful economies (Japan, Sweden) are among those having low income disparities and low incidence of poverty, while others (the USA, France) are among those having high income disparities and incidence of poverty. In principle, these differences provide an opportunity for testing the theory that inequality of income is associated with the prevalence of psychosocial disorders. In the case of crime and suicide, the cross-national data are good enough to warrant an analysis of this kind in future, although none has yet been reported.

While the long-term historic trend in the advanced economies has been towards greater equality of income, this trend has clearly been reversed in a number of these countries, notably the USA, the UK, and Germany, in recent years. Future research should aim to establish whether this reversal in the 1980s of the earlier trend towards greater equality was associated with a change in the time trends for psychosocial disorders.

Of course, over the longer term, the major increase in psychosocial disorders appears to have occurred during a period of increasing equality of incomes and declining poverty. However, without a clearer theoretical foundation it is difficult to know what to make of this. It is possible, for example, that in the postwar boom period the causes of increasing psychosocial disorders were unconnected with inequality, but that in a period of economic stagnation, increasing inequality becomes a significant factor: an increased number of formerly affluent people descending into poverty might be expected to cause an increase in stress and hence disorder.

MIGRATION

The last 50 years have seen a substantial increase in the migration to many European countries of people often from developing countries whose cultures are substantially different from European ones (see Chapter 5). Accordingly, it is necessary to consider whether any aspects of migration could have played a part in the rise of psychosocial disorders in young people. Clearly the rise cannot be explained in terms of high rates of disorder in immigrant groups if only because the proportion of immigrants in all countries is far too low for that to be possible. Alternatively the mechanism could lie in the disruptive changes to the host community associated with a sudden massive in-migration.

Again, that explanation can be rejected because the rises in psychosocial disorders have not followed the ebbs and flows over time or between countries in rates of migration. Alternatively, the mechanism could lie in the effects of ethnic and cultural diversity. It cannot be said that this possibility has been subjected to adequate systematic research. However, it is not a strong contender as a major influence on psychosocial disorder for several different reasons. To begin with, it has not been shown that the effects of such diversity are predominantly negative. However, it is also relevant that the rises in psychosocial disorder are not apparently any less in countries (such as those in Scandinavia) where ethnic diversity may be less. Similarly, within countries (such as the UK), the rise in crime (little is known about patterns of other disorders) has been as great in rural areas (where there tends to be less ethnic diversity) as in the cities where the influx of ethnic minorities has been greatest. There is a need for further study of the effects, both positive and negative, of cultural and ethnic diversity, but it does not seem likely that this accounts for the rise in psychosocial disorders in young people over the last half-century.

FAMILY FUNCTIONING

In many but not all developed countries, there have been striking changes in family structures over the past 50 years (see Chapter 5). Because of a decline in fertility, an increasing proportion of families have only one or two children; an increasing proportion of mothers, even of young children, go out to work; large increases in divorce and remarriage mean that children are decreasingly likely to grow up within a stable family unit; an increasing number of people live alone for a greater portion of their lives (either before uniting with their partner or in their extended old age); an increasing proportion cohabit as an alternative to marriage, or else postpone marriage, or refuse to marry and have children; and an increasing proportion of women choose planned single motherhood outside marriage.

These changes are far advanced in Northern European countries (Denmark, Finland, Norway, and Sweden) followed fairly closely by a larger number of countries outside Southern Europe (Austria, Belgium, France, Germany, the Netherlands, Switzerland, England and Wales). They are far less advanced in Southern European countries (Greece, Italy, Portugal, Spain), and also in Ireland. Whether the Southern European countries will follow the path marked out by Northern Europe remains to be seen.

A vast array of research demonstrates the many links between various aspects of family functioning and child development. The general principle underlying these relationships is that adolescents develop positively when their parents provide them with strong emotional support and a sense of belonging to the family, while at the same time recognising their increasing maturation and independence. Parental involvement, as well as emotional warmth, is shown to be important.

Some, though not all, of the changes in family structures make it less likely that parents will be able to provide the necessary support to their children, and therefore increase the risk that developmental transitions will not be successfully accomplished, and that psychosocial disorders will develop. The change towards smaller family sizes is probably on balance a positive influence, since children in large families are more at risk of failure in achievement or adjustment. However, a large number of (mainly American) studies consistently show that marital dissolution and reorganization places children and adolescents at significantly higher risk for short-term problems in psychosocial well-being, and for long-term difficulties in forming and maintaining families of their own. The effects of being raised by a mother who has chosen single parenthood are not yet well understood, because the growth of single parenthood by choice is such a new phenomenon. However, a substantial proportion of single parents are poor, even in countries with highly developed social welfare systems. It seems likely that the economic hardship associated with single parenthood may have adverse effects on the children because it makes parenting more difficult. Also, a single mother will tend to have less time and energy to devote to her children than a couple, especially where (as is usual) she has to go out to work.

While these findings are compelling, it is more difficult than might at first appear to move from them to a prediction of the effects of the changes in family structure. Adolescent development depends on detailed family functioning rather than family structure: on whether or not the parents are involved with their children, and whether they provide stability, support, and the required level of independence. The research on adolescent development shows that, at any given time, children within unstable family units tend to be at a disadvantage compared to those in more stable ones. However, it is just possible (albeit unlikely) that family functioning (in the respects that affect children and adolescents) has on balance improved throughout the period when divorce and remarriage has increased. This could happen if, for example, the conflicts within families that used to stick together were more destructive than the effects of family breakups. In fact, there is a considerable body of research to show that children are adversely affected by family conflict *before* a family breakup occurs, and independently of it. However, the evidence (limited though it is) that the adverse effects on children associated with parental divorce are as great today as they were a generation ago suggests that the rise in divorce *has* been accompanied by a parallel rise in family conflict.

For such reasons, the evidence summarized in Chapter 5 does not *demonstrate* that the changes in family structure are a cause of the increase in psychosocial disorders. However, it is enough to make this a highly plausible hypothesis. In addition, the hypothesis is consistent with the timing of change in family structures on the one hand, and psychosocial disorders on the other. Both types of change began in the 1950s and gathered pace from the 1960s onwards.

The opportunity for a critical test of the hypothesis is provided by the radical difference in the timing of change in family structures in different European countries. Cross-national differences in crime and suicide may well be consistent with the hypothesis, but because changes in family structures are interrelated with so many other social changes, a full investigation must be a project for future research.

A more serious risk factor than divorce is provided by the abuse of children. There is no doubt that there has been a great increase in the number of cases of abuse *recognized* by societies and it has often been supposed that the true frequency of abuse must also have increased. Because adequate data on rates of abuse 50 years ago are lacking, it is not possible to be sure whether or not there has been a true increase. However, the evidence suggests that it is *un*likely that there has been an increase in sexual abuse. A modest rise in physical abuse may have occurred but it is improbable that it has been very large and, because of this, probably it can have played only a minor contributory role in the rise of disorders (if it has played any part at all).

ADOLESCENT TRANSITIONS

Adolescence involves a process of development from relative dependence to relative independence, and an associated series of transitions in various domains. There has been a long-term change in the patterning of these transitions and possibly a lengthening of the period over which some of these transitions occur. This has happened because, on the one hand, puberty has tended to come at an increasingly early age, while, on the other hand, the length of full-time education has tended to increase, and young people have tended to become economically independent and to leave the parental home at an increasingly late age (see Chapter 4). Both changes have been substantial. Among European girls, the average age of first menstruation has reduced from approximately 16 to 12 over the past 100 years, while among boys the age of voice deepening has decreased from about 18 to 14 years. Over the same period there has been an increase of around four years in the average number of years of full-time education. However, whether or not the period of transition is viewed as having lengthened or shortened depends crucially on which transitions are considered. Thus, the average time from puberty to finishing education has lengthened over this century, but the time from starting work to getting married and setting up one's own home has substantially shortened (Modell et al., 1976). What is clear is that the *pattern* of transitions has greatly altered.

Some have suggested (for example, Hurrelmann, 1989: see Chapter 4, this volume) that the lengthening period of adolescence increases the stresses involved in accomplishing the transitions and, therefore, the risk of psychosocial disorders. The underlying theory tends to be expressed in metaphorical language: the transitions are said to be 'stretched' and 'uncoordinated'. In more concrete terms, this may be interpreted in one of two ways. First, lengthened adolescence might mean the prolongation of an insecure status, and of an uncertain personal identity. Second, it might lead to internal conflicts and to clashes with parental or other authority because autonomy is achieved much sooner in some domains than in others.

Against all this, it may be argued that a high level of stress would be caused if all of the transitions occurred at or around the same time: for example, it would be stressful to begin work and start an independent family at the same time. On this view, successful transition to adulthood might best be achieved step by step, building confidence gradually at each stage. This would fit with a large body of evidence on the conditions for successful social learning.

Thus, plausible reasons can be advanced in theory for expecting lengthening adolescence to cause either an increase or a decrease in psychosocial disorders. Perhaps surprisingly, in view of the importance given to lengthening adolescence in sociological writings, there seems to be no evidence that individuals who go through a long transitional period experience greater problems than others. The age at which they reach puberty relative to their peers has contrasting implications for boys and girls. Early-maturing boys, compared with those who mature later, are more self-confident and popular, have higher aspirations, and rank higher on standardized achievement tests. Broadly the opposite is true for girls. The mechanisms underlying these differences are almost certainly unconnected with the length of the adolescent period. There seems to be no evidence that those who *complete* the transitions to adulthood at a late age are worse off than others.

The evidence on secular change does not support the hypothesis of a link with psychosocial disorders. Both the reduction in the age of puberty and the increase in the length of education began in the last century and proceeded steadily thereafter. Hence much of the lengthening of adolescence happened long before the known increase in psychosocial disorders of youth.

A more promising approach is to concentrate on changes in the status of adolescents that have occurred in the postwar period. What seems most striking is the growth of a youth culture and of youth markets (for music, fashion, and places of entertainment) which mark off adolescents as a separate group in a more decisive way than earlier in the century. These changes, combined with the lengthening of youth and the postponement of economic independence, may tend to insulate young people from the influence of adults, in particular their parents, and increase the influence of the peer group. It may therefore be that it is an isolated youth culture that leads to the increase in psychosocial disorders. That theory seems worth investigating in future research.

STRESSORS

Another possibility is that young people today have a greater number of stress experiences than their counterparts in the past. There are no satisfactory measures of secular trends in stress and any examination of such trends would have to make questionable assumptions about the relative severity of very different experiences. The generally improved living conditions, at least up to the 1980s, presumably meant a reduction in some sorts of stressors. Similarly, the increasing longevity of the population would have meant that fewer young people will have experienced the death of a parent, or a sibling. On the other hand, undoubtedly there has been a very great increase in the proportion experiencing breakdown of their parents' marriage, a period of single parent upbringing and the further potentially stressful adaptation involved in parental remarriage. The prolongation of education will have meant that a higher proportion of young people will have experienced the stresses of major examinations and perhaps more will have had to cope with exam failure or a rejection from some chosen source of tertiary education. The major rise in crime will have meant an increase in the proportion of the population who are victims of crime. The massive increase in the availability of drugs will also have involved young people in potentially stressful decision-making on whether to engage in drug-taking and how to stop taking drugs when it may have been part of their peer culture. The increasing openness in society's approaches to sexuality and marriage will have meant an increasing need for young people to take their own decisions, a freedom certainly but one that is not free of stress. Finally, the increasing tendency to cohabit before marriage may well have involved a substantial rise in the proportion of young people experiencing a breakdown in cohabiting love-relationships – a potent source of stress (see Chapter 5). Putting together these trends, it is possible (but uncertain and certainly not proven) that there has been an increase in the stressors experienced by young people; if so, that may have played a contributory role in the rise in disorders. The possibility warrants study but will require research focused on those stressors that may have increased, that combines individual and aggregate data, and which examines possible effects on the overall liability to disorder and not just on its timing.

THE MASS MEDIA

Although radio and cinema first became established in the 1930s, the explosion of the mass media happened in the 'golden era' of economic growth starting in 1950. Television – easily the most powerful medium, and the one taking up the largest portion of people's time – became established in the mid-1950s and from that point grew very rapidly. Therefore, the growth of the mass media coincided closely with the increase in psychosocial disorders of youth.

As set out in Chapter 7, a large body of evidence, mostly from American studies, supports the theory that exposure to violent television programmes predisposes to violent behaviour. Many of these studies are experiments of some kind, and can be criticized on the ground that the circumstances of the experiment were remote from conditions of real life. However, experimental manipulation has been important in the development of detailed and well-supported theories describing the psychological processes involved and showing which elements of the scenario are important in producing an effect on behaviour. In addition, a considerable number of longitudinal studies, some of them cross-national, have demonstrated an effect of television watching in real life on later behaviour. These effects, of modest degree everywhere, have probably been considerably greater in the USA than in Europe, because American television throughout most of the postwar period was much more violent than European television. However, with increasing deregulation, the level of violence in European television is now rising.

Of course, the behaviour of young people is influenced by a wide range of factors, and the relative importance of exposure to television violence compared with other factors is not known. Moreover, it is important to recognize that the content of television reflects the mores of the day, making it difficult to determine the independent effect of the media. It seems unlikely, on general grounds, that the media have played a major role in the rise of crime, but they may well have played a significant contributory role in enhancing other negative influences.

A number of studies have found statistical relationships between media coverage of suicides and suicide rates: for example, Phillips (1974) (see Chapter 7) found that a week after Marilyn Monroe killed herself, the US suicide rate temporarily jumped by 12 per cent.

It seems possible, although undemonstrated, that television plays some role in the predisposition to eating disorders. There is evidence that adolescents who watch a great deal of television are more likely to be obese and unfit than those who watch less, although these studies have not been able to establish the direction of causation. Experimental studies show that exposure to television images of slim women portrayed as role models can cause young women to be dissatisfied with their body shape; and content analysis of television programmes shows that they are populated by thin people eating fattening food. However, no research has yet demonstrated that exposure to media images is, in fact, a cause of eating disorders.

There is no evidence that the media have contributed to the rise in depressive disorders or in drug abuse.

MORAL CONCEPTS AND VALUES

Psychosocial disorders might have increased because of a decline in self-control arising from a change in moral concepts or a weakening of internalized moral values. Long-run data on this subject are not available, but Chapter 8 contains an analysis of three surveys going back to 1969. These analyses highlight a number of important shifts in moral values and perceptions; the pattern of change is complex, and its interpretation remains controversial. These changes do not amount to a 'decline in standards': in fact, they are a move towards giving greater emphasis to a wider range of 'standards'. However, they may be associated with the increase in psychosocial disorders.

The 1981 European Values Survey showed that young people across a large number of countries were more tolerant than older people, less respectful of traditional values, and more demanding of autonomy and control. These differences may have reflected an age effect rather than a secular change in values over the period prior to 1981. However, when the survey was repeated in 1990, the findings suggested that secular change occurred after 1981. There was a shift towards greater tolerance in personal-sexual morality, and towards greater tolerance of self-interest and minor illegality, again repeated across a large number of European countries. The youngest generation showed the most divergent and tolerant attitudes, but over a ten-year period they tended to grow rapidly out of their earlier anti-civic attitudes. A different survey series shows a large secular change over a longer period (1969-90) in the proportion of people who approve of keeping a lost article one has found. However, the same survey showed no change in levels of disapproval of more serious illegal acts.

Between 1981 and 1990, there was a modest shift away from traditional religious beliefs and attitudes. On the whole, however, religious beliefs were highly resilient, considering the low level of religious observance.

On the basis of attitude data from the Eurobarometer surveys, it has been argued by Inglehart and others that there has been a secular change towards 'postmaterialism': that is, an increasing emphasis on non-material values, such as freedom of speech, as compared with material ones, such as low inflation. There is a difference of this kind between the attitudes of successive generations, which remain stable as the people grow older. However, this interpretation of the data has proved controversial. It is possible to argue, instead, that younger generations are no less concerned than older generations with material values, but are in addition more concerned with non-material values such as freedom of speech. In practice, they may not be prepared to place a higher priority on these non-material values.

A safer generalization is that there has been an increase in individualism, as shown, for example, by an increasing willingness to protest, and a decline of confidence in major institutions (such as the police, the government, and the army). More generally, there is an emerging emphasis on individual empowerment, equitable remuneration, and a broader and more sceptical political awareness. It is plausible that increasing individualism leads to increased risks, especially for young people at moments of transition. Future research should aim to test whether cross-national differences, especially in crime rates and abuse of drugs, are related to differences in moral values on these dimensions.

The shift towards tolerance in personal and sexual morality, and towards individualism in the private and informal sphere, is contrasted with an expansion of formalized rules and sanctions, and with a tendency for rules to become more universal, and to take in relationships with distant people and abstract entities (say, the European Court). This universalizing tendency is reflected, for example, in an increase between 1969 and 1990 in the proportion of Europeans who are prepared to pay higher taxes to help poorer countries outside Europe, or poorer regions within the EC. It is possible that an expansion of formal regulation is associated with a decline in the efficacy of informal controls and internalized values.

RISING EXPECTATIONS

It was suggested in an earlier section that increasing education may be associated with widening awareness and rising expectations. There is specific evidence to support the theory that expectations are rising, especially in relation to work. The 1981 European Values Survey found that the young expected more of a job than older people, and the 1990 survey shows a trend towards still higher expectations. If anything, people are becoming more concerned about the material aspects of work, such as pay and promotion, and less concerned about its usefulness to society. However, these changes are overshadowed by the rapidly increasing emphasis given to intrinsic interest, personal development, and responsibility. In addition, people give increasing emphasis to equitable remuneration, or in other words pay for performance. Because of these rising expectations, Europeans have become less satisfied with their work.

It is plausible that rising demands will lead to psychosocial disorders to the extent that those demands cannot be met.

FUTURE RESEARCH PRIORITIES

This report has made a start towards describing the rising cross-national trends in psychosocial disorders and testing possible explanations. In spite of the enormous difficulties, this field of research has considerable potential. In order to make further progress, it will be important to specify in some detail the mechanisms that may link societal changes with psychosocial disorders, so that critical tests of hypotheses can be set up.

The review of possible explanations of the rising trend in psychosocial disorders has thrown up a number of questions that need to be tackled by future research. The relationship between the unprecedented economic growth of the postwar period and the increase in disorders is perhaps the chief of these. This is a case where the specific mechanisms – such as increasing opportunity for theft associated with economic growth – need to be specified and tested. It seems likely that economic growth brought about a large number of changes which had complex and partly compensating effects on opportunity and motivation, so there is a need for econometric modelling.

Far more effective use can be made in future of cross-national differences in testing possible explanations. Japan will provide a crucial test of most generalizations. For example, in spite of explosive economic growth in Japan between 1950 and 1973, the crime rate there remained level although it was rising fast in other developed countries.

As well as understanding the role of economic growth, it is also important to explore the significance of the switch from agriculture to industry and, later, services, and the historic trend towards urbanization. The link between crime and urbanization is fairly well established, but less is known about any links with the other disorders. The theory that rates of disorder are lower in late-industrialising countries merits closer examination.

Cross-national differences should be used to test the theory that inequality of income is a cause of psychosocial disorders. The reversal of the long-term trend towards greater income equality in certain countries in the 1980s provides an opportunity for a critical test of the theory.

It seems likely that changes in family structure and the increase in family breakup are a cause of increasing psychosocial disorder, but what is missing is an account of changes in quality of parenting as they relate to changes in family structure. It is particularly important to establish whether single parents manage to supervise and support their children as well as couples. The timing of changes in family structure varies substantially between European countries, and this provides the opportunity for a critical test of the theory that family structure changes are an important cause of increases in disorders.

There is no support for the idea that changes in the timing of puberty or the increase in the length of the adolescent phase is a cause of increasing disorders. However, an associated development is that adolescents may have become more insulated from adult influence, more subject to the influences of the peer group and youth culture and possibly more subject to psychosocial stressors.

It is worth investigating whether these changes are an important cause of increases in psychosocial disorders.

There is considerable evidence, mostly from the USA, that the mass media have had some influence on violent crime, suicide, and eating disorders. It is important to collect more evidence on this in Europe, through longitudinal research in the field rather than laboratory experiments.

It is striking that the rise in psychosocial disorders over the last 50 years is a phenomenon that applies to adolescents and young adults and not to older people. The explanation therefore, has to lie in social, psychological or biological changes that particularly impinge on younger age groups. Greater use in research needs to be made of this age contrast and on the various sex differences in secular trends. The evidence that we have amassed on secular trends as shown in different European countries clearly emphasizes the reality and importance of the rise in psychosocial disorders in young people that has taken place since the Second World War. It has been possible to rule out several popular explanations and to point out a number of remaining strong contenders. The challenge now is to devise effective tests of the likely hypotheses, to determine the probable causal mechanisms and by so doing provide the basis for effective policies of prevention and intervention.

Finally, the theory that certain shifts in moral concepts and values are among the causes of increased psychosocial disorder is worth further investigation. In particular, the shift towards individualistic values, the increasing emphasis on self-realization and fulfilment, and the consequent rise in expectations, should be studied as possible causes of disorders.

In order to tackle these problems, there is a need for a strengthening of the research infrastructure. For example, cross-national comparisons of crime are seriously hampered by lack of comparability between national statistics of recorded crime. A substantial further investment is needed to produce more useful harmonized statistics. Victim surveys and self-report surveys, especially when they are organized cross-nationally, add substantially to the information available from recorded crime statistics. If cross-national time series can be built up from victim surveys or self-report studies, then the study of crime will be established on an entirely new footing.

In each of the other fields, there is a similar need to collate and harmonize statistics, and to carry out local, national, and cross-national surveys. For example, more reliable information on secular trends in depression and other mental disorders will only become available as a time series of general population surveys begins to build up.

More generally, there is a need to develop a better cross-national database of social indicators to supplement the economic indicators which tend, so far, to be much more highly developed. In the next ten years, bodies such as OECD and Eurostat should shift the emphasis of their work from economic to social indicators. Developments of this kind would gradually establish the infrastructure on which more ambitious research programmes could be based.

REFERENCES

Diekstra, R. F. W. (1989). Suicidal behavior in adolescents and young adults: The international picture. *Crisis 10*, 16-35.

Field, S. (1990). *Trends in crime and their interpretation: A study of recorded crime in postwar England and Wales*. Home Office Research Study 119. London: HMSO.

Hurrelmann, K. (1989). The social world of adolescents: A sociological perspective. In K. Hurrelmann & U. Engel (eds.) *The social world of adolescents: International perspectives*, 3-26. Berlin/New York: Walter de Gruyter.

Modell, J., Furstenberg Jr., F. F. & Hershberg, T. (1976). Social change and transitions to adulthood in historical perspective. *Journal of Family History 1*, 7-32.

Phillips, D. P. (1974). The influence of suggestion on suicide: Substantive and theoretical implications of the Werther effect. *American Sociological Review 39*, 340-354.

Sartorius, N., Nielsen, J. A. & Stromgren, E. (1989). Changes in frequency of mental disorder over time: Results of repeated surveys of mental disorders in the general population. *Acta Psychiatrica Scandinavica 79, Supplement 248*, 5-6.

Index

Index prepared by Barbara Nash and Janet Smy

Related titles of interest...

Developmental Psychopathology
Volume 1: Theory and Methods
Volume 2: Risk, Disorder and Adaptation
Edited by Dante Cicchetti and Donald J. Cohen

Two complementary volumes - Volume 1 covers the history, theory and methods; Volume 2 deals with assessment, classification and diagnosis; risk factors such as maltreatment, family discord etc; and specific disorders eg. addictions, schizophrenia, all from the developmental point of view.

0-471-53243-6   1995   850pp   Vol 1
0-471-53244-4   1995   850pp   Vol 2
0-471 53257-6   1995   1700pp   2 Vol Set

Temperament in Childhood
Edited by G.A. Kohnstamm, J.E. Bates and M.K. Rothbart

Covers all the current major issues on temperament in childhood, including biological processes; development; cross-cultural; socioeconomic status, sex and other group differences, historical and international perspectives.

0-471-95583-3   1995   660pp   Paperback

Parenting and Psychopathology
Edited by Carlo Perris, Willem A. Arrindell and Martin Eisemann

Presents the result of a long term multinational research project which suggests that there is a link betwen parental attitudes to child rearing and various psychopathological disorders.

0-471-94226-X   1994   360pp

Precursors and Causes in Development and Psychopathology
Edited by Dale F. Hay

Explores precursors and causes of intelligence, theory of mind, empathy and cooperation, attachment and peer relationships, conduct disorder and criminal offending.

0-471-92211-0   1993   334pp

WILEY